Human ethology

Claims and limits of a new discipline

This book is published as part of the joint publishing agreement established in 1977 between the Fondation de la Maison des Sciences de l'Homme and the Press Syndicate of the University of Cambridge. Titles published under this arrangement may appear in any European language or, in the case of volumes of collected essays, in several languages.

New books will appear either as individual titles or in one of the series which the Maison des Sciences de l'Homme and the Cambridge University Press have jointly agreed to publish. All books published jointly by the Maison des Sciences de l'Homme and the Cambridge University Press will be distributed by the Press throughout the world.

Human ethology

Claims and limits of a new discipline

Contributions to the Colloquium sponsored by the Werner-Reimers-Stiftung

Edited by M. von Cranach, K. Foppa W. Lepenies and D. Ploog

Cambridge University Press
Cambridge
London   New York   New Rochelle   Melbourne   Sydney

Editions de la Maison des Sciences de l'Homme
Paris

Published by the Press Syndicate of the University of Cambridge
The Pitt Building, Trumpington Street, Cambridge CB2 1RP
32 East 57th Street, New York, NY 10022, USA
296 Beaconsfield Parade, Middle Park, Melbourne 3206, Australia
and Editions de la Maison des Sciences de l'Homme
54 Boulevard Raspail, 75270 Paris Cedex 06

First published 1979

Phototypeset by
Western Printing Services Ltd, Bristol
Printed in Great Britain at the
University Press, Cambridge

Library of Congress Cataloguing in Publication Data

Main entry under title:

Human ethology.

Includes bibliographies and index.

1. Psychology, Comparative.   2. Social psychology.
I. Cranach, Mario von.
BF671.H86   155   78–27330
ISBN 0 521 22320 2 hard covers
ISBN 0 521 29591 2 paperback

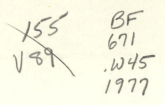

155
V89

BF
671
.W45
1977

Contents

6   Intra- and intergroup relationships in primates

PART III. ONTOGENY OF PRIMATE BEHAVIOUR

7   Development of social interaction

8   Cognitive development

11 Language development

To the memory of
Professor Dr Konrad Müller,
Chairman of the Werner-Reimers-Stiftung 1968–1979

Participants at the Werner-Reimers-Stiftung Conference on Human Ethology, Bad Homburg, West Germany, October 1977

Irwin Altman, *Department of Psychology, University of Utah*

Anthony J. Ambrose

Jürgen Aschoff, *Max-Planck-Institut für Verhaltensphysiologie, Erling-Andechs*

Albert Bandura, *Department of Psychology, Stanford University*

Dalbir Bindra, *Department of Psychology, McGill University*

William R. Charlesworth, *Institute of Child Development, University of Minnesota*

Mario von Cranach, *Psychologisches Institut, Universität Bern*

John H. Crook, *Department of Psychology, Bristol University*

Judy Dunn, *Sub-Department of Animal Behaviour, University of Cambridge*

Irenäus Eibl-Eibesfeldt, *Forschungsstelle für Humanethologie, Max-Planck-Institut für Verhaltensphysiologie, Seewiesen*

Paul Ekman, *Human Interaction Laboratory, Department of Psychiatry, University of California, San Francisco*

John P. Flynn, *Department of Psychiatry, Yale University*

Klaus Foppa, *Psychologisches Institut, Universität Bern*

James J. Fox, *Department of Anthropology and Sociology, Australian National University*

Derek Freeman, *Department of Anthropology and Sociology, Australian National University*

Maurice Godelier, *Laboratoire d'Anthropologie Sociale, Collège de France*

Erving Goffman, *Department of Anthropology and Sociology, University of Pennsylvania*

Jürgen Habermas, *Max-Planck-Institut zur Erforschung der Lebensbedingungen der wissenschaftlich-technischen Welt, Starnberg*

Rom Harré, *Sub-Faculty of Philosophy, University of Oxford*
Eckhard Hess, *Department of Behavioral Sciences, University of Chicago*
Robert A. Hinde, *Sub-Department of Animal Behaviour, University of Cambridge*
Adam Kendon, *Department of Anthropology and Sociology, Australian National University*
Hans Kummer, *Zoologisches Institut, Universität Zürich*
Wolf Lepenies, *Institut für Soziologie, Freie Universität Berlin*
Willem J. M. Levelt, *Projektgruppe für Psycholinguistik, Max-Planck-Gesellschaft zur Förderung der Wissenschaften e.V., Nijmegen*
Paul Leyhausen, *Arbeitsgruppe Wuppertal, Max-Planck-Institut für Verhaltensphysiologie, Wuppertal*
Alvin M. Liberman, *Haskins Laboratories, New Haven*
Thomas Luckmann, *Fachbereich Psychologie und Soziologie, Universität Konstanz*
Aubrey Manning, *Department of Zoology, University of Edinburgh*
Peter Marler, *Field Research Center, The Rockefeller University*
William A. Mason, *Department of Psychology, University of California, Davis*
Roger D. Masters, *Department of Government, Dartmouth College*
Glen McBride, *Animal Behaviour Unit, Department of Psychology, University of Queensland*
David McNeill, *Department of Behavioral Sciences, University of Chicago*
Konrad Müller, *Werner-Reimers-Stiftung, Bad Homburg*
Hanuš Papoušek, *Max-Planck-Institut für Psychiatrie, Munich*
Detlev Ploog, *Max-Planck-Institut für Psychiatrie, Munich*
Peter C. Reynolds, *Department of Anthropology and Sociology, Australian National University*
Vernon Reynolds, *Department of Biological Anthropology, University of Oxford*
Harriet L. Rheingold, *Department of Psychology, University of North Carolina*
Eric A. Salzen, *Department of Psychology, University of Aberdeen*
Henri Tajfel, *Department of Psychology, University of Bristol*
Lionel Tiger, *The Harry Frank Guggenheim Foundation, New York*
Colwyn Trevarthen, *Department of Psychology, University of Edinburgh*
Christian Vogel, *Institut für Anthropologie, Universität Göttingen*

Introduction

According to two of its most prominent founders, Konrad Lorenz and Nikolaas Tinbergen, the field of ethology can be defined as 'the Biology of Behaviour'. It places emphasis on the notion that the behaviour of animals and its physiological basis has evolved phylogenetically and should be studied as one aspect of evolution. The success of this endeavour led to the further attempt to apply ethological methods and the evolutionary perspective to psychological and sociological phenomena of human behaviour. However, the possibilities and limitations of 'Human Ethology', and the question of whether it may rightly be called a new discipline, are still a subject of debate. To mention only a few issues under discussion: What is the logic of inference from animal to human behaviour? Do culture and history provide the same conditions (in principal) for the development and determination of human behaviour as does the natural environment for animal behaviour? Are there typically human forms of behaviour which cannot be dealt with adequately in terms of (animal) ethology?

In view both of the interest shown in this field by scientists from many disciplines and its undoubted importance for a science of man, the Werner-Reimers-Stiftung – with the generous support of the Stiftung Volkswagenwerk – decided in 1975 to sponsor an international symposium under the title 'Human ethology – claims and limits of a new discipline'. Its main purpose was to bring together representatives from various fields of research with a common interest in analysing human behaviour who, at the same time, might not share the same basic assumptions or methodology, or place the same confidence in the usefulness of an ethological approach. The scientific board of the Werner-Reimers-

Stiftung asked Professors Jürgen Aschoff (Behavioural Physiology), chairman, Mario von Cranach (Social Psychology), Irenäus Eibl-Eibesfeldt (Human Ethology), Klaus Foppa (Psychology), Wolf Lepenies (Sociology) and Detlev Ploog (Neuro-Ethology) to act as members of an organizing committee. The committee agreed to focus the conference on three allied subjects for which eleven topics in all were selected (see the table of contents). For each topic, two contributors, whose viewpoints were expected to diverge, were asked to submit papers, and these were distributed to all participants in advance. In addition, a referee was asked to prepare a critical comment on the two papers. At the conference itself, the referee opened the discussion by commenting on the papers and by giving his own views. After short replies from the contributors, the general discussion began. This volume presents the papers of all contributors and referees but omits the discussions. Since the contents of the volume are therefore very rich and at the same time relatively diverse, it is not possible in this introduction to offer a synthesis, or even a simple outline; instead, we shall develop some very general ideas on the book's three parts, and on the field of human ethology in general.

1. Let us look then, in this way, at part I. The higher we place an organism on the evolutionary scale, the more we find that its behaviour is intimately connected with social affairs and is intrinsically social. It is therefore inevitable that a central concern in human ethology, both for the social and for the life sciences, is social behaviour. Although it is clear that we have not yet come to the point where an agreement about the relevance of ethological research for several other disciplines could easily be reached, it may nevertheless be useful to indicate the prospects for the social sciences of cooperation with human ethology and to formulate some 'results'. First of all, the debate over a possible theory of cultural or societal evolution, which plays such an important role in the social sciences today, makes it necessary to define the parallels, the distinctions and the relations between biological evolution and cultural evolution as precisely as possible. The conference, and especially the discussions, made it clear that human ethology is far from presenting a unified view of this problem, but it also became obvious that the frontier dividing those who believe in a theory of cultural evolution and those who believe that the term 'evolution' has only a biological application is not in any way identical with the frontier separating human ethologists and social scientists. It has, perhaps, been one of the most surprising, yet promising, results of the conference that lines of agreement and disagreement on

central topics of research are not necessarily those which form the boundaries of scientific disciplines.

Throughout the conference it became clear that human ethology, whether or not it is regarded as a discipline in the proper sense of the term, may well serve as a link between other disciplines, e.g. sociology and (cultural or social) anthropology. In the discussions on 'Property and territoriality', especially, human ethology at least seemed to provide some sort of common language, in which results from rather different disciplines might be 'translated' and thus fruitful comparisons made.

It is obvious that there are problem areas in the social sciences where ethological results must be taken into consideration. A sociological analysis of rituals, for instance, will have to rely at least on both ethnological and ethological research. There are areas of research in which such interdisciplinary relations would seem to be less necessary. The conference demonstrated, however, that even in regard to those problems which form the core of a well-defined disciplinary problem area, the perspective of human ethology might be useful – at least for a reformulation and perhaps more appropriate definition of central categories of research. In sociology, for instance, this holds true for the theory of action. On the other hand, it should be mentioned that throughout the conference a basic need for conceptual clarification was felt which could only partially be satisfied.

2. Although social topics play an important role in the papers of parts I and III of this volume, social behaviour and social organization are the specific topics of part II.

Clearly, only a selection from a tremendous range of possible problems could be presented in the programme. Strikingly (the more so perhaps because it was unintended), the focus is at the level of the individual; in all three sections of part II, interaction and particularly social organization are considered mainly in so far as they reflect the individual input into the social situation. The emphasis is on 'the organization of individual social behaviour'. This may represent a current trend in ethological thinking; it certainly reflects the line of contact and debate between ethology and the human behavioural and social sciences.

With regard to basic organizing principles of individual social behaviour, there was some agreement in the assumption that both social behaviour and social organization emerge from basic approach–avoidance tendencies, namely aggression, fear and attachment. These tendencies constitute, in their complicated structure and interplay, basic social needs in the individual animal, including man. On the other hand, it was also apparent that the disciplines concerned were often neither in agreement nor disagreement, since they have yet to meet on common ground. As the discussion on aggression (section 5) made clear, there was no common viewpoint between, for example, psychological and ethological behaviour analysis and the possibilities of neurophysiology, or – and this constitutes the more important example – between a behavioural and social science, where at this moment a unifying principle is emerging in cognition, and an ethology in which, due to its traditions and methods, cognition cannot yet play a major role. Thus, in section 6, which was concerned with social relationship, the influence of sociobiology was made clear in the elaboration of the benefits an individuum gains from his partner in the perspective of primatology. On the other hand, the role of cognitive processes was emphasized when a research strategy for human intergroup conflict was developed in which a 'distal' analysis of the historical, economic and biological basis of intergroup conflict was replaced by a so-called 'proximal' analysis.

Looking back at part II, we see that the approach of ethology and the other behavioural sciences to problems of social behaviour and organization is still far from integrated, but that the borders of this field are emerging and that some of the future lines of debate are becoming clearer. Again, the role of cognition will be one of the important issues in the organization of human individual and social behaviour.

3. Ethology has contributed in two particular ways to our understanding of the ontogeny of behaviour in man and ape. This has resulted, first, from the application of techniques for the precise observation, description and classification of naturally occurring behaviour and, secondly, from the ethological approach to the study of behaviour, especially the development of behaviour in terms of evolution. Of particular interest to the ethologist are questions relating to the function of a particular kind of behaviour, e.g. attachment behaviour, and its adaptive value. The description of the behavioural repertoire of a species, the recognition of patterns of behavioural development and the classification of established behavioural patterns are prerequisites for any comparison between different species or between organisms of a single species. The ethological approach is to study the interaction between the organism with certain innate species-specific structures and the environment for which the organism is genetically programmed. It can be regarded as an established fact today that the human infant has cognitive abilities at birth and

interacts with environmental stimuli even in his first days of life in ways which he cannot have learned, just as it is now considered a fact that within the framework of his innate abilities the newborn immediately begins to learn to adapt to different environmental conditions. The contributions to part III on ontogeny demonstrate convincingly the methodological and theoretical difficulties confronting the student of human behaviour interested in determining where behaviour shows plasticity and variability and where there are invariant behaviour patterns.

It must be assumed that invariant behaviour patterns – those which remain relatively stable in the presence of variations in environment – have a morphological basis, mainly in neuronal structures, which is common to all members of a species and, depending on the kind of behaviour, may also be common to a genus or family or a whole order, e.g. the primates, or even to a whole class, e.g. the vertebrates. In such structures we can retrace and follow the evolutionary process by which the environment has produced structures, especially nervous systems and brains, which generate adaptive behaviour. In organisms with a high level of organization, the processes in which the ethologist is especially interested are those genetically preprogrammed motor and perceptual processes that facilitate social interaction and communication, such as facial expression and vocalization. If we consider the most highly developed means of communication, language and speech, which is found in man alone, the question arises as to the biological foundation of this species-specific behaviour and perceptual skill. The ethologist examines this question primarily from the point of view of ontogenetic development.

In the preceding paragraphs, we have already referred to some of the merits and also the shortcomings of human ethology. Are the claims of the new discipline justified, and what are its limits? We are scarcely in a position to act as arbiters, yet it may be considered our duty to attempt a restricted and cautious evaluation.

The main strength of human ethology is that its approach to old problems is a new one; from the basis of theories, concepts and methods that have proved successful in animal ethology, it has looked at man from a new viewpoint. The essence of this is of course the evolutionary perspective; but since ethologists have been relatively unaffected by the long history of the humanities, they have often referred to facts and interpretations, perhaps obvious, but neglected by other social sciences, in an apparently naive but very effective manner. Another strength seems to lie in its integrative power. If we look back at the history of the relationship between the life sciences and the social sciences, we find two prevailing modes of theoretical orientation: on the one hand, reductionism, i.e. attempts to reduce human action to animal-like behaviour; and on the other, attempts to separate human action and human society completely from the animal world. The advent of evolutionism in the nineteenth century brought no easy solution to the traditional nature–nurture problem, since it could still be 'solved' in either a continuous or discontinuous manner. It seems as if human ethology, more perhaps than any other 'discipline', has significantly contributed to the disappearance of such simple dichotomies.

However, the contributions of human ethology may give rise to certain dangerous fallacies. First, the desire to make a fresh start can easily lead to the neglect of methods and findings of other disciplines which have their own validity. Consequently, human ethologists may sometimes simply ignore earlier findings about a particular problem, and the methods that have been developed to study it; this can result in the other disciplines concerned overreacting and discarding completely the ethological viewpoint. The second and major difficulty, which has still to be overcome, is a related problem. After all, human behaviour is specific and cannot be considered without taking into consideration, for example, cognitive and cultural processes. It is, therefore, essential to integrate these specifically human characteristics and the general biological human nature, which will only be possible if both these viewpoints and their findings are taken seriously and studied as an integrated system. The emerging descriptions and explanations will be neither truly psychological, sociological, ethnological not ethological, but something new. This integration has as yet hardly been attempted; if it should ever be successful, human ethology will be no longer ethology applied to man, but a science of its own: a new discipline.

A meeting of scientists who differ widely in their opinions and the ways in which they pursue their research certainly runs the risk of achieving little through lack of communication. In fact, the papers as they are published in this volume may appear to the reader a fairly diverse collection. However, attention should be paid to where reconciliation emerges. The general feeling one gets from the sum of the contributions is that some of the areas of misunderstanding have been clarified, and that interdisciplinary cooperation can contribute substantially to a better understanding of a science of man – even if there are no definite answers to the many questions asked at the conference and to the main question stated in its title.

The editors wish to thank Agnes von Cranach for her invaluable help in preparing and editing this book.

Part I

Phylogenetic and cultural ritualization

1. Functions of rituals

1.1. Ritual and ritualization from a biological perspective[1]

IRENÄUS EIBL–EIBESFELDT

I. The use of the term 'ritual' in biological and anthropological science

'Exhibited by all known societies, ritual is a specific, observable kind of behaviour based upon established or traditional rules. It is thus possible to view ritual as a way of defining or describing man' (*Encyclopaedia Britannica*, vol. 15, 1974).

Ethologists, however, have also spoken of ritual and ritualization ever since the term was introduced into biology by Huxley (1914, 1923)[2] to describe a particular class of animal behavior patterns and the process by which they originated. Is this procedure justified? Does what is called ritual behavior in man share common features with that in animals and are both governed by similar laws associated with analogous functions? Our thesis is that this is indeed the case.

Ritual behavior in man was first attributed by anthropologists to the realm of religion and myth. A characteristic of ritual in this more general sense is its symbolic nature. It can be considered as a system of acts which are structured according to rules of convention between actor and addressee. And it is this particular symbolic nature which modern social

---

[1] This paper will often refer to the concepts of ethology, but lack of space means that such references must be sketchy. A more detailed discussion, with particular reference to their relevance for the study of human behavior, may be found in Eibl-Eibesfeldt (in press; see also 1975a). These publications contain numerous references to works in human ethology. However a recent work by Morris (1977), which came to my attention after this paper was completed, is of particular relevance to the subject under discussion (expressive behavior).

[2] In these papers Huxley describes the courtship movements of the birds which he studied for ceremonies and rituals. In 1966 he organized a 'Discussion on ritualization of behavior in animals and man' in which the term ritualization and ritual was applied to both.

3

anthropologists refer to when they speak of greeting rituals, rituals of encounter, and the like (Goffman 1963).

When biologists started to use the term, they had this symbolic characteristic in mind, as they still do. Rituals (*Symbolhandlungen* in German) are behavior patterns which serve the function of communication and which undergo changes in the service of this function that enhance their communicative value. In other words, rituals have a signalling function which they acquire by a process called ritualization. When we speak of courtship rituals, greeting rituals, fighting rituals etc., we thus refer to a complex set of behavior patterns structured according to certain rules, whereas when we speak of the single acts involved in such a ritual we refer to expressive patterns or expressive movements. For all levels of organization the term ritualization is used when we refer to the process by which these patterns originate.

II. Adaptation and function – two key terms of biology

Any structure (morphological structure, behavior pattern etc.) which contributes in terms of reproductive success to the survival of the species is by definition adaptive. For the process of phylogenetic evolution mutations provide the variability of the phenotype on which selection operates, variants in behavior being often pace-makers in evolution (Mayr 1970).

In the process of evolution organisms 'adapt' themselves to features of the external world. The features which affect the organisms make up reality and since the organisms are shaped by selective pressure to fit them to this reality, it follows that organisms reflect or depict certain features of the outer world in their adaptations. The hoof of a horse, as Lorenz (1973) pointed out, depicts certain features of the steppe.

Adaptation can take place during phylogeny. The process can be considered as a process of information-acquisition by the adapting system. The information is stored in the genome and decoded during ontogeny. An analogous process takes place in man during cultural evolution in historical dimensions. Since similar selection pressures operate in both processes, phylogenetic and cultural evolution share a number of features.

Biological and cultural evolution proceed on the basis of balanced interplay of progressive and conservative principles. Mutations only affect a minute percentage of the genetic heritage. Experimentation is limited in each generation and thus most of what has been so far proved to be adaptive remains the same. Similarly, humans are fond of traditional ways. They do not like to throw overboard the beloved customs which provide subjective security. It takes the dynamic of the young to push through new ideas and lifestyles, particularly where our social conduct is concerned. The clear advantage of technical improvements is taken over with less hesitation.

The fear, often superstitious, of discarding completely ingrained customs is adaptive since the majority of traditional customs certainly do not lose adaptedness from one generation to the next (see Campbell 1975 and Lorenz 1973), and a complete break in tradition would very probably be maladaptive.

The term function, widely used in biology, relates to adaptation. The question used to be asked: What function does a structure (behavior pattern) fulfil? And it meant: In what ways does the structure contribute to the survival of the species? This is not just a matter of speculation, but can be tested empirically (Tinbergen 1965, Tinbergen *et al.* 1962, 1967). A functional approach also exists in anthropology which tries to explain – along very similar lines – a behavior in relation to the maintenance of a society. We can indeed ask what function a greeting ritual fulfils and can check it by experimentation.[3]

III. The nature–nurture issue

The nature–nurture issue centers on the question of whether a structure owes its *specific adaptedness* to a process of phylogenetic, cultural or individual adaptation. In the realm of behavior the traditional ethologists of the Lorenzian–Tinbergen group stress the importance of such a distinction, but some ethologists, calling themselves interactionists, argue that such a distinction is only theoretical. Phylogenetically and individually acquired patterns are said to intermingle in such a way that neither can be distinguished and the term 'innate', as applied to behavior patterns, can therefore be of no heuristic value. Finally individual adaptation of behavior by learning from experience takes place. Specific phylogenetic adaptations are a prerequisite for learning with the result of adaptation taking place, which determines, for example, what is rewarding for a species (see learning disposition, p. 8). Lorenz (1966b) has argued

---

[3] The intended and actual function of cultural rituals have to be distinguished. The intended function of the Hopi rain dance is certainly fictive. The observer can, nonetheless, distinguish actual functions that the ritual fulfils, e.g. it contributes to the group cohesion and helps to reinforce group identity.

against this point of view, by pointing to the adaptedness of the observed behavior patterns. If we find in an organism a structure which mimics an environmental feature, we have to assume, as mentioned above, that the former acquired information about the feature which it depicts. We know that there are only limited ways by which such acquisition of information can take place. If the organism is deprived of patterned information concerning the environmental feature, and it nonetheless continues to manifest the adaptation in question, then phylogenetic adaptation is proven. For example, if we want to know whether the species-specific songs of a bird-species are individually or phylogenetically acquired, we must just raise the bird in social isolation in a sound-proof chamber. If, at onset of sexual maturity, the bird nonetheless sings the species-specific songs, it has been proved that this specific patterning is a result of phylogenetic adaptation. The network of neurons in connection with sensory and effector organs which is responsible for this patterned motor output develops in a process of selfdifferentiation according to the recipes (or blueprint) encoded in the genome of the species. For brevity we call the resulting pattern innate. Of course, there are environmental prerequisites necessary for such a development to take place, for example, oxygen and nutrition. But these do not contain the patterned information concerning the adaptation in question.

If our discussants argue that strictly speaking there are no innate behavior patterns, we would agree. The term is sloppy. Behavior patterns develop, but what must be recognized is that they do so within a range of variability determined by the genome.

IV. Phylogenetic adaptations in behavior

Behavior is determined in various ways by phylogenetic adaptations.

1. Inborn motor patterns (fixed action patterns)

Animals are as a rule born or hatched with a number of functional motor patterns. Newly hatched ducks walk, swim, grease their feathers, dabble mud and they do so even when brooded by a hen. Gnus can run shortly after being born and newborn whales swim perfectly well.

A number of patterns mature during ontogeny, e.g. the complicated and highly specific courtship movements of the mallards. They show up at sexual maturity even if the animal is deprived of any opportunity to learn them from a conspecific.

Fixed action patterns are often linked to orientation movements (taxis; Lorenz and Tinbergen 1938). Innate and learned movement patterns are often integrated to form a functional whole, as can be demonstrated in the nut-opening technique of the squirrel (Eibl-Eibesfeldt 1963).

2. *Innate releasing mechanisms, key stimuli and releasers*

Behavior patterns are, as a rule, released by specific stimuli. Visual stimuli release the prey-catching response of a frog, mating calls of the male frogs orient the female toward them.

It has been demonstrated by a great number of experiments that the capacity to respond to specific environmental stimuli in such a way can take place without prior conditioning. Thus the newly metamorphosed frog will launch its tongue at any small moving object. In an experimental situation this response can be released by moving a small pebble. In order for such selective responses to occur, it must be assumed that animals possess detector devices tuned during phylogeny toward the perception of specific stimuli. These data processing mechanisms have been termed innate releasing mechanisms or innate templates (Lorenz 1943, Tinbergen 1951). The studies of Maturana *et al.* (1960) and Ewert (1973, 1974a, 1974b) provide well-grounded data about the basic features of such mechanisms.

If it is of mutual importance for both participants in an interaction that particular responses in one are triggered by signals of the other, then mutual adaptations between the sender and the receiver of a signal develop. The sender develops structures and behavior patterns which serve as signals and the receiver tunes his receiving mechanisms toward them. The signals thus evolved are called releasers. The process by which behavior patterns acquire their signalling function is called ritualization (p. 14).

3. *Drives (internal motivating mechanisms)*

Drive is first of all a descriptive term. Its use does not imply unitary motivating mechanisms but simply refers to the fact that an internal variable in addition to external factors causes fluctuations in the individual's readiness to act. Inner sensory stimuli, hormones and neurogenic activity may cause an animal to seek in appetitive behavior the release of stimulus situations allowing the performance of particular behaviors. Animals as a rule do not just wait for events to happen, but seek actively for a mate, prey, rival, nesting material etc. It is therefore customary to speak of hunger, thirst and the like, referring to the motivational state of an animal, or to speak of sexual or aggressive drive.

Because the same terms are used to describe a motivational state of two animals as different as a blowfly and a dog, one might get the misleading impression that the mechanisms involved are homologous. This is certainly not always the case. The internal motivating mechanisms behind food intake are in fact constructed very differently in the blowfly and in the dog.

4. Learning disposition

According to Skinner, reward and punishment shape an organism's behavior, and thus it should be possible to extinguish any habit through punishment. This is often the case, but not always. If a cock is punished by an electric shock whenever it displays aggression, its aggressive behavior will be dropped and, as a consequence, the cock will assume a low-ranking position within his group. However, if a cock is punished with the same electric shock whenever it shows low-ranking submissive behavior, its submissive behavior will not simply be dropped, but rather it will show even more submission (Euler, in press).

It is well known to ethologists that animals do not learn everything with the same ease and at the same time. They learn what contributes to their survival and this differs from species to species; animals thereby demonstrate particular species-specific learning dispositions. To modify behavior individually in an adaptive way seems to require complicated programs, which in part explains why this capacity develops comparatively late in evolution, lower animals showing a more limited capacity to adapt individually.

A learning disposition which has been thoroughly studied is 'imprinting', first described by Lorenz (1935; see also Immelmann 1966, 1967, 1970).

V. The comparative approach

One important characteristic of the ethological approach is the comparative method. A number of excellent publications have dealt with the subject (Wickler 1967, von Cranach 1976), but not all behavioral scientists have yet reached agreement as to what can be compared and what can be derived from such comparisons. This is obvious from the frequent comments that ethologists make 'unjustified' extrapolations from animal to human behavior.

The comparative method in behavioral sciences dates back to Darwin. But he was much in advance of his time and only decades later were similar methods rediscovered. Heinroth (1910) studied the taxonomy of ducks and thereby found that movement patterns of courtship could be used for grouping the species according to closeness of relationship (Lorenz 1941).

Indeed, inborn motor patterns can be studied as characteristics of taxonomic groups like organs. By applying the criteria of homology as elaborated by morphologists (see Remane 1952),[4] students of animal behavior are in a position to find out whether a similar behavior pattern, observed to exist in two or more species, is based on a common heritage from a shared ancestral form or evolved independently. In the former case we classify the patterns as homologous, in the latter as analogous.

As far as man–animal comparison is concerned, it is often argued that only the study of our closely related primates can be of any explanatory value, and that nothing worthwhile will be achieved from the study of distantly related species such as greylag geese or cichlid fishes. Such arguments are certainly based on the mistaken assumption that it is only worthwhile studying homologies. The study of analogies, however, as Wickler has emphasized, can sometimes contribute more to the understanding of behavior than the study of homologies. Analogies inform us about the selection pressures that independently shape patterns along similar lines. We thus learn what rules derived from function govern the evolution of a certain structure or behavior pattern independently of any phylogenetic relationship. For example: If a functional morphologist is interested in finding out which laws govern the construction of wings, he is certainly justified in studying wings in as many different species as possible, particularly unrelated ones. Nobody will question, I believe, that the correct procedure in this case is to study insect wings, which are constructed from ancuticular folds, and bird and bat wings, which are modified vertebrate extremities. And he may even proceed to compare these organs with the man-made wing of an aeroplane. The well-established field of biotechnics flourishes from such comparison and has promoted technical developments. Turning to behavior, it is certainly legitimate to ask what selection pressures bring about monogamy or

---

[4] The main criteria are (a) criterion of the specific form, (b) criterion of specific position within the contextual patterning, (c) linkage by intermediate form. Remane also lists a number of auxiliary criteria.

ranking behavior in various species and what laws govern their development and their specific patterning. Thus, it is certainly advisable to study a phenomenon in its manifestations in as many different species as possible and not just in closely related primates.

VI. Expressive movements and their origin – the process of ritualization

Expressive movements are behavior patterns which have signal functions. The threat posture of a mantis, the lateral display of a cichlid fish, the courtship display of a pheasant cock and the smile of a human being fall into this category. These behavioral elements are usually incorporated into more complex behavioral events for which the term ritual is customary (courtship rituals, fighting rituals, greeting rituals and the like).[5] Expressive movements and rituals thus refer to different levels of integration. In a ritual expressive movements are integrated in a more complex event which is structured in a rule-governed way.

As to the origin of these patterns we can distinguish between phylogenetically evolved, culturally acquired, and individually invented signals. The criteria of homology are applicable to phylogenetically as well as to culturally evolved signals. The method of tracing homologies in language is in principle the same as that applied by morphologists. We distinguish between phylogenetic homologies and homologies of tradition (Wickler 1967).

In reconstructing the phylogeny of behavior patterns we have to rely primarily on the comparison of living species since fossil evidence is lacking. This is less of a disadvantage than it may at first seem, once we realize that morphologists must often apply the same method when reconstructing the phylogeny of organs made from soft tissue, which rarely leaves fossil evidence. The process of evolution was in fact discovered by comparing living species, following Darwin's observations on the variability of species in the living Galápagos Island finches. Even if fossil evidence were not available, the process of evolution could be determined by the often finely graded similarity of species allowing comparisons to be made between advanced and primitive features in the development of organs. Comparative embryology is another source of information since aspects of embryology or ontogeny often repeat phylogeny.

Expressive behavior serves the function of communication. This does

[5] 'Ceremony' is often used synonymously.

not mean that a message is necessarily consciously intended by the sender of the signal. If someone shivers, as he does not necessarily intend to communicate 'I am cold' or 'afraid', but the perceiver of the behavior may recognize the mood of the sender and either learn to attach significance to it or phylogenetically adapt to it.

In order for a signal to acquire the function of communication, it is necessary that its precursor should consistently accompany a certain emotional state providing a fairly reliable indicator of it. It is thus the receiver who attaches a 'meaning' to a given pattern (signal). If it is actually advantageous for him to read and interpret a signal, his detector devices will be tuned appropriately. If it is advantageous for the signal sender to be more thoroughly understood, the selection pressure exerted by his partner will lead to mutual adaptation, and the sender will then adapt too by developing more easily comprehensible signals. There are a variety of preadaptations from which the evolution of signals may originate. They range from (a) functional acts which change in their function, to (b) movements expressing intention which precede an act, (c) displacement activities, and (d) pure epiphenomena of excitation. A few examples may illustrate the above.

1. Examples of functional acts which change in their function can be seen in developments from parental behavior. Since parental behavior clearly indicates friendly intent, it is not particularly surprising that such patterns are repeatedly and independently used to establish contact or strengthen a bond between adults, thereby changing or extending their function to one of creating bonds. More specifically, infantile appeals which release such actions as parental feeding are used in birds and mammals during courtship and in greeting rituals, although in these cases it is the friendly intent, not the actual transferral of food, which is most important.

It has been observed in many species of finches that courting males behave 'childishly'. They flutter their wings, gape and utter begging sounds as if they were nestlings begging for food, and, indeed, the response of the prospective mate is feeding. In the course of evolution this behavior was often modified into a symbolic act: bullfinches do not feed each other during courtship, but often just nibble at each other's beak (*Schnabelflirt*; Nicolai 1956). And in a similar way the mouth to mouth feeding, a form of parental feeding in some mammals, developed into various forms of kissfeeding or muzzling and finally, in man and chimpanzees, into the act of kissing (see p. 21).

Schenkel (1956) provided an illuminating example of this stepwise change into a more symbolic act in his analysis of pheasant courtship which is based upon food-enticing.

In a similar fashion, elaborate displays serving the function of bonding have evolved from patterns of nestbuilding or grooming. Grooming is an important part of parental behavior and therefore preadapted for use when adults want to express friendly intent. It occurs in this context either in its original form, such as licking, combing another's fur with one's teeth, etc., or in a more ritualized form, such as that used by the Mongoz lemur, who, when greeting a conspecific, performs licking movements and fur combing movements of the lower jaw in the air, without establishing bodily contact. Ritualized nestbuilding behavior plays a most important role in many birds who present each other with nesting material, or perform nestbuilding movements in a stylized form. The blue-footed booby of the Galápagos Islands no longer engages in nestbuilding but in nuptial displays still uses a ceremony of passing nesting material (Eibl-Eibesfeldt 1977a).

Functional patterns like, for example, female presentation before copulation in mammals, also developed signalling characteristics which came to be used in a wider context. These are accompanied by morphological changes which have been investigated in primates by Wickler (1966). In some primates the skin around the vaginal orifice becomes swollen and conspicuously colored during oestrus. Since female presenting buffers aggression in males, the presentation pattern in many species expands to include the more generalized function of appeasing and is incorporated into greeting behavior. The pattern has subsequently become incorporated into the males' behavioral repertoire: low-ranking baboons, for example, present in front of high-ranking ones. Hamadryas male baboons imitate the females' swellings in nearly perfect mimicry. The males' hairless buttocks are as brilliantly red-colored as those of females in oestrus.

2. Intention movements are usually understood as behavior patterns which regularly precede an act. For example, before a bird takes off, it performs movements with its neck, aiming in the direction of intended flight; before a hamster attacks, it often raises itself on its hind legs; and before biting, many mammals open their mouths to display their intention. Many threat displays are derived from the latter. Cats open their mouth and expose their teeth when threatening. Marine iguanas, when displaying in front of a rival, open their mouths widely to show they intend to bite. Teeth-threatening displays can be seen to have evolved, in further ritualization, into submissive and even friendly signals, e.g.

silent display of bared teeth, fear grin and friendly smile (van Hooff 1971).

Since in an encounter situation intentions of both approach and with-drawal are frequently released (see p. 49), we often find both combined in an expressive pattern. In the stickleback a head-down posture results from the conflict of the tendencies to approach and retreat, since the animal retreats in front, but continues to propel his body with his tail. The courtship display of the stickleback, the so-called 'zigzag dance', evolved from the simultaneously motivated tendency to approach the female and to swim to the nest prepared beforehand. In convergent evolution the nuptial display of the male damselfish (*Dascyllus aruanus*) evolved from the tendencies to approach the female and to swim toward the coral. The same is true for the dance by which the cleaner fish (*Labroides dimidiatus*) invites his host-fishes to stay and to be cleaned. The more fear-motivated the cleaner fish is, the more the downward component of his dance is emphasized, showing that the downward component is clearly a flight-motivated behavior. Other examples in which two conflicting intention movements are combined in a new behavior pattern of expression are described in the literature, the most famous example, perhaps, being the inciting display of ducks as analyzed by Lorenz (1941).

3. Behavior patterns which occur out of context, when one specific activity of an animal is thwarted, are termed displacement activities. Cocks, for example, who threaten each other but are too inhibited to attack, vigorously peck the ground as if searching for food. In many species of mammals preening movements occur when other behavior is thwarted. The original explanation for the occurrence of behavior patterns not conforming to the function of the originally activated drive, was that central energy, inhibited from discharging normally, flared over into another activity and thus found its outlet. Although some cases may be explained thus, other explanations have been provided, for example, that the conflict of two drives blocking each other liberates a third drive which has so far been blocked. What may wrongly be called 'displacement nesting' could, upon closer examination, prove to be a demonstration of locality ownership and thus indicate to the addressee a stronger motivation to fight. Whatever the processes underlying displacement activities may be, such out-of-context activities with no apparent function do occur with great regularity, and often presumably as a by-process of neuronic events. Numerous examples of such displacement activities being changed into expressive patterns are provided in the literature. Displacement preening occurs as a regular courtship movement in male

ducks. With increasing ritualization, special wing feathers have evolved as an organ of vanity to be preened in front of the female.

4. Displacement activities can already be considered as epiphenomena accompanying a state of excitation. Other epiphenomena are trembling from excitation, blushing, sweating, changes in the secretory activity of external glands and the like. If they accompany an event regularly enough, they can serve as indicators and then be changed into signals. In many rodents, for example, the tail trembles when the animal is aggressively excited. In a number of species the movement has become independently ritualized into a signal of threat, as in the porcupine which developed hollow spines that beat together during display, producing a loud rattling sound. Darwin, who provided the example, also traces the evolution of the rattlesnake's rattle back to an analogous epiphenomenon widespread among snakes. In a similar fashion blushing has led to the development of highly vasculated skin parts and special presenting movements. Further examples can be found in Morris (1956) and Eibl-Eibesfeldt (1956).

VII. Analogous changes of behavior during biological and cultural ritualization

Ritualization is the process by which non-communicative behavior patterns evolve into signals. The term 'semantization' has been proposed by Wickler (1967) to encompass all processes which lead to an improvement of communication. This can take place from the sender (semantization from the sender) which is then called ritualization.

As mentioned above, during the process of ritualization behavior patterns *change in their function*. Food-enticing in the various *Phasianids* becomes a signal, the movements of swimming toward the female and toward the nest in the stickleback become a courtship dance. Furthermore, a *change of motivation* can be observed; in baboons, for example, the female sexual presenting posture is incorporated in the male repertoire of behavior and used as a greeting ritual. In addition, movements experience a number of changes directly related to the signalling function. Signals have to be conspicuous and at the same time simple and precise so as not to be misunderstood. This is achieved by the following changes:

1. The movements become *exaggerated* in frequency and amplitude.
2. They become *stereotyped* and *simplified* by the dropping of some of the original components and the exaggeration of others.
3. *Variable movement sequences* of often antithetic intent *become fused* into a

stereotyped single movement pattern (invitation dance of the cleaner fish, zigzag dance of the male stickleback).

4. *Rhythmic repetition* enhances the visual effectiveness of the pattern.
5. Components of *orientation* are sometimes changed (inciting in ducks).
6. Sometimes movement patterns are performed with a constant *typical intensity*. In this manner the behavior patterns become less ambiguous (Morris 1957). Some courtship movements of ducks illustrate this principle.
7. Movements may *'freeze'* into postures: attacking movements, for example, often have developed into threat postures.
8. The *threshold values* for the stimuli releasing the pattern often *change* in such a way that the more ritualized the behavior, the more easily it is released (Daanje 1950, Oehlert 1958).
9. Along with the above, behavioral changes frequently cause the development of additional bodily structures which emphasize the display, for examples plumes, manes, brightly coloured skin patches or fins which unfold to sails.
10. Expressive patterns with opposing intentionality in emphasis of contrast get ritualized in clear antithesis. A marine iguana will raise itself on all its feet and make itself as large as possible in aggressive display, but will drop flat on its belly in submission. This principle of antithesis was discovered by Darwin.
11. Several expressive patterns can be combined, each in varying stages of intensity, thus giving rise to a great variety of expressions, which nonetheless can be reduced to a few variables (Lorenz 1953). Simultaneous combination results in superposition. In cases of alternative combination the animal (or man, see p. 49) may oscillate between the antithetic patterns.

There are similarities between phylogenetically and culturally evolved patterns of expression, which is not particularly surprising. The selection pressures in both cases operate along similar lines. In general these patterns have to fulfil the criteria of being conspicuous, unmistakable and at the same time fairly simple as signals. Mimic exaggeration by emphasis of movement amplitude, simplification, rhythmic repetition, fusion of elements into new patterns and emphasis by additional structures of adornment are also principles in the cultural evolution of ritualistic behavior. An example of this can be seen in the courtship ritual 'Tanim Het', for which film records were carefully analyzed by Pitcairn and Schleidt (1976). This courtship ritual of the Mbowamb of New Guinea serves the function of synchronizing prospective marriage partners and establishing closer acquaintanceships much as we do at a dance. For this occasion the couples, beautifully painted in patterns typical of the tribe and adorned with plumes of birds of paradise and the green leaves of the sacred Cordyline plant, sit side by side in one of the houses. Relatives of the girls sit in attendance as 'chaperones'. The males sway their bodies in slow motion to a chant and as they address the girls faster head-swaying motions are superimposed. A girl thus addressed will finally answer by a similar swaying. The young man then will try to establish contact between his forehead and hers. If she reacts to this by maintaining contact both will bow deeply twice, in almost perfect synchrony. Then they turn towards each other, establish contact with their foreheads and turn their heads to left and right while remaining in contact, rubbing noses together. Immediately after the couple will twice bow again, and so on, in a smooth uninterrupted sequence. The elements of bowing and turning are fused together in a stereotyped sequence, emphasized in amplitude of movement and by rhythmic repetition, and accentuated by the movement of their head plumage. Bowing and head-turning may be repeated as often as twenty-five times. Then, if the girl wants to indicate her more intimate engagement, she will bow several times in succession. Pitcairn and Schleidt (1976) analyzed in detail the principle by which the synchronization of the couple takes place. The derivation of the single movements is only partly known. Head-turning appears to be very much related to the nose-rubbing which occurs as a sign of affection in many parts of the Malayan-Melanesian, Papuan and Polynesian regions and which in turn appears to be derived from sniffing (Eibl-Eibesfeldt 1973). The origin of bowing cannot be reconstructed, however, because intermediate stages have not yet been discovered. We can only speculate about its possible origin. It could, for example, have had its origin in a bow of consent.

Similar regularities of rhythmic repetitions can be observed in many other rituals: dancing, funeral or military parades. Ritualization at all levels seems to share these features. The way in our society pallbearers march carrying a coffin is highly stylized, and the same is true for the way people walk at an inauguration ceremony. At the river Ganges in India I was impressed by the highly stylized washing rituals of the pilgrims. The elements – some of which were clearly recognizable as simplified washing patterns – were amalgamated with those of other origins into a religious ceremony. Rhythmic repetition of the elements as well as exaggeration and simplification of the movement patterns were again basic characteristics.

Aside from these more general similarities, detailed analogies reflecting the same principles at a more specific level are to be found. Rituals which fulfil more specific, everyday functions provide comparable examples.

Let us take rituals of intended friendly encounter, which we call greeting rituals. The flightless cormorant, for example, engages in such a ritual by passing over nesting material to its mate; other birds achieve the same by passing food. The European stork turns his beak toward his back and clatters, a behavior that is just the opposite of a threat, where the beak as a weapon is turned toward the opponent. Sometimes, however, even patterns of threat are used in greeting rituals, but usually with a new orientation demonstrating again peaceful intent. Greylag geese greet each other with a special triumph ceremony which is basically a threat posture. The necks outstretched as if in threat do not however point toward each other, but in a course past each other, as if both were displaying at a third imagined enemy. The anthropomorphic translation of this would be that they are united in threat against a joint enemy. To provide a final example, low-ranking male Barbary macaques, who want to establish friendly contact with a high-ranking male or strangers, or who want to be adopted into another group, both situations where there is danger of attack, will borrow a baby monkey and carry it with them during approach (Deag and Crook 1971). It appears that the signals sent by the child buffer the aggression of the others and acquaintanceship is thus established.

I can demonstrate that we can find analogies to all these rituals in human greeting rituals (Eibl-Eibesfeldt 1973). In the more elaborated rituals, several of the appeals just mentioned often occur in a stylized form. A visitor of state is first greeted by ritualized aggression: he is given a ten-gun salute and the guard of honor presents arms before him. At the same time the visitor is greeted by a child (a formal documentation of peaceful intent) who presents him with a bouquet of flowers. Finally the visitor may be embraced and kissed on the cheek by his host. These cultural rituals start from similar preadaptations in both man and animals and have evolved along similar lines, due to analogous selection pressures.

VIII. Phylogenetic and culturally evolved signals in man

1. Phylogenetic roots of human expressive behavior

Over a hundred years ago Darwin pointed to the possibility that a number of facial expressions are inborn in man, but his statements as to this possibility have been ignored. Until quite recently a number of psychologists and anthropologists representing the environmentalist position emphasized that nothing is inborn in man 'except perhaps a few reflexes of the newborn' (Montagu 1962). This viewpoint is also expressed in the well-known work of LaBarre, who wrote: 'The anthropologist is wary of those who speak of an "instinctive" gesture on the part of a human being' (LaBarre 1947:49). He consolidates this statement by pointing out variables which have to be accepted as cultural, and finally includes in this list even laughing and smiling.

Smiling, indeed [he writes], I have found may almost be mapped after the fashion of any other culture trait; and laughter is in some senses a geographic variable. On a map of the Southwest Pacific one could perhaps even draw lines between areas of 'Papuan hilarity' and others where a Cobuan, Melanesian dourness reigned. In Africa Gorer noted that laughter is used by the negro to express surprise, wonder, embarrassment and even discomfiture; it is not necessarily, or even often, a sign of amusement; the significance given to 'black laughter' is due to a mistake of supposing that similar symbols have identical meaning. Thus it is that even if the physiological behavior be present, its cultural and emotional functions may differ. Indeed, even within the same culture, the laughter of adolescent girls and the laughter of corporation presidents can be functionally different things. (p. 52)

On p. 55 LaBarre finally writes: 'There is no natural language of emotional gesture.'

To date I have been unable to locate data, apart from these anecdotal remarks, which back this statement. LaBarre does not provide any statistical data on Papuan or Melanesian laughter; he evidently depended on his subjective impression.

Probably there are differences in the spectrum of meanings of certain expressions from culture to culture but, in order to find out, a statistical analysis based on data is needed. This is not provided by LaBarre and, to my knowledge, has not been provided for any culture so far. The cross-cultural evidence, however, indicates that aside perhaps from minor cultural differences there exists basic agreement about certain meanings of an expression across cultures. People may cry in a situation of extreme enjoyment in some cultures, but in all cultures children cry in distress (e.g. when they hurt themselves) and, even though people may smile sardonically, in most cultures they express friendly feelings this way. The studies of Ekman and Friesen (1971) clearly show that these expressions are cross-culturally understood. Illiterate Papuans were perfectly capable of correctly interpreting the videotape recordings of numerous facial expressions from another culture which they were shown. To illustrate the extent of detail for which there is agreement, I will provide some examples from our cross-cultural studies, but first I would like to present evidence from ontogenic investigations which support the hypothesis of the innateness of some of the patterns in question.

The evidence is derived from the study of those born deaf and blind, who are deprived by their handicap of visual and auditory knowledge about the facial expressions of their fellow men, and who, nonetheless, exhibit the patterns of crying, laughing, smiling. The argument that there is a high probability that these patterns will occur accidentally (because there are only a limited number of muscles that can contract) does not hold up under examination. If we consider the twenty-three facial muscles (taking those occurring in pairs on the left and right side of the face as one) involved in facial expressions, and if we allow only two stages of contraction for each, the number of possible combinations already amounts to 253. The probability of accidental occurrence of a particular pattern in a given situational context is practically nil.

The possibility remains, of course, that behavioral shaping occurred because the mother or caretaker was responsive, for example, to patterns of smile. But again, in order for such shaping to take place without conscious intent, the pattern must first of all occur at least in a recognizable fashion to release attention. Furthermore, it is hard to imagine how responses to neglect, like the anger-syndrome accompanied by clenching of fists, stamping of feet, clenching and exposing of teeth and vertical frown, should be acquired this way. The further possibility remains that the child born deaf and blind, although growing up in eternal silence and darkness, nonetheless acquires patterned information about other peoples' behavior by his remaining sense of touch. We can exclude this possibility, however, because thalidomide children born deaf and blind (see Eibl-Eibesfeldt 1973), who have no arms with which to touch their mothers' faces, nonetheless develop the typical expressions listed above. Thus these facial expressions can be classified as fixed action patterns.

Besides the ontogenetic studies of the deprived children, evidence for phylogenetic adaptations in human expressive behavior is provided by cross-cultural studies and primate comparison (van Hooff 1971, Jolly 1972, van Lawick-Goodall 1968). Before we turn to discuss some examples we have to provide some methodological framework for the evaluation of similarities. As far as comparison is concerned, the criteria of homology, as discussed, are usefully applied. The same can be said for cross-cultural comparisons. However, as we all know, a universally found pattern need not necessarily be a result of a phylogenetic homology. For example, universally similar experiences during early childhood may shape behavior along parallel lines. Darwin, speculating as to the origin of head-shaking as a gesture of refusal and 'no', suggested that it could have been derived from the behavior of the nursing infant who, when satiated, turns his head sideways and lets go of the nipple. This would explain why this pattern is found all over the world in cultures as different as those of the Papuans, the Yanomami Indians, the Bushmen and most Europeans, although certainly not in all cultures. The universal similarity of such a pattern could alternatively be functionally explained. If such an explanation is evident, phylogenetic homology should not be assumed unless proved by ontogenetic studies. In a similar fashion no archaeologist or ethnologist should assume that the similar shape in two different cultures of a stone-ax blade implies a common origin. It could have developed independently in each culture as a result of the function of the ax. There appear to be some exceptions to this, however; peculiarities in ornamentation or language are much less open to parallel developments and this is certainly also true for patterns of non-verbal expressive behavior. Here cross-cultural universality is itself a strong indicator for phylogenetic homology within the different subspecies of man, since culturally acquired symbols for communication tend to change rapidly in cultural evolution, as the evolution of language clearly demonstrates.

The comparison of non-human primates and man reveals a great number of homologies in expressive behavior, as for example the relaxed-open-mouth display. Playing monkeys and apes exhibit this expression, which may be interpreted as an intention movement of playful biting, and which is often accompanied by the sounds of hectic breathing. This 'playface' can also be frequently observed in playfully aggressive children. I have documentary film evidence of the children of Papuans, Bushmen, Europeans, Yanomami and Himba, among others,[6] who all exhibit the identical relaxed-open-mouth display. Van Hooff (1971) shows that a young chimpanzee and a boy when playfully wrestling exhibited this same expression and evidently understood each other correctly.

[6] We are at present engaged in a program of cross-cultural documentation of unstaged social interactions and rituals. So far 120 km of 16 mm films have been collected (published in the Humanethologisches Filmarchiv der Max-Planck-Gesellschaft; cf. Eibl-Eibesfeldt 1971c for further details). I only want to emphasize here that every filmed event is accompanied by a protocol which gives the social context in which the pattern occurred as well as those behavior patterns which were observed before and after. This alone allows an objective correlation analysis.

The hypothesis that certain behavior patterns are innate[7] is further strengthened by cross-cultural and comparative primate studies of kiss-feeding and the corresponding kissing in man. It has been known for a long time that chimpanzees and orang-utangs feed their young with premasticated food and that this parental feeding occurs as kissfeeding between adults during friendly encounters (Rothmann and Teuber 1915, Bilz 1944). This is confirmed by Goodall's (1965) observations in the wild. Friendly chimpanzees greet each other on meeting by embracing and pressing the lips together, sometimes passing food thereby, but at others simply performing the movements without feeding.

My cross-cultural documentation contains many examples of mouth to mouth feeding as an expression of friendly affection, mostly between children and babies or adults and babies, but sometimes also between older children and adults as well. Documentary film exists of Papuans, Yanomami Indians and two Bushman linguistic groups. Sometimes food or water is passed, but even when it is not, tongue movements often occur which indicate the feeding intention. All stages between kissfeeding and kissing can be found, and kissing is in fact a universal pattern between mother and child although not always between adults.

In man, as well as in some other primates, a fixating look (full gaze) is perceived as a threat, if not interrupted by periodic cut-offs and if not accompanied by other signals of friendly intent (Argyle and Dean 1965, Chance 1962). Looking at a person is a behavior which signals readiness for contact and attentiveness. But the looking must not be prolonged or it is perceived as an attempt to dominate or even threaten. I filmed children in several cultures during threat stare duels. These normally end with one child giving up, turning away and leaving the scene. Often the loser lowers his gaze and head in a clear cut-off movement while pouting. Interestingly enough this response usually inhibits further attacks by the other child, to the extent that he may even try to comfort his pouting opponent. It should be noted, in this context, that experiment has demonstrated that most arousal is caused by eyes presented in a horizontal plane, with arousal gradually diminishing as they are tilted (Coss 1972). It is also relevant, perhaps, that eye patterns are often used in amulets and other devices which serve the function of warding off evil spirits (Koenig 1975).

There are numerous other patterns of human expressive behavior where homologies in other primates can be found (Jolly 1972, van Lawick-Goodall 1975).

[7] 'Innate' and 'phylogenetically adapted' are used as synonyms.

2. Expressive patterns shaped by inborn receptor biases

A number of universals in human behavior occur only in a very generalized form. In some cases the behavior patterns themselves vary considerably from culture to culture, but there are certain universal features. Some of these seem to have their origin in the fact that, due to innate releasing mechanisms, people react to certain stimuli in the same way all over the world. Certain features of a small child release, for example, friendly caretaking behavior and thus are adapted to buffer aggression (Lorenz 1943, Hückstedt 1965, Gardner and Wallach 1965). It is not surprising therefore that appeals via a child are often used in rituals of encounter. It has already been mentioned that state visitors are often welcomed by a child. Likewise, when the aborigines of central Australia want to establish friendly contact with the whites, they frequently bring a small child with them. Basedow (1906) described how an old man used to put his hands upon the shoulders of a small child when approaching the camp of white settlers. A further example comes from the Yanomami, who are fairly belligerent and customarily establish and strengthen village alliances through feasts. The male guests, on entering the village of the host dressed in full armor and festively decorated with feathers and body paint, first dance one circle around the open place of the village with full aggressive display. Children, however, accompany the warriors. They dance with them holding green leaves in their hands, and thus provide the appeasing part of the ritual. Innate releasing mechanisms in this case provide a guiding norm.

These may also be responsible for the use of phallic figurines as scare devils and guardians. Ploog *et al.* (1963) were the first to describe phallic displays in the squirrel monkey, and Wickler (1967) drew attention to the fact that phallic displays are quite common amongst primates. Their prime function is that of spacing. When, for example, a group of squirrel monkeys forage, some males will sit guard with their backs to the group exposing their brilliantly red (penis) and blue (scrotum) colored external genitalia. When a member of another group approaches, erection occurs, apparently as a ritualized threat to mount. Mounting as a demonstration of dominance is quite widespread amongst mammals, and occurs in man in some aggressive encounters (Eibl-Eibesfeldt and Wickler 1968). For example, the Eipo in aggressive phallic display loose the tip of their penis gourd and jump up and down making the gourd swing vertically in a most conspicuous way (for further details see Eibl-Eibesfeldt 1976a, and see also Schiefenhövel, 1976). More commonly in man, however, figurines and amulets are used rather than direct phallic display to ward off all sorts of evil. The evil is feared in the form of bad spirits with basically human and mischievous characteristics (Eibl-Eibesfeldt and Wickler 1968, Eibl-Eibesfeldt 1970).

The thesis that such universals are often the result of a shared receptor bias is supported by other examples concerning similarities in male body-decoration and female fashion and art (Eibl-Eibesfeldt 1975b, Wickler 1967, Schlosser 1952).

3. Innate motor patterns with derived cultural meaning

The motor patterns which accompany or act as a substitute for a verbal 'yes' and 'no' vary from culture to culture. It is well known that the Greeks, Turks and other inhabitants of the Near East–Mediterranean border accompany a factual 'no' with a vertical tilting of their heads often accompanied by a sideways motion. At the same time they close their eyes and raise their eyebrows. In the Ayoréo (Paraguay) we filmed another movement pattern signalling 'no': they close their eyes tightly and at the same time wrinkle their noses and purse their lips. The most widely spread 'no'-pattern is, however, horizontal head-shaking. We filmed it among Yanomami Indians, some Papuan tribes (Eipo, Woitap-min, Kukukuku, Biami), the Balinese, some Australian tribes (Gidjingali, Pintubi, Walbiri), Samoans, Kalahari Bushmen (G/wi, !Ko), Himba of South West Africa and, of course, among Europeans, where it is the most common movement pattern accompanying 'no'.

How should this finding be interpreted? It is, of course, a clear example of cross-cultural difference, but closer examination reveals that cultural convention has taken advantage of already existing motor patterns which may very probably be innate. Thus the same movement pattern which the Greeks use to underline a factual 'no' is also used, in a more limited way, by other nationalities. When central Europeans emphatically deny some-thing, particularly some misdemeanor, or when they indignantly refuse some request, we observe that the head is moved backwards in the vertical plane, the brows are raised, sometimes the eyes are closed and the hands raised with the palms toward the opponent as if to ward him off. The backward movement of the head appears to be an intention movement of withdrawal. The same movement is used as an expression of haughtiness. In other words, this particular behavior pattern is used in a social context of refusal, and in this context we observe that similar patterns occur cross-culturally. Among the Eipo in New Guinea this expression of slight indignation is combined with a pouting or pursing of the lips.

The different movement by which the Ayoréo indicate 'no' is also found in other cultures in a related context. When disturbing visual and olfactory stimuli are perceived, people all over the world close their eyes tightly and wrinkle their nose. They shut themselves off, they refuse to accept these stimuli. The Ayoréo indicate a factual 'no' in this way. In the Yanomami the same patterns are used when refusing social contact.

Finally, the head-shake may be related to a universally found shaking-off movement, which is probably of an older mammalian heritage and not necessarily derived as Darwin proposed. Any conclusions on this have to wait, however, since a study of the corresponding ontogeny is still lacking.

The movements which in different cultures accompany a 'no'-statement thus appear to be derived from patterns which already existed essentially as negations, either for warding off noxious stimuli, or for refusing further social contact by ritualized withdrawal and cut-off behaviors. By cultural conventions these primary means of refusal were able to take on the more generalized meaning of 'no'. The fact that head-shaking is the more widely generalized expression may be explained by its primary use outside social contexts; the other movements indicated refusal of social contact and may thus be less suited to express a factual 'no'.

IX. Basic strategies of social interaction: some organizing principles of ritualistic behavior

When Craig (1918) introduced the concept of appetitive behavior his model of behavioral events was simple: appetitive behavior leads to a stimulus-releasing situation and this allows the consummatory act to occur. This, however, is a special case. Normally a whole sequence of acts must occur before a consummatory act brings about a change of the animal's motivational state.

Behavioral events are often organized in a hierarchical way. Starting from the highest level of integration the range of behavior open to an animal narrows each time he chooses a certain act. For example, in spring the male stickleback migrates in schools from the deep water into the shallow waters. Here he chooses a territory and this results in a change of his behavioral state. He changes coloration, and from now on he is responsive to stimuli which release either courtship, nestbuilding, fighting or parental behaviors. Each of these encompasses a number of behavior patterns, mostly specific for reproduction, and the set of behavior patterns observed in each case is, except for a few *Werkzeughand-lungen* like swimming,[8] exclusive, i.e. once the behavior patterns of fighting are released, courting, nestbuilding and parental behaviors are inhibited. The occurrence of particular patterns depends upon the specific signals perceived. On the whole the sequences are generally orderly. Where two individuals communicate, their behavior is interdependent, each one triggering the response of the other in turn. The appearance of the female stickleback will release the zigzag dance, a courtship behavior. This in turn elicits female courting, through a presenting posture, which causes the male to turn around and swim toward the nest (leading). When the female follows, the male points with his snout to the entrance of the nest, whereupon the female enters and the male, again in response to her behavior, trembles with his snout against the base of her tail, thereby causing spawning. She immediately leaves the nest, he enters, fertilizes the eggs and, after fertilization, fans the eggs to provide fresh water, and attacks females who come near the nest.[9] A new set of behavior has set in.

External stimuli at this level play a decisive role, but already here, and more so at the next level down, coordination by internal stimuli, or even central coordination without the need of any sensory feedback, controls the events (von Holst 1935, Taub, Perella and Barro 1973; for further examples see Fentress 1976).

Lorenz provides a classic example. He observed a tame well-fed starling which from time to time flew from its branch to catch something invisible, then returned to its perch, performed killing movements as if it had caught prey, and finally swallowed. The chain of acts was fairly fixed and seemed independent of guiding external influences. Similar events can be observed in mammals. A squirrel buries a nut by digging a hole, depositing the nut, tamping it down with his snout and finally covering the nut with sweeping movements of his fore-paws. An inexperienced squirrel raised in social isolation will do the same when first presented with a nut, searching for a hiding place and performing scratching movements. Should he have chosen a place where no hole can be dug, he will still deposit the nut after a certain number of scratching movements,

[8] Swimming occurs in the 'service' of fighting, courting, nestbuilding etc.
[9] The stimulus that brings a behavior sequence to an end varies. It can be an achieved stimulus situation, e.g. the consummatory situation where the enemy is no longer present after the fight. It may, however, also be internal feedback or, finally, changes on the motor neuron level.

tamp it down with his snout and finally perform, in the air since no earth has been dug up, the covering movements with his paws.

Rituals serve the function of communication. They release responses which in turn are answered; this leads to an orderly sequence of patterns of expression. But in ritualistic events behavior patterns are sometimes also linked rigidly with each other, without the sequence being determined by external stimuli. Thus in the courtship of the Galápagos albatross, the courtship pattern of preening his shoulder-feathers is always followed by a rather stereotyped sky-pointing of the beak.

Events which follow the stimulus-response principle may also be observed in the rituals of man. A smile is usually responded to by a smile, a nod by a nod and a handwave in a distance greeting with a similar handwave. In addition, however, acts are fused into longer sequences. The Tanim Het ritual described above is an example. Linking of patterns according to preprogrammed sequences can be observed too. One universal pattern of distance greeting begins with eye contact, followed by a head toss combined with a rapid raising of the eyebrows for approximately one-sixth of a second. The greeting is terminated with one or a few nods. A smile is usually, but not always, superimposed upon the whole sequence after eye contact has been established.[10]

Furthermore there exists a clear tendency of response matching which provides that basis for the development of the first mother–child rituals (dialogues, see p. 47). In addition, we can find universal rules along which ritualistic events are structured on a higher level of integration.

Let me first provide a simple example (figure 1), an illustration taken from a 16 mm film showing a Yanomami girl. She is playing by a pole supporting the roof of a house. A boy approaches with the intention of chasing the girl away. The girl smiles, clearly in an attempt to appease. This strategy fails,[11] and the boy hits the girl who, in response now lowers her gaze, pouts and turns her head away. This clear combination of cut-off and pouting inhibits aggression. The boy turns away and leaves the girl in peace.

Our cross-cultural studies revealed that the strategy of agonistic buffer-

---

[10] The eyebrow flash illustrates well the basis on which we consider a universal pattern to be homologous. Both its general features and its structural relationship with other behavior patterns (head-tossing, nodding, smiling, leading finally to approach or invitation to approach) remain similar in specific examples. Furthermore the social context in which it occurs and the fact that its basic 'meaning' is universal also support the assumption of cross-cultural homology.

[11] We use the term strategy if a set of actions is available for the achievement of a particular goal, e.g. agonistic buffering.

1. A Yanomami girl is approached by a boy with the aggressive intent to take over the pole which she was climbing. They had already been engaged in such a competition (or struggle) before. The girl attempts to block the aggression by smiling, but her attempts are in vain. The boy hits her, she lowers her gaze in a clear cut-off, and pouts. Thereupon he withdraws.

ing just described is universally employed. Pouting and cut-off efficiently block aggression everywhere and, in addition, initiate strategies of bond-repair since the insulter is eager to re-establish friendly contact. A cut-off is, indeed, a serious threat for a gregarious being.

We may observe these strategies at different levels, in interactions between individuals but also between groups; and while children act out the strategy, adults often verbalize it ('I can't see any further point in our talking!') with the same result. Verbalized behavior in this case follows the same rules which are preprogrammed by phylogenetic adaptations.[12] A sentence acts as a functional equivalent of gaze-aversion and lowering of the head plus pouting. It is a verbal cut-off. That functional equivalents may be substituted for one another is a characteristic of human ritual-events. These can be inborn motor patterns as well as cultural ones. They are substituted according to a deep structure given as phylogenetic adaptation. It is my hypothesis that many of the diverse cultural rituals are based upon elementary strategies of social interactions which in their original form are acted out in child behavior. The strategies of requesting, sharing and giving are another example which we have studied recently (Heeschen, Schiefenhövel and Eibl-Eibesfeldt, in press; figure 2).

How functional equivalents can be substituted for each other according to a deep structure can be observed in greeting rituals and feasts, which both serve the function of re-establishing or reinforcing a friendly bond. Three phases characterize such a ritual of friendly encounter (Eibl-Eibesfeldt 1971a, 1971b, 1973, Ghosh 1972):

a. the opening phase (phase of salutation)
b. the phase of interaction
c. the phase of parting

Each of these three phases is characterized by a set of verbal and non-verbal behavior patterns which correlate with a specific functional aspect of each of the phases; the encounter phase being characterized by patterns of display and appeasing serving the function of opening the channels for communication, the interaction phase by patterns which primarily reinforce bonding and the parting phase by patterns of appeasing and reinforcing the bond for the future. Cultural factors and the relations of the particular individuals involved in the encounter ritual cause variation of the pattern, but the principle structure remains univer-

---

[12] Trevarthen's observation (chapter 8.2 below) that two-month-old children show cut-off behavior as a result of a short period of being ignored by their mothers supports my hypothesis.

2. Two Yanomami girls are eating berries while engaged in friendly conversation. The girl to the left shows her friend her blue tongue. After she has finished eating her berries, she tries to grasp some berries from her friend. Her friend refuses to relinquish them by withdrawing her hand. Thereupon the other girl waits to be given her share.

Children share readily provided that the request is made in such a way as to demonstrate respect for possession. This is 'polite' behavior. As in other strategies of social interaction, verbalized requesting and sharing obey the same rules.

sally the same. Let us illustrate this by describing a greeting ritual[13] as we may observe it in everyday life.

a. The *opening phase* begins with eye contact or, more precisely, with looking at each other's face. It will be followed by some pattern of distance greetings which may already combine patterns of aggressive display with appeasing appeals signalling friendly intent; in this function we may observe universals in form and principle as well as cultural emblems. Readiness for contact is signalled by appeasing smiles following eye contact, by the eyebrow flash and nod, by raising the open palm and by shouted phrases like 'hello', mostly acts signalling friendly recognition and thus the willingness to contact. But display may occur if the encounter is more formalized. For example among the Bedouin the host will receive a visitor with quite an aggressive display, including sham attack on horses during which rifles are fired so that bullets hit the ground in front of the visitor. Similar displays with arrow-showing are known in South American forest tribes. Australian aborigines also exhibit ritualized aggressive display when two groups meet, as do the Mbowamb on the occasion of mourning rituals when they welcome visitors (Eibl-Eibesfeldt 1975b). In our culture guests of honour are welcomed on the occasion of a state visit by a military salute.

The display serves the function of protecting one's identity against possible domination by others. In our everyday life we are very careful indeed not to show any signs of weakness and we are on constant guard.[14] The aggressive display in a greeting situation can be dropped when the people know each other very well but it usually occurs even if reduced to just a firm handshake. In all cultures when a greeting opens with aggressive display, this is always performed in such a way that the person or group received will understand that no hostile intent is behind it. When a group of Mbowamb rushes with raised spears toward a group of visitors, women run with them holding green Cordyline branches in their hands.

Manly display during greeting encounter does not necessarily consist in a threat to others. For example, when a Yanomami visitor enters a village, he may stand motionless on the open place, in full view of the villagers, who sometimes behave as if intending to attack, ignoring any

---

[13] The term 'greeting' is used here, in its wider sense, for the whole encounter. It may well be restricted to the opening phase (distance greeting upon perception of the partner and followed by close greeting), as in the excellent paper by Kendon and Ferber (1973).

[14] Goffman's 'response cries' contain a number of illustrative examples (see chapter 3.2 below).

such threats. To expose oneself to full view in such a society contains an element of danger, since there is always a chance that someone in the host village harbors an old grudge arising from the continuous feuding which is customary amongst the Yanomami (Eibl-Eibesfeldt 1973).

A most important part of the opening phase of greeting consists of rituals which primarily serve the function of appeasing and thus pave the way for friendly communication – the main objective of the second interactional phase. This goal is achieved by patterns of submissive behavior and by the demonstration of peaceful intent which are in part inborn, in part culturally specific. One of the universal patterns of distance greeting – smiling, head-tossing, eyebrow flashing and nodding following visual contact – has already been described. Cultural specifications are deep bowing, raising of the open hand with the palm facing the other, lifting of the hat (which in Europe derived from lifting off the helmet, a clear demonstration of peaceful intent; as is the disposing of arms, e.g. by putting them on the ground, which also occurs occasionally). Sometimes presents are made visible as are branches with green leaves, or, in the case of visitors, the accompanying children or women, both of whom are always a clear indication of peaceful intention.

Distance greeting is often accompanied by a verbal utterance ('Good morning!') expressing peaceful intent and good wishes, which may be interpreted as a verbal opening gift. The expression of peaceful intent in one way or another is obligatory in the opening phase. Sex, status of the persons meeting, whether it is an accidental encounter or a planned visit, all lead to different patterns within one culture. Cultural variation has also produced a multitude of customs, but essentially these have evolved along the same lines (Eibl-Eibesfeldt 1971a, 1971b).

After this distance greeting, one is permitted to approach; during approach the partners usually do not stare fixedly at each other, but interrupt eye contact (Kendon and Ferber 1973, Pitcairn and Eibl-Eibesfeldt 1976). Once they are close, eye contact is re-established, full orientation of the greeting partners toward each other takes place, and in this facing position patterns of contact greeting (*Kontaktgruss*) occur. The patterns of contact greeting continue to serve the same function as distance greeting: contact readiness and appeasement are expressed by smiling, embracing, kissing, bowing, patting and the like. All the patterns just mentioned appear to have biological roots, but patterns like kissing and embracing, although universal, cannot occur everywhere in a greeting encounter. This is a matter of cultural variation. In addition, contact greeting patterns which have clearly evolved culturally may be observed.

The handshake is a good example. It demonstrates in Europe peaceful intent as well as manly strength. The former is indicated by the old habit of removing one's glove beforehand, which appears to have been derived from the medieval custom of knights removing their gauntlets as a sign of peace. In addition, however, the handshake serves the function of aggressive display when, in the pressure of their hands, the partners demonstrate their firmness and strength. Similar rituals can be observed in other parts of the world (Eibl-Eibesfeldt 1973). Verbal utterances like 'How do you do?' initiate the next phase.

b. The *phase of interaction* is characterized by the mutual efforts to establish and strengthen the bond. This is mostly done verbally, but as in every verbal interaction non-verbal signals (nods, smiles, possibly touching and patting) play a very important role. Verbal expressions first of all demonstrate *concern* and *interest* in the partner: 'How are you?' is a widespread phrase. If the stranger is not familiar he will first be asked from where he comes, what his background is (family, trade, etc.) and what are his objectives. This serves to define the relationship (see Goffman 1971). If the people meeting already know each other, this phase of becoming basically acquainted is of course not necessary. The interactants can start with the exchange of courtesies beginning with demonstration of concern. Inquiries about the well-being of the partner are followed by similar inquiries about his family; this exchange is reciprocal because the other partner will ask the same questions.

Furthermore, basic *agreement* is demonstrated. An opening statement, 'Nice day today!', will, for example, receive the reply 'Oh yes, lovely!' The other may continue, 'But a bit too dry, we could do with some rain!'; again agreement is expected. The factual information exchanged in such a dialogue is redundant. But such common-places for which Morris (1968) aptly coined the term 'grooming talk' contain the all-important message that the channels are open for communication and that both parties think and feel in the same way. And this feeling of sameness and thus unity creates a strong bond. This verbal exchange will not be informally disrupted but formally concluded by the phase of departure.

c. The *departure phase* will be initiated by intention movements of departure which change the position of the interactants toward each other. As Deutsch (1977) recently emphasized, people always face each other at a certain angle during verbal exchange. The intention to depart is signalled by slightly turning away. This is usually accompanied by the verbal comment that a person has to go, and quite often this is the only thing said by the departing person. 'I go' is the usual phrase with the

Yanomami, the !Ko Bushmen and the Eipo, and the reply may be a farewell-wish, as is the case with the Yanomami and !Ko.[15] Often touching, patting or handshaking occur as a gesture of reassurance and in many cultures good wishes are mutually exchanged, which are, in fact, a verbal gift exchange.

A departure must be characterized in such a way that it is not misinterpreted as a cut-off. We have mentioned that in agonistic encounters cut-offs serve to control aggression. Both departure and cut-off indicate termination of an encounter. In the case of a cut-off the termination is to be interpreted as a threat to end the bond (p. 28), but in the case of departure the termination should be understood as transitory and the bond should be understood to remain intact during the separation. In a cut-off the threat is expressed non-verbally by abrupt turning away and by facial expressions like pouting or anger frown, depending on the particular nature of the relation of the individuals involved. The non-verbal expression of departure is a gradual shift of orientation (Deutsch 1977), and verbal behavior can serve as a functional equivalent.

Sometimes behavior patterns of submission occur, indicating that the departure phase is critical. In moving away the interactants are no longer in full control of their partner, the bond is loosened, and, should there have been any previous hostilities, the departing person may be attacked now inhibitions are being lost. Those who withdraw backwards, repeatedly bowing, clearly indicate fear motivation. In this aspect the departure phase is in some ways analogous to the post-copulatory displays so characteristic of many birds. After copulation a change of motivation takes place, and aggression which was inhibited by the sexual drive may break through and disrupt the pair-bond. The post-copulatory displays are basically appeasing (Eibl-Eibesfeldt 1975b). In so far as the departure phase provides reassurance of a future bond it is typically human.

The comparison of greeting rituals with feasts clearly shows that feasts are basically patterned in the same way – although feasts are more elaborate. Let us take the 'reaho' of the Yanomami as an example. The Yanomami are belligerent people engaged in protracted village feuds. The survival of village units depends on their skill in forming and keeping alliances with other villages. The feasts, which are generally celebrated when the palm fruit (*Guilielma gasipaes*) is ripening, show the following pattern. Weeks before, the inviting village informs the inhabitants of the

[15] On departing a Yanomami says 'Jako' or 'Jakohamuja' ('I go') and the addressee responds 'Adacobeheri' ('Well you go'). In the Eipo the corresponding utterances are 'Na binam' ('I will go') and 'Ur binalam' ('All right, you will go') (Eibl-Eibesfeldt 1971a, 1977b).

other village of its intention to perform a 'reaho'. A formal invitation is extended. The hosts prepare themselves for the visitors by hunting, gathering palm fruits, bananas and other food, so that they are able to feed their visitors and to give them presents. The visitors in turn bring presents along for exchange.

The *opening phase* begins with the actual arrival of the visitors in the vicinity of the hosts' village. Even though the arrival will be known to the hosts, it will be announced in a formalized chanting by an emissary from the visitors, who will come in full body-decoration (feathers, paint) and present himself on the open place in the village. He will be given food as a present for his group, who are resting in the vicinity and preparing for the reception by washing and decorating. This done, the visitors will enter the village one by one, men first. Each man is fully decorated with feathers and body paint. The pattern of painting is in part the pattern used on the occasion of war. Parts of the body, in particular the face, are blackened, which functionally serves as a camouflage during a raid. In contrast, however, peaceful intent is demonstrated by white plumes glued to the hair or to their fur headband decoration.

Each man dances around on the open place in warrior's display. Arms are displayed and often the dancers aim with bow and arrow at their hosts, who stand guard commenting and yelling in response to the visitors' performance.

The aggressive display of the guests is balanced by a friendly display (p. 17). Children dance along with the warriors waving green palm leaves; thus, as in greeting, aggressive displays and friendly appeals are combined. Sometimes presents which are going to be exchanged between guests and visitors are displayed during the dance. Finally all visitors including children and women dance in a group, and the same is done by the hosts. When the salutation by the village as a whole has taken place, it is continued by individuals. The guests will put up their hammocks beneath the roofs of their relatives and friends and retire. This rest is also partly a display. The visitors will lie completely quiet for a while as if ignoring what is going on around them, but eventually they will loosen up and start to talk to their friends, thus starting the *phase of interaction* on an individual basis.

In the meantime the hosts will have prepared banana soup which is poured into a trough. This meal is given by the village community to their guests, who will help themselves freely to it. Next the men, visitors and hosts alike, engage in drug-sniffing. The drug is mutually blown with a blowpipe into the other's nose. It has a strong intoxicating effect and the men experience hallucinations of strength and feel supernatural power. In this state of intoxication they believe themselves to be able to cure sickness. And it is a common occurrence that particularly gifted individuals (medicine-men of the hosts' village but sometimes also visiting individuals) engage in mutual curing as a token of friendship. The intoxicated men may also unite in sending spirits, over which they now believe they have power, to enemy villages which they will supposedly harm. It is a sort of ritual fighting on the same side through which unity is created. Sometimes, particularly if old grudges have to be buried, visitors and hosts may engage in tournament-like fighting, occasionally even using their hardwood clubs. Finally, shared common concern is demonstrated by mourning for those who have recently died. This is an event in which women also take part. The pulverized bone-ash of those that have been cremated is consumed in banana soup. This phase of intensive communal interaction is continued on an individual basis. Pairs, composed of one visitor and one host, will engage in contract singing, mostly in the evening and at night. In a highly stylized way, they sing a duet, each assuring the other of his friendship and each demanding and promising gifts in exchange. They finally get down to real business. A visitor usually makes his round singing with every adult man in the village. The contract singing can be heard throughout the night.

The following morning the *phase of parting* usually begins. Guests and hosts exchange presents for practical use (reed for arrow-shafts, dogs for hunting, bush-knives), for decoration (plumes, etc.) and for consumption (smoked game, palm fruits, bananas). These presents are given on a village basis and are exhibited before being passed on. Once again both groups may mourn the deceased, and before departure males will sit opposite each other on the ground or even on each other's laps, embracing each other and once again engaging in a song dialogue of mutual friendship. Then, when the exchange is complete, the guests will depart laden with gifts.

Feasts all over the world follow a similar pattern. A Bavarian 'Schützenfest' opens with a quasi military display (*Aufmarsch der Schützen*), but girls and children take part in the 'Festzug'. A phase of interaction follows during which shared interest and friendship are emphasized in speeches. The participants will also demonstrate their mutual concern by standing in honor of those who have recently died, and by laying a wreath at the war memorial. The people enjoy the shared experience of dining and drinking, and they will then engage in the competitive sport of shooting. After this emotional preparation, as it were, they will begin to discuss business and political matters.[16] The end consists of a formalized 'Abschied' during which all participants assure each other of lasting friendship.

Each of these phases is characterized by a set of behavior patterns. They are repetitive in that the same intention, e.g. the willingness to form a bond, is repeatedly communicated in a variety of ways. Leach has mentioned this point:

> One feature, however, is very plain and virtually universal. A ritual sequence when performed 'in full' tends to be very repetitive; whatever the message may be that is supposed to be conveyed, the redundancy factor is very high. Here it is worth reflecting on a general point of communication theory. If a sender seeks to transmit a message to a distant receiver against a background of noise, ambiguity is reduced if the same message is repeated over and over again by different channels and in different forms.   (Leach 1966:404)

It is clear from the above description that 'greetings' and 'feasts' share many features. Both are rituals of friendly encounter. The main difference is the number of persons involved. Greeting is often a dyadic relationship, feasts involve one or more groups. The structural characteristics of rituals of friendly encounter are summarized in table 1.

Greeting rituals and feasts provide a good example of the fact that, in spite of great cultural variation as far as the particular elaboration of the events is concerned, the basic strategies of these particular types of interaction remain cross-culturally the same. We may hypothesize that phylogenetic adaptations determine this basic structure in a fashion analogous to that by which they determine the deep grammar of language. We have yet to clarify, however, whether in this particular case necessary structural elements determine the conditions of the event. One does not need to postulate the existence of a universal grammatical rule to explain, for example, the universal existence of the personal pronouns 'I, you and he'.[17] This results from necessity once one speaks about someone to someone. A ritual has to begin and has to end. Our ambivalent attitudes toward our fellow men (the conflict of approach and withdrawal, see §XIII), which derive from our motivational structure, necessarily lead to a combination of patterns of display as a means of attention-seeking and of establishing individual identity with patterns of appeasement to allow bonding to occur. But we seem to be adapted to act

---

[16] Our modern matter-of-factness often causes us to omit this emotional preparation. We want to get down to business in a hurry and fail to achieve our goals, since sympathy and friendship have not been achieved beforehand.

[17] Although this does not rule it out either.

Table 1. *Rituals of friendly encounter (greeting ritual, feast).*

(a) *Opening phase (salutation)*	
Assumed function:	appeasement and display to impress as a means of identity reassurance; expression of readiness to contact in order to allow approach and to open the channels for communication
Some patterns of display (selected examples of functional equivalents):	display dance; handshake; military salute; displaying arms
Some patterns of appeasement and contact readiness (functional equivalents):	smile, eyebrow flash, nod, eye contact, embrace, kiss, lifting of the hat, raising of the hand; appealing via a child or woman; showing gifts
(b) *Phase of interaction*	
Assumed function:	emotional preparation by bonding, often as preparation for coming down to business
Some patterns of interaction:	dialogues expressing concern and agreement; demonstration of shared interests; exchange of promises; joint cooperative activities which emphasize unity (dining, dancing, ritualistic combat against shared enemies, mourning)
(c) *Phase of parting*	
Assumed function:	appeasing and strengthening of the bond for the future
Patterns observed:	exchange of good wishes; gift exchange; patterns of retreat in submission

thus without much individual trial and error learning. In part this is certainly due to culturally evolved rules, as Goffman (1971) has emphasized. The opening greeting marks a period of contact, the closing salutation ends the encounter, and it is expected that the two partners will not meet again immediately after this. An unexpected return contradicts this expectation and spoils the departure. Even very small children, meeting a stranger and trying to make friends, run through all the stages just described with great spontaneity. They put themselves in the focus of attention by display, and they offer their toys or other objects with friendly smiles, as tokens of friendship. Once the bond is established, they will engage in play, mutually imitating each other and so forth. The spontaneity and security which eighteen-month-old children already exhibit in their performance seem to indicate that basic features of this strategy of interaction constitute part of an inherited program.

So far little is known about the 'grammar' of other basic strategies of social interaction. How does one proceed to achieve 'rank'? What strategies are available to resolve a conflict? How does one acquire an object which is in the possession of another person? How does one gain access to a group of strangers? As far as we know from our comparative studies, there is only a limited number of patterns available to achieve such things and cross-cultural studies of child behavior reveal that the strategies are in part universal. Thus, in order to achieve rank, one must by some means bring oneself into the focus of attention of a group. This alone is certainly not sufficient (a murderer, after all, bringing himself into the focus of attention does not achieve rank), but it is a prerequisite. Mutual giving and taking is another strategy which can be universally observed. It recurs regularly between mother and child and can be observed in all cultures studied so far even among very young children. Cultural ritualization can elaborate upon this disposition which is apparently innate in man, e.g. in the verbalized give and take ritual of contract singing mentioned above. Giving and showing off objects is one of the basic strategies by which small children initiate contact (Eibl-Eibesfeldt 1972b, 1973; Stanjek 1978).

X. Verbal communication as a ritual event

'In ritual the verbal part and the behavioural part are not separable' (Leach 1966:408). In his speech to the Royal Society Meeting on Ritualized Behaviour, Leach emphasized that 'speech itself is a form of ritual'; this certainly accords with our definition. Of the many aspects of language, I want to stress two outstanding ones. Gehlen (1940) was to my knowledge the first to emphasize one characteristic of language, the fact that it need have no basis in human emotions. It is this characteristic which allows us to pass on factual information about the outer world in a detached, objective way. There also exists, of course, emotionally laden language, which we encounter when two people quarrel, and yell at or curse each other, or when lovers engage in love-talk. Among other things speaking can be ritualized aggression or courtship. Man verbalizes what animals perform in non-verbal engagements both ritually or non-ritually. Man can fight in words, which is certainly the most elaborate ritualization of aggressive behavior, and it is easy to see the selective advantage of such a ritualization. This type of speech is not detached from emotions but is a ritualization of behaviors with a phylogenetic background – people all over the world say basically the same things in specific situations. The vocabulary is different, but the verbal clichés are the same. Infantile and parental behavior are translated into verbal appeals during courtship and, as was mentioned above, what people say during the interaction phase of greeting is practically the same cross-culturally. The discovery that verbal and non-verbal behavior can substitute for each other as functional equivalents bridges the gap between them and also provides a unifying theory for the study of a grammar of human social behavior. The basic strategies of social interactions indeed prove to follow the same rules whether verbalized or acted out non-verbally.

XI. Functions of rituals

Rituals serve the function of communication. They thus release responses. According to these responses we can classify rituals. Here we will present only some main categories of rituals and restrict ourselves to a few examples from animal and human behavior.

1. Bonding

We have already had cause to mention the functional aspect of bonding and the interesting fact that individualized bonds evolved independently in birds and mammals from the mother–child relationship. Behavior patterns that serve bonding in the adult are derived from mother–child signals (p. 21). Kissing, derived from kissfeeding, was given as an example of a parental behavior used to express affection and thus strengthen the bond between adults of opposite sex. Infantile appeals are used to attract friendly attention. It is well known that persons who feel neglected regress to childish behavior. Direct appeals via the child as a bonding agent can be observed too. In the Christian religion the Christ child undoubtedly serves as a uniting symbol.

Rituals of bonding may be classified in various ways, according to the agents involved or the method by which the bonding is achieved. *Courtship rituals* as for example the Tanim Het described above refer to the establishment of pair-bonds. *Greeting rituals* and *feasts* refer to bond formation and reinforcement outside the context of pair formation, feasts particularly on the level of groups.

If classification is by method, a particular type of bonding ritual might be categorized under the heading *rituals of synchronization*. The Tanim Het again provides a good example and so do dances in many cultures. The melon ball game of the Bushwomen could be mentioned as another example. It is a game played by women and girls when groups meet, e.g. at the water hole or within the village community particularly during the cooler morning and late afternoon hours. Women and girls line up during this melon ball game and clap a rhythm with their hands. The one holding the melon steps in front and performs a number of dancing steps to the rhythm; when finished she throws the melon to the next woman in line who catches it and repeats the sequence, and thus the ball is passed on. The only interruption occurs when a woman is not skilful and drops the ball. If a girl or woman makes a mistake too often, she is teased and sometimes even scolded (Sbrzesny 1976, Eibl-Eibesfeldt 1972a, 1976a). There is an apposite German saying which refers to such a disruption of harmony: 'Wenn einer aus der Reihe tanzt' (if you step out of line).

Bonding, furthermore, can be achieved by rituals which express a *shared concern* (mourning rituals) or which unite the group ritualized by acts of *joint aggression* against a common enemy. An example of this is found among the Yanomami who, as described above, send harmful spirits to their enemies when intoxicated by drugs at their feasts. The trance dance of the Bushmen could serve as another example. Here the group unites in fighting ghosts (p. 35). The threat symbol of the raised fist unites those who fight for the same goals.

Rituals of *gift exchange* are another category of bonding patterns. This subject has been well covered in a monograph by Mauss (1966). Among the more recent monographs dealing with gift exchange Wiessner's (1977) investigation of the !Kung should be mentioned. (For further discussion and references see Eibl-Eibesfeldt 1972b, 1975b.) The party accepting a gift is usually obliged to give a gift of at least the same value in return. Sometimes, however, he is obliged to give more. In such cases escalation may take place, the exchange taking on the character of a ritualized fight, each party competing with the other. Primarily, however, presents are tokens of friendship. The inclination to establish or reinforce a bond by giving something is even shown by toddlers, who first offer food and toys to their mother and thus initiate dialogues of give and take. Small children also use the same strategy when they want to establish friendly relations with a visitor. Often they offer morsels and actually feed the person (Eibl-Eibesfeldt 1973, Stanjek 1978).

2. Spacing and competing

Spacing is achieved by fighting and display. Spacing via aggression can occur on the individual level as well as on the group level, and each level is distinguished by a number of characteristics.

Individual aggression, as it has been observed in members of the same group, basically follows the pattern of intraspecific aggression in animals, which is only destructive in exceptional cases. In most vertebrates that are potentially capable of hurting each other, special inhibitions and fighting rules have evolved which prevent the destruction of the conspecific. Well-known examples are the ritualized fights of marine iguanas, rattle-snakes and the various antelopes (Eibl-Eibesfeldt 1955, 1972b, Lorenz 1966b, Shaw 1948, Walther 1961).

Individual aggression in members of the same human group follows the same basic pattern. Special inhibitions, released by appeals of sub-mission (crying, pouting with cut-off and lowering of the head), prevent escalation into destruction. The appeals are the same universally. In addition, fighting by display occurs, one universal form being the threat stare duel (Eibl-Eibesfeldt 1972a, 1976a).

With the development of armor, cultural codes of conduct evolved again designed to prevent killing, e.g. special rules for duelling. The use of destructive weapons may be forbidden and rivals may have to settle their matter in ritualized matches (one extreme example is the song duel of the Eskimos).

Intragroup aggression often leads to the establishment of ranking orders which are certainly advantageous for those that achieve a high-ranking position but may also be so for the group. Leaders are selected not simply because of their aggression but according to their particular social abilities, for example as peacemakers, organizers, etc. The struggle for rank-position is often carried out in a subtle and highly ritualized form without the use of any force at all. Display plays a most important role. Since the struggle for a rank-position is usually not just between two persons competing for rank, but depends on the decision of an impartial group, many of the display patterns do not really derive from patterns of aggression. A person may achieve a high-ranking (in the focus of atten-tion) position by graciously distributing presents, which may well esca-late into a competition, a 'fighting with gifts'. Such is the case with the Potlatch of the Kwakiutl, where the chiefs of different groups compete for rank by outdoing each other in wasting and destroying property (Boas 1897). Here, in a strange way, patterns of bonding (to entertain, to give a gift) change their original function. Since wealth may be seen as an indication of ability, it can serve among the more 'advanced' pastoralists and agriculturists as display to achieve and to defend rank and power.

Chance (1967) discovered that high-ranking monkeys are always those that are in the focus of attention in the group, i.e. which are most looked at by the others. To put oneself into the focus of attention still serves to achieve or keep rank in man. The etiquette of seating at a formal dinner clearly reflects this focus of attention criterion.

I want to conclude the discussion of phenomena related to intragroup aggression by drawing attention to a category of rituals which German ethnologists have termed 'Ventilsitten', and which apparently serve the function of neutralizing aggression by allowing it to have an outlet in contests which 'let off steam'. In this context I should mention that Bushmen, who rarely engage in war, compete in a great variety of games. In contrast the Eipo (West Irian) and the Yanomami (upper Orinoko), who regularly engage in warfare, do not play any ritualized games. The boys play at raids and thus exercise the strategies of warfare, and also play at club fighting in a tournament-like way, but more ritualistic games, by which a party wins according to rules, have not been observed. Adult males hardly play at all. They are often engaged in warfare and fighting and thus have no need to let off steam.

Intergroup aggression differs from intragroup aggression in that it is primarily destructive. This is achieved by special cultural adaptations which take advantage of some inherited dispositions, in particular the inclination to form closed territorial groups and to fear strangers. The latter disposition matures during infancy even if the child has not experienced anything disagreeable from strangers.

The destructive aspect of intergroup aggression, however, is cultural. War can be defined as a culturally evolved mechanism of spacing between groups. It fulfils basically territorial functions (Eibl-Eibesfeldt 1975b). Human groups tend to define themselves as the only real human beings and to speak of their neighbors in derogatory terms. Neighbors are also not considered to be fully human and sometimes are even spoken of as if they were not people at all. The neighbor is thus dehumanized and in this process of self-indoctrination man shuts himself off from those signals which release pity. In addition, armament, which allows killing at a distance (arrows, throwing spears), is an effective shield from those signals which release inhibitions to aggression. Furthermore it is made a cultural virtue to kill those who are enemies. A cultural filter is superimposed upon the biological filter which commands 'thou shalt not kill'.

As long as the enemy is not seen as human, as is the case in aggression at a distance, there is no apparent contradiction between the biological and the cultural. In face-to-face encounter, however, signals are perceived which appeal to our inbuilt reactions and then a conflict is experienced and felt as bad conscience. The biological filter of norms is after all inborn and cannot easily be eradicated by culturally evolved mechanisms.

Mutual self-interest is another factor that lessens the destructiveness of wars, since neither side wants to sustain heavy losses. But certainly the emotional component of sympathy exerts a very strong pressure toward humane conduct. This derives from the fact that in order to fight an enemy, sympathy must be fought first, and sympathy, in the original meaning of the word, is expressed already in very small babies, who cry when listening to tapes of crying, in what is presumably inborn response. In my opinion it is primarily the discomforting bad conscience resulting from the conflict of norms that guides the cultural evolution of war to a less destructive, more humane encounter. Conventions are established to restrict killing to the combatants, to spare the civilians, to allow a warrior to surrender and to ban particularly destructive weapons. This is not just an invention of the 'civilized'. The Tsembaga in the Highlands of New Guinea fight wars with their neighbors, but try to avoid escalation into bloodshed if possible. According to Rappaport (1968) there are several stages of the war. At the beginning both parties rely mainly on display. After having cleared the traditional battle ground, they face each other, shouting insults and shooting at each other with arrows which lack the feathers and therefore easily miss the target. Since the parties are communicating verbally a release of tension may occur and reconciliation may result, particularly since a neutral third party is commenting on the event. Standing on a hill nearby, its members shout to the fighting parties how bad it is for brothers to fight, and that the dispute should be settled by an arrangement.

Only if this fails does an escalation take place. The groups will decide to put the nets with the sacred stones, which have so far hung under the roof of the communal men's hut, on the ground. This is the formal declaration of destructive war. But there are rules by which an armistice can be achieved and there are conventions which allow the formal establishment of peace. In addition, should one party lose, this does not mean that the evacuated area will immediately be taken over by the victors. It is believed that the ancestral spirits of the losers will still dwell there and guard the area until they start to plant the sacred Cordyline trees in their new area of refuge. This will then be taken as a signal that the area is given up and that the ancestral spirits will move to the new place. The evacuated area may then be taken into possession by the victors.

Where territories have already been staked out and where people have already implemented measures to achieve population control (post-partem taboo, infanticide) so as to establish an equilibrium between population number and available resources, war tends to get ritualized into a sort of territorial display, to retain one's territory, and confirm one's group identity, but not to acquire new land. A further prerequisite is of course a certain ecological stability. If droughts and other climatic fluctuations force people to migrate, peaceful coexistence is not easily reestablished. Of particular interest are the ritualizations by which most Australian tribes resolve disputes over territories. By myth, they trace ownership of tribal land back to a totemic ancestor, half animal, half man, who guards their territory. Features of their landscape are interpreted as traces of the totemic ancestor's activities. Fear of the totemic ancestors of other groups prevents territorial acquisition. In addition the different groups have mutual obligations. The totemic animals are of economic importance to all groups and since every group, by performing rituals at their 'sacred sites', makes their own totemic animals prosper, it would certainly be inopportune to destroy a neighboring group.

The modern armament race (*Wettrüsten*) of the superpowers could be interpreted as intimidation display, and has in fact achieved military successes without bloodshed (for example during the Cuba crisis). But it is certainly a risky game since safeguards against large scale escalations still seem insufficient.

3. Appeasing

Appeasing is directly related functionally to aggression. Without the ability to appease, community life for potentially aggressive individuals would scarcely be possible. The simplest way to appease is by deflecting aggression-releasing signals. In man, signals which act as unconditioned aggression inhibitors are the signals which constitute the baby schema (*Kindchenschema*) and appeals through children have been mentioned as part of the rituals of friendly encounter. Behaving like a child may serve as an appeal as well. Experiments have shown that pictures of women inhibited aggression in males (Baron 1974, Baron and Bell 1977), and we may therefore assume that some of their actual characteristics similarly buffer aggression.

Among the patterns of expressive behavior which inhibit aggression may be included smiling, pouting, ritualized cut-off (p. 28) and crying. Behavior patterns derived from parental and child behavior have an appeasing value, as is the case with all patterns of bonding, including verbalized appeals.

4. *The conquest of fear*

Man as a rational being seeks for causal explanations of events. Events which he cannot explain cause fear. In an attempt to conquer fear man invents explanations for events caused by factors which are not accessible to his direct observation. He structures his world view according to these assumptions, providing security as well as a logical framework within which to act.

The trance dance of the Bushmen may serve as an example. According to Bushman lore, a person falls ill when the ancestral spirits try to carry him off into the realm of the supernatural (Katz 1976). In the state of trance induced by dance, some men and occasionally also women are capable of struggling with these spirits and of eliciting the help of other ancestral spirits to prevent the sick person from being carried off. Another explanation for sickness is that invisible arrows sent by spirits or enemies as black magic have entered the body of the person and have made him ill. In this case the trance dancer extracts the arrows from the victim's body (Eibl-Eibesfeldt 1976a).

The trance dance usually starts in the evening and may last through the night with short interruptions. The women sit in a circle around the fire, clap a rhythm with their hands and sing a complex melody without words. The men, with rattles on their feet, dance to this song around the women, occasionally touching them as they pass by. After a while some of the men will go into a trance. A man in trance will cry out in pain, experience X-ray vision, hallucinations and convulsions, as his 'medicine' warms up, rises from his stomach up his spine to his skull and takes him beyond his ordinary self (Katz 1976). Finally he may fall into a state of unconsciousness. Helpers assist him, giving support and preventing his getting hurt. By massage and other means they try to bring him back to consciousness. The women then increase the intensity of their song to support him in his struggle. It is during this state of trance that the trance dancer has special powers. He touches the women and bystanders, chants and looks into each person for sickness. If a person is sick, he concentrates his attention on him or her. The trance dancer massages the person, rubs him with sweat, etc., while sharing his medicine with him. Sometimes he also tries to suck out the disease, and he will then spit the disease out or throw it away. Although versions of what exactly is done to locate and cure a sickness vary considerably from healer to healer, the main burden of the healing is basically the same. The healer, in trance, struggles with the ghosts to prevent them from carrying away the sick person to the realm of the supernatural. He pleads for help from his dead relatives saying that the community wants and needs the sick person and does not want him to be taken away. The healer is further supported in his struggle by the women's singing and the concern of all present. The sick person himself is relieved of fear and anxiety and feels wanted, all of which have therapeutic effects. In addition, the shared experience of combating sickness serves as a bond between all those participating in the ceremony. Thus, rituals provide security at the same time as removing fear. It is for that reason that we are reluctant to do away with our old beloved customs.

5. Rituals to keep 'discipline'

When I worked among the Himba, a pastoralist Bantu group to the south of Angola, it struck me that every morning after milking the cows, all members of the group came to the headman and offered their milk. He tasted it – or just touched the pots – and only after this ritual had been performed could the milk be used. It was a demonstration of his authority and certainly conditioned those who accepted it for further obedience. I observed nothing like that among the Bushmen or among the Yanomami Indians, but it would seem a sensible procedure for the Himba, who survived only by their capability for concerted, disciplined military action during their frequent exposure to raids and consequent moves to new pastures, which thus caused continuous conflict with their neighbors. An authoritarian structure on the small community level was thus certainly functional; even its maintenance in peacetime was dependent on every-day rituals, which necessitated daily obedience, and meant that rebels would be spotted immediately by the community. Such a military attitude was furthermore fostered by songs of praise which hailed the heroic deeds of ancestors, and were sung at social gatherings, particularly with visiting friends. In the military circles of our culture similar rituals of obedience can be observed (raising and saluting the flag in the morning and evening), and it was not very long ago that in England the national anthem was sung at the end of a theater or cinema performance.

XII. Ontogeny of ritual and cultural pseudospeciation

One of the basic principles of ritualistic behavior is the mutuality of recognition. Erikson emphasized that

man is born with the need of such regular and mutual affirmation and certification, we know at any rate that its absence can harm an infant radically by diminishing or extinguishing his search for impressions which will verify his senses, but once aroused this need will reassert itself in every stage of life as a hunger for ever new, formalized and more widely shared ritualization and rituals, which repeat such face-to-face 'recognition' of the hoped for. (Erikson 1966:338)

Indeed, the first rituals between mother and child are a manifestation of the principle and both partners are certainly programmed for such a dialogue. The baby starts to be outfitted with his smile, which triggers strong response in the mother (Ambrose 1961, 1966). Later repetitive actions like give and take develop into rituals of dyadic communication, long before verbal communication is possible. It is in fact fascinating to see how small children enjoy such games. To conform is an expression and reassurance of unity, and small children often start to form a bond by such simple rituals which they also spontaneously invent. When a pair of two year olds meet they will, after an initial phase of ambivalence, start to establish friendly contact, e.g. by approach and showing off toys. Once the first shyness is overcome, one may invent a simple game, e.g. banging with an object against the table, or dancing around. The other child will respond with the same behavior pattern, and by alternate repetition it becomes a ritual of bonding. I have seen this not only in European children, but also in many other cultures (e.g. Himba, Bushman, Yanomami). There exists a tendency, probably inborn to man, of response matching. Babies less than a week old will imitate some behaviors like eyelid-fluttering or tongue-showing (Meltzoff and Moore 1977). Rosenfeld (1967) reported response matching as a typical pattern of the dyadic interaction. Subjects smiled and nodded more in response to a smiling and nodding partner.

Erikson (1966) drew our attention to the fact that man has the inclination to form groups which are demarcated from other groups by customs. Dialects evolve, and formerly uniform groups divide and a divergent development sets in. In this way human languages and cultures evolved diversely, a process which Erikson terms 'cultural pseudospeciation' because to a certain degree cultures behave like species. There is an adaptive radiation in that cultures developed different strategies of survival. Until recently groups must also have been made up of fairly closed gene-pools. This would have allowed the rapid biological subspeciation which has resulted in the numerous races that we can distinguish today. This racial diversity is particularly astonishing if one considers the fact that at the most man produces only five generations every hundred years. Culture until quite recently seems to have been the pace-maker of biological evolution in man. Now, with fusing cultures, the trend may have reversed.

Man's inclination to subspeciate culturally still manifests itself in many ways in everyday life. Many of the subcultures and groups with specific rituals which form part of the same culture will demarcate themselves from others, as if there were an urge to go new ways, to experiment in cultural pseudospeciation. Avant-gardists, for example, consciously want to try out new personal lifestyles and to free themselves from the old ways and the rules imposed upon them, simply to subjugate themselves, but this time voluntarily, to the even more rigid rules of their newly formed groups. It could well be that this urge to try new ways has been selected to speed up cultural evolution, to cause mutations, so to speak, on the cultural level.

Even children engage in such experimentation. I well remember that in our classroom friends used to form clubs long before puberty. One characteristic was a shared secret, often accompanied by a special language created simply by the addition of an extra syllable to each word. It was play – but it resulted in closed groups being formed which banded against others.

Man as a cultural being shows a strong inclination to mould his behavior culturally, thus enhancing cultural pseudospeciation, and evolution. There is practically no aspect of life which man does not cultivate, and those which characterize his own group he considers as 'good manners'.

It's right and legitimate that we should consider as 'good' the manners which parents taught us, that we should hold sacred the social norms and rites handed down to us by cultural tradition. What we must guard against, with all the power of rational responsibility, is our natural inclination to regard social norms and rites of other cultures as inferior.   (Lorenz 1966a:284)

Deviation from ritualized behavior is accompanied by feelings of shame and guilt. It is our second nature for ritualized behavior to conform with our cultural norm, and it is certainly a mistake to consider patterns like those of courtesy as nothing but a superficial 'whitewash' covering our real feelings (see Lorenz 1973).

XIII. Medical aspects of communicative behavior

The ambivalence of approach and withdrawal in everyday encounters and disturbances of communicative behavior derived from it

In many mammals and birds the conspecific is perceived with ambivalence since he emits not only signals which initiate friendly approach but also others which activate agonistic behaviors (aggression and flight). Thus, for example, the black face mask of the blackheaded gull is a signal which releases aggression. Both sexes bear this signal and for this reason they have difficulties in establishing the pair-bond. Special rituals are needed to establish contact. One is that, as males and females approach each other, they have to 'face away'. During the ceremony, which Tinbergen (1959) called headflagging, the birds turn the backs of their heads toward each other in a demonstrative fashion and, at the beginning of their acquaintance, they practically never face each other fully, but look at each other only from the corners of their eye. Nonetheless the female often gets attacked and has to appease by begging behavior, a ritualized infantile response. Once the birds know each other individually, the aggression-releasing effect of the black face is diminished and the birds can now face each other without the risk of being attacked. Similar observations have been made of many other animals; the similar ambivalence of man in his reaction to a fellow man has already been mentioned. At the age of approximately six to eight months this fear of strangers already manifests itself. One of the stimuli releasing fear are the eyes. It is for this reason that we have to avoid staring into another person's face. When we are obliged to face someone, as we do during a conversation, we intersperse cut-offs at fairly regular intervals by looking away (Argyle and Cook 1976, Cook and Smith 1975, Ellsworth, Carlsmith and Henson 1972).

The ambivalence of approach and withdrawal manifests itself in many ways in everyday encounters. Coy behavior is one clear expression of it and manifests itself cross-culturally in much the same way. If we address a child or girl in a friendly way, she will indicate by a number of signals that she accepts the invitation for friendly contact. She will smile, look at you and even signal an eyebrow flash. At the same time, however, reactions of flight and aggression are released which manifest themselves either simultaneously or in successive ambivalence. While smiling the girl may inhibit the smile by the activation of antagonistic muscles, which results in a coy smile with lips pressed together, sometimes even slightly pursed as if pouting. Often the lower part of her face is hidden behind her hand as if to shield off the friendly expression. An eyebrow flash may be combined with a cut-off by lowering the lids, while face orientation may still indicate readiness for contact, or the flight motivation may be indicated by turning one shoulder away. In the case of successive ambivalence the person may oscillate between facing and facing away. The girl may look with a smile, then turn the head away, lower the gaze while the smile fades, look back from the corners of her eyes or even turn the face back to full face contact and so forth. Patterns of aggression finally may be turned against her own self, e.g. by biting the lips or the fingernails. Sometimes, a girl will push or hit a friend standing close by while smiling at the man who initiated contact; sometimes she stamps her feet. In short, motor patterns of approach, withdrawal and aggression are combined in various ways, resulting in a great variability of expression which nonetheless derives from the combination of a few constants (p. 15). It is for this reason that we understand this expression wherever we encounter it, even in a stone age Papuan girl, who has had no previous contact with people from the outside world. It is clear from these and many other observations (p. 36) that man to a certain extent fears his fellow man, and the more so if he is a stranger. Personal acquaintance buffers this fear.

Until people started to live in large cities, man lived in individualized groups where everyone knew each other. Contact with strangers was a rare event. Most of the time people lived with others they knew well. This has changed in modern times where the majority of people spend their daily life within anonymous groups, meeting mostly strangers and depending on them, whereas their individualized group of relatives and friends is geographically scattered.

People certainly like close contact with others, but mainly with those they know well. Strangers are reacted to with a certain amount of avoidance, if we are not somehow 'introduced' to them. To demonstrate this, we need only watch people who do not know each other, in an elevator for example (see Goffman 1963). They avoid looking at each other and look at the floor indicator instead. This tension may be dissipated by a friendly remark but it is certainly present at first. This is why constant exposure to strangers is experienced as a stress. Most people can cope with it, but they do complain about too many contacts of this sort, and also of the loneliness felt within an impersonal crowd, because they are not embedded in an individualized group. Living with strangers in an anonymous society shifts our behavior more towards mistrust and avoidance since there is more agonistic arousal (mistrust and flight system) than within an individualized community where mutual trust predominates.

We adapt to strangers in various ways. One pattern is to mask our emotions by controlling our expressive behavior. This builds up a communication barrier which may be considered as a protective device. If we allow others to read our emotions we become vulnerable and expose ourselves to the danger of exploitation, since aggressions are less inhibited with strangers. The 'mask' is therefore adaptive; it keeps the stranger at a distance. Constant avoidance of this sort, however, may establish such an atmosphere of mistrust that individuals are unable to get rid of their mask, even when within their individualized group. The defensive attitude becomes strongly embedded in everyday life. Once established it may continue as a family tradition. It seems to me that the contact avoidant mothers whom Main (1977) described are the result of such habitual masking of emotions in response to the anonymous society. These mothers do not get rid of their masks and pass this habit on to their children, in a vicious cycle. Modern group therapies mainly deal with disturbances of this sort, and the therapy consists of training people in communicative strategies which allow them to express themselves and take off their masks. These strategies include physical contact, group activities, rituals of synchronization, all allowing the participants to overcome barriers between themselves.

Therapy corrects disturbances that already exist. But what can be done actually to prevent the development of such communication difficulties? We shall certainly have to continue to live within an anonymous society, and I am sure we can do so without problems, if we are also allowed to enjoy the warmth of the individualized group. At the moment our cities are built as if neighbors were our greatest enemies, whom we must screen off. City planners do their best to isolate families from each other.

Children and adults alike need facilities in our cities where local groups can meet and create individualized communities within the anonymous mass society. This seems feasible if we consider the amount of money spent on the automobile, which is after all just an artificial organ of locomotion. The future of our children should be worth the same expenditure, but at the moment only a small fraction of the money spent on cars is invested for this purpose.

In some individuals the fear of conspecifics is never overcome and even personal acquaintance does not seem to help. This is the case in autistic children who are unable to establish a bond since communication is seriously disturbed by the individual's anxiety. Tinbergen and Tinbergen

(1972) have shown in their study that fear of people is the cause of autistic withdrawal. This fear makes it impossible for them to look into another person's face and to respond to another person's expressions and so the person withdraws completely. Whereas behavior therapists reward the child for every eye contact, Tinbergen proposes a more subtle approach where the child is first gradually accustomed to physical contact and then eye contact is reinforced. If we knew more about the basic strategies of interaction which are part of our inborn behavioral repertory, we could certainly take advantage of such knowledge in all therapies concerned with communication disturbances.

There are many more pathologies in human communication. For example, failure to signal in the accepted way, even though this failure may be accidental, may lead to rejection. I know someone who, due to an eye ailment, always looked at people with his head slightly tilted backwards. This gave him an expression of haughtiness which, combined with his impressive height, made it difficult for him to make friends. In cases like this it becomes clear how blindly man responds to the expressive pattern of his fellow man.

Other communication disturbances result from the adherence to a role which is supposedly no longer suitable. Regression, for example, is a common phenomenon. An adult's regression into infantile behavior serves as an appeal to establish or strengthen a bond. Lovers use childish talk and behavior, and so do people who are in need of friendly, comforting attention. Similar behavior has been observed in the seriously ill, whether old or young. Soldiers who have experienced a breakdown after a battle have been seen to seek refuge at a comrade's breast, burying their head and clinging like babies. Regression into infantile patterns is part of the normal behavioral repertoire. Only if an adult fails to come out of his regressive phase does the phenomenon become pathological. When the rules underlying communicative strategies are clarified, we shall be in a position to understand and thus treat such pathological behavior.

XIV. Aims and objectives of human ethology

According to Shafton: 'What human ethologists take as their legitimate domain . . . are the "primitive animal-like" design features of behavior, which still exist in us, but subserviently to higher levels of organisation not to be approached by ethological methods' (1976:15).

There evidently exists some misconception about what human ethologists consider their field of research. Certainly the search for phylogenetically adapted behavior patterns is a major issue, but even these are not necessarily ' "animal-like" design features' since many of the programs inborn in us have no homologous equivalent in animal behavior and are typical only for our species.

In addition, the question to what extent man's behavior is pre-programmed by phylogenetic adaptations is not the only one ethologists seek to answer. The present investigation should illustrate quite clearly that we are interested in the phenomena of cultural evolution, which can be examined and understood by applying the methods and the theoretical background of biology. It is certainly not the only approach for ethologists, nor are we the first to search for the function of a pattern and for universals. The field of ethology is specifically characterized by the theoretical background and the methodological approach. The final aim is to understand human behavior in all its different facets in order to answer the question why man behaves in the way he does. This question has an historical aspect, and psychologists and anthropologists have mainly concentrated on cultural history and individual history (ontogeny), while ethologists have added to it the phylogenetic dimension. The question also has a functional aspect. We are asking whether a behavior fulfils any function which contributes to the survival of the species. This question can be asked both for culturally as well as for phylogenetically evolved behavior. Certainly not all observable patterns fulfil functions, but in most cases they do. Finally the question of why a human being behaves in a particular way can also be examined in relation both to external and internal causes. Here the field of ethology merges with behavioral physiology.

As to the methodology, emphasis is put upon observation in the natural setting and the comparative approach (see p. 8). Objective observation by sampling data on film and tape is one of the main methods of ethology, since when encounters are filmed, the data provide a good basis for cross-cultural comparisons. The protocols accompanying such film strips describe what the people did before and afterwards as well as the actual reactions of the interactants. Behavior can then be analyzed objectively and correlated by a number of observers. This is not always possible when the observer actually participates in the events and may introduce subjective impressions. My own team tapes verbal communication and also cooperates with ethologists who answer verbal inquiries which supplement our data, a method which has proved very satisfactory. However this needs to be further supplemented by other methods of data retrieval, which it cannot wholly replace. From our observations in the natural setting we proceed to experimental analyses.

In our attempt to answer the question why we behave in the way we do, we certainly do not restrict ourselves to the 'primitive' design features of behavior, and Shafton's statement that the higher levels of organization cannot be approached by ethological methods is invalid. In this paper alone we have discussed complex rituals of communication-bonding, spacing and competing, appeasing, conquering fear, maintaining discipline etc., all rituals which are certainly not 'primitive' design features. In this context Lorenz's book, *Die Rückseite des Spiegels* (The other side of the mirror, 1973) is of importance, for here he presented a biological theory of cognition.

In summary, human ethology is the biology of human behavior. Its emphasis lies in morphology, phylogeny, ecology, developmental biology and physiology. Our field of research overlaps other disciplines of human behavior such as developmental and social psychology or social anthropology, which in part also employ similar strategies of research.

When ethologists emphasize the importance of a shared inheritance as a determinant of human behavior, they are also emphasizing the possible danger of developing educational programs which assume that man's behavior is easily malleable, and run the risk therefore of being 'inhuman', since they fail to consider the possibility that man has some given inclinations, which should be at least respected if frustration is to be avoided. Of course, we have to educate man, and often against his inborn inclinations; knowing these, however, will help to develop humane strategies of education. As Lorenz emphasizes:

Wherever man has achieved the power of voluntarily guiding a natural phenomenon in a certain direction, he has owed it to his understanding of the chain of causes which formed it. Physiology, the science concerned with the normal life processes and how they fulfill their species-preserving function, forms the essential foundation for pathology, the science investigating their disturbances.   (Lorenz 1966b:30)

The fact that we share a common inheritance, and that we remain biologically one species, allows us to share concern on a basic emotional base. If it were not so – if it were indeed true, for example, that ethical norms are all culturally derived and that these are what contribute to the survival of a specific culture, as Skinner once suggested – then the representatives of different cultures would be totally different men and accordingly would act as if they were different species. Fortunately our heritage sets limits to our cultural indoctrinability. We may be taught that others are our enemies, and indeed that they are not human at all, but our conscience will not believe it and therein rests our hope. It rests in our heritage *and* also in our education. I find it very comforting that there exists a nature of man.

1.2. Personal identity as an evolutionary and historical problem

THOMAS LUCKMANN

The birds and the bees do it, too?
(Punch-line from an Austro-Hungarian joke)

I. On invasions, rituals and institutions

When new intellectual ventures begin developing into academic disciplines they seem quite regularly to follow a natural inclination to colonize neighboring territories. The established occupants of these territories appear to have an equally natural conservative bent. They oppose resolutely, and sometimes – if the threat is serious – violently, the immoderate jurisdictional claims of the upstarts. The disputes are usually resolved in the end, but not before there has been much talking and shouting by all concerned. It is the talking rather than the shouting that decides how such claims and counterclaims are adjudicated. This, I suppose, is the point which the organizers of the conference had in mind.

The expeditions into the territory of the social sciences which were inspired by many sources, from Darwin to the modern geneticists, but most particularly by Jakob von Uexküll, were continued by Konrad Lorenz and now, prominently among many others, Eibl-Eibesfeldt. These incursions led not only to ritualized duelling among gentlemen scholars in the time of Darwin and Spencer but in recent decades also to unrestrained mortal combat between some of the more ambitious invaders and some of the most worried self-appointed defenders. Ethologists will surely be able to tell us whether biological analogies and, in this case, perhaps also homologies could help us to understand these all-too-human set-to's and to-do's. In fact, I wonder whether an instructive comparison of various traditions of the comparative method so beloved of

56

ethology should not be arranged. What would a primatologist conversant with the procedures by which rank is established in a troop of baboons, a historian of science contemplating the long series of partly successful and partly disastrous importations of biological ideas and models into social science, and a sociologist of knowledge familiar with the ways by which social institutions reinforce the theoreticians' bent toward cognitive totalitarianism, make of the latest episodes of intellectual incursion? Speaking of territorial invasions, it may be salutary for those of us who assume that the topic of this volume is not merely a minor but an important and particularly promising crossing of the borders, to remember not only what happened to China after the Mongols crossed the Great Wall in the Middle Ages but also what happened to the Mongols after they invaded China. Can we see the conference as a signpost pointing to the sinification of our vigorous latter day intellectual Mongols?

If that is indeed the case, I may express my hope that ever larger segments of the Mongol elite will acquaint themselves with the vast body of Chinese literature. It is in keeping with historical precedent that in the first phases of such an invasion the invaders try to seal themselves off from the decadent civilization of the local inhabitants. But in order to understand the rather quaint customs of a people of whom they so far had only superficial knowledge, a different attitude on the part of the newcomers eventually becomes necessary. Shall we say that sinification is a matter of adaptive behavior?

In trying to offer a contribution of my own to the discussion of the question how far ethological approaches can be taken in the systematic study of human affairs, I could follow one of several paths. For one, I could bypass the fascinating substantive parts of chapter 1.1 by Eibl-Eibesfeldt and directly start a debate of certain key methodological issues which he raises. These issues concern more than the problem of ritualization; they go beyond the ethological approach. But it would surely be premature to engage in abstract argument on what constitutes an *explanatory* law and what is merely a *descriptive* regularity; what levels of interest can be legitimately satisfied in the systematic explanation of the complex structures of behavior that are involved in human affairs; how different levels of analysis can be reasonably connected in an encompassing yet non-reductionist theory that satisfies both practical and philosophical dimensions of our curiosity about the world; the limits of *functionalism* in general (i.e. in the context of any systems theory) and the specific problems of functionalist explanation in the study of human cultures; the proper uses of the comparative method in dealing with data on human affairs, data that have a peculiar (inter-) subjective, (linguistic-) symbolic and (narrative-) historical dimension. I am confident that there will be time and opportunity to discuss these matters at a later date.

An obvious alternative was to take the paper by Eibl-Eibesfeldt as a whole and discuss it in detail from the point of view of a sociologist. I should like to stress that I find Eibl-Eibesfeldt's exposition of the key concepts of ethology instructive, the summary of his far-ranging empirical work on the universality of basic expressive movements and certain rituals in face-to-face interaction wholly admirable, and the programmatic statement of his views on what he calls cultural evolution and on the presumed selective pressures operating on cultural patterns, sufficiently wrong-headed to provoke me into resolute opposition. I do not believe that anyone who has dealt systematically with the complexities of social organization and cultural process in history could accept such a view of 'cultural' evolution. The notions of selective pressure, reproductive success, group fitness and the like cannot be transferred, without danger of simplification as well as confusion, from one explanatory level to another. The social sciences have been blessed by misleadingly vague biological analogies before! Incidentally, this probably explains why so many social scientists block off with prejudice any contribution to the human sciences from biology that goes beyond anatomical structure and physiological function. With Eibl-Eibesfeldt and other adherents of the position for which he stands one should very carefully debate the question to what extent explanations of structures and functions on one organizational level can be integrated into explanations of structures and functions on a higher level: higher in the sense that it evolved from the preceding level *and* that it still contains many of the elements of the preceding level (cf. Jonas 1976).

None the less I shall not choose this second path to enter the discussion either. I do not plan to argue directly against what I think is a mistaken and unproductive view of social historical processes. I intend to approach the general question of how evolutionary explanations of human behavior can be integrated from a different direction. With Eibl-Eibesfeldt I share the modern, historically not always obvious, creed that *human* life is a matter of *life*, and I suppose that most social scientists today will agree with him that this means that it is a product of evolution. I also agree with him that ritualization (in the ethological meaning of the term) shapes and determines much of what are the 'building blocks', the constituent behavioral elements of face-to-face social interaction. Although it is probably premature to worry now about exactly *how* much, the possibilities of some kind of measurement on such matters may improve in the future and the question may be *then* answerable more accurately (cf. Jolly 1972:138ff). Following Eibl-Eibesfeldt, I shall take ritualization to refer to 'the process by which non-communicative behavior patterns evolve' into communicative ones (see above, p. 14). I shall assume that the expressive movements of which rituals consist are indeed 'integrated in a more complex event which is structured in a rule-governed way' (see above, p. 10). I shall further assume that the regularities which he finds in these events are pretty much as he describes them and that for non-human species at least they are sufficient to account for these events.

It seems to me fairly obvious, however, that these events, being necessarily face-to-face, consist of continuous or near-continuous short-term sequences of social interaction. The ethological meaning of the term 'ritual' does *not* include the full range of regularities in social interaction which the proverbial man in the street wants to understand for practical purposes, and which social anthropologists and sociologists as well as historians and other social scientists try to describe and explain systematically. Although the term overlaps to some extent the anthropological notions of ritual, it does not reach as far as the sociological concept of institution. It does not account for regularities in long-term behavioral sequences of individuals nor does it connect these to basic principles of human social organization as successfully as does the concept of institution – nor, of course, was it designed to do so. I do not wish to try my hand at an abstract comparison of the explanatory power of 'ritual' and 'institution', picking up here and there illustrations (from the Peloponnesian War to the rise of modern bureaucracy) favorable to the point to be made. Instead I should like to take up a problem that is on the borders of our various disciplines and that has been – with the mostly inglorious exception of psychology – neglected by all of them, despite the fact (or what I think is a fact) that it clearly demonstrates the interplay of evolutionary and historical determinants of human behavior: the problem of personal identity. It may be highly unusual to think of personal identity rather than specific traits (phenotypes), as having evolved and it may be even more unusual for a sociologist with historical interests to speculate on evolutionary matters – but the Great Wall can be pierced in *both* directions.

II. On the evolution of personal identity

What I have to say about personal identity rests on several connected assumptions. To the best of my knowledge these assumptions are compatible with present information on human phylogeny and ontogeny. I consider the argument to which I am led by these assumptions in agreement with whatever historical knowledge is available on the subject. None the less it will be prudent to admit immediately that my argument contains speculative elements. This is due to two circumstances. Leaving aside for the moment the possibility that my knowledge of the specifics of human phylogeny and ontogeny is inadequate to support my assumptions, the argument that is derived from these assumptions is rather sweeping. It is formulated on such a high level of abstraction that several intermediate steps of conceptualization and operationalization are required before the argument's corroboration or refutation by an identifiable set of empirical data can be established definitely. It should therefore be considered, perhaps, as a paradigmatic venture rather than as a hypothesis. Furthermore, the argument is formulated with prejudice; which proposition about the nature of human beings offered by a human being is not? In my case the argument is evidently rooted in a philosophical and a social-theoretical position. These are the assumptions.

1. The species to which we belong is characterized by a somewhat unusual form of life. This form of life, i.e. the human level of behavioral integration, is most aptly described by the concept of personal identity. Personal identity refers to *central long-range control of its behavior by an individual organism.*

2. This form of life emerged in the *interaction* of several analytically distinct dimensions of the evolutionary process: of the anatomical and physiological evolution of the body; of the evolution of individual consciousness; and the the evolution of social organization. In theoretical reconstructions, at least, ethologists and palaeo-anthropologists should be able to account for the emergence of this level of behavioral organization by tracing its adaptive value to a species forced from foraging to cooperative and food-sharing hunting (cf., e.g., Kummer 1971, Lancaster 1968, Schaller and Lowther 1969, Tiger and Fox 1971, Washburn and Lancaster 1968). At all events, it seems highly implausible to assume that anything like human language, technology and culture could have evolved without a roughly corresponding development of strongly individualized social relations and a central control of individual behavior.

3. The high measure of individualization in social relations was only possible in a species with extraordinary intra-specific behavioral variability. Cultural 'sub-speciation', so important for the development of historical social structures, presupposes a high degree of individualization (cf. Jelínek 1969).

4. The evolution of personal identity presupposes an especially high measure of the individual organism's detachment from the situational 'here and now' of the environment as well as from the immediacy of its experiences of self. In other words, it presupposes the beginnings of some sort of reflective consciousness and an initial stage of 'excentric positionality', if I may use a term coined by Plessner (1965) to refer to what he considered the basic mode of human existence. After the last decades of field investigation and experimental study of primates we must no longer cherish the (neo-Cartesian?) notion that all species, save ours, live in closed worlds. It may well be that the transition between the positionality of other species and the excentricity of ours is less abrupt than former generations of scholars imagined. None the less it seems reasonably certain that the conditions necessary for a high measure of individual detachment are not fully present – nor all available in the necessary combination – in other species, not even other primates.

5. The main conditions for such detachment are as follows:

(a) With regard to the body: the physiological evolution of the organism, and especially of the brain, must enable the organism to experience the environment through a rich ('redundant') variety of senses as a reasonably stable and predictable structure of objects and events (cf. Jonas and Jonas 1974). Reconstructions of the phylogeny of the brain in relation to the phylogeny of the entire organism, and of the phylogeny of the species in relation to ecologically variable and climatically and otherwise changeable environments, show the emergence of increasingly more complicated synthetic performances. Multi-modal informations about the environment can be grasped 'holistically'; they are consistently related to temporally and spatially identifiable stimuli in the environment; eventually, they can even be labeled in some fashion and stored for centrally controlled re-use (Ebbecke 1959, Count 1970, 1974, Jerison 1973). This is of course an essential condition for the emergence of face-to-face symbol systems and, eventually, notation (cf. Marshack 1976).

(b) With regard to consciousness: the results of the physiological evolution of the body which were just described can also be put in different terms. The extraordinary measure of synthetic ability (synthesizing synchronically *and* diachronically; cf. Premack 1977) meant that the individual could experience changing environments as a structure of typical objects and qualities, as a 'world'; and that he could integrate sequences of situations to a 'history' of typical events. This cognitive development has obvious pragmatic functions. It is a necessary condition for the ability to *delay* responses to immediate situational stimuli and, eventually, to suppress some responses altogether for the sake of fictively anticipated and volitionally *projected* trans-situational ends. The ability of the individual to locate himself in a 'historical world' enables him to engage in *actions* over long and discontinuous sequences of behavior. It is surely plausible to assume that this ability must have been advantageous to individuals, groups and the species as a whole.

(c) With regard to social organization: detachment from the immediacy of the experiences of self rests on attentiveness to others and the ability to recognize the reflection of one's own self in the behavior and actions of others. Protracted and intensive attention to the behavior of other individuals and a reasonably coherent assessment of their reactions emerged in social systems which were based on highly individualized and already somewhat 'historicized' relations among the members of a group. The assumed ritual cannibalism of Peking man and the Neanderthal burial of the dead are symptoms of 'historicization' (Clark 1967). There seem to be considerable differences in this respect even among primates and the importance of the degree of individualization of social relations for ranking and sexual bonding (all the way to the avoidance of incest) seemed to vary significantly (cf. Kummer 1971, Reynolds 1966). It is likely that cooperative hunting and food-sharing, in which *Homo* differs from other primates but shows interesting analogies to the carnivores, furthered what is already a high degree of individualization of social bonds among primates and especially among chimpanzees. But the most important factor seems to be the long dependence of the child on the mother. This process, need I add, should not be considered as a purely cognitive or pragmatic one. It has an important emotional component (cf. Eibl-Eibesfeldt 1972b, Hamburg 1963). In any case, it is difficult to imagine that the highly individualized human recollection of the actions of others and the reciprocal long-term and trans-situational imputation of responsibility for past actions should not have evolved from these or similar pre-human and proto-human circumstances.

6. The phylogenetically evolved structures of body and consciousness continue to determine basic elements of individual behavior. They also set recognizable limits to the varieties of human social organization. But personal identity is the regulatory principle for the integration of basic behavioral elements into long-term sequences of social interaction.

Furthermore, the influence of many of the phylogenetically evolved structures of body and consciousness upon behavior is no longer direct but mediated by personal identity.

7. The evolution of a continuous central organization of individual behavior, linked to the evolution of individualized long-term structuring of social interaction, are the main sources of the 'historicization' of individual consciousness and social organization. Evolution in the strict sense ceases to determine human affairs as specifically human, i.e. subjectively and collectively meaningful affairs. Social interaction, beginning with the rituals of face-to-face encounters, over the complex patterning of social relations in relatively small groups (as, for example, in archaic kinship systems), all the way to the bureaucratic political economies of modern industrial societies, are regulated by 'norms' and 'traditions', i.e. by *social institutions*. The individual lives in a historical world; his actions have strong trans-situational and trans-individual components. Human beings develop into political and (im-)moral actors.

To put it briefly: *personal identity, itself a product of* a few million to several hundred thousand years of *natural history*, mediates between the phylogenetic and ontogenetic determinants of human existence and those determinants which are the result of the artificial, self-made history that can be measured in tens of thousands and hundreds of years.

It is from these assumptions that I come to my argument. I shall try to show how personal identity, an evolutionary emergent, becomes a *historical* form of life. The constituent elements of personal identity, the human body, the elementary structures of consciousness and the basic determinants of social interaction are established in the *'biogram'* of the species. The concrete development of any individual personal identity, however, depends upon a *socio-historical a priori*. That socio-historical *a priori* is linked to the evolutionary 'biogram' of the species inasmuch as it cannot transgress the limits set by it. It cannot be derived from the 'biogram', however; it is only one of the many possible human historical constructions which is compatible with it.

In my attempt to show how personal identity becomes a historical form of life I shall take three steps. I shall present a basic sketch of the social ontogeny of personal identity in face-to-face interaction which systematizes models developed by Mead (1934) and Cooley (1967). Then I shall discuss the ways in which face-to-face interaction is determined by historically specific forms of social organization, a social structure; and by historically specific, symbolically transmitted systems of orientation in reality, a culture. Finally, I shall use a crude typology ('archaic' versus 'modern') of socio-historical *a priori*'s to illustrate the variety of factors that make for historically distinct kinds of personal identity.

III. On the historical ontogeny of personal identity

It is an elementary fact of our life that we are born as individual organisms of a particular species. Another elementary fact of our life is that we are born into a unique historical society. For an individual organism it is as much part of its fate that it starts life as a twentieth-century Ulster man rather than a first-century Bedouin or Upper Palaeolithic hunter, as is its birth as *Homo* rather than *Papio* or *Hylobates*. Twentieth-century Ulster society and first-century Bedouin tribes are objective realities for the individuals living in them. No doubt such realities have a peculiar objectivity that is not quite the same as the objectivity of a tree or a rock. It does not merely rest on perceptual constancy in the environment of an organism; it rests on an intersubjective, *communicatively* established and socially transmitted organization of subjective experience. Such realities are peculiar for an additional reason. They confront the individual in the *actions* of other individuals. Anyone can see that things are so and not otherwise because of the past actions of forefathers, past and present actions of contemporaries, and perhaps because of the past and present actions of the gods. In other words, the peculiar nature of such realities resides in the fact that they are human creations – although they are not creations *ex nihilo*. This applies as much to language and religion as to kinship, politics and economics. The prohibition of joking with mother-in-law is as much part of such a reality as the belief that yams walk at night, the discovery of the wheel as much as the construction of the atom bomb, hydraulic despotism as much as parliamentary bureaucracy.

The human child is born with a body that is the result of phylogeny, leaving aside some pre-natal accidents. It is born with a phylogenetically determined potential for the development of elementary structures of consciousness ranging from basic emotions and hemispheric specialization to a certain level of 'intelligence'. It is also born with a set range of social requirements and inclinations. The child's ontogeny has a natural history. But although this determines the *nature* of its life, in some respects inexorably and in others as a limit to alternative possibilities, it does not simply determine the *historical* course of its life. None the less, the course of the child's life is not simply a sequence of open possibilities to choose from. There is a second, a socially superimposed level of existential determination which is a product of history and only very indirectly of evolution.

The individual organism, although by no means a *tabula rasa* in which learning processes happen to occur, is none the less the highly malleable material for an historically specific language, culture and social structure. Historical socialization is superimposed upon maturation. Evidently, this does not mean that language, culture and social structure should be considered arbitrary from a biological point of view; it *does* mean that they cannot be derived from biological processes except in the purely metaphorical sense in which 'history' is an off-spring of 'evolution'. To paraphrase Plessner: their artificiality is natural. *The human organism and human society are not simple structural or functional correlates.* They are not the two sides of one coin nor are they moments of a dialectical process. *The human organism is an evolutionary rather than an historical individual; human societies are historical collectivities rather than evolutionary sub-species or varieties.* Their relation is established in a complicated process in which the individual organism acquires an historical personal identity in a social process that presupposes *both* phylogenetic and historical structures.

A historically specific social structure and an historically specific world view (i.e. a language and a culture viewed from 'within' as formal but subject-centered systems of orientation and communication) influence the course of human life by way of institutional 'norms'. Individual action and orientation are geared to these 'norms' as the individual comes to know them and he comes to know them in communicative and, most importantly, symbolic processes. The individual's behavior is increasingly not only governed by rules – it also follows rules, and, a circumstance that should not be overlooked, breaks rules.

The norms of a historical social structure and world view determine, to begin with, the character of the *primary social relations* into which the child is placed from its birth. They define the child's kinship position (first-born son) and its legal status (heir) and they also influence its survival chances (infanticide; modern hospitals). These norms shape the way in which the child is likely to be treated (authoritatively and affectionately; or authoritatively and coldly; or permissively and affectionately, etc.). They are translated into direct injunctions (don't scream; don't steal; sit straight, etc.). In sum, a historical social structure and a historical world view shape the most intricate aspects of the social relations in which the child matures. At the same time, a world of typical objects and events, and of connections between them, a world of smiles, words and actions is being established in these relations for the child.

And this is of course not the end of it. Historical social structures and world views continue to influence individual existence by determining the character of social interactions in later life. The social division of labor and a system of stratification determine work and leisure and private and public conduct. All of these are evidently historical categories. Face-to-face encounters as, for example, religious rituals or flirting as well as indirect forms of social interaction such as the filling out of income tax declarations are determined by social structures rather than biological individuals. Social interaction is rule-governed intentional behavior geared into known and anticipated rule-governed behavior of others, but the rules are perceived and followed as social rather than individual entities.

Personal identity does not 'mature' in the same sense in which a biological individual matures. It is the sedimentation of actions and impositions in a synthesizing, interpreting 'memory'. It does not develop from 'within' as does the biological individual; it comes from 'without'. Historical sedimentations are not transmitted genetically but socially, symbolically.

Except for bodily functions, lusts and pains, the individual does not experience himself directly; what he does experience directly is a structured and changing environment. Not only rocks and trees and dogs and fishes but other individuals, too, are a functionally essential part of this environment. They are experienced directly, by means of their body. The body of fellow-men is experienced as the field of expression of their consciousness: their feelings, moods, intentions and projects. Inasmuch as fellow-men experience an individual as a significant part of their environment, the individual experiences directly another's experience of him. He comes to experience himself indirectly. In a manner of speaking, personal identity is a result of social *learning*. Cooley (1967) spoke of the 'looking-glass effect'. This image aptly represents the process in which one individual is reflected in another's experience. In face-to-face encounters the *experience* (and not, to begin with, the more complex reflective consciousness) of one's self is built up in experiences of another.

Reciprocal mirroring is an elementary condition for the formation of personal identities. But reciprocal mirroring in the 'here and now' of face-to-face encounter is a necessary but not a sufficient condition. A second condition is the mutual recollection of the actions of the other in past face-to-face situations and the reciprocal imposition of responsibility for past actions. The other fellow in the encounter is the same one as yesterday, and vice versa. Personal identity originates in the reciprocity of face-to-face encounters and as the individual matures from 'within' it is imposed from 'without' in collective memory. To put it somewhat differently, personal identity is intersubjective and has a situational and biographical dimension.

It is clear without much further elaboration that personal identities are not 'things' but regulatory principles of the intentional structures of subjective consciousness *and* of the intersubjective rather than instinctive organization of social interaction. Personal identities are not closed and definitive. Although informed consensus will have it that the most important elements of personal identity are established in the early phases of socialization, later social interactions, from face-to-face encounters to purely symbolic and mediated forms of 'mirroring', support, reinforce, modify or threaten personal identities or, in extreme cases, destroy them.

Let us return to the earliest forms of intersubjective 'mirroring'. The earliest social relations of the child rest upon an assumption of reciprocity, although that assumption is perhaps in part fictive. In a manner of speaking, this assumption imposes reciprocity on the child and, given the phylogenetic make-up of the human child, full reciprocity will *normally* develop.[1] If socialization fails to produce full reciprocity (for psychological, social-psychological and communicative or social-structural reasons or some combination thereof) and the human being does not attain this form of life, a host of everyday difficulties, legal problems, psychiatric or religious questions and moral dilemmas arise.

Intersubjective 'mirroring' is a concept which refers to the formal properties of a process which in fact is the encounter of physically and historically concrete individuals. This is merely one way of saying that the fellow-men involved in the earliest social relations of the child have formed personal identities in their own earlier and earliest social relations which again were not with mere biological organisms and mere sociological *homunculi* but with historically unique individuals. A historical world view, i.e. a particular sediment of past interpretations of reality, shaped *their* knowledge of the world and a historical social structure with specific institutions and 'norms', i.e. the sediment of a *particular* enchainment of past actions, influenced their own actions. No more and no less is meant by the statement that a historical social structure and a historical world view form a socio-historical *a priori* for the child which is superimposed on its biological maturation. I am aware of the fact that

---

[1] Along with most sociologists I may have underestimated the degree of biological sociality and perceptual-cognitive achievement present in the newborn and young infant. Cf. chapters 7.2, 8.2, 9.2, 11.2 below; cf. also Rheingold 1969.

superimposition may be a poor term for the kind of interdependence that characterizes the biological and socio-historical dimensions of *unitary* process.

The socio-historical *a priori* which guides the actions of the adults vis-à-vis the child, actions which the child experiences as reflections of itself, determines the specific way in which the child learns to think of itself and to act as a person. Sociologists like to use the conceptual apparatus of role theory to analyze the details of this process, but the use of this apparatus is by no means essential. It is important to see that the basic processes of intersubjective 'mirroring' are always concretely determined by a socio-historical *a priori*. Human socialization is a historical process.

IV. Personal identity in primitive and modern society

Let us now consider the historical social conditions for the development of varied elementary types of personal identity in primitive societies. In a second step, we shall compare these conditions to the requirements of socialization that characterize modern industrial societies and the kind of personal identities to which they lead. I shall have to neglect the ancient civilizations which, from a historical point of view, were an equally important frame of human socialization and which represented not only transitional forms between primitive and modern societies but long-lived, fully 'adopted' social systems.

Primitive societies determine nearly all the individual's social actions directly by way of – and in terms of – the kinship system. Actions which have primarily economic, political, kinship and religious functions do not form separate and distinct sets of institutions. Indeed, these different functions are merged in activities *subjectively* regarded as having unitary significance. In other words, the social structure of primitive societies is not organized into separate sectors with functionally specialized institutions. A hunt, for example, is not only a behavior complex that is relevant to the economic basis of the society, it also embodies aspects of the kinship system, and is a representation of religiously significant action as well as of the structure of authority. Furthermore, the institutional norms which determine behavior are subordinated to an extraordinary level of reality which is connected to experiences of death, seasonal and life-cycle transformations, dreams, fertility, and the like and which is represented symbolically and treated ritually.

The world view is transmitted almost exclusively through direct social interactions in which the validity and 'reality' of linguistically and symbolically transmitted meanings, values and 'solutions' are concretely exemplified. These social interactions are structured by social, mostly kinship, roles. In primitive societies the nature of reality is therefore something which is *relatively* easy to grasp. Individual action in such a reality does not constitute a problem which normally demands great 'originality'. This of course does not mean that life is easy, behavior unproblematic, and individuals generally dull and non-creative, but it does mean that the adult who has been socialized into the reality of a primitive society is rather more than less competent to cope with all the problems which are assumed to be soluble within the framework of that society's world view. This contributes to the stability and unity of personal identity as a central regulatory principle of action and behavior as it is typically formed in primitive society.

In sum, the socialization process in primitive societies is almost always embedded in the most important of the systems underlying the social structure – kinship. Personal identity evolves almost exclusively in *direct* face-to-face social relationships. These relationships are familiar, stable, highly individualized *and* they are systematically connected. The connections, i.e. the structure of kinship, make sense subjectively, they are articulated as elements of a symbolic universe. The maximum congruence of meaning in processes of intersubjective mirroring is, as it were, already provided for in the social structure itself. The individual's assumption that he lives in the 'same' reality as his fellows is corroborated concretely time and again in direct social relationships from the earliest stages of socialization to adult life. This assumption is probably of decisive importance for the stability of the self.

Contrary to this, one of the most important characteristics of *modern* societies is the segmenting of the total structure into institutional domains which are organized to meet the main requirements of separate functions. In *primitive* society, economic, political, religious and kinship functions are simply aspects of more or less unitary activities. In *modern* society, the economy, government, religion and the family form patterns of activity which are institutionalized as specialized systems. These component systems of the social structure are of course not completely independent of each other, but they work essentially according to their own norms. This means that the norms of behavior inherent in one system at any one time are not directly transferable to other component systems. The structures of meaning belonging to different component systems are not related to personal identities, but to institutions. The behavioral norms belonging to different sectors are primarily determined by requirements which derive from their basic function (e.g. production, social control and authority, procreation, rearing and socialization). The norms tend to be functionally rational, i.e. 'rational' in terms of the several primary functions. In consequence, they are more or less emancipated from 'religious' meanings, i.e. overarching symbolic universes that attempt to link social structure to individual existence and connect everyday life and crisis situations to an extraordinary, transcendent level of reality.

The segmentation of the social structure into specialized institutional sectors is accompanied by a far-reaching change in the relationship of the individual to institutions and to the social order as a whole. The social existence of the individual in modern society is made up in high measure of behavior in functionally specialized roles, which are not related to special institutions and are nearly completely anonymous in some measure. Highly specialized economic and political institutions, far removed from the immediate face-to-face social relationships of the majority of the population, determine the distribution of the very chances of access to social roles. By virtue of the continuous control of functionally important role-performances, they also shape the contents of large parts of everyday life.

Whereas primitive society consisted of a network of primary social relationships, classical civilizations had centralized political institutions. In spite of their symbolic incorporation into personalized dynastic, feudal and similar forms, these institutions had a more or less strongly marked bureaucratic and anonymous character. Economic processes, too, were generally more impersonal in the civilizations of antiquity than in primitive society, although they were still rooted in the kinship order and especially in the family as a production and consumption unit. None the less, social relationships in villages or clannish communities remained for the majority of the population exclusively face-to-face. They were linked to the superimposed political structure by clearly designated points of contact and then only from time to time (tax collectors, corvée labor, and the like).

In modern society, by contrast, the impersonal and pre-defined obligations attached to roles have priority in the business of everyday life; the actor's self plays an increasingly smaller part. As long as the specialized obligations of a role are 'adequately' performed in the proper institutional context, the role-player is, so to speak, free to 'choose' his personal identity. That identity must of course remain in the background of his role-performance or must be even denied completely. The course of institutionalized social interaction is 'objectively' defined. This means that it is determined by its place in the 'rational' organization of a social function in its relevant institutional sector.

But whether that course of social interaction makes sense to the human individual, whether it fits into the 'subjective' organization of his person, becomes a structurally negligible issue. The objective meanings of action in most sectors of everyday life are important to the stability of the society, but they are no longer equally 'important' to the personal identity of an individual. They lose their primary significance for his life. This is why in modern societies the determination of personal identity by social roles is turning into something of a mass subjective problem. Social roles which are necessary structural elements of all societies inevitably become anonymous in some measure. It hardly needs to be stressed that social roles are a necessary constituent of modern industrial societies. But when *most* social roles become highly anonymous and thereby de-personalized, the individual's personal identity is no longer clearly shaped by the social order in which he lives. Whether the non-production of personal identities by modern societies or the production system of industrial capitalism is responsible for a certain degree of alienation is a moot question.

In primitive society there is a socially objectivated world view which is transmitted through socialization processes common to all. In modern societies there is no *unitary* and *obligatory* form of world view as there is in pre-literate small communities. To the highly developed division of labor and the specialization and bureaucratization of political and economic decision-making processes there corresponds a highly differentiated social *a priori* within society. Formation of personal identity takes place in a context which not only varies historically but is also socially unequal. To put it more precisely, even the opportunities for access to the no longer quite so common stock of knowledge are structurally 'preconditioned'. Socially differentiated 'unequal' systems of how an individual orients himself in reality contain the categories by which an individual learns to see himself and others. They play an important role in the development of personal identity.

After primary socialization no version of the world view has an absolute monopoly. Although in modern society there is a multiplicity of world views, the individual is not completely 'free to choose'. Primary socialization already forms attitudes and inclinations which influence choices at a later stage. Furthermore, the constraints on behavior in institutionally specialized role-systems are not without consequence for the consolidation of character, for the development of personal identity. And yet primary and secondary socialization in modern society are not linked together by cogent structural constraints, 'pre-selecting' for the individual a cohesive (sub-)cultural model. This means that achieving a stable personal identity becomes a subjective and indeed an essentially private enterprise. This is the socio-psychological correlate of the so-called pluralism of modern societies: no common social reality, no socially produced stable structure of personal identity!

Beginning from childhood, in all societies the self is placed in social relations in which, by virtue of intersubjective mirroring, it is beginning to form a personal identity. So far, all societies have provided their members with the means to do so. In modern industrial societies, however, the processes of intersubjective mirroring do not have uniform parameters of meaning. Modern societies typically produce a relatively high measure of 'contradictory' aspects of the apperception of self and environment. The most important source of potential incongruence in the formation of personal identity is the gap between primary and secondary socialization. There is something of a break between the home and the more or less anonymous and bureaucratized social structure into which the young person is pushed and pulled. In addition to this 'longitudinal' gap there are typical problems of 'horizontal' integration: between work and private life, between the half-real, half-fictive world of the mass media and the social reality of a neighborhood, etc. There are many ruptures or at least inconsistencies which make it difficult for the typical person to create – or recreate – a reasonably satisfactory and cohesive frame in which to place its experiences and actions. The individual cannot discover cohesiveness of meaning in his social experiences and actions as such; the meaning of these actions is *system*- rather than *person*-oriented. With all due caution one might say that the social structure of modern industrial societies does not provide – as other types of human social orders do – a firm basis for the development of personal identity as a consistent principle of the individual organization of human life.

In this respect modern society not only differs from primitive societies, but also from traditional pre-industrial cultures. The world view – no longer firmly based on the social structure – now consists of a supply of items from which individuals may add on to the basic inventory that was built up in primary socialization. No particular version of the world view is strictly obligatory or inescapably predetermined by the social structure. Personal identity is not a matter of the socio-historic *a priori* to quite the same extent as in other forms of society. Personal identity of course continues to emerge from social processes, but the social *production* of cohesive models of personal identity is largely abandoned by the social system. The production of personal identity thus increasingly becomes the business of the most private *petit entrepreneur*, the human individual.

As in all other forms of society, thus also in modern societies the central aspects of the world view (among them language), the most important patterns ('rituals') of behavior, the basic vocabularies of motives, and people's orientation within nature and the social world are transmitted through primary socialization. Here again the family works as a 'filter' to the societal 'in-put'. Here again the basis of personal identity is laid down in the primary socialization process. But in *no other* type of society are there so many and such important aspects of personal identity articulated and determined through social relationships developed *after* primary socialization. Nowhere else is it possible for so many of the elements of personal identity formed in primary socialization to be modified subsequently. And the connection between secondary and primary socialization was never so weak as in modern industrial societies. In no other society does orientation to social reality and social action depend so strongly on *secondary* socialization.

The acquisition of specialized knowledge occurs during secondary socialization. Specialized knowledge renders possible action in the different institutional sub-systems. For most members of society who are recruited into the occupational system, only those specialized parts of expert knowledge are transmitted which are relevant to performance in their roles in sharply defined areas of institutionalized activity. Thus in modern society everyone, or nearly everyone, becomes a 'specialist'. Expertness is, however, definitely limited to clearly designated operations in specialized institutional sectors. In societies in which there is a relatively simple social distribution of knowledge, the bulk of the population consists of 'laymen' – but these 'laymen' are persons who are competent to deal with practically all the problems they meet in ordinary life. In modern society nearly everyone is an 'expert', but mostly in an extraordinarily restricted, functionally specialized and *impersonal* area of activity.

In all societies, at all times, personal identity is formed in processes of intersubjective mirroring. The basic structure of this process is surely 'biological' but its specific operations are determined by the historically varied social structures. Modern industrial societies have significant effects on the formation of personal identity. The specialization of institutional systems, the weakening or severing of subjectively meaningful ties between experiences and actions which are determined by these systems, the growing anonymity of many social roles, the break between primary and secondary socialization; all these circumstances combine to form a rather new type of socio-historical *a priori* for human organisms that happen to be born now rather than 400, 4000 or 40 000 years ago. The construction of personal identity has become entrusted in some measure to an 'institution' which, by its very nature, is *not* an institution, the individual subject. This does not mean that society and personal identity in our time have made something like an evolutionary leap. But it does mean that they have changed significantly. And they have changed primarily because of a historically fateful degree of independence of specialized institutional systems from the cultural organization of personal identity in face-to-face communities. The institutional 'second nature' which man made for himself in history is far removed from the structure that evolved from 'nature' as a uniquely historical form of *life*.

Comments on papers by Eibl-Eibesfeldt and Luckmann

ROM HARRÉ

Introduction

The mass of examples assembled by Eibl-Eibesfeldt forces us to a much deeper probing of the parallels between animal and human forms of action than we have hitherto undertaken, to go beyond such distinctions as that between analogy and homology. I shall follow Luckmann in turning my attention mostly to Eibl-Eibesfeldt's paper, though I shall have some comments to make on Luckmann's contribution.

The patterns in nature are rarely thrust upon us. We need conceptual preparation to see them. Part of the interest in our deliberations lies in the fact that the ethologists brought to their examination of animal social life their intuitions of human social life. Controlled anthropomorphism was a stroke of genius and now we are here to contemplate a reciprocal trade. Can we partition the complex activities of social life into elements forming a structure using the ethologists' frame of reference? I shall argue that we can do this only by making use of prior intuitions of the social force of interactions. These intuitions must be grounded by reference to our human social beliefs and theories of sociality. Thus the behavioural elements of action can be identified only in a taxonomy which essentially involves human social knowledge.

A central topic of our discussions will surely be social universals, since only if we have reason to believe in them is there even the slightest support for ethological parallels in the *identifications* of behaviour and even action being extended to include genetic *explanations* of the existence and persistence of social practices, the second leg, as it were, of an ethological contribution to the study of human social practices.

75

I

This leads me to my first elaboration of the conceptual basis of Eibl-Eibesfeldt's paper. He notices the fact of cultural diversity of means with respect to social ends without, I think, fully acknowledging the consequences for the problem of universality and explanation. The ethogenic approach distinguishes the following:

(1) Acts which are socially defined with respect to the tasks of maintaining and recreating collectives by producing coordinated commitments in individuals. In the human case commitments are created by a wide variety of processes, from occasional collusion to ceremonial illocutionary means. For example, insulting, apologizing, triumphing, greeting, marrying, conferring degrees, are acts.

(2) Actions which are locally current forms of behaviour in whose performance acts are achieved, as for instance the sayings and doings by which an invasion of privacy is remedied while maintaining the relative dignity of all involved. Action-sequences are partitioned into elementary components and structures of components with respect to act interpretations. For example, a unit element in an introduction ceremonial is identified with respect to unit act criteria, for example, the 'How do you do' exchange is identified as the action-unit in which the mutual recognition of personhood is affirmed. Thus by reference to the act it is distinguished from an enquiry. Notice the assumptions of understanding in Eibl-Eibesfeldt's analysis of introductions and the more detailed studies of Kendon and De Waele and myself (Harré and De Waele 1976).

(3) Finally, there are movements and utterances which are the 'substance' of action. Here we must distinguish ethological *bricolage* such as smiles, bows, etc., for which a convincing case for phylogenetic origin could be made out, from movements specifically created and promulgated for the purpose at hand, for example, signing of the cross, victory rolls, and other symbolic aerobatics devised by fighter pilots, signs essentially sociogenically formed.

The issue of universality appears in quite different form at each level, coupled with a very diverse range of possible couplings between biogenic and sociogenic components at each level of analysis. The complexity of the issue can be approached by separating the questions,

(i) 'Why do humans greet, marry, apologize to, upstage, confer honorary degrees upon, etc. each other?'

(ii) 'How do humans . . . ?'

Both questions admit two kinds of answers, the one essentially bio-social, the other culturo-historical. The question 'Why do people marry each other?' could be given a bio-social answer – such as 'To provide the social conditions for the biological task of raising a neotenic infant' – while 'Why do people give each other honorary degrees?' requires a culturo-historical answer. We are tempted to assume that

(a) the universality of the early items in my list, such as marrying, apologizing, and so on, implies a biologically based carrier of the social pattern at both levels of analysis, that is it includes a genetically carried, and perhaps epigenetically modified, action and act.

(b) But, cultural diversity – that is non-universality – of the answers to questions concerning the actions locally taken to be performances of acts, with respect to any one social practice defined at the act level, suggests a culturo-historical explanation both of the origin of the practice and of its transmission from generation to generation. Yet Eibl-Eibesfeldt offers us dozens of examples of ethological parallels (by this term I avoid a premature decision on the analogy–homology issue) among animal social practices to human patterns of behaviour, suggesting a bio-social account. But if this is taken seriously it implies a bio-evolutionary origin and a genetic transmission which seems to me to run counter to the observed cultural diversity of actions as means for the performance of specific social acts.

So far as I can see, the only possible solution to this apparent paradox is the hypothesis of ethological *bricolage* – that genetic endowment provides us with behavioural routines which can be differentiated semantically as the means for specific social acts differentiated by reference to the histori-cally conditioned necessities of human society, e.g. bowing in ceremonies conferring honorary degrees. The focus of interest then shifts to the question of the universality of acts, the way they originate and the means of their maintenance, propagation and promulgation. Again, it seems to me that for some, for example the act of apologizing, a bio-evolutionary origin is plausible. But for others, say the conferring of degrees, the signing of cheques, etc., a sociogenic account seems called for.

I detect a tendency in ethologists to assume that an act accounted for biogenically must be performed by biogenically explained actions, and to assume a similar link between sociogenic acts and their action-performance patterns. If this assumption were true a clear path for future development could lie before us – but I offer as counter-examples the sociogenic signals of fighter pilots (the climbing roll) as the action-pattern to realize the biogenic act of triumphing over one's adversary, while the biogenic head-touching actions of Vice-Chancellors are the ethological *bricolage* brought into action to perform the sociogenic act of degree-giving. These examples pose problems for studies as diverse as those of Eibl-Eibesfeldt and of Trevarthen (chapter 8.2 below), should they accept too uncritically the unifying tendency of ethology in the explanatory task.

Finally, I would define a ritual as an action-sequence *conventionally* associated with the social act which is its meaning. Thus, ritual*ization* is the transfer of an action from the role of a natural to a conventional sign (or, as in Goffman's paper (chapter 3.2 below), across frames), or the invention of an action-sign for an act for which we have no *bricolage*. The important point is the standardization of the action-sequence as a local means for the performance of the act which is its meaning. Thus, ritualization in the ethological sense requires the act–action distinction, that acts are the meanings of actions, and opens up the possibility for the biogenic–sociogenic cross-connections I pointed to as paradoxical in the context of too simple-minded a human ethology.

II

Eibl-Eibesfeldt defines rituals in terms of communication. I want to break that down into two deeper ideas.

1. The requirement to satisfy coordination conditions so that we each put in our bit to complete a ceremony properly and, as far as human beings (and chimpanzees) go, to thus make public commitment. Explanation of the future efficacy of commitments made in this case is not required for people, since there are institutions which remind us of our duties and the demands others may properly make upon us if we have performed the ceremony properly – *Bruderschaft*, or marriage, for example. I am not happy about generalizing Eibl-Eibesfeldt's concept of communication in the context of ritual, since it seems to me proper for some animals but inadequate to man. I distinguish (i) communication proper, which to be effective requires both sender's intentions and receiver's interpretations, from (ii) manifestations, which to be effective require only receiver's interpretations. Thus, waving is a communication since we must assume the sender's intention to farewell, whereas blushing is a manifestation, since we do not generally assume the sender's intention to show embarrassment. This roughly corresponds to the traditional distinction between natural and conventional signs and partly to Austin's important distinction between locutionary and illocutionary

forces of socially effective utterances. Illocutionary forces exist independently of intention.

2. In human ritual, communication seems to me to be involved only in the coordination of activities, not in the explanation of their social effects. Simply by playing a part in the ceremony we acquire commitments and incur expectations, often publicly enforced. Thus, taking part in a farewell ceremony may not be the occasion for any communication between participants. Rather by experiencing the symbolic actions of others and performing one's own, one makes a public commitment to the revival of civility next time one meets those people, and they will demand it of one.

III

I suppose next to its contribution to our capacity to perceive the social lives of animals, the most important aspect of ethology has been the precision of its application of an evolutionary explanatory framework, enabling exact questions of adaptation and gene selection to be posed, but in transposing the explanatory framework to the human case we have reinvented the idea of cultural evolution. I believe it is the right idea, but it needs more careful analysis than Eibl-Eibesfeldt gives it in his paper, since he cheerfully juxtaposes both applications in a simple conjunction.

An evolutionary theory in general consists of two components: a theory of transmission and a theory of mutation and selection. To formulate a good theory of cultural evolution on the analogy of bio-evolution, both components must be modified. The mechanism of transmission is partly genetic (ethological *bricolage*) and partly by other means. To understand these we must introduce the distinction between intrinsic carriers – carriers of social patterns which are proper parts of individual members, like genes are for bio-evolution – and extrinsic carriers – not proper parts of individuals. Dawkin's (1977) term 'memes' (concept, knowledge, belief, etc.) refers to an intrinsic carrier, for without that knowledge an individual would not be an adequate member of the relevant collective. But many social patterns are transmitted by public and relatively extrinsic templates such as manuals of instruction, the memories of designated experts, mnemonic picture-sequences, and so on. Extrinsic carriers are subject to mutation in ways very different from the ways intrinsic carriers mutate. I would assimilate Marx's idea of the role of the means of production in social replication to an evolutionary theory as an extrinsic carrier or transmitter.

The second component – the mutation-selection mechanism – needs careful discussion in the cultural application. If we define a 'Darwinian' process as one in which there is an absolute independence between mechanisms of mutation and mechanisms of selection, and a 'Lamarckian' process as one in which the mechanisms are coupled, there is obviously a spectrum of possible processes between pure Darwinian and pure Lamarckian. The process of cultural evolution is likely to be somewhere between, since mutant practices may be introduced to cope with a specific selection environment (e.g. obsequious behaviour to foreign conquerors) while a selection environment may be manipulated to favour a certain mutant (control of the money supply to favour local manufacturers). More important still, historical and anthropological knowledge (even at the folk level) can feed into the system making the actual process of social and cultural evolution more Lamarckian, since that kind of knowledge enables us to improve our design of mutants for given selection environments and of environments to favour specific mutants. This conference itself has changed the actual processes of cultural evolution.

IV

While, in general, I am in complete agreement with the outline argument of Thomas Luckmann's paper, I have some fairly substantial points of detail to disagree with him about.

He does not maintain a clear distinction between the fact of personal identity and the sense of personal identity. Without that distinction the question of whether a sense of personal identity is a necessary (or even a sufficient) condition of the fact of personal identity, cannot be asked. Unless this question can be asked, the place of consciousness, action-monitoring and self-consciousness (monitoring plus action-control and monitoring) among the necessary palaeo-anthropological developments, cannot be discussed.

Luckmann offers three theses about personal identity and its necessary role in the development of specifically human conditions of life. In my view each needs supplementing in rather substantial ways.

Thesis 1: Personal identity requires that an individual have agency – particularly in the sense of being able to conceive and execute alterations and alternatives to traditional courses of action. I do not believe that agency alone is sufficient to define the fact of personal identity, nor does it provide an adequate grounding for the possibility of a sense of this important property. I would argue that it is necessary further that the human being have a point of view in both space and time and that that point of view be connected with the body through which, as body-agent, he performs his actions. I believe the arguments of Hampshire (1959) and Strawson (1964) to be decisive on this point.

Thesis 2: The sense of personal identity is the product of social inter-action. Again, I am disposed to agree with this as a necessary condition for the development of a sense of personal identity. However, it seems that a second necessary condition is required – namely the capacity to carry out second-order self-monitoring to become aware of oneself as an actor and particularly as one who prepared for action by rehearsal in the mind preparatory to taking part in action in the world.

Thesis 3: Only if personal identity is distinct from social identity is there the possibility of mutant social practices and theories and hence the possibility of social change. I have rather amplified Thomas Luckmann's notions at this point, since I think he needs to distinguish personal from social identity to get his argument going. Further, it seems apparent that unless this thesis is embedded in some form of evolutionary conception of social change, namely some form of mutation-selection theory, the fact of personal identity would be sufficient to create mavericks and deviants, not social change.

I. EIBL-EIBESFELDT: REPLY TO HARRÉ'S COMMENTS

The issue of universality appears indeed in different forms at different levels. Triumphing and greeting can take different forms. The victory rolls introduced by Harré to illustrate the fact are well chosen. I see the problem in a similar way. What strikes me is the finding that there appear to be universal strategies of interactions and not just some universal movement patterns. The slides of the Yanomami girl who, after failing to block an attack by a smile, resorted to cut-off and pouting, provided a fairly simple example. Again what strikes me is not only the universality of the pattern, but the fact that in adults the whole encounter may be verbalized. If one verbally expresses the intention to stop further verbal interaction, this has the same effect as a cut-off by looking away. Verbal behavior can substitute as a functional equivalent for non-verbal motor patterns. This is also true for the patterns of requesting, sharing and giving.

The analysis of greeting and feasts which I presented in my contribu-tion illustrates how cultural patterns of behavior can substitute for inborn patterns in a variety of ways. For example, a variety of actions can serve the function of display, and may substitute for each other as functional equivalents, but the whole string of events is universally the same, structured according to universal rules. From this it should be clear that I do not assume that acts like insulting, triumphing, greeting etc., when accounted for biogenically, must result from biogenically explained actions.

I am in agreement with Harré that the two kinds of questions 'Why do humans greet' and 'How do humans greet' can be answered along a biosocial and cultural–historical line. For the moment we are concentrating upon the elucidation of the former, not because we underestimate the importance of the latter, but for reasons of research strategy.

As to the definition of the term 'ritual', I pointed out that rituals are based upon conventions, but I included phylogenetically evolved conventions. For the moment I can see no advantage in narrowing the definition down to encompass only actions which changed from a natural to a conventional signal. As long as we can show that movement patterns were particularly selected to serve as signals for the function of communication, and are thus 'ritualized' to enhance their signalling value, we speak of ritualized movement patterns. We do not refer to intentions, in the subjective meaning of the term – a smile may occur non-intentionally in a reflex-like fashion. It nonetheless serves the signalling function and it is a ritualized movement pattern. But we distinguish between adaptations which occur mutually in the sender and in the receiver, from adaptations in the receiver alone, which can be tuned in to its receptor mechanisms to interpret occurrences of the environment as 'signals', e.g. signalling prey. In this case it is readily understood that the 'sender' of the signal does not 'intend' to signal. Where communication is advantageous to both parts, they mutually adapt, and conventions evolve either culturally or biologically. In spite of our different terminologies we are aware of the same problems. As far as cultural evolution is concerned I can accept Harré's position. Cultural evolution could free itself from the Darwinian mechanisms of selection and follow a more Lamarckian process of adaptation guided by insight and reason. For the moment, however, much of cultural evolution remains a sort of groping by trial and error; even in the realm of economic and technical planning investment is dictated by the immediately expected reward and it is the same strategy of opportunistic maximizing which also governed biological evolution. Organisms at the biological level as a rule tend to maximize their propagative success, exploiting every opportunistic possibility up to the point where nature sets limits, e.g. when the resources are over-exploited. A population break-down may be the result, but this strategy of evolution has its own dynamics; to coin a metaphor, the stream of life at times of flood seeks out many channels where it will be able to continue to flow. Technical evolution seems to be guided by a similar principle and not by far-sighted planning; one wonders whether it would work in any other way. By opportunistic maximizing and experimentation in numerous trials we achieve a broad range of adaptability which certainly would be narrower if reason alone were responsible. An evolution guided by reason would hardly produce 'hopeful monsters'. But unless the future demands exerted upon us by the environment can be exactly predicted, we might need them in order to survive. Nonetheless cultural evolution opened a new dimension of life with consequences which cannot be predicted for the moment. Derek Freeman, in discussion, was certainly right to emphasize this point and he was in agreement with Konrad Lorenz in this respect.

T. LUCKMANN: REPLY TO HARRÉ'S COMMENTS

Having read the other papers in this volume I feel there is no need to apologize for the speculative character of my own. Except for the most precisely descriptive-minded among us (for whom I have the greatest respect and admiration), it is quite obvious that we are all speculating together or against each other. Harré comments critically and extensively on that part of Eibl-Eibesfeldt's paper which I also think deserves critical discussion: his notion of cultural evolution. Let me merely add to what I said in my paper that I am not only sceptical about this particular way of talking about human affairs but of *all* models – some of them of great sophistication – that have tried to interpret human history or, if you wish, the *stories* of human history. I do not find the Christian-Augustinian account of history compelling; I consider the Marxist version to be wrong and I am convinced that cultural evolutionism, in all the variants known to me, is beyond repair. Here I disagree with Harré.

In order to try to make sense of human history, agnosticism may be more appropriate and much safer than any of the major creeds foisted upon us. A way of talking about socio-cultural processes that I do think is adequate is that of a sociology of knowledge – but evidently I am *parti pris* in this respect.

Human history is a determining factor of individual life and social processes. The generic historicity of human affairs is something that emerged in the evolution of life: its origin must be understood in evolutionary terms. But the specific historical determination of human life and society cannot be so understood. Social philosophers from Aristotle to Thomas Aquinas and sociologists from Comte and Marx, Durkheim and Max Weber to the structural-functionalists of yesterday and today have used, in one way or another, the notion of *social institution* as an explanatory category in order to account for the peculiarly historical character of human social interaction. Again, as Gehlen and others have shown, social institutions are principles of social interaction that have, as it were, an evolutionary past; their origin must be explained in an evolutionary account. But their functioning, the way they actually determine human social interaction, cannot.

And now I come to the point. In order to understand social interaction as a *determining* element of historical processes and as *determined* by historical processes we need an *additional*, systematic category of explanation – additional, that is, to *social institution* and the related concepts of social role and the like. That category, I suggest, is that of *personal identity*. In analogy to what can be said about social institutions, personal identity, too, is an evolutionary emergent – but once it has emerged it becomes a relatively independent structure and, correspondingly, an explanatory category on the level of historical process.

We all employ it as a matter of course in this way when we account for our own actions to ourselves and to others and whenever we act in relation to others. Historians use it in *their* accounts, social scientists use the category implicitly, as a *presupposition* of their talk of social structure, linguistic codes, cultural forms, etc.

What I am arguing for is:

(1) that the use of this category be made explicit;
(2) that the evolutionary origin of the phenomenon to which this category refers be investigated systematically and
(3) that the category be used as a legitimate explanatory device rather than as a taken-for-granted and unclarified background assumption in the accounts of human history, social organization and social interaction.

And now I will answer some specific points raised by Harré.

I do not make much of the fact, if it is a fact, that personal identity as a central principle of the organization of action is specifically human. After all, it does have an evolutionary past. But so has human language, to take a related example.

In their full development, as *relatively* autonomous structures, however, both *are* specifically human. The concept of self, on the other hand, is less than specifically human, it is historically very limited if not unique. Bruno

Snell argued convincingly that pre-homeric Greeks did not have a *concept* of self.

As to the distinction suggested between personal and social identity, it does not seem to be a very useful one on *our* level of discussion. My case is that personal identity is socially produced; it is not my case that personal identity is all there is to a concrete, living human being. And I can see the point of distinguishing, with Goffman and others, those elements of a self that are publicly presented and those that are not. But that, I suppose, is not what Harré found missing from my argument.

References

Ambrose, J. A. 1961. The development of the smiling response in early infancy. In B. M. Foss (ed.), *Determinants of infant behaviour*. London: Methuen.

1966. Ritualization in the human infant–mother bond. In Huxley 1966:359–62.

Argyle, M. 1969. *Social interaction*. London: Methuen.

1973. *Social encounters*. Harmondsworth: Penguin.

Argyle, M. and Cook, M. 1976. *Gaze and mutual gaze*. Cambridge: Cambridge University Press.

Argyle, M. and Dean, J. 1965. Eye contact, distance and affiliation. *Sociometry*, 28:289–304.

Baerends, G. P., Brower, R. and Waterbolk, H. T. 1955. Ethological studies on *Lebistes reticulatus Peter*: I. Analysis of the male courtship pattern. *Behaviour*, 8:249–334.

Baron, R. A. 1974. Sexual arousal and physical aggression: the inhibiting influence of 'cheesecake' and nudes. *Bulletin of the Psychonomic Society*, 3:337–9.

Baron, R. A. and Bell, P. A. 1977. Sexual arousal and aggression by males: effects of type of erotic stimuli and prior provocation. *Journal of Personality and Social Psychology*, 35:79–87.

Basedow, H. 1906. Anthropological notes on the Western coastal tribes of the Northern Territory of South Australia. *Transactions of the Royal Society of South Australia*, 31:1–62.

Berger, Peter and Luckmann, Thomas. 1966. *The social construction of reality*. New York: Doubleday.

Bilz, R. 1944. Zur Grundlegung einer Paläopsychologie. I. Paläophysiologie. II. Paläopsychologie. *Schweizerische Zeitschrift für Psychologie*, 3:202–12, 272–80.

Boas, F. 1897. The social organization and secret societies of the Kwakiutl Indians. *Report of the U.S. National Museum for 1895* (Washington), 311–738.

Borst, Arno. 1973. *Lebensformen im Mittelalter*. Berlin: Propyläen.

Bronowski, J. and Bellugi, U. 1970. Language, name and concept. *Science*, 168:669–73.

Campbell, D. T. 1975. On the conflicts between biological and social evolution and between psychology and moral tradition. *American Psychologists*, 30:1103–26.

Chance, M. R. A. 1962. The interpretation of some agonistic postures: the role of

'cut-off' acts and postures. *Symposia of the Zoological Society of London*, 8:71–89.
1967. Attention structures as the basis of primate rank orders: *Man*, N.S.
2:503–18.
Clark, Grahame. 1967. *The stone age hunters*. London: Thames and Hudson.
Cook, M. and Smith, J. M. C. 1975. The role of gaze in impression formation.
British Journal of Social and Clinical Psychology, 14:19–25.
Cooley, Charles H. 1967. *Human nature and the social order*. First published 1902.
New York: Schocken.
Coss, R. G. 1972. Eye-like schemata: their effect on behaviour. Unpublished
Ph.D. thesis, University of Reading.
Count, Earl W. 1970. *Das Biogramm. Anthropologische Studien*. Frankfurt am Main:
S. Fischer.
1974. On the phylogenesis of speech. *Current Anthropology*, 15(1):14–16.
Craig, W. 1918. Appetites and aversions as constituents of instincts. *Biological
Bulletin of Woods Hole*, 34:91–107.
von Cranach, M. (ed.) 1976. *Methods of inference from animal to human behaviour*. The
Hague/Paris: Mouton.
von Cranach, Mario and Vine, Ian (eds.) 1973. *Social communication and movement*.
London/New York: Academic Press.
Cullen, E. 1960. Experiments on the effects of social isolation on reproductive
behaviour in the three-spined stickleback. *Animal Behaviour*, 8:235.
Daanje, A. 1950. On the locomotory movements in birds and the intention
movements derived from it. *Behaviour*, 3:48–98.
Dawkins, R. 1977. *The selfish gene*. Oxford: Oxford University Press.
Deag, J. M. and Crook, J. H. 1971. Social behaviour and 'agonistic buffering' in the
wild Barbary macaque *Macaca sylvana L. Folia primatologica*, 15:183–200.
Deutsch, R. 1977. *Spatial structurings in everyday face-to-face behavior: a neurocyber-
netic model*. Orangeburg/New York: Asmer.
Ebbecke, U. 1959. *Physiologie des Bewusstseins in entwicklungsgeschichtlicher Betrach-
tung*. Stuttgart: Georg Thieme.
Eibl-Eibesfeldt, I. 1955. Der Kommentkampf der Meerechse (*Amblyrhynchus
cristatus Bell*) nebst einigen Notizen zur Biologie dieser Art. *Zeitschrift für
Tierpsychologie*, 12:49–62.
1956. Einige Bemerkungen über den Ursprung von Ausdrucksbewegungen bei
Säugetieren. *Zeitschrift für Säugetierkunde*, 21:29–43.
1961. The interaction of unlearned behavior patterns and learning in mammals.
Symposium on brain mechanisms and learning. Oxford: Blackwell.
1963. Angeborenes und Erworbenes im Verhalten einiger Säuger. *Zeitschrift
für Tierpsychologie*, 20:705–54.
1970. Männliche und weibliche Schutzamulette im modernen Japan. *Homo*,
21:175–88.
1971a. Zur Ethologie menschlichen Grussverhaltens. II. Das Grussverhalten
und einige andere Muster freundlicher Kontaktaufnahme der Waika-
Indianer (Yanoama). *Zeitschrift für Tierpsychologie*, 29:196–213.
1971b. Eine ethologische Interpretation des Palmfruchtfestes der Waika-
Indianer (Yanoama) nebst Bemerkungen über die bindende Funktion des
Zwiegespräches. *Anthropos*, 66:767–78.
1971c. Das Humanethologische Filmarchiv der Max-Planck-Gesellschaft.
Homo, 22:252–6.

1972a. *Die !Ko-Buschmanngesellschaft: Aggressionskontrolle und Gruppenbindung.* Monographien zur Humanethologie 1. Munich: Piper.

1972b. *Love and hate. The natural history of behavior patterns.* New York: Holt, Rinehart and Winston.

1973. *Der vorprogrammierte Mensch: Das Ererbte als bestimmender Faktor im menschlichen Verhalten.* Vienna: Molden. English translation (in press), *The preprogrammed man*, New York: Viking Press.

1975a. *Ethology, the biology of behavior.* 2nd edn. New York: Holt, Rinehart and Winston.

1975b. *Krieg und Frieden aus der Sicht der Verhaltensforschung.* Munich: Piper. English translation (in press), *The biology of peace and war*, New York: Viking Press.

1976a. *Menschenforschung auf neuen Wegen.* Vienna: Molden.

1976b. Phylogenetic and cultural adaptations in human behavior. In George Serban and Arthur King (eds.), *Animal models in human psychobiology.* New York: Plenum Press.

1977a. *Galapagos.* Munich: Piper.

1977b. Patterns of greeting in New Guinea. In S. A. Wurm (ed.), *New Guinea area languages and language study*, vol. 3, *Language, culture, society, the modern world.* The Hague: Mouton.

In press. Human ethology – concepts and implications for the sciences of man. *Behavioral and Brain Sciences.*

In press. Strategies of social interaction.

Eibl-Eibesfeldt, I. and Wickler, W. 1968. Die ethologische Deutung einiger Wächterfiguren auf Bali. *Zeitschrift für Tierpsychologie*, 25:719–26.

Ekman, P. and Friesen, W. 1971. Constants across cultures in the face and emotions. *Journal of Personality and Social Structure*, 17:124–9.

Eliade, Mircea. 1974. On prehistoric religions. *History of Religions*, 14(2):140–7.

Ellsworth, P. C., Carlsmith, J. M. and Henson, A. 1972. The state as a stimulus to flight in human subjects: a series of field experiments. *Journal of Personality and Social Psychology*, 21:302–11.

Erikson, E. H. 1966. Ontogeny of ritualisation in man. *Philosophical Transactions of the Royal Society of London, Series B*, 251:337–49.

Euler, H. A. In press. Der Effekt von aggressionsabhängiger Strafreizung (Elektroschock) auf das Kampfverhalten von Leghorn-Hähnen. 28.Kongress der Deutschen Gesellschaft für Psychologie, October 1972.

In preparation. Effect of contingent electric shock on submissive responses in white leghorn cockerels.

Ewert, J. P. 1973. Lokalisation und Identifikation im visuellen System der Wirbeltiere. *Fortschritte der Zoologie*, 21:307–33.

1974a. Neurobiologie und System-Theorie eines visuellen Muster-Erkennungsmechanismus bei Kröten. *Kybernetik*, 14:167–83.

1974b. The neural basis of visually guided behavior. *Scientific American*, 230(3):34–42.

Fentress, J. C. (ed.) 1976. *Simpler networks and behavior.* Sunderland, Mass.: Sinauer Associates Inc.

Firth, Raymond. 1972. Verbal and bodily rituals of greeting and parting. In J. S. La Fontaine (ed.), *The interpretation of ritual.* London: Tavistock Publications.

Gardner, B. T. and Wallach, L. 1965. Shapes of figures identified as a baby's head. *Perceptual and Motor Skills*, 20:135–42.

Gardner, R. A. and Gardner, B. T. 1969. Teaching sign language to a chimpanzee. *Science*, 165:664–72.

Gehlen, Arnold. 1940. *Der Mensch, seine Natur und seine Stellung in der Welt*. 8th edn, 1966. Frankfurt am Main: Athenaeum.

1964a. *Urmensch und Spätkultur*. Frankfurt am Main: Athenaeum.

1964b. *Die Seele im technischen Zeitalter*. Hamburg: Rowohlt.

Ghosh, S. 1972. Towards a grammar of greetings. In L. Heilmann (ed.), *Proceedings of the 11th International Congress of Linguistics*, vol. I. Bologna: Il Mulino.

Goffman, E. 1963. *Behavior in public places*. Glencoe: Illinois. Free Press.

1971. *Relations in public*. London: Allen Lane.

Goodall, J. 1965. Chimpanzees of the Gombe Stream Reserve. In I. DeVore (ed.), *Primate behavior*. New York: Holt, Rinehart and Winston.

Halbwachs, Maurice. 1976. *Les cadres sociaux de la mémoire*. First published 1925. Paris: Mouton.

Hamburg, David A. 1963. Emotions in the perspective of human evolution. In P. Knapp (ed.), *Expressions of the emotions in man*. New York: International Universities Press.

Hamilton, W. D. 1964. The genetical evolution of social behavior. *Journal of Theoretical Biology*, 7:1–52.

Hampshire, S. 1959. *Thought and action*. London: Chatto and Windus.

Harré, R. and De Waele, J. P. 1976. The incorporation of a stranger. In R. Harré (ed.), *Life sentences*. London: Wiley.

Heeschen, V., Schiefenhövel, W. and Eibl-Eibesfeldt, I. (in press). Requesting, giving and taking. The relationship between verbal and nonverbal behavior in speech community of the Eipo, Irian Jaya (West New Guinea). In R. Key (ed.), *Verbal and nonverbal communication*. The Hague: Mouton.

Heinroth, O. 1910. Beiträge zur Biologie, insbesondere Psychologie und Ethologie der Anatiden. *Verhandlungen des 5. Int. Ornith. Kongr., Berlin*, 589–702.

Hinde, Robert A. (ed.). 1972. *Non-verbal communication*. Cambridge: Cambridge University Press.

1974. *Biological bases of human social behavior*. New York: McGraw-Hill.

Hockett, Charles F. and Ascher, R. 1964. The human revolution. *Current Anthropology*, 5(3):135–68.

Hold, B. and Schleidt, M. 1977. The importance of human odour in non-verbal communication. *Zeitschrift für Tierpsychologie*, 43:225–38.

von Holst, E. 1935. Über den Prozess der zentralen Koordination. *Archiv für die Gesamte Physiologie*, 236:149–58.

1969. *Zur Verhaltensphysiologie bei Tieren und Menschen*. 2 vols. Munich: Piper.

Holzkamp-Osterkamp, U. 1975. *Grundlagen der psychologischen Motivationsforschung*. Frankfurt: Campus.

van Hooff, J.A.R.A.M. 1971. *Aspecten van Het Sociale Gedrag En De Communicatie Bij Humane En Hogere Niet-Humane Primaten*. (Aspects of the social behaviour and communication in human and higher nonhuman primates). Rotterdam: Bronder Offset.

Hückstedt, B. 1965. Experimentelle Untersuchungen zum 'Kindchenschema'. *Zeitschrift für experimentelle und angewandte Psychologie*, 12:421–50.

Huxley, J. S. 1914. The courtship-habits of the Great Crested Grebe (*Podiceps cristatus*) with an addition to the theory of sexual selection. *Proceedings of the Zoological Society of London*, 491–562.

1923. Courtship activities in the Red-Throated Diver (*Colymbus stellatus Pontopp*): together with a discussion of the evolution of courtship in birds. *Journal of the Linnean Society of London, Zoology*, 53:253–92.

1966. A discussion on ritualization of behaviour in animals and man. *Philosophical Transactions of the Royal Society of London, Series B*, 251:247–526.

Immelmann, K. 1966. Zur Irreversibilität der Prägung. *Die Naturwissenschaften*, 53:209.

1967. Zur ontogenetischen Gesangsentwicklung bei Prachtfinken. *Zoologischer Anzeiger*, Supplement, 30:320–32.

1970. Zur ökologischen Bedeutung prägungsbedingter Isolationsmechanismen. *Verhandlungen der Deutschen Zoologischen Gesellschaft*, 64:304–14.

Jelínek, Jan. 1969. Neanderthal man and homo sapiens in central and eastern Europe. *Current Anthropology*, 10(5):475–503.

Jerison, Harry J. 1973. *Evolution of the brain and intelligence*. New York: Academic Press.

Jolly, Alison. 1972. *The evolution of primate behavior*. New York/Toronto: Macmillan.

Jonas, Doris F. 1976. On an 'alternative paleobiology' and the concept of a scavenging phase. *Current Anthropology*, 17(1):144–5.

Jonas, Doris F. and Jonas, A. David. 1974. More on 'assumption and inference on human origins'. *Current Anthropology*, 15(4):457–8.

Katz, R. 1976. Education for transcendence: !Kia-healing with the Kalahari !Kung. In R. B. Lee and I. DeVore (eds.), *Kalahari hunter-gatherer*. Cambridge, Mass./London: Harvard University Press.

Kawamura, Syunzo. 1959. The process of sub-culture propagation among Japanese macaques. *Primates*, 2:43–55.

Kendon, A. and Ferber, A. 1973. A description of some human greetings. In R. P. M. Michael and J. H. Crook (eds.), *Comparative ecology and behavior of primates*. London: Academic Press.

Koenig, O. 1968. Biologie der Uniform. *Naturwisschaft und Medizin*, 5(22):3–19 and 5(23):40–50.

1975. *Urmotiv Auge. Neuentdeckte Grundzüge menschlichen Verhaltens*. Munich: Piper.

Kummer, Hans. 1971. *Primate societies, group techniques of ecological adaptation*. Chicago/New York: Aldine.

LaBarre, W. 1947. The cultural basis of emotions and gestures. *Journal of Personality*, 16:49–68.

Lancaster, Jane B. 1975. *Primate behavior and the emergence of human culture*. First published 1935. New York/Chicago: Holt, Rinehart and Winston.

1968. Primate communication systems and the emergence of human language. In Phyllis C. Jay (ed.), *Primates, studies in adaptations and variability*. New York/Chicago: Holt, Rinehart and Winston.

van Lawick-Goodall, Jane. 1968. The behaviour of freeliving chimpanzees in the Gombe Stream Reserve. *Animal Behaviour Monographs*, 1:161–311.

1971. *In the shadow of man*. New York: Houghton Mifflin.

1975. The behaviour of the chimpanzee. In G. Kurth and I. Eibl-Eibesfeldt (eds.), *Hominisation und Verhalten*. Stuttgart: G. Fischer.

Leach, E. R. 1966. Ritualization in man in relation to conceptual and social development. In Huxley 1966:403–8.

1972. The influence of cultural context on non-verbal communication in man. In Hinde 1972.

Lévi-Strauss, Claude. 1966. *The savage mind.* London: Weidenfeld and Nicolson.

Lorenz, K. 1935. Der Kumpan in der Umwelt des Vogels. *Journal für Ornithologie,* 83:137–413.

1941. Vergleichende Bewegungsstudien bei Anatiden. *Journal für Ornithologie,* 89:194–294.

1943. Die angeborenen Formen möglicher Erfahrung. *Zeitschrift für Tierpsychologie,* 5:235–409.

1953. Die Entwicklung der vergleichenden Verhaltensforschung in den letzten 12 Jahren. *Zoologischer Anzeiger,* Supplement, 16:36–58.

1966a. Evolution of ritualization in the biological and cultural spheres. In Huxley 1966:273–84.

1966b. *On aggression.* New York/London: Methuen.

1973. *Die Rückseite des Spiegels.* Munich: Piper. English translation, *Behind the mirror,* New York: Harcourt Brace Jovanovich, 1977.

Lorenz, K. and Tinbergen, N. 1938. Taxis und Instinkthandlung in der Eirollbewegung der Graugans. *Zeitschrift für Tierpsychologie,* 2:1–29.

Luckmann, Thomas. 1967. *The invisible religion.* New York: Macmillan.

1972. Zwänge und Freiheiten im Wandel der Gesellschaftsstruktur. In Hans-Georg Gadamer and Paul Vogler (eds.), *Neue Anthropologie,* vol. III. Stuttgart/Hamburg: Thieme und Deutscher Taschenbuch Verlag.

1973. Aspekte der Sozialkommunikation. In *Lexikon der germanistischen Linguistik.* Tübingen: Niemeyer.

1975. On the rationality of institutions in modern life. *European Journal of Sociology,* 1:3–15.

McPhall, J. D. 1969. Predation and the evolution of a stickleback (*Gasterosteus*). *Journal of the Fisheries Research Board of Canada,* 26:3183–208.

Main, M. 1977. Avoidance of the mother in young children, implications for daycare. In R. A. Webb (ed.), *Social development in childhood: daycare programs and research.* Baltimore: Johns Hopkins.

Marshack, Alexander. 1971. *The roots of civilization.* New York: McGraw-Hill.

1976. Some implications of the paleolithic symbolic evidence for the origin of language. *Current Anthropology,* 17(2):274–82.

Maturana, H. R., Lettvin, J. Y., McCulloch, W. S. and Pitts, W. H. 1960. Anatomy and physiology of vision in the frog (*Rana pipiens*). *Journal of General Physiology,* 43(6):129–75.

Mauss, M. 1966. *The gift. Terms and functions of exchange in archaic societies.* First published 1925. London: Cohen and West.

Mayr, E. 1970. Evolution und Verhalten, *Verhandlungen der Deutschen Zoologischen Gesellschaft,* 64:322–36.

Mead, George H. 1967. *Mind, self and society.* First published 1934. Chicago: University of Chicago Press.

Meltzoff, A. N. and Moore, M. K. 1977. Imitation of facial and manual gestures by human neonates. *Science,* 198:75–8.

Montagu, M. F. A. 1962. *Culture and the evolution of man.* New York: Oxford University Press.

92   Functions of rituals

Morris, D. 1956. The feather postures of birds and the problem of the origin of social signals. *Behaviour*, 9:75–113.
   1957. 'Typical intensity' and its relation to the problem of ritualization. *Behaviour*, 11:1–12.
   1968. *Der nackte Affe*. Munich: Droemer. *The naked ape*. New York: McGraw-Hill.
   1977. Manwatching. London: Elsevier and Jonathan Cape.
Nicolai, J. 1956. Zur Biologie und Ethologie des Gimpels. *Zeitschrift für Tierpsychologie*, 13:93–132.
Oehlert, B. 1958. Kampf und Paarbildung einiger Cichliden. *Zeitschrift für Tierpsychologie*, 15:141–74.
Piaget, Jean. 1967. *Biologie et connaissance – essai sur les relations entre les régulations organiques et les processus cognitifs*. Paris: Gallimard.
Pitcairn, T. K. and Eibl-Eibesfeldt, I. 1976. Concerning the evolution of nonverbal communication in man. In M. E. Hahn and E. C. Simmel (eds.), *Communicative behavior and evolution*. London: Academic Press.
Pitcairn, T. K. and Schleidt, M. 1976. Dance and decision. An analysis of a courtship dance of the Medlpa, New Guinea. *Behaviour*, 58:298–316.
Plessner, Helmuth. 1965. *Die Stufen des Organischen und der Mensch – Einleitung in die philosophische Anthropologie*. Berlin: de Gruyter
Ploog, D. W., Blitz, J., and Ploog, F. 1963. Studies on social and sexual behavior of the squirrel monkey (*Saimiri sciureus*). *Folia Primatologica*, 1:29–66.
Portmann, Adolf. 1970. *Entlässt die Natur den Menschen? Gesammelte Aufsätze zur Biologie und Anthropologie*. Munich: Piper.
Premack, David. 1977. *Intelligence in ape and man*. New York: Halsted.
Rappaport, R. A. 1968. *Pigs for the ancestors*. New Haven/London: Yale University Press.
Redfield, James M. 1975. *Nature and culture in the Iliad*. Chicago: University of Chicago Press.
Redfield, Robert. 1953. *The primitive world and its transformations*. Ithaca, New York: Cornell University Press.
Remane, A. 1952. *Die Grundlagen des natürlichen Systems der vergleichenden Anatomie und der Phylogenetik*. Leipzig: Geest und Portig.
Reynolds, Vernon. 1966. Open groups in hominid evolution. *Man*, 1(4):441–52.
   1976. *The biology of human action*. Reading/San Francisco: W. H. Freeman.
Rheingold, Harriet L. 1969. The social and socializing infant. In David A. Goslin (ed.), *Handbook of socialization theory and research*. New York: Rand McNally.
Rosenfeld, H. M. 1967. Non-verbal reciprocation of approval: an experimental analysis. *Journal of Experimental Psychology*, 3:102–11.
Rothmann, M. and Teuber, E. 1915. Einzelausgabe der Anthropoidenstation auf Teneriffa: I. Ziele und Aufgaben der Station sowie erste Beobachtungen an den auf ihr gehaltenen Schimpansen. *Abhandlungen der k. Preussischen Akademie d. Wissenschaften zu Berlin*, 1–20.
Sbrzesny, H. 1976. *Die Spiele der !Ko-Buschleute unter besonderer Berücksichtigung ihrer sozialisierenden und gruppenbindenden Funktion*. Monographien zur Humanethologie 2. Munich: Piper.
Schaller, George B. and Lowther, Gordon R. 1969. The relevance of carnivore behavior to the study of early hominids. *Southwestern Journal of Anthropology*, 25(4):307–41.
Schenkel, R. 1947. Ausdrucksstudien an Wölfen. *Behaviour*, 1:81–129.

1956. Zur Deutung der Phasianidenbalz. *Der Ornithologische Beobachter, 53*: 182–201.

Schiefenhövel, W. 1976. Die Eipo-Leute des Berglands von Indonesisch Neuguinea. *Homo*, 24:263–75.

Schlosser, K. 1952. *Der Signalismus in der Kunst der Naturvölker*. Kiel: Kommissionsverlag Walter, G. Mühlau.

Shafton, A. 1976. *Conditions of awareness. Subjective factors in the social adaptations of man and other primates*. Portland, Oregon: Riverston Press.

Shaw, C. E. 1948. The male combat 'dance' of some Crotalid snakes. *Herpetologica*, 4:137–45.

Seitz, A. 1940. Die Paarbildung bei einigen Zichliden I. *Zeitschrift für Tierpsychologie*, 4:40–84.

Stanjek, K. 1978. Das Überreichen von Gaben: Funktion und Entwicklung einer menschlichen Verhaltensstrategie. *Zeitschrift für Entwicklungspsychologie und pädagogische Psychologie*, 10:103–13.

Strawson, P. F. 1964. *Individuals*. London: Methuen.

Taub, E., Perella, P., and Barro, G. 1973. Behavioral development after forelimb deafferentiation on day of birth in monkeys with and without blinding. *Science*, 181:959–60.

Tiger, Lionel and Fox, Robin. 1971. *The imperial animal*. New York: Holt, Rinehart and Winston.

Tinbergen, N. 1951. *The study of instinct*. New York/London: Oxford University Press.

 1959. Einige Gedanken über 'Beschwichtigungsgebärden'. *Zeitschrift für Tierpsychologie*, 16:651–65.

 1965. Behavior and natural selection. In J. A. Moore (ed.), *Ideas in modern biology*. New York: Doubleday.

Tinbergen, N., Broekhuysen, G. J., Feekes, F., Houghton, J. C. W., Kruuk, H. and Szulc, E. 1962. Egg-shell removal by the black-headed Gull *Larus ridibundus* L.: a behaviour component of camouflage. *Behaviour*, 19:74–118.

Tinbergen, N., Impekoven, M. and Frank, D. 1967. An experiment on spacing-out as a defence against predation. *Behaviour*, 28:307–21.

Tinbergen, W. A. and Tinbergen, N. 1972. Early childhood autism: an ethological approach. *Zeitschrift für Tierpsychologie, Suppl.*, 10:1–53.

Trivers, R. L. 1971. The evolution of reciprocal altruism. *Quarterly Review of Biology*, 46:35–57.

Walther, F. R. 1961. Entwicklungszüge im Kampf- und Paarungsverhalten der Horntiere. *Jahrbuch des G.v.Opel – Freigeheges für Tierforschung*, 3:90–115.

Washburn, Sherwood L. and Lancaster, C. S. 1968. The evolution of hunting. In Richard B. Lee and Irven DeVore (eds.), *Man the hunter*. Chicago: Aldine.

Weber, Max. 1968. *Gesammelte Aufsätze zur Wissenschaftslehre*, ed. J. Winckelmann. First published 1922. Tübingen: J.C.B.Mohr (Paul Siebeck).

 1972. *Wirtschaft und Gesellschaft*, ed. Johannes Winckelmann. First published 1925. Tübingen: J.C.B. Mohr (Paul Siebeck).

Wickler, W. 1966. Ursprung und biologische Deutung des Genitalpräsentierens männlicher Primaten. *Zeitschrift für Tierpsychologie*, 23:422–37.

 1967. Vergleichende Verhaltensforschung und Phylogenetik. In G. Heberer (ed.), *Die Evolution der Organismen*, vol. I. 3rd edn. Jena: G. Fischer.

Wiessner, P. 1977. Hxaro: a regional system of reciprocity for reducing risk among the !Kung-San. Unpublished Ph.D. thesis, University of Michigan.

2. Property and territoriality

2.1 Privacy as an interpersonal boundary process

IRWIN ALTMAN

Introduction

This paper deals with privacy as a central concept in the human environment and behavior field. It addresses (1) the properties of privacy and its relationship to other concepts such as territoriality and personal space, (2) the cultural universality of privacy, and (3) conceptual, methodological and philosophical implications of privacy for human environmental research.

The first section of the paper describes privacy as a self–other boundary regulation process. Privacy is conceptualized as a dialectic, dynamic, multilevel process that is crucial to an understanding of human behavior in relation to the physical and social environment. Given the importance of privacy in human functioning, the second part of the paper explores privacy regulation as a culturally universal process, based on cross-cultural and ethnographic research.

The third section of the paper presents a preliminary model of human boundary regulation that includes biological, sociological, interpersonal and social system levels. In this model privacy is the key concept associated with interpersonal boundary processes. The thesis is offered that territorial behavior in humans is one of several behavioral mechanisms that people use in the service of privacy regulation. As such, privacy is a central aspect of human behavior whereas territory may be a more situationally, individually and culturally specific process that functions in the service of privacy.

The final section of the paper deals with some conceptual, philosophical and methodological issues that derive from the earlier discussion and that have import for future environment–behavior research. I propose an analysis of environment–behavior relationships in terms of (1) a focus on the individual and social group as a unit of analysis; (2) a dialectic perspective on human behavior; (3) an assumption system that includes equilibrium, consistency, balance *and* disequilibrium, inconsistency and imbalance as central human processes, not one or the other alone; and (4) an interactional perspective on the nature–nurture issue, rather than a strictly reductionist or strictly environmental deterministic stance.

Parts of this paper, especially those sections concerned with philosophical issues, are sometimes speculative and occasionally value laden. However, my goal is not only to examine research related to privacy, territory, and other concepts but also to explore the philosophical underpinnings of these concepts.

Privacy: a fundamental concept

A major thesis of this paper is that privacy is a central construct concerned with the regulation of self–other boundaries. This section explores this theme in terms of (1) properties of privacy regulation and their relation to concepts of territory, personal space, crowding, etc., and (2) functions of privacy, including the maintenance of psychological viability.

Some properties of privacy regulation

In the past fifteen years, research on environment and human behavior has captured the attention of social and behavioral scientists. This work has been heavily influenced by studies of animal ethology, particularly in relation to such concepts as personal space or individual distancing, territory and crowding. There are about 300 empirical, psychological studies of human distancing; over 100 studies of human crowding; and numerous studies of human territorial behavior. Further, there are a number of descriptive anthropological and sociological analyses of territory and crowding behavior. (See Altman 1975, Altman and Vinsel 1977, Baum and Epstein 1977, and Evans and Howard 1973 for reviews of social psychologically oriented research on these topics.) Interestingly, privacy has received little research attention, perhaps because it is a distinctively human construct and has little history in the animal ethology literature. In other writings (Altman 1975, 1976b), I have described privacy as a vehicle for integrating research and theory on personal space, territory, crowding and related concepts.

Privacy as a dialectic, boundary regulation process. Some previous analyses of privacy contain a number of implicit assumptions that I question. For example, a traditional approach has been to view privacy as a 'keep out' or 'keep in' process, whereby people attempted to prevent outside stimulation from reaching them or personal information about themselves from becoming available to others. Thus designers build walls, sound-reducing features, etc. into environments to 'keep out' undesired stimulation; and political scientists, lawyers and philosophers have been concerned with privacy invasion in the form of inappropriate access to personal information. My view is that these approaches are incomplete; consequently I decided to play the game of the character in *Alice in Wonderland* who essentially said, 'I can make words mean anything I want them to mean.' To that end, I defined the concept of privacy as 'the selective control of access to the self' (Altman 1975). There are several implications of this definition, the most important being that I see privacy as a boundary regulation process concerned with the interface of the person or group and the social and physical environment. The idea of 'selective control' means that people do not act in a singular way toward their environment, i.e., only shutting it off, but that they selectively close or open themselves to social and physical stimulation. Thus, privacy regulation is a process whereby people make their self–other boundaries permeable on some occasions and impermeable on other occasions.

A related property is that privacy is a dialectic process. That is, I assume the operation of oppositional forces in people to be open and closed to contact with others. This idea draws from the ancient Chinese notion of yin–yang or dialectics, and the many variants of this way of thinking that have appeared through history. Three features of dialectics are explicit in my analysis. First, oppositional forces to be open or closed vary in strength from time to time and from circumstance to circumstance. One force may dominate at one time and the other force may prevail at another time, but neither is totally, absolutely, or permanently dominant. Thus, people rarely wish to avoid all contact with others or, conversely, to be in constant contact on a permanent basis. Rather, forces toward accessibility or inaccessibility vary, depending upon internal states and characteristics of the physical and environmental setting.

A second feature of a dialectic approach is that privacy regulation is a dynamic, changing process. The *I Ching*, the ancient Chinese philosophical treatise built around a dialectic approach, literally means 'Book of Changes'. It illustrates how oppositional forces, physical and social, are in a continual state of change – day and night, leadership and follow-ership, strength and weakness, and the like. In the same way I view privacy regulation as a changing process. Third, to be with or without contact and stimulation from others does not involve separate processes. They are two sides of the same coin and their opposition yields a unity concerned with differential accessibility to social contacts.

Privacy as a multilevel behavioral process. Figure 1 illustrates the dialectic quality of privacy, with the yin–yang circles reflecting oppositional forces to be open or closed and the dashed lines around the circles indicating the changing permeability of self–other boundaries. A second class of assumptions I make is that people use a variety of behavioral mechanisms to control openness–closedness. As shown in the small circles of figure 1,

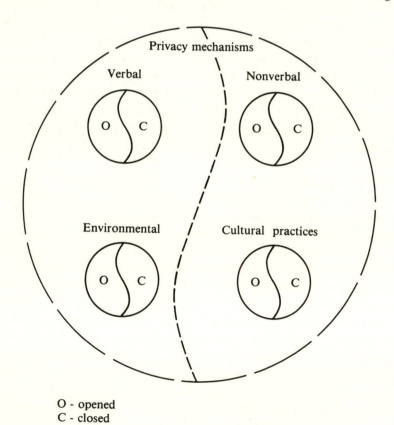

O - opened
C - closed

1. Model of privacy regulation (adopted from Altman 1977a).

these mechanisms include verbal, nonverbal, environmental and culture styles of behavior.

Some approaches to privacy emphasize environmental mechanisms such as walls, fences, acoustic and visual barriers as the primary means for achieving privacy. My opinion is that privacy regulation is managed through a variety of behaviors, not by one or the other alone. These mechanisms include verbal behavior, whereby we let others know of our desire to interact or not to interact, e.g. 'Let's talk', 'Can I raise an issue with you?', 'Sorry, I'm too busy now'. Or through use of a 'cool' or 'warm' way of speaking, so-called paraverbal communication cues, we convey our accessibility or inaccessibility to others. People also use nonverbal behaviors to reflect openness or closedness – nodding the head, smiling, leaning forward, relaxed body postures, frowning, looking away, rigid symmetrical body positions. Personal space also serves as a boundary regulation mechanism, as we move away from or toward others. Territories, or places over which a person has control, also assist in privacy regulation. We invite others to our territories; we shut off places from others; we open or close doors; we use signs that say 'keep out' or 'welcome', and so on. Finally, as the fourth circle in the figure indicates, cultures have customs, rules, and norms for regulating accessibility. In the present-day United States, we do not 'drop in' on friends too early in the morning or too late in the evening. We generally do not barge through locked doors; we are careful not to intrude on others; we have cultural practices to reflect dissatisfaction with intruders.

The various privacy mechanisms work in profiles and patterns, not separately. People use various mixes or combinations of behaviors to reflect desires for interaction or withdrawal. Sometimes emphasis is placed on verbal behaviors, sometimes on nonverbal behaviors, sometimes on a combination of two or three classes of mechanisms. Thus, as illustrated by the large circle, there are a variety of patterns of behavior that people use to reflect accessibility or inaccessibility, with particular combinations of behaviors varying according to settings, social relationships and other factors.

Privacy as a psychological and behavioral process. A third class of assumptions I make is that privacy regulation involves both psychological and behavioral processes, and that these function as an interdependent system. Beyond the behavioral mechanisms just discussed, there are psychological processes associated with *desired* and *achieved* privacy (Altman 1975, 1976b). A person sets forth a desired psychologically ideal or appropriate level of openness–closedness in a given circumstance. Overt behavioral mechanisms are then used to help achieve the desired level of accessibility. This process is monitored psychologically, in terms of the fit between the desired level of privacy and the achieved level of privacy or outcome. A form of 'crowding' exists when the achieved level of contact is greater than the desired level, that is, the behavioral mechanisms under- shoot the desired level of interaction. 'Social isolation' exists when the system overshoots the mark, that is, achieved privacy is greater than desired privacy. Thus, psychological and behavioral aspects of bound- ary regulation are linked with one another and with other environ- mental concepts such as crowding, social isolation, territory and personal space.

A further implication of my analysis is that the causal relationship between psychological and behavioral aspects of privacy regulation does not operate solely in one direction or the other. A desired level of privacy may sometimes 'cause' the use of particular behavioral mechanisms in certain settings, but the operation of behavioral mechanisms can also 'cause' changes in psychological processes.

Privacy as an optimization process. A fourth assumption underlying my approach is that privacy regulation is an optimization or nonmonotonic process. Although the ideal level of openness–closedness may shift in the dialectic way described earlier, deviation or outcomes in either direction around a momentary ideal point, i.e. too much or too little contact, are unsatisfactory. Thus, unlike some traditional ways of thinking about privacy, where a more-the-better attitude prevails, I view privacy as a two-way nonmonotonic or optimization process.

Privacy as a changing, dynamic 'growth' process. Another set of assumptions is that privacy is a cumulative growth-oriented process. While it is true that, at any interval in time, boundary regulation processes are directed at a balance between desired or achieved levels of openness, I do not assume any long-term movement towards a generic, ideal or ultimate equilibrium state. Rather, using a dialectic approach, I presume that there is a flux between change and stability. Thus, change, growth and move- ment exist alongside forces toward matching actual and desired out- comes. To use a physical analogy, day and night are a dialectic system involving change and movement, with day dominating at one time and night dominating at another time, but with both in a continual process of change. So it is with privacy. While a particular mix of accessibility–inaccessibility is appropriate in a given circumstance, and while equilibrium or balance is thereby momentarily sought, there are also internal and external forces to change the balance of openness–closedness.

To summarize, I propose an approach that views privacy as a dialectic, boundary regulation process involving differential self–other permeability to the social and physical environment. Furthermore, I assume that privacy regulation involves the interplay of verbal, nonverbal, environmental and cultural behaviors that are designed to optimize momentarily a relationship between desired and achieved privacy. I also assume that privacy regulation is geared toward both change and stability, not one or the other alone. Within this framework, territory and personal space, two important environmental concepts, are behavioral mechanisms that function in the service of privacy regulation.

Privacy functions

Given that privacy operates as a dialectic, optimizing, multilevel boundary regulation process, the question arises: So what? Why is privacy so important? What functions does privacy serve?

As discussed earlier, one important function of privacy regulation is to regulate accessibility to others, so that we can pace, control, and manage our social contacts. But there is much more at stake, and I hypothesize that psychological viability, self identity and self worth are affected by people's ability to manage privacy. My view is that self identity and a sense of self worth partly involve an understanding and control of one's boundaries and distinctiveness from others. Such self–other boundary identity probably derives in part from a successful history of regulating one's contact with others. It is often said that crucial phases in child development occur when the child learns to distinguish between the self and nonself. The infant who learns that the mother is 'different' from the self; the child who learns that the world is more than where he or she is 'at' at the moment; the child who can conceptualize directionality in a coordinated system of reference, rather than from an egocentric reference system, all reflect aspects of the learning of self–other boundaries.

Examples of unsuccessful or poor self–other boundary definitions illustrate the importance of privacy regulation in relation to self identity and viability. For example, Blatt and Wild (1976) conceptualized schizophrenia as involving malfunctioning self–other boundary processes. They state that schizophrenics are not able, cognitively or emotionally, to distinguish between the self and the nonself; the world is part of them and they are part of the world, with little separation between the two. The self–other boundary of the schizophrenic seems to have an uncontrolled and inconsistent permeability and thus operates in a helter skelter fashion, both from the point of view of the person and of others.

People who are relatively successful at regulating boundary openness–closedness not only come to know where they begin and end but are also able to develop an actual and perceived sense of competence to control their lives. If a person cannot reasonably achieve interaction when desired and/or is more lonely and isolated than desired, or if a person cannot prevent intrusions to a moderate extent, then it is difficult to see how she or he can have a very clear or articulate sense of self. If someone grows up with people always intruding on his or her places, possessions and person, and if she or he is unable to prevent or control such boundary intrusions, then it is unlikely that such a person will have a very favorable or even clearcut sense of self. Research on 'learned helplessness' illustrates these ideas in a different context (Seligman 1975). In some of these studies, animals are exposed to negative stimulation, such as shock, that appears sporadically and inconsistently. They cannot control it in a predictable fashion and therefore they cannot regulate transactions with the environment. A history of failing to regulate such self–other boundaries often results, subsequently, in poor functioning.

The essence of this discussion is that:

privacy mechanisms define the limits and boundary of the self. When the permeability of these boundaries is under the control of the person, a sense of individuality develops. But it is not the inclusion or exclusion of others that is vital to self definition; it is the ability to regulate contact when desired. If I can control what is me and not me, if I can define what is me and not me, and if I can observe the limits and scope of my control, then I have taken major steps toward understanding and defining what I am. Thus, privacy mechanisms serve to help me define me.   (Altman 1975:50)

The cultural universality of privacy regulation

The line of reasoning pursued thus far led me to consider the possibility of privacy regulation as a culturally pervasive and perhaps even universal phenomenon. That is, if privacy regulation is so important to human functioning, then it should be present in all societies – from technologically complex urban societies to technologically simple rural societies.

But how is it, one must ask, that some cultures do not seem to have privacy? They live in crowded conditions where several families may reside in a common dwelling, there may be no doors or walls to separate people, one's affairs and relationships seem accessible to others, and so on. Based on the earlier discussion of privacy as a multilevel process, I reasoned that the absence of *environmental* privacy mechanisms does not necessarily mean that a culture has no privacy mechanisms whatsoever. If one looked 'properly' at a given culture, one might uncover other behavioral mechanisms that people use to make themselves more or less accessible to others. Thus, I hypothesize that all societies have systems that permit their members to control self–other boundaries. However, societies differ in the particular mechanisms that they use. What varies among cultures may be *how* they regulate privacy, not whether they do or do not possess a generic capability for self–other boundary control.

To assess the cultural universality of privacy regulation, I examined different types of anthropological material: cultures that appeared to have either no privacy or maximum privacy in social relationships among strangers, acquaintances, in-laws and family members.[1]

Cultures with apparently minimum privacy

Consider a few examples of cultures with apparently little ability to make self–other boundaries impermeable or closed. Gregor and Roberts did a dialectic, multimodal analysis of privacy regulation in the Mehinacu indians, a tribal group who live in the jungles of Central Brazil (Gregor 1970, 1974, Roberts and Gregor 1971). In one village, houses were located around a plaza where everyone could see and be seen by others. In each building several families lived communally, although families had their

---

[1] There are many difficulties with the analysis of privacy as a cultural universal. (See Lonner 1979 for a detailed analysis of this question.) One issue is related to an emic–etic distinction. Cultural relativism holds that cultures are unique and must be understood in their own terms, i.e. from an emic perspective, not through imposition of the perspective of another culture. According to this thinking the search for cultural universals may be subject to an etic flaw, and one might misperceive how a culture really works if one approaches it only from the perspective on one's own culture. On the other side of the coin, however, a purely relativistic approach may ignore similarities among people, and some believe that there is utility in searching for commonalities across cultures while still maintaining sensitivity to cultural uniqueness.

Another issue concerns the level of abstraction used to describe cultural universals. Surely, people eat, sleep and procreate in all cultures. But one must do more than assert the existence of such activities. Lonner (1978) suggests that one should also examine how a particular universal relates to a society's institutions and how it fits within a theoretical or conceptual system.

own areas for sleeping and eating. People could see and hear what was happening in other parts of the dwelling unit; they entered the residence without announcement; the thatched walls were not very effective sound reducers. Furthermore, paths leading into the plaza were long and straight so that people could be observed at great distances. Villagers were also able to recognize one another's footprints in the sandy paths around the village; agricultural fields outside of the village were right next to one another, so that everyone knew a great deal about others' whereabouts.

Although it appears that people had very little privacy, Roberts and Gregor stated that the Mehinacu did, in fact, have a variety of means to regulate their contacts. For example, there was a maze of twisting paths and secret clearings beyond the village that was used to avoid others. Families also left the village for lengthy periods, and some even had houses and gardens miles away, to which they retreated for extended stays. Furthermore, people did not enter other dwelling units without permission, and even those who lived in the same building were careful not to intrude on another family's space. The Mehinacu also avoided exposing others' misconduct, and they were careful not to ask embarrassing questions of one another. If such information was revealed then the Mehinacu deliberately lied to one another. So, side by side, in a dialectic sense, we see mechanisms that the Mehinacu used to make themselves more or less accessible to one another.

A vivid aspect of Mehinacu society concerns practices of seclusion and isolation that spanned many stages of a person's life. One period of seclusion began when a husband and wife had their first child. At this time the mother, father and child lived behind a wooden partition in the dwelling and remained isolated from the rest of the village for several weeks. The child continued to be secluded until it reached the age of one or one and a half years. Another period of isolation often lasted for two years and occurred when boys reached nine or ten years of age. At this time a boy remained inside the home behind a wooden partition and rarely had contact with others. Even food and bathing water were brought to him, and he urinated through a wooden tube that was pushed through the thatched wall of the dwelling. During this period the boy was taught to speak quietly, to refrain from play, and to avoid emotional displays. Girls were also isolated following their first menstruation. Other instances of seclusion occurred on the death of a spouse or when men learned to become religious leaders. It was possible, theoretically, for a Mehinacu villager to spend up to eight years of life in seclusion.

Roberts and Gregor interpreted this pattern of seclusion and openness in a dialectic fashion, to the effect that the Mehinacu culture had evolved mechanisms that permitted regulation of interaction, with different mechanisms and levels of accessibility shifting over time and with circumstances. Furthermore, this ethnographic analysis illustrates the importance of treating privacy as a multimodal process, involving a mixture of environmental, verbal, nonverbal and cultural practices. By focusing only on one aspect of behavior, one would have obtained a distorted view of the Mehinacu privacy regulation system.

Another anthropologist, Geertz (cited in Westin 1970), described certain groups in Javanese culture who also apparently had little environmental privacy. Family homes were constructed out of bamboo, had thin walls and were not tightly built, so that sounds could be heard easily and there was some visual access. Furthermore, many homes did not have doors and there often were no fences or other barriers around houses. It was customary for people to wander freely in and out of houses; inside, people moved about from room to room without announcing themselves. So, once again, people seemed to have little privacy, at least in physical terms. But Geertz observed that the Javanese actually had a variety of means for regulating their contacts with others, decorum was elaborate, politeness was widely practiced, people spoke softly and, as Geertz stated, 'Javanese shut people out with a wall of etiquette' (Westin 1970:16). Thus, the Javanese, like the Mehinacu, used a variety of behavioral mechanisms, not just environmental ones, to regulate their social interaction.

Turnbull (1961) described Pygmy groups who live in heavily vegetated rain forests in Zaire, Africa. This hunting and gathering people establish temporary camps in an arrangement where everyone can see and hear what others are doing. Seemingly, they possess little privacy. Yet these people reflect some of the principles enunciated earlier. Huts were built out of large leaves and were repaired and rearranged frequently. Turnbull noted that the arrival of a new family or person in a camp might result in a door being moved from one side of the hut to the other, especially if the new arrival was disliked. One could almost keep track of arguments, jealousies and conflicts as the directions of the huts were rearranged. People also sometimes built 'spite fences' between one another's huts during serious disagreements. Thus, constant shifting and modifying of the environment served as a symbol of people's changing self–other boundaries. The Pygmies also illustrate a long-term dialectic quality of privacy regulation. Periodically, single families lived apart from a main group for months at a time. However, Turnbull observed that, eventually, they began to long for communal life and sought out the larger encampments. It was as if the Pygmies oscillated between periods of separateness and togetherness, a cycle that they followed year after year. Thus, once again, a society that apparently had little ability to regulate privacy because of a communal lifestyle actually did have behavioral mechanisms – some environmental, some involving long-term withdrawal – to regulate social interaction.[2]

In the cases presented thus far people live in arrangements where others can easily see, hear and know about one's life. Yet in all the examples we were able to cull the presence of a variety of behavioral mechanisms that enabled people to regulate their interaction with each other. Sometimes these compensatory mechanisms were cultural customs; sometimes they involved space use and allocation; sometimes they involved physical withdrawal and distancing.

Cultures with apparently maximim privacy

Now consider the other side of the coin, namely, cultures where people apparently have maximum privacy and minimum contact. Geertz (cited

[2] There are many other examples of societies that seemingly have minimal privacy. In some of these cultures close living arrangements are coupled with freedom to enter and leave groups easily, along with other techniques for controlling social contacts. Among the Ngadju Dayaks of Borneo, people live in communal houses that typically contain two to three families (Miles 1970). Living arrangements are flexible and people come and go easily, joining new communities and not being obligated to long-term residential commitments. So, while people live communally and seemingly have little privacy from one another, it was easy to regulate contacts simply by staying or leaving. Also, when families lived together, territorial behavior was quite prevalent. For example, everyone had their own sleeping mats and sleeping areas, families had private storage areas and ate at different times, people left if a husband and wife were arguing, and it was customary not to interfere in other families' child rearing and discipline. Thus, in some respects there was minimum privacy and considerable openness of people to one another. Yet in other ways cultural practices were available to control excessive interaction.

An analogous lifestyle characterizes the Choco Indians of Panama (Faron 1962). They also live communally and with little evident privacy. Sleeping, eating and relaxing also occurred visibly, and with the exception of sexual activity, life was quite public. Yet Faron observed an easy exit and entry system from communal residences, with people coming and going freely. Residential composition changed often so that withdrawal may have served as a compensatory system for regulating interaction. Similar practices were reported by Draper (1973), who studied the !Kung Bushmen of Southwest Africa. Members of this hunting and gathering society lived in groups of about 150, in densely packed villages, with extensive contact among people. According to Draper, the !Kung seemed to enjoy such intense interaction and seeming lack of privacy. Yet they also had a norm of easy entry and withdrawal from villages, so that people had a readily available mechanism to shut off interaction and to avoid conflict whenever they desired.

in Westin 1970) described Balinese families who live in homes surrounded by high walls, where entranceways to yards are through narrow doorways that are often locked, and where it is customary only for family and friends to enter houseyards without invitation. On the face of it this is an isolated, private existence. Yet, Geertz pointed out that there was, at the same time, 'a tremendous warmth, humor and openness' among the Balinese, reflecting a dialectic interplay of openness and closedness to others.

Another example comes from the Tuareg, a Moslem people who live in Northern Africa (Murphy 1964). Adult males wear a long, flowing outer garment that reaches from the shoulder to the ankle, and a turban and veil. The veil covers their whole face except for a narrow slit around the eyes, making it difficult for anyone to see the forehead, nose and mouth. The veil, coupled with the flowing loose quality of the robe, gives the impression of the Tuareg male as a fairly inaccessible and unknowable person. Moreover, the veil is worn at all times – when eating, sleeping, traveling and the like. Maximum privacy? No, says Murphy, because the veil actually serves as a sensitive boundary regulation mechanism. It is slightly raised or lowered to fit various social relationships. For example, higher status males expose more of their face when interacting with lower status people, as if to signal their lack of psychological vulnerability. Moreover, the Tuareg are sensitive to slight eye movements and to changes in body postures. So, the Tuareg achieve different degrees of accessibility through a variety of behavioral mechanisms that are played out in different profiles.

Another example comes from Galt's (1973) description of Pantelleria, a town in Sicily. Life in this town seemed to be characterized by separation and even animosity among people. People were uncooperative, jealous, and mistrustful; there was a strong norm of individuality and little evident warmth among people. A closed, private, inaccessible lifestyle seemed prevalent. But, Galt observed, there was also a long-established custom of an annual, week-long carnival that contrasted with the generally uncooperative lifestyle of these people. For example, a few months prior to carnival week people were pressured into participating in the planning process. A group *esprit* gradually developed and the generally hostile and uncooperative townspeople evolved a sense of unity of purpose. During the carnival itself behavior was quite different from that during the rest of the year, and people exhibited warmth, openness and good will. They danced with strangers, joked and teased good naturedly, and men could ask women to dance without first obtaining permission from their husbands. So, in spite of a typically closed lifestyle, the Pantellerian culture used the carnival as a vehicle for people to interact in a positive way. Note the dialectic occurrence of openness and closedness – this time on a long-term basis over the course of a year – along with various behavioral mechanisms that people used to regulate openness–closedness.

We could continue this cross-cultural analysis in terms of relationships between strangers, acquaintances, in-laws and family members, to illustrate the dialectic interplay of openness–closedness and the use of a variety of behavioral mechanisms in the service of privacy regulation. However, space does not permit a full presentation and the reader is referred to other sources (Altman 1977a, Altman and Chemers, in press, 1979) and to related analyses of Pygmies (Turnbull 1961); Lapps (Paine 1970); Chinese (Anderson 1972); rural Thai groups (Tambiah 1969); African polygamous societies (LeVine 1962); and cross-cultural analyses of in-law avoidance (Murdock 1971) and adolescent rituals (Whiting, Kluckhohn and Anthony 1958).

Based on this analysis I hypothesize that the capability of privacy regulation may be a culturally universal phenomenon. What differs among cultures is not the presence or absence of privacy regulation capabilities but the particular set of behavioral mechanisms used to control self–other boundaries. For a host of reasons – environmental, cultural, political, etc. – cultures may differ in how their members regulate contact with one another. Some societies may rely heavily on environmental mechanisms; some may use mixes of verbal and nonverbal behaviors; some may use these and environmental mechanisms, and so on. While I recognize the conceptual and empirical difficulties of establishing cultural universals, the possibility of privacy as culturally pervasive underscores its potentially central role in human functioning.

Boundary regulation: a basic human process

Thus far I have considered privacy as a specific boundary regulation process and as a culturally universal phenomenon. Now I will proceed further up the ladder of abstraction and speculation, to examine privacy in relation to other boundary regulation systems that govern human functioning. Let me state some general themes of the discussion:

(1) The functioning and viability of individuals and groups involve

a series of boundary regulation processes or systems. These boundary processes function partly independently and partly interdependently.

(2) Privacy regulation is one of several such human boundary systems. Its focus is on *interpersonal* self–other processes; other boundary systems deal with biological, psychological and social system levels of functioning.

(3) These boundary systems involve dialectic processes of stability–change and permeability–impermeability. Furthermore, they do not move toward a particular end-state, but function in a continuous growth-like way through endless cycles of stability and change, and permeability and impermeability.

Figure 2 identifies four boundary regulation systems: biological, psychological, interpersonal and social. One might be tempted to equate these systems with disciplines in the life sciences, psychology, social psychology, and sociology, respectively; and to some extent this is valid. However, I will examine these systems specifically in relation to boundary regulation.

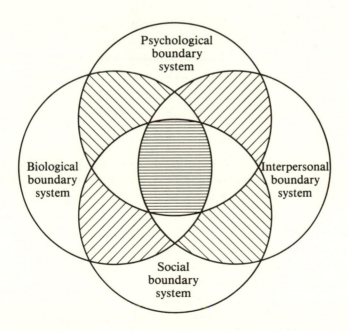

2. A framework of human boundary regulation systems.

Biological boundary systems

One series of boundary events essential to human viability concerns biological processes, for example, irritability and response to stimulation, neuron activity, organ system functioning, digestive processes, food intake, etc. Although these boundary processes vary on a molarity–molecularity dimension, all involve biologically based regulation of exchange with the environment. Perhaps the simplest boundary regulation process is that of biological irritability, which involves moving toward or away from environmental stimuli. At a higher level, the firing of neurons in response to stimulation and their shutdown in the refractory phase reflect basic processes of openness–closedness of biological systems. At an even more complex level, changes in organ system functioning in response to external and internal conditions can also be interpreted in terms of boundary processes.

As the figure indicates, the biological boundary system is not located in a hierarchical arrangement (subordinate or superior) in relation to other systems but operates partly independently and partly in a complementary, interactive fashion. Thus biological and other systems function somewhat separately, as traditional disciplinary lines suggest, but also in consort with one another. Since my interest is primarily in interpersonal boundary systems, I wish merely to indicate that several levels of human functioning, including biological, can be examined in terms of boundary regulation processes.

Psychological boundary systems

Another level of human functioning involves psychological boundary relations between individuals and the environment. For example, a major aspect of child development, particularly evident in Piagetian analyses, is a child's progress through various stages of differentiated relations with the physical and social environment. An early stage of development involves few psychological boundaries between the child and the world; the environment is part of the child and the child is part of the environment. Eventually a more sophisticated orientation evolves as the child distinguishes between the self and nonself, and as the child gains skill at being open or closed to the world. Thus, child development includes psychological development and acquisition (or maturation) of boundary regulation skills.

Another example involves progress from an egocentric spatial orientation system to a fixed coordinate system to a coordinated frame of reference system. Thus Piaget (Hart and Moore 1973) suggests that children initially locate themselves spatially from the perspective of their own bodies as psychological and physical centers of the world. Later, a remote object, often the home, serves as the spatial and psychological center from which all else is located. Still later, at the most sophisticated stage of development, a child can orient spatially using any of a series of locations as central reference points. Thus, with development, the child's relationship to the world becomes successively more finely tuned, and self–other boundaries become increasingly articulated and differentiated.

These examples also point to the relationship between boundary systems. The progress of children's development from egocentric to coordinated systems of spatial reference involves an interplay of biological and psychological boundary systems. Physical maturation of the child's sensory, perceptual and motor behaviors is a precursor of psychological development. Yet learning and experience with the spatial world is necessary for the biological system to achieve its full potential. Thus, various boundary systems operate somewhat independently and somewhat interdependently. As reflected in figure 2, the various system levels are also not arranged hierarchically (with the biological at the top or bottom, and successive levels derived from it). Instead, I wish to adopt the perspective that, while the biological system may be *chronologically* more fundamental, it operates as an interactive, interdependent partner with other systems. I further assume that each system also operates partly independently, perhaps according to different functional rules. Thus, I adopt explicitly a nonreductionist approach to boundary processes. More on this issue later.

Another example of psychological boundary processes involves research on 'learned helplessness', described earlier (Seligman 1975). Here, an organism is placed in a situation where it cannot control environmental stimulation. Aversive events appear in an unpredictable and uncontrollable fashion and are not contingent on the organism's responses. Thus normal boundary regulation is rendered ineffective. In some experiments animals almost 'give up', fail to regulate well their self–environment boundaries, and perform poorly on subsequent learning tasks. Such research illustrates the crucial role of boundary regulation and the negative implications of failure to regulate transactions with the environment.

Another example, also mentioned earlier, is the recent theorizing of

Blatt and Wild (1976), who view schizophrenia in terms of malfunctioning psychological boundary processes. While this idea has appeared in earlier analyses of schizophrenia, Blatt and Wild's goal is to link their analysis with child development. They hypothesize that schizophrenia involves malfunctioning boundary regulation systems at many levels – cognitive, perceptual and interpersonal. In contrast, they state that 'healthy' functioning, absent in schizophrenics, involves the following:

By boundary differentiation we mean the capacity to maintain a separation between independent objects and between representations of independent objects. Perception is sufficiently articulated and attention sufficiently focused so that ordinary segments of reality are perceived and represented as separate from other segments of reality that have similar properties or that are temporally or spatially contiguous. We also mean the maintenance of a separation between an object and its representation, as well as between self and nonself, and between internal experience and external objects and events. We also use the term to refer to the capacity to maintain a stable representation of the self as separate and distinct from representations of others, so that interpersonal relationships are not disrupted by extreme wishes for, or fears of, fusion and merging or both. (p. 6)

Interpersonal boundary systems

The interpersonal boundary system, the next level of analysis, is of particular importance to this paper and involves the concept of privacy regulation. There are several illustrations of boundary regulation in the social psychological literature, although they have not always been identified as such. All focus on the relationship between people and the management of various typical interpersonal exchanges.

Reactance to loss of freedom. This topic deals with responses to perceived infringement on freedom to act (Brehm 1966). Research demonstrates that perceptions of restrictions on one's freedom often lead to 'reactance', including a psychological state of stress, a drive to restore one's options, and behaviors that are aimed at reestablishing perceived freedom. Reactance states and associated behaviors are, therefore, responses to psychological and interpersonal intrusions of self–other boundaries. And, just as biological and psychological systems respond by avoidance, shutdowns and adjustments, so do people in interpersonal situations respond to unacceptable boundary transactions with various reactance behaviors. In fact, much of the earlier discussion of privacy can be applied to this topic.

Self disclosure. Another research area deals with the development, management, and deterioration of interpersonal relationships from stranger-ship to friendship and beyond (Altman and Taylor 1973). Studies investigate changes in intimacy that people exhibit toward others as a function of a variety of factors that propel or delay development of mutual openness. For example, increased self disclosure under interpersonal conditions and the shutdown of accessibility in conflict have been extensively studied. After having written about and done research into this topic for over a decade, I now view the development and deterioration of interpersonal relationships as a mutual boundary process, with many of the features described earlier applicable to its dynamics. That is, the growth of an interpersonal relationship can be depicted as a boundary regulation process, with self–other permeability being responsive to rewards and costs, setting features, personal characteristics of participants, and the stage of a relationship. Thus shifting self–other accessibility depends on internal and external circumstances, in much the same generic way that occurs for biological, psychological and other interpersonal systems.

Personal space. Perhaps even closer to the issues of this paper are the environmentally oriented concepts of personal space and territory. Personal space has been described as a personal bubble, an invisible boundary, a series of spatial zones whereby people relate to one another. Different zones are used as a function of settings, relationships between people, cultural factors and so on (Altman 1975, Hall 1966). Research also demonstrates that emotionally disturbed people have abnormal personal space practices, findings compatible with the earlier discussion of schizophrenia as involving confused boundary systems between the self and others. In addition, there is a body of research on personal space intrusion that parallels the reactance literature described earlier. For example, people avoid being intruded upon; they react negatively to intrusions; they attempt to reestablish appropriate boundaries between themselves and others when intrusion occurs (see Altman 1975, Altman and Vinsel 1977 for reviews of this research). Groups also have personal boundaries and they respond in similar ways as individuals. Personal space boundaries are, therefore, similar to the psychological and biological boundaries described earlier, in that they are focused on the relation between the individual and the external world, in this case the social environment. Personal space involves proximal boundaries, literally involving the skin and minds of people themselves. It is also focused on interpersonal interaction and therefore falls within the interpersonal boundary regulation systems described above.

Human territorial behavior. The concept of animal territoriality is not new. It has been observed in a variety of species for centuries (Eibl-Eibesfeldt 1970, Wynne-Edwards 1962). Although anthropological and sociological descriptions of human territoriality have been available for some years, it is only within the past ten years, perhaps spurred on by popularized writings, that social psychological work on human territoriality has begun to appear with regularity.

Based on an analysis of several meanings I proposed the following definition of human territoriality (Altman 1975):

Territorial behavior is a self–other boundary regulation mechanism that involves personalization of or marking of a place or object and communication that it is 'owned' by a person or group. Personalization and ownership are designed to regulate social interaction and to help satisfy various social and physical motives. Defense responses may sometimes occur when territorial boundaries are violated.   (p. 107)

There are several features of this definition that are worth noting. First, I view territory as a boundary regulation process whereby individuals or a group attempt to control access to and use of a place they occupy or own. However, territorial behavior is focused on areas and objects in the environment whereas privacy is a generic boundary regulation process that encompasses, but is not restricted to, places and objects. Territorial behavior, according to the definition, also involves personalization or marking of a place. In animals this is often accomplished by body secretions and excretions, sounds, etc. In humans, marking and personalization frequently involve artifacts, such as fences, signs and other symbols (natural boundaries such as rivers and landmarks may also be used). The definition also states that territoriality often serves social motives in humans, such as status, dominance and power, along with more fundamental biological processes. Finally, the definition allows for active defense of territories in response to intrusion.

There have been several taxonomies of human territoriality, perhaps in recognition of its diverse and complex qualities (Brower 1965, Goffman 1971, Lyman and Scott 1967). My taxonomy involves three types of human territories: primary, secondary and public. Three social psychological dimensions underlie this classification. One dimension refers to the psychological centrality, personal involvement or importance of a place to a person or group in everyday life. Thus a home or bedroom is more important to a person or family than a seat on the bus or place in line. A second, related, dimension is duration of permanence of territories. Human territories vary in their permanence from short-term to long-term use and occupancy. Some places, like a table in a restaurant, are short-term; others, like homes, are used on a relatively long-term basis. A third dimension involves the degree of control that occupants have over a place. Control over access and use of a home by residents is normally quite extensive; control over access to a private country club is somewhat less pervasive; the ability to control use of a public street in one's neighborhood is relatively limited.

These three dimensions, while not strictly orthogonal, provide one basis for distinguishing between types of human territoriality in terms of social psychological dimensions. For example, *primary territories* are exemplified by places such as family homes, a person's bedroom and bed, and so on. Primary territories are usually central to the lives of occupants, are used on a long-term basis and are under the relatively exclusive control of users. Brower (1965) referred to these as personal territories; Goffman (1961) observed the existence of places in a mental hospital that were under the strict control of staff. Since primary territories are central, invasion and intrusion can be a serious affront to well-being. Among humans, violations of primary territories are probably infrequent, although there is little research on this issue.

Secondary territories are less central to occupants, although they are important and people often have a strong identity with such places. A country club, a neighborhood pub, a community swimming pool are secondary territories. While there are some public aspects to secondary territories, use is often restricted, formally or informally, to a select group of people. While one cannot legally prevent a person from using a public thoroughfare or a public restaurant, it often happens that users who are 'regulars' often feel a sense of ownership of the place and do, in fact, attempt to keep outsiders away.

Lyman and Scott (1967) used the terms home territory and interactional territory to reflect a blend of public and private use of certain places; Brower (1965) spoke of community occupancy places; Goffman (1961, 1971) referred to surveillance space and group territories. Because their use and control has a mixture of public and private access, secondary territories are likely to be a source of conflict. Research by Newman (1972) confirms this idea, with crime and conflict more evident in secondary territories, particularly where markings and design features do not clearly specify restricted use and occupancy. This is a little researched area of human territorial behavior.

Public territories are exemplified by seats on a bus or train, places on a public beach, positions in a queue, places at a table in a library. They are temporarily owned, are not central to a person's life, and control is limited to the time that the place is occupied. Anyone has reasonable access to public territories, as long as a few basic societal rules are observed. Such places have been described as occupancy-by-society or free places (Brower 1965); public territories (Lyman and Scott 1967); free spaces (Goffman 1961); stalls, turns, use space (Goffman 1971).

Beyond providing a taxonomy for its own sake, this three-fold categorization has utility for framing a variety of research questions. What human functions are associated with each type of territory? Do all human societies have one or the other type of territory? What factors enter into the establishment of one or the other type of territory? What are the probabilities and implications of invasion of different types of territories? What modes of control and/or response to intrusion occur in different territories?

The issue of human territoriality has become a *cause célèbre* among social and behavioral scientists and human ethologists, and there is often a rush to deal with the 'nature–nurture' issue. The environmental determinists, usually social scientists, hasten to defend the learned, culturally specific aspects of territorial behavior, whereas ethological researchers are equally ready to search out the biological and evolutionary roots of such behavior. In their mutual polarization, each side glosses over the need for careful taxonomy and descriptive work, the need to distinguish between different types of territoriality and the need to assemble a far greater amount of empirical research than is now available. My opinion is that we have yet to appreciate the crucial dimensions of human territoriality and that considerable empirical and taxonomic work is required. The simple three-fold classification presented here points to the complexity of the phenomenon in humans. The following cursory review of research further substantiates the point that empirical knowledge about human territorial behavior is at a rudimentary level, and that the rush to seek a simple (simplistic?) answer – learned or innate – is premature.

Present-day research can be grouped into the following categories: studies of marking behavior, studies of the relationship between dominance and territorial behavior, studies of the regulation of social systems; anthropological and sociological research on present-day and earlier cultures. Anthropological and sociological analyses have spanned several decades; research by social psychologists has only appeared within the past fifteen years. A review of all of this work would require too much space, so let me summarize some general themes. First, as ethologists have found with animals, humans actively mark or personalize territories and such markings serve to protect or hold territories (Altman 1975; Edney 1974). The more personalized the marker, the more markers that are used, the less crowded and less desirable the space, the more effectively do markers protect places. Such findings have been illustrated in a variety of public settings, such as cafeterias, bars, libraries, etc. Thus, territorial marking is an effective boundary regulation mechanism.

A second area of research suggests that territoriality ties in with social systems. While there are some inconsistencies, research generally indicates that, in stable social systems, the higher people are in the dominance hierarchy of a group the more they have exclusive use of certain places, and the places they control are generally more desirable. In less stable social systems, where there are membership changes, such relationships do not appear as systematically. Research also demonstrates that 'the home team wins', i.e. people are more influential and dominant on their own territories than on others' territories. Thus, there is evidence that territorial behavior helps regulate transactions between group members. A third body of research on humans relates to the maintenance of social systems. Several studies have demonstrated that groups with established territories among members function more effectively than groups in which members do not have territories. In addition, Newman's (1972) work on crime, although controversial, points to the possibility that the clarity of territorial boundaries in urban settings may be associated with lower crime rates. Thus, territorial behavior seems related to individual and group well-being.

It is evident from everyday knowledge that human territoriality is widespread. However, anthropological research, especially that conducted on hunter-gatherer societies, is, to my reading, somewhat unclear about the universality of territoriality. It seems that one can marshal arguments on either side of the issue, that early hunter-gatherer and/or nomadic groups all exhibited territoriality versus the idea that many such groups lacked territoriality (Lee and DeVore 1968, Peterson 1975, Reynolds 1966, 1972, Tringham 1972). While my understanding of this literature is incomplete, a sampling suggests a few themes. First, territorial behavior, including the occupancy, control and even defense of geographical areas, was not apparently prevalent or central to all hunter-gatherer societies. While such groups were often located in specific geographic locales, there is some evidence that they were frequently flexible and open in their use of such areas. Other groups were often permitted entry, band membership changed readily, social organization was quite variable, conflicts were often resolved by avoiding and fleeing from others rather than by territorial defense. According to some writers, human territorial behavior was a later historical development and occurred when people settled down and became agricultural or herding cultures. It was then that geographical boundary regulations, control over property etc. evolved, and this practice is apparently a rather recent development in the history of mankind. But, aside from its origins or pervasiveness, the data are clear to the point that territoriality in humans is a crucial form of boundary regulation, which assists in the management of transactions between people and groups.

In summary, self disclosure, personal space, territory, and other processes function as part of a generic interpersonal boundary system that I have labeled 'privacy regulation'.

Social systems

Referring again to figure 2, boundary regulation systems also occur in larger social systems. My experience here is quite limited, as it was at the level of biological boundary systems, but a few examples may suffice to illustrate the point. Large social systems often contain various practices applicable to a society at large or to segments of a culture. Formal and informal role relationships among males and females, acquaintances and friends, superiors and subordinates, and others, involve consensually accepted and/or imposed modes of relating and responding to others that serve as boundary regulation vehicles. Playing out various role relationships provides mutually understandable ways of being open or closed to others, and serves to regulate people's transactions. As another example, Goffman's (1959) description of front and back regions of homes and other settings can be viewed in relation to boundary regulation processes, the design of human and office settings often serves to regulate contacts between people, etc. Another social systems level of boundary regulation is evident in many institutions – political, religious, etc. – where certain rules and regulations about behavior prevail. Many such rules relate to boundary regulation, e.g. property and ownership customs, access by different strata of society to various facilities, to different classes of membership in groups and so on. Although these examples only touch on facets of social systems in relation to boundary regulation, they illustrate how such systems can be viewed in terms of the model proposed earlier.

Some general issues

In this paper I initially described privacy as a specific concept in the environment and behavior field, and then examined it in a cross-cultural context. I also discussed how privacy encompasses other concepts, including personal space and territoriality. Finally, I cast privacy within a general model of human boundary regulation processes. Throughout the paper I alluded to some philosophical, conceptual and methodological issues, but either failed to discuss them or only referred to them in passing. In this final section of the paper, I will address the following rather knotty matters: (1) the relationship between privacy and territory; (2) methodological and philosophical issues associated with human environmental research; and (3) biological versus learned bases of privacy and territory. I must admit uncertainty about some of this issues, especially the nature–nurture question. However, I raise them for heuristic purposes and to bring to the forefront matters that need to be addressed in environmental research.

Privacy and territory: which is the more central concept?

I have theorized that privacy is a central boundary regulation process and that territory is a specific behavioral mechanism used in the service of privacy regulation. Within the general model of the previous section, privacy was depicted as the generic process of the interpersonal boundary system, involving regulation of contact between a person or group and others. Like other aspects of boundary control, privacy was hypothesized to involve dialectic openness–closedness, optimization and multiple behavioral mechanisms. Territory, along with verbal and nonverbal behaviors, personal space and cultural practices, represented a specific behavioral mechanism that facilitated a desired level of accessibility or privacy. Within such a framework, therefore, territory is a less focal concept than privacy.

Another aspect of privacy relates to its cultural universality. I hypothesized that an 'appropriate' perspective would reveal complex, dialectic patterns of privacy regulation in all cultures, with the differences between cultures reflected in their particular regulatory mechanisms. However, there is a question about the universality of territory, at least when defined in terms of occupancy and control of specific geographic regions.

On conceptual grounds alone I would not necessarily expect territorial behavior to be culturally pervasive. As only one of several privacy mechanisms, its appearance should depend on the life circumstances of a culture. For example, one might expect territoriality to be more important for permanently settled societies with complex governance and interpersonal relationships than for loosely organized nomadic or hunter-gatherer cultures. Or, cultures in environments that are plentiful in food and other resources might be less likely to exhibit extensive territorial behaviors compared with societies who live in more marginal circumstances. Thus, in my theoretical framework, privacy is generic to all humans whereas territory operates only in specific circumstances. Whether this reasoning will prove empirically valid is another question.

Another facet of my thinking is that privacy regulation involves the person or group more directly than territoriality. As I have defined privacy, it can include the individual directly – his or her immediate contact with others. Territoriality seems to involve more remote spatial relationships with others. Space or geography is controlled and occupied *in order* to help regulate contact with others. Thus it is an indirect vehicle, a spatially distal one. For privacy the focus is on the self; for territory the focus is on a place that bears indirectly on the self. Also, by definition, privacy regulation is a multichanneled process that can involve various combinations of mechanisms to regulate contact, including space. Territoriality, on the other hand, must have distal space and geography as one of its components and, in this sense, is a less generic process than privacy. Finally, my analysis suggested that boundary regulation, including interpersonal boundary regulation, is an historically 'old' process. Regardless of the particular means by which it has been achieved, the process of biological, psychological and interpersonal boundary regulation is a long-standing aspect of human functioning. I glean from the anthropological literature that territorial behavior in humans is a relatively recent historical phenomenon and came into play when people formed geographically stable communities.

Does it really matter whether privacy or territory is more generic? I think so. Psychological and ethological research often conveys the idea that territoriality is a central feature of human behavior and that it is almost independent of and/or subsumes other environmental processes. Instead, my conceptual framework attempts to cast human territorial behavior in relation to other constructs, and portrays it as part of a focal human process of interpersonal boundary regulation. By placing territorial behavior in such a context, we may better come to appreciate its relation to other facets of human environmental processes and thereby more effectively guide theory and research.

Philosophical perspectives on human environmental research

There are several philosophical values expressed in this paper that have implications for research and theory on behavior–environment relationships. And some of these ideas may not fit with current practices in parts of the social and behavioral sciences, especially in my parent field of social psychology. In particular I refer to (1) a social unit perspective and (2) a dialectic approach to human social behavior.

A social unit perspective. In previous writings (Altman 1976a, 1977b), I called for social psychology to expand its perspective from a focus on single behavioral dimensions to one that includes 'social units'. Social units refer to intact, holistic entities, such as individuals, couples, and families. I stated that a legitimate goal of research was to understand such social units and to make them an end-product of our analyses and generalizations. Most present-day social psychological research is not directed at social units but is focused on specific single behaviors. We have 'sliced up' the intact organism and become expert in understanding one or the other behavior taken alone, but we have not 'put it all together' to understand the 'whole' organism. We have become experts in analysis but we have fallen short in synthesis. While it is necessary to adopt a single behavior emphasis, it is as legitimate a goal, scientifically, to seek conclusions and generalizations about couples, families and teams as it is to make conclusions about behaviors X, Y or Z. It is important, therefore, for a science of human behavior–environment relationships (as it has been traditionally for anthropology and animal ethology) to attempt to understand 'whole' social entities.

How does one accomplish a social unit analysis? My analysis of privacy and the framework of human boundary processes presented in this paper contain the elements of a social unit perspective. First, it assumes that understanding a person, group or social system requires tapping into several levels of behavior – verbal, nonverbal, environmental and so on. No single level can completely portray a system's functioning, and my analysis of privacy as a cultural universal reflects this principle. I examined how cultures used a variety of levels of behavior to regulate self–other interaction. Had we examined only one type of behavior, e.g.

use of environmental barriers, we would have missed a great deal. Second, a social unit perspective assumes that various levels of behavior occur in coherent patterns. Thus our analysis of privacy indicated that different profiles or sets of behaviors were called into play by different cultures. The clinical psychologist, the cultural anthropologist, and the animal ethologist usually tap many different facets of organisms, persons and cultures to identify profiles of functioning. So is it also necessary that we adopt a similar strategy in human environmental research.

A third feature of a social unit orientation concerns the need to re-examine current values about 'causation'. In social psychology's attempt to fit within the mainstream of psychology, we have gone along with a model of causation adapted from earlier periods in the history of physics and chemistry, i.e. a linear model of causation. Our research designs, strategies and theories are based on both 'horizontal' and 'vertical' linearity of causation. On the horizontal level, we seek out chains of relationship between variables, such that $A \rightarrow B \rightarrow C$, rarely admitting in practice that C might cause B in some circumstances. As part of this approach we also assume a strong value of environmental determinism, manipulating experimental variables to demonstrate changes in behavior. Rarely do we examine the reverberatory and cycling effects of behavior on the environment. Along a 'vertical' dimension we are equally linear in our thinking, adopting a reductionist style of theorizing. We are ever ready to search for 'the' underlying cause of behavior, e.g. we often assume that biological processes 'cause' or are the underlying foundations of psychological phenomena, or that we must understand individual processes as the bedrock of social phenomena. Infrequently do we admit to the possibility of causal effects in the reverse direction, or in all directions at one time or another.

A social unit perspective does not deny causal relations between variables, but it assumes a complex interplay of effects, with any variable theoretically capable of affecting any other variable. It also assumes that, because we are dealing with complex social systems, it may not always be impossible to unravel a long history of reverberating relationships between variables. Thus, can we really specify precisely how a particular society's privacy regulation system originated? Probably not. Yet, we might identify circumstances in which one or the other set of mechanisms comes into play, which ones trip off others in particular situations, and so on.

As a related issue, I discussed boundary processes at biological, psychological, interpersonal and social systems levels. These levels were presented as interrelated, not hierarchical, levels of functioning. By so doing I intended to indicate explicitly that no level is necessarily more important or more basic than any other level. Rather, they were depicted as operating in a nonlinear, multidirectional causal fashion. Thus, social unit analysis neither denies causal relations between or within system levels, nor does it rule out research on specific cause–effect relations. However, it states that the fact that A → B does not preclude the possibility that B → A or that networks of causation may be complex and nonlinear in both horizontal and vertical directions.

A fourth aspect of a social unit orientation concerns the issue of description versus explanation. This is a matter that is hardly ever addressed any longer in social psychology, since the field has operated implicitly according to the value that 'explanation' is the desired mode of science, i.e. identify causal relationships between variables, and use the experiment as the *sine qua non* of science. A social unit orientation is as accepting of a descriptive approach as it is of an explanatory approach. It calls for the collection of baseline, normative data about social behavior – the size of social groups, their distribution and locations, their sex composition, the incidence of altruism and aggression in the general population, etc. In the environmental area, for example, we need much more descriptive and actuarial information about primary, secondary, and public territories, their nature and distribution, aspects of conflict associated with each, where and how they are used, etc. Similarly, we know little about the nature, distribution and use of various privacy mechanisms. Thus we have also not catalogued basic descriptive data about our subject matter, as the biological and natural sciences did at comparable periods in their history. Rather, we have sought primarily theoretically derived hypotheses and tests of causal relations between variables. A social unit orientation calls for more emphasis than heretofore on a descriptive, normative approach to human processes alongside the traditional explanatory approach. Here we can take a lesson from our colleagues in animal ethology, biology and the natural sciences, and from the work of Roger Barker (1968), who has carefully catalogued for decades the properties of human behavior in naturalistic settings.

The social unit orientation I propose is not a substitute for a behavioral emphasis; it is complementary. It is also not restricted to a particular methodology nor does it favor one research strategy over another. Rather, it calls for an expansion of our methodological and philosophical perspectives to include a focus on intact social units as an end-product of research. Put another way, psychologists interested in human environmental research need to move in the direction of ethological and anthropological philosophies of research. On the other hand, ethologists and anthropologists interested in environmental phenomena might also ask whether their perspectives require expansion in the direction of traditional psychological models.

A dialectic perspective. The concept of dialectics is central to my analysis of privacy as involving oppositional forces to be open versus closed to others. Rychlak (1976), in a very useful article, described the various meanings of dialectics, and his analysis sets the stage nicely for the present discussion (see also Adler (1927) for an historical analysis of dialectics).

The oldest meaning of dialectics involves elements in opposition or contradiction, e.g. fire and water, love and hate, activity and passivity, and so on. According to this view, dichotomies, oppositions, and contradictions are inherent in human affairs and in the nature of the universe. This approach to dialectics also often includes the idea of 'many in one', or the unity of oppositional processes. That is, each polar opposite – day and night, harmony and conflict, strength and weakness – gains meaning insofar as the other pole exists, and each oppositional quality serves to define the other pole. Harmony has no meaning without conflict; leadership is meaningless without followership, and so on.

The idea of opposition as unity occasionally appears in social science writings. For example, Georg Simmel (1950), a sociologist at the turn of the century, observed that social relationships are best understood as a dialectic interplay of opposite social processes: intimacy and triviality, conflict and harmony, togetherness and withdrawal. A social relationship, Simmel stated, cannot be understood without appreciating the simultaneous existence of such contradictory processes and, together, they provide unified meaning to social bonds. Sigmund Freud also used dialectic notions in facets of his theorizing (Rychlak 1968). For example, the primitive id, in its search for hedonistic pleasure, functions in opposition to societal norms represented in the superego; the executive ego works toward a reasonable balance and unification of these opposite forces. Interestingly, the id–superego tension is also symbolic of a long-standing topic of interest to philosophers concerning the conflict of individual needs versus societal demands.

A dialectic perspective has not been used explicitly very often in theorizing or research in the social and behavioral sciences, especially in social psychology. For example, altruism is treated as a separate topic from aggression; conflict and harmony are researched independently; leadership studies typically ignore followership; conformity is studied independently of freedom, and so on. Although my analysis of privacy as a dialectic process may or may not prove to be wholly 'valid', the attempt to cast it within a dialectical perspective has, at least for me, opened up some new lines of thinking. Thus, dialectic analysis may provide a valuable approach for research and theory on environment and behavior.

An aspect of my analysis of privacy that also appears in some dialectic approaches concerns *change, process* and *dynamics.* According to this view opposition forces are in a continual state of flux, change and growth, as their strength shifts vis-à-vis one another. Thus, the relationships between day and night, love and hate, harmony and conflict, intimacy and triviality, openness and closedness are not fixed or static. Rather, the strength of each force ebbs and flows in relation to its oppositional counterpart; one force is dominant at one time and in one situation and the other is dominant in other circumstances. And, the more one dominates, the greater the probability that the contradictory force will gain strength at a later time. Thus, at the instant that day, for example, is at its greatest strength (noon), it begins to wane, and night gathers strength. So, one oppositional force never dominates completely, but each has a 'seed' of itself in the other, so that neither force is ever in permanent control. For privacy, therefore, openness and closedness are in a continuous state of change, one force powerful at one time and the other strong at another time, but neither totally and permanently dominating. In fact, if either extreme of an opposition prevails too long or too intensively, we are prone to view the situation as abnormal. Thus, both the person who is always out of contact (the hermit) and the person who can never be alone are considered deviants. Instead, most people exhibit reasonable variation in openness and closedness over time, with extreme contact followed by noncontact and so on. So, the idea of change and dynamics as central to dialectic thinking suggests the importance of tracking behavior–environment relationships over time.

A related issue concerns the conceptual model that has dominated the social and behavioral sciences for decades, namely, a balance, equilibrium or drive reduction approach to human functioning. Much social psychological theory and research has operated out of so-called cognitive consistency or balance models. In fact, psychological research in general has been anchored around drive reduction or equilibrium concepts of one form or another. This philosophical view assumes that people strive primarily toward reduction of ambiguity, elimination of imbalances, removal of inconsistencies, and avoidance of disequilibria of all kinds. Furthermore, we have assumed that balance, order and consistency are ultimately desirable or ideal states of affairs. However, it is recognized that such equilibrium is not always possible, in part because behavioral and biological systems overshoot or undershoot the mark, so that there is a constant state of adjustment and readjustment as we strive toward a hypothetical equilibrium state. Furthermore, it is acknowledged that external events often impinge upon and upset balanced conditions. Such internal and external factors produce, therefore, a system in dynamic change. But the central assumption is that people, animals, psychological and biological systems strive toward balance and equilibrium as ultimate goals and as optimum end-states. As a result, psychological research is directed towards such questions as: What factors generate disequilibrium? How do people react to imbalances? What do they do to restore balance? In short, by assuming an 'ultimate' human need for consistency and equilibrium, we have directed our research in a particular way.

A dialectic approach might offer a somewhat different assumption system about basic human drives. Thus, one could assume the simultaneous existence of opposing forces to achieve balance and equilibrium and to achieve imbalance or change. According to this way of thinking people are 'driven' by a dialectic interplay of stability or balanced end-states and instability or change. It might be argued that, having achieved momentary equilibrium of one type or another, forces mount to seek change, and vice versa. Thus there would be a continuous and dynamic movement between equilibrium and disequilibrium, each present at different times and each something toward which people actively move. In privacy regulation I assume such movement between openness and closedness toward others. In social relationships one might also hypothesize alternation between harmony and conflict; in animal behavior one might postulate a dynamic blend of exploratory behavior and preferences for stable environments. A dialectic perspective suggests that balance *and* imbalance, equilibrium *and* disequilibrium, consistency *and* contradiction are equally central human motivations, each as important as the other, each leading to the other, together forming a unity, and neither operating as singular goals toward which humans strive. Such an assumption framework seems to me to be radically different from current views of organisms striving toward some ultimate, stable, equilibrium state.

Although I have only touched briefly on philosophical issues associated with ideas of balance and equilibrium versus change and instability, the point is that a dialectic approach may permit an analysis of human environmental issues from a somewhat different assumption base than that which currently dominates social science thinking. Given the fact that we are involved in a new interdisciplinary field, it behooves us, in my opinion, to examine seriously the philosophical underpinnings of the fields from which we come and to be explicit about the assumptions that guide our theory and research. For me, a dialectic strategy provides an alternative assumption system that has considerable promise.

The nature–nurture issue

The thorny matter of biological–evolutionary versus cultural–learned origins of human behavior is not an issue that I have previously worried about very much, since it was tangential to my research and theorizing. Furthermore, as an American social psychologist reared in the tradition of environmental determinism, I tended to treat lightly and critically what appeared to be extreme generalizations and oversimplifications made by some writers about the biological roots of social behavior. I saw extensive and scholarly analyses of animal behavior built on a biological and evolutionary base that were then applied in a simplistic and freewheeling way to complex human social behaviors without much empirical evidence, and without seeming recognition of the dangers of over-generalization. It was easy for me to dismiss such proposals casually as speculation and/or as poor science. But, with the line of thinking I have expressed in this paper, I can no longer avoid the issue nor can I dismiss the matter lightly.

To put matters in perspective I have found it helpful to review a few historical and philosophical roots of analyses of human behavior. For example, there were the reductionistic and materialistic philosophies of the past – from the early Greeks, notably Democritus, through the Frenchman LaMettrie in the eighteenth century, to present-day ideas of human ethology and sociobiology. For Democritus the universe consisted of ultimately indivisible basic units upon which all else was built, including the soul. Mental processes could be reduced to and derived from physical things (atoms, perhaps genes?). This doctrine, repeated in a variety of forms over the centuries, argued that the complex could be reduced to the simple and that a building block approach, from the physical and biological to the mental, was the way to proceed. Need I say how often this doctrine has been restated, reproposed, reaccepted and rejected throughout history? It has been found too simple, it has not always handled the complexities of social behavior very well, although it did provide a neat, logically tight and parsimonious framework.

On another part of the philosophical fence there was the equally oft-reappearing doctrine of dualism, that argued for the separate functioning and governing principles of mental and physical realms. Many varieties of this approach have existed throughout history, including pluralism, which argues that neither mind nor body is more fundamental; they are equal in importance but they operate according to separate rules. Here was a way to separate humanity from animals and to liberate human functioning from a reductionistic style of thinking. But, again, the rise and fall in popularity of dualism and its variants throughout history suggests that it too did not always seem to work.

As to current philosophical trends in psychology, MacLeod (1975) stated it well, namely, that modern-day psychologists are largely materialistic and reductionist in their attitudes:

Whether we use the language of stimuli and responses, the language of cell assembly and reverberating circuits or some new language still to be invented, it is part of the faith of the materialists that physical science can ultimately be extended to include all the phenomena of human behavior and experience.   (p. 56)

The point of this brief historical note is merely to remind us that the problem of the evolutionary and genetic versus learned basis of intelligence, altruism, aggression, territoriality, etc. is an age-old problem. It is an important problem, to be sure, and it involves deeply rooted philosophical issues that have been with us since the beginning of science and philosophy. It may well be that the issue is not resolvable and that we are dealing more with arbitrary, workaday assumptions systems than with some 'ultimate' truth.

Where do I stand on this issue in relation to privacy and boundary regulation? I cannot answer this question unequivocally, partly because I am not well versed in biological and evolutionary concepts, and partly because I have been able to work until now without bothering to deal with the question. But the chain of thinking reflected in this paper has brought me to the brink of having to deal with the issue, and my present thoughts can best be described as 'in progress'.

It should be evident that the development of my thinking from an analysis of the properties of privacy, to its presentation as a cultural universal, to a sketchy model of privacy as part of a multilevel boundary regulation system that includes biological, psychological, interpersonal and social levels, comes close to suggesting (a) a linkage of social and biological processes and (b) the possibility of mapping between social and biological processes, or at least discovering their isomorphic relations. It might also be noted that the progression of these ideas flowed from social to biological levels of functioning, rather than in the usual ethologically oriented direction of biological to social.

Most important to my thinking, and explicit in the generic boundary regulation model summarized in figure 2, is my discomfort with a materialistic or reductionist assumption set. I deliberately avoided saying 'the social models the biological' or, conversely, 'the biological models and social'. Rather, I stated that biological, psychological, interpersonal and social levels of boundary regulation are not arranged hierarchically, with any level more fundamental than any other level. As such, I have not subscribed to the classic reductionist idea that the biological serves as the bedrock of all other levels of system functioning, historically or con-temporaneously. Instead, I assumed multiple levels of explanation and effect, such that different phenomena need to be understood, at least partly, at their own level of unit definition. Just as I do not think that we can 'build up' an understanding of families solely from analyzing their individual members, so it is that I do not believe that we can develop a complete understanding of social behavior from the bedrock of biology alone. Of course, this position has been articulated earlier in the history of psychology by the Gestalt school and by Kurt Lewin, the latter in regard to social psychology. He stated the point well, to the effect that phenomena must be partially understood at their own level of analysis and that undue translation up or down in a reductionist hierarchy is not profitable. So, I adopted the stance that privacy regulation and boundary regulation at other levels of functioning must be partly understood at their own levels of analysis, with concepts uniquely developed to fit particular domains. However, the framework I proposed also suggests that there are linkages and isomorphic commonalities between system levels (although I was not able to specify them exactly). So I believe that there are both unique and common aspects of various levels of boundary regulation. In addition, my approach assumes interdependency among system levels, with any system or subsystem capable of affecting any other, although here again I gave only a few examples of such relation-ships. Thus, I do not view one system to be more basic than any other system, and, therefore, I am not comfortable with an analysis that attempts to strictly and hierarchically arrange levels of human functioning.

In short, I proposed a construct of boundary regulation as a fundamental human process that is manifested at several levels of human functioning, from biological to human social system levels. While there are unique features of boundary processes at various levels, there are also linkages between levels and isomorphic operating principles. All of this is to say that there is undoubtedly some representation of boundary regulation capabilities in the evolutionary history of people and nonhuman species, but I am not yet able to specify the nature of this representation or its relation to cultural events.

A 'gene' for boundary regulation is too simplistic for me and smacks of 'simple and sovereign' instinct theories of the earlier days of social psychology (Allport 1968). Here instincts were posited for every facet of human behavior, usually in a circular fashion, and there was great competition about which instincts were more fundamental. A 'broad propensity' is a softer way of saying it, but also too easily slips into a reductionist, materialistic style of logic. My present views are simply that (1) boundary regulation is a central human process, (2) it occurs at many levels of human and animal functioning, (3) it involves widespread variation in its phenotypic operation but seems to be a generic process, (4) it involves the idea of separate but related, and nonhierarchically arranged, boundary systems, and (5) the exact contribution and interplay of biological–evolutionary versus learned–culturally specific facets of boundary regulation needs analysis. But such an analysis is, in my opinion, not likely to prove fruitful if it is done from the perspective of a polarizing and imperialistic stance on either side.

Summary

This paper analyzed privacy as a central concept in the environment and behavior field and as a specific aspect of human boundary regulation processes. I first considered privacy as a dialectic, multilevel, dynamic, interpersonal boundary process. Privacy was viewed in terms of oppositional forces to be open and accessible to others versus forces to be closed and inaccessible to social contacts. The balance of these forces was hypothesized to shift with circumstances, yielding a dialectically based variation in self–other permeability. I also described privacy regulation as a multilevel behavioral process involving many different aspects of behavior, e.g. verbal, nonverbal, environmental and cultural. Behaviors from these domains were hypothesized to combine in various profiles to yield a large repertoire of behavioral mechanisms. The paper also considered privacy functions, the most crucial one involving the development and maintenance of self identity and self worth. It was argued that the ability to regulate satisfactorily one's exchange with others, and to increase and to lessen social contacts when desired, were important components of self worth and self identity.

An extension of this analysis examined privacy regulation in a cross-cultural context, to consider the proposition that privacy functions as a culturally universal process. This idea was examined in cultures that, on the face of it, had minimum or maximum privacy, and in various social relationships. The analysis was based on the premise that, while the capability for privacy regulation was generic to all cultures, specific behavioral vehicles for achieving privacy varied from society to society.

The paper also examined privacy as one of a series of generic human processes involving boundary regulation. Here I described several levels of human functioning that seem to involve management of accessibility and inaccessibility or permeability in respect to self–other transactions. These boundary regulation processes were hypothesized to occur at biological, psychological, interpersonal and social system levels of functioning. Privacy regulation was depicted as the generic process associated with interpersonal boundary regulation, with personal space and territorial behavior functioning as environmentally oriented aspects of the privacy boundary system.

The final section of the paper addressed some philosophical issues concerning human behavior and the environment: (1) I proposed that research adopt a social unit orientation, which means (a) an emphasis on holistic, intact social units in addition to the current focus, at least in social psychology, on single behaviors; (b) analysis of several levels of functioning and an understanding of their relationship; (c) a greater willingness to describe and catalogue social events along with the present explanatory emphasis in the social sciences; and (d) a nonlinear approach to causal relations between variables. (2) I also proposed a dialectically oriented analysis of human behavior in relation to the environment, with recognition of the importance of oppositional processes such as openness–closedness, their functioning as part of a single unity, and an appreciation of changing relations between oppositional processes over time. In addition, I suggested that we consider reformulating our widespread assumption of human behavior as based on an equilibrium, balance principle, to one that assumes the simultaneous operation of forces toward balance *and* imbalance, equilibrium *and* disequilibrium, stability *and* change. Finally, the paper addressed briefly the nature–nurture issue in relation to environmental processes. Here I called for an analysis based on several levels of system functioning that are simultaneously interdependent and independent in their operation.

2.2. Territory and property in primitive society

MAURICE GODELIER

Introduction

1. I should like to start by clearing up a certain number of *ambiguities* surrounding the term 'primitive society'. There are no *theoretical* criteria defining the *boundaries* of anthropology. Anthropology is concerned in the first place with *all* those societies that historians and economists *neglect*. The latter ignore these societies because we have no written records concerning them. Anthropology is a sort of trashcan of history; it deals with all those societies that demand *personal acquaintance* in order to be able to study them; that require that the researcher go and see for himself – requiring participatory observation if he is to understand something of their functioning. There are, then, no theoretical criteria; but there are two practical ones. The first reflects a concrete state of affairs, namely the absence of written records, while the second constitutes a methodological imperative, namely the obligation to employ a method known as participatory observation. This is why we anthropologists are confronted with an immensely diverse field, from the last bands of Bushmen roaming the Kalahari desert, to the Masai, pastoral nomads of East Africa, to the village communities of Peru, India or Java. This broad diversity offers one advantage: it constitutes an outstanding vantage point from which to observe the evolution of the human species in its social forms and its various habitats.

2. Property of territory is a specific form of property. We shall be discussing different forms of property of tracts of land and water whose resources, whether natural or transformed by man, are claimed by societies or by fractions of societies, or by certain groups making up societies. We

133

must therefore sort out a second ambiguity by defining what we mean by property in general.

I. Abstract property and concrete appropriation

1. Property in the first place takes the form of a series of *abstract rules* which determine access, control, utilization, transfer and transmission of any form of social reality susceptible to dispute. Formally speaking, the concept of property may be applied to any material or intangible reality, land, water, masks, ritual knowledge, magic spells for the fertility of plants and women, names of the dead, etc. In 1928, Robert Lowie emphasized this point in an article entitled 'Incorporeal property in primitive society'. But any reality is susceptible to dispute if it is or if it *appears* to be a *condition* of the reproduction of human life. For example, among the So of Uganda, only the older members of the different patrilineal lineages making up this society are authorized to *know* and to *utter* the names of the dead ancestors; these are seen as intermediaries between men and Bergen, the god controlling rain, and hence life of livestock and men alike. The other men, non-initiates, and all women, are forbidden to utter these names, on pain of death by sorcery or other forms of punishment inflicted by the ancestors and spirits, ghosts and gods.

2. Hence, the rules of property take the form of normative rules *prescribing* certain *forms of behaviour* while *prohibiting* others on pain of *repression* or sanctions. The rules of property are thus normative and are applicable either to all members of a society, or else to a certain number of them only. But even when they apply to all members of a society, they generally tend to exclude members of other societies, whether neighbouring or not, from the same rights and duties. As a result, the rules of property are simultaneously prescriptive, proscriptive and repressive (threats of death, various types of punishment, whether human or divine, physical or psychological, direct or indirect, immediate or different). But even if these rules only apply to certain members of a society, they *must be known to all* in order to be respected, and so they must be *taught* to all members. Many legal systems have a principle similar to the Latin *ignorantia legibus neminem excusat*.

The forms taken by this teaching process vary greatly. Among Australian aborigines, for instance, young men learned to identify the different tracts of land and water belonging to their own kinship group or section; on the occasion of their great initiation journey, made in company with the elders of all the sections over a period of several months, these young men would explore their tribal territory in every direction and their guides would teach them the boundaries of their territory and of the territory of each kinship group as well as all the resources (vegetable, animal, water) that they could (usually) expect from each tract of land. They would also teach them the directions to be taken in order to find water and other resources in times of exceptional drought in one portion or another of the tribal territory. But their education also encompassed supernatural realities, such as totemic sites where the spirits of dead ancestors dwelt. Topographical features – mountains, water-holes, etc. – were all taught, being described as transformed ancestors who, in the course of the Dreaming Times, had been changed into a stone or lake, pond, snake, etc. The great initiation journey across the territory thus served as the occasion for learning all the *productive* possibilities of this territory and at the same time for *transmitting* from one generation to the next the *rights* of the community over certain fractions of these resources.

3. It is vital to bear in mind that rules of property are *systems* of rights founded *simultaneously* upon *several distinct* principles. Malinowski went to great lengths to stress this in his critique of so-called 'primitive communism' which, in the nineteenth century, was presented as a system based on a single principle that everything belongs to everyone. In all societies, however, there exist, as Malinowski has put it, 'combined systems' of rights, combining collective forms and individual forms of appropriation depending on the nature of the 'reality' appropriated. To illustrate the notion of combined systems or systems embracing several different principles, I shall take the example of the Siane, a New Guinean tribe that has been studied by Richard Salisbury. This society is divided into patrilineal clans, themselves divided into lineages placed under the authority of the eldest brother of the oldest generation. There is no centralized power, and government works through reciprocal relations between the clans and their representatives. The economy is based on the cultivation of sweet potatoes and taro, the gathering of plants in the bush, and on small-scale wild-pig hunting. The rules of property of the Siane are of two different types.

A person has rights over an object in the same way as a 'father' (*merafo*) has rights over his children. He is responsible for them before the community and before his ancestors. This rule governs the appropriation of land, sacred flutes, ritual knowledge and objects over which authority is not transferable.

A person has rights over objects as though he were their 'shadow' (*amfonka*). These objects may be pigs, clothing, needles, implements, planted trees; they are personal property and may be transferred.

There is a hierarchical relationship between these two types of rule: only if one has a *merafo* relationship with the land does the work involved in planting trees give one the right to individual appropriation (*amfonka*). Interpreting the data related by Richard Salisbury, we may say that this hierarchical relationship, in which *merafo* dominates *amfonka*, means that the system of rights is founded upon membership of a group, and that the underlying principle governing this system is the pre-eminence of wider groups over smaller ones (tribe over clan, clan over lineage, etc.). This then gives us a series of dovetailing systems (a little like a Russian doll) of rights invested in hierarchically organized groups in descending order of size. As a member of a tribe, an individual has the right to hunt and gather on the entire territory of the tribe. As a member of a clan, he has the right to cultivate on the clan's territory. As a member of a men's house, he has rights over certain portions of his clan's territory. As a member of a lineage, he has priority over the members of other lineages in his own men's house regarding the use of certain plots of land. When conflict breaks out between two individuals regarding the use of a plot of land, the individual with the greatest number of use-rights accruing to him takes precedence over the other. But when a group claims land attributed to another group or an individual, precedence goes to the largest group:

clan > men's house > lineage > individual

The distinction between tribal use-rights (hunting, gathering) and clan rights (farming) shows clearly that agriculture supplies the basic permanent resources, and that the basic social unit is the clan.

The hierarchical relationship between *merafo* and *amfonka* relations thus ensures free access for all to land and food and protects – inside the limits prescribed by the reciprocal solidarity and obligations of clan-members – the rights of each person to the fruit of his personal labour. The purpose of the complex of *merafo* and *amfonka* rights would seem to be to harmonize the interests of the group with those of the individual by limiting – through the granting of absolute priority to groups over the individual – the contradictions which arise between individuals and between clans.

Not only do we find combined systems of rights concerning different objects, but we also encounter different rights concerning the 'same' object or reality. For example, the Incas expropriated tribes that they conquered, depriving them of their property rights over land. The latter became the eminent property of the Inca (the sovereign), Son of the Sun.

Local communities retained permanent use-rights. Many languages have several terms to distinguish the different types of rights that pile up on top of a given reality. In French, we distinguish 'propriété' (right of alienation) and 'possession' (right to permanent use); in English 'property', 'ownership' and 'possession'; in German, 'Eigentum' and 'Besitzung'. The theoretical problem raised here is to discover why the existence of several different principles should be necessary and why a hierarchy should have grown up among them in the reproduction of social life.

4. Systems of property always define – with greater or less precision – *the nature and the number of those who have rights* (who, and how many?). In other words, what is defined here is *the equality or inequality of rights* among the members of a society. For example, among the Baruya of New Guinea, hunting territories and cultivation areas are the joint property of patrilineal lineages. But this property may only be transmitted by men, women being excluded. Women retain the right to use the land of their ancestors after their marriage, and for their life-time; but they may not transmit it to their descendants, as the latter belong to a different lineage (patrilineal descent). But women may transmit the magic spells for the fertility of pigs to their daughters, and at the same time they transmit the names of these pigs. Men, on the other hand, are alone in possessing the magic bundles used in the male initiation rituals for the reproduction of the warriors' strength. Women are forbidden to touch or see these sacred objects. In matrilineal societies, on the other hand, rights to the land are transmitted through the women. To these inequalities between sexes and generations are added – in a great many primitive societies – unequal rights between aristocratic groups and the remainder of the population. In the Trobriand Islands, the aristocracy alone has the right to practise the rituals that reproduce the fertility of the land and the water. Instead of individuals (chiefs of lineages) possessing this monopoly, as with the So (Uganda), we find whole lineages possessing this monopoly to the exclusion of commoner lineages. Here, kinship groups making up society are no longer equal but hierarchized in terms of both status and rights.

5. But property only exists fully in a concrete activity of appropriation. Property cannot therefore be *reduced* to an existing body of abstract rules, and only exists when made effective in an appropriative process.

These five points having been made, we may now go on to analyse that particular form of property referred to as 'territorial property'.

II. Society and territory

1. Territory: a tentative definition

The term 'territory' is used to designate a portion of nature and space that is claimed by a given society, this society guaranteeing for all, or only some, of its members stable rights of access to control and use of all or part of the resources found therein, and which it (the society) is capable of exploiting.

By space we in fact mean a stretch of land, a stretch of water, and nowadays airspace as well; within these spaces, 'exploitable' resources may be found on the ground, underground, and on the surface of the water as well as below the surface. We all know too that a natural phenomenon is not *en soi*, in itself, a 'resource' for man: I am referring, for example, to the 'force' of the wind, or water, not to mention atomic 'energy'. It becomes so at a specific moment in the evolution of mankind and for a specific period, after which it is either exhausted, or else abandoned because it has been replaced by another one. But in all such cases, a natural phenomenon only becomes a resource through a combination of two conditions: it must be either directly or indirectly capable of satisfying a human need; and it must possess some utility within some form of social life, a 'social' utility. In addition, man must have the technical means to *extract* it from the rest of nature and to *make it serve* his needs. This implies that a society must possess a certain 'interpretation' of the surrounding nature, and that it is capable of combining these intellectual means with material means in order to act upon this portion of nature and to make it serve its own physical and social reproduction.

What nature endows man with is then, first of all, and needless to say, his own nature, i.e. an animal species having a body – a specific organism – obliged to live in society in order to reproduce itself. But in addition, nature also provides him with material resources capable of serving as means of (a) subsistence; (b) labour and production (tools, or raw materials with which to manufacture them); and (c) reproduction of the material aspect of his social relations, those that make up the specific structure of a society (kinship relations, politico-religious relations, etc.). This last category embraces both the irridescent feathers of birds of paradise and the clays or mineral powders used to decorate the body and to communicate with ancestors or the spirits, both sculpted wooden masks and temples and their stone altars where the gods dwell. It hardly needs to be pointed out here that the resources that man extracts from nature are rarely usable in their immediate form, and that they *have to* undergo a certain number of *changes in form and state* before being trans- formed, finally, into 'consumable' goods (for example, wild tubers or bitter domestic manioc whose venomous juices have to be pressed out before they become edible). Nor need we insist on the fact that once they have been consumed, the whole process of production has to be started all over again.

Seen from man's point of view,then, nature is two complementary though distinct *realities* (we might equally have said, is two aspects of a single reality): man's *'organic' body*, that is his reality as a social species of animal, and, secondly, the environment in which he finds his means of social reproduction; this environment forms, so to speak, man's *'inor- ganic' body*, to borrow Marx's perceptive observation in his *Grundrisse*. I shall thus use 'territory' to refer to that portion of nature and of space which a society claims as the place where its members shall always enjoy the material conditions and means necessary for their existence.

Of course, in no society, including our own (which has come up with a number of different materialist visions of nature), can natural phenomena be reduced to their ostensible, tangible aspects alone. Wherever we look, man represents them as consisting also of forces and powers that are *refractory* to the senses, constituting their least visible part, although in his own eyes they are the *most important* part for his own reproduction. This is why all those forms of concrete activity invented by man in order to appropriate natural phenomena necessarily combine 'material' gestures and forms of conduct, designed to act upon their visible and tangible aspects, with gestures and forms of conduct that we nowadays call 'symbolic', designed to act upon their hidden depths (rituals connected with the sharing out of game killed in hunting, soil or female fertility rites, etc.).

What a society claims, when appropriating a territory, is access, con- trol, and use of *the visible realities and the invisible powers* composing it; powers apparently wielding joint mastery over the conditions of the reproduction of human life, i.e. of human reproduction and of reproduc- tion of the resources upon which they depend. This, then, is what seems to be entailed by the notion of 'ownership of a territory'. But this 'owner- ship' only fully exists when the members of a society employ it to govern their *concrete* forms of appropriation of its resources. These forms of action are always social, whether individual or collective; and they take the form of what we call hunting, gathering, fishing, stockbreeding, farming, crafts or industry. In our society, we call these activities 'labour', and we term the organized development of each of these activities the 'labour process'. Logically, in this case, we ought to consider as 'labour' – and as an essential aspect of each labour process – the 'symbolic' moments and behavior it contains, through which man seeks to act upon the invisible forces controlling the visible phenomena he is seeking to appropriate (rain, heat, game, plants, etc.).

But it should be pointed out here that a good many languages do not have a word for labour, because they have no representations corresponding to it. According to the Maenge, New-Britain horticulturists, gardening activities are seen as an 'exchange' with the dead and with the gods. There is no idea of a transformation of nature and still less of any transformation of 'man's' nature. This is a common enough idea in the west today, but it only made its appearance relatively recently, although no one knows exactly when (eighteenth century?). Neither ancient Greek nor Latin possessed words equivalent to 'labour' and to 'work'.

Forms of ownership of a territory are thus an essential part of the 'economic' structure of any society, since they constitute the 'legal', though not necessarily the 'legitimate', condition of access to resources and to the means of production. These have combined with the specific forms of organization of the labour process and of the distribution of the fruits of this process to form the economic structure of society, the social framework of its productive activities, its 'mode of production', its 'economic system'.

To describe and account for the different forms of ownership of nature thus entails combining history with anthropology and economics in order to produce a reasonably plausible reconstructed history of the different economic systems that have arisen throughout the course of man's evolution.

Territorial ownership forms exist both as a relationship with nature and as a twofold relationship between men. For this relationship holds simultaneously between societies and within each society, between the individuals and groups making it up. Usually, these are neighbouring societies, but not always and not necessarily so (for example, former 'colonial' territories belonging to France, Great Britain, Germany or Russia). This is why, whatever the form, individual or collective, of any given concrete process of appropriation of nature (individual or collective hunting, for example), this form is always a social relation, a product of the structure of a society.

This leads us to one fundamental theoretical conclusion: the idea that the individual as such, as a being distinct from the social group to which

he belongs, may be the source of property rights over nature is utterly
devoid of any scientific basis. Of course, one does find it in the ideology of
certain societies, at certain periods in history including our own, but this
is merely an expression of the fact that the individual in such societies and
at such moments enjoys certain rights over a portion of nature, but not
that he is the source and the ultimate justification of these rights. This has
been remarkably expressed by Carl Brinkmann in his article 'Land tenure'
(1933):[1]

The vesting of land tenure in an individual as distinct from a social group,
whether of contemporaries or of successive generations is a very modern concept
incapable of complete fulfilment even in a capitalist economy. But so also is land
tenure as an individual right exclusive of other concurrent rights. What must
seem a contradiction in terms to the property notion of Roman or of modern civil
law – namely that there may be two or more property rights in the same thing – is
evidently the most general rule in the institutions governing the tenure of land.

(p. 74)

Nowhere, not even in the most highly developed capitalist society, does
one find a case of individual ownership of land in which the individual is
totally free to use and misuse it. Wherever one looks one finds some form
or other of limitation on his right founded upon some priority community
right, the state, nation, crown, etc. The *jus uti et abutendi* spells out an ideal
principle, one that actually exists nowhere.

When, in the course of history, individuals did possess some priority
rights over an entire territory and over all a society's resources, as in the
case of the Pharaoh in ancient Egypt, or the Inca, they did not possess
these rights as individuals but as the highest personification of the capitalist state and of the power of a dominant class over all the other groups and
classes of that society. In these examples, the 'property' of a superior
individual was both the form and effect of a concentration of land ownership in the hands of a single class and/or the state.

I shall now go on to describe briefly some forms of territory ownership
encountered in pre-capitalist societies.

2. *Territory as a relationship between societies*

We find:

a. Societies which apparently possess no territory of their own. Such is
the case with the WoDaaBe Peuls, shepherd nomads now living in Niger.

[1] See also, on the same topic, the articles of R. Lowie, F. Heichelheim, H. Cunow, D.
Mitrany, P. Struve, R. Mukerjee, Y. Takekoshi, G. McBride, *Encyclopaedia of the social
sciences*, vol. VI (New York, Macmillan, 1933).

They have slowly infiltrated the territory of sedentary farming populations, the Hausas, who have allowed them to use their bush and their
fallow land in return for taxes in the form of animals or services. Sometimes, when the Touareg, who were formerly themselves nomads, controlled sedentary populations on the territory over which the Peuls move,
the latter were obliged to pay taxes in animals and services both to the
Touareg and to the sedentary peoples. This form of common trans-
humance thus implies no exclusive appropriation of pasture land, and
one thus finds a criss-crossing of several distinct pastoral populations,
Peul, Bella, Touareg, over the same portion of agricultural land, their
movements being synchronized by custom in order to avoid conflicts.

b. There are cases of several pastoral societies using the same territory in
turn. This is the case with the Bassari, studied by Frédéric Barth. In these
nomadic pastoral societies in the south of Iran, each tribe in turn exploits
the same tract of land and the same wells in orderly succession. Tribes
with the largest flocks go to the top of the queue. Owen Lattimore has
shown that this system also existed among the Mongol shepherds and
that the power of the Khans rested partly on the capacity of their own
tribe to regulate the order of passage of the other tribes over pasture land
and around wells, these being the joint property of the confederation they
composed.

c. We also find in southern Iran societies that coexist within a single
ecosystem, the different societies utilizing parts situated at different
altitudes. In the upper region of the Zagros chain, the Turkish-speaking
tribes raise Bactrian camels, which are well adapted to the rigours of this
altitude. In the hills below, the Iranian-speaking tribes raise horses and
small livestock, while in the foothills, Arabic-speaking tribes make their
living from the extensive breeding of dromedaries.

d. In addition to these societies inhabiting adjoining territories, mention
should also be made of societies that simultaneously exploit several
disconnected territories. John Murra has shown this for Inca and pre-Inca
Andine societies. He has shown that the economies of these societies
were founded on the complex exploitation of several ecological layers,
sometimes separated by large distances. For example, the Chupaychu
community described by the royal visitor Inigo Ortiz, who visited the
Huanuco region in 1559, was spread over three disconnected areas. The
core of the population lived at 3200 metres, growing corn and tubers as
stable crops. This was the centre. At 4000 metres, in the Puna, small
groups worked to produce salt and bred llamas and alpacas extensively.
In the Montana, lying some hundreds of metres above the Amazon basin,

other families grew cotton and exploited the area's wood and coca resources. The population of these peripheral centres was multi-ethnic and the land was simultaneously exploited by groups belonging to several different tribes. However, members of the community permanently living in these peripheral centres, three or four days' walk from the central core, nevertheless retained all their rights over the land of the central village. This society thus formed a string of ecologico-economic islands scattered around a single centre.

Still more complicated was the structure of the kingdoms of the Altiplano, around lake Titicaca. Basing his account on Garcia Diez de San Miguel's visit in 1557, J. Murra has shown that the kingdom of Lupaka, whose population numbered around 20 000 households and spoke Aymara and Uru, exploited several territories lying on both the western and eastern slopes of the Andes, whilst keeping the zone around lake Titicaca as its political and economic centre. This kingdom exploited the resources of the Amazon forest as well as those of the Pacific Ocean and the irrigated valleys of the littoral. But the distance between the central territory and its peripheral elements was now ten to fifteen days' walk across foreign territories. On the whole, the territorial structure of the kingdom of Lupaka was the same as that of the Chupaychu community.

A series of ecologico-economic islands are thus strung out at different altitudes around a centre, in which two ethnic groups, the Aymara and the Uru, lived sharing the resources among them. In addition to tribal organization and ethnic differences, though, we now have the difference between a hereditary aristocracy and the mass of common people, a difference that appears to be a 'class difference'. It was within this new social framework that problems concerning access to resources both at the centre and at the periphery were settled, and that the conduct of a policy of war and peace, and questions of conflicts and alliances between ethnic groups or kingdoms, were dealt with.

At the same time, the economic structure of the society was diversified and, in addition to farmers and stockbreeders, specialized groups of people were engaged in the production of ceramics as well as in working copper, silver and gold.

With the appearance of Tawantinsuyu, the Inca empire of the 'Four Quarters of the Universe', the Andine territorial model underwent a fresh transformation. The state deported entire populations in order to smash their resistance, or else transferred military colonies (*mitmaq*), selected from among the most loyal tribes, over vast distances, settling them in strategic positions among populations that dared to rebel against the conquering Inca. Entire human communities were henceforth cut off from their traditional ecological environment and from their original ethnic group, being placed directly in the service of the state, and forced to cooperate in the reproduction of relations of political domination. This reorganization of territorial space reflected a new way of exploiting nature and the peasants' labour force, since the limitations imposed by the diversity of regional ecosystems and by the local character of forms of social organization and production were henceforward partially transcended.

These examples offer a particularly sharp illustration of the continuity and the discontinuities that have characterized the definition and use of nature as territory over the course of the evolution that transformed classless societies into class societies and into state formations. And archaeologists now tell us that this process first occurred in a handful of areas of the globe: Meso-America, Peru, Mesopotamia, northern India and ancient China.

3. Territory as a relation between groups and between the individuals making up society: territory, object and source of conflict in connection with its distribution within societies

a. Forms of property and social relations of production

We have already seen that individuals and groups making up a given society always obtain access to the resources of nature and appropriate them *within* and *through* a *social* form of ownership (or stable use) of a territory, which form legitimizes this access and this appropriation. Now, we can show that in all societies the forms of ownership of its territory *take* the form of social relations, in whatever form they may happen to take, and that they function as systems of production, as social relations of production.

Take for example the Australian aborigines. For them, it was legitimate for any individual belonging to one of the descent-groups forming his tribe (half, section, or sub-section) to hunt over all the territory belonging to his kinship group. In case of need, he was also permitted to hunt on the land of his allies, i.e. land belonging to his mother's section or to the section that had given him a wife in exchange for one of his classificatory or real sisters. Here, rights of 'access', of control, usage and transmission of various fractions of a tribal territory were attached to kinship groups which, through reciprocal relations, formed what is rather imprecisely called a tribe (a practically endogamous group, recognizing itself as having common interests and territory which it was prepared to defend by force of arms if necessary). Ownership of nature took the form of an attribute of kinship relations because these functioned as a social framework for 'production', as social relations of production.

Things are in fact much more complex, and this complexity sheds light on current controversy among anthropologists concerning the notion of territory among the Australian aborigines. Radcliffe-Brown (1931) claimed that each patriclan had an 'exclusive' right over its territory and exploited it exclusively. According to him, each local band was a patrilineal group jointly exploiting the territory of its ancestors. Unfortunately, and this accounts for the controversy, the accumulated work of Elkin, Rose, Hiatt, Meggitt, Turner, etc., since 1930 has shown that local Australian bands were made up of members of *several* patriclans and not of one only, and that they exploited several territories, theirs and those of certain of their allies. Our analysis of the difference between abstract ownership of a territory and concrete appropriation may (perhaps) enable us to clear up this discussion. What seems to have happened was that each kinship group functioned as the unit of 'abstract' appropriation of territory, but did not function as a *direct*, *everyday* unit of 'concrete' appropriation. The units of direct production and consumption were the local bands, consisting of a restricted number of families and individuals. Several kinship groups came together for the purpose of exploiting the resources of several territories. Descent relations thus may have served as a basis for abstract and juridical appropriation of resources from generation to generation, whereas relations of *alliance* may have served as a basis for concrete appropriation and for cooperation in everyday, non-ceremonial life. Thus, both aspects of kinship relations, descent and alliance, served as a social framework for 'production' (a not entirely suitable term, since the essence of economic activities was to appropriate wild resources, *unproduced* by man). Once again, this would appear to be a point of fundamental theoretical importance. For we are dealing here with kinship relations which, as in all societies, are relations regulating marriage, descent, sometimes even the place of residence of the individuals forming society; but at the same time here they are what we in our western culture would call the economic structure of society, the social relations that organize production. At the risk of surprising and shocking both Marxists and non-Marxists alike, both of them being victims of the same *ethnocentrism* in this respect, the *distinction between infrastructure and superstructure*, economy and kinship or religion, *is a distinction between functions and not between institutions.* Some institutions may function as both economy and kinship, and we are going to have to accept, as an analytical principle, that social relations *are what they do*, or better still what they make men do, and not what they seem to us to be. In support of my demonstration, I shall take two examples of forms of land ownership, which in one case (Assur) occurs as an aspect of *religious* relations, and in the other (Athens) occurs as an aspect of *political* relations. In Assur, the land 'belonged' to the god Assur, whose house (the temple) stood in the centre of the city-state. Production was carried out under the authority of the priests, and the economy was organized along centralized and bureaucratic lines. Thus the social form of appropriation of natural resources was that of the relation of subordination of a community of the faithful to its god and to the priests, his servants. The high priest himself was called 'the slave' of god, and the community as a whole considered itself as dependent on the god and on the priests for the reproduction of its life – as their slaves.

In Athens, another city-state, all citizens, i.e. all free men born of Athenian parents, had the right to two forms of usage of the land belonging to his community. On the one hand he was allowed to use state lands of which, along with all the other members of the community (*politeia*), he was a co-owner; on the other hand, he also owned land separate from the public land, which he used for his own private purposes. Until the fourth century, this portion of land (*kleros*) was the inalienable property of a kinship group. It is important to note, first, that this portion was not private property in the modern sense of the term, since it remained the undivided property of a kinship group and, secondly, that it was considered as having been originally separated from the common land (in archaic Greek, the word *temonos*, from the verb *temnein* 'to cut'; in Latin, the word *privatus* also means 'cut off from' the *ager publicus*).

As we can see, the study of forms of ownership can only advance if progress is also made in our knowledge of the *conditions* and the *reasons* that have made economic structures, *relations of production, change their locus and, in changing their locus, change their form and consequences* over the course of historical evolution. I shall be returning to this problem in the last part of this paper. Beforehand, I should like to take a brief look at a number of forms of internal sharing of territory, selecting my examples from among hunters, shepherds and farmers, i.e. the different systems of exploitation of nature.

b. Some forms of ownership of a territory

Hunter-gatherer societies. It is worth comparing three societies living in very different ecosystems: a generalized equatorial forest ecosystem (the Pygmies of Zaire); two specialized ecosystems, the arboreal grassland of the Kalahari (Bushmen) and the desert wastes of Southern Australia (Aranda). Among the Bushmen, one finds territories that are common to several bands, who share access to permanent wells. This complex of associated bands constitutes a 'nexus'. These bands are not kinship groups (lineages, etc.) and they roam over the entire territory, consulting mutually about their movements. The arid wastes between two 'complexes' of bands constitute a desert no-man's-land which serves as a boundary. While an individual is free to use the resources of the territory of the group of bands to which he belongs, he is forbidden to go and hunt on the territory of another group of bands after having crossed the no-man's-land separating them. Richard Lee and H. J. Heinz are currently in disagreement on this point. According to Lee (1976), there is no such thing as ownership of territory among the Bushmen, there is no aggression or warfare among them, etc. According to Heinz (1972), on the other hand, the Bushmen do have territory, which they defend with weapons if necessary. In fact, I think, Lee and Heinz are talking about two different things. Lee is looking at the way individuals and groups use resources within a *given territory*, while Heinz is looking at relations between two 'global societies', two 'complexes' of local bands.

Among the Pygmies, who hunt antelope herds with nets (these animals not being very mobile), the forest is divided up into distinct territories belonging to local bands. These bands, as with the Bushmen, are not really kinship groups. Individuals may change bands and hence territories, provided they are accepted by all the members of the band they are visiting. Bands and territories, then, are fixed, while individuals are mobile. In the heart of the forest, there lies a no-man's-land, which no band whatsoever is permitted to appropriate. This exclusion is based on tacit agreement and is justified by the idea that the god of the forest lives in this heart. I would suggest that this zone remaining unappropriated by the local bands functions to the advantage of all simultaneously, as a sanctuary in which the game may breed in peace. It is as if the Forest, a benevolent divinity, sent out from this sacred and protected place the game necessary to the survival of the Pygmies, its children.

Among the Australian aborigines, as we have seen, there was, as with the Pygmies, an internal division of the 'tribal' territory into portions belonging to closed kinship groups. The local bands which exploited these resources did not coincide with these kinship groups. They were composite and mobile over several different fixed territories, whereas with the Pygmies the bands and the territories were fixed, while the individuals were mobile.

It would be well worthwhile expanding this typology of forms of territory among hunter-gatherers, although unfortunately there is no room to do so here.

Pastoral societies. It seems that there are two forms of appropriation of resources among nomadic shepherds. Animals are appropriated 'privately' by domestic groups constituting autonomous production units. But pastures and wells are appropriated on a broader 'community basis'. This generally implies that local and kinship groups have equivalent rights over resources. However, the evolution of pastoral society shows the emergence of aristocracies and in some cases (the Mongols, Mauritania) the formation of states. In such cases, the equivalence of kinship groups with regard to common resources disappears, but a tribe or a clan manages the use of common resources by each local group, and thus controls their conditions of existence. These two main forms of ownership of resources, domestic ownership of livestock and tribal or inter-tribal ownership of pasture land, tended both to be mutually reinforcing and at the same time mutually exclusive. Domestic 'appropriation' of livestock encourages the development of inequality between lineages, clans, and tribes, while the common appropriation of pasture land re-imposes equality.

Farmers. Turning now to farmers, we shall take the case of the Rumanian village communities analysed by H. H. Stahl. Stahl's historical and anthropological study (1969), which combines observation of the last surviving archaic communities of Rumania with a study of historical documents dating back to the high Middle Ages, shows that forms of community can be classified into four groups expressing the different stages of historical evolution.

In the older communities, using extensive agro-pastoral techniques to exploit mountain forests, it would seem that there was equality of access for all families to all resources within each community. Herds and fields moved through the forest at their users' *concerted* will. Here, there was not even a rule of 'particular' appropriation of land. Stahl has shown that this archaic model rapidly gave way to communities of what he calls the 'genealogical' type. Under the pressure of increasing population, and in order to preserve equality of access to the good land (which was unevenly spread over the area of the territory), communities divided their territory into two equal parts. The larger part was freely accessible to all for stockbreeding, gathering, etc., as in the older system, but the good agricultural land and sites for the planting of fruit trees were divided up equally among all the families on the basis of their genealogical links with other common ancestors, and each group of families descending from a given ancestor received an equal portion. The principle of equivalence was thus maintained. But with uneven rates of increase in the size of families, some found themselves with far more land per member than others. The application of a principle of equality in the appropriation of land and its resources resulted in an unequal distribution. These two types of community were 'free' communities. However, a study of their historical evolution shows that two different types of subjection slowly arose in succession. Around the tenth century, certain communities (Wallachia) gradually came under the sway of an aristocracy of boyards and warlords (*voievode*); these boyards themselves lived in family communities and shared out the titles and the forced-labour which they raised from the peasant communities. This sharing followed the same pattern as for the distribution of good farmland between the families in a peasant community. Then, gradually, the development of capitalism in the west and of the European cereals market encouraged the boyards to appropriate the best farmland personally and to oblige the peasants to grow wheat for export. The peasants gradually lost their individual liberty, and thus were bound to the soil. The villages' community pattern of exploitation was in this way transformed into a quasi-feudal form, and the boyard became an individual landowner within these communities, the latter progressively losing community control over their land. But for this to happen, commercial production and the capitalist system in western Europe (England, France, the Netherlands, etc.) needed to develop.

The Incas provide another example. When they conquered tribes or local village communities, they totally expropriated the land which then became the 'eminent' domain of the Inca. The latter then divided each community's land into three portions; one was reserved for his 'father', the Sun, whose produce served to support the priests and the religion; another he reserved for himself and for the state (in its non-religious activities); and a third he 'graciously' *returned* to the local communities to enable them to *live*; they were *henceforth under the obligation* to give priority to cultivation of the two parts of their territory which they had lost and which the Inca state had appropriated. Here we have an example of exploitation of one community by another community that is far more complex than that of the Rumanian boyards. Once again we should note the extreme diversity of forms of property encountered in history due to the fact that these forms reflect not only an evolution of relations with nature, but also of relations between men. The question that now arises is: can we discover some of the principles governing this evolution of forms of territorial ownership?

III. Hypotheses concerning the reasons for the diversity and for the transformation of forms of ownership of nature

When seeking the reasons for the appearance, the more or less long-term maintenance, and the disappearance of forms of ownership of nature, we should examine three different types of analysis.

1. The study of relations between productive forces, forms of material exploitation of nature, and forms of its appropriation

If we take the case of hunter-gatherers, it will be observed that they are heavily dependent on the spontaneous reproduction of natural resources, and that their capacity for acting upon this reproduction, while not exactly nil, is limited. These limits force groups to *split up* and to *scatter* across the land in order to exploit its natural resources which are themselves spontaneously scattered and limited in quantity; these limits also oblige local bands to *coordinate* their use of the territory. In view of the vagaries and the precariousness of natural resources, cooperation is essential not only within groups but between them. This has certain consequences upon forms of territorial appropriation. On the one hand, natural resources are appropriated on a *communal* basis, and on the other hand this communal appropriation does not entirely *exclude* other groups from the sharing out of resources in case of drought, famine, etc.

This dispersal and precariousness of resources is matched by the *numerical limits* of local bands (which are the direct units of production and consumption), by the *social* diversity of their *internal composition*, the *flexibility* of the concrete labour processes and their *nomadic* way of life. This dispersal and precariousness is also matched by the *common* and *non-exclusive* form of ownership of nature, which guarantees the *continuous* appropriation and repeated sharing out of resources obtained through individual or collective 'labour' both within each group and among different groups. In hunter-gatherer societies, where territory is jointly appropriated, tools are owned individually and the product of hunting and gathering likewise, this being the condition of the functioning of complex systems of *personal* gifts and counter-gifts forming the network of mutual obligations.

Taking the example of nomadic shepherds, it will be observed that their capacity for acting upon nature is far greater. A part of nature, their livestock, is no longer wild and can only reproduce itself through man's intervention. Here, human intervention means guiding flocks along pre-established routes, arranging watering-places, protecting animals against predators and sickness. Grass and water do remain 'natural' resources upon which man may act, however, by burning grass to revive pastures, and by the intensity of use and the selection of pastures which modify the structure of the vegetation, and by sinking wells. But in the main, the reproduction of these resources depends on the vicissitudes of nature. It is interesting to note that two forms of property correspond to these two aspects of nature. The domesticated part, livestock, is appropriated in a 'particular' manner, almost 'privately', by domestic groups which constitute units of direct production. The undomesticated part, grass and water, is appropriated and managed on a community basis. We may perceive an internal link between productive capacities and the forms of appropriation of nature and of social organization. As with hunters, nomadic pastoral socities are obliged to split up into units of direct production separately exploiting joint resources. Here too, kinship relations function as relations of production. But at the same time, in order for all these groups to reproduce their common conditions of existence, their *particular* use of common resources first has to be *organized* socially. One of the most usual responses is the institution of a rule governing the order of access of groups and flocks to the same areas. Each group thus *cooperates* with the others by *abstaining from presence* on the fraction of territory being exploited by the others. This is a form of indirect negative cooperation which implies an *absence* of *personal* relations with other groups while engaged in *productive activities*. On the other hand, all groups cooperate directly, positively and personally, whenever they need to defend common interests, for purposes of warfare, religious sacrifice, etc. In the first case, the community is one of the conditions of production, operating more or less through the exclusion of personal relations between groups, whereas for political and religious activities the community exists in the form of personal relations between these groups.

The structure of nomadic pastoral societies seems therefore to rest upon a contradiction that is linked, in the last analysis, to their capacities to act upon nature and to their conditions of production. On the one hand, private ownership of livestock facilitates the considerable development of social inequality, but on the other hand, the obligation incumbent on all groups to preserve equal access to joint resources acts constantly to re-establish social equality between the groups. Under certain cir- cumstances, which need to be theorized, equality of access to joint resources vanishes and a hierarchy of classes emerges within pastoral societies. The example of the Mongols has shown us that the ruling class arose by gradually taking over the management of joint resources and by controlling each group's access to them, coming to personify in their eyes the interests of all, the common interest.

2. Relations between forms of ownership of nature and the development of social inequalities

If we now try to obtain a global view of the evolution of systems of property which, as we have seen, always consist of combinations of different principles adjusted to different realities (joint appropriation of territory, personal appropriation of tools and products, for example), we may formulate the hypothesis that evolution has travelled from forms of inequality that first and foremost manifested themselves in the control of products, to forms of inequality in the control of land and means of production.

In examining this evolution we should take as our point of departure the fact that, in primitive societies, local groups not only produce for their immediate everyday needs, but that from time to time they *also* produce in order to defend their common interests (real or imaginary in our own eyes), for example to organize big religious ceremonies and initiations, which immobilize the entire population for several days or even several weeks, keeping them absent from immediate production.

Evolution has led to a number of changes in the use of this surplus labour which, instead of exclusively serving common interests, gradually came to serve in the reproduction of a social minority *who appeared to possess a monopoly* of creating fertility, wealth and life for everyone. In this context, 'community' forms of territorial appropriation gradually became transformed into forms of personal property attached to a social minority that 'represented', 'personified', 'identified with' the common interests of society. At the same time the principles of 'personal' appropriation, which in the first place applied only to the instruments of production and to the personal product of hunting and gathering, gradually came to apply to the control of land and of 'domesticated' natural resources.

3. Relations between forms of exploitation of nature and forms of exploitation of man

Finally, we are beginning to perceive an intimate and profound link between forms of exploitation of nature and forms of exploitation of man by man. To return to my example of the city-state of ancient Greece and Rome, the fact that a citizen enjoyed dual access to the land provided a basis for the considerable development of that form of exploitation of man by man which we know as slavery. Whereas the slave of high antiquity was treated almost as 'one of the family' (albeit the lowliest member of the family), with the development of private property and commercial agriculture slavery began to expand out of all proportion to the archaic forms and was transformed into a generally pitiless system of exploitation of man by man. The existence of private property alone is not sufficient to account for this transformation. All it does is to help us understand the struggles that went on among free men, between rich and poor; for to lose one's 'private' land was to lose the economic basis of one's independence; it meant becoming dependent on someone else and gradually losing one's status as a 'free' man. What was required in addition was that the exploitation of nature – farming, animal husbandry, handicrafts and so on – instead of being concerned solely with the production of useful objects, of use-values, increasingly became concerned with the production of commodities, of exchange-values. It was under this combination of conditions that intensive, productive slavery developed, signifying simultaneously the pillage of the populations of hundreds of barbarian tribes, the pillage of a very special natural resource: human labour.

This example (as with that of the Incas who *expropriated* communities' property rights, *leaving* them only possession rights and *rights restricted by forced-labour obligations*, i.e. of surplus labour) shows us that the *secret of the evolution of forms of property always, in the last analysis, resides in the genesis of the relation between those who possess a monopoly of access to nature and those who exploit that nature directly*. In farming societies, this contradiction takes the form of the relation between the landowner and the direct producer (serf or tenant-farmer, etc.). The history of forms of property in pre-capitalist societies will be clearer when we know more about the reasons for the historic *separation between property and use of the earth and of natural resources*.

It should be observed that the effects of this separation are always contradictory. On the one hand, we have the concern to *administer* the exploitation of man by man and the exploitation of nature carefully so as to ensure the reproduction of the conditions of existence of the dominant minorities, while at the same time there is a *wastage* of natural resources and human labour as soon as this wastage becomes beneficial to the development of the conditions of existence and of the power of these minorities. Now that mass industrial production is increasingly taking the place of agrarian or pastoral production, and is organized purely along the lines of a logic based on commodity exchange and monetary profit, we may also observe the contradictory phenomenon of a management that claims to be 'economical' as regards conditions of production combined with senseless 'waste' both of natural resources and of the productive force of the producers. Ecology and economy are intimately interwoven, and the present crisis is in the first place one of society, of a mode of social organization and of its objectives, which determine the logic of its mode of action upon nature.

Conclusion

I need hardly point out that this paper contains many serious omissions. Nothing has been said about the dimension of territories, about population/resources ratios, about the *espace vital* of a society, about war as a way of preserving its own resources or of appropriating other people's resources. It should be even more apparent that to try to list the manifold forms of ownership of nature and to attempt to arrange them in order or to extract principles of evolution from them is a task that is way beyond the capacities of a single person: it is an undertaking that in any case could not be fully completed at the present time in view of the patchy, contradictory, and inadequate nature of our information.

All I set out to do was: (a) to construct a framework of definitions capable of helping us to embark upon an analysis of concrete forms of appropriation of nature; in themselves, these abstract definitions teach us *nothing*, for there is no such thing as property in general, and their sole interest is that they serve as an analytical framework for concrete phenomena; (b) to shed light on the diversity of concrete forms of property and to seek in the nature of the productive capacities of societies some of the reasons for the diversity of forms of appropriation. The controversy between collective appropriation, particular appropriation, individual appropriation and finally private appropriation points to some of the trends characterizing their evolution. However, we cannot account for these trends purely by the emergence of new capacities to exploit nature; they are also explained by the emergence of new capacities to exploit man's labour force.

Nor does it strike me that a discussion of this kind concerning primitive and pre-capitalist societies is all that far removed from the most up-to-the-minute, controversial problems now facing our industrial societies, whether capitalist or socialist. Anthropology is not a waste of time. It may possibly be a detour, but it is one that takes us right back to the heart of everyday contemporary life. Plato said that theoretical work was a *periodos*, a road leading to one side, and he called philosophy the *macroteros periodos*, the grand detour taking us right back to the essence of things. Today, for the social and for the natural sciences, the problem is neither to emerge from our cave in order to discover 'reality', nor to submit our sciences to some abstract philosophy in order to comprehend this reality. What we are concerned to do is to work *together* to devise a complex analytical instrument capable of carrying us from one level of reality to another, of penetrating appearances and of revealing, beneath the diversity and confusion of social forms, the foundations of their logic and their evolution.

Comments on papers by Altman and Godelier

Territory, property, and privacy

LIONEL TIGER

There is a considerable history of political controversy about the status of biological influences on human territoriality and property use. There is a pattern of guilt-by-association between proponents of a biological view of the motivation of behavior and generally right wing political positions. Why this should be is perhaps historically understandable but not scientifically or intellectually clear. Kropotkin's explanation of the biology of mutual aid is no less plausible than Herbert Spencer's conception of a strong strain of economic individualism in the human system. In an important way the central scientific issue about the subject under discussion here has been confounded, obscured, and indeed corrupted by political controversies.

One early rendition of the problem was by John Stuart Mill, who argued that for political purposes it was unwise to study 'human nature' because such study could reveal limits which would then be placed on the political process of making social options. Yet he first used the term 'ethology', and his concept of the greatest good for the greatest number is clearly a profoundly ethological concept, rooted in both a sense of the needs of whole populations and of individual organisms' well being within these populations.

Yet of course 'is' does not imply 'ought' and analysis is different from moral recommendation. It is possible that ethological knowledge could be put to political use, but conversely so could its absence. As the English economist Marshall once said, 'the most reckless theorist is he who

156

presumes to let the facts speak for themselves'. In this context, then, a discussion of the technical status of property and territory as biological concepts, and of privacy, which is an interesting amalgam of them both, is in order.

A note on some historical antecedents. The French sociologist Durkheim is generally held responsible for enunciating a set of rules, of sociological method, which formalized the distinction between the biological and the social sciences. It was Durkheim's view that social events should be explicable by other social events and not by lower order, physiological or even psychological events. In part his antipathy to the use of biology was professional. It had to do with the establishment of sociology in French academia. But his position was also, like Mill's, that knowledge of biological components of behavior could interfere with the development of that socialism in which he was interested. Curiously enough, as one of the major students of the biologist Espinas, Durkheim employed many terminological and technical devices of biology even in his biology-free social science.

The more radical socialist, Karl Marx, had no such antipathy as Durkheim's to the use of biology, and, as we know, Engels in his funeral oration at Marx's graveside claimed that Marx had tried to do for social science what Darwin did for biology. Subsequently, however, in the Marxist tradition there has emerged an extraordinarily forceful antipathy to the use of biology in social science with the most earnest expression of this being the extreme environmentalism of Lysenko. (It is always sobering at least to me to recall that Lysenko remained effectively in scientific power in the Soviet Union until 1964, and there has been scarcely time for a generation of non-Lysenko-afflicted scientists to equip themselves in the Soviet Union to deal constructively with modern social biology.) In any event, Marx was of course deeply concerned about resources and their disposition. Nevertheless, the concept of property became identified in the Communist world as well as in the non-Communist with keeping rather than sharing. But as we see from Godelier's discussion, and as we know from many ethnographies of hunter-gatherers, the important feature of resources is their public sharing rather than private retention. It is quite possible that humans adapted to the hunting-gathering way were seriously disrupted by the shift to agricultural production, with its very long period of 'deferred gratification' between planting and reaping and with the highly elaborated social structures which the existence of increasingly intensive agriculture permitted – again, see Godelier's description.

I will from here focus more on property than territory, if only because a fairly considerable literature exists in biology about territory and the social behaviors associated with it – though not, of course, in the complex psychological sense which emerges from Altman's paper on privacy, with its pattern of boundary-maintenance. The 'ethology of property' has been considerably less well developed and there are fewer clear hypotheses than there are about territory, such as for example that in a variety of species one can relate reproductive to territorial behavior. Such a link with property is more difficult to make.

Having said this, I nevertheless want to raise a few ethological questions about property. How indeed does property affect the reproductive system? There are several important vectors of property transfer related to this in most societies. Perhaps the most general involves a transfer of resources from old to young – old being parents, young being children. The next most significant general pattern of sharing property, taking a global picture, is from the male group to the group of females and young. So an industrial worker in Frankfurt or Cleveland or Leicester even today gives nearly all his life's earnings to his wife and family. In ethological terms this is quite an intriguing transfer payment and raises very interesting questions about why males do this.

It is probably wrong to underestimate the relationship between property and the reproductive system, as Engels was among the first to point out. In contemporary terms one sees a clear if somewhat negative relationship: in the United States, for example, many women, as many as 45%, are in the labor force, and the association of this with a very low birth rate is probably not accidental. There is, given these property arrangements, relatively less reason for maintaining the family system than even twenty years ago, when female participation in the labor force was more limited, episodic and less seriously treated as a source of both income and psychological benefit to the female. Of newly minted marriages in the USA, the prediction is that of ten, four will end in divorce, which involves an unprecedented and quite massive change in the expectations of certainty and stability which people may have about their reproductive careers; presumably in part the birth rate reflects females' decisions to forgo or delay producing offspring unless or until they are certain of some reliable male assistance in what is still a demanding and economically costly process. In any event, the disruptions are immense. Consider how quickly governments would ban any other activity which so consistently and importantly ended badly (e.g. taxi rides in accidents or hamburgers in food poisoning). It may well be that the shifts in marriage patterns are quite closely connected to changes in pattern of property use; one can well imagine in, for example, some of the societies to which Godelier refers that changes of a major kind in the distribution of income between males and females would be bound to have equally major repercussions for the conduct of the kinship system. That is to say, the basic connection between 'the natural', which has to do with the reproduction of the species in this context, and 'the economic', which has to do with the production and use of resources, is a profound one. One of the contributions of an ethology to the study of this connection can now be made by appreciating the links between kinship and genetics – if not in the way some socio-biologists have argued at least in some way which suitably accounts for the centrality of the connection.

Godelier comments on the 'intimate and profound link between forms of exploitation of nature and forms of exploitation of man'. This becomes an interesting matter to cast in the light of the socio-biological argument about 'the selfish gene' and the relationship between males and females as mutually involved co-producers of genetic and possibly economic resources – children – who have different strategies to follow in this co-production. A critical shift must arise from female control of contraception; we may surmise that such an innovation in mammalian species is of quite unprecedented importance. It is intriguing to recall that prior to fifteen or so years ago the principal form of contraception employed by contraceptive users was the condom. The shift to contraceptive techniques controlled by females such as the diaphragm, the pill, and the i.u.d. constitutes a fundamental revision of the way in which forms of exploitation of male by female or female by male takes place. It is quite possible, as I've already noted, that a reason for the striking decline in birth rates now marking most of the technologically sophisticated world has to do with females' decisions that the males with whom they are consorting are inadequate co-producers in the reproductive system. That is to say further, that females can now be more precise in their reproductive decisions, and one result of this precision is a decline in their general confidence in and enthusiasm for the particular males available to them for reproductive purposes – hence the decline in birth rate. While this is in part a far fetched explanation, nevertheless, to return to Godelier again, if one sees females as 'those who possess a monopoly of access to nature' in the form of their own reproductive capacity, and 'those who exploit that nature directly' their males, then one can begin to perceive legitimate if nonetheless still confusing links between resources in the form of property or even territory and basic human biology. I recognize that this is an extension from Godelier's argument which he might himself not make nor indeed wish to see made; nevertheless since the ultimate natural resource is the body it is perhaps appropriate to consider it particularly in the context of reproduction, as a central analytical unit for anthropological purposes.

Perhaps this comes dramatically into focus when one considers the evidently rising incident of sterilization as a form of contraception among Americans. Westoff estimates that among Americans from their late twenties on sterilization is now almost as widely used for contraceptive purposes as the pill, and is furthermore increasing in popularity. This raises a serious question about the availability of the 'resource of the body' to partners, particularly in view of the relatively high divorce rate in this very same culture. The point is that it is precisely that culture with an extremely high divorce rate in which people elect to sterilize themselves, perhaps on the basis that they have already completed a child-producing cycle with their partner and hence can withdraw from that process permanently. However, the divorce rate being high, this is a mere surmise, and the possibility exists that sterilized individuals will find themselves consorts to new partners who may wish to reproduce but who cannot do so with these now sterile people. This may further abet the increasing divorce rate and we should be able to see more directly the links between the body as resource in reproductive terms, the overall system of kinship, and the economic system within which this is in turn embedded.

Of course, I am not claiming that there is a 'gene for property'. The relationship between resources and biology isn't at all simple or clear cut. Yet a particular virtue of Altman's analysis in this context is how resourcefully it suggests what connections are made and how, between individual organisms, their groups, and wider structures. The notion of 'boundary systems' permits us to see how the interaction works at the various levels of sociability which Altman discusses. The connection is also strong between Altman's notion of boundaries and their pattern and Godelier's emphasis on some of the symbolic aspects of the use of property and territory.

Restricted though these comments must be, I should conclude with a brief point about an issue which concerns both papers and which is also likely to be a central one in the years of human ethological research to come. I refer to the function of cognition in expressing, articulating, stimulating and institutionalizing the variety of valences and barriers which individual people sustain and which together make up a social system. Both Altman and Godelier show the socially consensual character of social regulation as it affects the area around the body, privacy, and the use of resources. How both privacy and resources are defined is critical, particularly in the societies beyond the minimal subsistence level, where the principal concerns of members of societies will be not with struggling with the real problem of 'too little' but rather with the symbolic problem of allocating and using 'too much'.

Clearly the bridge between individual and space/resource is created by the brain. The brain more than any other organ stimulates the movement of property and the exchange of space – the prototype process here is of the behavior of children who routinely but enthusiastically engage in complex forms of trading which serve no useful purpose, e.g. in cards picturing sports heroes, military equipment, etc. Cognitive interpretation or assessment of resources becomes critical, of course, beyond the hunting-gathering stage when the problem of disposable surplus emerges. An animal with the motivational and physical structure of a hunter-gatherer designed to cope with 'not enough' translates the same characteristics into the situation of 'too much'. And there is consequent escalation of wants and needs, now on a species-wide level because of modern communication technology.

The recurrently appetitive nature of the hunting-gathering adaptation has had, I believe, the effect of creating difficulties for *Homo sapiens* involved in industrial societies. The set of capacities useful for securing perishable animals and foods have an entirely different meaning when employed for the acquisition of durable goods and services involving other persons. The escalation of demand for goods and services appears to remain relatively immune to socio-political blandishment – even the Chinese, post-Mao, have seen fit to emphasize more consumer consumption at the expense of those communal investments which nearly thirty years of fairly stringent socialization have claimed were preferable to private ones. As well, the passionate concern for consumer artifacts in eastern European countries belies a clear endorsement of the view that, for example, state ownership of means of production necessarily causes disappearance of commitment to private control over resources. Once the cooperative hunting scheme is broken and immediate clearly perceived cooperation is no longer essential for communal survival, then the possibility for economic privacy appears to have a volatile effect on the overall level of self seeking behavior, even in social systems committed to highly egalitarian ethics.

I do not, of course, claim that inequality is 'natural'; indeed the consistent occurrence of the dream of equity as a modern phenomenon suggests how powerfully large in the human cognitive capacity is the notion of equity. Be that as it may, there may well be interesting insights about the conduct of economic systems which come from employing the ethological lens and bearing firmly in mind economic aspects of human phylogeny.

References

Adler, M. J. 1927. *Dialectic*. New York: Harcourt Brace.

Alland, A. 1975. Adaptation. *Annual Review of Anthropology*, 4:59–73.

Allport, G. 1968. The historical background of modern social psychology. In G. Lindzey and E. Aronson (eds.), *The handbook of social psychology*, vol. I. Reading, Mass.: Addison-Wesley.

Altman, I. 1975. *The environment and social behavior: Privacy, personal space, territory and crowding*. Monterey, California: Brooks/Cole.

  1976a. Environmental psychology and social psychology. *Personality and Social Psychology Bulletin*, 2:96–113.

  1976b. Privacy: a conceptual analysis. *Environment and Behavior*, 8(1):7–29.

  1977a. Privacy regulation: culturally universal or culturally specific? *Journal of Social Issues*, 3:66–84.

  1977b. Research on environment and behavior: A personal statement of strategy. In D. Stokols (ed.), *Perspectives on environment and behavior: Theory, research and applications*. New York: Plenum.

Altman, I. and Chemers, M. M. 1979 (in press). *Culture and environment*. Monterey, California: Brooks/Cole.

Altman, I. and Taylor, D. A. 1973. *Social penetration: the development of interpersonal relationships*. New York: Holt, Rinehart and Winston.

Altman, I. and Vinsel, A. M. 1977. Personal space: an analysis of E. T. Hall's proxemics framework. In I. Altman and J. F. Wohlwill (eds.), *Human behavior and environment: Advances in theory and research*, vol. II. New York: Plenum.

Anderson, E. N. Jr. 1972. Some Chinese methods of dealing with crowding. *Urban Anthropology*, 1(2):141–50.

Barker, R. 1968. *Ecological psychology*. Stanford, California: Stanford University Press.

Barth, F. 1959–60. The land use patterns of migratory tribes of South Persia. *Norsk Geografisk Tidskrift*, 17:1–11.

Baum, A. and Epstein, Y. (eds.) 1977. *Human response to crowding*. Hillsdale, New Jersey: Erlbaum.

Bennett, R., Osborne, R. and Miller, R. 1975. Biocultural ecology. *Annual Review of Anthropology*, 4:163–81.

Berg, R. 1975. Land: an extension of the peasant's ego. *Anthropological Quarterly* (Jan.), 4–13.

Berndt, R. (ed.) 1970. *Australian aboriginal anthropology*. Nedlands, Western Australia: Australian Institute of Aboriginal Studies.

Birdsell, J. 1953. Some environmental and cultural factors influencing the structuring of Australian aboriginal populations. *The American Naturist*, 834:171–207.

1958. On population structure in generalized hunting and collecting populations. *Evolution*, 12(2):189–205.

Blatt, S. J. and Wild, C. M. 1976. *Schizophrenia: a developmental analysis*. New York: Academic Press.

Bonte, P. 1973. Etudes sur les sociétés de pasteurs nomades. *Cahiers du CERM*, 6–32.

Brehm, J. W. 1966. *A theory of psychological reactance*. New York: Academic Press.

Brinkmann, C. 1933. Land tenure, *Encyclopaedia of the Social Sciences*, vol. VI. New York: Macmillan.

Brower, S. N. 1965. Territoriality, the exterior spaces, the signs we learn to read. *Landscape*, 15:9–12.

Digard, J.-P. 1973. Histoire et anthropologie des sociétés nomades. *Annales ESC*, 6:1423–35.

Draper, P. 1973. Crowding among hunter-gatherers: The !Kung Bushmen. *Science*, 182:301–3.

Dupire, M. 1970. *Organisation sociale des Peul, étude d'ethnographie comparée*. Paris: Plon.

1975. Exploitation du sol, communautés résidentielles et organisation lignagère des pasteurs WoDaaBe (Niger). In T. Monod (ed.), *Les Sociétés pastorales en Afrique tropicale*. Oxford: Oxford University Press.

Edney, J. J. 1974. Human territoriality. *Psychological Bulletin*, 81:959–75.

Eibl-Eibesfeldt, I. 1970. *Ethology: the biology of behavior*. New York: Holt, Rinehart and Winston.

1974. The myth of the aggression-free hunter and gatherer society. In Ralph Halloway (ed.), *Primate aggression, territoriality and xenophobia*. New York: Academic Press.

Evans, G. W. and Howard, R. B. 1973. Personal space. *Psychological Bulletin*, 80(4):334–44.

Faron, L. C. 1962. Marriage, residence, and domestic groups among the Panamanian Choco. *Ethnology*, 1(1):13–38.

Forde, D. 1971. Ecology and social structure. In *The Huxley Memorial Lecture*. Proceedings of the Royal Anthropological Institute, 15–29.

Fox, R. and Pleishing, U. 1976. Human ethology. *Annual Review of Anthropology*, 5:265–88.

Galt, A. H. 1973. Carnival on the island of Pantelleria: ritualized community solidarity in an atomistic society. *Ethnology*, 12(3):325–41.

Gluckmann, M. 1965. *Politics, law and ritual in tribal society*. London: Blackwell

1972. *The ideas in Barotse jurisprudence*. Manchester: Manchester University Press.

Godelier, M. 1972. *Rationality and irrationality in economics*. London: New Left Books.

1975. Modes of production, kinship and demographic structures. In M. Bloch (ed.), *Marxist analyses and social anthropology.* London: Malaby Press.

1977. *Perspectives in Marxist anthropology.* Cambridge: Cambridge University Press.

Goffman, E. 1959. *The presentation of self in everyday life.* New York: Doubleday.

1961. *Asylums.* New York: Doubleday.

1971. *Relations in public.* New York: Basic Books.

Gregor, T. A. 1970. Exposure and seclusion: a study of institutionalized isolation among the Mehinacu Indians of Brazil. *Ethnology, 9*(3), 234–50.

1974. Publicity, privacy, and Mehinacu marriage. *Ethnology, 13*(3), 333–49.

Hall, E. T. 1966. *The hidden dimension.* New York: Doubleday.

Harris, D. 1978. Settling down: An evolutionary model for the transformation of mobile bands into sedentary communities. In *Evolution of social systems.* London: Duckworth.

Hart, R. A. and Moore, G. T. 1973. The development of spatial cognition. In R. M. Downs and D. Stea (eds.), *Image and environment.* Chicago: Aldine.

Heider, K. 1972. Environment, subsistence and society. *Annual Review of Anthropology, 1*:207–26.

Heinz, H. J. 1972. Territoriality among the bushmen in general and the !Ko in particular. *Anthropos, 67*:405–16.

Hobhouse, L. T. 1922. The historical evolution of property, in fact and in idea. In *Property, its duties and rights, historically, philosophically, and religiously regarded.* First published 1918. New York: Macmillan.

Keenan, J. 1977. The concept of the mode of production in hunter-gatherer societies. *African Studies, 36*:57–69.

King, G. 1975. Socioterritorial units among carnivores and early hominids. *Journal of Anthropological Research, 31*:69–87.

Lattimore, O. 1951. The steppes of Mongolia and the characteristics of steppe nomadism. In *Inner Asian frontiers of China.* New York: American Geographical Society, Capital Publishing Co.

Leacock, E. 1955. Matrilocality in a simple hunting economy: Montagnais-Nadkapi. *Southwestern Journal of Anthropology, 2*:31–47.

Lee, R. and DeVore, I. (eds.) 1968. *Man the hunter.* Chicago: Aldine.

1976. *Kalahari hunter-gatherers.* Cambridge, Mass.: Harvard University Press.

LeVine, R. A. 1962. Witchcraft and co-wife proximity in southwestern Kenya. *Ethnology, 1*(1), 39–45.

Lévi-Strauss, C. 1948. *Les Structures élémentaires de la parenté.* Paris: Presses Universitaires de France.

1973. Structuralism and ecology. *Social Science Information, 12*(1):7–23.

Lonner, W. J. 1979 (in press). The search for psychological universals. In H. C. Triandis (ed.), *Handbook of cross-cultural psychology.* Boston: Allyn and Bacon.

Lowie, R. 1928. Incorporeal property in primitive society. *Yale Law Journal, 5*:551–63.

1943. Property rights and coercive powers of plains Indian military societies. *Journal of Legal and Political Sociology, 3*:59–71.

Lyman, S. M. and Scott, M. B. 1967. Territoriality: a neglected sociological dimension. *Social Problems, 15*:235–49.

MacLeod, R. B. 1975. *The persistent problems of psychology.* Pittsburgh, Pa.: Duquesne University Press.

Malinowski, B. 1926. *Crime and custom in savage society*. London/New York: Library of Psychology, Philosophy and Scientific Method.

Marx, K. 1953. Formen, die der kapitalistischen Produktion vorhergehn. In *Grundrisse der Kritik der politischen Ökonomie*. Berlin: Dietz Verlag.

Meggitt, M. 1972. Understanding Australian aboriginal society: Kinship systems or cultural categories. In Paul Reining (ed.), *Kinship studies in the Morgan centennial year*. Washington, DC: The Anthropological Society of Washington.

Miles, D. 1970. The Ngadju Dayaks of Central Kalimantan, with special reference to the Upper Mentaya. *Behavior Science Notes*, 5(4):291–319.

Murdock, G. P. 1971. Cross-sex patterns of kin behavior. *Ethnology*, 10(3):359–68.

Murphy, R. F. 1964. Social distance and the veil. *American Anthropologist*, 66:1257–74.

Murra, J. 1958. On Inca political structure. In *Systems of political control and bureaucracy in human societies*. Seattle, Wash.: University of Washington Press.

    1972. El 'control vertical' de un maximo de pisos ecologicos en la economía de las sociedades andinas. In *Visita de Pedro de Leon*. Peru: Universidad de Huanuco.

Newman, O. 1972. *Defensible space*. New York: Macmillan.

Paine, R. 1970. Lappish decisions, partnerships, information management, and sanctions – A nomadic pastoral adaptation. *Ethnology*, 9(1):52–67.

Peterson, N. 1972. Totemism yesterday: Sentiment and local organization among the Australian aborigines. *Man*, 31:12–32.

    1975. Hunter-gatherer territoriality: The perspective from Australia. *American Anthropologist*, 77:53–68.

Powell, H. A. 1969. Territory, hierarchy and kinship in Kiriwina. *Man*, 4(4):580–604.

Radcliffe-Brown, A. R. 1931. The social organization of Australian tribes. *Oceania*, 1:34–63, 206–46, 322–41, 426–56.

Reichel-Dolmatoff, G. 1976. Cosmology as ecological analysis. *Man*, 11(3):307–18.

Reynolds, V. 1966. Open groups in hominid evolution. *Man*, 1:441–52.

    1972. Ethology of urban life. In P. J. Ucko (ed.), *Man, settlement and urbanism*. London: Duckworth.

Rigby, P. 1969. *Cattle and kinship among the Goyo*. Ithaca, New York: Cornell University Press.

Roberts, J. M. and Gregor, T. A. 1971. Privacy: a cultural view. In J. R. Pennock and J. W. Chapman (eds.), *Privacy*. New York: Atherton Press.

Rychlak, J. F. 1968. *A philosophy of science for personality theory*. Boston: Houghton Mifflin.

    1976. The multiple meanings of dialectic. In *Dialectic: Humanistic rationale for behavior and development*. Basel, Switzerland: S. Karger.

Sahlins, M. 1972. *Stone-age economies*. New York: Aldine.

Salisbury, R. 1962. *From stone to steel*. Melbourne: Melbourne University Press.

Seligman, M. E. P. 1975. *Helplessness: on depression, development, and death*. San Francisco: Freeman.

Simmel, G. 1950. *The sociology of Georg Simmel*, trans. K. H. Wolff. New York: Free Press.

Stahl, H. H. 1969. *Les anciennes communautés villageoises roumaines*. Paris: CNRS.

Steward, J. 1955. *Theory of culture change*. Urbana/Chicago/London: University of Illinois Press.

Strehlow, T. G. 1970. Geography and the totemic landscape in Central Australia. In Berndt 1970:92–140.

Tambiah, S. J. 1969. Animals are good to think and good to prohibit. *Ethnology*, 8(4):423–60.

Tringham, R. 1972. Territorial demarcation of prehistoric settlements. In P. J. Ucko (ed.), *Man, settlement and urbanism*. London: Duckworth.

Turnbull, C. 1961. *The forest people*. New York: Simon and Schuster.

 1965. *Wayward servants*. London: Eyre-Spottiswoode.

Ucko, P. and Dimbleby, F. 1969. *The domestication and exploitation of plants and animals*. Chicago: Aldine.

Vayda, A. and McCay, B. 1975. New directions in ecology and ecological anthropology. *Annual Review of Anthropology*, 4:293–306.

Westin, A. 1970. *Privacy and freedom*. New York: Atheneum Press.

Whiting, J. M., Kluckhohn, F. and Anthony, A. 1958. The function of male initiation ceremonies at puberty. In E. E. Maccoby, T. M. Newcomb and E. L. Hartley (eds.), *Readings in social psychology*. New York: Holt.

Wilmsen, E. 1973. Interaction, spacing behavior and the organization of hunting bands. *Journal of Anthropological Research*, 29(1):1–31.

Woodburn, J. 1968. An introduction to Hadza ecology. In Lee and DeVore 1968: 49–55.

Wynne-Edwards, V. C. 1962. *Animal dispersion in relation to social behavior*. New York: Hafner.

Yengoyan, A. 1968. Demographic and ecological influences on aboriginal Australian marriage sections. In Lee and DeVore 1968: 185–99.

 1972. Biological and demographic components in aboriginal Australian socio-economic organization. *Oceania*, 43:85–95.

3. Non-verbal and verbal rituals in interaction

3.1. About brows: emotional and conversational signals[1]

PAUL EKMAN

Introduction

We will distinguish two types of facial social signals – emotional expressions and conversational actions. Many of the same facial movements are recruited into each type of signal, although certain facial movements which appear in emotional expressions are rarely seen in conversational actions. To discuss these facial signals (and to study them), it is necessary to have an accurate way of characterizing the great number of movements which can flash across the face.

We will begin by explaining the advantages of an anatomically based system for describing facial action. How such a system works will be illustrated by considering the actions of the eyebrows. These movements have been chosen because the musculature is simpler and the number of distinguishable actions smaller than for other regions of the face. Another advantage of focusing just upon the eyebrows is that we need not worry about whether these actions are required by the process of speech articulation when later we consider the role of facial actions in conversation. The choice of eyebrow movements is also appropriate to a discussion of the origin of facial signals and the adaptive function of facial actions, since eyebrow movements have been the subject of somewhat divergent com-

The research I report and much of the speculations are the product of collaborative work over the last twelve years with Wallace V. Friesen. This research has been supported by a grant MH 11976, and a Research Scientist Award MH 06092, from the National Institute of Mental Health, and a grant from the Harry Frank Guggenheim Foundation. I am indebted to Wally Friesen and Harriet Oster for their many criticisms and suggestions about this paper, and also to Linda Camras, Joe Hager, Maureen O'Sullivan and Rainer Krause for their comments.

169

mentary by ethologists (Blurton Jones and Konner 1971, Eibl-Eibesfeldt 1970, 1972).

There are but seven visibly distinctive eyebrow actions. This may seem a small repertoire, but it is larger than was recognized by previous students of facial movement. Each of these actions is the result of different muscles or combinations of muscles. The seven brow actions represent the repertoire allowed by the equipment. Each of these seven actions can be considered a candidate for recruitment into a social signal. Not all are. Five of the eyebrow actions are involved in emotional expressions. Two of the eyebrow actions play a major role in a variety of conversational signals.

We will describe what is known about the eyebrow actions in emotional expression. We will consider the controversy over universality, and attempt to reconcile contradictory claims. This will include a discussion of the problematic dichotomies of voluntary versus involuntary, deliberate versus automatic actions.

A number of conversational eyebrow signals will be described. We will ask why certain actions more than others are recruited into these conversational signals. Visual contrasts among the various eyebrow movements, and differences in ease of performance, are relevant but do not provide the answer. We will also explain our rationale for distinguishing conversational from emotional signals.

Finally, we will address the question of why certain actions are selected for certain signals. For example, why are the eyebrows typically not raised in anger and lowered in surprise; and why have there not been reports of lowered brows in greetings, but only of raised brows? We will consider the evolutionary view that these movements originally had some biologically adaptive value to our progenitors and were selected and modified for their role as signals. Our discussion will reveal problems in applying this explanation to the role of eyebrow actions in emotional expressions. While we will not resolve the issue of the origin of these facial actions, our discussion will draw attention to the type of evidence that is needed to discover the relative contribution of biological and cultural processes to the development of facial signals.

Before proceeding, we should note that in limiting the focus of this paper to the eyebrows we do not imply that these actions should be studied in isolation from the rest of facial action. It would be equally misguided to study facial action in isolation from head movement, other facial sign systems,[2] body movement, vocalizations and speech, and all

_____

[2] Elsewhere (Ekman 1977a) we have distinguished among static, slow and rapid facial signs, describing the different information provided by each. Rapid signs include changes in

the usually unspecified phenomena which slip so easily under the rubric 'social context'. The focus upon eyebrow movements is a heuristic for exposition, not a recommendation for research.

Describing facial action

With few exceptions, present-day students of animal communication seem unaware of the criteria that they, themselves, have used in establishing catalogues of behavior units. Each catalogue is presented as a *fait accompli*, with little or no justification for the particular choice of behavioral units or elements. Yet, what stage in our research could be more crucial than this initial choosing of behavioral units! Upon it rest all of our subsequent records of communication interactions and any conclusions that we may draw from them, as well as any attempt by others to replicate our results.   (Altmann 1968: 501)

These comments apply with equal force to students of human communication, and in particular to those who have proposed ways to measure facial action. The descriptive systems have been incomplete, without an explanation of what has been left out or why. The units or categories have sometimes specified a single action, sometimes included complex actions due to a number of muscles, often without acknowledgment of this difference. Descriptions have often been contaminated with inference about meaning, so that it is not possible to use the descriptions to test whether the meanings are indeed so associated.[3] The specification of units has sometimes been so vague that investigators cannot know if they are cataloguing the same actions. Descriptions of actions have occasionally been anatomically incorrect.[4] And, these systems have not dealt with the ways in which individual or age-related differences in physiognomy may confuse the recognition of certain actions. (See Ekman and Friesen 1976 for a review of facial measurement systems.)

These problems can be avoided or diminished by an approach based on the anatomy of facial action. Inspection of facial movement can be in-

vascular supply, temperature, coloration and non-visible muscle tonus, as well as the muscular actions which are discussed here.

[3] Examples of contaminating inference with description are 'aggressive frown' (Grant 1969); 'lower lip pout' (Blurton Jones 1971); 'smile tight-loose o' (Birdwhistell 1970); 'low frown' (McGrew 1972); 'sad frown' (Brannigan and Humphries 1972).

[4] While noting that the inner corners of the brows move up in the sad frown, in describing this category, Brannigan and Humphries (1972) wrote that the brows are 'drawn down at their outer end'. This cannot happen. The oblique slope of the brows is produced either by the action of the inner portion of the *frontalis* muscle, or by that action together with the *corrugator* muscle. Once such anatomically incorrect descriptions are made available, they can spread. For example, Lewis, Brooks and Haviland (1978) adapted Brannigan and Humphries' scoring categories in their research on infant facial behavior, incorporating this fallacious account of the 'sad frown'.

formed by knowledge of the mechanics of facial action.[5] How the equipment works – how single muscles and combinations of muscles change appearance – provides only part of the basis for a descriptive system. It is necessary also to take into account which variations in performance observers can distinguish. Otherwise the descriptive system would be unreliable.

When we turned to the literature on the neuroanatomy of facial movement, we expected to find muscles distinguished one from another on the basis of:

differences in how they change appearance;

capability for independent action;

feedback circuits (through proprioception or cutaneous means) which allow a person to become aware of what has moved on his face.

These issues have been considered but not studied systematically for the entire face. Anatomists have named muscles in the face largely on the basis of the appearance of different strands or bundles of muscle fibers when the skin was removed (S. Washburn, personal communication, 1975). Duchenne (1862), Hjorstjö (1970), and Lightoller (1925) are exceptions who were interested in how muscles change appearance.

Building upon their findings, and incorporating the descriptions scattered in many anatomy texts, Friesen and I took the following steps to determine the independent units of facial action. Over the course of two years, we learned how to move our own facial muscles by studying anatomy texts, palpating our muscles, and comparing what we would see in a mirror with the descriptions of others. We observed the changes in the surface of our own faces when a needle placed into a muscle delivered electrical current. And, with a needle in place, we voluntarily moved a muscle to see if there was a change in the electrical activity. (The work with the needle insertions was painful and we pursued it only with the few muscles about which we were in doubt.) We studied the facial actions of fourteen other people who learned how to control specific muscles following our instructions. Also, we studied the spontaneous facial actions found in the records of hundreds of persons from a number of cultures, to seek movements not previously identified.[6] This work provided the basis for specifying what the equipment can do.

[5] Blurton Jones (1971) was much more concerned and knowledgeable about the anatomy of facial action than other human ethologists, although he decided not to base his descriptive system on anatomical units or criteria.

[6] We did not uncover any evidence of new muscular actions when studying the records of non-western people, although we did note certain combinations of actions which are not commonly seen in western cultures. Our work on the anatomy of facial action was guided

We also considered what the perceiver can reliably distinguish. We carefully studied through repeated viewing and slow motion more than 5000 different combinations of specific muscular actions. We taught eight people how to recognize facial actions, and then determined what they could reliably distinguish. Based on these findings, we then wrote a manual (Ekman and Friesen 1978) on how to score facial behavior. Using this manual six other people learned to distinguish facial actions in the terms we proposed, achieving high reliability.

The descriptive units are called Action Units rather than muscle units. They are the product of what the muscular equipment can do and what the perceiver can distinguish under optimal viewing circumstances. For most of the units there is a one-to-one correspondence with what most, but not all, anatomists distinguish in the naming of muscles. Occasionally more than one Action Unit is provided for what anatomists describe as a single muscle. This is because we have found that visibly different actions are produced by different parts of that muscle. In one instance, described below, we have combined into a single Action Unit what anatomists distinguish as three separate muscles.

Consider now what this blending of anatomy (for the person who makes the facial action) and perceptual capability (for the observer of the action) provides for one part of facial action, the movement of the eyebrows. There are three elemental Action Units, which can occur singly or can combine to produce four other movements. Figure 1 shows a tracing from photographs of these Action Units and a baseline example of no action. Action Unit 1 designates the appearance changes when just the medial portion of the *frontalis* muscle contracts. The inner corner of the eyebrow is raised, and the skin in the middle of the forehead is pulled up, which may cause short wrinkles to appear or deepen in the center of the forehead.

Action Unit 2 designates the appearance changes when just the lateral portions of the *frontalis* muscle contract. The outer corners of the eyebrows are raised, and the skin in the lateral portions of the forehead is pulled up, which may cause short wrinkles to appear or deepen in the lateral portions of the forehead.

Action Unit 4 designates the appearance changes when the *corrugator, depressor glabella* and/or *depressor supercilli* contract. The eyebrows are

by German, French, Swedish, English and American anatomists. We also studied Burkitt and Lightoller's (1926–7) and Huber's (1931) accounts of the differences in facial anatomy in other racial groups. Their work suggests some anatomical variations, but not ones which would produce unique movements.

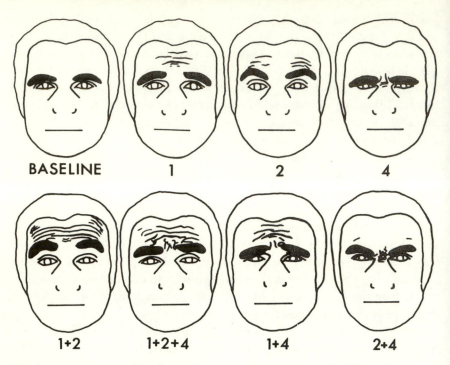

1. Action Units for the brow/forehead.

pulled down and drawn together, the skin between the brows is bunched, often wrinkling or deepening a wrinkle between the brows. These three muscles are combined into one Action Unit because we have rarely observed their separate occurrence, and observers cannot reliably distinguish one from another.[7]

Let us consider three other muscles which can have an influence on the eyebrows. The *occipitalis* muscle reaches down from the scalp. It pulls the forehead skin upwards, pulls the scalp backwards and sometimes produces a very slight lift to the eyebrows. We will not further consider this

[7] Oster (1978) believes it is possible to distinguish *corrugator* from *depressor glabella* in young infants, and that they are differentially related to subsequent smiling and crying. In one child with a cranio-facial malformation, we found that the action of the *depressor glabella* was quite evident, probably because the child did not appear to have a functioning *corrugator* muscle. In children and adults we believe it is not useful to distinguish *corrugator* from *depressor glabella*, because they often co-occur and when they do not are difficult to distinguish. If further empirical work suggests they can be reliably distinguished, this would easily be done within our measurement system. Action Unit number 3 has been left vacant in our system so it could be later used if it proves necessary to separate *corrugator* and *depressor glabella*.

action since its influence on the eyebrows is minor and often not visible. No one has observed this muscular action as a social signal, although Birdwhistell (1970) claimed that the basal position of this muscle varies among social groups.[8] The *levator labii superioris alaeque nasi* can lower the brows, particularly the inner corners, in addition to wrinkling the nose, pulling the nostril wings upwards, and lifting the upper lip. This action is scored in our measurement system, but need not concern us here, since it involves a change across the entire face, not just an eyebrow movement. Finally, the outer portion of the *orbicularis oculi* muscle (*pars orbitalis*) can slightly lower the eyebrows as part of an action which draws skin surrounding the eye orbit inwards, producing crow's-feet wrinkles, and narrowing the eye fissure. This action is also scored in our measurement system, but will not be of concern here since it produces changes in the eye region as well as in the brows. It should be noted that in focusing just upon actions which change the appearance of one region of the face – eyebrows and forehead – we must be cognizant of the influence of these other facial actions. Otherwise we might draw spurious conclusions about the relationship between eyebrow movement and changes in the eye region, nose or lips.

Return now to consider the three single Action Units which change the appearance of just the eyebrows and forehead. Each of them can occur unilaterally or bilaterally. The extent of action may vary for each. Often bilateral actions are asymmetrical, stronger on one side of the face than the other. These three Action Units are the building blocks for the four combinations shown in figure 1. Together the three single actions and the four combinations provide a complete picture of the repertoire of distinguishable movement in this region of the face.

The other well known systems for describing facial action provide only partial coverage of these seven possibilities. Birdwhistell (1970) included only two; Blurton Jones (1971) and McGrew (1972) each distinguished three; Grant (1969) and also Brannigan and Humphries (1972) each distinguished four of the seven possibilities. None allowed for Action Unit 2, an infrequent action. When it occurred, it was probably unwittingly categorized with 1+2. Only Brannigan and Humphries allowed for Action Unit 1; the others probably included it with 1+4 which they did include. None allowed for 2+4, an infrequent action. Only Grant men-

---

[8] While this may be so it is documented only by Birdwhistell's impressive performances using his own face. The issue of social or psychological differences in the baseline muscle tonus of the face is a rich area for research, which is just now beginning (cf. Schwartz *et al.*, 1976).

tioned 1+2+4, although it was not one of his scoring categories. This is a frequent action, and it is not clear what these investigators did when they saw it.

Omission of some behaviors from a system for describing facial action is not necessarily problematic, although a complete system is preferable. The problem arises if the omissions were unwitting, and even worse if what was omitted is unwittingly combined with other different actions. Combining into one functional category a 1+2 and a 2, or a 1 with a 1+4, should rest upon evidence on how these are used, which can never be obtained if the distinctions are collapsed in the initial description.[9]

The seven eyebrow actions shown in figure 1 are candidates for a role in social signals. First, we will consider which actions are recruited in emotional expressions, then which function as conversational signals.

Emotional expressions[10]

There is now a large body of evidence that specific patterns of facial actions universally signify particular emotions. Quantitative studies have provided evidence in more than thirteen literate cultures and two visually isolated preliterate cultures. Qualitative studies support this evidence in a great number of visually isolated cultures. These studies include the work of anthropologists, ethologists, pediatricians, psychologists and sociologists. The people studied have included neonates, children and adults; mostly sighted but some blind persons. Naturalistic observations and laboratory experiments have been conducted. Spontaneous and contrived facial expressions have been measured in various contexts, and the interpretations of faces by members of different cultures have been compared (see Ekman 1973 for a review of this work).

Despite such evidence some still argue that there are no universals in facial expressions of emotion. 'Since natural languages do not in general

[9] Throughout the rest of this report we will refer to these seven eyebrow actions in terms of their Action Unit numbers. This will require the reader to consult figure 1 to recall the designated movements. Admittedly, the figure gives only a partial representation of the movements, as it is only a tracing of a still picture. In our *Facial action coding system* manual each Action Unit and combination is depicted in cinema and described in considerable detail. The alternatives for describing facial action are cumbersome and vague. The Latin names are long and provide little idea about the movement's appearance. Terms such as oblique slope, entire brow raise, inner corner brow raise, are just as cumbersome, and may mislead by over-simplifying the range of changes in appearance which occur for each Action Unit.

[10] Although differing in detail, the account of the interrelationship between facial expression and other responses described here was first most explicitly and systematically presented by Tomkins (1962–3). He offered a different, but not contradictory, view of the characteristics common to the elicitors of each emotion.

associate particular sounds or combinations of sounds with particular meanings, the linguistic analogy does not suggest there will be any consistent relationship between nonverbal signal and response when such signals are observed in differing cultural environments' (Leach 1972: 329). That same view has been most vigorously argued by Birdwhistell (1970) and most recently by Mead (1975). Elsewhere (Ekman 1977b), we have explained how a linguistic analogy is misleading about facial expressions of emotion, although useful in describing the function of facial conversational signals. We have attempted to explain the basis for the disagreement between those who argue from a linguistic analogy and those who argue an evolutionary view, offering a theoretical framework which attempts to embrace both, to reconcile the disagreement. Here, we will only summarize some of the main issues.

One major source of disagreement has been the failure of many of the universalists to explain what they mean by emotion terms such as anger, fear, surprise, sadness, disgust, happiness, etc. We (Ekman 1977b) have suggested that these terms imply a complex package of information. Consider only three components of this package: elicitors, co-occurring responses, and subsequent interpersonal behavior. Elicitors refer to the stimulus events, external or internal, which precede and appear to regularly call forth an emotional expression. The co-occurring responses refer to skeletal muscular actions, vocalizations, autonomic nervous system changes, memories, images, expectations and other cognitions which occur simultaneously with the emotional expression. Subsequent interpersonal responses refer to a more complex pattern of activity which describes how a person copes with the source of emotional arousal. There is both universality and cultural variation in regard to each of these components of emotion. We will use just a few examples.

Consider the elicitors of surprise. Universally, surprise elicitors are novel, unexpected and sudden. This characterization requires that the specific stimuli for surprise must vary since what is expected will vary with particular social contexts. Therefore, surprise elicitors cannot be uniform for any one person, social group or culture. Whether an investigator finds evidence of universality or cultural variation in elicitors of emotional expression will depend, in part, upon the level of abstraction employed in his analysis.

The co-occurring responses for surprise which are likely to be universal[11] include muscular movements which orient the person towards the

---

[11] Not all of the co-occurring responses should show universality; e.g. memories, images, expectations should be quite variable.

surprising event, a quick inhalation, and if a sound is made, one that is abrupt in onset and offset like 'wow', 'oh', 'whew'. By contrast, in disgust the muscular responses orient the person away from the source, an exhalation is likely, and the sound is likely to resemble a regurgitation noise, so that 'yucch' would be more probable than 'mmhmm'. These immediate responses are probable, common, but not likely to be fixed. While there is no evidence directly pertaining to this matter, casual observation suggests that people can interfere with these immediate responses. In line with Hamburg's (1963) view of the evolution of emotion, it seems reasonable to propose that social learning could be organized to inhibit or replace these responses, but such learning might be a bit harder than experiences which support, amplify or extend these responses.

The same potential for variability exists when it comes to the subsequent coping responses, although here individual and group differences loom larger. We cannot use the example of surprise, since we know of no common coping response subsequent to surprise; it depends upon how the surprising event was evaluated. One might say that fighting, verbally or physically, is a coping response in anger, and flight, physically or through social withdrawal, is a coping pattern in fear. Yet it is only by ignoring enormous variations that one could argue for universality here. How an individual copes with anger depends upon his own past experiences and how he evaluates the particular occasion. Subsequent coping responses are not subject to random variations. There are some commonalities across divergent social groups due to biologically based predispositions and constraints, but clearly social learning, which can be quite variable, plays a major role.

Thus when we begin to specify just what is meant by emotion, what it may be that a facial expression signifies, it is clear that it is neither universal nor totally variable. There are commonalities and variability in different respects and to a different extent depending upon which aspect of emotion is considered.

Another major source of confusion and contradiction about emotional expressions has to do with the issue of whether facial expression is voluntary or involuntary. The accounts of the cultural relativists have suggested or implied that facial expressions are deliberate, feigned, chosen, employed as masks, unreliable indicators of feelings, the product of social conventions about which feelings should be shown in what context. Some of those arguing for the universalist position have implied that facial expressions are involuntary, occur without awareness or choice, are difficult to control, and may reveal information the person is trying to inhibit. Both views are partially right; neither offers a satisfactory account.

Neurological studies of deficits in facial activity associated with different brain lesions have suggested that facial expression has dual control (Myers 1969). While the neural mechanisms which govern facial activity are still far from understood, it seems clear that we cannot consider facial action as the exclusive product of the 'old' or 'new' brain, of hypothalamic or cortical activity. The distinction between voluntary and involuntary has merit, but it is too simple.

One problem with this distinction is that it does not deal with many voluntary actions which become well established habits and automatic in their occurrence. Many of the facial conversational signals that we will describe later are just such instances. Using the eyebrows to mark emphasis during speech can be done voluntarily, but usually it is done with little awareness or seeming choice. A person who customarily uses a particular eyebrow emphasis marker can, if he focuses his attention upon it, interfere with such a habit, but it will reappear when he stops thinking about it. Later when we discuss the differences between emotional and conversational facial signals we will speculate about the neural basis of these two types of signals.

Even when considering just the emotional expressions, the distinction between voluntary and involuntary misses some of the complexities. Consider a few pieces of evidence which come from our studies of the facial actions observed when people attempt to conceal how they feel (Ekman and Friesen 1969a, 1974). Some people are quite capable of inhibiting facial expressions of emotion when they feel disgusted, pained, afraid, or distressed. Many others cannot manage to do so and report a struggle to control facial action. Many people can put on facial expressions which mask how they feel and do this so well that they successfully mislead others. While there are suggestions that these false expressions differ from felt ones, the differences are subtle and typically go unnoticed.

There are not only such individual differences but also systematic group differences in facial expressions of emotion. We (Ekman and Friesen 1969b, 1975) proposed the term 'display rules' to describe social norms which specify who can show what emotion to whom, when. Some of these rules are learned so well that they operate automatically, without choice or even awareness. Others are known but not acquired as habits; they are ideals to be followed, but not well practiced. These display rules cover many signs of emotion, not just the face, although facial expression receives attention as a very visible, easily decipherable cue. We (Ekman 1972, Friesen 1972) found evidence to support our expectation that cultural differences in facial expressions sometimes may be due to different display rules overlying and disguising universals. When alone, Japanese and Americans showed virtually the same facial actions while viewing a stressful film. The very same measurements of facial action revealed marked differences between members of these two cultures when the stressful film was viewed in the presence of an authority figure. The Japanese, more than the Americans, controlled facial expressions of disgust, pain, distress and fear and masked those actions with smiling.

The observations by cultural relativists of variations in facial actions associated with emotion may be the consequence of their observing social occasions where different display rules were operative. The universalists may have focused upon those occasions where display rules to disguise were not operative, or where the same display rule was followed in the cultures compared. The universal facial expression of anger (or any other emotion) will not invariably signify that the person observed is angry. It may just as well mean that he wants to be viewed as angry. And the failure to observe a facial expression of anger does not necessarily mean that the person is not angry. The system is not that simple.

Elsewhere (Ekman 1973, 1977b) we have discussed these and other issues which had led to confusion about universality and cultural differences in facial expression, and we attempted a more explicit description of how cultural and biological influences contribute to facial expression. Now, having indicated some of what we mean by emotion and the constraints on what is meant by saying expressions are in any way universal, let us consider the seven eyebrow movements. We will consider their role in only a few emotions, just those emotions about which there is evidence that the facial actions have some universal association with either an emotion term, an elicitor, or co-occurring responses.

In sadness, either Action Unit 1 or the combination 1+4 occurs, together with the relaxation of the upper eyelid (probably *levator palpebralis superioris*), sometimes a pulling in of the skin around the eye and slight raising of the cheeks (*orbicularis oculi, pars orbitalis* and *zygomatic minor*), a slight depression of the angle of the mouth (*triangularis*), sometimes also a pushing up of the chin (*mentalis*) and lowering of the lower lip (*depressor labii inferioris*). In the distress cry some of the facial actions change. Action Unit 4 is most important in the eyebrows, with less evidence of Action Unit 1. This is joined by the inner and outer portions of *orbicularis oculi*, raising the cheeks, pulling in skin towards the eyes, and tightening the eyelids. Around the mouth the actions described for sadness are joined by horizontal stretching of the lips (*risorius* and/or *platysma*), lowering of the mandible, lowering of the lower lip (*depressor labii inferioris*) and raising of the upper lip (*levator labii superioris*).

In surprise, the combination 1+2 is accompanied by raising the upper eyelid (*levator palpebralis superioris*) and dropping the jaw (relaxation of the *masseter*).

In fear, the combination 1+2+4 is accompanied by raising the upper eyelid and tightening the lower eyelids (*orbicularis oculi, pars palpebralis*), and by horizontal stretching of the lips (*risorius* and/or *platysma*).

In anger, Action Unit 4 without any brow raising is accompanied by the same actions around the eyes as described for fear, with the lips either pressed firmly together (*orbicularis oris* and perhaps *mentalis*), or squared and tightened (some combination of *orbicularis oris*, *levator labii superioris quadratus*, and *depressor labii inferioris*).

For two emotions – disgust and happinesss – no specific eyebrow actions are recruited. (It may appear that the brows are lowered in disgust, but this is due to the involvement of either *orbicularis oculi* or *levator labii superioris alaeque nasi* action recruiting *depressor glabella*.) There may be other facial expressions of emotion, but those we have described – fear, surprise, anger, sadness, disgust and happiness – are the only ones for which there is evidence of some kind of universality.

Table 1 recasts this description of the involvement of eyebrow actions in the emotional expressions, to highlight the role of each Action Unit and combination. We have not found a simple way to describe or explain which actions are involved in emotional expressions and which are not. Some single Action Units signify emotion (when combined with lower face actions), some combinations also do so, but not every possible single action, nor every possible combination. At the end of this paper we will show how consideration of the adaptive consequence of some of these eyebrow actions may account for their involvement in particular emotions; but that line of reasoning does not explain the role of all the eyebrow actions in emotional expression.

Let us consider briefly whether any of the eyebrow actions signify emotion when they stand alone without any other muscular action visible in the face. It is common for some of these eyebrow actions to occur without any other facial movement. There has been very little study of such isolated eyebrow actions, although we have made a few studies within the United States and are just beginning a cross cultural study. We

Table 1. *Role of eyebrow actions in*
emotional expression

Action Unit 1	With eye region and lower face actions
without other brow actions	SADNESS
with Action Unit 4 (1+4)	SADNESS
with Action Unit 2 (1+2)	SURPRISE
with Action Units 2+4 (1+2+4)	FEAR
Action Unit 2	
without other brow actions	
with Action Unit 1 (1+2)	SURPRISE
with Action Unit 4 (2+4)	
with Action Units 1+4 (1+2+4)	FEAR
Action Unit 4	
without other brow actions	ANGER or DISTRESS
with Action Unit 1 (1+4)	SADNESS
with Action Unit 2 (2+4)	
with Action Units 1+2 (1+2+4)	FEAR

expect that when the eyebrow actions are not joined by other facial movements they may still convey information about emotion, but that the information is less precise, that it is about a family of related emotions not specific to a single emotion. And we expect to find much more variability across cultures in precisely what is signified when only the eyebrows are active. What follows are best viewed as hypotheses, supported only in one culture by a limited number of studies.

The combination 1+2 will be associated with positive rather than negative emotions, but could be a surprise or interest signal. It will also be confused with conversational signals which employ this action (questioning, doubting, greeting, emphasizing).

Action Unit 1, and the combinations 1+4 and 1+2+4 will be associated with either fear or sadness but not with anger or disgust, or with positive emotions.

Action Unit 4 will be associated with anger, disgust, perplexity and more generally with difficulty of any kind. It will also be confused with the variety of conversational signals which employ this action.

Two of the seven eyebrow actions appear to play no role in emotional expression: 2 and 2+4. Hjorstjö (1970) said 2+4 was a sign of rage, and Eibl-Eibesfeldt (1972) noted that this action is shown in Japanese theatrical masks depicting anger or rage. We have seen this eyebrow action in Etruscan, early Roman, and Renaissance art as well as in comic strips. Yet we know of no evidence showing that this action is often employed in spontaneous or even posed facial expressions. Action Unit 2 is also rare in emotional expression, and there has been little commentary of any kind on this eyebrow movement.

Conversational signals

Compared to the emotional expressions, relatively little is known about conversational signals. We do not know of any quantitative studies of these actions. There have only been scattered observations, unsubstantiated by careful description, without systematic cross cultural comparisons. We began to observe these actions a few years ago, and started systematic study only in the last year. What we report must be considered preliminary, tentative, and only a suggestion about what may be found. First, we will consider facial actions shown while speaking, then the facial actions shown while listening, and finally actions which may occur when people converse without words. Again our focus will be upon eyebrow actions, which are probably among the most frequent facial actions employed as conversational signals.

Speaker conversational signals

Baton. Efron (1941) proposed this term for hand movements which appear to accent a particular word as it is spoken. We have noted that batons appear to coincide with primary voice stress, or more simply with a word that is spoken more loudly. When we have asked people to place the voice stress on one word and put the baton on another word, most cannot do so. Usually the voice emphasis shifts to the locus of the baton. The neural mechanisms responsible for emphasis apparently send impulses to both voice and skeletal (or facial) muscles simultaneously when both modalities are employed. We expect this relationship between baton and voice emphasis to be maintained across languages and cultures, but have no data as yet.

Birdwhistell (1970) and Eibl-Eibesfeldt (1972) have commented that facial actions can emphasize speech, but neither distinguished between a baton and what we next describe as an underliner. Birdwhistell did not specify any particular facial emphasis action; Eibl-Eibesfeldt mentioned only what we call 1+2. In both systematic and casual observations of Americans we find that 1+2 is the most frequent baton. Next most common is Action Unit 4. Much more rare is the combination 1+4, although some people frequently employ this action as a baton. (The

American actors Woody Allen and Zero Mostel are examples who do so.) Almost any other facial action could be employed as a baton, but few are. The upper eyelid raise is sometimes used, as is nose-wrinkling, although the latter is more typical of females than males.

Most people show both 1+2 and 4 batons, more of the former than the latter, but some of each. We are beginning a study to test our hypothesis that when Action Unit 4 is employed as the baton there is some evidence of uncertainty, perplexity, doubt or difficulty of some kind. This will not always be so, but sufficiently to reject the notion that the occurrence of 4 versus 1+2 is random.

Underliner. We have proposed (Ekman 1977b) this term to describe a movement which also provides emphasis, but in this case the emphasis stretches out over more than a single word. Underliners coincide with one of a variety of speech changes which provide emphasis – sustained loudness, increased pauses between each word spoken, stretching out the words as they are spoken.

Hand movements, postural leans, sustained gaze or facial action may function as underliners. As with the baton, Action Units 1+2 and 4 are the most common, and here too we expect to be able to show that the conversational context in which each is shown differs at least some of the time. As with batons, some people show a preponderance of 1+2 or of 4, and a few people primarily employ 1+4.

There are many occasions when people mark emphasis in their speech without either a baton or an underliner. We are not optimistic about being able to predict when a baton or underliner will be used and when emphasis will be carried just by voice, although perhaps there might be some weak relationship with overall involvement in what is said. There may well be differences between social groups in the frequency of batons or underliners, conceivably also in the type of action employed.

Punctuation. Both 1+2 and 4 appear to be employed as punctuation marks. When a person describes a series of events, either of these actions may sometimes be placed in a pause after each event in the series, much as a comma would be located if the speech was written.

Either 1+2 or 4 may be placed in a juncture pause at the end of a phonemic clause much as if it was a period or exclamation point. Our hunch is that there again is a difference in the semantic context if 1+2 or 4 is so located. With the 1+2 the context seems to be more of an exclamation over something amazing, incredible, etc. If the 4 is placed at a juncture pause, the semantic implication appears to be one of seriousness, importance, doubt, perplexity, or difficulty.

The question mark, another punctuation action, has been subject to more commentary and some preliminary study, so we describe it separately.

Question mark. Birdwhistell (1970), Blurton Jones (1967), Darwin (1872), and Eibl-Eibesfeldt (1972) all commented on the use of brow raises (probably 1+2, not 2) to indicate a question. Linda Camras, a post-doctoral research fellow at our laboratory, has begun to examine eyebrow actions in the course of conversations between mothers and their five year old children. Her preliminary findings suggest that both 1+2 and 4 are used in question statements, although 1+2 is more common than 4. Her findings support our prediction that (just as with batons and underliners) there is a difference in the context in which 1+2 or 4 occur. If the mother is less certain about the answer to her question, more in doubt or perplexed, then 4 is more likely to occur than 1+2. When observers were allowed to listen to and watch the context which immediately preceded the use of either 1+2 or 4 in a question, they were able to do better than chance in guessing which eyebrow action occurred, although often they could not explain their guess.

Camras also has preliminary evidence which may suggest when a brow action is most likely to be recruited to signal a question mark. A 1+2 is more likely to occur in a question when the words do not provide a clue that a question is being asked. For example, if the statement does not begin with a 'what, where, who, when or which', a 1+2 is more likely than in a statement that has such a verbal or syntactic indication of questioning.

Word search. Goffman (chapter 3.2 below) interpreted the speaker's 'ah' or 'uh' as making 'it evident that although he does not have the word or phrase he wants, he is giving his attention to the matter . . . assuring that something worse than a temporary loss of words has not happened, and incidentally holding the speaker's claim to the floor'. We have noted (Ekman 1977b) that hand movements (e.g., finger-snapping or movements which seem to be trying to pluck the word from space) occur in just this conversational location and may also serve to help hold the floor. In a similar way Action Unit 4 may indicate also that word search is occurring, and incidentally hold the speaker's claim on the floor. This action often occurs during one of the 'ah' or 'uh' word search pauses. Another common action during word search is 1+2 with the eyes looking up as if the word was to be found on the ceiling. Apart from the brow action, during word searches it is typical for the gaze to be directed at an immobile spot, reducing visual input. This visual inattention may increase the risk of losing the floor, and the brow actions may serve to signal the listener not to interrupt or take over the speaker turn.

Other speaker conversational signals. We see many other eyebrow actions during speech which we do not yet know how to characterize. There may be actions which are employed as signals for turn-taking. And there may be facial actions which serve syntactic functions.[12] So far these remain elusive, but our search has just begun.

Listener's responses

Dittmann (1972) described how the listener provides head-nods, smiles and 'um-humms' during conversation. He found that these actions occur at specific locations in relation to the structure of the speaker's words. In classroom exercises we have found that students find it hard to withhold listener responses, doing so only as long as they concentrate on this task. When they succeed, the speaker usually inquires whether something is wrong, whether they are listening, etc.

What Dittmann described can be termed *agreement* responses, indicating not only that the listener is attending, but that he understands and does not disagree with what is being said. 1+2 with either a smile, a head-nod, or an agreement word is also an agreement listener response.

Eyebrow actions also function as calls for information. The listener may show Action Unit 4 when he does not understand what the speaker has said. Or the 4 may be more of a metaphorical comment that he finds what the speaker has said to be figuratively, not literally, incomprehensible. Another call for information is the question mark 1+2 shown by the listener much as it is performed by the speaker. As with Action Unit 4, 1+2 may indicate that the listener does not understand, or metaphorically it may signal his incredulity at what the speaker has said. If the latter is the signal, it will be more explicit when joined by other facial actions described below for the disbelief message.

---

[12] Liddell (1975), working in Bellugi's laboratory, used an early version of our facial measurement system to isolate a particular set of facial actions which mark the occurrence of a relative clause when deaf people use American Sign Language.

Some people make movements around the mouth which seem preparatory to speaking. Such movements conceivably might also signal to the speaker when the listener wants his turn to speak. We have not noticed eyebrow actions serving this function.

The listener could use eyebrow movements to emphasize the speaker's words. We have observed this rarely, only between people very intimately involved.

There are probably other eyebrow listener responses but we have not focused as much on these in our research.

Conversational signals without speech (emblems)

So far we have considered only facial actions which occur during spoken conversation. These actions are usually ambiguous outside of the context of talk in which they occur. Their role is known by examining what is being said, intonations, pauses, turns, etc. Now consider facial actions which can occur when there is no talk yet communication is intended. We have used Efron's (1941) term *emblem* to refer to such actions with specific semantic meaning; most of our previous work on emblems has focused on hand movements.

When the burden for communication is totally on other than the verbal, we have not found eyebrow actions to carry the message without the recruitment of other facial actions, head movements, gaze direction, or vocalizations. An isolated facial action could be an emblem (e.g. the wink is such an instance using an eye muscle), but we do not know of such single muscle eyebrow emblems.

All of the signals described below are also shown by speaker and listener during spoken conversation. What distinguishes them, however, is that these actions can be used with little ambiguity when the participants choose not to use any words at all.

Flash. Although Eibl-Eibesfeldt's account of this facial action emphasized a repeated brow raise (1+2), he also mentioned an upwards tilt of the head, a smile, and an upper eyelid raise as part of the greeting signal. Our own observations of the flash in New Guinea suggest the flash typically involves one or another of these actions in addition to 1+2. We disagree with Eibl-Eibesfeldt about the universality of this action as a greeting signal. It is widespread, but our own studies of symbolic gestures and those of our students (see Ekman 1976 for a review) suggest that it is not employed as a greeting in a number of cultures.

(Since discussion of the flash occurred at the conference, let me add some comments to amplify our view of this action. We do not believe that any specific conversational facial signal is innately programmed and therefore none is likely to be universal. We do believe there are reasons (explained later in this paper) why it would be more likely for 1+2 to be chosen as the brow movement for a greeting than 4 or 1+4 *if* a culture did have a brow movement for a greeting. Not believing that this brow action is built into the organism to signal greetings, we do not agree with Eibl-Eibesfeldt's reasoning in discussion that the failure to use it represents an instance of cultural suppression.

Why would our distinguished colleague believe he has seen this brow movement universally as a greeting when we do not? In part this may be because the movement of raising the brow is a frequent action occurring in many different conversational signals – emphasis, yes/no, question marks, exclamation marks, etc. In part it may be because the brow raise can be part of a surprise emotional expression. It would not be uncommon for people to be surprised or to show mock surprise when first seeing another person. Nor would it be uncommon that a person might show a question mark or an exclamation mark upon first seeing another unexpected person arrive. It would be necessary to rule out these uses of the brow raise, in order to be certain that all appearances of the brow raise during initial encounter are truly greetings.)

Disbelief. In Americans (and probably therefore in at least some European countries), when the combination 1+2 is joined by pulling the corners of the lips down (*triangularis*), relaxing the upper eyelid, pushing up the lower lip (*mentalis*), raising the upper lip, and /or rocking the head from side to side, the message is disbelief or incredulousness.

Mock astonishment. The performance for this signal involves the combination of 1+2 accompanied by raised upper eyelid, dropped open jaw, and an exaggerated element to the performance noticeable in an abrupt onset followed by a longer duration than occurs for actual surprise. Often the head will be tilted to the side and the eyes will sharply point away.

Affirmation and negation. Darwin described an affirmation signal among Abyssinians in which the head is thrown back and the eyebrows raised for an instant. Eibl-Eibesfeldt commented also on this signal, particularly among Samoans. He also noted the brow raise as a statement 'no' among Greeks. Our observations in Turkey, where it also signals negation, suggest that in this case it involves an eyelid movement and sharp upward movement of the head and raising of the chin. Darwin also noted that the Dyaks of Borneo show affirmation with brow raise and negation with the lowering and drawing together of the brows (Action Unit 4) 'with a peculiar look from the eyes' (1872: 274).

Sophisticated skepticism. In Hollywood movies circa 1930–40, sophisticated and attractive women would sometimes employ Action Unit 2 on one side of their face (sometimes with 4 on the other side) to signal sophisticated skepticism. In those days teenagers would try to make this movement, admiring those who could do so. We have rarely seen this movement in any natural situation. This action is used also by villains in melodramas.

These are the only well documented instances of eyebrow emblems – actions which, with other actions, provide unambiguous signals if utilized when people choose to converse without words. Certainly there are other emblems, some involving the face, and many which utilize the hands, but no others in which the eyebrows play a central role.

Let us consider why it is that sometimes people totally unfamiliar with an emblem may accurately describe what it signifies upon first seeing it, for such instances have been incorrectly interpreted as evidence of universality. In emblems the relationship between an action and what it signifies is often iconic, so that the form, rhythm, or what the action does, resembles the message it stands for. Such emblems can be interpreted without any previous familiarity. There are also emblems which appear to be arbitrarily coded, with no obvious relationship between the appearance of the movement and what it signifies. These arbitrary emblems may have little meaning to people outside the social group who customarily employ them. Yet even such an arbitrary emblem may be understood by an outsider if it is placed within a social context where the norms about what is transpiring are so explicit as to suggest what any signal in that locus would mean. We have found it possible for Americans totally unfamiliar with the flash to understand that it signals a greeting, if we place the flash within the context of first response upon noting the presence of a familiar person – precisely where we ordinarily would put a hand-wave emblem.

We and our students have used a standardized method for surveying the repertoire of emblems in five cultures. Our findings agree with Efron's prediction that for the most part these actions are not shared among groups who have not had contact. In the final section, when we consider the origin of the facial social signals, we will suggest that, while not universal, the use of the eyebrows in some of these emblematic conversational signals is not arbitrary.

Our descriptions of conversational eyebrow signals reveal that two of the eyebrow actions are used again and again: 1+2 and 4. Let us inquire why these actions, rather than any of the other five eyebrow actions, occur in so many conversational signals. These two actions represent the extremes in how the brows can be moved, from raised high to lowered and drawn together. While the research has not yet been done, we expect studies would show that these two actions are the most visually contrasting for the perceiver, the most easily distinguishable of the seven eyebrow actions. The next most contrasting actions are probably 1+4 versus 2+4 which angle the brows up or down in opposite directions. Action Unit 1 may often be confused with 1+4 or with 1+2; 2 may not be easy to distinguish from either 1+2 or 2+4, and the combination of 1+2+4 is probably often confused with 1+2, 4 or 1+4. If research bears out these predictions, then the observation that 1+2 and 4 are the eyebrow actions most often recruited as conversational signals would fit with the hypotheses that the most contrastive actions are selected to become signals.

These two eyebrow actions also differ from the other five brow actions in being the easiest to perform. While a few people seem unusually gifted in being able to move voluntarily any facial muscle, our efforts to teach people to do so suggests – in agreement with Duchenne (1862) – that some facial actions are easier to perform than others. Gowen Roper (1977) has recently completed a developmental study on this topic, using our methods to define and measure facial actions. He asked children of six, nine and thirteen years to imitate a series of facial Action Units and combinations depicted on motion picture film. His results confirmed our prediction: 1+2 and 4 were successfully performed by the majority regardless of their age, while the other five eyebrow actions were successfully performed by less than one-third of the children even at the oldest age.

It is tempting to suggest that 1+2 and 4 are recruited into conversational signals, in part, because they are the easiest to perform. Of course the data do not prove that. They might be the easiest to perform just because they are prevalent social signals. We believe that differences in ease of performance could be shown to predate the use of these eyebrow actions in conversational signals. But there is no evidence as yet to suggest that we are correct in attributing such differences to the neural basis of facial actions rather than to social learning.

Even if such evidence existed, we would only be able to say that the eyebrow actions which are most often employed as conversational signals are the easiest to do and the most visually contrasting. These factors would not explain why one action rather than the other is deployed in a particular social signal. For example, why is 4 not commonly used in greetings, only 1+2? Similarly, why does there appear to be some negative implication in the conversational context when 4 is used rather than 1+2 as a baton, underliner, or question mark? To address this question we will consider the origin of facial actions; but first let us discuss the rationale for distinguishing conversational from emotional signals.

Distinguishing between emotional and conversational facial signals

It may seem strange or artificial to have divided facial movements into emotional and conversational signals. Both occur in the presence of others, both occur during conversation, and some writers have argued that the facial expressions evolved specifically for their role in communication. Let us now consider some differences between these two classes of facial social signals.

The emotional expressions are coherent, organized and systematic in their occurrence earlier in life than most of the conversational signals. Just how early an organized pattern of facial actions can be considered to be emotional is a subject of some argument. For our purposes here we need not be concerned with whether the emotional expressions appear in the first, fifth, or the twelfth month of life. They occur before language and before the emergence of symbolic processes. While some of the conversational signals appear early, not many do. By definition the speaker conversational signals cannot appear before at least the rudiments of intentional spoken language. (There may be precursors of such facial speaker conversational signals as Trevarthen has suggested (chapter 8.2 below) for hand movements.) The listener responses probably do not occur with much regularity very early in speech acquisition, if we define a listener response as one that reflects an understanding of the meaning and syntactic structure of the speaker's words. Dittmann observed that the agreement listener responses are infrequent at age five. (Of course, the child may show attention to the parent's speech much earlier.) While a few emblematic conversational signals may develop prior to speech, the repertoire is limited. For the most part emotional expressions precede conversational facial signals.

The difference in the age at which these two classes of social signals appear implies something about a difference in the neural mechanisms which direct each set of signals. We hypothesize that diseases and lesions which impair voluntary facial action will also tend to impair the conversational facial signals more than the facial expressions. The social control of the facial expressions through display rules also may show impairment in such cases. And the converse should be so; disorders which impair spontaneous expression but not voluntary facial action will not be accompanied by as many deficits in the conversational facial signals as in the emotional expressions. While this is probably an oversimplification, we are proposing different, if overlapping, neural mechanisms in the direction of these two signal systems.[13]

Such a difference in neural mechanisms would be consistent also with hypothesized differences between emotional and conversational facial signals in the ease with which a person may interfere with each. Some people appear to easily control facial emotional expressions, but most find it a struggle. Some conversational facial signals are so habitual that a person must concentrate to prevent them, yet we think it is easier to interfere with these than the emotional expressions.

Conversational facial signals and emotional expressions differ also in their accessibility to voluntary performance. The conversational facial actions we described are easy to perform; not so with all the emotional expressions. Furthermore, the performance of the conversational or emotional actions has very different consequences. A person can elect to make a conversational facial signal, to utilize even one he has never previously employed. By the performance he succeeds in producing the phenomenon – a greeting has been made, a word or phrase emphasized, a question indicated, etc. Tomkins (1962–3:I) drew attention to how the performance of a facial action or pattern of facial actions does not produce the phenomenon of which it is a part. We cannot so easily generate our own emotional experience. Making an emotional expression if done correctly may fool someone else, but rarely would produce the experience of the emotion.[14]

The referents for the emotional expressions and conversational signals also differ. Earlier we described some of what we mean by emotion, what

[13] Myers agrees with this extrapolation based on his studies, as does Tomkins (personal communication, 1977), who wrote extensively about the complexities of voluntary and involuntary facial expressions.

[14] Because Tomkins emphasized the centrality of the face in his account of emotion, some have misunderstood him on just this point, leading to studies and even therapeutic efforts which have tried to show if you move the muscles you experience the emotion. Tomkins (personal communication, 1977) views this as a fundamental misinterpretation of his theory.

these facial actions signify. It is considerably more complex than what is signified by most conversational facial signals. The emblematic conversational facial signals (those which can be employed when people choose to communicate without words) may refer to simple or complex matters; they are not constrained to just the package of information signified by the emotional expression.

There are a series of differences between emotional and conversational facial signals which have to do with when each is shown. It is rare for conversational signals to occur when a person believes himself unobserved, although they may occur in rehearsals or replays of an encounter. We and other hidden observers have found that emotional expressions occur with regularity when a person thinks he is unobserved. Both types of facial signals occur during conversation, but are related to different aspects of the conversation. Earlier we suggested a number of very specific ways in which the speaker and listener conversational facial signals are related to the words spoken. The emotional expressions during conversation are more related to the affective content of what is said or implied. They also occur in conjunction with the speaker's or listener's feelings about the process of conversing. For example, they may show anger at not finding a word, excitement in speaking fluently, fear of not understanding what is being said, etc. When the emblematic conversational social signals occur in conversation they may repeat, precede or be simultaneous with a spoken word. Sometimes they replace a word, often at the beginning of a conversational turn.

The actual facial behavior may also differ, even when the same Action Units are recruited. For example, when 1+2 occurs as part of an emotional expression, we expect the onset, duration and offset to differ from when it is used as a baton or underliner. Also, if it is an emotional expression it is more likely that it will be accompanied by a specific set of other facial actions, simultaneous or consequent, than if it is a baton or underliner.

The only difference between emotional and conversational facial signals about which there is much evidence is universality. This is, we believe, well established for the emotional expressions – if differences due to display rules and elicitors are taken into account as described above. While the conversational facial signals have been much less studied, what is known suggests they are more widespread than simply an arbitrary use of facial action might suggest, but there are probably no universals.

Admittedly the distinction between emotional and conversational social signals is not always clear cut. We may have misclassified certain conversational signals; for example, research may show that the word search facial signal (Action Unit 4) should be considered an emotional expression of perplexity. While the distinction must be considered as only provisional, we find it useful since it draws attention to a series of differences which can be investigated. Now let us consider a fundamental issue about both the emotional and conversational facial signals – why some actions rather than others are recruited into particular signals.

The origin of facial social signals

We have described consistencies in the particular facial actions employed in particular social signals. In the emotional expressions, five of the seven eyebrow actions play a role in one or another emotion. Here we ask why they have been 'selected' for their particular role, i.e. what is the nature of the selection process? How can we explain why 1+2 is used in surprise rather than 4, why is 1+4 rather than 2+4 employed in sadness? Parallel questions can be asked about the participation of the eyebrow actions in the conversational signals, for here too consistency was noted. Why is 1+2 rather than 4 employed in a greeting, why is there a (hypothesized) negative implication if 4 is the baton or underliner rather than 1+2?

Most of those who have considered this question (Andrew 1963, Darwin 1872, Eibl-Eibesfeldt 1970) focused only on the emotional expressions. According to these investigators the facial actions seen in emotional expressions originally served some purely biological or instrumental function in our progenitors. In addition, these actions conveyed information to others about an individual's possible future behavior, or what might have happened to elicit the action. Because this (at first incidental) communicative value was also adaptive, the facial actions were maintained in the repertoire even if the original function was lost, or the facial actions were modified as a result of natural selection, to enhance their efficacy as signals.

Ethologists use the term *ritualization* to describe the process by which a behavior is modified through genetic evolution to enhance its efficacy as a signal. If we ask why 1+2 rather than 4 is shown as part of the expression of surprise, an evolutionary explanation might go as follows: the 1+2 may have been adaptive for our progenitors in dealing with unexpected events. This action was maintained in the repertoire and modified to become a better signal because the ability to communicate surprise had survival value for both sender and receiver. Note that ritualization does not imply that the 1+2 action is still adaptive (other than in terms of communication), but only that 1+2 may have been selected for this signal rather than another action because 1+2 was adaptive for our progenitors. Those who have employed the concept of ritualization to explain the origin of facial social signals have attempted to buttress their argument by postulating a present adaptive value for these facial actions in *Homo sapiens*.

We will review the various claims that have been made about the adaptive value of different eyebrow actions. While many of the claims that have survived in the literature are not supported by current knowledge, some of these brow actions do seem to serve some biological function apart from communication. This possibility opens the door to an alternative explanation to ritualization, one which emphasizes ontogenetic development rather than genetic evolution.

The adaptive value of 1+2. In discussing this action all commentators have emphasized that it increases visual input. Some have more specifically noted that this movement increases the superior portion of the visual field. Blurton Jones and Konner (1971) found that children show this action in visual search and when looking upwards at an adult, although children show 1+2 on other occasions as well. Peiper (1963) pointed out that when a newborn's head is bent forward strongly, 1+2 is part of a reflexive response, together with eye opening and neck movements.

The 1+2 action does increase the superior visual field, yet this influence of 1+2 is probably not uniform for all members of our species. The benefit of 1+2 would depend upon how deeply set the eyes are in the bony socket, the prominence of the brow ridge, and how well endowed with hair the eyebrows are. Generally, there should be more benefit for males, Caucasians, and adults,[15] although obviously there will be individual differences as well.

A number of other related functions of 1+2 have been described which are not supported by current knowledge of the neuroanatomy of vision.[16] Darwin wrote that 1+2 helps to raise the upper eyelid quickly, and raising the upper eyelid helps to increase vision. There is no reason to believe that speed of upper lid action is enhanced by 1+2 unless the person has enormously drooping eye-cover folds, which hang down so far as to place pressure on the upper eyelid. Furthermore, the upper eyelid rarely comes down so far as to block vision unless the person is nodding off to sleep, or *orbicularis oculi* has been contracted. Darwin noted that when someone

[15] Oster suggests that infants' eyes are not deeply set and brow hair is sparse, so 1+2 should have less benefit.
[16] I am grateful for the help of Ed Engle, University of Kentucky, for his advice on how muscle actions influence vision and for directing me to literature on this topic.

becomes drowsy, he may use 1+2 to counteract the involuntary relaxation of the upper eyelid. This could provide the basis for a learned association between 1+2 and wanting to see. Less plausibly, Darwin suggested (and Andrew repeated) the idea that 1+2 helps to free the eyeball so that it can be moved around more quickly.

The adaptive value of 4. In explaining the origin of 4 in emotional expressions Darwin listed many different functions. Most now seem to be incorrect. The two functions which he correctly described he considered unimportant.

Action Unit 4 can act as a sunshade. It is often shown by people subject to bright glaring light, who don't have sunglasses. 'It seems probable that this shading action would not have become habitual until men had assumed a completely upright position, for monkeys do not frown when exposed to a glaring light' (Darwin 1872: 226). Action Unit 4 decreases the superior visual field, the extent of influence depending on the variables mentioned earlier with respect to the value of 1+2 in increasing the superior visual field. Since mental activity and vision are closely related Darwin thought this use of 4 to decrease light and narrow the field of view explained why we come to use 4 whenever we encounter something difficult. Since Darwin, a number of writers have supported his observation (often without crediting him), finding that 4 occurs during concentration, determination, or when difficulty of some kind is encountered. Oster (1978) reports what seems to be a precursor of 4 in concentration in one to three month old infants gazing at their mothers' faces.

Another explanation, mentioned but considered unimportant by Darwin, was that 4 helps to protect the eyeball from blows. Neither he nor anyone else has made much of this possibility, although it is undoubtedly true, even if 4 may afford little such protection.

Darwin placed greatest emphasis on Bell's (1872) claim that 4 along with *orbicularis oculi* serves to protect the eyeball from becoming engorged with blood during violent expirations in screaming, crying, etc. Lersch (1932) and Peiper (1963) were doubtful of this. This explanation has survived and continues to appear in accounts of the basis of facial expression. Current understanding of the eye suggests that Bell was wrong. It is plausible, but not proven, that *orbicularis oculi* could by mechanical pressure on the eyeball sufficiently increase the pressure of the vitreous fluid to counteract vasodilation. But even if *orbicularis oculi* does serve this protective function, there is no need for 4 to be involved. *Orbicularis oculi* and the muscles involved in 4 can and often do act independently. In fact,

Darwin noted that 4 often precedes *orbicularis oculi* before infants begin to cry. By itself, however, 4 cannot exert any pressure on the eyeball and thus cannot protect the blood vessels in the eyes. In sum, while Darwin was correct in observing that 4 is virtually always present in crying, along with extreme *orbicularis oculi* contraction, his explanation of what function it serves fails.

Darwin mentioned another explanation of the origin of 4 which he attributed to a famous specialist on optics, Dr Donders. The muscles involved in 4, along with the action of *orbicularis oculi*, were said to cause the eyeball to advance 'in accommodation for proximity', converging the optical axes. Darwin did not emphasize Donders' idea in his account of the origin of 4, although Andrew did. Neither 4 nor *orbicularis oculi* can advance the eyeball. In any case, the eyes do not focus by advancing the eyeball but by changing the shape of the lens and cornea. Squinting, caused by a strong action of *orbicularis oculi*, can help to sharpen vision by exerting pressure on the cornea, but again this action need not involve 4, and 4 alone could not have any effect on sharpening vision. A related idea was put forward by van Hooff (1969). The muscles involved in 4 were said to steady the eye in visual fixation. If facial muscles could so steady the eye, it would be *orbicularis oculi*, not 4, that would do so.

The adaptive value of 1 +4. Based on Duchenne's (1862) observation that the muscles involved in 4 are difficult to inhibit, Darwin offered an explanation of the 1+4 in sadness. When we learn to inhibit crying, the only way we can counteract the involuntary involvement of *depressor glabellae* which lowers the inner portion of the brows is by the upwards counterforce of Action Unit 1. However, the *corrugator* muscle which draws the brows together cannot be prevented from acting by Action Unit 1. As a result, we see the combined action of strongly drawn together brows raised at their inner ends – 1+4. This is a clever explanation, and may be true. It builds upon the involvement of 4 in crying, which though not to be doubted, itself is not explained. Moreover, it has not been demonstrated that contraction of Action Unit 1 in expressions of sadness represents a voluntary effort to control crying. No one else has even discussed the origin of 1+4 in sadness.

The adaptive value of 1 +2 +4. No one has speculated about the origin of this facial action in fear, so we will mention two possibilities. Perhaps this eyebrow action should be considered the consequence of merging two actions seen in other primates during threat: 1+2 and 4. Alternatively, if we consider fear as an anticipatory response, it might make sense to explain 1+2+4 as a movement relevant to attention and increased visual input (1+2), occasioned by a novel object, with 4 providing the clue as to what is anticipated, a distress experience. Considering fear as an anticipation of distress is consistent with the thinking of most developmental psychologists who believe infants do not show fear until late in the first year of life when they develop the cognitive abilities necessary to anticipate. The viability of this explanation awaits longitudinal study of the occurrence of 1+2+4 in fear situations.

To *summarize* this review of the adaptive value of the eyebrow actions, 1+2 and 4 have opposite effects on vision. The former increases and the latter decreases the superior visual field. In addition, 1+2 may make the eyeball more vulnerable to blows, cinders, and the like while 4 may afford some protection.

Even though some of the claims for the adaptive value of 1+2 and 4 no longer seem credible, these facial actions do seem to have opposite effects on vision and these effects can be used as the basis for an explanation of their role in emotional expression. Presumably 1+2 is the action involved in a surprise expression rather than 4 because 1+2 increases visual input. Similarly (although less convincingly), 4 is involved in an anger or distress expression because this action protects the eyeball from blows, decreases glare, and decreases visual input.

By this logic the selection of 1+2 and 4 for their respective signals could have been the product of genetic evolution (ritualization) or through a process of learning (what Smith (1977) calls conventionalization). Two problems weaken the ritualization explanation.

1. Ritualization presumes that selection of actions for their role as signals occurred through phylogenetic evolution. The implication is that these signals can be traced to other primates, i.e. they do not exist *de novo* in *Homo sapiens*. One might expect to see 1+2 in contexts of surprise and 4 in anger in other primates. Chevalier-Skolnikoff's (1973) and Redican's (1975) reviews, and study of some of the literature they cite, suggest that the matter is ambiguous. In threat, for example, some primates show both 1+2 and 4. No one, to our knowledge, has yet done the type of analysis which would reveal whether something different is happening within a threat episode when those two actions occur, although Redican suggested that possibility. Furthermore, we are not certain whether the actions of 1+2 and 4 have the same influence on vision in other primates as they do in humans, although non-human primates do have the muscular equipment to raise and lower the eyebrows. The prominence of the

eyebrow ridge may lessen the influence of these actions on vision in some species.

Some might argue that we should not expect to be able to trace the origin of facial actions to other primates, yet wide credence is given to just such an account of the smile by van Hooff (1971). The lack of evidence regarding homologous eyebrow actions in non-human primates does not rule out an evolutionary account of the role of these actions in emotional expression, although the presence of such evidence would be supportive. By raising this issue perhaps we can encourage primatologists to examine these eyebrow actions in more detail, for the evidence might be there.

2. Implicit in the assertion that facial expressions are innate species-specific signals (cf. chapter 1.1 above) is the assumption that they were shaped into specialized communicative signals by the process of natural selection; i.e. that their function as signals is innate and cannot be explained on the basis of some purely biological function in present-day *Homo sapiens*, either in adults or in children. Yet those eyebrow actions for which we can specify an adaptive function (1+2 and 4) continue to serve this function for contemporary man (as noted by Allport 1924, Blurton Jones 1971, Lersch 1932, Peiper 1963). The fact that these actions have current adaptive value allows for the *possibility* that ontogeny may play more of a role than phylogeny in shaping these actions into expressive signals. The genes may transmit only information about how the equipment works (1+2 increases the visual field). The signal value of such an action and its association with emotion (surprise) may depend primarily upon early experience, experience common to all members of the species who have a functioning visual apparatus.

Such reasoning would go as follows:

Infants encounter unexpected events in which they would raise their brow to see what is happening above them. (One could even argue that the unexpected is more likely to be above than below the infant.) Over time, perhaps abetted by the signal value of the movement, brow raising and surprise would become associated. In the strictest version of this explanation, the infant would have to learn, presumably by trial and error, that brow raising increases his visual field. Alternatively, that might be given, and what he learns is to make this movement when trying to see what has unexpectedly happened. To grant even more to biology, the infant could be born equipped to raise his brows when visually scanning unexpected sudden visual events. What he needs to learn is to generalize this response to any unexpected event, regardless of whether it is visual.
(Ekman 1977b)

We do not mean to suggest that this type of species-constant learning *is* the correct explanation, only that it is just as plausible as an explanation based on phylogenetic evolution. There is no clear evidential base for making a choice between conventionalization (species-constant learning) and ritualization (phylogenetic evolution) in explaining the role of eyebrow actions in emotional expression. The origin of 1+2 in surprise could be resolved by developmental data. If blind infants do not show 1+2 to sudden unexpected sounds or touches, then at least we could assume that the brow raise is not wired in for surprise, nor for scanning, if the eyes are not operative. Unfortunately, that data is equivocal (cf. Charlesworth 1970, Eibl-Eibesfeldt 1972, Lersch 1932, Goodenough 1932, Peiper 1963). No one has yet done a detailed descriptive study of the repertoire of facial behavior in the first year of life, for either blind or sighted infants.

The role of Action Unit 4 in both anger and distress is similarly open to multiple interpretations. There is no evidence as yet to rule out the possibility that species-constant learning experiences are decisive, with phylogenetic evolution contributing only the basic biological function (4 narrows the visual field and protects the eyeball). A conventionalization explanation for this action in distress seems less plausible, but the choice between explanations should rest upon data, not just plausibility.

Now let us consider a different type of problem with explaining the origins of facial actions as instances of ritualization. This view stresses the biological adaptive value of these actions for our progenitors. This explanation does not apply to three of the eyebrow actions: 1 and 1+4 in sadness, and 1+2+4 in fear – since it is not possible to show (or at least no one has shown) a biological function for these actions for humans or to imagine one for our progenitors. It might be argued that it is not necessary to find specific adaptive value for each of the eyebrow configurations. Rather, once certain actions became part of the behavioral repertoire via their adaptive value (1+2 and 4), they could have been shaped by evolution into specialized displays. The new communicative function of 1, 1+4 or 1+2+4 need not be linked to any purely biological function. While we would be more satisfied to find some plausible phylogenetic scenario to explain why 1+2+4 occurs in fear and 1+4 in sadness rather than vice versa, this is not necessary, one might argue. Darwin's principle of antithesis might be invoked here, but if it is we should be able to demonstrate how a given action is antithetical to another. Here again, data on these actions in non-human primates, and on their ontogeny in blind and sighted infants, would help to clarify the matter.

We have been discussing the origins of the facial actions in emotional expressions. Now let us consider the origin of the facial conversational signals. For those that involve 1+2 more than 4, and vice versa, it seems most conservative to assume that the selection of one or another action is based upon socio-cultural or ontogenetic processes (conventionalization) rather than on natural selection. If the selection were exclusively or largely the result of phylogenetic evolution, the actions employed in these conversational signals should be more uniform across cultures than we believe the evidence suggests. The socio-cultural or ontogenetic processes might be based either on the role of these actions in emotional expressions, or on the adaptive consequences of these actions for humans.

It could be said that 1+2 as a component of surprise (which entails unexpected, novel, sudden events and likely orientation towards the source), is a more sensible candidate for a greeting than 4, which is seen in anger or distress. Certainly the connotations of 1+2 should be less disruptive of greeting than would be the connotations of 4. With respect to the use of 1+2 or 4 as batons or underliners, such reasoning would suggest that 4, which is employed in a variety of negative emotions (fear, sadness, distress, anger) should carry an implication of something negative, whereas 1+2 would be more likely to suggest surprise or interest. Alternatively, the role played by these two actions in conversational signals may be selected on the basis of their current biological function: 1+2 increasing and 4 decreasing visual input. Their role in conversational signals would thus be viewed as analogues to their biological adaptive value. Either possibility could be true. Careful description of facial actions in longitudinal studies of blind and sighted infants extending through the point in childhood where these actions appear as conversational signals is needed to resolve the issue. Relevant also would be study of the occurrence of conversational as compared to emotional facial signals in individuals suffering from lesions in different brain areas.

We do not mean to deny the likelihood that evolution played a major role in emotional expression. This must be the case for at least some facial actions in some of the facial expressions of emotion. But which ones, and on what basis, is not known. Certain facial actions may have served a crucial adaptive function in our evolutionary precursors or during ontogenetic development. Species-constant learning may be important in explaining some facial expressions, certainly not all. (Smiling is an example of an expression which cannot be explained by species-constant learning.) Again, with few exceptions we do not know which ones. The problem with accepting ritualization as the explanation of the origin of facial social signals at this point in our knowledge is that it forecloses investigation of issues which should be explored, it leads away from rather than toward research which needs to be done. Competing explanations should be considered and ambiguities emphasized to motivate the research which is needed on facial social signals.

Conclusion

By focusing just upon the eyebrows we were able to demonstrate how an anatomically based descriptive system provides a powerful tool for distinguishing among facial movements. Hundreds of visibly different facial actions occur, and thousands are possible. Yet, each can be recognized and described using our *Facial action coding system*.

The questions that we raised about the origin of both emotional and conversational signals involving the eyebrows can and should be raised about other facial actions. We believe such consideration will reveal similar ambiguities, and point to the type of research which is needed. The distinction between emotional and conversational signals applies to the entirety of facial action, not just the brows. While the brows play an important role in conversational signals, we expect that study will show some conversational signals using the eyelids and movements around the mouth.

The student of emotional expression needs to understand the conversational signals as well. These actions occur often and if they are not recognized will confuse the study of emotional expressions. The student of conversation must understand the emotional expressions if he is to disentangle them from actions that are directly guided by conversational processes. Further, the particular facial action employed in a particular conversational signal (e.g. in batons, underliners, question marks, etc.) may be related to the role played by that action in emotional expression. The student of human communication will, of course, want to understand the full complexity of behaviors which provide social signals, including both emotional and conversational facial signals, as well as body movement and speech.

3.2. Response cries[1]

ERVING GOFFMAN

Utterances are not housed in paragraphs but in turns at talk, occasions implying a temporary taking of the floor as well as an alternation of takers. Turns themselves are naturally coupled into two-party inter-changes. Interchanges are linked in runs marked off by some sort of topicality. One or more of these topical runs make up the body of a conversation. This interactionist view assumes that every utterance is either a statement establishing the next speaker's words as a reply, or a reply to what the prior speaker has just established, or a mixture of both. Utterances, then, do not stand by themselves, indeed, often make no sense when so heard, but are constructed and timed to support the close social collaboration of speech turn-taking. In nature, the spoken word is only to be found in verbal interplay, being integrally designed for such collective habitats. This paper considers some roguish utterances that appear to violate this interdependence, entering the stream of behavior at peculiar and unnatural places, producing communicative effects but no dialogue. The paper begins with a special class of spoken sentences and ends with a special class of vocalizations, the first failing to qualify as communication, the second failing not to.

I

To be all alone, to be a *solitary* in the sense of being out of sight and sound

[1] Without specific acknowledgement I have incorporated a very large number of sugges-tions, both general and specific, provided by John Carey, Lee Ann Draud, John Fought, Rochel Gelman, Allen Grimshaw, Gail Jefferson, William Labov, Gillian Sankoff, Joel Sherzer, W. John Smith, and an anonymous reviewer. I am grateful to this community of help; with it I have been able to progress from theft to pillage. Comments on broadcasters' talk are based on a study in progress.

of everyone, is not to be alone in another way, namely, as a *single*, a party of one, a person not in a *with*, a person unaccompanied 'socially' by others in some public undertaking (itself often crowded), such as sidewalk traffic, shopping in stores and restaurant dining.[2]

Allowing the locution 'in our society', and, incidentally, the use of *we* as a means of referring to the individual without specifying gender, it can be said that when we members of society are solitary, or at least assume we are, we can have occasion to make passing comments aloud. We kibitz our own undertakings, rehearse or relive a run-in with someone, speak to ourselves judgmentally about our own doings, offering words of encouragement or blame in an editorial voice that seems to be that of an overseer more than ourselves, and verbally mark junctures in our physical doings. Speaking audibly, we address ourselves, constituting ourselves the sole intended recipient of our own remarks. Or, speaking in our own name, we address a remark to someone who isn't present to receive it. This is self-communication, specifically, *self-talk*. Although a conversation-like exchange of speaker–hearer roles may sometimes occur, this seems unusual. Either we address an absent other or address ourselves in the name of some standard-bearing voice. Self-talk of one type seems rarely replied to by self-talk of the other. I might add that the voice or name in which we address a remark to ourselves can be just what we might properly use in addressing a remark to someone else or what another might properly use in talking to us. It is not the perspective and standards that are peculiar or the words and phrases through which they are realized, but only that there are more roles than persons. To talk to oneself is to generate a full complement of two communication roles – speaker and hearer – without a full complement of role-performers, and which of the two roles – speaker or hearer – is the one without its own real performer is not the first issue.

Self-talk could, of course, be characterized as a form of egocentricity, developmentally appropriate in childhood years and only reappearing later 'in certain men and women of a puerile disposition' (Piaget 1974:40). Common sense, after all, recommends that the purpose of speech is to convey thoughts to others, and a self-talker necessarily conveys them to someone who already knows them. To interrogate, inform, beseech, persuade, threaten, or command oneself is to push against oneself or at

---

[2] This easy contrast conceals some complications. For a *with* – a party of more than one – can be solitary, too, as when a lone couple picnics on a deserted beach. Strictly speaking, then, a *single* is a party of one present among other parties, whereas a solitary individual is a party of one with no other parties present.

best to get to where one already is, in either case with small chance of achieving movement. To say something to someone who isn't there to hear it seems equally footless.

Or worse, self-talk might appear to be a kind of perversion, a form of linguistic self-abuse. Solitary individuals who can be happily immersed in talking to themselves need not in that degree seek out the company of their fellows; they need not go abroad to find conversational company, a convenience that works to the general detriment of social life. Such home consumption in regard to the other kind of intercourse qualifies either as incest or masturbation.

A more serious argument would be that self-talk is merely an out-loud version of reverie, the latter being the original form. Such a view, however, misses the sense in which daydreaming is different from silent, fugue-like, well-reasoned discussion with oneself, let alone the point (on which Piaget (1962:7) and Vygotsky (1962:19–20) seem to agree) that the out-loud version of reverie and of constructive thought may precede the silent versions developmentally. And misses, too, the idea that both the autistic and constructive forms of 'inner speech' are considerably removed from facially animated talk in which the speaker overtly gives the appearance of being actively engrossed in a spirited exchange with invisible others, his eyes and lips alive with the proceedings.

In any case, in our society at least, self-talk is not dignified as constituting an official claim upon its sender-recipient – true, incidentally, also of fantasy, 'wool gathering', and the like. There are no circumstances in which we can say, 'I'm sorry, I can't come right now, I'm busy talking to myself'. And anyway, hearers ordinarily would not *reply* to our self-talk any more than they would to the words spoken by an actor on the stage, although they might otherwise *react* to both. Were a hearer to say, 'What?', that would stand as a rebuke to conduct, not a request for a rerun, much as is the case when a teacher uses that response to squelch chatter occurring at the back of the room; or, with a different intonation, that the self-talk had been misheard as the ordinary kind, a possibility which could induce a reply such as 'Sorry, I was only talking to myself'.

Indeed, in our society a taboo is placed on self-talk. Thus, it is mainly through self-observation and hearsay that one can find out that a considerable amount goes on. And, admittedly, the matter has a Lewis Carroll touch. For the offense seems to be created by the very person who catches the offender out, it being the witnessing of the deed which transforms it into an improper one. (Solitary self-talkers may occasionally find themselves terminating a spate of self-talk with a self-directed reproach, but in doing so would seem to be catching *themselves* out – sometimes employing self-talk to do so.) In point of fact, the misdoing is not so much tied up with doing it in public as *continuing* to do it in public. We are all, it seems, allowed to be caught stopping talking to ourselves on one occasion or another.

It is to be expected that questions of frames and their limits will arise. Strictly speaking, dictating a letter to a machine, rehearsing a play to a mirror, and praying aloud at our bedside are not examples of self-talk, but should others unexpectedly enter the scene of this sort of solitary labor, we might still feel a little uneasy and look for another type of work. Similarly, there are comedy routines in which the butt is made vulnerable by having to sustain a full-blown discussion with someone who is hidden from general view. And there are well-known comic gestures by which someone caught out talking to himself attempts to transform the delict into a yawn or into the just-acceptable vocalizations of whistling, humming, or singing.[3] But behind these risible issues of frame is the serious fact that an adult who fails to attempt to conceal his self-talk, or at least to stop smartly on the appearance of another person, is in trouble. Under the term verbal hallucination we attribute failure in decorum here to 'mental illness'.[4]

Given the solitary's recourse to self-addressed remarks well into adult life, and that such talk is not merely a transitional feature of primary socialization (if, indeed, a natural phase of childhood development), one is encouraged to shift from a developmental to an interactional approach. Self-talk, when performed in its apparently permissible habitat – the self-talker all alone – is by way of being a mimicry of something that has its initial and natural provenance in speech between persons, this in turn implying a social encounter and the arrangement of participants through which encounters are sustained. (Such transplantation, note, is certainly not restricted to deviant activity; for example, a writer does it when he quotes in the body of his own single sentence an entire paragraph from a

---

[3] Nor should the opposite framing issue be neglected. A man talking to himself at a bar may cause the bartender to think him drunk, not peculiar, and if he wants to continue drinking may suffer more hardship from the first imputation than the second. (An instance is reported to me of a barroom self-talker being misframed as always having had too much and temporarily solving this threat to his drinking rights by retreating to the tavern's telephone booth to do his self-talking.)

[4] I mean to leave open the question of whether the individual who engages in verbal hallucination does so in order to create an impression of arcaneness, or for other reasons, and is merely indifferent to the impression of derangement created, or carries on in spite of some concern for the proprieties. And open, too, the question of whether in treating unabashed self-talk as a natural index of alienation, we have (in our society) any good grounds for our induction.

cited text, thereby pseudomorphically depositing in one form something that in nature belongs to another.)

With self-talk, then, one might want to say that a sort of impersonation is occurring, for, after all, we can best compliment or upbraid ourselves in the name of someone other than the self to whom the comments are directed. But what is intended here is not so much the mere citation or recording of what a monitoring voice might say, or what we would say to another if given a chance, but the stage-acting of a version of the delivery, albeit only vaguely a version of its reception. What is set into the text is not merely words, but their animator also – indeed, the whole interactional arrangement in which such words might get spoken. And to this end we briefly split ourselves in two, projecting the character who talks and the character to whom such words could be appropriately directed. Or we summon up the presence of others in order to say something to them. Self-talk, then, involves the lifting of a form of interaction from its natural place and its employment in a special way.

Self-talk described in this way recommends consideration of the soliloquy, long a feature of western drama, although not currently fashionable.[5] An actor comes stage center and harangues himself, sometimes at enormous length, divulging his inner thoughts on a pertinent matter with well-projected audibility. This behavior, of course, is not really an exception to the application of the rule against public self-talk. Your soliloquizer is really talking to self when no one is around; we members of the audience are supernatural, out-of-frame eavesdroppers. Were a character from the dramatized world to approach, our speaker would audibly (to us) self-direct a warning:

But soft, I see that Jeffrey even now doth come. To the appearance of innocent business then.

and would stop soliloquizing. Were he to continue to self-talk, it would be because the script has instructed him to fail to notice the figure all the rest of us have seen approach.

Now, if talking to oneself in private involves a mocking-up of conversation and a recasting of its complementarity, then the production of this recasting on the stage in the bloated format of a soliloquy obviously involves a further insetting, and a transformation of what has already

[5] Never necessary in novels and comics where the author has the right to open up a character's head so the reader can peer into the ideas it contains, and technologically no longer necessary in the competing modes of commercial make-believe – movies and television plays. In these latter a voice-over effect allows us to enter into the inner thoughts of a character who is shown silently musing.

been transformed. The same could be said, incidentally, about a printed advertisement which features realistically posed live models whose sentiments are cast into well-articulated inner speech in broken-line balloons above their heads, providing a text that the other figures in the pictured world can't see but we real people can, to be distinguished from the continuous-line balloon for containing words that one figure openly states to another.

Here, I believe, is a crucial feature of human communication. Behavior and appearance are ritualized – in the ethological sense – through such ethologically defined processes as exaggeration, stereotyping, standardization of intensity, loosening of contextual requirements, and so forth. In the case under question, however, these transformations occur to a form of interaction, a communication arrangement, a standard set of participant alignments. I believe that any analysis of self-talk (or for that matter, any other form of communication) that does not attend to this nonlinguistic sense of embedding and transformation is unlikely to be satisfactory.

II

These parables about self-talk provide entrance to a mundane text. First, definitions: by a *social situation* I will mean any physical area anywhere within which two or more persons find themselves in visual and aural range of one another. The term *gathering* can be used to refer to the bodies that are thus present. No restriction is implied about the relationship of those in the situation: they may all be involved in the same conversational encounter, in the sense of being ratified participants of the same state of talk; some may be in an encounter while others are not, or are, but in a different one; or no talk may be occurring. Some, all, or none of those present may be definable as together in terms of social participation, that is, in a *with*.

Although almost every kind of mayhem can be committed in social situations, one class of breaches bears specifically on social situations as such, that is, on the social organization common to face-to-face gatherings of all kinds. In a word, although many delicts are *situated*, only some are *situational*. As for social situations as such, we owe any one in which we might find ourselves evidence that we are reasonably alive to what is already in it, and furthermore to what might arise, whether on schedule or unexpectedly. Should need for immediate action be required of us, we will be ready; if not mobilized, then able to mobilize. A sort of communication tonus is implied. If addressed by anyone in the situation we should not have far to go to respond, if not to reply. All in all, a certain respect and regard is to be shown to the situation at large. And these demonstrations confirm that we are able and willing to enter into the perspective of the others present, even if by no more than is required to collaborate in the intricacies of talk and pedestrian traffic. In our society, then, it is generally taboo in public to be drunken, to belch or pass wind perceptibly, to daydream or doze, or to be disarrayed with respect to clothing and cosmetics – and all these for the same reason. These acts comprise our conventional repertoire, our prescribed stock of 'symptoms', for demonstrating a lack of respectful alertness in and to the situation, their inhibition our way of 'doing' presence, and thereby self-respect. And the demonstration can be made with sound; audible indicators are involved as well as visual ones.

It is plain, then, that self-talk, in a central sense, is situational in character, not merely situated. Its occurrence strikes directly at our sense of the orientation of the speaker to the situation as a whole. Self-talk is taken to involve the talker in a situationally inappropriate way. Differently put, our self-talk – like other 'mental symptoms' – is a threat to intersubjectivity, warning others that they might be wrong in assuming a jointly maintained base of ready mutual intelligibility among all persons present. Understandably, self-talk is less an offense in private than in public; after all, the sort of self-mobilization and readiness it is taken to disprove is not much required when one is all alone.

This general argument makes sense of a considerable number of minor details: in a waiting room or public means of transportation, where it is evident that little personal attention to pedestrian traffic is required, and therefore less than a usual amount of aliveness to the surround, reading is allowed in our society, along with such self-withdrawal to a printed world as this makes possible. (Observe that reading itself is institutionalized as something that can be set aside in a moment should a reason present itself, something that can be picked up and put down without ceremony, a definition that does not hold for all of our pleasures.) However, chuckling aloud to ourselves in response to what we are reading is suspect, for this can imply that we are too freely immersed in the scene we are reading about to retain dissociated concern for the scene in which our reading occurs. Interestingly, should we mouth the read words to ourselves and in the process make the mouthings audible, we will be taken to be unschooled, not unhinged – unless, of course, our general appearance implies a high educational status and therefore no 'natural' reason for uncontained reading. (This is not to deny that some mumbled reading gives the impression of too much effort invested in the sheer task of reading to allow a seemly reserve for the situation at large.)

When in public, we are allowed to become fairly deeply involved in talk with others we are with, providing this does not lead us to block traffic or intrude on the sound preserve of others; presumably our capacity to share talk with one other implies we are able to share it with those who see us talking. So, too, we can conduct a conversation aloud over an unboothed street phone while either turning our back to the flow of pedestrian traffic or watching it in an abstracted way, without the words being thought improper; for even though our co-participant is not visually present, a natural one can be taken to exist, and an accounting is available as to where, cognitively speaking, we have gone, and, moreover, that this 'where' is a familiar place to which the others could see themselves traveling, and one from which we could be duly recalled should events warrant.[6]

Observe also that we can with some impunity address words in public to a pet, presumably on the grounds that the animal can appreciate the affective element of the talk, if nothing else; in any case, although on these occasions a full-fledged recipient isn't present to reply to our words, it is clear that no imagined person or alien agency has captured our attention. On the other hand, to be seen walking down the street alone while *silently* gesticulating a conversation with an absent other is as much a breach as talking aloud to ourselves – for it is correctly taken as equal evidence of the alienation which the aloud version suggests.

Finally, there are the words we emit (sometimes very loudly) to summon another into talk. Although such a speaking begins by being outside of talk with actual others, its intended recipient is likely quickly to confirm – by ritualized orientation, if not by a verbal reply – the existence of the required environment, doing so before our utterance is completed.[7] A

[6] I once saw an adolescent black girl collapse her male companion in laughter on a busy downtown street by moving away from him to a litter can in which she had spied a plastic toy phone. Holding the phone up to her mouth and ear while letting the cord remain in the can, and then, half-turning as if to view the passing parade in a dissociated manner (as one does when anchored to an open telephone kiosk), she projected a loud and lively conversation into the mouthpiece. Such an act 'puts on' public order in a rather deep way, striking at its accommodative close readings, ones we all ordinarily support without much awareness.

[7] A pet or a small child can be repeatedly summoned with a loud cry when it is not in sight, with some disturbance to persons in range; but a 'mental' condition is not ordinarily imputed. Typically it is understood that the words are merely a signal – a toy whistle

summons that is openly snubbed or apparently undetected, however, can leave us feeling that we have been caught engaging in something like talking to ourselves, and moreover very noticeably.[8]

To say that self-talk is a situational impropriety is not to say that it is a *conversational* delict, no more, that is, than any other sounded breach of decorum, such as an uncovered, audible yawn. Desisting from self-talk is not something we owe our fellow conversationalists as such; that is, it is not owed to them in their capacity as co-participants in a specific encounter and thus to them only. Clearly it is owed to all those in sight and sound of us, precisely as we owe them avoidance of the other kinds of improper soundings. The individual who begins to talk to himself while in a conversational encounter will cause the other participants in the encounter to think him odd; but for the same reason and in the same way those not in the encounter but within range of it will think him odd, too. Clearly, here the conversational circle is not the relevant unit; the social situation is. Like catching a snail outside its shell, words are here caught outside of conversations, outside of ratified states of talk; one is only saved from the linguistic horror of this fact because the words themselves ought not to have been spoken. In fact, here talk is no more conversational than is a belch; it merely lasts longer and reflects adversely on a different part of personality.

So a rule: *No talking to oneself in public.* But, of course, the lay formulation of a rule never gets to the bone, it merely tells us where to start digging. In linguistic phrasing, *No talking to oneself in public* is a prescriptive rule of communication; the descriptive rule – the practice – is likely to be less neat and is certainly to be less ready to hand, allowing, if not encouraging, variously grounded exceptions. The framework of normative understandings that *is* involved is not recorded, or cited, or available in summary form from informants. It must be pieced out by the student, in part by uncovering, collecting, collating, and interpreting all possible exceptions to the stated rule.

---

would do – to come home, or to come into view to receive a message, not to come into protracted conversation from wherever the signal is heard.

[8] Such an occurrence is but one instance of the deplorable class of occasions when we throw ourselves full face into an encounter where none can be developed, as when, for example, we respond to a summons that was meant for someone behind us, or warmly greet a total stranger mistakenly taken to be someone we know well, or (as already mentioned) mistakenly reply to someone's self-talk. The standard statement by which the individual whom we have improperly entangled sets us right, for example, 'Sorry, I'm afraid you've . . .', itself has a very uneasy existence. Such a remark is fully housed within a conversational exchange that was never properly established, and its purpose is to deny a relationship that is itself required for the remark to be made.

III

An unaccompanied man – a single – is walking down the street past others. His general dress and manner have given anyone who views him evidence of his sobriety, innocent intent, suitable aliveness to the situation, and general social competency. His left foot strikes an obtruding piece of pavement and he stumbles. He instantly catches himself, rights himself more or less efficiently, and continues on.

Up to this point his competence at walking had been taken for granted by those who witnessed him, confirming their assessment of him in this connection. His tripping casts these imputations suddenly into doubt. Therefore, before he continues he may well engage in some actions that have nothing to do with the laws of mechanics. The remedial work he performs is likely to be aimed at correcting the threat to his reputation, as well as his posture. He can pause for a moment to examine the walk, as if intellectually concerned (as competent persons with their wits about them would be) to discover what in the world could possibly have caused him to falter, the implication being that anyone else would certainly have stumbled, too. Or he can appear to address a wry little smile to himself to show that he himself takes the whole incident as a joke, something quite uncharacteristic, something that can hardly touch the security he feels in his own manifest competency and therefore warranting no serious account. Or he can 'overplay' his lurch, comically extending the disequilibrium, thereby concealing the actual deviation from normal ambulatory orientation with clowning movements, implying a *persona* obviously not his serious one.

In brief, our subject externalizes a presumed inward state and acts so as to make discernible the special circumstances which presumably produced it. He tells a little story to the situation. He renders himself easy to assess by all those in the gathering, even as he guides what is to be their assessment. He presents an act specialized in a conventional way for providing information – a *display* – a communication in the ethological, not the linguistic, sense. The behavior here is very animal-like, except that what the human animal seems to be responding to is not so much an obvious biological threat as a threat to the reputation it would ordinarily try to maintain in matters of social competence. Nor is it hard to catch the individual in a very standard look – the hasty, surreptitious survey sometimes made right after committing a fleeting discreditable deed, the purpose being to see whether witnessing has occurred and remedial action is therefore necessary, this assessment itself done quickly enough so that a remedy, if necessary, can be provided with the same dispatch as occurs when there is no doubt from the start that it will be necessary.

However, instead of (or as a supplement to) engaging in a choreographed accounting that is visually available, our subject may utter a cry of wonderment, such as *What in the world!* Again he renders readily accessible to witnesses what he chooses to assign to his inward state, along with directing attention to what produced it, but this time the display is largely auditory. Moreover, if nonvocal gestures in conjunction with the visible and audible scene can't conveniently provide the required information, then self-talk will be the indicated alternative. Suddenly stopping in his tracks, the individual need only grimace and clutch at his heart if there is an open manhole at his feet; the same stopping consequent on his remembering that he was supposed to be somewhere else is more likely to be accounted for by words. (Presumably the more obscure the matter, the more extended the self-remarks will have to be and perhaps the less likely is the individual to offer them.)

I am arguing here that what in some sense is part of the subject matter of linguistics can require the examination of our relation to social situations at large, not merely our relation to conversations. For apparently verbalizations quite in the absence of conversations can play much the same role as a choreographed bit of nonvocal behavior. Both together are like other situational acts of propriety and impropriety in that they are accessible to the entire surround and in a sense designed for it. They are like clothing more than like speech. However, unlike clothing or cosmetics, these displays – be they vocal or pantomime – are to be interpreted as bearing on a passing event, an event with a limited course in time. (What we wear can certainly be taken as an indication of our attitude to the social occasion at hand but hardly to specific events occurring during the occasion.) Necessarily, if unanticipated passing events are to be addressed, a marker must be employed that can be introduced just at the moment the event occurs, and withdrawn when concern for the event has been.

IV

It has been argued that there is a prohibition against public self-talk and that breachings of this rule have a display character; but also that there are social situations in which one could expect self-talk. Indeed, I think that the very force which leads us to refrain from self-talk in almost all situations might itself cause us to indulge in self-talk during certain exceptional ones. In this light, consider now in greater detail a few environments in which exposed self-talk is frequently found.

On being 'informed' of the death of a loved one (only by accident are we 'told', this latter verb implying that the news might be conveyed in passing), a brief flooding out into tears would certainly not be amiss in our society. As might be expected, it is just then that public self-talk is also sanctioned. Thus Sudnow (1967:141) describes the giving of bad news in hospitals:

While no sympathy gestures are made, neither does the doctor withdraw from the scene altogether by leaving the room, as, for example, does the telegram delivery boy. The doctor is concerned that the scene be contained and that he have some control over its progress, that it not, for example, follow him out into the hall. In nearly all cases the first genuine interchange of remarks was initiated by the relative. During the period of crying, if there is any, relatives frequently 'talk'. Examples are: 'I can't believe it', 'It's just not fair', 'Goddamn', 'Not John . . . no . . .'. These remarks are not responded to as they are not addressed to anyone. Frequently, they are punctuated by crying. The physician remains silent.

The commonsense explanation here is that such informings strike at our self so violently that self-involvement immediately thereafter is reasonable, an excusable imposition of our own concerns upon everyone else in the gathering. Whatever the case, convention seems to establish a class of 'all-too-human' crises that are to be treated as something anyone not directly involved ought yet to appreciate, giving us victims the passing right to be momentary centers of sympathetic attention and providing a legitimate place for anything we do during the occasion. Indeed, our utter self-containment during such moments might create uneasiness in others concerning our psychological habitat, causing them to wonder how responsive we might be to ordinary situated concerns directly involving them.

Not all environments which favor self-talk are conventionally understood to do so. For example, podium speakers who suddenly find themselves with a page or line missing from their texts or faulty microphones will sometimes elect to switch from talking to the audience to talking to themselves, addressing a full sentence of bewilderment, chagrin, or anger for their own ears and (apparently) their own benefit, albeit half-audibly to the room. Even in broadcast talk, speakers who lose their places, misplace their scripts, or find themselves with incoherent texts or improperly functioning equipment, may radically break frame in this way, apparently suddenly turning their backs on their obligations to sustain the role of speaker-to-an-audience. It is highly unprofessional, of course, to engage in *sotto voce*, self-directed remarks under just those microphonic conditions which ensure their audibility; but broadcasters may be more concerned at this point to show that some part of them is shocked by the hitch and in some way not responsible for it than to maintain broadcasting decorum. Also, being the sole source of meaningful events for their listeners, they may feel that the full text of their subjective response is better than no text at all. Note, there are other social situations which provide a speaker with an audience that is captive and concerned, and which thereby encourage self-talk. Drivers of buses, taxis, and private cars can shout unflattering judgments of other motorists and pedestrians when these have passed out of range, and feel no compunction about talking aloud to themselves in the presence of their passengers. After all, there is a sense in which their contretemps in traffic visibly and identically impinge on everyone in the vehicle simultaneously.[9]

That drivers may actually wait until the apparent target of their remarks cannot hear them points to another location for self-talk, this also suggested by the lay term *muttering*. Frustrated by someone's authority, we can mutter words of complaint under the breath as the target turns away out of apparent conversational earshot. (Here is a structural equivalent of what children do when they stick out their tongues or put their thumbs to their noses just as their admonisher turns away.) For these sub-vocalizations reside in the very interstice between a state of talk and mere copresence, more specifically, in the transition from the first to the second. And here function seems plain. In muttering we convey that although we are now going along with the line established by the speaker (and authority), our spirit has not been won over, and compliance is not to be counted on. The display is aimed either at third parties or at the authority itself, but in such a way that we can deny our intent and the authority can feign not hearing what we have said about him. Again a form of communication that hardly fits the linguistic model of speaker and addressed recipient; for here we provide a reply to the speaker that is displaced from him to third parties or to ourselves. Instead of being the

[9] And, of course, there will be occasions of equivalent license for nonverbal signs, both vocal and gesticulatory. In trying on a shoe we can engage in all manner of grimaces and obscure soundings, for these signs provide running evidence of fit, and such information is the official, chief concern at that moment of all parties to the transaction, including the shoe clerk. Similarly, a sportsman or athlete is free to perform an enormous flailing about when he flubs; among other reasons for this license, he can be sure (if anyone can) that his circumstances are fully attended and appreciated by everyone who is watching the action. After all, such clarity of intent is what sports are all about.

recipient of our reply, the initial speaker becomes merely the object or target of our response. Observe, as with tongue-sticking, muttering is a time-limited communication, entering as a 'last word', a post-terminal dollop to a just-terminated encounter, and thus escapes for incidental reasons the injunction against persisting in public self-talk.

Consideration of self-talk in one kind of interstice recommends consideration of self-talk in others. For example, if we are stopped for a moment's friendly chat just before entering or leaving an establishment or turning down a street, we may provide a one-sentence description of the business we are about to turn to, this account serving as a rationale for our withdrawing and as evidence that there are other calls upon our time. Interestingly enough, this utterance is sometimes postponed until the moment when the encounter has just finished, in which case we may mumble the account half-aloud and somewhat to ourselves. Here again is self-talk that is located transitionally between a state of talk and mere copresence, and again self-communication that is self-terminating, although this time because the communicator, not the hearer, is moving away. Here it is inescapably clear that the self-talker is providing information verbally to others present, merely not using the standard arrangement – a ratified state of talk – for doing so.

Finally, it must be allowed that when circumstances conspire to thrust us into a course of action whose appearance might raise questions about our moral character or self-respect, we often elect to be seen as self-talkers in preference. If we stoop to pick up a coin on a busy street, we might well be inclined to identify its denomination to ourselves aloud, simultaneously expressing surprise, even though we ourselves are no longer in need of the information. For the street is to be framed as a place of passage not – as it might be to a child or a vagrant – a hunting ground for bits of refuse. If what we thought was a coin turns out to be a worthless slug, then we might feel urged to externalize through sound and pantomime that we can laugh at the fools we have made of ourselves.[10] Trying the doorhandle of a car we have mistaken for our own and discovering our mistake, we are careful to blurt out a self-directed remark that prop-

---

[10] Picking money off the street is, of course, a complicated matter. Pennies and even nickels we might well forgo, the doubt cast on our conduct of more concern to us than the money. (We accept the same small sums in change when paying for something in a shop, but there a money transaction is the official business at hand.) Should another in our sight drop such a coin, we might well be inclined to retrieve and return it, for we are allowed a distractive orientation to the ground we walk on so long as this is patently in the interests of others. (If we don't retrieve our own small coins, then we run the risk of others doing so for us and the necessity, therefore, of showing gratitude.) If the sum is large enough to qualify as beyond the rule of finders keepers, we might quickly glance around to see if we

erly frames our act for those who witness it, advertising inadequate attentiveness to deny we are a thief.

With these suggestions of where self-talk is to be found, one can return and take a second look at the conventional argument that children engage in it because they aren't yet socialized into the modesties of self-containment, the proprieties of persondom. Vygotsky, responding to what he took to be Piaget's position, long ago provided a lead:

In order to determine what causes egocentric talk, what circumstances provoke it, we organized the children's activities in much the same way Piaget did, but we added a series of frustrations and difficulties. For instance, when a child was getting ready to draw, he would suddenly find that there was no paper, or no pencil of the color he needed. In other words, by obstructing his free activity we made him face problems.

We found that in these difficult situations the coefficient of egocentric speech almost doubled, in comparison with Piaget's normal figure for the same age and also in comparison with our figure for children not facing these problems. The child would try to grasp and to remedy the situation in talking to himself: 'Where's the pencil? I need a blue pencil. Never mind, I'll draw with the red one and wet it with water; it will become dark and look like blue.'[11]   (1962:16)

The implication is that for children the contingencies are so great in undertaking any task, and the likelihood so strong that they will be entirely discounted as reasonably intentioned persons if they fail (or indeed that they will be seen as just idling or fooling around anyway), that some voicing of what they are about is something they are always prepared to offer. An adult attempting to learn to skate might be equally self-talkative.

Some loose generalizations might be drawn from these descriptions of places for self-talk. First, when we address a remark to ourselves in public, we are likely to be in sudden need of reestablishing ourselves in

have been seen, carefully refraining from saying or gesturing anything else. Covert also may be our act whenever we spy a coin of any denomination to see if any others are not to be found, too.

[11] Recently Jenny Cook-Gumperz and William Corsaro have offered a more compelling account (1976:29): 'We have found that children consistently provide verbal descriptions of their behavior at various points in spontaneous fantasy in that it cues other interactants to what is presently occurring as well as provides possibilities for plugging into and expanding upon the emerging social event.' The authors imply that if a fantasy world is to be built up during *joint* play, then words alone are likely to be the resource that will have to be employed, and an open recourse to self-talk then becomes an effective way to flesh out what is supposed to be unfolding for all the participants in the fantasy.

A purely cognitive interpretation of certain action-oriented, self-directed words ('non-nominal expressions') has also been recently recommended by Alison Gopnik (1977:15–20).

the eyes and ears of witnesses as honest, competent persons not to be trifled with, and an expression of chagrin, wonderment, anger, and so forth would seem to help in this – at least establishing what our expectations for ourselves are, even if in this case they can't be sustained. Second, one could argue that self-talk occurs right at the moment when the predicament of the speaker is evident to the whole gathering in a flash or can be made so, assuring that the utterance will come as an understandable reaction to an understood event; it will come from a mind that has not drifted from the situation, a mind readily tracked. The alien world reflected in hallucinatory talk is therefore specifically avoided, and so, too, therefore, some of the impropriety of talking outside the precincts of a ratified conversation. Nor is 'understandable' here merely a matter of cognition. To appreciate quickly another's circumstances (it seems) is to be able to place ourselves in them empathetically. Correspondingly, the best assurance another can have that we will understand him is to offer himself to us in a version with which we can identify. Instead, then, of thinking of self-talk as something blurted out under pressure, it might better be thought of as a mode of response constantly readied for those circumstances in which it is excusable. Indeed, the time and place when our private reaction is what strangers present *need* to know about is the occasion when self-talk is more than excusable.[12]

V

Earlier it was suggested that when an unaccompanied man stumbles, he may present his case by means of self-talk instead of silent gesture. However, there is another route to the advertisement of self-respect. He can emit one or two words of exclamatory imprecation, such as *hell* or *shit*. Observe, these ejaculatory expressions are nothing like the pointed shout of warning one individual might utter to and for another, nor even like an openly directed broadcast to all-in-hearing, such as a street vendor's cry or a shriek for help. Talk in the ordinary sense is apparently not at issue. In no immediate way do such utterances belong to a conversational encounter, a ritually ratified state of talk embracing ratified participants, nor to a summoning to one. First speaker's utterance does not officially establish a slot which second speaker is under some obligation to fill, for there is no ratified speaker and recipient – not even imaginary ones –

---

[12] Understandably, stage soliloquies occur only when the character's personal feelings about his circumstances are exactly what we members of the audience require to be privy to if we are to be properly positioned in the drama unfolding.

merely actor and witness. To be sure, an interjection is involved, but one that interrupts a course of physical action, not an utterance.

When, unaccompanied, we trip and curse ourselves (or the walk, or the whole wide world), we curse *to* ourselves, we appear to address ourselves. Therefore, a kind of self-remarking seems to be involved. Thus, like the publicly tolerated self-talk already considered, imprecations seem to be styled to be overheard in a gathering. Indeed, the styling is specific in this regard. With no one present in the individual's surround, I believe the expression is quite likely to be omitted. If women and children are present, your male self-communicator is quite likely to censor his cries accordingly – a man who utters *fuck* when he stumbles in a foundry is quite likely to avoid that particular expletive should he trip in a day-nursery. If we can see that persons very close by can see what we have just done (or failed to do) then whispered expletives are possible; if witnesses are far away, then shouted sounds will be required. 'Recipient design' is involved (to use Sacks' term) and so quickly applied as to suggest that continuous monitoring of the situation was being sustained, enabling just this adjustment to take place when the moment requiring it came. Of course, in any case we will have taken the time to encode our vocalization in the conventional lexicon of our language (which is, incidentally, likely to be the local one), a feat that is instantaneously accomplished even sometimes by bilinguals who in addition must generally select their imprecations from the language of their witnesses.[13] (This is not to say that bilinguals won't use a harsh imprecation from one language in place of a less harsh one drawn from the language in use, foreignness apparently serving as a mitigation of strength.) Significantly, here is a form of behavior whose very meaning is that it is something blurted out, something that has escaped control, and so such behavior very often is and has; but this impulsive feature does not mark the limits to which the utterance is socially processed, rather the conventionalized styling to which it is obliged to adhere.

It is plain that singles use imprecations in a variety of circumstances. Racing unsuccessfully to enter a turnstile before it automatically closes or a door before it is locked for the evening may do it; coming up to what has just now become a brick wall, we may exhibit frustration and chagrin, often with a curse. (Others, having formulated a possible reading of the precipitous rush we have made, can find that our imprecations are a way of confirming their interpretation, putting a period to the behavioral

[13] It would be interesting to know whether or not bilingual children who self-talk select the code likely to be employed by others in their presence.

sentence we have played out, bringing the little vignette to a close, and reverting us to someone easily disattendable.) Precariously carrying too many parcels, we may curse at the moment they fall. The horse we have bet on being nosed out at the finish line, we may damn our misfortune while tearing up our tickets; our cause for disappointment, anger, and chagrin being amply evident, or at least easily surmisable, we have license to wail to the world. Walking along a wintry street that carries a record-breaking snow now turned to slush, we are in a position to cry *God* in open private response, but as it happens we do so just at the point of passing another, the cause of our remark and the state of our mind perfectly plain and understandable. It might be added that the particular imprecations I have so far used as illustrations seem in our society to be the special domain of males – females, traditionally at least, employing softer expressions. Nor, as is now well known, is this gender convention impervious to rapid politically inspired change.

Finally, I want to recommend that although imprecations and extended self-remarks can be found in much the same slot, do much the same work, and indeed often appear together, raising the question as to why they should be described separately, judgment should be reserved concerning their equivalence. However, other questions must be considered first.

VI

The functioning of imprecations raises the question of an allied set of acts that can be performed by singles: *response cries*, namely, exclamatory interjections which are not full-fledged words. *Oops!* is an example. These nonlexicalized, discrete interjections, like certain unsegmented, tonal, prosodic features of speech, comport neatly with our doctrine of human nature. We see such 'expression' as a natural overflowing, a flooding up of previously contained feeling, a bursting of normal restraints, a case of being caught off guard. That is what would be learned by asking the man in the street if he uses these forms and, if so, what he means by them.

I am assuming, of course, that this commonsense view of response cries should give way to the co-occurrence analysis that sociolinguists have brought to their problems. But although this naturalistic method is encouraged by sociolinguists, here the subject matter moves one away from their traditional concern. For a response cry doesn't seem to be a statement in the linguistic sense (even a heavily elided one), purportedly doing its work through the concatenated semantic reference of words. A remark is not being addressed to another, not even, it seems, to the self. So, on the face of it at least, even self-communication is not involved, only a simpler sign process whereby emissions from a source inform us about the state of the source – a case of exuded expressions, not intentionally sent messages. One might better refer to a 'vocalizer' or 'sounder' than to a speaker. Which, of course, is not to deny the capacity of a well-formed, conventionally directed sentence to inform us about the state of the protagonist who serves as its subject, nor that the speaker and protagonist can be the 'same' – for indeed through the use of first-person pronouns they routinely are. Only that this latter arrangement brings us information through a message, not an expression, a route fundamentally different from and less direct than the one apparently employed in response cries, even though admittedly such cries routinely come to be employed solely in order to give a desired impression. Witnesses can seize the occasion of certain response cries to shake their heads in sympathy, cluck, and generally feel that the way has been made easy for them to initiate passing remarks attesting to fellow-feeling; but they aren't obliged to do so. A response cry may be uttered in the hope that this half-license it gives to hearers to strike up a conversation will be exercised; but, of course, this stratagem for getting talk going could not work were an innocent reading not the official one. As might be expected, the circumstances which allow us to utter a response cry are often just the ones that mitigate the impropriety of a different tack we could take, that of opening up an encounter by addressing a remark to an unacquainted other; but that fact, too, doesn't relieve one of the necessity to distinguish between this fully social sort of comment and the kind that is apparently not even directed to the self.

A response cry is (if anything is) a ritualized act in the ethological sense of that term. Unable to shape the world the way we want to, we displace our manipulation of it to the verbal channel, displaying evidence of the alignment we take to events, the display taking the condensed, truncated form of a discretely articulated, nonlexicalized expression. Or, suddenly able to manage a tricky, threatening set of circumstances, we deflect into nonlexicalized sound a dramatization of our relief and self-congratulation in the achievement.

VII

Consider now some standard cries.

1. There is the *transition display*. Entering or leaving from what can be

taken as a state of marked natural discomfort – wind, rain, heat, or cold – we seem to have the license (in our society) to externalize an expression of our inner state. *Brr* is a standard term for wind and cold upon leaving such an atmosphere. (Other choices are less easily reproduced in print.) *Ahh* and *phew* are also heard, this time when leaving a hot place for a cool one. Function is not clear. Perhaps the sounding gives us a moment to orient ourselves to the new climatic circumstances and to fall into cadence with the others in the room, these requirements not ordinarily a taxing matter and not ordinarily needful, therefore, of a pause for their accomplishment. Perhaps the concentration, the 'holding ourselves in' sometimes employed in inclement places (as a sort of support for the body), gets released with a flourish on our escaping from such environments. In any case, we can be presumed to be in a state of mind that any and all those already safe might well appreciate – for, after all, weather envelops everyone in the vicinity – and so self-expression concerning our feelings does not take us to a place that is mysterious to our hearers. Incidentally, it appears that, unlike strong imprecations, transition displays in our society are not particularly sex-typed.

2. There is the *spill cry*. This time the central examples, *oops* and *whoops*, are well-formed sounds, although not in every sense words, and again something as much (perhaps even more) the practice of females as males. Spill cries are a sound we emit to follow along with our having for a moment lost guiding control of some feature of the world around us, including ourselves. Thus a woman, rapidly walking to a museum exit, passes the door, catches her mistake, utters *oops*, and backtracks to the right place. A man, dropping a piece of meat through the grill to coals below, utters *oops* and then spears the meat to safety with his grill fork.

On the face of it, the sound advertises our loss of control, raising the question of why we should want to defame ourselves through this publicity. An obvious possibility is that the *oops* defines the event as a mere accident, shows we know it has happened, and hopefully insulates it from the rest of our behavior, recommending that failure of control was not generated by some obscure intent unfamiliar to humanity or some general defect in competence. Behind this possibility is another: that the expression is presumably used for *minor* failings of environmental control, and so in the face of a more serious failure, the *oops* has the effect of downplaying import and hence implication as evidence of our incompetence. (It follows that to show we take a mishap *very* seriously we might feel constrained to omit the cry.) Another reason for – and function of – spill crying is that, a specific vocalization being involved, we necessarily demonstrate that at least our vocal channel is functioning and, behind this, at least some presence of mind. A part of us proves to be organized and standing watch over the part of us that apparently isn't watchful. Finally, and significantly, the sound can provide a warning to others present that a piece of the world has gotten loose and that they might best be advised to take care. Indeed, close observation shows that the *oo* in *oops* may be nicely prolonged to cover the period of time during which that which got out of control is out of control.

Note, when we utter *oops* as we slip on the ice, we can be making a plea to the closest other for a steadying hand and simultaneously warning others as to what they themselves should watch out for, these circumstances surely opening up our surround for vocalizations. When in fact there is no danger to the self, we may respond to *another's* momentary loss of control with an *oops* also, providing him a warning that he is in trouble, a readied framework within which he can define the mishap, and a collectively established cadence for his anticipated response. That some sort of help for others is thus intended seems to be borne out by the fact that apparently men are more likely to *oops* for another when that other is a child or a female, and thus definable as someone for whom responsibility can be taken. Indeed, when a parent plucks up a toddler and rapidly shifts it from one point to another or 'playfully' swings or tosses it in the air, the prime mover may utter an *oopsadaisy*, stretched out to cover the child's period of groundlessness, counteracting its feeling of being out of control, and at the same time instructing the child in the terminology and role of spill cries. In any case, it is apparent that *oopsing* is an adaptive practice with some survival value. And the fact that individuals prove (when the occasion does arise) to have been ready all along to *oops* for themselves or an appropriate other suggests that when nothing eventful is occurring, persons in one another's presence are still nonetheless tracking one another and acting so as to make themselves trackable.

3. There is the *threat startle*, notably *eek* and *yipe*. Perhaps here is a response cry sex-typed (or at least so believed) for feminine use. Surprise and fear are stated – in lay terms, 'expressed' – but surprise and fear that are very much under control, indeed nothing to be really concerned about. A very high open stairwell, or a walk that leads to a precipice, can routinely evoke *yipes* from us as we survey what might have been our doom, but from a position of support we have had ample time to secure. A notion of what a fear response would be is used as a pattern for mimicry. A sort of overplaying occurs that covers any actual concern by extending with obvious unseriousness the expressed form this concern

would take. And we demonstrate that we are alive to the fearsome implications of the event, albeit not overthrown by them, that we have seen the trouble and by implication will assuredly control for it, and are, therefore, in need of no warning, all of this releasing others from closely tracking us. And the moment it takes to say the sound is a moment we can use actually to compose ourselves in the circumstances. In a very subtle way, then, a verbal 'expression' of our state is a means of rising above it – and a release of concern now no longer necessary, coming after the emergency is really over.

Here an argument made earlier about multiple transformations can be taken up. Precipitous drops are the sorts of things that an individual can be very close to without the slightest danger of dropping over or intent to do so. In these circumstances it would seem that imagery of accident would come to the fore or at least be very readily available. It is this easily achieved mental set that the response cry in question would seem to participate in. Thus the uncompelling character of the actual circumstances can be nicely reflected in the light and almost relaxed character of the cry. One has, then, a warning-*like* signal in dangerous-*like* circumstances. And ritualization begins to give way to a copy of itself, a playful version of what is already a formalized version, a display that has been retransformed and reset, a second order ritualization.

4. There are *revulsion sounds*, such as *eeuw*, these heard from a person who has by necessity or inadvertence come in contact with something that is contaminating. Females in our society, being defined as more vulnerable in this way than males, might seem to have a special claim on the expression. Often once we make the sound, we can be excused for a moment while decontamination is attempted. At other times, our voice performs what our physical behavior can't, as when our hands must keep busy cleaning a fish, leaving only the auditory and other unrequired channels to correct the picture – to show that indelicate, dirty work need not define the person who is besmeared by it. Observe, again there is an unserious note, a hint of hyperritualization. For often the contamination that calls forth an *eeuw* is not *really* believed to contaminate. Perhaps only germ contamination retains that literal power in our secular world. So again a protective-like cry is uttered in response to a contaminating-like contact.

VIII

So far response crying has been largely considered as something that could be available to someone who is present to others but not 'with' any of them. If one picks accompanied individuals, not singles, the behavior is still to be found; indeed, response crying is, if anything, encouraged in the circumstances. So, also, response cries are commonly found among persons in an *open state of talk*, persons having the right but not the obligation to address remarks to the other participants, this being a condition that commonly prevails among individuals jointly engaged in a common task (or even similarly engaged in like ones) when this work situates them in immediate reach of one another.

One example is the *strain grunt*: lifting or pushing something heavy, or wielding a sledge hammer with all our might, we emit a grunt at the presumed peak and consummation of our fully extended exertion, the grunt so attesting. The sound seems to serve as a warning that at the moment nothing else can claim our concern, and, sometimes, as a reminder that others should stand clear. No doubt the cry also serves as a means by which joint efforts can be temporally coordinated, as is said to be true of work songs. Observe that these sounds are felt to be entirely unintentional, even though the glottis must be partially closed off to produce them and presumably could be fully opened or closed to avoid doing so. In any case, it could be argued that the expression of ultimate exertion these sounds provide may be essentially overstated. I might add that strain grunts are routinely guyed, employed in what is to be taken as an unserious way, often as a cover for a task that is reckoned as undemanding but may indeed require some exertion, another case of retransformation. Note, too, that strain grunts are also employed during solitary doings that can be construed as involving a peaking of effort. The rise and falling away of effort contoured in sound dramatizes our acts, filling out the setting with their execution. I suppose the common example is the vocal accompaniment we sometimes provide ourselves on the occasion of the passing of a hard stool.

Secondly, there is the *pain cry*, *oww* (or *ouch*).[14] Here the functioning of this exclamation is rather clear. Ensconced in a dentist's chair, we use a pain cry as a warning that the drill has begun to hurt. Or when a finger is firmly held by a nurse, we *ouch* when the needle probing for a sliver goes too deep. Plainly the cry in these cases can serve as a self-regulated

[14] Solitarily experiencing a bout of intense pain, we sometimes follow its course with a half-moaned, half-grunted sound tracing, as though casting the experience in a sort of dialogic form were a way of getting through the moment and maintaining morale. We sometimes also employ such sound tracings when witnesses are perceivedly present, producing in these circumstances a real scene-stopper, implying that our current inner acutely painful state is the business everyone should be hanging on.

indicator of what is happening, providing a reading for the instigator of the pain, who might not otherwise have access to the information needed. The meaning, then, may not be 'I have been hurt', but rather, 'You are just now coming to hurt me'. This meaning, incidentally, may also be true of the response that a dog or cat gives us when we have begun to step accidentally on its tail, although *that* cry often seems to come too late. In any case, these are good examples of how closely a vocalizer can collaborate with another person in the situation.

Consider, too, the *sexual moan*, the sub-vocal tracking of the course of sexually climactic experience, a display available to both sexes, but said to be increasingly fashionable for females – amongst whom, of course, the sound tracing can be strategically employed to delineate an ideal development in the marked absence of anything like the real thing.

Next, there are *floor cues*: a typist in a typing pool makes a mistake on a clean copy and emits an imprecation, this leading to, and apparently designed to lead to, a colleague's query as to what went wrong. A fully communicated statement of disgust and displeasure can then be introduced, but now ostensibly as a reply to a request for information. A husband reading the evening paper suddenly brays out a laugh or a *good God*, thereby causing his wife to orient her listening and even to ease the transition into talk by asking what is it. (A middle-class wife might be less successful in having her floor cues picked up.) Wanting to avoid being thought, for example, self-centered, intrusive, garrulous, or whatever, and in consequence feeling uneasy about making an open request for a hearing in the particular circumstances, we act so as to encourage our putative listeners to make the initial move, inviting us to let them in on what we are experiencing. Interestingly, although in our society married couples may come to breach many of the standard situational proprieties routinely when alone together – this marking the gradual extension of symmetrical ritual license between them – the rule against persisting in public self-talk may be retained, with the incidental consequence that the couple can continue to use response crying as a floor cue.

Finally, there are varieties of audible glee. A lower-middle-class adolescent girl sitting with four friends at a table in a crowded creperie is brought her order, a large crepe covered with ice cream and nuts. As the dish is set before her, she is transfixed for a moment, and wonder and pleasure escape with an *oooooo*. In a casino an elderly woman playing the slots alongside two friends hits a twenty dollar payoff, and above the sound of silver dropping in her tray peeps out a *wheee*. Tarzan, besting a lion, roars out a Hollywood version of the human version of a lay version of a mammalian triumph call.

IX

It is important, I believe, to examine the functioning of response cries when the crier is a ratified participant in talk – being a participant of a conversational social encounter, as opposed to a task-structured one. Walking along saying something to a friend, we can, tripping, unceremoniously interrupt our words to utter *oops*, even as the hand of our friend comes out to support us; and as soon as this little flurry is passed, we revert back to our speaking. All that this reveals, of course, is that when we are present to others as a fellow conversationalist we are also present to them – as well as to all others in the situation – as fellow members of the gathering. The conversational role (short of what the telephone allows) can never be the only accessible one in which we are active.

So response cries can function in work encounters and can obtrude into conversational ones. Now let us move on to a closer issue. If these responses are to be seen as ritualized expressions, and some as standardized vocal comments on circumstances that are not, or no longer, beyond our emotional and physical control, then there is reason to expect that such cries will be used at still further remove, this time in response to a *verbally presented* review of something settled long ago at a place quite removed. A broker tells a client over the phone that his stock has dropped, and the client, well socialized in this sort of thing, says *yipe* or *eek*. (The comedian Jack Benny made a specialty of this response cry.) A plumber tells us what our bill will be and we say *ouch*. Indeed, response cries are often employed thrice removed from the crisis to which they are supposed to be a blurted response: a friend tells us about something startling and costly that happened to him and at the point of disclosure we utter a response cry on his behalf, as it were, out of sympathetic identification and as a sign that we are fully following his exposition. In fact, we may offer a response cry when he recounts something that happened to someone *else*. In these latter cases, we are certainly far removed from the exigent event that is being replayed, and just as far removed from its consequences, including any question of having to take immediate rescuing action. Interestingly, there are some cries which seem to occur more commonly in our response to another's fate (good or bad) as it is recounted to us than they do in our response to our own. *Oh wow* is an example.

And we can play all of these response games because our choice of vocalization allows the recipient, or rather hearer, to treat the sound as something to which a specific spoken reply is not required. To the plumber we are precisely not saying: 'Does the bill have to be that high?' – *that* statement being something that would require a reply, to the possible embarrassment of all.

Having started with response cries in the street, the topic has been moved into the shelter of conversations. But it should not be assumed from this that the behaviors in question – response cries – have somehow been transmuted into full-fledged creatures of discourse. That is not the way they function. These cries are conventionalized utterances which are specialized for an informative role, but in the linguistic and propositional sense they are not statements. Obviously, information is provided when we utter response cries in the presence of others, whether or not we are in a state of talk at the time. That is about the only reason why we utter them in the first place and the reason why they are worth studying. But to understand how these sounds function in social situations, particularly during talk, one must first understand where the prototype of which they are designed to be a recognizable version is seated. What comes to be made of a particular individual's show of 'natural emotional expression' on any occasion is a considerably awesome thing not dependent on the existence anywhere of natural emotional expressions in the first place. But whatever is made of such an act by its maker and its witnesses is different from what is made of openly designed and openly directed communication.

X

At the beginning of this paper it was argued that extended self-talk, if discovered, reflects badly on the talker. Then it was recommended that elements in the situation can considerably mitigate the impropriety of talking to ourselves publicly, and that in any case we are prepared to breach the injunction against public self-talk when, in effect, to sustain this particular propriety would go even harder on our reputation. Much the same position could be taken with respect to interjected imprecations. In both cases, one can point to some hitch in the well-managed flow of controlled events and the quick application of an ostensibly self-directed pronouncement to establish evidence – a veneer – of control, poise, and competency. And although response cries do not on the surface involve words uttered even to oneself, being *in prototype* merely a matter of nonsymbolic emotional expression, they apparently come to function as a means of striking a self-defensible posture in the face of extraordinary events – much as does exposed self-talk.

However, there is one source of trouble in the management of the world which is routine, and that, interestingly enough, is in the management of talk itself. So again response cries occur, but this time ones that are constantly uttered. First, there is the well-known filled pause (usually written *ah* or *uh* or *um*) employed by speakers when they have lost their places, can't find a word, are momentarily distracted, or otherwise find they are departing from fluently sustained speech. Response *cries* seems an awkward term for such unblurted sub-vocalizations, but nonetheless they do, I think, function like response cries, if only in that they facilitate tracking. In effect, speakers make it evident that although they do not now have the word or phrase they want, they are giving their attention to the matter and have not cut themselves adrift from the effort at hand. A word search, invisible and inaudible in itself, is thus voluntarily accompanied by a sound shadow – a sound, incidentally, that could easily be withheld merely by otherwise managing the larynx – all to the end of assuring that something worse than a temporary loss of words has not happened, and incidentally holding the speaker's claim on the floor.[15] (Interestingly, in radio broadcasting, where visual facial signs of a word search can't be effective, the filling of pauses by a search sound or a prolongation of a vowel has much to recommend it, for speakers are under obligation to confirm that nothing has gone wrong with the studio's equipment, as well as their own, the floor in this case being a station. And if only inexperienced broadcasters employ filled pauses frequently, it is because professionals can manage speech flow, especially aloud reading, without the hitches in encoding which, were they to occur, would equally give professionals reasons to ritualize evidence of what was occurring.)

In addition to the filled pause phenomenon, consider the very standard form of self-correction which involves the breaking off of a word or phrase that is apparently not the one we wanted, and our hammering home of a corrected version with increased loudness and tempo, as if to

---

[15] A case can be made that in some English-speaking circles the familiar hesitation markers are systematically employed in slightly different ways, so that, for example, *uh* might be heard when the speaker had forgotten a proper name, *oh* when he knew a series of facts but was trying to decide which of them could be appropriately cited or best described for the hearers. The unfilled or silent pause participates in this specialization, giving one reason, alas, to think of it as a response cry, too. Here see the useful paper by Deborah James, 'Some aspects of the syntax and semantics of interjections' (1972).

catch the error before it hit the ground and shattered the desired meaning. Here the effect is to show that we are very much alive to the way our words should have come out and are somewhat shocked and surprised at our failure to encode properly an appropriate formulation the first time round, the rapidity and force of the correct version presumably suggesting how much on our toes we really are. We display our concern and the mobilization of our effort at the expense of smooth speech production, electing to save a little of our reputation for presence of mind over and against that for fluency. Again, as with filled pauses, one has what is ostensibly a bit of pure expression, that is, a transmission providing direct evidence (not relayed through semantic reference) of the state of the transmitter, but now an expression that has been cut and polished into a standard shape to serve the reputational contingencies of its emitter.

XI

Earlier it was suggested that imprecations were somewhat like truncated, self-addressed statements but not wholly so. Later these lexicalized exclamations were shown to function not unlike response cries. Now it is time to try to settle on where they belong.

Say, for example, someone brings you the news that they have failed in a task you have seriously set them. Your response to the news can be: 'I knew it! Did you have to?' In the styling I have in mind, this turn at talk contains two moves and a change of 'footing': the first move (uttered half under the breath with the eyes turned upward) is a bit of self-talk, or something presented in that guise – the sort of open aside which adults are especially prone to employ in exasperated response to children, servants, foreigners, and other grades who easily qualify for moments of nonperson treatment. The second move (*Did you have to?*) is conventionally directed communication. Observe that such a turn at talk will oblige its recipient to offer an apology or a counter-account, locking the participants into an interchange. But although the recipient of the initial two-move turn will be understood to have overheard the self-addressed segment, he will have neither the right nor the obligation to reply to it specifically, at least in the sense that he does in regard to the conventionally communicated second portion.

Now shift from extended self-talk to the truncated form: imprecation. 'Shit! Did you have to?' Given the same histrionics, one again has a two-move turn with a first move that must be oriented to as something that can't be answered in a conventional way. If the recipient does address a remark to this blurted-out portion, it will be to the psychic state presumably indexed by it – much as when we comfort someone who has burst into tears or when we upbraid them for loss of self-control. Or the respondent may have to venture a frame ploy, attempting to counter a move by forcing its maker to change the interpretative conventions that apply to it – as in the snappy comeback, *not here*, injected immediately after the expletive. In all of this, and in the fact that standard lexicalizations are employed, *I knew it* and *shit* are similar. However, although *I knew it* follows grammatical constraints for well-formed sentences, *shit* need not, even if one appeals to the context in order to see how it might be expanded into a statement. *Shit* need no more elide a sentence than need a laugh, groan, sob, snicker, or giggle – all vocalizations that frequently occur except in the utterances ordinarily presented for analysis by linguists. Nor, I think, does it help understanding very much to define *shit* as a well-formed sentence with NP! as its structure. Here, of course, imprecations are exactly like response cries. For it is the essence of response cries that they be presented as if mere expression, and not recipient-directed, propositional-like statements, were involved, at least on the face of it.

Imprecations, then, might best be considered not as a form of self-talk at all, but rather as a type of response cry. Whereas unlexicalized cries have come to be somewhat conventionalized, imprecations have merely extended the tendency, further ritualizing ritualizations. Religious life already setting aside a class of words to be treated with reserve and ranked with respect to severity, response crying has borrowed them. Or so it would seem.

May I add that insofar as self-talk is structurally different from the normal kind, imprecatory utterances (like other response cries) are too, only more so. And because of this sharp underlying difference between conventionally directed statements and imprecatory interjections, the two can be given radically different roles in the functioning of particular interaction systems, serving close together in complementary distribution without confusion.

Take, for example, tennis. During the open state of talk sustained in such a game, a player who misses an 'easy' shot can response cry an imprecation loudly enough for opponents and partner to hear. On the other hand, a player making a 'good' shot is not likely to be surprised if an opponent offers a complimentary statement about him to him. (And as these two forms of social control help frame his own play, so he will participate in the two forms that frame his opponents'.) But, of course, good taste forbids a player addressing opponents in praise of his own efforts, just as they must allow him elbow room and not reply directly to his cries of self-disgust. A player may, however, use directed, full-fledged statements to convey self-castigation and (when directed to his partner) apology. Response cries and directed statements here comprise a closely working pair of practices, part of the ritual resources of a single interaction system. And their workings can be intermingled because of their structural difference, not in spite of it. Given this arrangement, it is understandable that a player will feel rather free to make a pass at ironically praising himself in statements made to opponents or partner, correctly sensing that his words could hardly be misframed as literal ones. (That he might employ this device just to induce others to communicate a mitigated view of his failure merely attests again to the various conveniences that can be made of forms of interaction.)

And just as response cries can form a complementary resource with conventionally directed statements, so they can with self-directed ones. For example, in casino craps, a shooter has a right to preface a roll, especially a 'come out', with self-encouraging statements of a traditional kind directed to the fates, the dice, or some other ethereal recipient, this grandstanding (as dignified gamblers call this self-talk) sometimes serving to bring the other players into a cadence and peaking of attention. When, shortly, the shooter 'craps out', he is allowed a well-fleshed imprecation coincidental with the dissolution of the table's coordinated involvement. So again there is complementarity and a division of labor, with self-talk located where collective hope is to be built up, and imprecatory response cry where it is to be abandoned.

Discussion

1. Written versions of response cries seem to have a speech-contaminating effect, consolidating and codifying actual response cries, so that, in many cases, reality begins to mimic artifice, as in 'ugh', 'pant pant', 'gulp', 'tsk tsk', this being a route to ritualization presumably unavailable to animal animals.[16] This easy change is only to be expected. For response cries themselves are by way of being second

---

[16] The carryback from the written to the spoken form is especially marked in the matter of punctuation marks, for here writing has something that speaking hasn't. Commonly used lexicalizations are: 'underline', 'footnote', 'period', 'question mark', 'quotes', 'parenthetically'. Written abbreviations (such as British *p* for *pence*) also enter the spoken domain. Moreover, there is a carryback to the spoken form of the pictorial-orthographic form of the presumed approximated sound effects of an action: *pow, bam* are examples.

order ritualizations, already part of an unserious, or less than serious, domain.

Here cartoons and comics are to be taken seriously. These printed pictures must present entire scenarios through a small number of 'panels' or frozen moments, sometimes only one. The cartoonist has great need, then, for expressions that will clearly document the presumed inner state of his figures and clearly display the point of the action. Thus, if individuals in real life need response cries to clarify the drama of their circumstances, cartoon figures need them even more. And so we obtain written versions of something that could be thought originally to have no set written form. Moreover, cartoon figures portrayed as all alone must be portrayed acting in such a way as to make their circumstances and inner states available to the viewer (much as real persons do when in the presence of others), and included in this situational-like behavior are found response cries. (So also in the case of movies showing persons ostensibly all alone.) In consequence, the practice of emitting response cries when all alone is tacitly assumed to be normal, presumably with at least some contaminating effect upon actual behavior when alone.

2. A point might be made about the utterances used in response cries. As suggested, they seem to be drawn from two sources: taboo but full-fledged words (involving blasphemy and – in English – Anglo-Saxon terms for bodily functions) and from the broad class of nonword vocalizations, 'vocal segregates', to employ Trager's term (1958:1–12), of which response cries are one, but only one, variety.

There is a nice division of linguistic labor here. Full-fledged words that are well formed *and* socially acceptable are allocated to communication in the openly directed sense, while taboo words and nonwords are specialized for the more ritualized kind of communication. In brief, the character of the word bears the mark of the use that is destined for it. And one has a case of complementary distribution on a grand scale.

I might add that nonwords as a class are not productive in the linguistic sense, their role as interjections being one of the few that has evolved for them. (Which is not to say that a particular vocal segregate can't have a very lively career, quickly spreading from one segment of a language community to others, the response cry *wow* providing a recent example.) Many taboo words, however, are considerably productive, especially in the tradition maintained in certain sub-cultures, some of these words occurring (if not functioning) in almost every syntactical position.[17]

[17] Admittedly, even in these productive cases, taboo words are not entirely vulnerable to syntactical analysis. Saying that *the fuck* in a sentence like *What the fuck are you doing?* is

Further, curse words are drawn from familiar scales of such words, and choice will sharply reflect (in the sense of display, negotiate, etc.) the terms of the relationship between speaker and hearer; nonwords don't function very effectively in this way.

Nonwords, note, can't quite be called part of a language. For example, there tends to be no canonical 'correct' spelling. When and where convention clearly does begin to establish a particular form and spelling, the term can continue to be thought of as not a word by its users, as if any written version simply conveys a rough and ready attempt at transcription. (I take it here that in our society a feature of what we think of as regular words is that we feel the written form is as 'real' a version as the spoken.) Further, although we have efficient means of reporting another's use of an expletive (either literally or by established paraphrastic form), this is not the case with nonwords. Yet the sound that covers any particular nonword can stand by itself, is standardized within a given language community, and varies from one language community to another, in each case as do full-fledged words.[18] And the nonwords of a particular language comply with and introduce certain of the same phonotactic constraints as do its regular words (Jefferson 1974:183–6). Yet admittedly, the voiced and orthographic realizations of some of these constructions do involve consonant clusters that are phonotactically irregular, and furthermore, their utterance can allow the speaker to chase after the course of an action analogically with stretches, glides, turns, and heights of pitch foreign to his ordinary speech. Interestingly, there is some evidence that what one language community handles with a nonword, other language communities do, too.

On the whole, then, nonword vocalizations might best be thought of as semi-words. Observe that the characterization provided here (and by linguists) of these half-caste expressions takes no note that some (such as *Uh?* and *Shh!*) are clearly part of directed speech, and often interchangeable with a well-formed word (here *What?* and *Hush!*), but others (such as the *uh* as filled pause) belong to a radically different species of action, namely, putatively pure expression, response crying. (Imprecations and some other well-formed interjections provide an even more extreme case, for exactly the same such word may sometimes serve as an ostensibly

adjectival in function, or that *bloody* in *What are you bloody well doing?* is an adverb, misses something of the point. Here specific syntactic location seems to be made a convenience of, for somehow the intensifying word is meant to color uniformly the whole of the utterance some place or other in which it occurs. Here see Quang Phuc Dong (1971).

[18] Quine (1959:6) has an example: ' "Ouch" is not independent of social training. One need only to prick a foreigner to appreciate that it is an English word.'

undirected cry and at other times be integrated directly into a recipient-directed sentence under a single intonation contour.) Here, again, one can see a surface similarity covering a deep underlying difference, but not the kind ordinarily addressed by transformationalists.

Apart from qualifying as semi-words, response cries can be identified in another way, namely, as articulated free-standing examples of the large class of presumed 'natural expressions', signs which are meant to be taken to index directly the state of the transmitter, some of which signs, like voice qualifiers, can paralinguistically ride roughshod across natural syntactical units of speech. I might add that although gender differences in the basic semantic features of speech do not seem very marked in our society, response cries and other paralinguistic features of communication are. Indeed, speech *as a whole* might not be a useful base to employ in considering gender differences, cancelling out sharp contrasts revealable in special components of discourse.

3. Earlier it was suggested that a response cry can draw on the cooperation of listeners, requiring that they hear and understand the cry but act as though it had not been uttered in their hearing. It is in this way that a form of behavior ostensibly not designed for directed linguistic communication at all can be injected into public life, in certain cases even into conversations and broadcasts. In brief, a form of response perceived as native to one set of circumstances is set into another. In the case of blasphemous cries, what is inserted is already something that has been borrowed from another realm, semantic communication, so the behavior can be said to have been returned to its natural place, but now so much transformed as to be little like a native.

This structural reflexivity is, I believe, a fundamental fact of our communicative life. What is ritualized here, in the last analysis, is not an expression but a self–other alignment – an interactional arrangement. Nor, as earlier suggested, is that the bottom of embedding. For example, when a speaker finds he has skated rather close to the edge of discretion or tact, he may give belated recognition to where his words have gone, marking a halt by uttering a plaintive *oops* that is meant to evoke the image of someone who has need of this particular response cry, the whole enactment having an unserious, openly theatrical character. Similarly, in the face of another's reminder that we have failed in fulfilling some obligation, we can utter *darn it* in an openly mock manner as a taunting, even insolent, denial of the imprecation we might normally be thought to employ in the circumstances. In brief, what is placed into the directed discourse in such cases is not a response cry but a mocked-up individual uttering a mocked-up response cry. (All of this is especially evident when the cry itself is a spoken version of the written version of the cry, as when a listener responds to the telling of another's near disaster by ungulpingly uttering the word *gulp*.) So, too, the filled pause *uh*, presumably a self-expression designed to allow hearers to track speaker's engagement in relevant (albeit silent) production work, can apparently be employed with malice aforethought to show that the word that does follow, and is ostensibly the one that was all along wanted, is to be heard as one about which the speaker wants it known that he himself might not be naturally inclined to employ it (Jefferson 1974:192–4). In this case a 'correction format' has been made a convenience of, its work set into an environment for which it was not originally designed. Similarly, on discovering that he has said *April the 21st* instead of *May the 21st*, an announcer may as one type of remedial work repeat the error immediately, this time with a quizzical, speaking-to-oneself tone of voice, as though this sort of error were enough of a rarity to cause him to break frame, but this response itself he may try to guy, satirizing self-talk (and self-talkers) even as he engages in it, the retransformation confirmed by the little laugh he gives thereafter to mark the end to error-making *and* playful correction.

The moral of the story is that what is sometimes put into a sentence may first have to be analyzed as something that could not occur naturally in such a setting, just as a solitary's self-comments may first have to be analyzed as something exclusively found in social intercourse. And the transformations these alien bits of saying undergo when set into their new milieu speak as much to the competence of ethologists as of grammarians.

A turn at talk that contains a directed statement *and* a segment of self-talk (or an imprecation or a nonlexicalized response cry) does not merely involve two different moves, but *moves of two different orders*. This is very clear, for example, when someone in or out of a conversation finds cause to blurt out *shit* and then, in apparent embarrassment, quickly adds *excuse me*, sometimes specifically directing the apology to the person most likely to have been offended. Here, patently, the first move is an exposed response cry, the second, a directed message whose implied referent happens to be the first. The two moves nicely fit together – indeed, some speakers essay an imprecation knowing that they will have a directed apology to compensate for it – but this fit pertains to how the two moves function as an action–response pair, self-contained within a single turn at talk, and not to any ultimate commonality of form. So, too, when an announcer coughs rather loudly, says *excuse me* with greater urgency of tone than he likes, and then follows with a well-designed giggle, he is giving us a three-move sequence of sounded interference, directed statement, and response cry, the second move a comment on the first, the third move a comment on the second move's comment. Any effort to analyze such strips of talk linguistically by trying to uncover a single deep structure that accounts for the surface sequence of words is destined to obscure the very archaeological issues which the generative approach was designed to develop. A blender makes a mush of apples and oranges; a student shouldn't.

And a student shouldn't even when there is no obvious segmentation to help with the sorting. For now it is to be admitted that through the *way* we say something that is part of our avowedly directed discourse, we can speak – ostensibly at least – for our own benefit at the same time, displaying our self-directed (and/or non-directed) response to what is occurring. And thereby we simultaneously cast an officially intended recipient of our propositional-like avowals into an overhearer of our self-talk. The issue is not merely that of the difference between what is said and what is meant, the issue, that is, of implicature; the issue is that one stream of information is conveyed as avowedly intended verbal communication, whilst simultaneously the other is conveyed through a structural ruse – our allowing witnesses a glimpse into the dealings we are having with ourselves. It is in this way that one can account for the apparently anomalous character of imprecations of the *fuck you* form. It might appear as if one person were making a directed verbal avowal to another by means of an imperative statement with deleted subject, but in fact the format is restricted to a relatively small list of expletives, such as *screw*, and none qualify as ordinary verbs, being constrained in regard to embedded and conjoined forms in ways in which standard verbs in the elided imperative form are not (Quang Phuc Dong 1971).

Nor is this analysis of the unconversational aspects of certain conversational utterances meant to deny the traditional conception of transformation and embedding; rather the power of the latter is displayed. Waiting with her husband and a friend for the casino cashier to count down her bucket of silver, a happy player says, 'And when I saw the third seven come up and stop, I just let out "Eeeee".' Here, through direct quotation, the speaker brings to a well-circumscribed, three-person talk what was, a few minutes ago, the broadly accessible eruption of a single. This shows clearly that what starts out as a response cry (or starts out, for that matter, as any sounded occurrence, human, animal, or inanimate) can be conversationally replayed – can be reset into ordinary directed discourse – through the infinite coverage of sound mimicry.

Conclusion

The public utterance of self-talk, imprecations, and response cries constitutes a special variety of impulsive, blurted actions, namely, vocalized ones. Our tacit theory of human nature recommends that these actions are 'purely expressive', 'primitive', 'unsocialized', violating in some way or other the self-control and self-possession we are expected to maintain in the presence of others, providing witnesses with a momentary glimpse behind our mask.

However, the point about these blurtings is not that they are particularly 'expressive'. Obviously, in this sense of that word, ordinary talk is necessarily expressive, too. Naked feelings can agitate a paragraph of discourse almost as well as they can a solitary imprecation. Indeed, it is impossible to utter a sentence without coloring the utterance with some kind of perceivable affect, even (in special cases) if only with the emotionally distinctive aura of affectlessness. Nor is the point about segmented blurtings that they are particularly unsocialized, for obviously they come to us as our language does and not from our own invention. Their point lies elsewhere. One must look to the light these ventings provide, not to the heat they dispel.

In every society one can contrast occasions and moments for silence and occasions and moments for talk. In our own, one can go on to say that by and large (and especially among the unacquainted) silence is the norm and talk something for which warrant must be present. Silence, after all, is very often the deference we will owe in a social situation to any and all others present. In holding our tongue, we give evidence that such thought as we are giving to our own concerns is not presumed by us to be of any moment to the others present, and that the feelings these concerns invoke in ourselves are owed no sympathy. Without such enjoined modesty, there could be no public life, only a babble of childish adults pulling at one another's sleeves for attention. The mother to whom we would be saying, 'Look, no hands', could not look or reply for she would be saying, 'Look, no hands', to someone else.

Talk, on the other hand, presumes that our thoughts and concerns will have some relevance or interest or weight for others, and in this can hardly but presume a little. Talk, of course, in binding others to us, can also do so for protracted periods of time. The compensation is that we can sharply restrict this demand to a small portion of those who are present, indeed, often to only one.

The fugitive communications I have been considering constitute a third possibility, minor no doubt, but of some significance if only because of what they tell us about silence and talk. Our blurtings make a claim of sorts upon the attention of everyone in the social situation, a claim that our inner concerns should be theirs, too, but unlike the claim made by talk, ours here is only for a limited period of attention. And, simply put, this invitation into our interiors tends to be made only when it will be easy for other persons present to see where the voyage takes them. What is precipitous about these expressions, then, is not the way they are emitted but rather the circumstances which render their occurrence acceptable. The invitation we are free to extend in these situations we would be insane to extend in others.

Just as most public arrangements oblige and induce us to be silent, and many other arrangements to talk, so a third set allows and obliges us momentarily to open up our thoughts and feelings and ourselves through sound to whomsoever is present. Response cries, then, do not mark a flooding of emotion outward, but a flooding of relevance in.

There is linguistic point to the consideration of this genre of behavior. Response cries such as *eek* might be seen as peripheral to the linguist's domain, but imprecations and self-talk are more germane, passing beyond semi-word vocal segregates to the traditional materials of linguistic analysis. And the point is that all three forms of this blurted vocalization – semi-word response cries, imprecations, and self-talk – are creatures of social situations, not states of talk. A closed circle of ratified participants oriented to engaging exclusively with one another in avowedly directed communications is not the base; a gathering, with its variously oriented, often silent and unacquainted members, is. Further, all three varieties of this ejaculatory expression are conventionalized as to form, occasion of occurrence, and social function. Finally, these utterances are too commonly met with in daily life, surely, to justify scholarly neglect.

Once it is recognized that there is a set of conventionalized expressions that must be referred to social situations, not conversations, once, that is, it is appreciated that there are communications specifically designed for use outside states of talk, it is but a step to seeing that ritualized versions of these expressions may themselves be embedded in the conventionally directed talk to be found in standard conversational encounters. And appreciating this, then to go on to see that even though these interjections come to be employed in conversational environments, they cannot there be adequately analyzed without reference to their original functioning outside of states of talk.

It is recommended, then, that linguists have reason to broaden their net, reason to bring in uttering that is not talking, reason to deal with social situations, not merely with jointly sustained talk. Incidentally, linguists might then be better able to countenance inroads that others can be expected to make into their conventional domain. For I believe that talk itself is intimately regulated and closely geared to its context through nonvocal gestures which are very differently distributed than the particular language and subcodes employed by any set of participants – although just where these boundaries of gesture-use *are* to be drawn remains an unstudied question.

Comments on papers by Ekman and Goffman

JÜRGEN HABERMAS

The central topic of both papers is nonverbal expressive reactions or gestures. Paul Ekman analyzes a well defined set of facial expressions. Five of seven units of eyebrow movements are involved in emotional expressions. Three of them, and four combinations of the three, form the repertoire of eyebrow movements in emotional expression. Erving Goffman covers a wider range of phenomena a bit more rhapsodically. We can, however, take 'response cries' as one focus of his paper. These are nonverbalized exclamatory interjections with an emotional meaning such as transition displays (brr, aah); threat startles (eek, yipe); revulsion sounds (eeuw), pain cries (ouch) etc. Emotional gestures have played a prominent role in anthropological research for centuries; the main reason is, I suppose, that gestures do have archaic roots in the prelinguistic behavior of infants and of nonhuman animals, and that they nonetheless can become an integrated part of linguistic communication. These are, at the same time, the two main aspects under which emotional gestures have been analyzed so far.

Under the *first* aspect we are mainly interested (a) in establishing the cultural universality of sets of basic gestures and (b) in explaining the origin of these symbolic universals. Ekman has clarified in what sense his seven eyebrow movements (as far as they function in emotional expressions) can be interpreted as symbolic universals; he has, in the last part of his paper, discussed two main genetic hypotheses: the hypothesis on species-constant learning versus the usual phylogenetic account; and he has proposed a research design with blind infants as a route on which we might reach a better founded decision between the competing theoretical claims. This is not my field; I personally find Ekman's position plausible but I cannot seriously argue for or against it and leave this part for others to discuss. I will try to add a few remarks on the *second* aspect under which emotional gestures attract our interest. Let me briefly deal with two questions: (a) how do these expressions differ from their linguistic equivalents and (b) how do they function as linguistic substitutes? We connect facial movements, response cries, and other gestures with emotional meanings such as fear, anger, surprise, sadness, revulsion, etc. The standard speech-acts by which we can utter equivalent meanings have the form: 'I am afraid (I am angry, surprised, sad, etc.) that p', where 'I' is self-referential for the speaker and 'p' stands for any propositional content (not necessarily related to the speech situation). 'Erlebnissätze' of this type are normally not linked with an explicit illocutionary component of the form 'I hereby express that p', where p now stands for a complex sentence (*Erlebnissatz*). The illocutionary component must be made explicit in the case of avowals, when the speaker discloses what he had or could have concealed before the eyes of others: 'I (hereby) confess (avow, disclose, tell you) that I hate his seemingly kind behavior yesterday.' Take this as an example of a standard expressive speech-act $M_e p$, with explicit illocutionary and propositional components, which is a linguistic equivalent of corresponding expressive gestures.

The main difference between the two is, of course, the context-independence of gestural meanings on elicitors and subsequent interpersonal behavior. This difference is due to the propositional structure of speech. But there are further differences which seem to be even more instructive; let me mention the following four:

Expressive speech-acts principally have *communicative function*. If expressive speech-acts are performed by solitary actors, they are items of deviant self-talk which violates Goffman's rule: 'No talking to oneself in public'. They may then count as mental symptoms with a function for the psycho-dynamics of repressed material (that is, for a communication between different parts of one and the same ego). But these linguistic utterances differ from response cries, from gestures in general, in that they demand a communicative setting with at least one other person involved. Expressive gestures, on the other hand, often have communicative functions but they can legitimately occur outside of communications.

Expressive speech-acts principally can be negated by standards of *veracity*. Participants in communicative action expect each other to be truthful, but they will know that the speaker while expressing his needs and feelings may say what he does *not* mean. Expressive gestures, again, often become part of linguistic communication to such an extent that the speakers can instrumentally handle them for deceiving other people (or for role-playing in fictional contexts). But it requires a particular training to get that sort of control over gestures exercised whenever we produce speech-acts. If it comes to doubts about validity, in this case of the veracity of an intention expressed, gestures normally count as more reliable than speech-acts.

Expressive utterances, as is the case with actions in general, are principally submitted to *regulations by social norms*. This is true for both expressive speech-acts and gestures (as Ekman's American–Japanese movie experiment indicates, p. 180 above). But normative regulations pertain to a lesser degree to gestures than to speech-acts, due to the difficulties in learning how to achieve control over the former. This is indicated, e.g. by gestures which replace speech-acts in those situations where participants wish to avoid open resistance and yet want to express their opposition (see Goffman on 'muttering', chapter 3.2 §IV above).

In performing expressive speech-acts we use sentences with *conventional meanings* while at least some basic gestures and their emotional meanings are linked in a non-conventional way. This does not mean that basic gestures with non-conventional meanings cannot acquire conventional meanings. Gestures will gain conventional meanings as soon as they serve as substitutes for linguistic devices in other than the expressive dimensions, that is when they enter into linguistic communication not only for the purpose of self-representation of the speaker's subjectivity.

To go on to the second question, if one leaves aside expressive gestures in their role as speech-associated *emphasizers*, the distinction which I want to make is similar to Ekman's distinction between emotional and conversational signals. Expressive gestures can assume nonexpressive linguistic functions and thereby acquire conventional meanings. From this point of view, Ekman's examples for the two eyebrow-movements discussed in this context (4 and 1+2) can be used for a reclassification:

such gestures can be used as illocutionary indicators (e.g. instead of a question mark);

they can be used by hearers to indicate yes/no attitudes towards validity claims (truth, veracity, rightness) and some of their variations (doubt, abstention);

they can be used for metacommunicative purposes, to give an extraverbal comment to what is explicitly said (either extending the manifest con-

tent of the speech-act, or in contrast to it – as is the case with an ironic variation of what is said);
they can be used in the place of verbal utterances which would elicit sanctions (mock, astonishment, sophisticated scepticisms etc.).

Having made these two remarks on expressive gestures as an extraverbal part of linguistic communication, let me turn to Goffman's paper with one further remark. Most of what Goffman writes on 'response cries' can be related to both the emotional-expressive and the linguistic-substitute function of eyebrow-movements, and of gestures in general. This does not hold, however, for what he discussed under the heading of 'self-talk'.

Self-talk, at least in the way it is introduced by Goffman, is in the first place, not an expressive, but a self-saving and facekeeping device. Goffman analyzes self-talk as a remedial device for situations in which the actor has partly lost control over his environment and his own behavior, where he faces a threat to his reputation and feels some need to reassure himself and others of his competences. You remember the examples. What we may utter in these cases, talking to ourselves but indirectly addressing ourselves to witnesses as well, is self-talk. It functions as a coping mechanism. Self-talk by no means simply gives expression to anger, fear or surprise or pain; self-talk serves as a defense against and a compensation for peculiar types of identity-threatening acts.

Among these utterances are also cries, spill cries or sounds 'we emit to follow along with our having for a moment lost guiding control of some feature of the world around us, including ourselves' (chapter 3.2 §VII above). Spill cries cannot be classified together with the other response cries, which are less complicated and more basic insofar as they express feelings and attitudes which human and nonhuman animals seem to share. Spill cries presuppose a symbolically structured social and personal identity which can be threatened, and highly organized controls by acting and speaking subjects which can break down. What, then, is Goffman's reason for discussing two types of utterances which are as different as self-talk and expressive gestures?

There are two interesting phenomena, which can only be analyzed in terms of a combination of emotional expressions *and* self-saving devices. Goffman deals with the first one: with imprecations and curses. The other one is laughter and weeping. Some decades ago Helmuth Plessner made an attempt to explain these extreme emotional reactions, which only occur among human beings, as ultimate devices for coping with situations of total loss of control. Where loss of control is not near to total we save the balance of our identity by imprecation and curses, thereby expressing our angry feelings, our sadness or despair, and yet signalling at the same time that a mischief, for which we are not really responsible, cannot cast any serious doubt on our competence and autonomy. In imprecations as in laughter and weeping, emotional cries and self-talk form a unified whole. Both phenomena, imprecations and laughter or weeping, reveal what their elements, emotional expressions and self-talk, have in common: they are indicative of a peculiar compulsion, of a restraint on the autonomy of actors which operates in normal linguistic communication. The compulsion of nonverbal emotional expressions is more of an impulsive kind, and that of self-talk more of a coercive kind. What this intuitive description means, however, is difficult to explain.

P. EKMAN: REPLY TO HABERMAS' COMMENTS

I will only reply to a few points where there is some possible ambiguity in Professor Habermas' interesting comments.

Our research suggests that some people are quite capable of using expressive gestures to mislead others without any specialized training, although Habermas is correct in saying that most people do not do so. The specialized training that he refers to as required for such control over expressive gesture may only be effective with people who are naturally talented in such control, and might be disastrous if applied to most people. One might wonder in this connection whether it is just control, by which I presume Habermas refers to the ability to inhibit an expressive gesture, or whether talent in deceit also requires the ability to perform convincingly an expressive gesture which is not felt.

I believe Habermas is correct in saying that gestures normally count for more than speech-acts when veracity is questioned, but there are obvious exceptions worth noting. Smiles are well known as untrustworthy, since they are used for so many purposes other than just as expressive of pleasure or happiness, and of course are a common mask. Folklore, in the United States at least, says that the eyes are the most trustworthy, although I know of no reason to believe that this is actually so.

References

Allport, F. M. 1924. *Social psychology*. Boston: Houghton Mifflin.

Altmann, S. 1968. Primates. In T. Sebeok (ed.), *Animal communication: techniques and results of research*. Bloomington: Indiana University Press.

Andrew, R. J. 1963. The origin and evolution of the calls and facial expressions of the primates. *Behaviour*, 20:1–109.

Bell, C. 1872. *Anatomy and philosophy of expression*. 6th edn. London.

Birdwhistell, R. L. 1970. *Kinesics and context*. Philadelphia: University of Pennsylvania Press.

Blurton Jones, N. G. 1967. An ethological study of some aspects of social behavior of children in nursery school. In D. Morris (ed.), *Primate ethology*, London: Weidenfeld and Nicolson.

   1971. Criteria for use in describing facial expressions in children. *Human Biology*, 41:365–413.

Blurton Jones, N. G. and Konner, M. J. 1971. An experiment on eyebrow-raising and visual searching in children. *Journal of Child Psychology and Psychiatry*, 11:233–40.

Brannigan, C. R. and Humphries, D. A. 1972. Human non-verbal behaviour, a means of communication. In N. G. Blurton Jones (ed.), *Ethological studies of child behaviour*. Cambridge: Cambridge University Press.

Burkitt, A. N. and Lightoller, G. S. 1926–7. The facial musculature of Australian Aboriginal. *Journal of Anatomy*, part I, 61:14–39, part II, 62:3–57.

Charlesworth, W. R. 1970. Surprise reactions in congenitally blind and sighted children. NIMH Progress Report.

Chevalier-Skolnikoff, S. 1973. Facial expression of emotion in non-human primates. In P. Ekman (ed.), *Darwin and facial expression: a century of research in review*. New York: Academic Press.

Cook-Gumperz, Jenny and Corsaro, William. 1976. Social-economical constraints on children's communicative strategies. In Jenny Cook-Gumperz and John Gumperz (eds.) *Papers on language and context*, Berkeley: Language Behavior Research Laboratory, University of California, Berkeley

Darwin, C. 1872. *The expression of the emotions in man and animals*. New York: Philosophical Library, 1955.

Dittmann, A. T. 1972. Developmental factors in conversational behavior. *Journal of Communication*, 22(4):404–23.

Duchenne, B. 1862. *Mécanisme de la physionomie humaine ou analyse électrophysiologique de l'expression des passions*. Paris: Baillière.

Efron, D. 1941. *Gesture and environment*. New York: King's Crown; reprinted as *Gesture, race and culture*. The Hague: Mouton, 1972.

Eibl-Eibesfeldt, I. 1970. *Ethology, the biology of behavior*. New York: Holt, Rinehart and Winston.

   1972. Similarities and differences between cultures in expressive movements. In R. A. Hinde (ed.), *Non-verbal communication*. Cambridge: Cambridge University Press.

Ekman, P. 1972. Universals and cultural differences in facial expressions of emotion. In J. Cole (ed.), *Nebraska symposium on motivation, 1971*. Lincoln: University of Nebraska Press.

   1973. Cross cultural studies of facial expression. In *Darwin and facial expression: a century of research in review*. New York: Academic Press.

   1976. Movements with precise meaning. *Journal of Communication*, 26(3):14–26.

   1977a. Facial signs. In T. Sebeok (ed.), *Sight, sound and sense*. Bloomington: University of Indiana Press.

   1977b. Biological and cultural contributions to body and facial movement. In John Blacking (ed.), *Anthropology of the body*. London: Academic Press.

Ekman, P. and Friesen, W. V. 1969a. Nonverbal leakage and clues to deception. *Psychiatry*, 32:88–105.

   1969b. The repertoire of nonverbal behavior: categories, origins, usage, and coding. *Semiotica*, 1(1):49–98.

   1974. Detecting deception from the body or face. *Journal of Personality and Social Psychology*, 29(3):288–98.

   1975. *Unmasking the face*. Englewood Cliffs, New Jersey: Prentice-Hall.

   1976. Measuring facial movement. *Environmental Psychology and Nonverbal Behavior*, 1(1):56–75.

   1978. *The facial action coding system*. Palo Alto, California: Consulting Psychologists' Press.

Friesen, W. V. 1972. Cultural differences in facial expressions in a social situation: an experimental test of the concept of display rules. Unpublished Ph.D. thesis, University of California, San Francisco.

Goodenough, F. 1932. Expressions of the emotions in a blind-deaf child. *Journal of Abnormal and Social Psychology*, 27:328–33.

Gopnik, Alison. 1977. No, there, more, and allgone: why the first words aren't about things. *Nottingham Linguistic Circular*, 6:15–20.

Grant, N. G. 1969. Human facial expression. *Man*, 4:525–36.

Hamburg, D. 1963. Emotions in the perspective of human evolution. In P. Knapp (ed.), *Expressions of emotions in man*. New York: International Universities Press.

Hjortsjö, C. H. 1970. *Man's face and mimic language*. Lund: Student-litteratur.

van Hooff, J. A. R. A. M. 1969. The facial displays of the catarrhine monkeys and apes. In D. Morris (ed.), *Primate ethology*. New York: Anchor Doubleday: 9–88.

   1971. *Aspecten van het sociale gedrage en de comunicatie bij humane en hogere niet-humane primaten*. Rotterdam: Bronder-Offset.

Huber, E. 1931. *Evolution of facial musculature and facial expression.* Baltimore: Johns Hopkins University Press.

James, Deborah. 1972. Some aspects of the syntax and semantics of inter-jections. In Paul M. Peranteau *et al.* (eds.), *Papers from the eighth regional meeting of the Chicago Linguistic Society.* Chicago: Chicago Linguistic Society.

Jefferson, Gail. 1974. Error correction as an interactional resource. *Language in Society*, 3:181–200.

Leach, E. 1972. The influence of cultural context on nonverbal communication in man. In R. A. Hinde (ed.), *Non-verbal Communication.* Cambridge: Cambridge University Press.

Lersch, P. 1932. *Gesicht und Seele.* Republished 1971. Munich: Ernst Reinhardt Verlag.

Lewis, M., Brooks, J. and Haviland, J. 1978. Hearts and faces: a study in the measurement of emotion. In M. Lewis and L. Rosenblum (eds.), *The development of affect.* New York: Plenum.

Liddell, S. K. 1975. Restrictive relative clauses in American Sign Language. Unpublished mimeo, Salk Institute.

Lightoller, G. H. S. 1925. Facial muscles: the modiolus and muscles surrounding the rima oris with some remarks about the panniculus adiposus. *Journal of Anatomy*, 60 part 1 (Oct.):1–84.

McGrew, W. C. 1972. *An ethological study of children's behavior.* New York: Academic Press.

Mead, M. 1975. Review of Darwin and facial expression. Ed. P. Ekman. *Journal of Communication*, 25(1):209–13.

Myers, R. E. 1969. Neurology of social communication in primates. *Proceedings of the Second International Congress of Primatology, Atlanta, Georgia*, vol. III. Basel/New York: Karger.

Oster, H. 1978. Facial expression and affect development. In M. Lewis and L. Rosenblum (eds.), *The development of affect.* New York: Plenum.

Oster, H. and Ekman, P. 1977. Facial behavior in child development. In A. Collins (ed.), *Minnesota Symposium on Child Development.* New York: Thomas A. Crowell.

Peiper, A. 1963. *Cerebral function in infancy and childhood*, New York: Consultants Bureau.

Piaget, Jean. 1962. *Comments on Vygotsky's critical remarks concerning 'The language and thought of the child', and 'Judgment and reasoning in the child'.* Cambridge, Mass.: MIT Press.

   1974. *The language and thought of the child.* Trans. Marjorie Gabain. New York: New American Library.

Quang Phuc Dong. 1971. English sentences without overt grammatical subject. In A. M. Zwicky *et al.* (eds.), *Studies out in left field.* Edmonton, Alta: Linguistic Research Inc.: 3–9.

Quine, W. V. 1959. *Word and object.* New York: John Wiley and Sons.

Redican, W. K. 1975. Facial expressions in nonhuman primates. In L. A. Rosenblum (ed.), *Primate behavior*, vol. IV. New York: Academic Press.

Roper, G. 1977. The development of voluntary facial imitation in children. Unpublished M.A. thesis, San Francisco State University.

Schwartz, G. E., Fair, P. L., Salt, P., Mandel, M. R. and Klerman, G. L. 1976.

Facial expression and imagery in depression: an electromyographic study. *Psychosomatic Medicine*, 38(5):337–47.

Smith, K. J. 1977. *The behavior of communicating*. Cambridge, Mass.: Harvard University Press.

Sudnow, David. 1967. *Passing on: the social organization of dying*. Englewood Cliffs, New Jersey: Prentice-Hall.

Tomkins, S. S. 1962–3. *Affect, imagery, consciousness*, 2 vols. New York: Springer Publishing Co.

Trager, George L. 1958. Paralanguage: a first approximation. *Studies in Linguistics*, 13:1–12.

Vygotsky, Lev Semenovich. 1962. *Thought and language*. Trans. Eugenia Hanfmann and Gertrude Vakar. First published 1934 in Russian. New York: MIT Press and John Wiley and Sons.

Part II

Organization of social behaviour

4. Functional aspects of aggression, fear and attachment

4.1. Aggression, fear and attachment: complexities and interdependencies

PAUL LEYHAUSEN

Prologue

Recent discussions on the nature of behaviour in man and other animals are full of controversy. Most of the controversial arguments, however, seem to arise from two sources: muddled thinking and confusion over semantics on the one hand, and, on the other, failure to realise that each observable and identifiable behavioural act or sequence of acts invariably has a threefold history. It is the latter which is going to concern us here.

Each individual of a given species owes its existence to the unbroken chain of generations, to the reproductive continuity of that species. All its structural and functional properties are due to this species' pre-history, even those in which it differs from other members of the same species; the capacity to differ, the range of differences and their quality are also species-specific. Yet this must not be understood to mean that the evolutionary processes of phylogeny directly produce the properties. Phylogenesis produces a blueprint, a prescription for 'constructing' or 'assembling' a new individual. The prescriptions are self-activating and develop mechanisms capable of building the new organism out of the material available according to blueprint specifications. It is exclusively the blueprint and the developmental mechanisms which are the result of phylogenesis.

The interaction of the blueprint and the developing mechanisms with the environment forms the second kind of history: ontogenesis. As in other cases, the blueprint in part is very strict and in part leaves the developing mechanisms some latitude in their interaction with environmental conditions. Accordingly, some of the characteristics of the indi-

253

vidual will show little or no variation within the population, while others may vary along with variations in some of the environmental conditions under which each individual develops. All the same, the environment can never add something to the individual's *potential*; it can only modify what is already provided for in the blueprint, i.e. it can change the direction and/or the degree of realisation of that potential. Only where the potential is for storing acquired information does the environment contribute in the literal sense the kind and amount of information *offered*; whether this is actually accepted and stored is quite another matter and certainly not entirely a function of the environment. In short, what we traditionally call the innate in behaviour is but an environmentally stable trait or characteristic in the sense of classical genetics, and what we call acquired or learned is environmentally labile. And it is the kind, direction and force of the operating selection pressures which determine what it is to be in each case.

Functional characteristics of an animal differ from its structural ones in that they are not manifest or observable all the time. Behavioural acts in particular are functional characteristics which are observable only inter-mittently, at more or less regular intervals. In their case, what ontogenesis provides is not 'the behaviour' – not, for instance, the notori-ous 'fixed action pattern' – but a mechanism or mechanisms which are capable of delivering a behavioural act or a sequence of such acts. The process by which the mechanism is activated and consequently produces an observable behaviour I call – borrowing from a well-known German school of psychology – actogenesis (*Aktualgenese*). For more detailed dis-cussion of the interrelationship between phylogenesis, ontogenesis and actogenesis, its implications and consequences, see Leyhausen (1974).

All these considerations apply to the various behaviour patterns of fighting (threat, attack, defence), avoidance (cut-off, submission, freez-ing, withdrawal, flight) and attachment (contact seeking, following, allogrooming) and the accompanying patterns of expressive movements, vocalisations and secretions.

The discussion of aggression in particular has proved unsuccessful and frustrating in the past because nearly every participant has insisted on defining aggression in his own way, and – worse – has interpreted the contributions of others along his own lines. A recent reviewer was thus able to list over fifty definitions of aggression!

In Lorenzian terms, aggression is defined as 'unprovoked intraspecific attack'. Adhering strictly to this definition would mean that in the eyes of many, perhaps even the majority, of participants at this conference, aggression does not exist at all, since they hold that the kind of spontaneous behaviour described here by 'unprovoked' does not exist. But even if one accepts the evidence for spontaneous behaviour, as I myself certainly do, it is clear that it seldom appears in 'pure' form, and what one normally observes is the complementary effect of spontaneous and reactive mechanisms. The problem, then, boils down to a question of ratio: is an observed behaviour fairly matched to the stimulus situation, or overdone, or too weak? This clearly asks for a judgment by the observer, who may then speak of defence, aggression, or cowardice respectively. Still others classify all kinds of attack as aggression and therefore believe they are able to study aggression by experimenting with a predator's attack on its prey. And, to give a final example from a quite endless list, some confuse aggression with violence, which it may of course lead to but need not.

From all this and more, I have long since concluded that the term aggression is so fraught with subjective assumptions, beliefs and even dogmatisms that it has become useless both for research and for serious scientific discussion. Observable is fighting behaviour which serves a number of purposes and involves various adversaries. An attack may serve offensive or defensive purposes, and it must be noted that one of the 'classic' examples of 'aggression' – a territorial attack – is, at least normally, in *defence* of a territory.

I. Teleonomic function

Fighting among conspecifics would result in rapid extinction of the species if it invariably led either to the stronger animal killing or seriously injuring the other, or merely to the animals scattering so far that they would never meet again.

Fear among conspecifics would result in rapid extinction of the species if it either rendered the animals incapable of active contact or caused them to scatter beyond mutual reach.

Attachment between conspecifics would result in rapid extinction of the species if it were not checked by forces of dispersion.

Hence, only animal species able to strike a 'workable' balance between dispersion and approach survived. Although there might have been other ways in which this could have been achieved, and indeed such has been the case in many lower animals, evolution has furnished all vertebrates with the behavioural equipment of fighting, fleeing and socialising; and there is some evidence to indicate that they also experience the emotions of anger, hate, fear, shyness, companionship, friendship, love, etc., associated with these behaviours in humans. In fact, vertebrate behaviour is so uniform in this respect that, when one such component is missing in a species, we are certain that this is due to secondary loss (e.g. the Anura).

If one should wonder why the vertebrates have evolved this method of regulating their densities rather than the methods employed by most invertebrates, there seems to be only a somewhat speculative answer. I believe this to have been the price – for the vertebrate way cannot be considered an unmitigated blessing! – they had to pay when evolving the various kinds of social organisation which are based on personal acquaintance of the members of a given social unit. This type of organisation permits a higher degree of role diversity, flexibility and efficiency in social units containing only a relatively small number of individuals.

In consequence, individuals are no longer interchangeable; there has to be some means by which they can assert and maintain their identity. However, the uniformity mentioned above extends only to the general behaviour. When, for example, fighting is analysed in different species, we find a great variety of movements, weapons, etc., which in part are due to anatomical differences but in part seem to be arbitrary. The uniformity lies in the variable fact that these movements are organised in such an order of intensities, synergisms and antagonisms that effective fighting results. Moreover, the order is not necessarily governed by external situations, cues or stimuli or, if so, only to a certain extent. The fact that there *is* order in the course of a fight, sometimes even a rather rigid order (ritualised fighting), but most certainly always some order, cannot be explained in terms of efficiency, stimulus field, success or failure to achieve the goal, or chance probability alone: there must be a mechanism within the animal's system which *produces* spatial and temporal order.

In the case of animals which possess a certain variety of behaviour elements which they may use in fighting, choice, sequence and intensity of these elements are largely determined by the purpose, kind of adversary and circumstances of the individual case. Some of the elements may occur in all contexts, others are specific to certain contexts and will not occur in others except, perhaps, under very exceptional circumstances. Threatening signals, for instance, will not normally be used in predatory attack. In many animals, threat signals indicating imminent attack are different from those that merely warn off, and there is often a difference between the signals used when confronting a conspecific or an enemy of another species.

II. 'Mechanisms' of functioning

Morris (1956) considered the mutual interdependence of three 'major drives': flight, attack and mating, which he called the FAM system. The concept of 'major drive' or 'major instinct' had been put forward by Tinbergen as a rough equivalent of von Uexküll's (1921) virtually untranslatable *Funktionskreis*. In the years that followed, however, this was more and more often misunderstood as representing nothing better than the older concept of instinct which ethology had abandoned from the beginning. It was subjected to heavy criticism by Hinde (1959) and others. One of the certainly unintended consequences of this criticism and the wide acceptance it received was that it discouraged further investigation of the kind of interdependencies analysed by Morris and the treatment of all the various and diverse internal motivational factors of an animal as one complex, highly but flexibly organised system, largely self-regulated and balanced *over time*.

The study of complex motivational systems was further confused by many researchers – including Lorenz and Tinbergen themselves – who failed to notice that the Lorenzian concept of instinct was not identical and was in fact incompatible with the Tinbergian concept of hierarchy of instinct. My first protest against this confusion passed unnoticed (1952).

In the fifties, Hinde (1956, 1958) and I (1955, 1956) simultaneously made a number of observations and experiments which proved that the major drives or instincts were not of a 'unitary' nature or even permanently stable systems but could at best be described as 'ad hoc' systems. Neither the 'drive' concept still used by Morris in his FAM analysis nor the rigid hierarchical structure of the 'major instinct' were tenable any longer. It must be emphasised here that, while we drew very different conclusions, there is no dispute over facts, although we worked with such widely different animals as canaries and cats. Very unfortunately, this discouraged further studies along the lines pioneered by Morris: if there are no drives in the sense of identifiable, monolithic entities, what use would it be to investigate the interrelationships of mere abstractions or constructs?

In figure 1, I have attempted to place the components of behaviour employed by cats in the context of the subsystems of fighting, withdrawal and attachment according to their respective functions. It must be noted that the listing is not complete but contains only the more important elements or units. In the subsystem 'fighting' there are four main elements: biting, pawing, kicking and pulling-toward, together with the

A. Fighting behaviour

Attack / Defence / Withdrawal	Motor activities				Head movements	Postures	Vocalisations
	Locomotion	Biting	Fore paw	Hind paw			
Attack	Rush toward	Nape	Pull toward		Wave	Erect	Caterwaul
	Walk erect	Neck	neck only opponent's hindlegs		Oblique squint	Hindquarter high	
							Snarl
	Stalking run	Back	body	Pull toward	Low	Front low	Growl
	Stalk	Elbow	Strike at sides, back head	Kick	Level	Arched back	Hiss
	Walk		opponent's paws			Hindquarter low	
Defence		Mouth to mouth		Push away	Withdrawn	Shrinking crouch	Spit
	Slink away					Roll over	Shriek
Withdrawal	Flight (gallop)						

B. Attachment

Activities derived from mother-infant and sexual behaviour	Play	Vocalisations	Resting positions
Suckle	Play fighting	Purr	Close
Allogrooming	'King of the castle'	Gurgle (*Gurren*)	Bodies touching
Rubbing	Chase	Low calls	Head rests on partner's body
heads	Predatory stalk and attack		
sides			
shoulders			
back under chin of partner			
tail over back of partner			
Head pushing (*Köpfchengeben*)			
Follow			

1. Vertical distances between items symbolise approximate placement of each item on a supposed continuum Attack–Defence–Withdrawal (A). No such grading is possible for (B) because the degree of attachment is expressed through frequency and intensity

preceding, accompanying and concluding manners of approach, postures, vocalisations and withdrawal. According to whether they are employed in attack, defence or avoidance, they differ in threshold, latencies
and orientation. Which element is activated at the outset depends on the
balance between the differential levels of readiness of them all at that
moment as well as on the situation. The threshold is determined (1) by the
'level of readiness' of the respective component or element, which constitutes the degree of 'spontaneity', and (2) by the 'sensitivity' of the releasing mechanism which sets the degree of 'reactive readiness'. Both change
independently of each other. However, in this the internal balance is
more decisive in so far as the animal – given the opportunity – may simply
opt out of the situation if its internal motivational balance is not up to it, or
it may – in the reverse case – actively seek out or even create a 'suitable'
situation. The same goes for the other two subsystems considered here,
or indeed for any such subsystem which may be either permanently
present or transiently formed in the animal. It is important to note that
subsystems share many components. Also, one must not infer that only
elements which have been arranged on the same horizontal level could be
combined in an event. It is quite possible for the cat to attack with the
forepaws and defend with the hindpaws. Thus, from left to right, almost
all combinations are possible. This fact also adds to the difficulties in
singling out certain events as 'aggression'. Only the more extreme cases
appear sufficiently clear-cut to lend themselves to unambiguous classification.

'Opting out' of one situation generally also means opting for another
one. Thus this marks the transition from one subsystem to the next. If our
model of relative hierarchy of moods and its operation by way of changes
or differentials in the internal balance of readiness levels of single components has any claim to coming near to the real workings of motivational
systems, it should follow that a component released in subsystem x
would already be lowered in threshold when the animal meets a situation
appropriate to x but opts out of it because the subsystem as a whole is not
ready for it. When subsequently subsystem y is activated, that particular
component should then be more prominent than it would have been if y
had been activated directly and not as a means of escaping from the
x-situation; and this does in fact happen. I shall give one example of this
which reaches beyond the scope of the motivational system under
scrutiny here. No such subsystem or group of systems can be considered
closed, and interaction with others is unavoidable.

Biting, apart from being the main component of all-out attack, is also part of two other systems: retrieving of young and mating. In these two it is, however, subsidiary, a part of the chain of appetitive behaviour leading respectively to carrying the young or successful copulation. In rival fighting as well as in prey-catching, however, biting is the consummatory act. According to the organising principle of the relative hierarchy of moods, it is the consummatory act which organises all appetitive behaviour so that it will lead up to this end. But the details of the sequence and order of appetitive acts are, in part at least, also determined not only by present situational factors and expediency but also by their 'availability', and thus, if they are instinct movements, by their momentary readiness level. As I have described in detail elsewhere, cats very often carry the prey they have killed for some distance and time before settling down to devour or abandon it. Female cats do this significantly more often and for longer durations than males. Carrying is more 'available' in their case because of their greater readiness for retrieving young. There are many other examples of this kind. A full publication is in preparation.

The foregoing will suffice to show (1) that a concept does not become scientifically useless because what formerly seemed a more or less indivisible, homogeneous unit turns out to be a rather complex (sub)system (witness the atom); (2) that an organised system need not be permanently traceable or fixed to be identifiable whenever it is reassembled 'ad hoc'. It will be submitted that 'aggression', fear and attachment are such subsystems governed by or organised along the principles of 'relative hierarchy of moods' as described and analysed by myself (1965), and that it is by the same mechanisms which govern the functioning of these subsystems that their mutual interactions are organised and controlled:

(1) changes in releasing threshold (level of specific readiness, *Aktual-spiegel*);
(2) changes in stimulus threshold effected (a) from within (specific sensitivity and attention intensity and span) and (b) from without (adaptation and habituation), (c) preference for discrete balance ratios (*ausgezeichnete Koaktionslage*; von Holst 1935).

III. Human applications

It is often maintained that inferences from animal to human behaviour are not legitimate because, for ethical and other reasons, some of the methods applied in the study of animals cannot be used in the study of people. While it is true that this places certain restrictions on the kind of conclusions which may be safely drawn, it is sheer ignorance to claim that it should invalidate all such conclusions. Safe conclusions may be drawn on the following grounds.

Firstly, they may be drawn on the grounds of general principles of vertebrate, homoeotherm, mammalian organisation. Hence, not only is it possible to draw a diagram like figure 1 for the human, but I have in fact used this in an experimental analysis of the postures and behavioural traits which convey 'threat' in humans.[1] It is also legitimate to survey the immense wealth of material on human psychological experience and behaviour in order to see how well it fits in with the theoretical framework furnished by ethological studies of higher animals, especially mammals. In doing so one will frequently find that facts which seemed paradoxical or even incompatible within the framework of other psychological or behavioural theories will suddenly fall into place and not only become compatible but have to be postulated on the grounds of ethological theory (cf. Leyhausen 1954). In contrast to a hypothesis, a theory is not tested by operational thinking and experimentation, but by the amount of available data it manages to harbour in logical order without intrinsic contradictions. A theory which serves this purpose best is also the one which presumably is the most promising when employed in the formulation of new working hypotheses. In the as yet very few cases where these two steps have been taken properly, as in the examples quoted, they have invariably proved successful. Therefore, I find it very hard to understand why so many researchers still flatly refuse to look at human behaviour in that way. Of course it may not always be successful, but why stay with a paradox or even a seemingly unsolvable factual contradiction rather than at least try the theory out? One reason which I suspect to be at the root of this attitude is that many people still firmly believe ethological interpretations or explanations to be simplistic. When one suggests that a certain element in human behaviour might be, for instance, an instinct and maybe homologous to the corresponding item in some other animal's repertoire, the answer all too often is: 'But in the human this cannot be simply an instinct!' – as if an instinct were something simple or uncomplicated and not a most complex (sub)system within the total behavioural system, the physiological and functional intricacies of which are still very incompletely understood. This apparently ineradicable contention that everything we call 'innate' in behaviour, i.e. the peristostable elements in behaviour, should be 'simple' seems to me to stem largely from the fact that most of the 'innate' is represented, if at all, only incompletely and vaguely in conscious experience, and that modern psychology and socio-

[1] 'Experimental analysis of a human releasing mechanism', in preparation.

logy still hold that only what is conscious in human experience really matters, and this in spite of all protestations to the contrary. I do not in any way attempt to belittle the fundamental importance of awareness, but I do think that at least since the advent of Freud we should all be aware that what we are aware of or may potentially become aware of is only the tip of the iceberg. Psychology and the study of human behaviour certainly must not neglect awareness and what it comprises; but it would be fatal to look to it as the explanation of all. It itself needs explaining as a biological phenomenon.

Secondly, conclusions about human behaviour may safely be drawn from animal behaviour on the basis of behavioural similarities which in detail as well as number go too far to leave any reasonable probability of their being due to mere convergence, let alone sheer chance. It is quite customary that scholars who normally tend to require the highest standard in scientific argument attempt to push aside even the most obvious and extraordinary resemblances between animal and human behaviour, or, to be correct, between human behaviour and that of other animals, as mere analogies. They are quick to point out that usually there is no stringent experimental or other evidence directly concerning the human behaviour in question which could be taken as direct and irrefutable proof of its homology with the corresponding behaviour of some other animal(s). This evasion is favoured by the fact that for ethical and other reasons it is very often impossible to employ the same method or a plausible equivalent to investigate the human behaviour as is used in studying other animals. This argument is particularly levelled at many of Eibl-Eibesfeldt's findings time and again, as well as at the attempts at re-interpretation of known facts about human behaviour in the light of ethological theory as described above. One cannot but feel pity at this kind of rearguard action. It can retain a semblance of justification only by employing the tactics of discussing each case of similarity in strict isolation. As soon as one considers one case after the other and all of them in combination, their number and undeniable interdependence are so overwhelming that even the most naive must admit the utter improbability of all this being due to chance and analogy instead of to the indubitable genetic, i.e. phylogenetic, relationship based on common descent and shared embryological, developmental mechanisms. One obstacle to accepting the inevitable seems to me to be the deplorable habit of thinking in alternatives. When the ethologist claims that kissing is an instinct movement, the cultural anthropologist will often reject this as he believes it to be a culturally controlled and often modified act because it is absent in

Objectively observable | Subjective experience

ALARM ('to all stations')

Tension → PANIC

Shyness, modesty
Watchfulness
Disquiet
Apprehension
Anxiety
Terror

Fright, Fear

Illusions

Hallucinations

'General' arousal
Substantia reticularis
Specified arousal

Specific propensities
(Differential levels
of readiness)

Perception 'Expectation'

Instinctive   Acquired
    Overt behaviour
Consummatory   Appetitive

Reticence
Reserved behaviour
Avoidance
Withdrawal
Flight
Hiding
'Freezing'
'Death feigning'
Defensive threat
Defence
Sham (counter) attack
Attack

Lowering of IRM
selectivity

IRM

ARM

Sudden and violent

Strange or
indeterminate

Unconditional

Conditional

Consummatory

STIMULI

ARM = acquired releasing mechanism

IRM = innate releasing mechanism

2. Objectively observable and subjective experience.

some cultures and employed in very different social contexts in others. But the one by no means excludes the other; among higher animals, it is the merest commonplace that one and the same instinct movement is performed in a variety of different behavioural contexts and is adaptable to these contexts and their purpose to various degrees.

Figure 2 undertakes to demonstrate the usefulness of this kind of interpretation for the motivational subsystem of 'fear'. Reactive fear and 'objectless' anxiety, panic and alarm, continuous wariness and focused attention to alerting stimuli together with all forms of their respective expressions and inhibitions, appetences and aversions are thus understood as differently balanced states or activities of the same complex system and its interactions with other such (sub)systems. The general principle is certainly mammalian, but the details are in part exclusively human and to fit other mammals would have to be changed accordingly. Some will have no equivalent in some other mammals and vice versa. But the subsystem as such is typical, as will become apparent as soon as one tries to fit it to a fish or bird: it will fit only in the parts which are the vertebrate in all of them and for the rest will be rather divergent.

Ethological theory, as I see it, is essentially an open system. It does not assume that everything in behaviour can be subsumed under any of the concepts developed by ethologists as long as these concepts and the facts on which they are based are given their due consideration. It does not try to reduce learning to instinct or something of that nature, but attempts to show how these and other functions and behavioural subsystems are linked up or interact in the causal networks of each of the three histories I discussed briefly in my introduction. Unlike other, competing theories in psychology and sociology, it has no need to explain away phenomena which do not fit; it is, for example, easily capable of incorporating the entire factual basis of learning theory without loss or contradiction, while learning theory cannot do the reverse. Therefore, of all the existing theories of behaviour I know of, ethological theory is the only one which can be built into a comprehensive 'general theory of behaviour' without strain in part or in toto. This is not to say there will never be anything better; but so far I fail to see anything of the kind on the horizon.

4.2. Beyond reductionism: five basic concepts in human ethology

ROGER D. MASTERS

Human ethology has generated widespread interest and controversy. Comparisons of our social behavior to that of other species seem to be threatening, attractive, or unsettling (depending on one's viewpoint). But here it is not worth debating whether, in principle, comparisons between animals and humans are possible; the question, rather, concerns the scientifically exact means of carrying them out.

This paper is an essay in theoretical clarification rather than a presentation of new data. I should like to suggest how the functional aspects of aggression, fear, and attachment can best be understood in the emerging field of human ethology. In so doing, both the limits of sociobiological or ethological approaches – and their tremendous promise – will be emphasized.

First, concepts which frequently generate confusion will be defined, and three typical errors in human ethology described in detail. On this basis, I will argue that aggression, fear and attachment serve as elements of social structures as well as of individual behavioral repertoires. While apparently self-evident, this functional approach to social organization suggests some interesting conclusions concerning the potential of human ethology and sociobiology.

I. Five basic concepts in human ethology

A number of scholars have discussed the methodology of behavioral comparisons between species and the legitimacy of extending them to *Homo sapiens* (von Cranach 1976, Lorenz 1974, Harlow, Gluck and Suomi 1972). In surveying this literature, I have argued that a careful specifica-

265

tion of the level of analysis is especially important if human ethology is to avoid serious errors (Masters 1976a). Here, it is useful to indicate five concepts which need definition when biological methods and hypotheses are used to analyze human social behavior. The notions of *cause* and *function*, of *emotion* and *behavior*, and of *social organization* have given rise to surprisingly frequent confusion. Perhaps if each of these concepts is shown to be distinct – and impossible to 'reduce' to the others – some of the most controversial (and doubtful) extrapolations from other species to humans could be avoided.

1. Cause and function

In recent sociobiology and ethology, many difficulties have arisen due to a confusion between *causes* and *functions*. A causal process or causal mechanism explains the material factors which produce phenotypical structures or behaviors. For example, one can say that, under stated conditions, a chromosomal sequence of nucleotide bases causes the production of a protein in particular cells. In contrast, *functions* refer to the effects of a structure or behavior, including the presumed selective advantages (functional adaptations) which might explain why the observed traits have evolved.

When a bird's wings are described as an evolutionary adaptation to flight, flying is presumed to be – or to have been – a selective advantage to the species. In such explanations, the functional relationship between wing structures and flight activity can be studied without knowing the precise genetic loci and cellular differentiation process that cause wing formation. As Anthony Ambrose puts it:

> Questions about the biological function of a piece of behaviour are thus questions about the part which this behaviour plays, or played, in contributing to species-survival in the type of environment in which the behaviour or capacity evolved. The answer refers not just to the immediate effect on the environment and its consequences for the behaving individual, but to the way these consequences contribute to the existence of species.   (von Cranach 1976:278)

The difference between a cause and a function seems at first trivial or merely definitional. But this distinction, while important for morphology, is often particularly critical in analyzing animal behavior (Kummer 1971). Much of the controversy over extrapolations from ethology or sociobiology to human behavior turns on a misunderstanding of these twin concepts. Moreover, this confusion has been shared by both proponents of analogies between other species and humans (e.g. Ardrey 1961) and their critics (e.g. Montagu 1968).

A given causal process may have originated for more than one functional 'reason' (even within a single species, not to mention in different species); as many scholars have remarked, biological processes are often overdetermined. Conversely, a similar function can be satisfied by the most diverse causal processes (as is manifest not only in comparing different species, but also in analyzing the behavioral repertoire of almost any complex vertebrate). Hence causal processes cannot be 'reduced' to their functional explanations, nor can functions be 'reduced' to their causes.

To be sure, this is a messy and intellectually unsatisfying statement. For many, the goal of science is a rigorous and complete account of nature, in which observed phenomena can be explained in terms of 'laws' that reduce complex and varying phenomena to simple and general rules (Hempel and Oppenheim 1969). Alas, nature is – as a leading contemporary biologist has wisely put it – a 'tinkerer' more than an engineer (Jacob 1977). Our research is motivated by the goal of providing causal explanations for presumed functional adaptations and functional explanations for observed causal processes. But a complete convergence between cause and function is not only unlikely in practice, but questionable in principle.

A concrete example will be more useful than these generalities. Much has been said of the applicability of sociobiological theories to human behavior. Models of population genetics, using the concept of 'inclusive fitness', have been proposed as explanations of 'altruism' and 'selfishness' in *Homo sapiens* (Wilson 1975, Wispé 1978). Both proponents and critics of this line of reasoning tend to interpret it as a causal explanation of why humans behave as they do. In fact, however, a theoretical prediction (or postdiction) of gene frequencies, based on population genetics, measures selective processes as they presumably operate on the gene pool; as such, this level of explanation is functional, unless of course the precise relationships between organisms and their environments through time have been specified.

Precisely speaking, therefore, a causal analysis of human altruism would have to specify neurological, developmental, and social factors involved in the behaviors so defined (for examples of such analysis, see chapters 5.1, 10.1 and 10.2 below). A functional analysis serves to explain the extent to which such behaviors – as well as the causal mechanisms related to them – might be adaptive (e.g. chapter 6.1 below). On the functional level, the concept of inclusive fitness is essential, because it permits the sociobiologist to go beyond intuitive hunches about the extent to which supposedly 'advantageous' traits can actually spread through the gene pool. But, in principle, the theories of sociobiology cannot in themselves provide a causal explanation of altruism – or any other aspect of human behavior.

This distinction between cause and function thus warns us against two errors which have mutually reinforced each other, generating acrimonious debates on the feasibility of human ethology as a scientific discipline. On the one hand, overly enthusiastic proponents of the new field have often treated functional hypotheses as causal explanations. And on the other, critics of sociobiology or ethology have attacked the 'reduction' of complex human behavior to 'biological' causes – ignoring the fact that the explanations offered are usually functional rather than causal.

The confusion of cause and function is especially dangerous because causal processes are generally viewed as deterministic laws, whereas the most that can be expected from functional analysis is a probabilistic and non-exclusive explanation. Functional analogies can only describe how or why a species came to behave in a given way; causal analysis usually suggests that – barring further evolutionary change – the behavior will persist. As a result, sociobiologists and ethologists sometimes seem to claim that observed behavior is inevitable and unchangeable, when all they are saying is that – under given conditions – it is probable. Conversely, critics of human ethology have again and again condemned the reductionist 'fallacy', without realizing that scientific research in this discipline must (and does) begin from a rejection of hasty inferences from presumed functions to causes.

I have stressed this problem because it is often ignored by some of our most thoughtful scientists on both sides of the issue. For example, even such outstanding sociobiologists as Trivers, Hamilton, or Wilson can discuss a supposed 'gene for altruism', without realizing that they view genes as causal and altruism as functional – and thereby confuse the two levels of analysis. Social scientists like Campbell, reading this literature, tend to make exactly the same mistake even if coming to opposed conclusions (for details, see Masters 1978). Happily, as Leyhausen illustrates in chapter 4.1 above, such a misunderstanding of the relation of causal and functional analysis is not inevitable.[1]

---

[1] More than one reader may object to the presentation, on the ground that the distinction between function and cause is not as clear and distinct as I have implied. This objection is all the more valid since these two terms refer to propositions about phenomena rather than

2. Emotion and behavior

The difference between a cause and a function is paralleled by the distinction between *emotion* and *behavior*. In general, the concept of 'emotion' refers to inner states (diversely called 'moods', 'tendencies', 'feelings' – not to mention 'drives' or even 'instincts'). In contrast, 'behavior' refers to observable actions of an organism. Crudely speaking, one can treat an emotion as 'subjective' (what an animal or human feels), whereas behavior seems more 'objective' (what others of the species – or human observers – see). But this way of putting the difference has often been misleading, especially because it can lead to the assumption that 'emotions' are always *causes* of 'behavior', whereas the relation between them is generally functional and not causal.

Once again, it is essential to be concrete. The terms 'aggression', 'fear', and 'attachment' have been chosen as the focus of this section. But these three concepts have been used in the literature to refer either to subjective states ('emotions' or moods), or to observed actions ('behavior' or motor coordinations). Quite obviously, inner feelings or emotions are not identical to observed behaviors. But failure to distinguish clearly between the two has muddled a great deal of research.

In no area has this confusion been more obvious than in discussions of aggression. What the layman calls 'aggression' is, in ethological terms, comprised of motor coordinations (*behavior*) and moods or feeling-states (which, in humans, seem to be closely related to *emotions*). When Lorenz proposed that aggression plays a functional role in the 'parliament of instincts' (Lorenz 1966), for most readers he was asserting that aggressive – if not violent – *behavior* is natural and inevitable. In fact, he merely suggested that the moods or *emotions* associated with aggression have been, in most vertebrates, highly adaptive; so much so, indeed, that

the phenomena themselves. Hence a statement about flying in birds may be functional or causal – but the phenomenon of the bird in flight is, strictly speaking, neither. Moreover, what is a functional proposition at one level of analysis may become, at a different level, a causal one . . . and vice versa. For example, the aggressive behaviors of rats and mice can be studied from a functional perspective (e.g. in relation to social organization, socialization of the young, etc.), or they can be analyzed in terms of the precise neurophysiological pathways causing observed responses (e.g. chapter 5.1 below). In the latter case, the discovery of causal relationships between neurophysiological processes and externally observable behavior does not *replace* or vitiate functional analysis, but merely operates on a different level. When shifting from functional to causal approaches, however, it is not infrequent for broad classificatory terms (which seem adequate in functional explanations) to be broken down into components. For a striking illustration, see Moyer 1969.

Lorenz argues against attempts to ignore these emotions or to reduce them entirely to cultural 'causes'.

As presented, Lorenz's hypothesis did not presume that aggressive or violent *behaviors*, such as murder, war, and rioting, are innate or desirable; quite the contrary, his intention was to show how aggressive *emotions* might be dissociated from human violence and redirected toward other behaviors. Apart from the tendency to confuse function and cause in popularized writing, Lorenz's thesis was misinterpreted by readers who assumed that his discussion of aggression referred primarily to behavior – or to behavior and emotion as a single unit. The result is that discussion of the supposedly 'natural' status of human aggressiveness was long bogged down in a confused morass, in which hypotheses about the *functionality* of aggressive *moods* were criticized using evidence of the *causation* of aggressive *behavior* (e.g. Montagu 1968).

As this example suggests, one must specify whether the terms aggression, fear, and attachment refer to behaviors or to emotions – or to both. Moreover, human ethology must always treat the relation of emotion to behavior as a scientific question, not a postulate. While it is often assumed that emotion 'causes' behavior, there are many cases where human behavior 'causes' the corresponding emotion. For example, the use of behavioral training to induce appropriate emotions is central to religious practice in faiths as diverse as medieval Catholicism and Zen Buddhism.

Indeed, this process plays a major role in most human socialization. When we teach our children to say 'thank you', it is usually presumed that the child who uses these polite formulas will come to have a corresponding emotion of gratitude; as the English have long said, 'Manners makyth the man.' Hence human ethology cannot treat emotion and behavior as a single unit in which the causal sequence moves invariably from one to another: just as emotion cannot be reduced to behavior, so behavior cannot be reduced to emotion.

3. Social organization

The fifth basic concept which deserves clarification is that of *social organization*. Here the problem concerns a mode of description and explanation rather than a confusion between two terms. All too often, there is a tendency to treat social interaction as a product, caused by the behavior of individuals. Hence, especially in social psychology and psychology, emotion and behavior are treated solely as traits of individual organisms. In this view, the organization of social behavior is entirely reducible to the

patterning of individual emotions and behaviors when animals interact
(cf. Krimerman 1969: part 7, Campbell 1965, 1972).

Obviously, there are some phenomena which are adequately described
in this way, just as sometimes emotions not only precede behavior but
can be shown to 'cause' it. But equally evident are cases in which social
organization is a 'cause' of individual emotions and behaviors (cf. chapter
6.2 below). We can all think of circumstances in which our own behavior
has been conditioned if not determined by the social roles in which we
find ourselves. And who does not know of individuals who were transformed by putting on a policeman's uniform or sitting behind a bureau-
crat's desk? The sociologist's concept of 'roles' (e.g. Levy 1952) – by
illuminating the way individual behavior is functionally adapted to the
needs of social structures – is as relevant to human ethology as the
psychologist's concept of 'emotion'.

The relation of social organizations to individual behavioral and emotional repertoires is therefore a scientific question, not a postulate. Just as
population genetics deals with a different level of phenomena from the
mapping of gene loci on individual chromosomes, so the organization of a
society is a systematic level which cannot be automatically equated or
reduced to individual behaviors and emotions. To be sure, particular
aspects of individual behavior or emotion may play a causal role in the
emergence and maintenance of social structure – or be functional adaptations to sociological patterns. But there is no reason to assume, as a
general rule, that the causal process always flows from the individual to
the group. Indeed, such a presumption echoes the social contract theory
of political theorists in the tradition of Hobbes, Locke, and Rousseau
(Masters 1977) – and if treated as a natural law, easily takes on an
ideological component.

II. The advantages of conceptual clarity: three typical errors in human ethology

To this point, the concepts of cause, function, emotion, behavior, and
social organization have been briefly distinguished. Even without universally accepted definitions of these five ideas, it should be clear that the
phenomena described by any one of them cannot be 'reduced' to the
others. Causal processes cannot be reduced to (or fully explained by) their
functional consequences. Functional adaptations cannot be reduced to
(or fully explained by) their causes. Emotions cannot be reduced to
objectively observable behaviors, to causal processes producing

behavior, or to social patterns of the group. Behavior cannot be reduced to subjectively felt emotion, to the causal processes eliciting it, or to the social organization in which it occurs. And social organization cannot be reduced to (or fully explained by) individual behavior or emotion, to causal processes, or to functional consequences.

This is an exceptionally 'messy' conclusion. On the one hand, human ethology – like all sociobiology – attempts to establish relationships between these five analytical concepts. And on the other, no one set of relations, however promising it may seem, is likely to generate a single and logically coherent explanation of the others. The global process of evolution is, by its very nature, capable of generating different consequences from similar factors – and similar consequences from different ones.

Biology thus seems to be a science in which the logic of reductionist explanation is only partially satisfactory. To be sure, I may be wrong. But the onus is on the reductionist to prove his theory, since all prior attempts in this direction seem empirically inaccurate. To demonstrate this point, let us reconsider three typical errors which have beset the extension of sociobiology and ethology to human aggression, fear, and attachment.

1. Confusion between functional and causal analysis

It has been argued that a distinction between causes and functions is necessary if one is to avoid confusion. Nowhere is this more evident than in discussions of aggression, fear, and attachment. As has already been remarked, the controversy triggered by the popularized works of Ardrey and Lorenz has rested on a mutual misunderstanding. Critics assume that aggression was being treated as a cause, whereas without genetic or neurological data all that can scientifically be proposed are functional analogies. Hence, when critics have denied that complex learned human behavior can be 'reduced' to animal instinct, they are quite right on the level of causal analysis – but also quite beside the point. And when human ethologists have replied that complex human behavior must be understood within a fundamental 'biogram' analogous to those of primates (Count 1967, Tiger and Fox 1971), they are quite right on the level of functional explanation – but cannot be understood without distinguishing between cause and function.

A first advantage of conceptual clarity is therefore negative. It is important to emphasize what functional analysis in human ethology is *not*. For example, when studying the role of aggression in social bonding, data from primates and other vertebrates can usefully be compared to human experience (e.g. Kaufman 1974). But since such comparisons do not rest on a complete examination of causal processes in every species considered, it need not follow that human emotions or behaviors of attachment are produced by exactly the same mechanisms as those of other species (cf. chapter 9.2 below). Human learning and cultural tradition may often satisfy functions which, in other species, are to a larger degree under genetic control.

For example, cultural symbols – whether verbal (words) or non-verbal (flags, insignia, etc.) – often serve as key stimuli or releasers among humans, yet such admittedly variable artifacts can have functional analogies to what Lorenz called 'innate releasing mechanisms' in other species. Human ethologists can therefore avoid a good deal of misunderstanding if they make it clear that their hypotheses do not involve causal reductionism, and are actually inconsistent with it. Conversely, social scientists must soon recognize that their categories of analysis – which seem unique when narrowly defined as causal variables – actually rest on functional concepts comparable to those of contemporary sociobiology and ethology.

Here, we are discussing functional aspects of aggression, fear, and attachment. By definition, this means that the precise causation of individual behaviors or emotions is not at issue. Aggressive behavior may be individually learned, socially transmitted, or genetically controlled – or a combination of all three – depending on the species and events being considered (cf. chapter 1.1 above). But the *functions* satisfied by such aggressive behaviors may be comparable – and, indeed, whenever we speak of adaptation and selection, we are at least implicitly making functional comparisons on this level (Masters 1976a).

2. Confusion between behavior and emotion

A second typical source of error in recent discussions of aggression, fear and attachment has arisen from confusion between emotion and behavior. Sometimes, these terms have behavioral referents: aggression is defined as violent behavior, such as killing or wounding conspecifics (e.g. chapter 5.2 below); fear as flight behavior or avoidance of danger; attachment as bonding behavior, whether male–female, mother–infant, or among peers. But at other times, the three basic terms are treated as emotions: aggression is defined as anger or competitive challenge directed toward conspecifics; fear as the mood or emotion of fright or withdrawal; attachment as feelings of love, friendship, or affection.

Insofar as emotion is a subjective feeling, obviously it is difficult to measure in others. Hence, both in research on humans and on other species, there is a tendency to seek behavioral correlates of emotion, such as non-verbal gestures (e.g. van Hooff 1969, Ekman, Friesen, and Ellsworth 1972, Ekman 1978). Although these motor coordinations can properly be treated as *signs* of emotional response, one must beware of popularized treatments that equate such signs of emotion with emotions themselves, not to mention with the entire range of behaviors associated with aggression, fear, or attachment (e.g. Morris 1977).

For example, the concept of displacement activity developed by ethologists of Lorenz's school (Lorenz 1970–1, Hass 1970) refers to motor coordinations which can be associated with different moods or emotions. When one primate male mounts another, we have learned to dissociate this behavior from sexual emotions, and to see its links with dominance relationships in the group; when a human politician kisses babies, we don't expect that he feels the same paternal emotions as a father kissing his own infant.

If emotions and behavior are confused, it is impossible to sort out the complex relationships between internal or felt states and externally observable behavior. Moreover, even in behavioral observation, the distinction is a useful reminder that components of a behavioral repertoire may be blended in a wide variety of combinations and permutations. In humans, not to mention rats and mice, virtually any motor coordination can apparently be conditioned; equally important, many internal states – once thought to be unconditioned responses – are also subject to behavioral regulation (Garcia, Hankins and Rusiniak 1974).

As a result, it is essential to distinguish precisely between emotional feelings or states, motor coordinations which signal them, and longer behavioral sequences which have a functional connection with emotions. Hitting or wrestling may be an action that results from anger and attack emotions when a complete sequence, generally identifiable as an aggressive interaction, takes place. But such 'aggressive' behaviors may take place without the corresponding emotions (as in pleasurable 'rough and tumble' play), just as aggressive emotions may arise without physical contact (as in each of us when 'containing' our 'anger' toward another).

Difficulties arise, of course, because the distinction between emotion and behavior is not always easy to make. For example, Ekman's studies of emotional display show how some facial and bodily gestures are cross-cultural signals of a given emotion. But the universal interpretation of a smiling face as signalling a happy emotion cannot be confused with a causal identity of smiling and happiness (Morris 1977); what adult has not learned to smile in order to disguise another emotion, be it fear, anger, or sexual desire?

An hypothesis concerning *emotions* of aggression, fear, or attachment thus cannot be tested solely by evidence derived from *behavior* – particularly if the test uses 'consummatory behaviors' which seem to the observer related to the corresponding emotions. Freudian psychologists would laugh at the argument that sexual desire is entirely cultural *because* ascetics have been known to die without experiencing sexual intercourse. Human ethologists have simply broadened the range of emotional and behavioral categories, showing that both emotion and behavior are normally composed of a number of components.

In studying aggression, fear, and attachment, this leads to two methodological complexities. Not only must one distinguish between emotion and behavior, but on either level it is to be expected that components of aggression, fear, and attachment will be combined in different ways, depending on the species and the event. As Desmond Morris argued long ago, for example, courtship behaviors in a wide variety of species can best be understood as mixtures of flight, attack, and mating components (Morris 1956). In much the same way, dominant humans as well as primates exhibit gestures which often include components associated with appeasement or subordination (e.g. Masters 1976b, Montagner 1977).

Again, therefore, we must focus on a negative conclusion. Findings related to emotion cannot be generalized to the corresponding behavioral sequences that 'seem' to 'go' together: insofar as aggression, fear, and attachment are used as functional categories, they cannot automatically be used to refer to emotions. Conversely, the emotions of aggression, fear, and attachment need not result in aggressive behavior, flight, or actual bonds with other individuals. Far from being a reductionist science, human ethology shows our behavior – and that of other species – to be far more complex than is commonly assumed.

3. *The reduction of social organization to individual behavior or emotion*

From the point of view of reductionist psychology, social behavior is the product of individual actions (Hull 1952, Skinner 1965). Such reductionism leads to an isolation of individual emotion and behavior from the social contexts in which it evolved and occurs. Hence behaviorist psychologists have devoted immense resources to very precise experimental designs, attempting to measure the way individual emotion and behavior is stimulated or conditioned – but until recently, have treated their research with little reference to the social causes and functions of individual responses in 'naturalistic' settings.

Such research methods often mask the adaptive functional consequences of individual behaviors of aggression, fear, and attachment. For example, in many primates, mothers respond aggressively to their maturing young; driven away from contact with the mother, the offspring engage in peer interactions which typically include a good deal of rough and tumble play, in which aggressive motor coordinations are frequently exhibited. In such sequences, the infant (and mother) often show a combination of aggressive, flight, and attachment behavior – and it is this *combination* which constitutes the socialization process in primates as well as humans.

It is misleading to treat aggression, fear, and attachment solely as individual emotions or drives which 'cause' the corresponding social behaviors of violence, flight, and bonding. There are complex and sometimes surprising relations *between* different kinds of emotion and behavior. For example, comparison between primate species has suggested the hypothesis that greater rejection of the young by their mothers is correlated with stronger bonds established by the young (Kaufman 1974). Here, then, the strength of attachment behaviors seems related to the aggressive behaviors of mothers toward their young (and the resulting frequency of the latter's flight from their mothers).

As these mother–infant interactions show, the behaviors that are usually classed as aggression, fear, or attachment are often closely interrelated in the social repertoire of a species. Moreover, at least some of these mixtures of aggression, fear, and attachment seem to reflect strategies of survival in response to the ecological setting. Hence Barash (1974), in a survey of the social behavior of marmots, has correlated different patterns of maternal rejection of the maturing young with the differences between the typical environments of Olympic marmots (who live in gregarious closed groups in high alpine meadows) and woodchucks (whose adults live as isolates in lowland forests and fields). As a similar range of differences within the intermediary yellow bellied marmot suggests, social patterns are often functional responses to the environment, and thus cannot be entirely reduced to traits of individuals taken in the abstract.

Once again, the first conclusion is essentially negative. Individuals are not atoms whose behavior is the sole factor generating social organization. Members of a single species sometimes behave differently in distinct environments, just as different species sometimes behave the same way if in similar settings. Moreover, social organization establishes a systematic level with its own constraints, at least some of which are impossible to reduce to evolutionary costs and benefits at the individual level. In terms of the equations of population genetics, for example, 'K selection' and 'r selection' are different variables – and species whose survival strategy emphasizes the one or the other will naturally tend to have quite different behavioral repertoires (Wilson 1975).

These general comments are directly relevant to the analysis of aggression, fear, and attachment. Behaviors described by these three terms often trigger social responses that are highly adaptive from a functional point of view (e.g. the primate mother's rejection of the young, leading to peer-group bonding and social maturation). In this case, does one say that social organization is caused by individual behavior – or that individual behavior is caused by social organization? Obviously, this is an impossible way of posing the problem (cf. Krimerman 1969: part 7). Social organization is not merely the product of individual emotions or behaviors, just as individual responses are not always narrowly determined by social structures.

III. A working hypothesis

To this point, my argument has been essentially negative. Precise use of the concepts of cause, function, behavior, emotion, and social organization can clarify many difficulties in human ethology and sociobiology. The conclusion that none of these five categories can be reduced to the others may seem trivial if not peevish. But this critical exercise makes possible a more positive statement in the form of a working hypothesis.

Broadly stated, I would suggest that aggression, fear, and attachment – both in emotion and behavior – can be traced in the social interactions of virtually all vertebrates. If so, aggression, fear, and attachment can be treated as components or building blocks of social organization. Just as genes are sequences of nucleotide bases, various patterns of social interaction could therefore be characterized as distinct combinations of these three categories of emotion and behavior.

Elsewhere, I have suggested that one can define a 'behavioral triangle' whose poles are attack, flight, and bonding (Masters 1976c). This triangle is illustrated in figure 1.[2] At each extreme is a form of behavior (or, in Lorenz's terms, a 'consummatory' action) associated with aggression (attack), fear (flight), and attachment (bonding or mating). But many other behaviors are mixtures of two or all three components. To cite but one crucial case, dominant individuals often approach subordinates with a mixture of aggressive and appeasement gestures. Indeed, over-emphasis on sporadic agonistic interactions has led some commentators to underestimate the mixture of attack, flight, and bonding components in the behavior of both dominant and subordinate individuals.

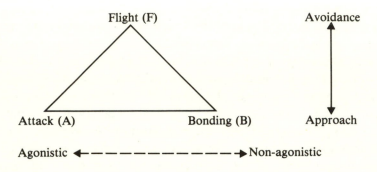

1. The behavioral triangle (from Masters 1976c).

Each behavioral action and sequence can thus be classified in terms of the weighting of attack, flight, and bonding components. If these three elements are denoted by their first letters (respectively A, F, B), for example, perhaps one could represent the dominant individual's behavior towards subordinates as BAf (where B indicates the primacy of bonding, A the strength of agonistic elements, and f the presence of some subordination or appeasement elements toward the avoidance end of the

[2] The generation of a triangular classification from two underlying and independent dimensions was suggested to me by Claude Lévi-Strauss' 'triangle culinaire' (Lévi-Strauss 1965). Although the dimensions used here – avoidance versus approach and agonistic versus non-agonistic behavior – may appear somewhat simplistic, they parallel Michael Chance's classification of primate social structures in terms of 'acentric' versus 'centric' and 'agonic' versus 'hedonic' attention structures (Chance 1976). The focus on flight, attack, and bonding should not, however, be treated as exhaustive; there are doubtless other dimensions of human behavior and emotion that equally deserve consideration. But given our stereoscopic vision humans seem adapted to explanations that transform a basic dualism (mind–body, being–becoming, subject–object) into a triadic classification like Freud's psychology (ego, superego, id), Plato's doctrine of the three parts of the soul (*Republic*, IV. 436a–444a), or the Hegelian dialectic. The deep structure of human thought may therefore be more complex than it at first appears (Masters 1977).

avoidance–approach dimension). Rather than speak of animals that are – or are not – 'aggressive', or 'fearful', or 'sociable', one would therefore focus on the relative saliency of attack, flight, and bonding in social behaviors. Hence various social roles could be defined in terms of *mixtures* of attack, flight and bonding behaviors, on the assumption that these elements do not always appear in pure or isolated form (cf. Goffman 1967, Chance 1976:326–7).

Previously, I have suggested how this approach might lead to a 'grammar' of behavior, in which complex social structures are described as constellations of roles, each of which is specified as a weighting of attack, flight, and bonding components (Masters 1976c). This approach was suggested by an economist's theory of human social behavior, according to which 'exit' (flight), 'voice' (agonistic challenge), and 'loyalty' (bonding) explain many of the observed responses of business firms, political parties, and states (Hirschman 1974). Hence my hypothesis may reflect a convergence of studies of animal behavior and of human social organization.

To be sure, the behavioral triangle of attack, flight, and bonding should not be confused with the emotions corresponding to these three poles of behavior. One could also develop an 'emotional triangle', whose poles of aggression, fear, and attachment define inner states or 'moods' of individuals. Like behaviors, emotions are often blends of two or more elements; like social interactions, emotional sequences often move from one combination to another in a predictable way. And since behaviors can be ritualized or conditioned to quite different emotional blends from those which originally (or 'normally') were associated with them, a complete specification of social organization would have to include both behavioral and emotional categorization.

When considered in detail, this will seem highly unwieldy. Even ignoring the emotional triangle, description of a complex social organization in terms of the behavioral triangle in figure 1 can seem lengthy and puzzling. For example, a structural description of the Soviet Communist Party using this schema might be:

$$A_{l\mapsto e}{}^{AB}{}_{l\to c}{}^{AB}{}_{l\mapsto m}{}^{B}{}_{l=m=c} + B_{m=l=c}{}^{AB}{}_{m\to c}{}^{FB}{}_{l\mapsto m} +$$

$$B_{c=m=l}{}^{FB}{}_{l+m\to c}{}^{A}{}_{c\to e}$$

(where the subscripts l, m, c, and e refer, respectively, to leaders, members of the Communist Party, citizens of the Soviet Union, and enemies designated by the leadership – for details, see Masters 1976c: note 31).[3] Granted that my notation is tentative and perhaps too complicated, there is no reason to presume that the social structure of an animal or human group should be more easily denoted than the structure of a hydrocarbon molecule.

The main point thus does not depend on questions of notation. Just as chemistry could hardly advance before substances were treated as compounds of basic elements, so human ethology is not likely to develop without a combinatorial approach to social organization. It is not yet possible to assess any particular approach to the combinations and permutations of aggression, fear, and attachment in both behavior and emotion. But there is good reason to believe that some such combinatorial scheme will be more economical than the ad hoc description of aggression, fear, and attachment as global or homogeneous terms. For example, it is not terribly useful to ask whether 'aggression' or aggressive behavior is 'natural'; since there is some aggressive component in most social interaction, it is far more important to know how these emotions and behaviors are related to other elements of an animal's response.

This way of approaching human ethology is closely parallel to Leyhausen's treatment of the 'balance' between fighting, fear, and attachment in other species. It leads to the conclusion that aggression, fear, and attachment provide the building blocks out of which individual behavioral repertoires and social structures are built. To be sure, this is a very broad functional consequence – so much so, that at first it will not seem very helpful. But remember: this functional explanation does not presume to provide a causal analysis like Leyhausen's 'relative hierarchy of moods'. What, then, have we accomplished by the hypothesis that all social organization is composed of a complex sequence of behavior and emotion, each stage of which combines aggression, fear, and attachment?

IV. A trivial conclusion: is aggression natural or cultural?

To begin with, the approach suggested here helps answer some frequently debated issues that are essentially trivial. Foremost among these questions is the old nature–nurture controversy: is aggression innate or acquired? Is sociability or bonding among humans natural or a cultural

[3] Discussion of this paper indicated that some readers took this *description* as a causal explanation. Nothing could have been further from my intention. Indeed, I am far from assuming that the *only* major categories of social behavior are flight, aggression, and bonding. For example, Kummer's paper (chapter 6.1 below) has convinced me that monitoring or attending to others is a vital factor in all social behavior – yet one that is not

artifact? Such questions can now be shown to resemble the impossible query: 'Is it longer to New York or by train?'

Consider aggressive emotions and behavior. Aggression is a *natural* component in human emotion, just as agonistic interaction is a *natural* component in human social behavior: apart from competitive rivalry, even sexual behaviors or submissive responses often have an aggressive element blended in them. Aggression is a *cultural* product in both emotion and behavior: cultures develop different combinations of aggression, fear, and attachment, producing societies with highly different frequencies of overtly competitive or hostile interactions. And aggression is a product of *individual life history*: within the range of cultural norms, personal experiences often reinforce aggressive emotions or behaviors for some, and redirect or extinguish them in others.

The nature–nurture controversy deals with a causal question. But aggression, fear, and attachment are functional categories, used to compare different species. And if functional categories cannot be 'reduced' to causal processes, is it any wonder that attempts to do so often founder? Yet as soon as these levels of analysis are distinguished, one can study the way different organisms acquire the information concerning appropriate objects and modes of behavior (e.g. chapters 7.1, 7.2, 8.2, 10.1 or 10.2 below). And once this causal question is distinguished from functional analysis, it is not hard to show that natural and cultural explanations of aggression, fear, and attachment can *both* be correct.

While perhaps interesting for some, this conclusion is essentially trivial. Leading biologists have been insisting for a generation that the nature–nurture dichotomy was no longer of the primary importance generally given it (Dobzhansky 1955). To be sure, social scientists have been slow to get the message. But since this is a phenomenon of interdisciplinary lag, frequently observed in the sociology of knowledge, it cannot generate a theoretically interesting problem for the emerging field of human ethology.

V. A non-trivial conclusion: the functional consequences of unnatural cultural patterns

The non-reductionist position set forth here thus leads to the admission

simply reducible to the three components of the behavioral triangle in figure 1. All that the above discussion claims is that social behavior seems difficult to *describe* without including *at least* the categories of attachment, flight, and bonding. Addition of further components would only strengthen my argument that a reductionist approach to complex social organization is not likely to succeed.

that natural and cultural explanations of human behavior are necessarily overlapping. The natural tendencies of human beings – whether deduced from comparison with primates and other vertebrates, or elaborated from analysis of the hominid life-way – presuppose if not require cultural variability from one population to another (see chapter 2.2 above). But this means that natural functions are fulfilled in our species by behavioral repertoires which have been modeled and transmitted by cultures (chapter 1.1 above).

It follows that ethology or sociobiology cannot say what is 'natural' for humans. Indeed, philosophers have long enjoyed the practice of negating generalizations about human behavior by discovering a single counterexample. Adequate for causal analysis, this procedure is not sufficient at a functional level – but it does remind us of the immense cultural variability of our species. Put another way, functional conceptions like 'inclusive fitness' can explain a multitude of sins – and for this very reason do not establish any *one* way of life as more 'natural' than all the others.

This apparently limited role of human ethology has, however, a converse. Ethology or sociobiology may not be able to say what is 'natural' – but it can specify combinations of behavior and emotion that are likely to be unstable and hence 'unnatural'. Although an individual can fast, a species which has no means of eating, drinking, or otherwise gaining nourishment is unlikely to persist. Similarly, it is unlikely that basic functional categories of behavior and emotion could disappear entirely from human social life. And wherever we discover causal processes that have been unchanged for millennia, it can be presumed that cultural practices which reverse species-specific traits only do so at the cost of behavioral or emotional tension elsewhere.

It seems highly unlikely, for example, that aggression, fear, or attachment – either at the behavioral or the emotional level – could be permanently eliminated from a human culture without unexpected negative consequences. Bonding, particularly between mother and infants, may be radically reduced if not eliminated among a people like the Ik. But even if anthropologists could not account for the historical pressures leading to this unpleasant result, human ethologists can suggest the functional disadvantages of the resulting social organization (e.g. difficulty in adopting complex technologies requiring a reliable form of social cooperation). In a functional sense, therefore, the Ik could be said to be 'unnatural' – even if the evolutionary and historical factors producing their culture are quite 'natural' and explicable.

Aggression, fear, and attachment thus seem to be very much part of human nature, just as they are part of the natural repertoire of other species. Our ways of combining the emotions and behaviors related to these three concepts are widely variable, but these variations are not without constraints. And since these limitations are often functional, the human ethologist can suggest and perhaps even predict difficulties which will arise when cultures attempt to eradicate aggression, fear, or attachment – or to exaggerate and expand one or more of these elements of emotion and behavior.

This conclusion is far from trivial. On the contrary, it has both theoretical and ideological consequences. Theoretically speaking, it indicates how the emerging field of human ethology can utilize existing work in the social sciences, which need not be rejected merely because it is focused on historical or cultural variables. Since most such work is descriptive or historical, it adds richness to our understanding of the complexity of human societies, and reminds us of the often unexpected results of relatively minor changes in behavior. From the point of view of human ethology, we should not be surprised that almost anything can have a noticeable impact on almost anything else in a human culture.

Ideologically, the consequences are even more significant. If all animal social organization combines elements of aggression, fear, and attachment, none of the three can be eliminated with impunity. On the contrary, human life – like that of other primate species – reflects complex balances between different emotions and behaviors. A political or social movement which promises to go beyond these natural tensions, for example by eliminating one or more of the basic manifestations of the behavioral triangle, is thus 'unnatural' in the particular sense used here – and as such likely to be an impractical or imprudent extension of ideological belief.

For example, dreams of a society with absolutely no element of aggression have often led to the reality of totalitarianism. Ironically enough, totalitarian societies tend to be highly aggressive and violent (both to external enemies and internal dissidents). Moreover, in such regimes all interpersonal attachments – except those to the party, the leader, or the state – are undermined by such institutions as secret police, informers, and concentration camps. Hence totalitarian regimes generate obedience through generalized fear and terror, enforced by multiple agencies of repression.

No one who has studied the history of our century would be so foolish as to say that totalitarian regimes are a natural impossibility: experience has shown them to be all too real. But no one who has the freedom to think and express his scientific findings can fail to admit that there is something unnatural about such social organizations in a primate like *Homo sapiens*. After living in small cooperative bands for over 3.5 million years, the mixture of aggression, fear, and attachment to which our species is functionally adapted is twisted and tortured by mass totalitarianism.

This example suggests that human ethology can confront political problems as well as those of early infancy or non-verbal communication. Although sometimes charged with ideological 'conservatism', in fact the approach of human ethology suggests the wisdom of traditions of compromise that are not associated with any party or movement. To be sure, we must expect extremists to attack this new field. In particular, utopians who actively seek heaven on earth, whether through revolution from below or state action from above, have good reason to detest those scholars who remind them of the limitations of humanity.

Comments on papers by Leyhausen and Masters

Functional aspects of aggression, fear and attachment in anthropological perspective

DEREK FREEMAN

By far the greatest contribution that anthropology has made to our understanding during the last century or so has been to establish the fundamental significance of the phenomenon of culture, and to demonstrate that the possession of an elaborately structured culture is a definitive characteristic of all known human populations.

This major advance was achieved mainly during the first four decades of this century, and frequently in the face of obdurate opposition from the biological determinists of the day. It is now commonplace, however, for well-informed evolutionary biologists to accept fully the profound and pervasive significance of culture in human history and action.

Many examples of this acceptance could be cited. C. H. Waddington, for example, in discussing 'the human evolutionary system' in 1975, wrote:

the salient feature about man – perhaps one might say that it is his defining characteristic – is that he has developed, to an enormously higher degree than is found in any other species, a method of passing information from one generation to the next which is alternative to the biological mechanism depending on genes. This human information-transmitting system is, of course, the process of social learning. This gives man a second evolutionary system superimposed on the biological one, and functioning by means of a different system of information transmission. (1975:288)

285

This 'second evolutionary system', or culture, as an anthropologist would say, is exosomatic, to employ Lotka's term (1945:188), and its main characteristics, as Medawar (1976:502) has pointed out, are:

Firstly, that it is Lamarckian in form; that is, what is invented or learned is passed on at once, and becomes part of the cultural heritage, this transfer being cumulative;

Secondly, cultural evolution is mediated through non-genetic channels; that is, it is carried mainly in symbolic systems; and

Thirdly, it is reversible.

As Dobzhansky (1972:127) has observed, this 'second evolutionary system' is 'indisputably the most potent method of adaptation that has emerged in the evolutionary history of the living world'. Furthermore, it is through possession of this 'second evolutionary system' that the human species principally, and ever increasingly, differs from other animals, for our evolutionary history is now, to a markedly preponderant extent, taking place exosomatically, by means of the growth of ideas, values and other human creations in the cultural domain, or in World Three, to use Popper's term (Elders 1974:108).

In 1963, in the course of his presidential address to the American Anthropological Association, Washburn (1963:528) remarked that 'our species only survives in culture, and, in a profound sense, we are the products of the new selection pressures that came with culture'.

From about that time onwards, there was among anthropologists an increasing concern with the nature of the feedback relationships between the cultural and the biological, and it soon became evident that humans, in the course of their evolutionary history, had developed biologically based capacities both to sustain and gradually transform their cultural systems.

In this way, anthropologists were becoming increasingly attentive to the evolutionary significance of the cognitive powers of *Homo sapiens* – cognition (in its broad dictionary sense) having to do with 'knowing or perceiving or conceiving'. Thus, in 1969, Washburn concluded his essay on 'The evolution of human behaviour' with these words:

Human evolution has produced a species in which learning, choice, and technical skills are developed more than in any other species and in which the adaptation is linked with slow growth and the long-continued care of growing individuals. The human way of life maximizes adaptation through awareness and choice, and these abilities depend on human biology.   (1969:188)

Kroeber, who, probably more than anyone else, was responsible for the recognition of the cultural dimension in human evolution, once defined a culture as being 'a way of habitual acting, feeling and thinking channeled by a society out of an infinite number and variety of potential ways of living' (1949:262). As Kroeber's definition suggests, every human culture as 'a cumulative selection from the spectrum of human possibility' (to use the words of Professor R. M. Keesing) stems from acts of imagination and choice, which, in the course of history, have been taken up, through social learning, by the members of a society.

Anthropology, then, has no alternative but to concern itself with the cognitive systems in terms of which almost all human behaviour is patterned. This, however, should cause no surprise to well-read evolutionary biologists, for as A. R. Wallace, co-discoverer of the process of natural selection, remarked, with the evolutionary emergence of *Homo sapiens* 'that subtle force we term *mind*, became of greater importance than . . . mere bodily structure' (1864:clxvii).

During the 1970s there has been a burgeoning of interest in the phenomenon of human consciousness (cf. Ornstein 1973), and an accompanying concern with the intentionality of human action (cf. Pribram 1976). So Harré and Secord view human beings as 'conscious social actors', capable, to a significant degree, of controlling their actions and commenting intelligently upon them (1972; cf. also Reynolds 1976). Dember recorded that psychology had 'gone cognitive' (1974); and Donald Griffin has cogently argued the case for a cognitive ethology (1976).

And so, the 'Naked Ape' who strutted through the pages of the mid-1960s, has, with the advent of biofeedback, the consciousness revolution and the emergence of effective techniques of self-regulation, begun to take on the persona of William Blake's Mental Traveller.

I note these developments because they are, in my judgment, crucially important indicators of a changing environment of understanding which is now taking place.

In the mid-1960s, persuaded of the pertinence to anthropology of the insights of ethology, I spent two years in the Samoan Islands with a community whose language, culture and history were very well known to me, using the method which, in chapter 9.2 below, Dr Judy Dunn has commended to us: that of 'sustained observation' in a 'normal habitat'. As a result of these and subsequent researches, I remain persuaded of the basically important contribution of ethology to a unified science of man, while, at the same time, being more cognizant than ever that, when it comes to humans, ethological study cannot, with any scientific justification, be divorced from cultural context, or from the self-awareness and intentionality by which human action is characterized.

I thus find myself in very much the same intellectual position as Dr Dunn, who, in chapter 9.2 below writes (p. 630): 'Humans are cultural creatures . . . Patterns of social behaviour, even with a very young baby, are part of a culture, and the idea that there is a biological pattern of relationships which can be divorced from culture is misleading.' She also comments (p. 637): '*Action* involves the idea of intentionality; whether or not it is possible to describe the behaviour of animals in a way that does not imply interpretation, there is no way of describing human behaviour without implying interpretation of it.' It is from this intellectual position then that I shall be commenting on the papers of Professors Leyhausen and Masters.

In the theoretical prologue to his paper, in discussing the processes of phylogenesis and ontogenesis, Professor Leyhausen states that 'the environment can never add something to the individual *potential*; it can only modify what is already provided for in the blueprint' produced by phylogenesis. This statement may well hold for infra-human animals, but I would question if it is true for humans. As I have already noted, it is characteristic of human populations that they possess elaborately structured cultures, and in the process of enculturation human individuals very definitely acquire behavioural, cognitive and other characteristics which distinguish them markedly from the individuals of other cultures.

Pointing out that evolution 'has furnished all vertebrates with the behavioural equipment of fighting, fleeing and socialising', Professor Leyhausen goes on to present an analysis, for the cat, of the 'components of behaviour employed by cats in the context of the subsystems of fighting, withdrawal and attachment according to their respective functions'. This analysis bears on issues in the theory of motivational systems in animal ethology that will, I feel sure, be of great interest to specialists in this field.

It is beyond my competence as an anthropologist properly to assess Professor Leyhausen's analysis, but I hope others may be able to explicate the relevance of Professor Leyhausen's model to the understanding of human behaviour. Unfortunately, Professor Leyhausen does not present us with any accounts of actual human behaviour of the kinds under discussion. Instead, we are assured that 'of all the existing theories of behaviour' of which Professor Leyhausen knows, 'ethological theory is the only one which can be built into a comprehensive "general theory of behaviour" without strain in part or in toto'. For my part, I would much prefer to be treated to an analysis of actual human behaviour in a series of fully documented cultural and historical situations.

I next turn to Professor Masters' paper. In its first part he stresses the need for conceptual clarity in our thinking about human behaviour. This, I suppose, is an ideal that none of us would wish to deny. Again, I fully accept Professor Masters' conclusion that the five concepts he discusses – function, cause, emotion, behaviour and social organization – ought not to be further reduced.

I would, however, like to comment briefly on the definition he offers, on p. 266), where function (a term of central importance to part II of this book) is made to refer to 'presumed selective advantages (functional adaptations) which might explain why the observed traits have evolved', with the flight of birds being given as an example.

This definition, it seems to me, is too narrowly biological in its emphasis to be useful in discussing most aspects of human action. Indeed, this emerges in Professor Masters' own paper when (on p. 271) he makes a reference to how individual behaviour, through the adoption of roles, is 'functionally adapted to the needs of social structures'. Here, function is being given a meaning virtually identical to the well-known usage of Radcliffe-Brown (1935:397), for whom function referred to 'the contribution which a partial activity makes to the total activity of which it is a part'.

My own preference, when it comes to the analysis of human action, is for the usage given in the *Dictionary of the social sciences*, compiled by Gould and Kolb (1964) under the auspices of UNESCO, where (p. 277) function is viewed as 'a consequence of some kind, of the existence and/or action (or motion) of persons or things, including . . . intangible items such as cultural patterns, group structure and attitudes'. I shall presently take this viewpoint in discussing some functional aspects of aggression, fear and attachment in Samoan society.

First, however, I must comment on the 'working hypothesis' of §III of Professor Masters' paper. It is Professor Masters' hypothesis (p. 280) that 'all social organization' as well as 'individual behavioral repertoires' are 'composed of a complex sequence of behavior and emotion, each stage of which combines aggression, fear, and attachment'. Together with this hypothesis Professor Masters presents a 'behavioral triangle', with attack, flight and bonding as its points, and then, using only these three concepts, a 'structural description' of the Soviet Communist Party.

At this juncture, I must confess to a niggling uncertainty as to whether or not Professor Masters is being entirely serious in featuring such a starkly simplified view of human behaviour in a paper entitled 'Beyond reductionism'. If he is serious, we here have, it seems to me, a telling example of the length to which a fervently ethological approach to human action can go.

A cursory glance at any competent survey of human psychology will show that the springs of human action are immensely more diverse than Professor Masters' triad of attack, flight and bonding; including, among other things, a concern with ethical values, as Waddington (1960) and others have made clear. Indeed, when I first encountered Professor Masters' 'behavioral triangle' I found myself contrasting its constricted form with the expansive range of Erik Erikson's schedule of the basic human virtues, first published in 1961.

In his illuminating paper 'The myth of the framework', Karl Popper (1976) recommends that we should compare the consequences of different intellectual frameworks. I shall merely comment that, in my judgment, Professor Masters' hypothesis is so limited in its scope as to have ideological consequences which are gravely distorting of fundamentally important aspects of the human condition.

In the few pages that remain to me I would like to present a succinct account of some of the functional relationships of aggression, fear and attachment as they exist in the society of the Samoans of western Polynesia. In so doing may I note that there are also very many other facets to Samoan social behaviour.

I shall begin by noting that an attachment between infant and mother (of the kind that has been described by Bowlby) is to be found among the Samoans. Recognizing the existence of this attachment, let me very briefly describe the way in which its character is shaped by the aggression and fear which have become endemic to Samoan culture.

Samoan culture is extremely authoritarian, its most lauded values, respect and obedience, being secured by a heavily punitive regime both within the family and within village communities.

The physical punishment of infants for acts of disobedience begins at about the end of the first year, continues throughout childhood, and, sometimes, into adulthood. Indeed, I once witnessed a chief (aged fifty-three) heavily beating his thirty year old daughter (who was about seven months pregnant) with a coconut frond midrib, for having failed to prepare food for him.

The beating of children is commonly heavy, and sometimes maiming, and takes a culturally patterned form. Thus, despite the severity of the punishment, the child is not permitted to express emotion. Should he persist in crying, additional punishment is inflicted, with shouts of 'Have done! Have done!', until the child, sitting with legs crossed, is physically coerced into stifling the expression of his feelings.

When I subsequently talked to children about how they felt about this kind of treatment, it was clearly evident that they experienced punishment as an attack, and, while being unable to flee, were suffused with fear. Further, they would sometimes confess to me feelings of intense anger and hatred towards their punishing mothers. So, while outwardly expressing nothing but respect and obedience, children of six or seven years would, when I afforded them the opportunity, depict the mothers to whom they were intensely attached as terrifying and threatening monsters. Figure 1 is an example in which a six year old girl depicts her mother as a *sau'ai*, or ogress, with her breast milk turning into child-devouring snakes. Samoan folklore, as this drawing indicates, is inhabited by towering and ferocious ogresses, with staring eyes and lolling tongues, who tear their victims apart as they devour them.

As the Samoans themselves recognize, the function of aggression and fear in their culturally patterned punitive treatment of misbehaving children is to produce highly respectful attitudes of mind towards chiefly and other authority. We are, they say, above all else a God-fearing people.

It must also be reported, however, that the attainment of these ends, through the use of aggression and fear, has, for all social attachments, accompanying consequences of a severe kind. The relationship between parents and children, in particular, is characterized by high ambivalence and tension; there is a general lack of trust, and deceptive behaviour is pervasive. Again, throughout Samoan society openly aggressive behaviour is exceedingly common, for its members tend to resort to direct attack on others in contention situations, even when the issues are of minor consequence.

My purpose in directing attention to these functional aspects of aggression, fear and attachment in Samoan society is to make the point that the ways in which aggression and fear enter into the social behaviour of human groups cannot be adequately understood in exclusively biological terms. In other cultures very well known to me as, for example, that of the Iban of Borneo, children are virtually never punished, and the characteristics I have described for Samoa are conspicuously absent.

The anthropological evidence, then, inescapably leads us to the conclusion that, in the case of *Homo sapiens*, the functional significance of aggression and fear in the attachment behaviour of groups is primarily the consequence of the social values which have become a part of their cultures in the course of their human histories.

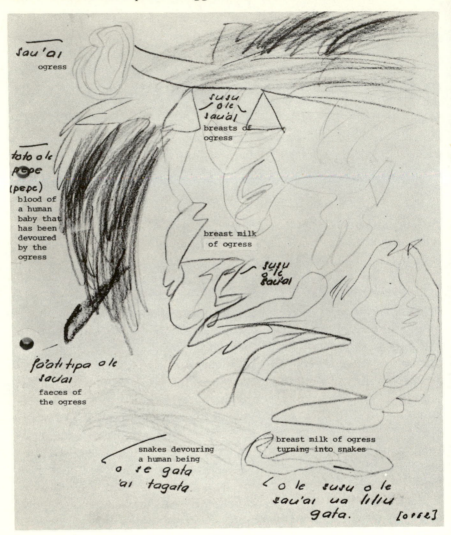

1. Drawings made by a six year old Samoan girl, in Samoa, western Polynesia, on 15 June 1966. The interpretations are those of the girl herself. The original drawing, which is in colour, is in the possession of the author.

Furthermore, these social values, being, in the end, socially sanctioned choices, are obviously susceptible to human agency, and so open to modification by wise and technically effective human action.

In the light of this evidence we are able to envisage the prospect of a scientifically based understanding that will promote the deliberate re-formation of human values and behaviour.

This, interestingly enough, is very much in accord with the kind of ethology of which John Stuart Mill conceived in 1843, and which, with exactitude, he defined as 'the science of the formation of character', it being Mill's view, as it is mine, that 'We are exactly as capable of making our own character, *if we will*, as others are of making it for us.'

In recent years with the founding of such scientifically well-informed periodicals as *Biofeedback and Self-Control*, and *Consciousness and Self-Regulation*, John Stuart Mill's vision is becoming a reality.

May I conclude then by expressing the hope that ethologists, in study-ing human behaviour, will increasingly join those behavioural scientists who are exploring not 'the limitations of humanity', but the means whereby human beings may further develop their sapient powers.

R. D. MASTERS: REPLY TO FREEMAN'S COMMENTS

The convergence between my paper and that of Paul Leyhausen was rather surprising. For example, we both independently cited the same paper by Morris (1956) as an indication of the combinations of the categories described as 'aggression, fear, and attachment'. For both of us, the specific behavioral actions and emotions grouped in these categories seem to be interdependent; hence none of the three can be reduced to the others.

Professor Freeman criticized my use of the 'triangle' of aggressive, flight and bonding elements. But then, when describing the Samoan case, he provided an excellent example of precisely the approach I had in mind. My main point was that some combinations of aggression, flight, and bonding – and especially attempts to suppress an entire category of behavior or motivation – may be 'unnatural' in a functional sense. As Freeman points out, among the Samoans the impact of aggressive behavior on mother–child bonds has 'accompanying consequences of a severe kind'.

Despite Freeman's implication, I never say that all aspects of a human culture can be described by the behavioral triangle, or that social organ-ization is reducible to it. My task was to relate the concepts of function, cause, aggression, fear, and attachment to social organization. And my argument is that these concepts are classificatory categories which do not seem reducible to primary elements. Of course, there are *other* categories which are also critically important in social life, such as values, intention, choice, and the like.

Freeman places particular emphasis on choice, citing Mill's view that 'We are exactly as capable of making our own character, *if we will*, as others are of making it for us.' In suggesting that the Communist Party of the Soviet Union could be described in terms of the categories of aggression, flight, and bonding, I was far from denying the reality of individual choice. But I did want to remind the meeting of the point well-stated by Bandura: 'The massive threats to human welfare are generally brought about by deliberate acts of principle rather than by unrestrained acts of impulse' (chapter 5.2 below, p. 356). It would be misleading in the extreme to conclude, from *individual* choice, that social groups have the same capacity or freedom to change 'if we will'.

In this case, as in others, there is a risk in slipping too readily from one level of analysis to another. On a number of occasions in our discussions – and in the literature – this sort of confusion has arisen. For crude purposes, I have found it useful to distinguish at least nine levels of analysis, based on three convenient cutting points in space (*individual*; *population*; *species*) and three in time (instantaneous cross-section or *structure*; short-term or reversible *behavior*; longer-term or irreversible change and *evolution*). While this schema (table 1) is an oversimplification, it reminds us that many of the categories discussed in earlier papers can neither be reduced to simpler levels nor used to generate, in a deterministic way, more complex levels.

One final example. Much has been said here of consciousness and intentionality in human behavior. It is generally assumed that our large brain, which makes possible these undeniable qualities, is unambiguously adaptive. For example, Freeman has mentioned Eccles' remark that the 'causal control potency' of the brain 'gives the phenomena of consciousness a use and a reason for being, and for having been evolved' (Eccles 1974:102). This is obviously a functional explanation – but it ignores the maladaptive consequences of the original mutation to larger hominid brain size.

It is too easily forgotten – especially by male scientists – that before the advent of modern medicine, childbirth was a frequent source of death for mother, fetus, or both. One cannot postulate the adaptiveness of large brains in human *adults* without considering the likelihood of a selection

Table 1. *Levels of analysis in human ethology*

Time	Space		
	Individual	*Population*	*Species*
Structure	Morphology (body and action pattern)	Group structure (or social structure)	Gene pool (breeding structure)
Function behavior	Action sequence	Interaction sequence	Behavioral repertoire
Irreversible change	Ontogeny	Tradition	Phylogeny

Source: Masters 1976a:88

pressure against this mutation at childbirth. Moreover, there is little in the known evolutionary record which correlates with the increase of brain size which occurred approximately 500 000 years ago: the hunting way, pebble tools, etc. can be traced back some three million years, whereas decisive evidence of symbolic use (e.g. cave paintings) is far more recent.

I have a very tentative hypothesis to offer (Masters 1978: appendix). Perhaps, in our evolutionary past, social cooperation slowly gave rise to the possibility that a female in childbirth could receive assistance if in difficulty. Such cooperation could of course counterbalance the selection pressure against a large brained fetus. In this way, the generally accepted advantages of larger brained adults – and therewith of consciousness – could eventually come into play.

This hypothesis, while impossible to prove, suggests that we might do well to revise the habitual way of relating our brain to our social life. Perhaps it is not true that humans have culture and social cooperation because we have big brains and consciousness. Rather, it could be that we have big brains and consciousness because we are social beings. Once again, it does not seem that complexity can be so readily reduced or explained in terms of any one of its components – even if that component is as awesome as the central nervous system of an individual human.

References

Ardrey, Robert. 1961. *African genesis*. New York: Atheneum.

Barash, David. 1974. The evolution of marmot societies: general theory. *Science*, *185*:415–20.

Biofeedback and Self Control. 1971–. Ed. T. X. Barber, J. Kamiya, N. E. Miller, D. Shapiro, J. Stoyva and L. B. DiCara. Chicago: Aldine Publishing Co.

Bowlby, John. 1969. *Attachment and loss*, vol. I, *Attachment*. London: Hogarth Press.

   1973. *Attachment and loss*, vol. II, *Separation, anger and anxiety*. London: Hogarth Press.

Campbell, Donald. 1965. Ethnocentric and other altruistic motives. In D. Levine (ed.), *Nebraska symposium on motivation*. Lincoln: University of Nebraska Press.

   1972. On the genetics of altruism and the counterhedonic components in human culture. *Journal of Social Issues*, *28*:21–37.

Chance, M. R. A. 1976. Social attention: society and mentality. In M. R. A. Chance and R. Larsen (eds.), *The social structure of attention*. New York: Wiley.

Consciousness and Self-Regulation. 1976–. Ed. Gary E. Schwartz and David Shapiro. New York and London: Plenum Press.

Count, Earl. 1967. The biological basis of human sociability. In M. F. A. Montagu (ed.), *Culture: man's adaptive dimension*. New York: Oxford University Press.

von Cranach, Mario (ed.) 1976. *Methods of inference from animal to human behaviour*. The Hague: Mouton.

Dember, William N. 1974. Motivation and the cognitive revolution. *American Psychologist*, *29*:161–8.

Dobzhansky, Theodosius. 1955. *Evolution, genetics and man*. New York: Wiley.

   1972. Unique aspects of man's evolution. In J. W. S. Pringle (ed.), *Biology and the human sciences*. Oxford: Clarendon Press.

Eccles, J. C. 1974. Cerebral activity and consciousness. In F. J. Ayala and T. Dobzhansky (eds.), *Studies in the philosophy of biology*. London: Macmillan.

Ekman, Paul. 1978. Biological and cultural contributions to body and facial movement. In John Blacking (ed.), *Anthropology of the body*. New York: Academic Press.

Ekman, Paul, Friesen, Wallace V. and Ellsworth, Phoebe. 1972. *Emotion in the human face*. New York: Pergamon.

Elders, Fons (ed.) 1974. *Reflexive water*. London: Souvenir Press.

Erikson, E. H. 1961. The roots of virtue. In Julian Huxley (ed.), *The humanist frame*. London: George Allen and Unwin.

Garcia, J., Hankins, W. G. and Rusiniak, K. W. 1974. Behavioral regulation of the milieu interne in man and rat. *Science*, 185:824–31.

Goffman, Erving. 1967. The nature of deference and demeanor. In *Interaction ritual*. New York: Anchor Doubleday.

Gould, J. and Kolb, W. L. (eds.), 1964. *A dictionary of the social sciences*. London: Tavistock Publications.

Griffin, Donald R. 1976. *The question of animal awareness: evolutionary continuity of mental experience*. New York: Rockefeller University Press.

Harlow, Harry P., Gluck, John P. and Suomi, Stephen J. 1972. Generalization of behavioral data between nonhuman and human animals. *American Psychologist*, 27 (August):709–16.

Harré, R. and Secord, P. F. 1972. *The explanation of human behaviour*. Oxford: Blackwell.

Hass, Hans. 1970. *The human animal*. London: Hodder and Stoughton.

Hempel, Carl G. and Oppenheim, Paul. 1969. The covering law analysis of scientific explanation. In Krimerman 1969: chapter 5.

Hinde, R. A. 1956. Ethological models and the concept of drive. *British Journal for the Philosophy of Science*, 6:321–31.

   1958. The nest-building behaviour of domesticated canaries. *Proceedings of the Zoological Society of London*, 131:1–48.

   1959. Unitary drives. *Animal Behaviour*, 7:130–41.

Hirschman, Albert O. 1974. *Exit, voice and loyalty*. Cambridge, Mass.: Harvard University Press.

von Holst, E. 1935. Alles oder nichts, Block, Alternans, Bigemini und verwandte Phänomene als Eigenschaften des Rückenmarks. *Pflügers Archiv*, 236.

van Hooff, J. A. R. A. M. 1969. The facial displays of the catarrhine monkeys and apes. In Desmond Morris (ed.), *Primate ethology*. New York: Anchor Doubleday.

Hull, C. L. 1952. *A behavior system*. New Haven: Yale University Press.

Jacob, François. 1977. Evolution and tinkering. *Science*, 196:1161–6.

Kaufman, I. C. 1974. Mother/infant relations in monkeys and humans: a reply to Professor Hinde. In N. F. White (ed.), *Ethology and psychiatry*. Toronto: University of Toronto Press.

Krimerman, Leonard I. 1969. *The nature and scope of social science*. New York: Appleton-Century-Crofts.

Kroeber, A. L. 1949. Values as a subject of Natural Science Inquiry. *Proceedings of the National Academy of Science*, 35:261–4.

Kummer, Hans. 1971. *Primate societies*. Chicago: Aldine-Atherton.

Lévi-Strauss, Claude. 1965. Le triangle culinaire. *L'Arc*, 26:19–29.

Levy, Marion J. Jr. 1952. *The structure of society*. Princeton: Princeton University Press.

Leyhausen, P. 1952. Theoretical considerations in criticism of the concept of the 'displacement movement'. In K. Lorenz and P. Leyhausen, *Motivation of human and animal behavior*. New York: Van Nostrand Reinhold, 1973.

1954. The discovery of relative coordination: a contribution toward bridging the gap between physiology and psychology. In K. Lorenz and P. Leyhausen, *Motivation of human and animal behavior*. New York: Van Nostrand Reinhold, 1973.

1955. Über relative Stimmungshierarchie bei Säugetieren. Paper given at the 3rd International Ethological Conference, Groningen.

1956. *Verhaltensstudien an Katzen*. Berlin: Verlag Paul Parey.

1965. On the function of the relative hierarchy of moods (as exemplified by the phylogenetic and ontogenetic development of prey-catching in carnivores). In K. Lorenz and P. Leyhausen, *Motivation of human and animal behavior*. New York: Van Nostrand Reinhold, 1973.

1974. The biological basis of ethics and morality. *Science, Medicine and Man*, 1:215–35.

Lorenz, K. 1937. Über den Begriff der Instinkthandlung. *Folia Biotheoretica Series B*, II: *Instinctus*: 17–50.

Lorenz, Konrad Z. 1966. *On aggression*. New York: Harcourt, Brace and World.

1970–1. *Studies in animal and human behavior*. 2 vols. Cambridge, Mass.: Harvard University Press.

1974. Analogy as a source of knowledge. *Science*, 185:229–34.

Lotka, Alfred J. 1945. The law of evolution as a maximal principle. *Human Biology*, 17:188.

Masters, Roger D. 1976a. Functional approaches to analogical comparisons between species. In von Cranach 1976.

1976b. The impact of ethology on political science. In Albert Somit (ed.), *Biology and politics*. The Hague: Mouton.

1976c. Exit, voice and loyalty in animal and human social behavior. *Social Science Information*, 15:855–78.

1977. Nature, human nature, and political thought. In Roland J. Pennock and John Chapman (eds.), *Human nature and politics – Nomos XVII*. New York: New York University Press.

1978. Of marmots and men: Animal behavior and human altruism. In Wispé 1978.

Medawar, Peter B. 1976. Does ethology throw any light on human behaviour? In P. P. G. Bateson and R. A. Hinde (eds.), *Growing points in ethology*. Cambridge: Cambridge University Press.

Mill, John Stuart, 1843. *On the logic of the moral sciences*. New York: Bobbs-Merrill Company, 1965.

Montagner, Hubert. 1977. Silent speech. *BBC2: Horizon*, 28 July.

Montagu, M. F. Ashley (ed.) 1968. *Man and aggression*. New York: Oxford University Press.

Morris, Desmond. 1956. The function and causation of courtship ceremonies. In *L'Instinct dans le comportement des animaux et de l'homme*. Paris: Masson.

1977. *Manwatching*. New York: Abrams.

Moyer, K. E. 1969. Internal impulses to aggression. *Transactions of the New York Academy of Sciences, Series 2*, 31 (February): 104–14.

Ornstein, Robert E. (ed.) 1973. *The nature of human consciousness*. San Francisco: W. H. Freeman and Co.

Popper, Karl. 1976. The myth of the framework. In Eugene Freeman (ed.), *The abdication of philosophy: essays in honor of Paul A. Schlipp*. Lasalle, Ill.: Open Court.

Pribram, Karl H. 1976. Self-consciousness and Intentionality. In Gary E. Schwart and David Shapiro (eds.), *Consciousness and self-regulation*, vol. I. New York and London: Plenum Press.

Radcliffe-Brown, A. R. 1935. On the concept of function in social science. *American Anthropologist*, 37:397.

Reynolds, Vernon. 1976. *The biology of human action*. San Francisco: W. H. Freeman and Co.

Skinner, B. F. 1965. *Science and human behavior*. New York: Free Press.

Tiger, Lionel and Fox, Robin. 1971. *The imperial animal*. New York: Holt, Rinehart and Winston.

Tinbergen, N. 1951. *The study of instinct*. Oxford: Oxford University Press.

von Uexküll, J. 1921. *Umwelt und Innenwelt der Tiere*. Berlin.

Waddington, C. H. 1960. *The ethical animal*. London: George Allen and Unwin.
   1975. *The evolution of an evolutionist*. Edinburgh: Edinburgh University Press.

Wallace, A. R. 1864. The origin of human races and the antiquity of man deduced from the theory of 'natural selection'. *Anthropological Review*, 2:clviii–clxxxvii.

Washburn, S. L. 1963. The study of race. *American Anthropologist*, 65:521–31.
   1969. The evolution of human behaviour. In J. D. Roslansky (ed.), *The uniqueness of man*. Amsterdam: North Holland Publishing Co.

Wilson, Edward O. 1975. *Sociobiology: The new synthesis*. Cambridge, Mass.: Harvard University Press.

Wispé, Lauren (ed.) 1978. *Altruism, sympathy, and helping behavior*. New York: Academic Press.

5. Neurobiological and psychological mechanisms of aggressive behavior

5.1. Anatomical pathways for attack behavior in cats

J. P. FLYNN, D. SMITH, K. COLEMAN AND
C. A. OPSAHL

This paper will consider the pathways associated with attack that descend from the forebrain and midbrain into the hindbrain. Even though ascending pathways exist, these will not be considered at length in this report.

Prior to the description of the anatomical pathways themselves, attack behavior in cats, the general anatomical procedure and an objection to it, as well as ways of determining the relevance of the anatomy to the behavior, will be presented.

Attack behavior

The particular behavior dealt with is quiet biting attack elicited by electrical stimulation of the brain (Wasman and Flynn 1962). This differs from the classical rage response which Hess (1928) first elicited, in that quiet attack lacks threat components, such as hissing, retraction of the lips, laying back the ears, and marked piloerection, which are prominent in the rage response.

Quiet attack is lethal, with a strong bite aimed usually at the back of the victim's neck (figure 1). The victims have customarily been anesthetized rats, but other cats may also be attacked. Most cats do not attack rats spontaneously. However, when a cat is stimulated electrically at appropriate sites in the hypothalamus or lower brain stem, the cat will attack a rat, bite its neck, and usually kill it. The cat's pupils are usually dilated, and moderate piloerection is often present. The cat selects its targets,

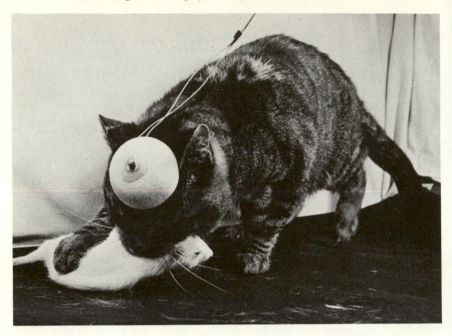

1. Quiet biting attack of a cat on a deeply anesthetized rat produced by electrical stimulation at a lateral hypothalamic site. Note crouched posture of cat, slight piloerection on back, positioning of attack object with right forepaw, and directed bite to rat's neck.

strongly preferring a rat to a comparable sized wooden or stryofoam block (Levison and Flynn 1965). Ordinarily it does not eat food or the rat it has killed (Flynn *et al.* 1970).

The terminal aspects of the behavior are a combination of reflexes that are present during the time of stimulation. These state-dependent reflexes include lunging at the rat (Bandler and Flynn 1971), striking it (Flynn, Edwards and Bandler 1971), placing a paw on it to position it (Bandler and Flynn 1972), positioning its own head to bite the rat, and the final act of biting (MacDonnell and Flynn 1966). The size of the receptive field for these reflexes varies with the intensity of the current to the brain, and at low intensities the effects elicited by stimulation of the hypothalamus or midbrain are usually more marked on the contralateral side than on the ipsilateral side.

Electrodes are implanted while the cat is unanesthetized, and capable of demonstrating the effects of stimulation. In cats that have had guides mounted on their skulls earlier, calibrated sterile electrodes are lowered step by step into the brain. The steps are less than a millimeter, frequently being of the order of a quarter of a millimeter. Monopolar and bipolar stimulating electrodes are used. The stimuli are biphasic constant current pulses lasting 2 msec. and delivered at 60 Hz in trains of 20 sec. or less. After suitable behavior is secured, the electrode is cemented in place. The behavior takes place during stimulation, occurs at a regular interval after the stimulation is started, and terminates with the end of stimulation. In the anatomical studies, ten additional trials are then given to describe the behavior elicited.

Anatomical procedures

The present anatomical studies differ from ordinary anatomical studies in that the sites from which attack can be elicited are the sites of interest rather than anatomically defined nuclei or regions which are of primary interest in anatomical studies.

Thus far two anatomical techniques have been employed. One is the Nauta stain or its modifications (Fink and Heimer 1967), which enables one to trace degenerating axons and terminals. The second method employs horseradish peroxidase (LaVail and LaVail 1972), and it enables one to determine the cells whose terminals or cut axons are in the region of the attack site.

The anatomical procedure which reveals degenerating fibers involves making a small lesion at the attack site, just sufficient to eliminate attack when the stimulating intensity is increased to twice its normal value. After three to ten days, the animal is killed and its brain perfused with 10% formalin. The brain is then removed, and frozen sections are cut and stained for degenerating fibers by modifications of Nauta's methods. From the site of the lesion one can trace degenerating fibers in an antero-grade direction. The lesion produces degeneration in fibers whose cell bodies were at the site of the lesion, and in fibers which originated elsewhere but pass through the site of the lesion. The injection of horse-radish peroxidase can reveal cells whose terminals or whose cut axons are in the area of injection. The general procedure is similar to that for making lesions, but a concentric bipolar electrode is used. After ten trials during which the behavior is described, the cat is anesthetized, placed in a stereotaxic apparatus, and the inner barrel of the bipolar electrode is removed. A calibrated pipette filled with a 33% solution of horseradish peroxidase in 0.1 M saline is lowered to the same place as the tip of the inner barrel, and the horseradish is ejected iontophoretically at 4 μA for 4 min. The cat is allowed to recover, and after 27 to 48 hours the cat is again anesthetized, and its brain perfused with 1% paraformaldehyde and 1%

gluteraldehyde. Frozen sections of the brain are cut, and the locations of the cells containing reaction products are determined with the aid of darkfield microscopy.

The fact that cut axons may take up the horseradish peroxidase, and the fact that degeneration takes place in fibers of passage are not a hindrance to the present work since electrical stimuli affect fibers as well as cells.

A major objection to tracing anatomical pathways from an attack site stems from the idea that the area immediately stimulated cannot be responsible for organizing the behavior since the cells and fibers in the immediate vicinity fire in accord with the rate of the stimuli and in hypersynchrony rather than at their natural rates.

The answer to this objection is that single units in the vicinity of the electrode that are directly driven are very few. Yung Huang and Flynn (1975) found that only 3.7% of the units in the hypothalamus were directly driven by the stimuli, and that units within 0.7 mm to 1.9 mm from the stimulating electrode were affected in the same way as units located within the range of 2.0 mm to 5.2 mm (figure 2). The rates of firing were also found to be within the rates of hypothalamic units responding to natural stimuli. In addition, the anatomical pathways revealed have led to investigations of previously unexplored sites which were found to yield attack.

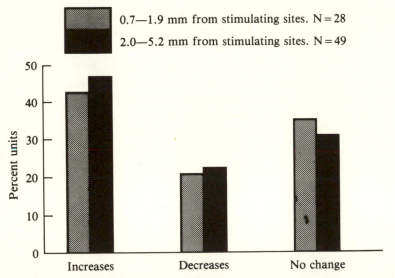

2. Percentage of single units in cat hypothalamus that increased, decreased, or showed no change in firing rates during simultaneous stimulation at hypothalamic attack sites that were 0.7–1.9 mm distant (striped bars) or 2.0–5.2 mm distant (filled bars).

Relationship of pathways to attack

The relevance of the anatomical pathways revealed by these methods cannot be assumed. At least three procedures can be used to determine their relevance.

One way is to explore the region in which the pathway terminates to see if attack can be elicited from it. For example, degeneration from hypothalamic attack sites terminated in the ventrolateral tegmentum of the midbrain. This region was explored with movable electrodes, and was found to yield attack. The site was not known previously to produce such results (Bandler, Chi and Flynn 1972).

A second way by which to verify the relevance of a pathway to attack is to implant two electrodes, one in the region from which the degeneration was originally obtained, the other in the region in which the degeneration terminated. Attack is elicited from each site, for example from the hypothalamus and from the ipsilateral midbrain. A lesion is then made at the midbrain site, and the effect of the lesion upon the hypothalamically elicited attack is assessed. The lesion eliminates or reduces the effects of stimulating the rostral hypothalamic attack site (Proshansky, Bandler and Flynn 1974).

A third way to verify the relevance of the anatomy to the behavior is to record single unit activity from these regions while the cat is attacking. Cats attack mice more frequently than they attack rats, and units whose locations are shown in figure 3 are ones that became active when the cat was viewing a mouse, approaching it, or striking at it. These are only fifteen units out of some 430 units recorded. While it is impossible to exhaust the controls, these fifteen units did not respond to any of the controls employed, while others responded to various controls or made no response (Opsahl and Flynn, in preparation).

In general, the relevance of the anatomy to the behavior cannot be assumed, but must be substantiated. In most of our cases this has consisted of eliciting attack at a given site.

Anatomical findings

Degeneration studies

Quiet attack sites in the hypothalamus have a tendency to occupy a dorsal position in the medial hypothalamus and move laterally towards a ventral position in the lateral hypothalamus.

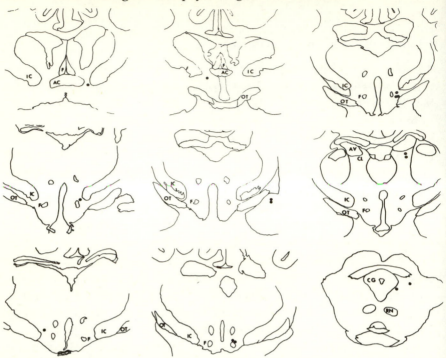

3. Anatomical locations of single units that selectively increased firing rates during components of naturally occurring quiet attack of an unrestrained cat on a mouse. In top right panel, cells responded when cat was approaching or striking mouse; in lower left panel cell responded when cat was pinning mouse with front paw; in middle right panel, cells responded when cat was 'searching' around an opaque partition for mouse. Cells in remaining panels responded when cat was viewing mouse. These cells did not respond when sensory (moving object, flashing lights, clicking noises, hand claps, odor of mouse urine, tactile stimulation on body, etc.) or motor (walking, turning head, dropping cat, etc.) controls were tested. AC = anterior commissure; AV = anterior ventral nucleus of the thalamus; CG = central grey; CL = central lateral nucleus of the thalamus; F = fornix; IC = internal capsule; OT = optic tract; RN = red nucleus.

Lesions at quiet attack sites produce degeneration in the lateral hypothalamus that descends caudally into the region ventral and lateral to the red nucleus, following the course of the medial forebrain bundle. From lateral sites, this is the primary pathway. From dorsal sites in medial hypothalamus, the degeneration takes the lateral path, but it also proceeds directly caudally into the central grey matter. A third pathway projects into the nucleus centralis medialis of the thalamus (Chi and Flynn 1971). The relevance of the ventrolateral tegmental pathway to attack was confirmed by the elicitation of attack from this site and by blocking hypothalamically elicited attack in the ventrolateral tegmentum (Bandler, Chi and Flynn 1972).

Degenerated fibers have been traced from lesions at attack sites in the lateral ventral tegmental area into the pons and medulla. The main findings were that degenerating fibers went into the immediate vicinity or actually into the motor nucleus, the principal sensory nucleus, and the spinal nucleus of the trigeminal nerve. Terminal degeneration could be found in the nucleus of the facial nerve and the spinal nucleus of the trigeminal nerve. Particles similar to those associated with terminal degeneration were found in the motor nucleus and the main sensory nucleus of the trigeminal nerve, but they were also found, although fewer in number, in the brains of two cats in which no electrodes or lesions were placed (Chi, Bandler and Flynn 1976).

The experimental animals had lesions which invaded the red nucleus which is known to project to the trigeminal sensory nuclei and to the facial nucleus. Against the possibility that damage to the red nucleus accounted for the findings is the poor correlation on the ipsilateral side between the degeneration in the rubrospinal tract and that in the other areas.

The projections from attack sites to the facial nucleus and the sensory and motor nuclei of the trigeminal nerve may be the anatomical substrate for the state-dependent reflexes of biting and for facial expression.

The lateral ventral tegmental area of the midbrain also projects to the central grey matter (figure 4). While sites yielding quiet biting attack have not been located along the entire course of the central grey matter, they have been found in the central grey matter at the level of the decussation of the brachium conjunctivum, and more rostrally in the region ventral and lateral to the central grey matter (Bandler 1975).

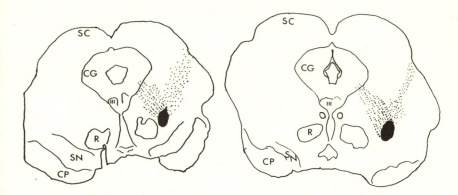

4. Coronal sections showing the lesions produced at quiet attack sites in the ventral tegmental area in two cats. Degenerated fibers were traced into the area of the central grey. CP = cerebral peduncle; F = facial nucleus; IC = inferior colliculus; R = red nucleus; SC = superior colliculus; SN = substantia nigra; III = third nerve.

308

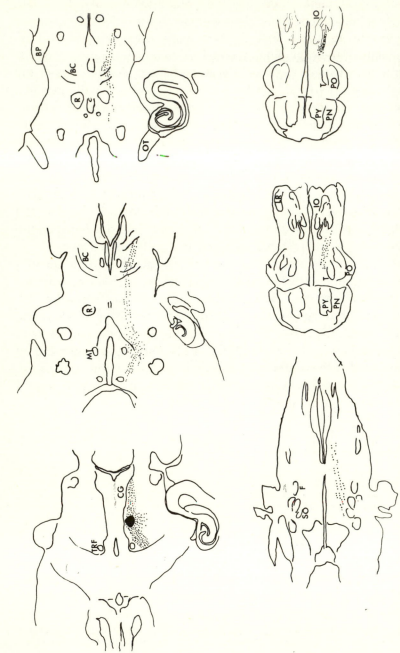

5. Horizontal sections showing lesion produced at a quiet attack site in the central tegmental field. Resulting degenerated fibers were traced rostrally into lateral hypothalamus. Degenerated fibers and terminals were found in the inferior olive. BC = brachium conjunctivum; BP = brachium pontis; IO = inferior olive; LR = lateral reticular nucleus; MT = mammilothalamic tract; PN = pons; PO = preolivary nucleus; PY = pyramidal tract; SO = superior olive; T = nucleus of the trapezoid body; TRF = retroflex bundle.

The degeneration resulting from a lesion at an attack site in the medial border of the central tegmental tract which lies ventral and lateral to the central grey matter illustrates a pathway that descends caudally to the region of the inferior olive (figure 5). Degeneration along this same pathway results from a lesion made at an attack site that is lateral to the decussation of the brachium conjunctivum, but impinges upon the brachium. This same pathway also results from a lesion at a more caudal attack site that invaded the brachium conjunctivum (figure 6), at the rostral pole of the nucleus reticularis pontis oralis.

The pathway embraces the parabrachial region, the paralemniscal region of the pontine tegmentum, proceeds ventrally and medially in the region of the superior olive, impinges upon the nucleus of the facial nerve and then proceeds to a region dorsal and lateral to the inferior olive (Coleman and Flynn, in preparation).

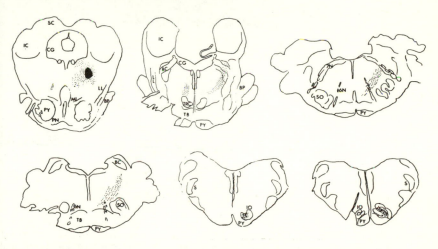

6. Coronal sections showing lesion produced at a quiet attack site in the parabrachial nucleus of the midbrain. Degenerated fibers were traced through the paralemniscal region and both degenerated fibers and terminals were found in the inferior olive. LL = lateral lemniscus; ML = medial lemniscus; S = spinal trigeminal tract; TB = trapezoid body; TRC = tegmental reticular nucleus; 6N = sixth nerve; 7N = seventh nerve.

The inferior olive itself contains terminal degeneration (figure 7). However, when electrodes have been put into the inferior olive, attack has not been elicited, but attack has been elicited from regions slightly rostral to the inferior olive and from a site lateral to the inferior olive. These data on attack sites at this caudal level are only preliminary.

An additional reason for being skeptical about the importance of the

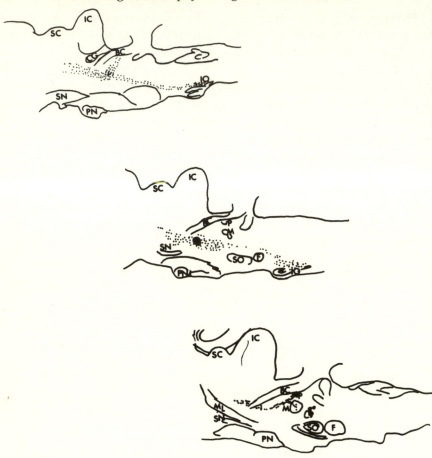

7. Sagittal sections showing lesion produced at a quiet attack site in the midbrain ventral to the brachium conjunctivum. Degenerated fibers were traced caudally to the level of the inferior olive, and a pathway of degenerated fibers was traced into the motor and principal sensory nuclei of the trigeminal nerve. M = motor nucleus of the trigeminal nerve; P = principal sensory nucleus of the trigeminal nerve.

inferior olive in attack behavior is the fact that attack elicited from this region is clearly guided by vision, and it is discriminate in character. This implies, on the basis of our earlier work, an influence on the visual system. Therefore it is likely that the behavior elicited at the level of inferior olive is mediated by pathways which ascend the brain stem. However, we have not done direct experiments, as yet, in which the effects of rostral lesions on attack elicited from more caudal sites have been demonstrated.

The major pathways suggested on the basis of the degeneration studies are summarized in figure 8. Table 1 provides sites at which degenerating fibers were found in individual cats.

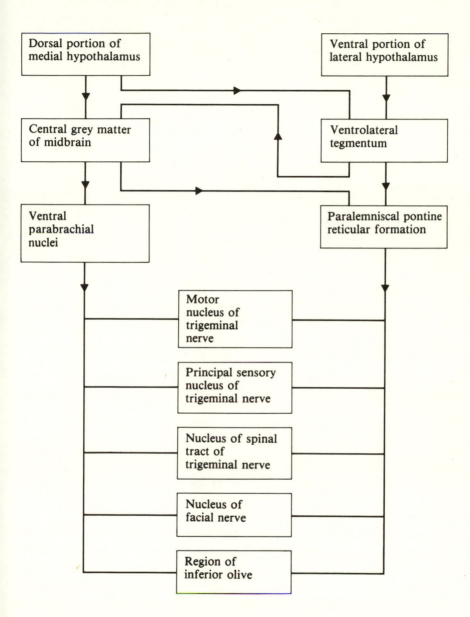

8. Descending neuroanatomical pathways implicated in quiet attack behavior on the basis of degeneration studies.

Table 1. *Common sites of degeneration from lesions at various attack sites in individual cats*

Cat number	06194	06114	06204	08214B	06175	01095	05275	07025	01075
Vicinity of inferior olive	Terminals found within the I.O.						Terminals found within the I.O.		
	+	−	⁓	−	NA	NA	+	+	NA
Medial and anterior to inferior olive	+	−	−	−	NA	NA	+	+	NA
Borders on Nucleus VII	+	+	−	−	NA	+	+	+	NA
Rostral and dorsal to superior olive	+	+	−	+	+	+	+	+	+
Paralemniscal pontine reticular formation	+	+	+	+	+	+	+	+	+
									Lesion is at this level
Nucleus of spinal tract of V	+	−	−	−	NA	NA	+	NA	+
Main sensory nucleus of V	+	−	−	NA	+	+	−	+	+
Motor nucleus of V	+	−	−	NA	+	+	+	+	+
Parabrachial region	+	−	−	+	+	+	+	+	+
Central grey	+	+	+	+	+	+	+	+	+

− no degeneration
+ degeneration
NA sections not available

Horseradish peroxidase studies

Cells have been located whose terminals and probably cut nerve fibers are at attack sites in the region of the parabrachial nuclei and in the paralemniscal region of the pontine reticular formation (Smith and Flynn, in preparation).

This method reveals more sites of origin and connections than were observed in the degeneration studies. In these last, degenerating fibers were not seen in pons and medulla unless lesions were made in the midbrain. In the case of injections made at attack sites in the region of the parabrachial nuclei or paralemniscal region, cells of origin were found as far rostral as frontal cortex.

The location of cells of origin are presented in figure 9. Those in the left

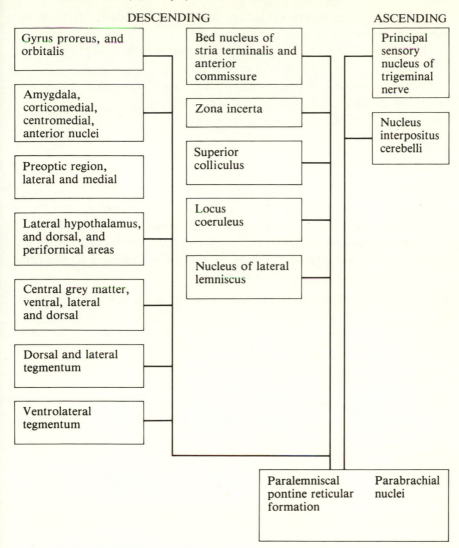

DESCENDING   ASCENDING

| Gyrus proreus, and orbitalis |
| Amygdala, corticomedial, centromedial, anterior nuclei |
| Preoptic region, lateral and medial |
| Lateral hypothalamus, and dorsal, and perifornical areas |
| Central grey matter, ventral, lateral and dorsal |
| Dorsal and lateral tegmentum |
| Ventrolateral tegmentum |

| Bed nucleus of stria terminalis and anterior commissure |
| Zona incerta |
| Superior colliculus |
| Locus coeruleus |
| Nucleus of lateral lemniscus |

| Principal sensory nucleus of trigeminal nerve |
| Nucleus interpositus cerebelli |

| Paralemniscal pontine reticular formation   Parabrachial nuclei |

9. Descending and ascending neuroanatomical pathways to parabrachial and paralemniscal attack sites revealed by horseradish peroxidase enzyme transport studies.

column are regions from which attack has either been elicited, or modulated. The second column in this figure denotes regions which either have not been explored or have not been associated with attack.

Table 2 shows the areas which have been found in individual cats to contain cells of origin. Some of the sites are in conformity with the findings of the degeneration studies and illustrate cells of origin in the central grey matter, and in the ventrolateral tegmentum.

The presence of cells of origin in the superior colliculus provides the possibility of visual guidance of attack behavior.

Another interesting finding indicates the possibility of direct trigeminal input into attack sites so that the act of biting could enter into the regulation of attack.

Ascending pathways

The data presented thus far deal primarily with pathways descending into the brain stem. The pathways were treated as motor systems or possibly modulators of some of the state-dependent reflexes mediated at brain stem or lower levels. However, ascending pathways go from the pons rostrally to the hypothalamus. It is not our intention to deny the

Table 2. *Sites of cells whose axons terminate in or traverse attack sites in the pons*

Cat number	12175	02106	03016	03166	05066	05076	05136
Gyrus proreus and orbitalis	NA	NA	NA	+	+	+	+
Amygdala, cortico-medial, centromedial, anterior	+	+	+	+	+	+	+
Preoptic region, lateral and medial	+	+	+	+	−	+	+
Lateral hypothalamus, dorsal and perifornical areas	+	+	+	+	+	+	+
Central grey matter, ventral, lateral and dorsal	+	+	+	+	+	+	+
Dorsal and lateral midbrain tegmentum	+	+	−	+	+	+	+
Ventrolateral midbrain tegmentum	−	−	+	+	+	+	+
Bed nucleus of stria terminalis and anterior commissure	+	+	+	+	+	+	+
Zona incerta	+	+	+	+	+	+	+
Superior colliculus	+	+	+	+	+	+	+
Locus coeruleus	−	+	+	+	+	+	+
Nucleus of the lateral lemniscus	+	+	+	−	+	−	+
Principal sensory nucleus of trigeminal nerve	+	+	−	−	+	−	−
Nucleus interpositus cerebelli	NA	NA	+	+	+	+	+

− cells not present
+ cells present
NA sections not available

possible influence of these ascending pathways. Injections of horseradish peroxidase into the hypothalamic attack sites demonstrated that cells of origin were located in the parabrachial nuclei, the nucleus of the lateral lemniscus, and the central grey matter, which also contained cells providing terminations at pontine attack sites. These regions with cells of origin to both hypothalamic and pontine tegmental attack sites could serve to integrate the entire axis from the hypothalamus to the medulla from which attack can be elicited. The axis would be constituted largely of pathways interconnecting various cell groups.

Possible significance for human ethology

What is the relevance of these findings to human aggression? The meager data available from human beings are in accord with the general findings in lower animals. However, these data are insufficient to establish the existence of mechanisms in man or in non-human primates similar to those in cats. Nonetheless, anatomists interested in the human nervous system have not been reluctant to incorporate anatomical findings from other animals into their accounts of the human nervous system.

   If one admits a neural basis for attack in man, or for eating, or for sexual behavior, the admission does not imply that the activities are uncontrollable. Eating, sexual behavior, and attack can be controlled, not only in human beings but even in cats. In fact, the cats upon which our research is based do not spontaneously attack rats or other cats. Man can and undoubtedly does exercise similar restraint.

5.2. Psychological mechanisms of aggression

ALBERT BANDURA[1]

Analysis of the determinants and mechanisms of aggression requires prior consideration of the phenomena the concept comprises. Differing conceptions of what constitutes aggression produce different lines of theorizing and research. Psychological theories of aggression have been largely concerned with individual physically injurious acts that are aversively motivated. In most of these accounts aggression is not only attributed to a narrow set of instigators but the purposes it presumably serves are limited. Inflicting injury and destruction is considered to be satisfying in its own right and hence the major aim of aggressive behavior. In actuality, aggression is a multifaceted phenomenon that has many determinants and serves diverse purposes. Therefore, theoretical formulations couched in terms of frustrating instigators and injurious aims have limited explanatory power (Bandura 1973). A complete theory of aggression must be sufficiently broad in scope to encompass a large set of variables governing diverse facets of aggression, whether individual or collective, personal or institutionally sanctioned.

Social labeling processes

Aggression is generally defined as behavior that results in personal injury and physical destruction. The injury may be physical or it may involve psychological impairment through disparagement and abusive exercise of coercive power. Not all injurious and destructive acts are judged

[1] The preparation of this paper and research by the author reported here was facilitated by Public Health Research Grant M–5162 from the National Institutes of Mental Health and by the James McKeen Cattell Award.

aggressive, however. Although injury is a major defining property, in fact, aggression refers to complex events that include not only injurious behavior, but judgmental factors that lead people to attach aggression labels to some forms of harmful conduct but not to others.

Whether injurious behavior will be perceived as aggressive or otherwise depends heavily on subjective judgments of intentions and causality. The greater the attribution of personal responsibility and injurious intent to the harm-doer, the higher the likelihood that the behavior will be judged as aggressive (Bandura 1973, Rule and Nesdale 1976b). The same harmful act is perceived differently depending on the sex, age, attractiveness, status, socioeconomic level, and ethnic background of the performer. As a general rule, people judge the harmful acts of favored individuals and groups as unintended and prompted by situational circumstances, but perceive the harmful acts of the disfavored as intentional and personally initiated. Value orientations of the labelers also influence their judgments of activities that cause harmful effects.

There are few disagreements over the labeling of direct assaultive behavior that is performed with explicit intent to injure or destroy. But people ordinarily do not aggress in conspicuous direct ways that reveal causal responsibility and carry high risk of retaliation. Rather, they tend to harm and destroy in ways that diffuse or obscure responsibility for detrimental actions, to reduce self-reproof and social reprisals. Most of the injurious consequences of major social concern are caused remotely, circuitously, and impersonally through social practices judged aggressive by the victims but not by those who benefit from them. Students of aggression examine direct assaultive behavior in minute detail, whereas remote circuitous acts, which produce widespread harm, receive comparatively little attention.

Disputes over the labeling of aggressive acts assume special significance in the case of collective behavior involving dissident and institutionally sanctioned aggression. Agencies of government are entrusted with considerable rewarding and coercive power. Either of these sources of power can be misused to produce detrimental social effects. Punitive and coercive means of control may be employed to maintain inequitable systems, to suppress legitimate dissent, and to victimize disadvantaged segments of society. People can similarly be harmed both physically and socially by arbitrary denial or discriminative administration of beneficial resources to which they are entitled.

Just as not all individual acts that produce injury are necessarily aggressive, nor are all institutional practices that cause harm expressions of aggression. Some social practices instituted with well-meaning intent create detrimental consequences that were unforeseen. Others are performed routinely and thoughtlessly through established custom. Judgments of institutional aggression are likely to be made in terms of indicants of injurious intent, deliberate negligence, and unwillingness to rectify detrimental conditions.

Dissident aggression is also judged in large part on the basis of factors external to the behavior. Some of these include the perceived legitimacy of the grievances, the appropriateness of coercive tactics, the professed aims and credibility of the challengers, and the ideological allegiances of the judges (Bandura 1973). People vary markedly in their perceptions of aggression for social control and for social change (Blumenthal et al. 1972). The more advantaged citizenry tend to view even extreme levels of violence for social control as lawful discharges of duty, whereas disadvantaged members regard such practices as expressions of institutional aggression. Conversely, aggression for social change, and even group protest without injury, is judged as violence by patriots of the system but not by dissidents. Thus, in conflicts of power, one person's violence is another person's benevolence. Whether a particular form of aggression is regarded as adaptive or destructive depends on who bears the consequences. As this brief review suggests, factors influencing the social labeling of different forms of injurious behavior merit more systematic investigation than they have received to date.

A complete theory of aggression must explain how aggressive patterns are developed, what provokes people to behave aggressively, and what sustains such actions after they have been initiated. Figure 1 summarizes the determinants of these three aspects of aggression within the framework of social learning theory.

Acquisition mechanisms

People are not born with preformed repertoires of aggressive behavior. They must learn them. Some of the elementary forms of aggression can be perfected with minimal guidance, but most aggressive activities – whether they be dueling with switchblade knives, sparring with opponents, military combat, or vengeful ridicule – entail intricate skills that require extensive learning.

Social learning analysis of aggression

Origins of aggression	Instigators of aggression	Regulators of aggression
Observational learning	Modeling influences	External reinforcement
Reinforced performance	Disinhibitory	Tangible rewards
Biological determinants	Facilitative	Social and status rewards
	Arousing	Expressions of injury
	Stimulus enhancing	Alleviation of aversive treatment
	Aversive treatment	Punishment
	Physical assaults	Inhibitory
	Verbal threats and insults	Informative
	Adverse reductions in reinforcement	Vicarious reinforcement
	Thwarting	Observed reward
	Incentive inducements	Observed punishment
	Instructional control	Self-reinforcement
	Bizarre symbolic control	Self-reward
		Self-punishment
		Neutralization of self-punishment
		Moral justification
		Palliative comparison
		Euphemistic labeling
		Displacement of responsibility
		Diffusion of responsibility
		Dehumanization of victims
		Attribution of blame to victims
		Misrepresentation of consequences

1. Schematic outline of the origins, instigators, and regulators of aggressive behavior in social learning theory.

Biological factors

New modes of behavior are not fashioned solely through experience. Biological factors, of course, set limits on the types of aggressive responses that can be developed, and influence the rate at which learning progresses. In addition to biological constraints on behavior, evolved biological systems predispose organisms to perceive and to learn critical features of their immediate environment.

The orchestration of aggressive actions, like other forms of visceral and motor responsiveness, depends on neurophysiological mechanisms. Research conducted with animals has identified subcortical structures, principally the hypothalamus and the limbic system, that mediate aggressive behavior (Goldstein 1974). But these neural systems are selectively activated and controlled by central processing of environmental stimulation. Research by Delgado (1967) illustrates how social learning factors influence the types of responses that are likely to be activated by stimulating the same neural structure. Hypothalamic stimulation of a dominant monkey in a colony prompted him to attack subordinate males but not the females with whom he was on friendly terms. In contrast, hypothalamic stimulation elicited submissiveness in a monkey when she occupied a low hierarchical position, but increased aggressiveness toward subordinates as her social rank was elevated by changing the membership of the colony. Thus, electrical stimulation of the same anatomical site produced markedly different behavior under different social conditions.

It is valuable to know how neurophysiological systems operate internally, but from the standpoint of explaining aggression it is especially important to understand how they are socially activated for different courses of action. In everyday life, biological systems are roused in humans by provocative external events and by ideational activation. A remark interpreted as an insult will generate activity in the hypothalamus, whereas the same comment viewed innocuously will leave the hypothalamus unperturbed. Given a negative interpretation, social and cognitive factors are likely to determine the nature of the response.

In the social learning view, people are endowed with neurophysiological mechanisms that enable them to behave aggressively, but the activation of these mechanisms depends on appropriate stimulation and is subject to cognitive control. Therefore, the specific forms that aggressive behavior takes, the frequency with which it is expressed, the situations in which it is displayed, and the specific targets selected for attack are largely determined by social learning factors. As we shall see, these factors are varied and complex.

The role played by biological factors in aggression will vary across species, circumstances, and types of aggressive behavior. In infrahuman organisms genetic and hormonal factors that affect neural organization and structural development figure prominently in aggressive responsiveness. Aggression in animals is largely determined by combat successes which depend on a robust physical build. The more powerfully developed members generally become belligerent fighters through victories; the physically less well-endowed become submissive through defeats. Because genetic and hormonal factors affect physical development, they are related to aggressiveness in animals.

People's capacity to devise and to use destructive weapons greatly reduces their dependence on biological structure to succeed in aggressive encounters. A puny person with a gun can easily triumph over powerfully built opponents who are unarmed. People's proclivity for social organization similarly reduces the importance of structural characteristics in aggressive attainments. At the social level, aggressive power derives from organized collective action. The chance of victory in aggressive confrontation is enhanced by the force of numbers acting in concert, and the physical stature of individual challengers does not much matter.

Structural characteristics related to aggressiveness also have different evolutionary and survival consequences for animals and humans. In many animal species, physical strength determines which males do the mating. Combat victors gain possession of females so that the most dominant males have the highest reproduction rates. In humans, mate selection is based more on such qualities as attractiveness, intelligence, parental arrangement, religious affiliation, and financial standing than on fighting prowess. Societal sanctions prohibit the brawny members of a social group from impregnating at will whomever they desire. Differential reproduction rates are primarily determined by religious beliefs, ideological commitments, socioeconomic factors, and birth control practices. For these reasons, one would not expect variations in human aggressiveness to be reflected in differential reproduction rates.

Observational learning

Psychological theories have traditionally assumed that learning can occur only by performing responses and experiencing their consequences. In fact, virtually all learning phenomena resulting from direct experience can occur on a vicarious basis by observing the behavior of others and its consequences for them. The capacity to learn by observation enables organisms to acquire large, integrated patterns of behavior without having to form them gradually by tedious trial and error.

The abbreviation of the acquisition process through observational learning is vital for both development and survival. Because errors can produce costly or even fatal outcomes, the prospects of survival would be slim indeed if organisms could learn solely by the consequences of their actions. The more costly and hazardous the possible mistakes, the heavier is the reliance on observational learning from competent models. This is particularly true of aggression, where the dangers of crippling or fatal consequences limit the value of learning through trial and error. By observing the aggressive conduct of others, one forms a conception of how the behavior is performed and on later occasions the symbolic representation can serve as a guide for action.

Learning by observation is governed by four interrelated subprocesses (Bandura 1977a). *Attentional* processes regulate exploration and perception of modeled activities. Organisms cannot be much influenced by observation of modeled behavior if they have no memory of it. Through coding into images, words, or other symbolic modes, transitory modeling influences are transformed for *memory representation* into enduring performance guides. The capacity for observational learning, whether assessed across species or over the course of development, increases with increasing capability to symbolize experience. Symbolic representations must eventually be transformed into appropriate actions. *Motor production* processes, the third component of modeling, govern the integration of constituent acts into new response patterns.

Social learning theory distinguishes between acquisition of behaviors that have destructive and injurious potential and factors that determine whether individuals will perform what they have learned. This distinction is important because not all the things learned are enacted. People can acquire, retain, and possess the capability to act aggressively, but the behavior may rarely be expressed if it has no functional value for them or is negatively sanctioned. Should appropriate inducements arise on later occasions, individuals put into practice what they have learned (Bandura 1965, Madsen 1968). *Incentive and motivational* processes regulate the performance of observationally learned responses.

Findings of numerous studies show that children can acquire entire repertoires of novel aggressive behavior from observing aggressive models, and retain such response patterns over extended periods (Bandura 1973, Hicks 1968). Factors that affect the four component processes influence the level of observational learning. In many instances the behavior being modeled is learned in essentially the same form. But models teach more general lessons as well. From observing the behavior of others, people can extract general tactics and strategies of behavior that enable them to go beyond what they have seen or heard. By synthesizing features of different modeled patterns into view amalgams, observers can evolve new forms of aggression.

In a modern society, aggressive styles of behavior can be adopted from three principal sources. One prominent origin is the aggression modeled and reinforced by family members. Studies of familial determinants of aggression show that parents who favor aggressive solutions to problems have children who tend to use similar aggressive tactics in dealing with others (Bandura and Walters 1959, Hoffman 1960). That familial violence breeds violent styles of conduct is further shown by similarities in child abuse practices across several generations (Silver, Dublin and Lourie 1969).

Although familial influences play a major role in setting the direction of social development, the family is embedded in a network of other social systems. The subculture in which people reside, and with which they have repeated contact, provides a second important source of aggression. Not surprisingly, the highest incidence of aggression is found in communities in which aggressive models abound and fighting prowess is regarded as a valued attribute (Short 1968, Wolfgang and Ferracuti 1967).

The third source of aggressive conduct is the abundant symbolic modeling provided by the mass media. The advent of television has greatly expanded the range of models available to a growing child. Whereas their predecessors rarely, if ever, observed brutal aggression in their everyday life, both children and adults today have unlimited opportunities to learn the whole gamut of violent conduct from televised modeling within the comfort of their homes.

A considerable amount of research has been conducted in recent years on the effects of televised influences on social behavior. The findings show that exposure to televised violence can have at least four different effects on viewers: (1) It teaches aggressive styles of conduct, (2) it alters restraints over aggressive behavior, (3) it desensitizes and habituates people to violence, and (4) it shapes people's images of reality upon which they base many of their actions. Let us review briefly each of these effects.

Television is an effective tutor. Both laboratory and controlled field studies, in which young children and adolescents are repeatedly shown either violent or nonviolent fare, disclose that exposure to filmed violence shapes the form of aggression and typically increases interpersonal aggressiveness in everyday life (Bandura 1973, Leyens *et al.* 1975, Liebert, Neale and Davidson 1973, Parke *et al.* 1977, Friedrich and Stein 1973, Steuer, Applefield and Smith 1971). Adults who pursue a life of crime improve their criminal skills by patterning their behavior after the ingenious styles portrayed in the mass media (Hendrick 1977). Being an influential tutor, television can foster humanitarian qualities, as well as injurious conduct. Programs that portray positive attitudes and social behavior foster cooperativeness, sharing, and reduce interpersonal aggression (Leifer, Gordon and Graves 1974).

Another line of research has examined how inhibitions over aggression are affected by exposure to televised violence. There are several characteristics of televised presentations that tend to weaken people's restraints over behaving aggressively. Physical aggression is often shown to be the preferred solution to interpersonal conflicts. It is portrayed as acceptable, unsullied, and relatively successful. Superheroes do most of the killing. When good triumphs over evil by violent means, viewers are more strongly influenced than when aggressive conduct is not morally sanctioned by prestigious figures. In experimental tests adults generally behave more punitively after they have seen others act aggressively than if they have not been exposed to aggressive modeling. This is especially true if the modeled aggressive conduct is legitimized by social justifications (Berkowitz 1970).

Desensitization and habituation to violence are reflected in decreases in physiological reactions to repeated exposure to displays of violence. Heavy viewers of television respond with less emotion to violence than do light viewers (Cline, Croft and Courrier 1973). In addition to emotional desensitization, violence viewing can create behavioral indifference to human aggression. In studies demonstrating the habituation effect, children who have had prior exposure to interpersonal violence are less likely to intervene in escalating aggression between children they are overseeing (Drabman and Thomas 1974, Thomas and Drabman 1975, Thomas *et al.* 1977).

During the course of their daily lives, people have direct contact with only a small sector of the physical and social environment. In their daily routines they travel the same routes, visit the same places, see essentially the same group of friends and work associates. Consequently, people form impressions of the social realities with which they have little or no contact partly from televised representations of society. Because the world of television is heavily populated with villainous and unscrupulous people it can distort knowledge about the real world. Indeed, communications researchers have found that heavy viewers of television are less trustful of others and overestimate their chances of being criminally victimized than do light viewers (Gerbner and Gross 1976). Heavy viewers see the society at large as more dangerous regardless of their educational level, sex, age, and amount of newspaper reading.

Many of the misconceptions that people develop about certain occupations, nationalities, ethnic groups, sex roles, social roles, and other aspects of life are cultivated through modeling of stereotypes by the media. Too often their actions are based on such misconceptions.

Symbolic modeling plays an especially significant role in the shaping and rapid spread of collective aggression. Social diffusion of new styles and tactics of aggression conforms to the generalized pattern of most other contagious activities: new behavior is introduced by a salient example, it spreads rapidly in a contagious fashion, and it then either stabilizes or is discarded depending on its functional value.

Modeled solutions to problems that achieve some success are not only adopted by people facing similar difficulties, but they tend to spread as well to other troublesome areas. The civil rights struggle, which itself was modeled after Gandhi's crusades of nonviolent resistance, in turn provided the example for other protest campaigns aimed at eliminating injustices and undesired social practices. The model of collective protest is now widely used as a means of forcing change.

Airline hijacking provides another recent example of the rapid diffusion and decline of aggressive tactics. Air piracy was unheard of in the United States until an airliner was hijacked to Havana in 1961. Prior to that incident Cubans were hijacking planes to Miami. These incidents were followed by a wave of hijackings both in the United States and abroad, eventually involving seventy-one different countries (figure 2). Just as aggressive strategies are widely modeled, so are the counter measures that prove effective in controlling modeled aggression.

Learning by direct experience

People rarely teach social behaviors that are never exemplified by anyone in their environment. Therefore, in behavior acquired under natural conditions it is often difficult to determine whether reinforcing experi-

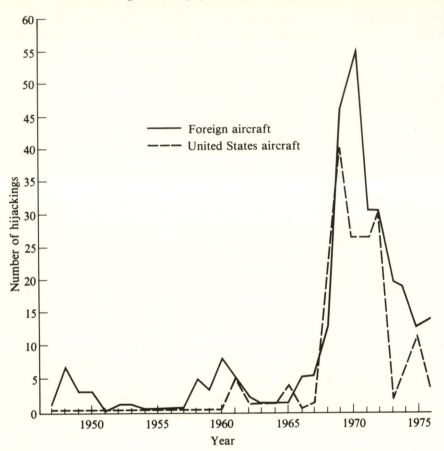

2. Incidence of hijackings over a span of thirty years. The rise in foreign hijackings during the 1948–50 period occurred in Slavic countries during the Hungarian uprisings, and the second flare-up in 1958–61 comprised almost entirely Cuban hijackings to Miami. A sudden widespread diffusion of hijackings occurred in 1969–70, involving airliners from a total of seventy-one different countries.

ences create the new responses or activate what was already partly learned by observation. Although modeling influences are universally present, patterns of behavior can be shaped through a more rudimentary form of learning relying on the consequences of trial-and-error performance.

Until recently, learning by reinforcement was portrayed as a mechanistic process in which responses are shaped automatically by their immediate consequences. In more recent theoretical analyses, learning from response consequences is conceived of largely as a cognitive process, especially in humans. Consequences serve as an unarticulated way of informing performers what they must do to gain beneficial outcomes and to avoid punishing ones. By observing the differential effects of their actions, individuals discern which responses are appropriate in which settings and behave accordingly. Although the empirical issue is not yet fully resolved, evidence that human behavior is not much affected by consequences until the point at which the contingencies are discerned, raises serious questions concerning the automaticity of reinforcement.

Viewed from the cognitive framework (Bandura 1977a), learning from differential outcomes becomes a special case of observational learning. In this mode of conveying response information, the conception of the appropriate behavior is gradually constructed from observing the effects of one's actions rather than from the synthesized examples provided by others. A vast amount of evidence lends validity to the view that reinforcement serves principally as an informative and motivational operation rather than as a mechanical response shaper.

There have been few experimental attempts to fashion novel forms of aggression by differential reinforcement alone. It would be foolhardy to instruct novices how to use lethal weapons or to fight dangerous opponents by selectively reinforcing trial-and-error efforts. Where the consequences of mistakes can be dangerous or fatal, demonstration rather than unguided experience is the best tutor.

Learning through combat experience has been explored to a limited extent in experiments with lower species designed to train docile animals into ferocious fighters (Ginsburg and Allee 1942, Scott and Marston 1953). This is achieved by arranging a series of bouts with progressively more experienced fighters under conditions where trainees can win fights without being hurt. As fighting skills are developed and reinforced through repeated victories, formerly noncombative animals become more and more vicious in their aggressive behavior. While successful fighting produces brutal aggressors, severe defeats create enduring submissiveness (Kahn 1951).

Patterson, Littman, and Bricker (1967) report a field study illustrating how passive children can be shaped into aggressors through a process of victimization and successful counteraggression. Passive children who were repeatedly victimized but occasionally succeeded in halting attacks by counteraggression, not only increased defensive fighting over time but began to initiate attacks of their own. Passive children who were seldom maltreated because they avoided others, and those whose counteraggression proved unsuccessful, remained submissive.

Modeling and reinforcement influences operate jointly in the social learning of aggression in everyday life. Styles of aggression are largely learned through observation, and refined through reinforced practice. The effects of these two determinants on the form and incidence of aggression are graphically revealed in ethnographic reports of societies that pursue a warlike way of life and those that follow a pacific style. In cultures lacking aggressive models and devaluing injurious conduct, people live peaceably (Alland 1972, Dentan 1968, Levy 1969, Mead 1935, Turnbull 1961). In other societies that provide extensive training in aggression, attach prestige to it, and make its use functional, people spend a great deal of time threatening, fighting, maiming, and killing each other (Bateson 1936, Chagnon 1968, Gardner and Heider 1969, Whiting 1941).

Instigation mechanisms

A theory must explain not only how aggressive patterns are acquired but also how they are activated and channeled. Social learning theory distinguishes between two broad classes of motivators of behavior. First, there are the biologically based motivators. These include internal aversive stimulation arising from tissue deficits and external sources of aversive stimulation that activate behavior through their painful effects. The second major source of response inducement involves cognitively based motivators. The capacity to represent future consequences in thought provides one cognitively based source of motivation. Through cognitive representation of future outcomes individuals can generate current motivators of behavior. The outcome expectations may be material (e.g. consummatory, physically painful), sensory (e.g. novel, enjoyable, or unpleasant sensory stimulation), or social (e.g. positive and negative evaluative reactions). Another cognitively based source of motivation operates through the intervening influences of goal setting and self-evaluative reactions. Self-motivation involves standards against which to evaluate performances. By making positive self-evaluation conditional on attaining a certain level of behavior, individuals create self-inducements to persist in their efforts until their performances match self-prescribed standards.

As will be shown shortly, some aggressive acts are motivated by painful stimulation. However, most of the events that lead people to aggress, such as insults, verbal challenges, status threats, and unjust treatment, gain this activating capacity through learning experiences. People learn to dislike and to attack certain types of individuals either through direct unpleasant encounters with them, or on the basis of symbolic and vicarious experiences that conjure up hatreds. Because of regularities in environmental events, antecedent cues come to signify events to come and the outcomes particular actions are likely to produce. Such uniformities create expectations about what leads to what. When aggressive behavior produces different results depending on the times, places, or persons toward whom it is directed, people use cues predictive of probable consequences in regulating their behavior. They tend to aggress toward persons and in contexts where it is relatively safe and rewarding to do so, but they are disinclined to act aggressively when it carries high risk of punishment. The different forms that aggression elicitors take are discussed separately in the sections that follow.

Aversive instigators

It has been traditionally assumed that aggressive behavior is activated by an aggressive drive. According to the instinct doctrine, organisms are innately endowed with an aggressive drive that automatically builds up and must be discharged periodically through some form of aggressive behavior. Despite intensive study, researchers have been unable to find an inborn autonomous drive of this type.

For years, aggression was viewed as a product of frustration. In this conception, frustration generates an aggressive drive which, in turn, motivates aggressive behavior. Frustration replaced instinct as the activating source, but the two theories are much alike in their social implications. Since frustration is ever present, in both approaches people are continuously burdened with aggressive energy that must be drained from time to time.

The frustration-aggression theory was widely accepted until its limited explanatory value became apparent from growing evidence. Frustration has varied effects on behavior; aggression does not require frustration. Frustration subsumes such a diverse set of conditions – physical assault, deprivation, insult, thwarting, harassment, and defeat – that it no longer has any specific meaning. As new instigators of aggression were identified, the definition of frustration was stretched to accommodate them. Not only is there great heterogeneity on the antecedent side of the relationship, but the consequence part of the formula, the aggressive behavior, also embraces a vast array of activities sifted through value judgments. One cannot expect a generalizable relationship to emerge from such a wide assortment of antecedents and behaviors.

The diverse events subsumed under the omnibus term frustration do have one feature in common – they are all aversive. In social learning theory, rather than frustration generating an aggressive drive that is reducible only by injurious behavior, aversive stimulation produces a general state of emotional arousal that can facilitate any number of responses (see figure 3). The type of behavior elicited will depend on how the source of arousal is cognitively appraised, the modes of response learned for coping with stress, and their relative effectiveness. When distressed some people seek help and support; others increase achievement efforts; others display withdrawal and resignation; some aggress; others experience heightened somatic reactivity; still others anesthetize themselves against a miserable existence with drugs or alcohol; and most intensify constructive efforts to overcome the source of distress.

Several lines of evidence, reviewed in detail elsewhere (Bandura 1973), lend greater validity to the *arousal-prepotent response* formulation than to the *frustration-aggression* view. Different emotions appear to have a similar physiological state (Ax 1953). The same physiological state can be experienced phenomenologically as different emotions, depending upon what people see as the incitements, and how they interpret them (Hunt, Cole and Reis 1958, Mandler 1975). In individuals who are prone to behave aggressively, different sources of emotional arousal can heighten their aggression (Rule and Nesdale 1976a, Tannenbaum and Zillmann 1975).

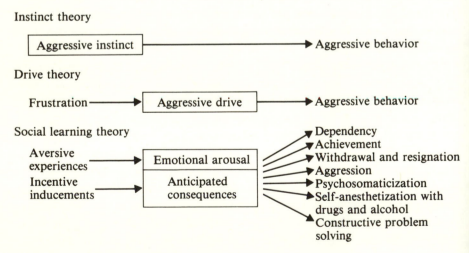

3. Schematization of alternative motivational analyses of aggression.

In drive theories, the aroused aggressive drive presumably remains active until discharged by some form of aggression. Actually, anger arousal dissipates rapidly, but it can be easily regenerated on later occasions through rumination on anger-provoking incidents. By thinking about past insulting treatment, people can work themselves into a rage long after their emotional reactions have subsided. Persistence of elevated anger stems from thought-produced arousal, rather than from an undischarged reservoir of aggressive energy. Consider the example of a person who becomes angered by an apparent exclusion from an important meeting only to receive the notice in the next day's mail. The person will show an immediate drop in anger arousal and aggressiveness without having to assault or denounce someone to drain a roused drive. Anger arousal decreased through cognitive means will reduce aggression as much, or even more, than will acting aggressively (Mallick and McCandless 1966). By varying anticipated consequences, the same aggressive acts can raise or lower physiological arousal (Hokanson, Willers and Koropsak 1968).

Frustration or anger arousal is a facilitative, rather than a necessary, condition for aggression. Frustration tends to provoke aggression mainly in people who have learned to respond to aversive experiences with aggressive attitudes and conduct. Thus, after being frustrated, aggressively trained children behave more aggressively, whereas cooperatively trained children behave more cooperatively (Davitz 1952).

There exists a large body of evidence that painful treatment, deprivation or delay of rewards, personal insults, failure experiences, and obstructions, all of which are aversive, do not have uniform behavioral effects (Bandura 1969). Some of these aversive antecedents convey injurious intent more clearly than others and therefore have greater aggression-provoking potential.

Physical assaults. If one wished to provoke aggression, one way to do so would be simply to hit another person, who is likely to oblige with a counterattack. To the extent that counteraggression discourages further assaults it is reinforced by pain reduction and thereby assumes high functional value in social interactions. Although naturally occurring contingencies favor the development of a pain-aggression relationship, there is some dispute over whether it is innate or acquired.

Azrin (1967) and Ulrich (1966) were major proponents of the nativistic view that pain-induced aggression is an unlearned reflexive behavior. As the determinants of pain-attack reactions were examined more closely, however, they began to lose their reflexive status. Young animals rarely, if ever, fight when shocked unless they have had some fighting experience, and in some studies shocks produce little or no fighting in 20 to 30% of mature animals (Hutchinson, Ulrich and Azrin 1965, Powell and Creer 1969). If aggression is an unlearned dominant response to pain, then initial shocks should produce attack, which is not generally the case (Azrin, Hutchinson and Hake 1963). Contrary to the reflexive elicitation hypothesis, when combative responses are shocked the pain reduces and eliminates rather than provokes fighting (Azrin 1970, Baenninger and Grossman 1969). The most striking evidence that pain-aggression reactions are determined more by situational factors than innate organization is the finding that in a small enclosure approximately 90% of the shocks provoke fighting, whereas in a larger chamber animals ignore each other and only 2% of the shocks elicit attack (Ulrich and Azrin 1962). As environmental constraints to fight are removed, avoidance and flight responses to painful stimulation take priority over attack (Knutson 1971, Logan and Boice 1969, Sbordone, Garcia and Carder 1977). Physically painful experiences may be facilitative but clearly not sufficient to provoke aggression in animals.

Pain stimulation is an even less consistent elicitor of aggression in humans. Nonsocial sources of pain rarely lead them to attack bystanders. Whether or not they counteraggress in the face of physical assaults depends upon their combat skill and the power of their assailant. Those who possess fighting prowess escalate counterattacks to subdue assailants (Edwards 1968, Peterson 1971). Given other alternatives, low aggressors are easily dissuaded from counterattacks under retaliative threats.

Verbal threats and insults. Social interchanges are typically escalated into physical aggression by verbal threats and insults. In analyzing dyadic interchanges of assault-prone individuals, Toch (1969) found that humiliating affronts and threats to reputation and manly status emerged as major precipitants of violence. High sensitivity to devaluation was usually combined with deficient verbal skills for resolving disputes and restoring self-esteem without having to dispose of antagonists physically. The counterattacks evoked by physical assaults are probably instigated more by humiliation than by physical pain. Indeed, it is not uncommon for individuals, groups, and even nations, to pay heavy injury costs in efforts to 'save face' by combat victory.

Insult alone is less effective in provoking attack in those who eschew aggression, but it does heighten their aggressiveness given hostile modeling and other disinhibitory influences (Hartmann 1969, Wheeler and Caggiula 1966). In subcultures in which social ranking is determined by fighting prowess, status threats from challengers within the group or rival outsiders are quick to provoke defensive aggression (Short 1968).

The most plausible explanation of how insults acquire aggression-eliciting potential is in terms of foreseen consequences. Affronts that are not counteracted can have far-reaching effects for victims. Not only do they become easy targets for further victimization, but they are apt to forfeit the rewards and privileges that go with social standing. To the extent that punishment of insults reduces the likelihood of future maltreatment, the insult-aggression reaction becomes well established.

Adverse reductions in conditions of life. Aversive changes in the conditions of life can also provoke people to aggressive action. Explanations of collective aggression usually invoke impoverishment and discontent arising from privations as principal causal factors. However, since most impoverished people do not aggress, the view that discontent breeds violence requires qualification. This issue is well illustrated in interpretations of urban riots in ghetto areas. Despite condemnation of their degrading and exploitive conditions of life, comparatively few of the disadvantaged took active measures to force warranted changes. Even in cities that experienced civil disturbances, only a small percentage of ghetto residents actively participated in the aggressive activities (Lieberson and Silverman 1965, McCord and Howard 1968, Sears and McConahay 1969).

The critical question for social scientists to answer is not why some people who are subjected to aversive conditions aggress, but rather why a sizable majority of them acquiesce to dismal living conditions in the midst of affluent styles of life. To invoke the frustration-aggression hypothesis, as is commonly done, is to disregard the more striking evidence that severe privation generally produces feelings of hopelessness and massive apathy. People give up trying when they lack a sense of personal efficacy and no longer expect their efforts to produce any beneficial results in an environment that is unresponsive or is consistently punishing (Bandura 1977b, Maier and Seligman 1976).

In accord with self-efficacy theory, comparative studies indicate that discontent produces aggression not in those who have lost hope, but in the more successful members whose assertive efforts at social and economic betterment have been periodically reinforced. Consequently, they have some reason to expect that they can effect change by coercive action (Caplan 1970, Crawford and Naditch 1970).

More recent explanations of violent protest emphasize relative deprivation rather than the actual level of aversive conditions as the instigator of collective aggression. In an analysis of conditions preceding major revolutions, Davies (1969) reports that revolutions are most likely to occur when a period of social and economic advances that instills rising expectations is followed by a sharp reversal. People judge their present gains not only in relation to those they secured in the past; they also compare their lot in life with the benefits accruing to others (Bandura 1977a). Inequities between observed and experienced outcomes tend to create discontent, whereas individuals may be satisfied with limited rewards as long as they are as good as what others are receiving.

Since most people who feel relatively deprived do not resort to violent action, aversive privation, like other forms of aversive treatment, is not in itself a sufficient cause of collective aggression. Additional social learning factors must be considered that determine whether discontent will take an aggressive form or some other behavioral expression. Using such a multideterminant approach, Gurr (1970) examined the magnitude of civil disorder in western nations as a function of three sets of factors. The first is the level of social discontent arising from economic decline, oppressive restrictions, and social inequities. The second factor is the traditional acceptance of force to achieve social change. Some societies disavow aggressive tactics, while others regard mass protests and coups d'états as acceptable means of change. The third factor is the balance of coercive power between the system and the challengers as measured by the amount of military, police, industrial, labor, and foreign support the protagonists can marshal on their side. The analysis reveals that when aggressive tactics are considered acceptable and challengers possess coercive power, they will use less extreme forms of collective aggression without requiring much discontent. Revolutionary violence, however, requires widespread discontent and strong coercive power by challengers, while tactical traditions are of less importance.

Although aggression is more likely to be provoked by relative than by absolute privation, clarification of the role of relative deprivation requires greater consideration of the multifaceted bases of comparative evaluation. People judge their life circumstances in relation to their aspirations, to their past conditions, and to the life situations of others whom they select for social comparison. Discontent created by raised aspirations, by reduction of rewards and privileges from accustomed levels, and by deceleration in the rate of improvement compared to others, undoubtedly has variant effects. Different sources of inequity (social, economic, political) may have differential aggression-activating potential. Response to inequitable deprivation is further influenced by mollifying social justifications and promise of social reforms. Considering the complex interplay of influences, it is hardly surprising that level of deprivation alone, whether defined in absolute or in relative terms, is a weak predictor of collective aggression (McPhail 1971).

Thwarting of goal-directed behavior. Proponents of the frustration-aggression theory define frustration in terms of interference or blocking of goal-seeking activities. In this view, people are provoked to aggression when obstructed, delayed, or otherwise thwarted from getting what they want. Research bearing on this issue shows that thwarting can lead people to intensify their efforts, which, if sufficiently vigorous, may be construed as aggressive. However, thwarting fails to provoke forceful action in people who have not experienced sufficient success to develop reward expectations, and in those who are blocked far enough from the goal so it appears unattainable (Bandura and Walters 1963, Longstreth 1966).

When thwarting provokes aggression it is probably attributable more to personal affront than to blocking of behavior. Consistent with this interpretation, people report more aggression to thwartings that appear unwarranted or suggest hostile intent than to those for which excusable reasons exist, even though both involve identical blocking of goal-directed behavior (Cohen 1955, Pastore 1952).

The overall evidence regarding the different forms of aversive instigators supports the conclusion that aversive antecedents, though they vary in their activating potential, are facilitative rather than necessary or sufficient conditions for aggression.

Incentive instigators

The preceding discussion was concerned solely with aversive instigators of aggression, which traditionally occupied a central role in psychological theorizing, often to the neglect of more important determinants. The cognitive capacity of humans to represent future consequences enables them to guide their behavior by outcomes extended forward in time. A great deal of human aggression, in fact, is prompted by anticipated positive consequences. Here, the instigator is the pull of expected benefits, rather than the push of painful treatment. This positive source of motivation for aggression represents the second component in the motivational analysis depicted schematically in figure 3.

The consequences that people anticipate for their actions are derived from, and therefore usually correspond to, prevailing conditions of reinforcement. The anticipatory activation and incentive regulation of aggression receive detailed consideration later. Expectation and actuality do not always coincide because anticipated consequences are also partly inferred from the observed outcomes of others, from what one reads or is told, and from other indicators of likely consequences. Because judgments are fallible, aggressive actions are sometimes prompted and temporarily sustained by erroneous anticipated consequences. Habitual offenders, for example, often err by overestimating the chances of success for transgressive behavior (Claster 1967). In social interchanges and collective protest, coercive actions are partly sustained, even in the face of punishing consequences, by expectations that continued pressure may eventually produce desired results.

Modeling instigators

Of the numerous antecedent cues that influence human behavior at any given moment, none is more common than the actions of others. Therefore, a reliable way to prompt people to aggress is to have others do it. Indeed, both children and adults are more likely to behave aggressively and with greater intensity if they have seen others act aggressively than if they have not been exposed to aggressive models (Bandura 1973, Liebert, Neale and Davidson 1973). The activation potential of modeling influences is enhanced if observers are angered (Berkowitz 1965, Hartmann 1969, Wheeler 1966), the modeled aggression is socially justified (Berkowitz 1965, Meyer 1972), or is shown to be successful in securing rewards (Bandura, Ross and Ross 1963), and the victim invites attack through prior association with aggression (Berkowitz 1970).

Social learning theory distinguishes four processes by which modeling influences can activate aggressive behavior. One mode of operation is in terms of the *directive function* of modeled actions. In many instances, behaving like others is advantageous because the prevalent modes have proven functional, whereas divergent courses of action may be less effective. After modeling cues acquire predictive value through correlated consequences they come to serve as informative prompts for others to behave in a similar fashion.

Aggressive behavior, especially when harsh and lacking justification, is socially censured if not self-condemned. Anticipated punishment exerts a restraining influence on injurious conduct. Seeing people respond approvingly or even indifferently toward aggressors conveys the impression that such behavior is an acceptable or normative mode of response. The same modeled aggression is much more effective in reducing restraints if it is socially legitimated than if it is portrayed as unjustified (Goranson 1970). In aggressive conduct that is unencumbered by restraints because it is regarded as emulative, aggressive modeling is primarily instigational, whereas it serves a *disinhibitory function* in injurious behavior that is fear- or guilt-provoking. Since physical aggression usually incurs some negative effects, both instigational and disinhibitory processes are likely to be involved.

Seeing others aggressive generates *emotional arousal* in observers. For individuals who are prone to behave aggressively, emotional arousal can enhance their aggressive response. Some of the instigative effects of modeling may well reflect the emotional facilitation of aggressive behavior.

Aggressive modeling can additionally increase the likelihood of aggressive behavior through its *stimulus enhancing effects*. Modeled activities inevitably direct observers' attention to the particular implements being used. This attentional focus may prompt observers to use the same instruments to a greater extent, though not necessarily in an imitative way. In one experiment (Bandura 1962), for example, children who had observed a model pummel a plastic figure with a mallet spent more time pounding other objects with a mallet than those who did not see it used for assaultive purposes. In sum, the combined evidence reveals that modeling influences, depending on their form and content, can function as teachers, as elicitors, as disinhibitors, as stimulus enhancers, and as emotion arousers.

Instructional instigators

During the process of socialization, people are trained to obey orders. By rewarding compliance and punishing disobedience, directives issued in the form of authoritative commands elicit obedient aggression. After this form of social control is established, legitimate authorities can secure obedient aggression from others, especially if the actions are presented as justified and necessary, and the issuers possess strong coercive power. As Snow (1961) has perceptively observed, 'When you think of the long and gloomy history of man, you will find more hideous crimes have been committed in the name of obedience than in the name of rebellion' (p. 24).

In studies of obedient aggression, Milgram (1974) and others (Kilham and Mann 1974, Mantell and Panzarella 1976), have shown that well-meaning adults will administer increasingly severe shocks on command despite their victims' desperate pleas. Adults find it difficult to resist peer pressures calling for increasingly harmful actions just as they are averse to defying legitimized authority. Seeing others carrying out punitive orders calmly likewise increases obedient aggression (Powers and Geen 1972).

It is less difficult to hurt people on command when their suffering is not visible and when causal actions seem physically or temporally remote from their deleterious effects. Mechanized forms of warfare, where masses of people can be put to death by destructive forces released remotely, illustrate such depersonalized aggression. When the injurious consequences of one's actions are fully evident, vicariously aroused distress and self-censure serve as restraining influences over aggressive conduct that is otherwise authoritatively sanctioned. Obedience declines as the harmful consequences of destructive acts become increasingly more salient and personalized (Milgram 1974). As the results of these and other studies to be cited later show, it requires conducive social conditions rather than monstrous people to produce heinous deeds.

Delusional instigators

In addition to the various external instigators, aggressive behavior can be prompted by bizarre beliefs. Every so often tragic episodes occur in which individuals are led by delusional beliefs to commit acts of violence. Some follow divine inner voices commanding them to murder. There are those who resort to self-protective attacks on paranoid suspicions that others are conspiring to harm them (Reich and Hepps 1972). Others kill for deranged sacrificial purposes. And still others are prompted by grandiose convictions that it is their heroic responsibility to eliminate evil individuals in positions of influence.

A study of American presidential assassins (Weisz and Taylor 1970) shows that, almost without exception, the murderous assaults were delusionally instigated. Assassins tend to be loners who are troubled by severe personal failure. They acted either under divine mandate, through alarm that the president was in conspiracy with treacherous foreign agents to overthrow the government, or on the conviction that their own adversities resulted from presidential persecution. Being unusually sec-

lusive, the assassins barred themselves from the type of confiding relationships needed to correct erroneous beliefs and to check autistically
generated resentments.

Maintaining mechanisms

So far we have discussed how aggressive behavior is learned and activated. The third major feature of the social learning formulation concerns
the conditions that sustain aggressive responding. It is amply
documented in psychological research that behavior is extensively regulated by its consequences. This principle applies equally to aggression.
Injurious modes of response, like other forms of social behavior, can be
increased, eliminated, and reinstated by altering the effects they produce.

People aggress for many different reasons. Similar aggressive actions
may thus have markedly different functional value for different individuals and for the same individual on different occasions. Traditional
behavior theories conceptualize reinforcement influences almost exclusively in terms of the effects of external outcomes impinging directly upon
performers. But external consequences, as influential as they often are,
are not the only kind of outcomes that regulate human behavior. People
partly guide their actions on the basis of observed consequences, and by
consequences they create for themselves. These three forms of outcomes
– external, vicarious, and self-produced – not only serve as separate
sources of influence, but they interact in ways that weaken or enhance
their effects on behavior (Bandura 1977a).

External reinforcement

As we have previously noted, consequences exert effects on behavior
largely through their informative and incentive functions. For the most
part, response consequences influence behavior antecedently by creating
expectations of similar outcomes on future occasions. The likelihood of
particular actions is increased by anticipated benefits and reduced by
anticipated punishment.

Aggression is strongly influenced by its consequences. Extrinsic
rewards assume special importance in interpersonal aggression because
such behavior, by its very nature, usually produces some costs among its
diverse effects. People who get into fights, for example, will suffer pain
and injury even though they eventually triumph over their opponents.
Under noncoercive conditions, positive incentives are needed to over-

come inhibitions arising from the aversive concomitants of aggression. The positive incentives take a variety of forms.

Tangible rewards. Aggression is often used by those lacking better alternatives because it is an effective means of securing desired tangible rewards. Ordinarily docile animals will fight when aggressive attacks produce food or drink (Azrin and Hutchinson 1967, Ulrich *et al.* 1963). Observation of children's interactions reveals that most of the assaultive actions of aggressors produce rewarding outcomes for them (Patterson, Littman and Bricker 1967). Given this high level of positive reinforcement of aggressive behavior, there is no need to invoke an aggressive drive to explain the prevalence of such actions. Aggressive behavior is especially persistent when it is reinforced only intermittently, which is usually the case under the variable conditions of everyday life (Walters and Brown 1963).

There are other forms of aggression that are sustained by their material consequences though, for obvious reasons, they are not easily subject to systematic analysis. Delinquents and adult transgressors can support themselves on income derived from aggressive pursuits; protesters can secure through forceful collective response social reforms that affect their lives materially; governments that rule by force are rewarded in using punitive control by the personal gains it brings to those in power and to supporters who benefit from the existing social arrangements; and nations are sometimes able to gain control over prized territories by military force.

Social and status rewards. Aggressive styles of behavior are often adopted because they win approval and status rewards. When people are commended for behaving punitively they become progressively more aggressive, whereas they display a relatively low level of aggression when it is not treated as praiseworthy (Geen and Stonner 1971, Staples and Walters 1964). Approval not only increases the specific aggressive responses that are socially reinforced but it tends to enhance other forms of aggression as well (Geen and Pigg 1970, Loew 1967, Slaby 1974).

Analyses of social reinforcement of aggressive behavior in natural settings are in general agreement with results of laboratory studies. Parents of assaultive children are generally nonpermissive for aggressive behavior in the home, but condone, actively encourage, and reinforce provocative and aggressive actions towards others in the community (Bandura 1960, Bandura and Walters 1959).

In aggressive gangs, members not only gain approval but achieve social status through their skills in fighting (Short 1968). In status rewards, performance of valued behavior gains one a social rank that carries with it multiple benefits as long as the position is occupied. A rank-contingent system of reward is more powerful than one in which specific responses are socially rewarded. If failure to behave aggressively deprives one of a specific reward, the negative consequence is limited and of no great importance. A demotion in rank, however, results in forfeiture of all the social and material benefits that go with it. The pressure for aggressive accomplishments is especially strong when status positions are limited and there are many eager competitors for them.

During wartime, societies offer medals, promotions, and social commendations on the basis of skill in killing. When reinforcement practices are instituted that favor inhuman forms of behavior, otherwise socialized people can be led to behave brutally and to take pride in such actions.

Reduction of aversive treatment. People are often treated aversively by others and so they seek relief. Coercive action that is not unduly hazardous is the most direct and the quickest means of alleviating maltreatment, if only temporarily. Defensive forms of aggression are frequently reinforced by their capacity to terminate humiliating and painful treatment. Reinforcement through pain reduction is well documented in studies cited earlier showing that children who are victimized but terminate the abuse by successful counteraggression eventually become highly aggressive in their behavior (Patterson, Littman and Bricker 1967).

Patterson's (1979) analysis of familial interactions of hyperaggressive children further documents the role of negative reinforcement in promoting aggressive styles of behavior. In such families children are inadvertently trained to use coercive behavior as the means of commanding parental attention or terminating social demands. The children's antagonistic behavior rapidly accelerates parental counteraggression in an escalating power struggle. By escalating reciprocal aggression each member provides aversive instigation for each other, and each member is periodically reinforced for behaving coercively by overpowering the other through more painful counteractions. Mutual coercion is most likely to appear as a prominent factor in families that find their children's control techniques painful and therefore seek relief from clinics. However, intrafamilial coercion is not a significant factor in families of pre-delinquent children who are forced to consult clinics because of legal threats rather than mutual torment (Reid and Patterson 1976).

A quite different view of aggression emerges if hyperaggressive children are selected from the population at large rather than from clinics. In one study (Bandura 1960), the most hyperaggressive children in an entire community were identified in school settings and their social behavior was systematically observed. Despite the fact that these children were highly belligerent, assaultive, and destructive of property, few of these families had ever consulted a clinic. This was because their training in aggression did not produce torment in the home. The parents modeled aggressive attitudes and, while nonpermissive and punitive for aggression toward themselves, they actively encouraged and rewarded aggression directed at others outside the home. As a result of this differential training, the children were reasonably well behaved at home but readily assaultive toward others. If their youngsters misbehaved, it was because others were at fault. The parents of these hyperaggressive children not only saw little reason to consult clinics, but many of them considered aggression to be a valued attribute. In these families, the development of aggression is better explained in terms of a positive, rather than a negative, reinforcement model. Samples of hyperaggressive children drawn from different sources may thus yield different theories on the familial determinants of aggression.

In the social learning analysis, defensive aggression is sustained to a greater extent by anticipated consequences than by its instantaneous effects. People will endure the pain of reprisals on expectations that their aggressive efforts will eventually remove deleterious conditions. Aggressive actions may also be partly maintained in the face of painful counterattack by anticipated costs of timidity. In aggression-oriented circles, failure to fight back can arouse fear of future victimization and humiliation. A physical pummeling may, therefore, be far less distressing than repeated social derision or increased likelihood of future abuse. In other words, humans do not behave like unthinking servomechanisms directed solely by immediate response feedback. Under aversive conditions of life, people will persist, at least for a time, in aggressive behavior that produces immediate pain but prospective relief from misery.

Expressions of injury. In the view of drive theorists the purpose of aggression is infliction of injury. Just as eating relieves hunger, hurting others presumably discharges the aggressive drive. It has therefore been widely assumed that aggressive behavior is reinforced by signs of suffering in the victim. According to Sears, Maccoby and Levin (1957), pain cues become rewarding because the pain produced by aggressive acts is repeatedly associated with tension relief and removal of frustrations. Feshbach (1970) interprets the rewarding value of pain expression in terms of self-esteem processes. Perception of pain in one's tormentors is experienced as satisfying because it signifies successful retaliation and thus restores the aggressor's self-esteem.

A contrasting view is that signs of suffering ordinarily function as inhibitors rather than as positive reinforcers of aggressive behavior. Because of the dangers of intragroup violence, all societies establish strong prohibitions against cruel and destructive acts, except under special circumstances. In the course of socialization most people adopt, for self-evaluation, standards that ruthless aggression is morally reprehensible. Consequently, aggression that produces evident suffering in others elicits both fear of punishment and self-censure which tend to inhibit injurious attacks.

Studies on how pain expressions affect assaults on suffering victims support the inhibitory effects. Aggressors behave less punitively when their victims express anguished cries than when they do not see or hear them suffer (Baron 1971a, 1971b, Sanders and Baron 1977). Contrary to drive theory, pain cues reduce aggression regardless of whether assailants are angered or not (Geen 1970, Rule and Leger 1976). People are even less inclined to behave cruelly when they see their suffering victims than when they merely hear the distress they have caused them (Milgram 1974).

The scope of the experimental treatments and the populations studied are too limited to warrant the strong conclusion that pain expressions never enhance aggressive behavior. A gratuitous insult from a stranger in a laboratory may not create sufficient animosity for the victim to derive satisfaction from injurious retaliation. It is a quite different matter when an antagonist repeatedly tyrannizes others or wields power in ways that make life miserable for them. In such instances news of the misfortune, serious illness, or death of an oppressor is joyfully received by people who ordinarily respond more compassionately to the adversities befalling others. However, the alleviation of aversive treatment from injured oppressors rather than their suffering may be the primary source of satisfaction. In experimental investigations pain expressions occur without the other extraneous rewards accompanying victory over antagonists.

From the standpoint of social learning theory, suffering of one's enemy is most apt to augment aggression when hurting them lessens maltreatment or benefits aggressors in other ways. When aggressors suffer reprisals or self-contempt for harming others, signs of suffering function as negative reinforcers that deter injurious attacks.

Findings of studies with infrahuman subjects are sometimes cited as evidence that fighting is inherently rewarding. Animals will perform responses that produce an attackable target, especially if they have been trained for aggression and are subjected to aversive stimulation. However, because of inadequate controls, this line of experimentation failed to clarify whether the animals were seeking combat, escape, or social contact (Bandura 1973). Studies including conditions in which animals perform responses to gain contact without opportunity to fight (Kelsey and Cassidy 1976) demonstrate that social contact rather than combat is the source of reward.

There are certain conditions under which pain expressions may assume reward value. Examples can be cited of societal practices in which brutal acts are regarded as praiseworthy by those in positions of power. Inhumane reinforcement contingencies can breed people who take pleasure in inflicting pain and humiliation. Additionally, clinical studies of sexual perversion have disclosed cases in which pain cues acquire powerful reward value through repeated association with sexual gratification. As a result, erotic pleasure is derived from inflicting pain on others or on oneself.

There are no conceptual or empirical grounds for regarding aggression maintained by certain effects as more genuine or important than others. A comprehensive theory must account for all aggressive actions, whatever purposes they serve. To restrict analysis of aggression to behavior that is supposedly reinforced by expressions of injury is to exclude from consideration some of the most violent activities where injury is an unavoidable concomitant rather than the major function of the behavior.

One might also question the distinction traditionally drawn between 'instrumental' aggression, which is supposedly aimed at securing extraneous rewards, and 'hostile' aggression, the sole purpose of which is presumably to inflict suffering (Feshbach 1970). Since, in all instances, the behavior is instrumental in producing certain desired outcomes, be they pain, approval, status, or material gain, it is more meaningful to differentiate aggressive behaviors in terms of their functional value rather than whether or not they are instrumental.

Punishing consequences

Restraints over injurious behavior arise from two different sources. *Social restraints* are rooted in threats of external punishment. *Personal restraints* operate through anticipatory self-condemning reactions toward one's own conduct. In developmental theories these two sources of restraint are traditionally characterized as fear control and guilt control, respectively. Punishing consequences that are observed or experienced directly convey information about the circumstances under which aggressive behavior is safe and when it is hazardous. Aggressive actions are therefore partly regulated on the basis of anticipated negative consequences. Being under cognitive and situational control, restraints arising from external threats vary in durability and in how widely they generalize beyond the prohibitive situations.

The effectiveness of punishment in controlling behavior is determined by a number of factors (Bandura 1969, Campbell and Church 1969). Of special importance are the benefits derived through aggressive actions and the availability of alternative means of securing desired goals. Other determinants of the suppressive power of punishment include the likelihood that aggression will be punished, the nature, severity, timing, and duration of aversive consequences. In addition, the level of instigation to aggression and the characteristics of the prohibitive agents influence how aggressors will respond under threat of punishment.

When alternative means are available for people to get what they seek, aggressive modes of behavior that carry high risk of punishment are rapidly discarded. Aggression control through punishment becomes more problematic when aggressive actions are socially or tangibly rewarded, and alternative means of securing desired outcomes are either unavailable, less effective in producing results, or not within the capabilities of the aggressor. Here, punishment must be applied with considerable force and consistency to outweigh the benefits of aggression. Even then it achieves, at best, temporary selective control in the threatening situation. Functional aggression is reinstated when threats are removed, and readily performed in settings in which the chance of punishment is low (Bandura and Walters 1959). Punishment is not only precarious as an external inhibitor of intermittently rewarded behavior, but its frequent use can inadvertently promote aggression by modeling punitive modes of control (Hoffman 1960).

Punishment, whether direct or observed, is informative as well as inhibitory. People can profit from witnessing the failures of others or from their own mistakes. Given strong instigation to aggression and limited options, threats lead people to adopt safer forms of aggression or to refine the prohibited behavior to improve its chances of success. For this reason, antisocial aggression is best prevented by combining deterrents with the cultivation of more functional alternatives. Most law-abiding behavior relies more on deterrence through preferable prosocial options than on threats of legal sanctions.

There are certain conditions under which aggression is escalated through punishment, at least in the short run. Individuals who recurrently engage in aggressive behavior have experienced some success in controlling others through force. In interpersonal encounters, they respond to counterattacks with progressively more punitive reactions to force acquiescence (Edwards 1968, Patterson 1979, Toch 1969). The use of punishment as a control technique also carries risks of escalating collective aggression when grievances are justifiable and challengers possess substantial coercive power (Bandura 1973, Gurr 1970). Under these circumstances, continued aggressive behavior eventually succeeds in changing social practices that lack sufficient justification to withstand concerted protest.

Vicarious reinforcement

In the course of everyday life there are numerous opportunities to observe the actions of others and the circumstances under which they are rewarded, ignored, or punished. Observed outcomes influence behavior in much the same way as directly experienced consequences. People can profit from the successes and mistakes of others as well as from their own experiences. As a general rule, seeing aggression rewarded in others increases, and seeing it punished decreases, the tendency to behave in similar ways (Bandura 1965, Bandura, Ross and Ross 1963). The more consistent the observed response consequences, the greater are the facilitatory and inhibitory effects on viewers (Rosekrans and Hartup 1967).

Vicarious reinforcement operates primarily through its informative function. Since observed outcomes convey different types of information, they can have diverse behavioral effects. Response consequences accruing to others convey contingency information about the types of actions likely to be rewarded or punished and the situations in which it is appropriate to perform them. A number of factors that enter into the process of social comparison can alter the customary effects of observed consequences. Models and observers often differ in distinguishable ways so that behavior considered approvable for one may be punishable for the other, depending on discrepancies in sex, age, and social status. When the same behavior produces unlike consequences for different members, observed reward may not enhance the level of imitative aggressiveness (Thelen and Soltz 1969).

When observed outcomes are judged personally attainable, they create incentive motivation. Seeing others' successes can function as a motivator by arousing in observers expectations that they can gain similar rewards for analogous performances. Some of the changes in responsiveness may also reflect vicarious acquisition or extinction of fears through the affective consequences accruing to models. Indeed, the legal system of deterrence rests heavily on the restraining function of exemplary punishment (Packer 1968, Zimring 1973). But observed outcomes also reduce the deterrent efficacy of threatened legal consequences. The chance of being caught and punished for criminal conduct is relatively low. In locales in which transgressions are common, people have personal knowledge of countless crimes being committed without detection. Such exposure to unpunished transgressions tends to reduce the force of legal deterrents.

In addition to the aforementioned effects, valuation of people and activities can be significantly altered on the basis of observed consequences. Ordinarily, observed punishment tends to devalue the models and their behavior, whereas the same models become a source of emulation when their actions are admired. However, aggressors may gain, rather than lose, status in the eyes of their peers when they are punished for a style of behavior valued by the group, or when they aggress against institutional practices that violate the professed values of society. It is for this reason that authoritative agencies are usually careful not to discipline challengers in ways that might martyr them.

Observed consequences can change observers' valuation of those who exercise power as well as of the recipients. Restrained and principled use of coercive power elicits respect. When societal agents misuse their power to reward and punish, they undermine the legitimacy of their authority and arouse opposition. Seeing inequitable punishment, rather than securing compliance, may foster aggressive reprisals. Indeed, activists sometimes attempt to rally supporters to their cause by selecting aggressive tactics calculated to provoke authorities to excessive counter measures.

The manner in which aggressors respond to the consequences of their behavior can also influence how observers later react when they themselves are rewarded for displaying similar responses. In one such study (Ditrichs, Simon and Greene 1967), children who observed models express progressively more hostility for social approval later increased their own output of hostile responses that brought praise. However, when models appeared oppositional by reducing hostile responses that brought them praise, or reacted in a random fashion as though they were uninfluenced, observers did not increase their expression of hostility even though they were praised whenever they did so. Thus, susceptibility to direct reinforcement was increased by observed willing responsiveness, but reduced by observed resistance.

Observed outcomes introduce comparative processes into the operation of reinforcement influences. The observed consequences accruing to others provide a standard for judging whether the outcomes one customarily receives are equitable, beneficent, or unfair. The same external outcome can function as a reward or as a punishment depending upon the observed consequences used for comparison. Relational properties of reinforcement affect not only behavior, but the level of personal satisfaction or discontent as well. Equitable treatment tends to promote a sense of well-being, whereas inequitable reinforcement generates resentments and dissatisfactions. The effects of perceived inequity on aggression were reviewed earlier in the discussion of relative deprivation.

Self-regulatory mechanisms

The discussion thus far has analyzed how behavior is regulated by external consequences that are either observed or experienced first-hand. People are not simply reactors to external influences. Through self-generated inducements and self-produced consequences they can exercise some influence over their own behavior. In this self-regulatory process, people adopt through tuition and modeling certain standards of behavior and respond to their own actions in self-rewarding or self-punishing ways. An act therefore includes among its determinants self-produced influences.

A detailed account of self-regulatory processes, which is presented elsewhere (Bandura 1976, 1978a), falls beyond the scope of this paper. In social learning theory, a self system is not a psychic agent that controls behavior. Rather, it refers to cognitive structures that provide the referential standards against which behavior is judged, and a set of subfunctions for the perception, evaluation, and regulation of action. Figure 4 presents a diagrammatic representation of three main subfunctions in the self-regulation of behavior by self-produced incentives. The first component concerns the selective observation of one's own behavior in terms of a

Self-observation	Judgmental process	Self-response
Performance dimensions	Personal standards	Self-evaluative reactions
Quality	Modeling sources	Positive
Rate	Reinforcement sources	Negative
Quantity	Tuition	
Originality	Referential performances	Tangible self-applied consequences
Authenticity		
Consequentialness	Standard norms	Rewarding
Deviancy	Social comparison	Punishing
Ethicalness	Personal comparison	
	Collective comparison	No self-response
	Valuation of activity	
	Regarded highly	
	Neutral	
	Devalued	
	Performance attribution	
	Personal locus	
	External locus	

4. Component processes in the self-regulation of behavior by self-produced consequences.

number of relevant dimensions. Behavior produces self-reactions through a judgmental function relying on several subsidiary processes which include referential comparisons of perceived conduct to internal standards, valuation of the activities in which one is engaged, and cognitive appraisal of the determinants of one's behavior. Performance appraisals set the occasion for self-produced consequences. Favorable judgments give rise to rewarding self-reactions, whereas unfavorable appraisals activate negative self-reactions.

Self-regulated incentives are conceptualized as motivational devices rather than as automatic strengtheners of preceding responses. By making self-reward and self-punishment contingent on designated performances, people motivate themselves to expend the effort needed to attain performances that give them self-satisfaction and they refrain from behaving in ways that result in self-censure. Because of self-reactive tendencies, aggressors must contend with themselves as well as with others when they behave in an injurious manner.

Self-reward for aggression. One can distinguish several ways in which self-generated consequences enter into the self-regulation of aggressive behavior. At one extreme are individuals who have adopted behavioral standards and codes that make aggressive feats a source of personal pride. Such individuals readily engage in aggressive activities and derive enhanced feelings of self-worth from physical conquests (Bandura and Walters 1959, Toch 1969, Yablonsky 1962). Lacking self-reprimands for hurtful conduct, they are deterred from cruel acts mainly by reprisal threats. Idiosyncratic self systems of morality are not confined to individuals or fighting gangs. In aggressive cultures where prestige is closely tied to fighting prowess, members take considerable pride in aggressive exploits.

Self-punishment for aggression. After ethical and moral standards of conduct are adopted, anticipatory self-condemning reactions for violating personal standards ordinarily serve as self-deterrents against reprehensible acts. Results of the study by Bandura and Walters (1959) reveal how anticipatory self-reproach for repudiated aggression serves as a motivating influence to keep behavior in line with adopted standards. Adolescents who were compassionate in their dealing with others responded with self-disapproval, remorse, and attempts at reparation even when their aggressive activities were minor in nature. In contrast, assaultive boys experienced relatively few negative self-reactions over serious aggressive activities. These differential self-reactive patterns are corrobo-rated by Perry and Bussey (1977) in laboratory tests. Highly aggressive boys reward themselves generously for inflicting suffering on another child, whereas those who display low aggressive tendencies react with self-denial for behaving injuriously. In studies of aggressive modeling, the more reprehensible children judge aggressive actions to be, the less likely they are to adopt them when they are later exemplified by a peer model (Hicks 1971).

Disengagement of internal control. Theories of internalization generally por-tray incorporated entities in the form of a conscience, superego, and moral codes as continuous internal overseers of conduct. Such theories encounter difficulties in explaining the variable operation of internal control and the perpetration of gross inhumanities by otherwise humane, compassionate people. Such concepts as 'superego lacunae', 'islands of superego', and various 'mental defense mechanisms' have been pro-posed as the explanatory factors.

In the social learning analysis, moral people perform culpable acts through processes that disengage evaluative self-reactions from such conduct, rather than because of defects in the development or the struc-ture of their superegos (Bandura 1973). Acquisition of self-regulatory capabilities does not create an invariant control mechanism within a person. Self-evaluative influences do not operate unless activated, and many situational dynamics influence their selective activation.

Self-deterring consequences are likely to be activated most strongly when the causal connection between conduct and the detrimental effects it produces is unambiguous. There are various means, however, by which self-evaluative consequences can be dissociated from censurable behavior. Figure 5 shows the several points in the process at which the disengagement can occur.

One set of disengagement practices operates at the level of the behavior. People do not ordinarily engage in reprehensible conduct until they have justified to themselves the morality of their actions. What is culpable can be made honorable through cognitive restructuring. In this process, reprehensible conduct is made personally and socially accept-able by portraying it in the service of moral ends. Over the years, much destructive and reprehensible conduct has been perpetrated by decent, moral people in the name of religious principles and righteous ideologies. Acting on moral or ideological imperative reflects not an unconscious defense mechanism, but a conscious offense mechanism.

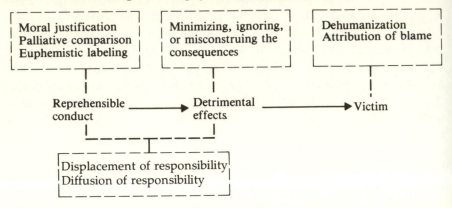

5. Mechanisms through which behavior is disengaged from self-evaluative consequences at different points in the behavioral process.

Self-deplored acts can also be made righteous by contrasting them with flagrant inhumanities. The more outrageous the comparison practices, the more likely are one's reprehensible acts to appear trifling or even benevolent. Euphemistic language provides an additional convenient device for disguising reprehensible activities and according them a respectable status. Through convoluted verbiage pernicious conduct is made benign and those who engage in it are relieved of a sense of personal agency (Gambino 1973). Moral justifications and palliative characterizations are especially effective disinhibitors because they not only eliminate self-generated deterrents, but engage self-reward in the service of injurious behavior. What was morally unacceptable becomes a source of self-pride.

Another set of dissociative practices operates by obscuring or distorting the relationship between actions and the effects they cause. People will behave in highly punitive ways they normally repudiate if a legitimate authority acknowledges responsibility for the consequences of the conduct (Diener *et al.* 1975, Milgram 1974). By displacing responsibility people do not see themselves as personally accountable for their actions and are thus spared self-prohibiting reactions. Nor is self-censure activated when the link between conduct and its consequences is obscured by diffusing responsibility. Through division of labor, diffusion of decision making, and collective action people can behave injuriously without anyone feeling personally responsible for culpable behavior. They therefore act more aggressively when responsibility is obscured by a collective instrumentality (Bandura, Underwood and Fromson 1975).

Additional ways of weakening self-deterring reactions operate by disregarding or obscuring the consequences of actions. When people embark on a self-disapproved course of action for personal gain, or because of other inducements, they avoid facing the harm they cause. Self-censuring reactions are unlikely to be activated as long as the detrimental effects of conduct are disregarded, minimized, or misjudged (Brock and Buss 1962, 1964).

The final set of disengagement practices operate at the level of the recipients of injurious effects. The strength of self-evaluative reactions partly depends on how the people toward whom actions are directed are viewed. Maltreatment of individuals who are regarded as subhuman or debased is less apt to arouse self-reproof than if they are seen as human beings with dignifying qualities (Bandura, Underwood and Fromson 1975, Zimbardo 1969). Analysis of the cognitive concomitants of injurious behavior reveals that dehumanization fosters a variety of self-exonerating maneuvers (Bandura, Underwood and Fromson 1975). People strongly disapprove of cruel behavior and rarely excuse its use when they interact with humanized individuals. By contrast, people seldom condemn punitive conduct, and generate self-disinhibiting justifications for it, when they direct their behavior toward individuals divested of humanness.

Many conditions of contemporary life are conducive to dehumanization. Bureaucratization, automation, urbanization, and high social mobility lead people to relate to each other in anonymous, impersonal ways. In addition, social practices that divide people into in-group and out-group members produce human estrangement that fosters dehumanization. Strangers can be more easily cast as unfeeling beings than can personal acquaintances.

Psychological research tends to focus on the disinhibiting effects of social practices that divest people of human qualities. This emphasis is understandable considering the prevalence and the serious consequences of people's inhumanities toward each other. Of equal theoretical and social significance is the power of humanization to counteract injurious conduct. Studies examining this process reveal that, even under conditions that ordinarily weaken self-deterrents, it is difficult for people to behave cruelly toward others when they are characterized in ways that personalize and humanize them (Bandura, Underwood and Fromson 1975).

Attributing blame to one's victims is still another expedient that can serve self-exonerative purposes. Detrimental interactions usually involve a series of reciprocally escalative actions in which the victims are rarely

Neurobiological and psychological mechanisms

faultless. One can always select from the chain of events an instance of defensive behavior by the adversary and view it as the original instigation. Victims then get blamed for bringing suffering on themselves, or extraordinary circumstances are invoked to vindicate irresponsible conduct. By blaming others, one's own actions are excusable. People are socially aided in dehumanizing and blaming groups held in disfavor by pejorative stereotyping and indoctrination.

Gradualism and disinhibition. The aforementioned practices will not instantaneously transform a gentle person into a brutal aggressor. Rather, the change is usually achieved through a gradual disinhibition process in which participants may not fully recognize the marked changes they are undergoing. Initially, individuals are prompted to perform aggressive acts they can tolerate without excessive self-censure. After their discomfort and self-reproof are diminished through repeated performance, the level of aggression is progressively increased in this manner until eventually gruesome deeds, originally regarded as abhorrent, can be performed without much distress.

As is evident from the preceding discussion, the development of self-regulatory functions does not create a mechanical servocontrol system wherein behavioral output is accurately monitored, compared against an internal standard and, if judged deviant, is promptly brought in line with the referent standard. Nor do situational influences exercise mechanical control. Personal judgments operating at each subfunction preclude the automaticity of the process. There is leeway in judging whether a given behavioral standard is applicable. Because of the complexity and inherent ambiguity of most events, there is even greater leeway in the judgment of behavior and its effects. To add further to the variability of the self-control process, most activities are performed under collective arrangements that obscure responsibility, thus permitting leeway in judging the degree of personal agency in the effects that are socially produced. In short, there exists considerable latitude for personal judgmental factors to affect whether or not self-regulatory influences will be engaged in any given activity.

Differing perspectives on disengagement of internal restraints

The preceding discussion analyzed reduction of internal control within the framework of social learning theory. Other researchers have addressed this issue from a different conceptual perspective. Zimbardo (1969) explains reduction of restraints over aggression in terms of deindividuation. Deindividuation is an internal state characterized by a loss of self-consciousness and self-evaluation coupled with a diminished concern for negative evaluation from others. According to this view, the altered perception of self and others weakens cognitive control over behavior, thus facilitating intense impulsive actions.

People can be deindividuated by a variety of external conditions, including anonymity, immersion in a group, diffusion of responsibility, high emotional arousal, intense sensory stimulation, and physiological factors that alter states of consciousness. Many of the postulated determinants of deindividuation remain to be investigated. However, the conditions that have been examined empirically, such as group presence, anonymity, and emotional arousal, have variable effects on behavior depending on the presence of other personal and situational factors conducive to aggression (Bandura 1973, Diener 1977, Zimbardo 1969). Verification of the deindividuation link in the causal process is a much more complicated matter because it requires independent assessment of the internal state. The initial attempts to link the indicants of deindividuation either to the situational conditions or to the disinhibited behavior have so far produced inconclusive results (Diener 1977).

It should be recognized that this line of research presents especially difficult methodological problems. One cannot keep interrupting unrestrained aggressors for their perceptions of themselves and others without aborting the disinhibitory process. To measure the cognitive concomitants of external disinhibitory conditions prior to performance is to alter the very phenomenon being studied. Judgments of the promise of a theory in this field must therefore rest heavily on its success in identifying determinants of behavioral disinhibition and in bringing order among diverse findings. In view of the important role played by self-justification processes in disinhibition, a full explanation of how aggression is freed from internal restraints must consider the self-regulatory mechanisms discussed earlier.

Although deindividuation and social learning theory posit some overlapping determinants and processes of internal disinhibition, they differ in certain important respects. Deindividuation views intense aggression as resulting mainly from loss of cognitive control. Social learning encompasses a broad range of disinhibitory factors designed to provide a unified theory for explaining both impulsive and principled aggressive conduct. As shown earlier, people frequently engage in violent activities not because of reduced self-control but because their cognitive skills and self-control are enlisted all too well through moral justifications and self-exonerative devices in the service of destructive causes. The massive threats to human welfare are generally brought about by deliberate acts of principle rather than by unrestrained acts of impulse. It is the principled resort to aggression that is of greatest social concern but most ignored in psychological theorizing and research.

Comments on papers by Flynn and Bandura

VERNON REYNOLDS

Bandura's aggression theory is, in large part, based on his general theory. People learn aggressive behaviour by observing the forms and circumstances in others. But they only act aggressively if, on balance, they feel it will be rewarding and not punishing to do so. Primary models on which attention is focussed and from which learning occurs are the family, the sub-culture, and the media, especially television. Where these positively sanction aggression, individuals learn from them how and when to act aggressively and then store the information for use on any subsequent occasion when such action will, they consider, lead to positive rewards.

There is no aggressive 'instinct' in Bandura's model, nor does he accept any 'drive' theory of aggression. Thus in the case of children taught to respond aggressively in frustrating situations, they respond that way, whereas children who have learned to respond cooperatively in the same circumstances respond by cooperation.

Bandura's theory goes beyond individual aggressiveness to group aggression but he does not feel the need to invoke any new process to explain group aggressions, such as institutionalised punishments or rewards. Such cases are to be seen as psychology at the collective level. Military social organisation is a large scale version of individual aggressive organisation, based, that is, on cognitive strategies about how and when to engage in conflict in order to achieve rewarding ends or avoid punishing ones.

The above represents Bandura's thesis as I understand it from reading his paper. The bulk of his paper is in fact given over to a detailed analysis of the processes involved in the social learning of modes of aggression,

357

the forms it takes and results it achieves. I shall now approach it from my own perspective, as referee, with two questions in mind:

(1) Is it a theory? and

(2) How does it relate to human ethology?

First, then, is it a theory? I should like to suggest that it is not so much a theory as a hypothesis. The *Oxford English Dictionary* definition of a 'theory' is a 'hypothesis that has been confirmed or established by observation or experiment'. I doubt whether enough has yet been achieved in psychology to dignify many, or even any, ideas about such weighty issues as human aggression with the status of 'theories'. It is safer to consider them as hypotheses.

A hypothesis should be able to predict, be verifiable, and preferably also falsifiable, by experiment or other empirical evidence. Bandura's hypothesis arises from a good deal of observational and experimental evidence. It has predictive power. It is verifiable. For instance, if a certain television programme shows a particularly ingenious method of committing a crime, and that method is then used in real life afterwards by an individual who watched the programme, and the individual (when caught) states that he got the idea from the programme, we then have good evidence in favour of Bandura's hypothesis. Bandura can (and *has*) been able successfully to predict new patterns of crime in areas in the USA by linking them to particularly suggestive television programmes.[1]

In such cases, the picture is clear enough. But we need to define the limits of predictability. For instance, if a person blames television programmes *generally* for his acts of aggressiveness, can we accept this? How specific a copy must an action be before we can accept that it is a case of social learning? And what are we to make of the fact that some models form the basis of social learning while others do not? What is the agency that selects which of all the various models we are presented with by television we use as a basis for our own actions, and which we reject? Clearly there is some such agency, some kind of a self-with-its-project, and I shall return to this later.

There remains the question of falsifiability. It seems unlikely that Bandura's hypothesis could be adequately falsified. Take the case where an individual acts aggressively (he hits his wife) and when asked why he says 'I don't know, I just lost my temper and lashed out'. He may never have done it before. He may never have seen anyone do it in real life, although he may have seen it on television or heard about it happening or read about it. He knows it happens, but he denies this influenced him, he

[1] Personal communication from A. Bandura.

just feels it was some sort of uncontrollable reaction that took over. In this case, is Bandura's hypothesis falsified or not? If it is, then, the hypothesis needs refining. If it is not, why not? Presumably because there could still be argument over whether the husband's statement was accurate – he may have forgotten the relevant past experience, or he may be denying it. This problem cannot be solved, because of the inevitably complex and unknowable life-history of individuals. So true falsification is not possible.

However, this raises an extremely important question concerning the whole issue of the scientific approach to cognitive processes. Are hypotheses about such processes, especially about their origins, *ever* falsifiable? The problem raised is the one facing all efforts to 'explain' human action, namely that action arises at any given time out of the history of the self, a complex history of interwoven strands of mental and physical experience, uncharted and undocumented, not understood by the actor himself let alone any other person. This is not to deny the possibility of going back over old memories, perhaps deep into infancy with a psychoanalyst as one's guide; but it *is* to doubt the chances of piecing together an accurate historical picture of anything but fragments of an individual's own personal history with respect to its role in determining present outcomes.

Further, even if it were possible to recover the relevant aspects of his history intact there are good reasons for saying that we still might not be able to produce predictive hypotheses. The reason is that in the process of self-construction that occurs during human ontogeny, the emergent self (that Bandura so rightly makes central to his concept of man) has an autonomy that to greater or lesser extent takes charge of and controls at every moment the forward movement in time of the personality. Otherwise there would be no difference between 'essence' (all that we are made of) and 'existence' (all that we make of ourselves).

This brings us to the second question we set out to ask about Bandura's social learning theory: the question of its relation to human ethology. Bandura is concerned with 'cognitive' man and for this we must be thankful, since man's actions are the outcome of his ideas and inner cognitive representations. Human ethology is concerned with the evolution and ontogeny of human behaviour. Bandura does not mention human evolution nor does he appear to consider it relevant to the understanding of human aggression. As regards behavioural ontogeny, Bandura does not use the word. His cognitive hypothesis of social learning must presumably imply neural equivalents of the ideational processes that enable both modelling and decision-making to take place. His neurophysiology is implicit but it is nevertheless there and it seems to be rather deterministic: given certain prior modelling, a certain decision process and a certain context, the result in human action is predictable. Thus an ethologist who was prepared to accept the very great learning component proposed by Bandura might still find something in his ideas, namely that the physical basis of the modelling process was part of the brain structure and perhaps genetically coded; also its links with a 'decision area' and the limbic system or any other lower brain structures associated with aggressive action.

There is no necessary conflict between Bandura's theory and how an ethologist might expect the human brain to be organised with respect to aggression, despite the extent of social learning stressed by Bandura. This does not of course affect the point made earlier, namely that the hypothesis relies heavily on a cognitive decision-process which cannot be validly assessed. But the problem he raises is not this: it is whether Bandura's ideas take sufficient account of man's ability to act at any time in new, unmodelled ways. The self has, besides its social constituents, an evolutionary and an ontogenetic-organic basis. It is concerned with its own integrity. We make ourselves out of what we are made of, and this constant process of internal reconstruction determines our actions. Modelling processes have their part to play in this, but are only one among a number of constituents underlying aggressive action.

Now we come on to a consideration of the paper by J. P. Flynn and his colleagues on 'Anatomical pathways for attack behavior in cats'. I have read this, together with a number of background papers and chapters written by Flynn over the last seven years, in order to try and understand the essentials of what a wholly neurophysiological approach can tell a non-neurophysiologist such as myself. The author has, with due caution, written nothing as far as I know about the neurophysiology of humans. He has confined himself to cats, on which he has worked extensively, and writes also about rats, mice and monkeys, though relatively little about the latter. In view of the topic of this volume, and in view of my own concerns as an anthropologist, I have a duty as referee to direct both his attention and that of others to the wider question of the relationship between his findings and the neurophysiology of man, and try and draw him out on this. Otherwise, his paper, despite its undoubted value as a research report, is not a contribution to the subject under discussion.

First, I should like to ask Flynn whether and to what extent he supposes that human neurophysiological processes are akin to those of the cat? This broad question can be narrowed down considerably on the lines of his own findings. He has distinguished for some years between two kinds of aggressive behaviour in cats. On the one hand there is the so-called 'classical rage response' of Hess (1928) in which the cat hisses, arches its back, displays piloerection, retracts its lips and lays back its ears, and which may lead to a defensive action in which the cat uses its claws to scratch the opponent (we have all seen cats do this when faced by a strange dog). On the other hand there is what Flynn calls 'quiet biting attack', which is a silent approach to the opponent, without the features mentioned above, leading to a strong bite on the back of the neck which usually is lethal.

Despite the fact that we can use the word 'aggression' for both these behaviour patterns, they are clearly very different from each other. To an ethologist, the former appears far more an intra-specific threat pattern while the latter looks like an inter-specific predatory pattern. My first question to Flynn is: do we now have a clear understanding of the neurophysiological differences between these two very different attack pathways? Stimulation of the hypothalamus appears to be the method used for producing both types of response, and Flynn has shown some of the pathways associated with quiet biting attack; are other pathways equally clearly associated with the threat display?

Let us assume they are, and the differences are clear at both the behavioural and the neurophysiological level. The next question, coming on to our present topic, must be: does Flynn suppose that in man, as in the cat, there are two 'systems' of aggression of the feline kind, one based on defensive threat with a lot of noisy display such as can be summed up by the word 'rage', and the other a silent process leading to a lethal act? Clearly such things occur in man. A study of family assaults (and it is in the close family that many if not most assaults do occur) often reveals a 'rage' basis, and the number of battered babies and battered wives is a good testimony of this. On the other hand the 'rage' approach would clearly be disadvantageous to the assassin, or for that matter to the hunter with his gun looking for a rabbit for the pot. But the question is: does Flynn suppose that, in a world where humans were available for neurophysiological experiments, stimulation of particular sites in the human hypothalamus, or neighbouring areas of the brain, would lead to the occurrence of *either* noisy violent rage *or* silent lethal killing depending on the site stimulated?

On the basis of ignorant supposition, let me propose the following rough hypothesis: that whereas the former, rage, response would be forthcoming in man, the latter, killing response would not (except perhaps in highly trained killers). My reason for this is that whereas rage is an intra-specific activity whose presence (together with adequate inhibitory mechanisms) has been selected for since early primate times some sixty to eighty million years ago if not before, silent killing has not been a part of man's behavioural system until much more recently, even, I would suggest, as recently as the invention of agriculture (despite the evidence of killing in monkeys, apes and *Australopithecus*). Certainly man has been killing both other species and perhaps also his own kind for a long time – perhaps five million years or more. But I do not think he has become a predator in the same way as a cat is a predator. His diet has never exclusively consisted of prey, except in a few marginal cases such as the Eskimos. And even in the Eskimos one can still today observe at first hand the extent of careful preparation of hunting weapons, the careful planning of hunting expeditions, the judicious choice of hunting times and places, the long wait at blowholes, and the calculated manner of killing that marks the climax of the endeavour, whether by large groups in the case of whales or by individuals in the case of seals. None of this looks like a well-programmed, stereotyped behaviour pattern with a neurophysiological programme underlying and steering it. Of course there is an underlying neurophysiology, but it is, I guess, of the same kind as that found in much of human action, namely a vastly complex and largely neo-cortical process involving mostly learned elements feeding to and from sensory and motor afferents and efferents, and leading to hypothalamic-limbic or other lower brain processes as part of its executive programme rather than the other way round.

If the above guesswork is right then I cannot see the direct relevance of Flynn's research on the quiet killing behaviour of cats to the understanding of human killing, though as I said, he may not think it is directly relevant either.

On the other hand, the study of rage reactions may be highly relevant in a direct way, and I invite his comments on this. How far, at the level of observation, does cat 'rage' look like human rage? Clearly we do not arch our backs, but do we piloerect? We may not spit, but do we shout? Do our pupils dilate? When attack follows, do we use our teeth or our nails? Some of these questions have already been tackled by ethologists. From the neurophysiological point of view we can ask: how well is the basis of this emotion understood? What is the evidence from so-called CNS 'tranquillising' drugs, i.e. where do they act and what do they do?

But I do not wish to conclude with the implication that, at the level of rage, man is to be placed alongside the cat, monkey, ape or any other species. There is nothing in the brain stem, limbic system, hypothalamus etc. that man cannot, with his neo-cortex, learn to control. In the words of the Buddha: 'Many do not know that we are here in this world to live in harmony. Those who know this do not fight against each other.' Flynn, judging from his final paragraph, agrees on this important point. Human ethologists and others interested in the neurophysiology of the human brain as related to aggression will eagerly await clarification of the extent to which our known ability to regulate body processes, even the so-called 'autonomic' ones, is reflected in particular anatomical structures and feedback mechanisms in the brain.

Having commented on the papers by Bandura and Flynn, the question finally arises as to the relation between the two approaches to the understanding of human aggression. Bandura emphasises the cognitive aspects of aggressive acts – the intentions, social norms, ideational context, and suppositions about outcomes of the person or group involved. He does not consider biological factors as important in determining actual levels of aggressiveness. There is no aggressive instinct, and no 'drive'. He accepts that there is such a thing as 'emotional arousal' (p. 330) but its expressions are the outcomes of social learning. By contrast, Flynn works with the idea that specific kinds of aggression are highly programmed not only at the behavioural but also at the neurophysiological level. A compromise could presumably be reached if we accepted that the physiological and behavioural organisation of rage were under the control, in man, of neo-cortical instructions deriving from social learning.

In this compromise, situations would be seen as rage-inducing rather than rage-producing. Messages would then pass to the neo-cortex requesting decisions whether rage behavior be given the go-ahead or inhibited. If given the go-ahead, it would proceed along a given set of neural pathways, if blocked these pathways would not be activated.

There is thus no essential difficulty in accepting both positions in suitably modified form. But inevitably perhaps, both of them present us with a crude vision of man. On account of the time-depth and complexity of our life experience, it is unlikely whether, even at the neurological level, people evaluate the majority of their future actions in the light of their past experiences. That would be too time consuming and too muddling. We have a self which, if well integrated, can act instantly and decisively even against social conditioning. It is this integration of the self, its self-adjusting and self-regulating property, that eludes Bandura. Flynn's rage mechanism likewise suffers from over-simplicity. Even if neurophysiological and behavioural 'rage' programmes exist in each of us, and even if they could be demonstrated by stimulation with suitably positioned electrodes, such behaviours and their physical origins are normally buried deep in the workings of the acting self and are not to be seen as contingent on the occurrence of *any* particular set of external circumstances.

J. P. FLYNN: REPLY TO REYNOLDS' COMMENTS

The paper submitted by me and my colleagues concerns attack elicited in cats by electrical stimulation of the brain. Ordinarily our cats do not attack rats spontaneously but only during stimulation. The anatomical pathways described in the paper are involved in the mediation of this attack. Dr Reynolds has referred to the two forms of attack, one which is marked by a display of rage including vocalization, the other which is quiet but lethal.

These actions are brought about by the direct activity of the nervous system. It does not appear necessary to invoke an intervening variable such as motivation. The elicitation of the behavior follows the same rules with respect to thresholds as does a single nerve fiber. The direct action on the nervous system itself is further substantiated by the fact that the behavior is more intense on the side contralateral to the site of the electrode. If the electrode is on the right side of the brain, the cat strikes a rat with its left paw.

The terminal aspects of attack are mediated by a combination of patterned or state-dependent reflexes, i.e. reflexes present when the cat is stimulated to attack or is attacking naturally, but not otherwise. These include lunging at a rat, positioning it, moving the head to bite it, and the actual bite itself. The receptive field for these reflexes increases with increasing stimulation to the brain. This again is understandable in terms of the activity of the nervous system, but not in terms of intervening psychological variables like rage. The material in the paper establishes some of the pathways in the brain by which attack and the combination of reflexes which constitute it are carried out.

Dr Reynolds has asked the broad question of the extension of our findings to man. I cannot give a firm answer to the question. The evidence is insufficient. However, what evidence exists conforms with the data from other animals. For example, a woman with a histologically verified tumor in the hypothalamus, involving the ventromedial nucleus, displayed symptoms, including irritability and rage, similar to those found in cats (Reeves and Plum 1969). Another woman with a history of uncontrollable anger was twice stimulated through electrodes in the amygdala. After stimulation when the electrical signs of seizure appeared, on one occasion she quickly and violently struck at the wall, and on the other occasion she swung her guitar, narrowly missing the head of the attending psychiatrist (Mark and Ervin 1970). In cats stimulation of some sites in the amygdala yields an explosive form of rage. If the findings made in cats were not found in monkeys, one would doubt their extension to man. In monkeys, attacks have been elicited in subordinate animals against dominant ones (Perachio and Alexander 1974). The data, however, are again sparse.

Dr Reynolds is inclined to accept the relevance of the work on rage to man, but he did have some specific questions. He wished to know if the pathways associated with the threat display and attack were known; and if so, were they different from those associated with quiet attack. The answer to that question is that some of the pathways are known. The degeneration from such attack sites in the hypothalamus has been determined (Chi and Flynn 1968) and the location of cells which project to attack sites in the hypothalamus are established (Smith and Flynn, in preparation). They are different from those associated with quiet attack, although some overlap occurs.

Dr Reynolds questions in particular the relevance to man of our findings about quiet attack. He puts forth a number of reasons why this behavior is unlikely to be similar to man's. Man is not a predator in the way a cat is. His diet has never consisted exclusively of prey. In reply it should be stated that this form of behavior is not restricted to carnivores: it has been found in omnivores such as the rat (Woodworth 1971, Panksepp 1971) and the opossum (Roberts, Steinberg and Means 1967). Furthermore, this behavior is not predation. It is killing without eating. Eating occurs in association with only a few attack sites. From the majority of attack sites, eating is not elicitable.

A second reason for doubting the relevance of quiet attack to man's behavior is that quiet attack is more like an interspecific assault than an intraspecific one. There is a form of threat in the cat that is offensive in nature. It is very different from the defensive display associated with rage. If attack occurs subsequent to offensive threat, it takes the same form as quiet attack. I find it hard to believe that different pathways would mediate the same form of attack depending upon the species encountered.

Another reason given by Dr Reynolds for regarding quiet attack as irrelevant to man's behavior is the planning and careful preparation involved in hunting as opposed to a well programmed stereotype behavior with a neurophysiological program underlying and steering it. My concept of how basic tendencies might manifest themselves in behavior differs from that of Dr Reynolds. He looks upon them as expressing themselves in well programmed stereotype behavior, whereas I view them as incorporating learned behavior into their execution. Such incorporation of learning in the process of quiet attack has been demonstrated (Roberts and Kiess 1964). As another example, I regard the subtleties of courtship as expressions of a basic sexual tendency. Pathways that may influence the neocortex and presumably planning do exist. In two different experiments cortical visual responses were demonstrated to be influenced by hypothalamic stimulation, apart from any influence mediated by the ascending reticular formation (Chi and Flynn 1968, Vanegas, Foote and Flynn 1969–70). In addition, cells in the preoptic region and substantia innominata as well as in the hypothalamus project to the frontal, postcentral, and parietal cortex. These projections permit hypothalamic cells to influence neocortical activity (Kievit and Kuypers 1975a, 1975b).

A. BANDURA: REPLY TO REYNOLDS' COMMENTS

The paper on the psychological mechanisms of aggression puts forth a complex set of interacting determinants and processes governing the development, instigation, and regulation of aggression. These complexities are lost in Professor Reynolds' abridgment of the conceptual system to the elementary proposition that people learn by observation and perform for extrinsic reinforcement. An extensive presentation of social learning theory was clearly beyond the scope of an analysis of aggression. Hence, in addressing the general issues raised by Reynolds, I shall refer to publications in which this theoretical perspective is discussed in some detail.

Modeling obviously is not the sole source of information for the development of behavior patterns. In a social learning analysis, conceptions of behavior and the environment are developed through four different means (Bandura 1977a). People gain some of their knowledge from direct experience of the effects produced by their actions. The capacity to learn by observation enables people to exploit a vast source of information mediated through the activities of others. A special virtue of modeling is that it can transmit knowledge of wide applicability to vast numbers of people simultaneously through the medium of symbolic modeling. There are many things we cannot come to know by direct or vicarious experience because of limited accessibility or because they involve matters that are not easily subject to objective confirmation. When experiential verification is either difficult or impossible, people develop and evaluate their conceptions of things in terms of judgments voiced by others. In addition to enactive, vicarious, and social sources of information, logical operations enter into the process. After people acquire some rules of inference they can derive from what they already know new knowledge about things that extends beyond their experiences.

Knowledge, however attained, does not ensure skilled performance. Skills are developed through a complex interplay between biological factors, cognitive processing of diverse sources of information, and informative feedback from enactment of response patterns.

The regulation of established behavior also involves a complex interplay between external, vicarious, and self-generated influences. External consequences, influential as they often are, are not the sole regulators of behavior, nor do they operate automatically. As social beings, people profit from observed consequences as well as from their own direct experience. Behavior is better explained by the relational influence of observed and direct consequences than by either factor alone.

I have argued elsewhere (Bandura 1974) that theories that seek to explain human behavior as the product of external rewards and punishments present a truncated image of human nature because people partly regulate their actions by self-produced consequences. Most value their self-respect above commodities. Anticipated self-evaluative reactions therefore often conflict with, and override, the influence of external rewards and punishments. When individuals invest their sense of self-worth in socially unpopular convictions they will submit to prolonged maltreatment rather than accede to what they regard as unjust or immoral.

In Reynolds' conceptual scheme, the emergent self is the prime mover of behavior. As he puts it succinctly, the self 'has an autonomy that to greater or lesser extent takes charge of and controls at every moment the forward movement in time of the personality'.

Self processes occupy a central role in a social learning analysis of thought and behavior. People are not only perceivers, knowers, and actors. They are also self-reactors with a capacity for reflective self-awareness. However, a self system does not function as an autonomous psychic agent that orchestrates activities. Behavior, internal factors, and environmental influences all operate as interlocking determinants of each other (Bandura 1978a). The process involves a triadic reciprocal interaction. Although environmental factors influence thought and behavior, the environment is partly of a person's own making. It is largely through their actions that people produce environmental conditions that affect their behavior in a reciprocal fashion. The experiences generated by behavior partly determine what individuals think, expect, and can do, which in turn affects their subsequent behavior. People activate different environmental reactions, apart from their behavior, by their physical characteristics (e.g. size, physiognomy, race, sex, attractiveness) and socially conferred attributes, roles, and status. The differential social treatment affects recipients' self-conceptions and actions in ways that either maintain or alter the environmental biases. The relative influence exerted by these three sets of interlocking factors will vary across individuals, activities, and situational circumstances.

Reciprocal determination of events has implications for ethological study of human behavior. Ethological methodology emphasizes the mutual interaction of organisms in their natural habitats. The emphasis on mutuality is a significant advance over unidirectional linear models of behavior. However, to the extent that analyses of human functioning are confined to sequential interchanges in behavior, but ignore the reciprocally contributing influences of cognitive factors, the resulting theories will sacrifice explanatory power.

Perhaps I might illustrate this point with an example of familial aggressive interchanges. In discordant families, aggressive behavior by one member tends to elicit aggressive counteractions from recipients in a mutual escalation of aggression. However, aggressive acts often do not produce aggressive counteractions. To increase the predictive power of a theory of behavior it is necessary to broaden the analysis to include cognitive factors that operate in the interlocking system. Counterresponses to antecedent acts are influenced, not only by their immediate effects, but also by judgments of later consequences for a given course of action. Thus, aggressive children will continue, or even escalate, aggressive behavior in the face of immediate punishment when they expect persistence eventually to gain them what they seek. But the same momentary punishment will serve as an inhibitor rather than as an enhancer of aggressive behavior when they expect continuance of the aggressive conduct to be ineffective.

In brief, people process and synthesize contextual and outcome information from sequences of events over long intervals about the action patterns that are necessary to produce given outcomes. Even in infra-human subjects, behavior is related to its effects at the level of aggregate rather than momentary effects. A comprehensive analysis of human behavior must therefore be extended in cognitive and temporal directions.

The contention that social learning theory fails to take sufficient account of the ability to act in new ways is at variance with the facts. In a social learning analysis, the various modes of influence (e.g. modeling, reinforcement, conditioning, tuition) are regarded as different ways of conveying information for constructing conceptions of behavior and the environment. We are dealing here with self-constructive rather than with reflexive processes. The conceptions that people form from these diverse experiences, and their capabilities for reflective thought and self-influence, enable them to act in new, unmodeled ways (Bandura 1977a, Rosenthal and Zimmerman 1978).

Our current research on self-efficacy sheds light on another important dimension of self-construction (Bandura 1977b). People develop and alter their self-conceptions by processing efficacy information resulting from their performance accomplishments, from observing the coping achievements of others, from social persuasion, and from inferences about their own physiological states. Perceived self-efficacy has proven to be a good predictor of behavior. Self processes, whether they involve symbolic constructions, self-regulatory operations, or self-conceptions, can be influenced by, but certainly not reduced to, modeling.

Theories can be construed in different ways. Given the substantive agenda of the conference I see little to be gained from debating the various meanings of the term 'theory', except to say that I regard a theory as a device for organizing diverse bodies of evidence and for guiding the search for more integrative generalizations.

Meaningful propositions about human behavior have verifiable consequences. Since theories are not free of imperfections, the experiments they suggest confirm the propositions under certain circumstances and disconfirm them under others. Like other approaches, social learning formulations are falsifiable on particulars. Experimental analyses identify limits of predictability and suggest refinements in theory that bring us nearer to an understanding of the object of study. Conceptual schemes that provide poor explanations of behavior are discarded not because they are proven false, but because they begin to take on so many limiting conditions that their explanatory and predictive value is severely limited. When better theoretical alternatives exist there is little interest in pursuing the final truth or falsity of a formulation that can, at best, be justifiably applied to an exceedingly narrow range of conditions.

Reynolds views a scientific approach to cognitive processes with considerable pessimism. The cited case of the assaultive husband certainly illustrates the problems of unraveling the determinants of an action that occurs under circumstances that are not easily ascertainable. It is for this very reason that theories are best tested and refined under controlled conditions that permit identification of determinants and the mechanisms through which they exert their effects. Our knowledge of how social learning factors influence thought and behavior has been expanded by such means rather than by probing people's rationalizations of their past actions.

The study of cognitive processes is of course fraught with difficulties because thought is not directly observable. Nevertheless, cognitively oriented theories make good use of indirect indices of cognitive events. Propositions are evaluated by varying hypothesized determinants, assessing their effects on thought processes, and examining the functional relationship between cognition and behavior.

It is commonly assumed that psychological approaches to social behavior view group processes reductively. It is true that there can be no group phenomena except through the actions of individuals. But social learning theory does not reduce group processes to those that operate at the individual level. Collective aggression might serve to illustrate this point. In seeking to explain why given individuals participate in aggressive activities one would analyze, among other things, the nature of their make-up, the inducements to aggression that impinge upon them, and how they process such influences.

By their collective actions, which have varied personal determinants, individuals create group processes, social effects, and social structures that transcend the totality of the individual processes (Bandura 1973). Although social structures can be represented in the cognitive structures of individuals, they are hardly analogous. In explaining intergroup aggression one would analyze the social conditions that breed discontent, societal doctrines that legitimize the victimization of disfavored classes of people, the structural mechanisms that exist for exercising reciprocal influence, and the relative coercive power possessed by the contending factions. The same external inducements to aggression can produce different levels and forms of intergroup aggression under different group structures.

A focus on the psychological mechanisms of behavior does not imply indifference to the evolutionary and ontological roots of those mechanisms. By way of example, consider observational learning. Theories of human development embrace the rudimentary form of learning based on direct experience but ignore the more pervasive and powerful mode of learning by observation or misconstrue it as simple response mimicry. Through a process of abstract modeling, observers can extract the principles governing specific performances for generating behavior that goes beyond what they have seen or heard (Bandura 1977a, Rosenthal and Zimmerman 1978). It is in humans, where the capacity for symbolizing experience has evolved to a high level, that observational learning is most abstract, versatile, and generative. As I noted in my paper, mistakes can be injurious or even fatal so it is most advantageous for a species to be able to learn through mediated experience.

Because observational learning involves four basic subfunctions (perceptual, representational, productive, and motivational) that evolve with maturation and experience, it depends on prior development. The ontogeny of observational learning is discussed at length elsewhere (Bandura 1977a, 1978b). The publications cited in this reply contain developmental analyses of other psychological functions and response systems.

References

Alland, A., Jr. 1972. *The human imperative*. New York: Columbia University Press.

Ax, A. F. 1953. The physiological differentiation between fear and anger in humans. *Psychosomatic Medicine*, 15:433–42.

Azrin, N. H. 1967. Pain and aggression. *Psychology Today*, 1:27–33.

1970. Punishment of elicited aggression. *Journal of the Experimental Analysis of Behavior*, 14:7–10.

Azrin, N. H. and Hutchinson, R. R. 1967. Conditioning of the aggressive behavior of pigeons by a fixed-interval schedule of reinforcement. *Journal of the Experimental Analysis of Behavior*, 10:395–402.

Azrin, N. H., Hutchinson, R. R. and Hake, D. F. 1963. Pain-induced fighting in the squirrel monkey. *Journal of the Experimental Analysis of Behavior*, 6:620.

Baenninger, R. and Grossman, J. C. 1969. Some effects of punishment on pain-elicited aggression. *Journal of the Experimental Analysis of Behavior*, 12:1017–22.

Bandler, R. J. 1975. Predatory aggression: midbrain-pontine junction rather than hypothalamus as the critical structure? *Aggressive Behavior*, 1:261–6.

Bandler, R. J., Chi, C. C. and Flynn, J. P. 1972. Biting attack elicited by stimulation of the ventral midbrain tegmentum of cats. *Science*, 177:364–6.

Bandler, R. J. and Flynn, J. P. 1971. Visual patterned reflex present during hypothalamically elicited attack. *Science*, 171:817–18.

1972. Control of somatosensory fields for striking during hypothalamically-elicited attack. *Brain Research*, 38:197–201.

Bandura, A. 1960. *Relationship of family patterns to child behavior disorders*. Progress Report, Stanford University Project no. M–1734, United States Public Health Service.

1962. Social learning through imitation. In M. R. Jones (ed.), *Nebraska symposium on motivation, 1962*. Lincoln: University of Nebraska Press.

1965. Influence of models' reinforcement contingencies on the acquisition of imitative responses. *Journal of Personality and Social Psychology*, 1:589–95.

1969. *Principles of behavior modification*. New York: Holt, Rinehart and Winston.

1973. *Aggression: a social learning analysis*. Englewood Cliffs, New Jersey: Prentice-Hall.

1974. Behavior theory and the models of man. *American Psychologist*, 29:859–69.

1976. Self-reinforcement: theoretical and methodological considerations. *Behaviorism*, 4:135–55.

1977a. *Social learning theory*. Englewood Cliffs, New Jersey: Prentice-Hall.

1977b. Self-efficacy: toward a unifying theory of behavioral change. *Psychological Review*, 84:191&215.

1978a. The self system in reciprocal determinism. *American Psychologist*, 33:344–58.

1978b. The ontogeny of observational learning. Unpublished manuscript, Stanford University.

Bandura, A. Ross, D. and Ross, S. A. 1963. Vicarious reinforcement and imitative learning. *Journal of Abnormal and Social Psychology*, 67:601–7.

Bandura, A., Underwood, B. and Fromson, M. E. 1975. Disinhibition of aggression through diffusion of responsibility and dehumanization of victims. *Journal of Research in Personality*, 9:253–69.

Bandura, A. and Walters, R. H. 1959. *Adolescent aggression*. New York: Ronald.

1963. *Social learning and personality development*. New York: Holt, Rinehart and Winston.

Baron, R. A. 1971a. Magnitude of victim's pain cues and level of prior anger arousal as determinants of adult aggressive behavior. *Journal of Personality and Social Psychology*, 17:236–43.

1971b. Aggression as a function of magnitude of victim's pain cues, level of prior anger arousal, and aggressor-victim similarity. *Journal of Personality and Social Psychology*, 18:48–54.

Bateson, G. 1936. *The naven*. Stanford, California: Stanford University Press.

Berkowitz, L. 1965. The concept of aggressive drive: Some additional considerations. In L. Berkowitz (ed.), *Advances in experimental social psychology*, vol. II. New York: Academic Press.

1970. The contagion of violence: An S–R mediational analysis of some effects of observed aggression. In W. J. Arnold and M. M. Page (eds.), *Nebraska symposium on motivation, 1970*. Lincoln: University of Nebraska Press.

Blumenthal, M., Kahn, R. L., Andrews, F. M. and Head, K. B. 1972. *Justifying violence: the attitudes of American men*. Ann Arbor: Institute for Social Research.

Brock, T. C. and Buss, A. H. 1962. Dissonance, aggression, and evaluation of pain. *Journal of Abnormal and Social Psychology*, 65:197–202.

1964. Effects of justification for aggression and communication with the victim on postaggression dissonance. *Journal of Abnormal and Social Psychology*, 68:403–12.

Campbell, B. A. and Church, R. M. 1969. *Punishment and aversive behavior*. New York: Appleton-Century-Crofts.

Caplan, N. 1970. The new ghetto man: a review of recent empirical studies. *Journal of Social Issues*, 26:59–73.

Chagnon, N. 1968. *Yanomamo: the fierce people*. New York: Holt, Rinehart and Winston.

Chi, C. C., Bandler, R. J. and Flynn, J. P. 1976. Neuroanatomic projections related to biting attack elicited from ventral midbrain in cats. *Brain, Behavior and Evolution*, 13:91–110.

Chi, C. C. and Flynn, J. P. 1968. The effects of hypothalamic and reticular stimulation on evoked responses in the visual system of the cat. *Electroencephalography and Clinical Neurophysiology*, 24:343–53.

1971. Neuroanatomic projections related to biting attack elicited from hypothalamus in cats. *Brain Research*, 35:49–66.

Claster, D. S. 1967. Comparison of risk perception between delinquents and non-delinquents. *Journal of Criminal Law, Criminology, and Police Science*, 58:80–6.

Cline, V. B., Croft, R. G. and Courrier, S. 1973. Desensitization of children to television violence. *Journal of Personality and Social Psychology*, 27:360–5.

Cohen, A. R. 1955. Social norms, arbitrariness of frustration, and status of the agent of frustration in the frustration-aggression hypothesis. *Journal of Abnormal and Social Psychology*, 51:222–6.

Coleman, K. and Flynn, J. P. In preparation.

Crawford, T. and Naditch, M. 1970. Relative deprivation, powerlessness, and militancy: the psychology of social protest. *Psychiatry*, 33:208–23.

Davies, J. C. 1969. The J-curve of rising and declining satisfactions as a cause of some revolutions and a contained rebellion. In H. D. Graham and T. R. Gurr (eds.), *Violence in America: historical and comparative perspectives*, vol. 2. Washington, DC: US Government Printing Office.

Davitz, J. R. 1952. The effects of previous training on postfrustration behavior. *Journal of Abnormal and Social Psychology*, 47:309–15.

Delgado, J. M. 1967. Social rank and radio-stimulated aggressiveness in monkeys. *Journal of Nervous and Mental Disease*, 144:383–90.

Dentan, R. K. 1968. *The Semai: a nonviolent people of Malaya*. New York: Holt, Rinehart and Winston.

Diener, E. 1977. Deindividuation: Causes and characteristics. *Social Behavior and Personality*, 5:143–56.

Diener, E., Dineen, J., Endresen, K., Beaman, A. L. and Fraser, S. C. 1975. Effects of altered responsibility, cognitive set, and modeling on physical aggression and deindividuation. *Journal of Personality and Social Psychology*, 31:328–37.

Ditrichs, R., Simon, S. and Greene, B. 1967. Effect of vicarious scheduling on the verbal conditioning of hostility in children. *Journal of Personality and Social Psychology*, 6:71–8.

Drabman, R. S. and Thomas, M. H. 1974. Does media violence increase children's toleration of real-life aggression? *Developmental Psychology*, 10:418–21.

Edwards, N. L. 1968. Aggressive expression under threat of retaliation. *Dissertation Abstracts*, 28:3470B.

Feshbach, S. 1970. Aggression. In P. H. Mussen (ed.), *Carmichael's manual of child psychology*, vol. 2. 2 vols., New York, Wiley.

Fink, R. P. and Heimer, L. 1967. Two methods for selective silver impregnation of degeneration axons and their synaptic endings in the central nervous system. *Brain Research*, 4:369–74.

Flynn, J. P., Edwards, S. B. and Bandler, R. J. 1971. Changes in sensory and motor systems during centrally elicited attack. *Behavioral Science*, 16:1–19.

Flynn, J. P., Vanegas, H., Foote, W. and Edwards, S. 1970. Neural mechanisms involved in a cat's attack on a rat. In R. Whalen (ed.), *The neural control of behavior*, New York: Academic Press.

Friedrich, L. K. and Stein, A. H. 1973. Aggressive and prosocial television programs and the natural behavior of preschool children. *Monographs of the Society for Research in Child Development*, 38(4), serial no. 151.

Gambino, R. 1973. Watergate lingo: a language of non-responsibility. *Freedom at Issue*, *22*.

Gardner, R. and Heider, K. G. 1969. *Gardens of war*. New York: Random House.

Geen, R. G. 1970. Perceived suffering of the victim as an inhibitor of attack-induced aggression. *Journal of Social Psychology*, *81*:209–16.

Geen, R. G. and Pigg, R. 1970. Acquisition of an aggressive response and its generalization to verbal behavior. *Journal of Personality and Social Psychology*, *15*:165–70.

Geen, R. G. and Stonner, D. 1971. Effects of aggressiveness habit strength on behavior in the presence of aggression-related stimuli. *Journal of Personality and Social Psychology*, *17*:149–53.

Gerbner, G. and Gross, L. 1976. Living with television: the violence profile. *Journal of Communication*, *26*:173–99.

Ginsburg, B. and Allee, W. C. 1942. Some effects of conditioning on social dominance and subordination in inbred strains of mice. *Physiological Zoology*, *15*:485–506.

Goldstein, M. 1974. Brain research and violent behavior. *Archives of Neurology*, *30*:1–34.

Goranson, R. E. 1970. Media violence and aggressive behavior: A review of experimental research. In L. Berkowitz (ed.), *Advances in experimental social psychology*, vol. V. New York: Academic Press.

Gurr, T. R. 1970. Sources of rebellion in Western societies: some quantitative evidence. *Annals of the American Academy of Political and Social Science*, *391*:128–44.

Hartmann, D. P. 1969. Influence of symbolically modeled instrumental aggression and pain cues on aggressive behavior. *Journal of Personality and Social Psychology*, *11*:280–8.

Hendrick, G. 1977. When television is a school for criminals. *TV Guide*, 29 January: 4–10.

Hess, W. R. 1928. Stammganglien-Reizversuche, 10. Tagung der Deutschen Physiologischen Gesellschaft, Frankfurt am Main. *Bericht Uber die Gesamte Physiologie und Experimentelle Pharmakologie*, *42*:554–5.

Hicks, D. J. 1968. Short- and long-term retention of affectively varied modeled behavior. *Psychonomic Science*, *11*:369–70.

1971. Girls' attitudes toward modeled behaviors and the content of imitative private play. *Child Development*, *42*:139–47.

Hoffman, M. L. 1960. Power assertion by the parent and its impact on the child. *Child Development*, *31*:129–43.

Hokanson, J. E., Willers, K. R. and Koropsak, E. 1968. The modification of autonomic responses during aggressive interchange. *Journal of Personality*, *36*:386–404.

Huang, Y. H. and Flynn, J. P. 1975. Unit activities in the hypothalamus and midbrain during stimulation of hypothalamic attack sites. *Brain Research*, *93*:415–40.

Hunt, J. M., Cole, M. W. and Reis, E. E. S. 1958. Situational cues distinguishing anger, fear, and sorrow. *American Journal of Psychology*, *71*:136–51.

Hutchinson, R. R., Ulrich, R. E. and Azrin, N. H. 1965. Effects of age and related factors on the pain-aggression reaction. *Journal of Comparative and Physiological Psychology*, *59*:365–9.

Kahn, M. W. 1951. The effect of severe defeat at various age levels on the aggressive behavior of mice. *Journal of Genetic Psychology*, 79:117–30.

Kelsey, J. E. and Cassidy, D. 1976. The reinforcing properties of aggressive vs. nonaggressive social interactions in isolated male ICR mice (*Mus Musculus*). *Aggressive Behavior*, 2:275–84.

Kievit, J. and Kuypers, H. G. J. M. 1975a. Basal forebrain and hypothalamic connections to frontal and perietal cortex in the rhesus monkey. *Science*, 187:660–2.

1975b. Subcortical afferents to the frontal lobe in the rhesus monkey studied by means of retrograde horseradish peroxidase transport. *Brain Research*, 85:261–6.

Kilham, W. and Mann, L. 1974. Level of destructive obedience as a function of transmitter and executant roles in the Milgram obedience paradigm. *Journal of Personality and Social Psychology*, 29:696–702.

Knutson, J. 1971. The effects of shocking one member of a pair of rats. *Psychonomic Science*, 22:265–6.

LaVail, J. H. and LaVail, M. M. 1972. The retrograde intraaxonal transport of horseradish peroxidase in the chick visual system: A light and electron microscope study. *Journal of Comparative Neurology*, 157:303–358.

Leifer, A. D., Gordon, N. J. and Graves, S. B. 1974. Children's television: more than mere entertainment. *Harvard Educational Review*, 44:213–45.

Levison, P. K. and Flynn, J. P. 1965. The objects attacked by cats during stimulation of the hypothalamus. *Animal Behavior*, 13:217–20.

Levy, R. I. 1969. On getting angry in the Society Islands. In W. Caudill and T. Y. Lin (eds.), *Mental health research in Asia and the Pacific*. Honolulu: East–West Center Press.

Leyens, J. P., Camino, L., Parke, R. D. and Berkowitz, L. 1975. Effects of movie violence on aggression in a field setting as a function of group dominance and cohesion. *Journal of Personality and Social Psychology*, 32:346–60.

Lieberson, S. and Silverman, A. R. 1965. The precipitants and underlying conditions of race riots. *American Sociological Review*, 30:887–98.

Liebert, R. M., Neale, J. M. and Davidson, E. S. 1973. *The early window: effects of television on children and youth*. New York: Pergamon.

Loew, C. A. 1967. Acquisition of a hostile attitude and its relationship to aggressive behavior. *Journal of Personality and Social Psychology*, 5:335–41.

Logan, F. A. and Boice, R. 1969. Aggressive behaviors of paired rodents in an avoidance context. *Behaviour*, 34:161–83.

Longstreth, L. E. 1966. Distance to goal and reinforcement schedule as determinants of human instrumental behavior. *Proceedings of the 74th Annual Convention of the American Psychological Association*, 39–40.

McCord, W. and Howard, J. 1968. Negro opinions in three riot cities. *American Behavioral Scientist*, 11:24–7.

MacDonnell, M. F. and Flynn, J. P. 1966. Control of sensory fields by stimulation of the hypothalamus. *Science*, 152:1406–8.

McPhail, C. 1971. Civil disorder participation: a critical examination of recent research. *American Sociological Review*, 36:1058–72.

Madsen, C., Jr. 1968. Nurturance and modeling in preschoolers. *Child Development*, 39:221–36.

Maier, S. F. and Seligman, M. E. 1976. Learned helplessness: theory and evidence. *Journal of Experimental Psychology*, 105:3–46.

Mallick, S. K. and McCandless, B. R. 1966. A study of catharsis of aggression. *Journal of Personality and Social Psychology*, 4:591–6.

Mandler, G. 1975. *Mind and emotion*. New York: Wiley.

Mantell, D. M. and Panzarella, R. 1976. Obedience and responsibility. *British Journal of Social and Clinical Psychology*, 15:239–46.

Mark, V. H. and Ervin, F. R. 1970. *Violence and the brain*. New York: Harper and Row.

Mead, M. 1935. *Sex and temperament in three savage tribes*. New York: Morrow.

Meyer, T. P. 1972. Effects of viewing justified and unjustified real film violence on aggressive behavior. *Journal of Personality and Social Psychology*, 23:21–9.

Milgram, S. 1974. *Obedience to authority: an experimental view*. New York: Harper and Row.

Opsahl, C. A. and Flynn, J. P. In preparation.

Packer, H. L. 1968. *The limits of the criminal sanction*. Stanford, California: Stanford University Press.

Panksepp, J. 1971. Aggression elicited by electrical stimulation of the hypothalamus in Albino rats. *Physiology and Behavior*, 6:321–9.

Parke, R. D., Berkowitz, L., Leyens, J. P. West, S. G. and Sebastian, R. J. 1977. Some effects of violent and nonviolent movies on the behavior of juvenile delinquents. In L. Berkowitz (ed.), *Advances in experimental social psychology*, vol. X. New York: Academic Press.

Pastore, N. 1952. The role of arbitrariness in the frustration-aggression hypothesis. *Journal of Abnormal and Social Psychology*, 47:728–31.

Patterson, G. R. 1979 (in press). A performance theory for coercive family interaction. In R. Cairns (ed.), *Social interaction: methods, analysis, and illustration. Monographs of the Society for Research in Child Development*.

Patterson, G. R., Littman, R. A. and Bricker, W. 1967. Assertive behavior in children: a step toward a theory of aggression. *Monographs of the Society for Research in Child Development*, 32(5), serial no. 113.

Perachio, A. A. and Alexander, M. 1974. The neural bases of aggression and sexual behavior in the rhesus monkey. In G. H. Bourne (ed.), *The rhesus monkey*. New York: Academic Press.

Perry, D. G. and Bussey, K. 1977. Self-reinforcement in high- and low-aggressive boys following acts of aggression. *Child Development*, 48:653–7.

Peterson, R. A. 1971. Aggression level as a function of expected retaliation and aggression level of target and aggressor. *Developmental Psychology*, 5:161–6.

Powell, D. A. and Creer, T. L. 1969. Interaction of developmental and environmental variables in shock-elicited aggression. *Journal of Comparative and Physiological Psychology*, 69:219–25.

Powers, P. C. and Geen, R. G. 1972. Effects of the behavior and the perceived arousal of a model on instrumental aggression. *Journal of Personality and Social Psychology*, 23:175–83.

Proshansky, E., Bandler, R. J. and Flynn, J. P. 1974. Elimination of hypothalamically-elicited biting attack by unilateral lesion of the ventral midbrain tegmentum of cats. *Brain Research*, 77:309–13.

Reeves, A. G. and Plum, F. 1969. Hyperphagia, rage, and dementia accompanying a ventromedial hypothalamic neoplasm. *Archives of Neurology*, 20:616–24.

Reich, P. and Hepps, R. B. 1972. Homicide during a psychosis induced by LSD. *Journal of the American Medical Association*, *219*:869–71.

Reid, J. B. and Patterson, G. R. 1976. The modification of aggression and stealing behavior of boys in the home setting. In E. Ribes-Inesta and A. Bandura (eds.), *Analysis of delinquency and aggression*. Hillsdale, New Jersey: Erlbaum.

Roberts, W. W. and Kiess, H. O. 1964. Motivational properties of hypothalamic aggression in cats. *Journal of Comparative and Physiological Psychology*, *58*:187–93.

Roberts, W. W., Steinberg, M. L. and Means, L. W. 1967. Hypothalamic mechanisms for sexual, aggressive, and other motivational behaviors in the opossum, *Didelphis virginiana*. *Journal of Comparative and Physiological Psychology*, *64*:1–15.

Rosekrans, M. A. and Hartup, W. W. 1967. Imitative influences of consistent and inconsistent response consequences to a model and aggressive behavior in children. *Journal of Personality and Social Psychology*, *7*:429–34.

Rosenthal, T. L. and Zimmerman, B. J. 1978. *Social learning and cognition*. New York: Academic Press.

Rule, B. G. and Leger, G. L. 1976. Pain cues and differing functions of aggression. *Canadian Journal of Behavioural Science*, *8*:213–23.

Rule, B. G. and Nesdale, A. R. 1976a. Emotional arousal and aggressive behavior. *Psychological Bulletin*, *83*:851–63.

1976b. Moral judgments of aggressive behavior. In R. G. Geen and E. O'Neal (eds.), *Prospectives on aggression*. New York: Academic Press.

Sanders, G. S. and Baron, R. S. 1977. Pain cues and uncertainty as determinants of aggression in a situation involving repeated instigation. *Journal of Personality and Social Psychology*, *32*:495–502.

Sbordone, R., Garcia, J. and Carder, B. 1977. Shock-elicited aggression: its displacement by a passive social orientation avoidance response. *Bulletin of the Psychonomic Society*, *9*:272–4.

Scott, J. P. and Marston, M. 1953. Nonadaptive behavior resulting from a series of defeats in fighting mice. *Journal of Abnormal and Social Psychology*, *48*:417–28.

Sears, D. O. and McConahay, J. B. 1969. Participation in the Los Angeles riot. *Social Problems*, *17*:3–20.

Sears, R. R., Maccoby, E. E. and Levin, H. 1957. *Patterns of child rearing*. Evanston, Ill.: Row, Peterson.

Short, J. F., Jr (ed.) 1968. *Gang delinquency and delinquent subcultures*. New York: Harper and Row.

Silver, L. B., Dublin, C. C. and Lourie, R. S. 1969. Does violence breed violence? Contributions from a study of the child abuse syndrome. *American Journal of Psychiatry*, *126*:404–7.

Slaby, R. 1974. Verbal regulation of aggression and altruism. In J. De Wit and W. Hartup (eds.), *Determinants and origins of aggressive behavior*. The Hague: Mouton Press.

Smith, D. and Flynn, J. P. In preparation. *Brain Research*.

Snow, C. P. 1961. Either-or. *Progressive*, *25*:24–5.

Staples, F. R. and Walters, R. H. 1964. Influence of positive reinforcement of aggression on subjects differing in initial aggressive level. *Journal of Consulting Psychology*, *28*:547–52.

Steuer, F. B., Applefield, J. M. and Smith, R. 1971. Televised aggression and the interpersonal aggression of preschool children. *Journal of Experimental Child Psychology*, 11:442–7.

Tannenbaum, P. H. and Zillmann, D. 1975. Emotional arousal in the facilitation of aggression through communication. In L. Berkowitz (ed.), *Advances in experimental social psychology*, vol. VIII. New York: Academic Press.

Thelen, M. H. and Soltz, W. 1969. The effect of vicarious reinforcement on imitation in two social racial groups. *Child Development*, 40:879–87.

Thomas, M. H. and Drabman, R. S. 1975. Toleration of real life aggression as a function of exposure to televised violence and age of subject. *Merrill-Palmer Quarterly of Behavior and Development*, 21:227–32.

Thomas, M. H., Horton, R. W., Lippincott, E. C. and Drabman, R. S. 1977. Desensitization to portrayals of real-life aggression as a function of exposure to television violence. *Journal of Personality and Social Psychology*, 35:450–8.

Toch, H. 1969. *Violent men*. Chicago: Aldine.

Turnbull, C. M. 1961. *The forest people*. New York: Simon and Schuster.

Ulrich, R. 1966. Pain as a cause of aggression. *American Zoologist*, 6:643–62.

Ulrich, R. E. and Azrin, N. H. 1962. Reflexive fighting in response to aversive stimulation. *Journal of the Experimental Analysis of Behavior*, 5:511–20.

Ulrich, R., Johnston, M., Richardson, J. and Wolff, P. 1963. The operant conditioning of fighting behavior in rats. *Psychological Record*, 13:465–70.

Vanegas, H., Foote, W. and Flynn, J. P. 1969–70. Hypothalamic influences upon activity of units of the visual cortex. *Yale Journal of Biology and Medicine*, 42:191–201.

Walters, R. H. and Brown, M. 1963. Studies of reinforcement of aggression: III. Transfer of responses to an interpersonal situation. *Child Development*, 34:563–71.

Wasman, M. and Flynn, J. P. 1962. Directed attack elicited from hypothalamus. *Archives of Neurology and Psychiatry*, 6:220–7.

Weisz, A. E. and Taylor, R. L. 1970. American presidential assassination. In D. N. Daniels, M. F. Gilula and F. M. Ochberg (eds.), *Violence and the struggle for existence*. Boston: Little, Brown.

Wheeler, L. 1966. Toward a theory of behavioral contagion. *Psychological Review*, 73:179–92.

Wheeler, L. and Caggiula, A. R. 1966. The contagion of aggression. *Journal of Experimental Social Psychology*, 2:1–10.

Whiting, J. W. M. 1941. *Becoming a Kwoma*. New Haven: Yale University Press.

Wolfgang, M. E. and Ferracuti, F. 1967. *The subculture of violence*. London: Tavistock.

Woodworth, C. H. 1971. Attack elicited in rats by electrical stimulation of the lateral hypothalamus. *Physiology and Behavior*, 6:345–53.

Yablonsky, L. 1962. *The violent gang*. New York: Macmillan.

Zimbardo, P. G. 1969. The human choice: individuation, reason, and order vs. deindividuation, impulse, and chaos. In W. J. Arnold and D. Levins (eds.), *Nebraska symposium on motivation, 1969*. Lincoln: University of Nebraska Press.

Zimring, F. 1973. *Deterrence: the legal threat in crime control*. Chicago: Chicago University Press.

6. Intra- and intergroup relationships in primates

6.1. On the value of social relationships to nonhuman primates: a heuristic scheme[1]

HANS KUMMER

Introduction

One of the basic questions society poses for biologists is: why does an individual put up with the time-consuming, frustrating and often harmful ado of group life rather than live in unhindered, but perhaps dangerous and uninformed, solitude? Why does he direct his attention to the behavior of the dominant males in his society, rather than to predators or food distribution; why does he groom and quarrel with group members rather than rest? The biologist's answer is that the gains must outweigh the costs, and that natural selection therefore produces individuals with social inclinations. But whereas the costs are obvious and partly measurable, e.g. in terms of wounds and time expended, the gains are not easily seen. Alexander (1974) even states that group life in nonhuman primates evolved only as a means for more efficient avoidance of predators through an accumulation of watchful eyes and sharp teeth.

Adaptive values of primate social systems have been much discussed (e.g. Crook 1970, Kummer 1971, Altmann 1974), but in my opinion such discussions are too often restricted to the level of entire groups. The benefits of social organization to the individual are not fully understood from group size and composition. They cannot be identified without a thorough understanding of a society's qualitatively unique element,

[1] I thank my collaborators J.-J. Abegglen, H. Sigg, A. Stolba and E. Stammbach for contributing their ideas to this paper. Its shortcomings are, however, exclusively mine.

which is the relationship between two individuals. What are the marks of valuable relationships? How do they benefit their members? And what can an individual do in order to establish and maintain them?

Concepts like dominance, familiarity and bond have long been used to describe isolated aspects of dyadic relationships. What is not clear is how these phenomena interrelate to make the relationship a profitable enterprise for one or both participants. In a recent paper, 'On describing relationships', Hinde (1976) has used his fine-grain studies on mother–infant pairs as a starting point toward a conceptual order. It involves three levels – interactions, relationships and social structure. At the data stage, a relationship is described by the number and types of its interactions (e.g. play and grooming), their quality (e.g. rough, gentle), and their temporal patterning. From such data emerge some of the dimensions along which relationships differ, such as reciprocity, control, or 'meshing', which is the degree to which the momentary goals of the two individuals are aligned.

In this paper, refinements of description are largely neglected in favor of the question asked at the outset: what does a primate gain from establishing social relationships? Interactions[2] are seen as means of building or preventing a particular aspect of a relationship; a relationship is seen as an investment which in some way, sooner or later, benefits the interactor.

These benefits, which ultimately are contributions to reproductive survival, are relatively clear only in male–female and in mother–infant relationships, which have obvious reproductive functions. But most primates live in groups much larger than nuclear families; they interact with companions of their own sex and age, and the intensity and the means with which they build such nonreproductive relationships is often comparable to those expended in a reproductive bond (e.g. Kummer 1975). In squirrel monkeys, dyadic relationships among adult females are actually given priority by their members over male–female dyads for most of the year (Vaitl, in press).

The emphasis in this paper will be on the possible functions of such nonreproductive relationships. A hypothetical picture of how they might be useful and what is done to make them so can be composed with the available fragments of observation. I believe that it is more worthwhile to attempt this than to present another review of established but discon-

---

[2] In the following, interactions are mainly seen as actions and cognitions within a dyadic relationship. However, interactions with a third object or partner may also be used to affect the relationship with a companion, especially when the latter is watching them.

nected facts. The picture will often lack sharp delineations and demands some tolerance of fuzziness, but I agree with Hinde that it is not appropriate at present to sacrifice complexity for precision.

However, it seems necessary to make two temporary simplifications. The first is to limit the discussion to the relationship of only two individuals. While at least triadic relationships have been demonstrated (e.g. Kummer, Götz and Angst 1974, Vaitl, in press), their analysis depends on a clear understanding of the component dyads. Secondly, interactions have often been analyzed as a ping-pong game between two individuals, the effect of a signal by A being analyzed in terms of B's immediate response signal, and so forth. This is a hindrance to the present attempt. We are interested not only in immediate responses, but in the long-term functions of A's social actions, i.e. the sum of their consequences that make it worthwhile for A to live with B rather than alone. Breaking the conceptual ping-pong circle of interaction is a useful simplification in that it allows temporary abstraction of the complications of feed-back effects and of conflicting goals of the two participants; furthermore, it is the behavior of individuals, not of dyads, that is subject to natural selection. We shall, therefore, focus on the acts and interests of only one animal, A, in a relationship, and we shall view his companion B as his social resource which, for the time being, must take care of itself. Eventually, both members of a dyad will have to be viewed in the position of A. Once the proximate goals and means of each A are well understood, their interaction in the dyad becomes accessible. It will eventually be important to distinguish between those functions of A's social behavior which increase his adaptation to his extraspecific environment (the resource and risk characters of his habitat) from those that adapt him to living in his group (such as meeting mates and avoiding rivals). Some of these intrasocietal adaptations merely alleviate the disadvantages inherent in social life and cannot explain why grouping evolved in the first place. The more complex a social structure, the more a member needs adaptive strategies for his career within that structure (Hausfater 1975, Abegglen 1976).

The value of the social partner

The assumption of evolutionary biology is that an individual A generally behaves so as to increase his chances of reproduction, to which his own survival is a means. A's conspecific B can, in various ways, increase or decrease A's success. In nonhuman primates the effects of B on the success of A, i.e. B's value to A, depend on at least the following factors:

(1) B's *qualities*, i.e. his lasting or long-term characteristics, e.g. sex and age, and, partially dependent on these, strength, skills, experience. For example, a B of the opposite sex is more valuable to A for reproduction but not necessarily as a discoverer of food. A powerful, skillful or experienced B is both a more dangerous opponent, a more useful social ally, and a more efficient leader or protector against predators.

(2) B's short-term and long-term *tendencies* (measured as probabilities) to perform acts that increase or decrease A's success, in a given context, e.g. fighting against A, or with him as an ally; bearing, caring for, defending or killing A's young; finding food, and communicating its location to or concealing it from A, defending or sharing the food with A. These tendencies can vary according to the context, e.g. who else participates in the event, or the desirability of the food. The more powerful and skilled B is, the more critical his tendencies are for A. To a considerable degree, B's value for A depends on what other group members *expect* B to do in a given situation.

(3) B's *availability*, i.e. external factors that induce or allow B to act according to his tendency. I am aware of two such factors: physical distance between A and B, and the presence of third parties that prevent B from acting. As distance increases A is less likely to induce B's attack, support, mating or grooming, and B's attack or support is less likely to become effective; on the other hand, B's discoveries may be most useful if the distance is great. The presence or intervening action of certain third parties may selectively suppress fighting, mating or grooming of B with A, thus altering the frequency profile of B's actions.

A sharp separation of the three factors is obviously not possible, nor is it, at present, very important.

Improving the value of the partner

Since the value of B to A can obviously be negative we expect that A will try to influence the effects of the above factors in his favor. He can do so in three ways:

(1) by *monitoring* the state of the factors and learning to predict them. A predictable B is both a more useful cooperator and a less dangerous competitor;

(2) by *selecting* the best available B;

(3) by *altering* the state of the factors in his favor, which includes the short- or long-term modification of B's behavior.

Some of these three kinds of activities are observable acts; others consist in omitting acts or in 'silent reading' of the environment. But all three activities are investments by A in his relationship with B.

We must now investigate the actual social behavior of nonhuman primates for hints about whether and how these functions are achieved. For obvious reasons, we know least about the content of the monitoring activity. Before proceeding to the examples, the difference between short- and long-term relationships should be clarified.

The social bond as an investment

Social relationships range from the anonymous to the individualized or personal. In an anonymous relationship, A either does not recognize B as an individual or does not care which particular individual of a B class he happens to deal with. In a large anonymous group, A may interact only shortly with each B and then lose contact with him. In such transient relationships A may profit from short-term monitoring and altering of B's qualities, tendencies and availability, but any action aimed at a long-term pay-off is a wasted investment. Long-term improvements of B's value are useful only if his continued availability is probable. In some species and stages of relationships, continued availability is assured by A's and B's attachment to the same object or locality, as Lamprecht's (1973) experiments have shown for the monogamous cichlid *Tilapia mariae*. The typical solution of mammals is the personal relationship based on individual recognition. A is thus in a position to focus his cumulative monitoring and altering efforts on one particular B. But this in itself does not insure that he will also harvest the benefits. Any long-term investment (such as a bird's nest or the food store of a digger wasp) may be destroyed by extraspecific factors, or conspecifics may become parasites. An A who has invested in a personal relationship must therefore be expected, within limits, to (1) insure B's spatial availability, at least whenever it is useful (e.g. of a female during her oestrus) by following B or by making B follow him, (2) defend B against extraspecific dangers and (3) defend B against a rival, A_1. The defence against rivals would be particularly important if an improvement of B's tendencies by A would improve B's tendencies to all individuals $A_{1, 2, \ldots}$. Such transfer of improved tendencies is known from grayling butterflies (Tinbergen 1948:46), for example, and must be suspected for species with communal courtship, such as *Capra ibex*, but it is an open question for research on nonhuman primate relationships.

Since many social interactions in primate groups are in fact concerned with maintaining proximity and warding off rivals, it is likely that many of their dyadic relationships are indeed long-term investments by either one or both members. Long-term effects of interactions are also suggested by the long social sessions, in which social interactions such as grooming are continued for an hour or more without being immediately followed by any action that is obviously useful or harmful to the interactor.

The tendency to respond to sign stimuli regardless of the sender's identity can be a problem as much as an aid to such a relationship, which requires of A that he restrict promiscuous responding in himself, in his partner B, and in his rival A_1. The mechanisms of such restriction should be a central topic of primate ethology.

Monitoring and improving the qualities of B

The study of an animal's *monitoring* of events in his environment is as important as it is difficult without experimentation in the natural group context (Menzel 1971). Even so, tentative inferences from observation alone are sometimes possible, first from the increasing selectivity of A's behavior as a new relationship develops, and secondly because non-human primates sometimes initiate interactions to no other apparent effect than to *test* B; monitoring then becomes observable. The following impressions are inferred from such qualitative evidence.

In what sequence does A recognize qualities of B from the moment he first perceives B? Sex, size and approximate age are most probably recognized within seconds, as suggested by the immediate choice of an A introduced to Bs that differ in these respects. Assessing B's strength takes more time. Primates of nearly equal size sometimes begin their relationship by a fight that has no apparent material object, which suggests that observational monitoring is here complemented by interactional testing of B's strength. The assessment of individual social skills and idiosyncrasies seems to require at least a week. Its effects are indirectly apparent when a newly formed group develops from an initial, rigidly sex-age-rank based structure to one in which personal relationships introduce an increasing number of exceptions to the initial regularity (Kummer 1975).

Circumstantial evidence leaves little doubt that a monkey can assess qualities of another from the latter's interactions with the environment. Rowell (1974) recounts how the *a*-male of her rhesus colony used to threaten her husband Hugh until, one day, *a* observed how Hugh caught and handled the β-male. From that day on, *a* treated Hugh with friendly gestures.

In nature, *selecting* the best B is generally limited to members of the group. By the time a young monkey or ape is capable of transferring independently to another group, he may already have invested so much in relationships within the native group that the transfer is a net loss (but see Kurland 1977:128). The mechanism that keeps him with his social investments is apparently the attractiveness of familiar conspecifics (cf. Zajonc 1971, Rosenblum and Lowe 1971, Erwin, Maple and Welles 1975, Bischof 1975). Nevertheless, transfer to other groups has been observed in both females at sexual maturity and males of post-juvenile age (Nishida and Kawanaka 1972, Drickamer and Vessey 1973, Abegglen 1976). Adult male yellow baboons seem to transfer more often (Altmann and Altmann 1970) than adult male hamadryas baboons (Abegglen 1976). As the latter seem to invest more in permanent bonds with females even at the sub-adult stage, one may hypothesize that the probability of intergroup transfer is inversely correlated with the investment in personal relationships.

Within the group, selection of and competition for Bs is pronounced. Dominant Bs are often preferred: for example, Seyfarth (1976) found that high-ranking female baboons are more attractive to other females than low-ranking ones. He assumes that the preference for high-ranking partners is related to their usefulness as allies. Other results suggest that rank is not the only criterion: Stammbach (1978) found that grooming among his female hamadryas baboons was correlated both with rank and with mutual preference established by a choice test. The preference in the choice test was not correlated with rank and must therefore be based on another quality.

There is little a nonhuman primate can do to *alter* the qualities of a companion. A can reduce B's health and strength by harassing or wounding him, or increase them by nursing, sharing food or information. By the latter, A may improve B's skills and experience and pass on a tradition. Whether such improving is in A's own interest or whether he should rather reduce B's strength and skill depends mainly on B's tendencies, which will now be examined.

Monitoring and improving B's tendencies

Increasing B's tendencies to act in favor of A and reducing B's tendencies for actions that harm A are probably the most typical long-term efforts which a nonhuman primate invests in his social relationships; their mechanisms are also the least known. In contrast, the short-term treatment of B's tendencies has been well analyzed in many animal species; a short list will therefore suffice. In a rapid dyadic exchange of communicative acts, A can release acts of B, monitor them, and favorably select and affect B's next acts by his own. Nonhuman primates are also skillful in avoiding the release of harmful acts by B. For example, a hamadryas baboon under threat can apparently avoid an actual attack simply by not attending (Kummer 1957). He also seems to suppress harmful tendencies of his own by 'cutting-off' the monitoring of B's acts (Kummer 1968). A primate can make short-term use of his monitoring of B's unaltered tendencies to obtain information on the extraspecific environment: Menzel's young chimpanzees inferred the location and desirability of a food source from the behavior of informed companions (Menzel 1971), and his adult Japanese macaques, when faced with a bucket of unknown content, left its exploration to juveniles, observed them, and acted on their responses (Menzel 1966).

Let us now turn to A's *monitoring of B's long-term tendencies* and their contextual dependence. Its effect is that A becomes familiar with B in the sense that he learns to predict what B will do under what circumstances. That familiarity is a useful investment is suggested by the higher number of young raised by bird parents in the second and third year of consortship than in the first (Coulson 1966). A rhesus monkey is more likely to learn which of four levers produces food from a familiar than from an unfamiliar companion (Mason and Hollis 1962). Communication is apparently more efficient among familiars than among aliens.

Long-term tendencies of a partner are also monitored by testing. In the first days after obtaining a juvenile female consort a young adult hamadryas male can be seen to lead her back and forth across the sleeping-cliff of the troop late in the evening. He incessantly checks the female's following response by looking back (Kummer 1968). Since there is no immediate ecological function in this activity – often, the other troop members are already asleep – it is likely that its function consists either in testing the female's following response, or in building up her following tendency, or both. Captive female hamadryas at menarche frequently tested their ability to provoke attacks by the dominant male against adult females without any apparent short-term goal (Kummer 1957). These attempts often back-fired. It seemed that the young females were inexperienced and explored the participants by testing their tendencies and their qualities. Their 'realism' improved within weeks.

These assumptions leave us with the task of deciding whether the goal of a given social act is mainly to test the companion's tendencies, or to use them here and now in a functional context. Does a juvenile cry wolf in order to explore who will help, or because it actually needs help? For some kinds of behavior the observer may feel confident enough to assess whether B's eventual response is useful or pointless in the given situation, but even so, this is at best a preliminary method. I am not aware of any study specifically aimed at this critical distinction.

Whether and how a primate *alters* a companion's long-term tendencies is also an open field for research, even though some hypotheses have recently been put forward and tested. Seyfarth (1976) found that female baboons with adjacent ranks both groomed and tended to ally more often. Genetic relationships were not known in his study. Rhesus macaques most often seem to form coalitions with relatives of adjacent rank (Sade 1967). Possibly, an A may use grooming to improve B's tendency to aid him as an ally.

Whether or not B's long-term tendencies toward A are improved by his familiarity with A, it seems a reasonable hypothesis that A furthers the improvement by his behavior toward B. One lead as to how A does this may be obtained from the sequence of his actions toward a B whom he meets for the first time. In this situation, captive adult gelada and hamadryas baboons go through an orderly sequence of steps, each marked by the first occurrence of a new type of behavior: the first fight, if it occurs, nearly always precedes the first presentation, which in turn precedes the first mounting. The final stage begins with the first grooming. The sequence is the same regardless of sex combination, but the speeds differ. A male–female dyad hurries through the sequence in a few minutes, two females take somewhat longer, and two males may take an hour or more to reach the first grooming (Kummer 1975, Abegglen *et al.*, unpublished data). Since the interactions of this sequence were not related to any momentary ecological goals, they may represent a long-term investment in a social bond. Fights may test the companion's strength; presenting and mounting appear as an acknowledgement of rank and as a reduction of agonistic tendencies that finally permits the intimate interaction of grooming. Grooming might be the most effective improver of the sequence. This agrees with Seyfarth's hypothesis that grooming recruits allies, the assumptions of which are somewhat elaborated in the following.

Social grooming removes ectoparasites and dirt, but in addition, the frequent invitations to be groomed and the postural abandon of the receiver during the act suggest that being groomed is pleasurable. If A frequently grooms B, we may expect that B eventually comes to seek A's proximity, to defend access to him against rivals, and perhaps to support him against opponents and to allow him to feed from the same food source. In order to be groomed, B would therefore treat A in the same way as A would treat B after having invested in improving his tendencies. Each would maintain and defend the availability of the other as a source of some benefits. There would, however, be two currencies of benefits: the hygiene, supported by the pleasure of being groomed, given by A to B, and assistance in interacting with the societal and extraspecific environment, given by B to A. According to Seyfarth, a dominant B has more assistance to offer than his lower-ranking partner A, and this may explain why the lower-ranking partner in a dyad often does more grooming than the higher-ranking member. Seyfarth's work is a promising start to the investigation of long-term improvements of a companion's tendencies. Its eventual success depends on a substantial progress in the understanding and measurement of the extraspecific benefits which A can derive from an association with B. Neither grooming (except for its hygienic function) nor intrasocietal alliance are possible ultimate functions of life in a permanent group.

The idea of a social reward is of course not new. The cultural anthropologist, W. Goldschmidt (1959),[3] postulates a general human 'need for social acceptance' as 'a motive for human acquiescence to the demands of social existence'. Ideally, such a reward should be energetically inexpensive and the appetite for it should not be easily saturated. Accordingly, food does not qualify, and gifts of food are in fact infrequently found among animal species, for example among social hymenoptera, or in the courtship behavior of empid flies and herring gulls. Low-intensity sexual interactions are relatively common among primates and possibly have tendency-improving effects, but saturation is relatively rapid. Social grooming, however, meets both qualifications.

Monitoring and improving B's availability

Monitoring, maintaining, defending and avoiding the availability of a partner are frequent goals of social acts in primates, and no other function of social behavior is as readily understood by the observer. Searching, following, pursuing, escaping and hiding are the most common

[3] Also personal communication from W. Goldschmidt, 1977.

examples. Herding (by punishing the companion for being too far away or in the wrong neighborhood), blocking a companion's access to another (by stepping between the two) and intervention (interrupting the interaction of two others by threat or guile) are more sophisticated techniques (e.g. Kummer 1968, 1975). Nonhuman primates obviously treat availability as if it were an important issue. We know that spatial proximity and the frequency of social interactions are highly correlated in primates, and we therefore use both as criteria for the definition of social groups (e.g. Altmann 1965). But when we compose sociograms of who-does-what-to-whom-how-often we generally do not concern ourselves with the questions of how a primate shapes the distribution of availability of each companion and whether, in turn, the distribution of availability differentially affects the distribution of different types of interaction. The study by Kurland (1977) addresses this problem.

More interesting than enumerating the known primate techniques of monitoring and manipulating availability is the still unanswered key question: what degree of B's availability makes him most valuable to A? For the sake of simplicity, I suggest we disregard the influence of a third party, C, on the availability. As far as we know, and keeping in mind our lack of attention to the question, C often decreases the availability of B to A. For example, sexual consort pairs of baboons and chimpanzees (Tutin 1975) temporarily leave the group and thus avoid interference from third parties. On the other hand, a mother C increases the mutual availability among her children A and B, and according to Deag and Crook's report (1971) male Barbary macaques carry an infant to a dominant male, apparently with the effect of reducing the latter's agonistic tendencies.

What is the optimal treatment of the distance component of availability? A simple assumption is that the manifestation of *all* tendencies of B, whether useful or harmful to A, increases as the distance between A and B decreases. If A behaved optimally, his preferred distance from B would then be an inverse measure of B's value to him. Correlations between the distance selected by A and the frequencies of B's acts times a rough estimate of the value of these acts to A could be investigated, but this, to my knowledge, has not been done. The choice of the optimal distance must be most difficult if B is powerful and skillful, i.e. potentially very useful and very harmful. A can choose the best distance only if his monitoring of B's tendencies toward him is precise and reliable. A dominant B should therefore be monitored intensely, and we would expect frequent conflict behavior in A.

The hypothesis of behavioral probabilities as a monotonous function of distance seems at least reasonable for those acts which B directs at A alone. However, we wish to know more about those acts that make group life profitable to A, and these must involve a third object, C, usually of the extraspecific environment. Here the hypothesis may be false. The distance at which B is most valuable as a discoverer of food or a predator presumably depends on many factors. If B communicates all that is relevant to A about what he has discovered, the greatest distance over which it can be communicated may be optimal. The less complete the message is, the more A depends on inspecting the discovery himself, and the shorter is the optimal distance among the exploring pair. If the object is mobile, the time available for A's response further complicates the matter. For a primate, the most relevant mobile object other than his conspecifics is a predator. A's distance from a discoverer should be sufficient to allow his escape, but within the range of B's discovering capacity. A might resolve the conflict as to what the optimal distance should be by keeping close to a B from which he can learn what parts of a plant are edible, e.g. his mother, and at the same time maintaining a larger distance from a potential discoverer of danger, e.g. a peripheral subadult male. Thus, the best possible relationship with a given companion is not necessarily the closest relationship. For example, two adult hamadryas males in their prime typically maintain a large distance and rarely interact at a stage higher than presenting. They are what we call incompatible, yet spatial behavior on the foraging march suggests that each may be most useful to the other for discoveries and for the protection of females when he is no less than about ten meters away. An A's optimal set of relationships consists of the right number of relationships at each degree of compatibility.

A special problem of availability arises when B moves out of A's range of perception. Qualitative experience suggests that nonhuman primates are poor predictors of each other's whereabouts once contact is broken. Their searching for a lost companion is often chaotic and excited, and it may fail to succeed for several days (van Lawick-Goodall 1971, Abegglen 1976) if the daily routine does not regularly touch on a place that may serve as a point of convening. This, however, may be a false impression since a calm and effective search is more likely to go unnoticed by the observer. Nevertheless, the danger of losing a companion is real but generally avoided by visual and auditory contact. Forest species evolved special loud calls for intergroup monitoring.

How can a companion be useful?

In saying that a social individual should monitor, select and alter the qualities, tendencies and availability of a companion in his own favor, we have started this discussion with what an observer sees and guesses most readily. I believe that this is acceptable as a beginning, but that it is ultimately of limited use unless we begin to concern ourselves with the precise nature of the benefits, especially the ecological ones, that A derives from his social bonds. The few valuable studies that demonstrate, for example, the beneficial effect of dominance on reproductive fitness (Hausfater 1975, Drickamer 1974), relate to adaptations of the individual to society, not to the habitat.

Social interaction with the environment involves at least a triad: A and B interact with a C, which is a conspecific, an extraspecific resource, a predator or a parasite. At least the following actions of B with regard to C should be considered as conceivably affecting the success of A:

Production: B can produce, increase, decrease or destroy C and thus alter the inventory or quality of A's environment. For example, B can build a nest for A, cultivate or destroy food for A, breed parasites or kill a predator. Such acts are not common among nonhuman primates.

Information: B can influence A's knowledge or monitoring of what there is in the environment. He can show him a waterhole, conceal a tidbit or fail to inform him of a danger. These effects are probably the most common among primates, but also the most difficult to demonstrate.

Motion: B can influence C's availability to A. He can lead A to or away from a resource, drive him into or away from danger, share, catch or bring food to A, or rescue and hide it, or take it away from him. Sharing (McGrew 1975, Teleki 1975, Strum 1975) and driving away from danger have been observed among free-living primates.

Motivation: B can conceivably affect A's tendencies to approach C in a particular way. He can caution or arouse him and encourage or reduce his tendency to explore. Most observations relevant to this class concern social facilitation of the allelomimetic type.

Nutrition: Finally and most proximally, B can intervene materially with A's metabolism. He might chew and digest food for A or even nurse him, or he might kill him, cannibalize him or offer himself as food.

It is obvious that nonhuman primates affect each others' success mainly in the classes of information, motion and motivation, whereas production and nutrition are human achievements, realized essentially by agriculture on one hand and medicine on the other.

The above list adds the third dimension to a biological concept of social relationship, the first two being the relevant factors presented by B and the means by which A improves them. A social activity of A should eventually be identified and demonstrated as being, for example, a monitoring of B's qualities with respect to his function as a discoverer of danger. The readily used concept of dominance, viewed in this way, assumes the complexity it deserves. We recognize B as being dominant over A because A reduces the availability of B by stepping out of B's way, and because A reduces B's tendency to attack him by submissive gestures, and we understand it as a result of A's monitoring B's qualities (strength) and long-term tendencies (aggressiveness), either through observing him or by testing him in a fight. This view neglects the possibility that A may have improved and monitored B's long-term tendencies toward himself, A, to a degree where he can profitably seek B's proximity rather than avoiding it (Kummer 1967). Also, an observant A might learn that B tends to assert and defend some rights of access but not others, and, in using such knowledge, become 'dominant' in some and 'submissive' in other situations.

Summary

I have chosen to present a tentative conceptual scheme for future research rather than another factual review for several reasons. The first is to illustrate the presently predominant vein of biological thinking to non-biologists. Secondly, it seems that research on primate social behavior has been in danger of crystallizing on a few traditional and disconnected concepts such as dominance, leaving large and important areas between them unattended, such as monitoring activities or the topic of availability. Thirdly, such a scheme may show what techniques of social life are theoretically conceivable but have not evolved among nonhuman primates. What we need is an intrinsically consistent conceptual framework that shows the connections between traditional concepts, and systematic studies that trace the chain of effects of social behavior from the proximate to the ultimate ones on which selection operates. These studies should link what we see primates do with what sociobiologists think they should do for their reproductive survival. At the present stage, the completeness of such an attempt seems more important than its accuracy in details.

In an attempt to facilitate our initial understanding, I have simplified the problem by focussing on the relationship between two animals, A and B, and I have broken the conceptual circle of their interaction by making A the subject whose goals and means are analyzed, while his companion B, for the time being, is merely A's social resource. The scheme suggests that A selects, monitors and alters B's qualities, tendencies and availability such as to increase B's value to him. In a typical relationship among nonhuman primates, A increases B's value to him over months and years; insofar as the returns are not immediate, B becomes an investment. A is therefore expected to insure B's continued availability: he will follow and defend B. Such a relationship is called a bond.

Our most acute and hindering ignorance concerns what a primate learns about and through his social companions in their natural environment. Perhaps the most disquieting and valuable insight gained from this heuristic scheme is that a single social act such as a scream may serve as widely differing goals as monitoring a companion's availability ('where are you?'), releasing his short-term tendency ('help me'), monitoring his long-term tendency by testing ('are you willing to help me?'), or selecting the companion with the most appropriate quality ('which of you is the most effective helper?'). While this is hardly news to anyone who knows primates, we have not usually had the courage to face the task of differentiating, but dutifully entered the act into our record sheet as what it clearly was: a carefully defined and carefully counted scream.

6.2. Human intergroup conflict: useful and less useful forms of analysis[1]

HENRI TAJFEL

I. The distal and the proximal analysis

The main question I wish to raise in this paper is a paraphrase of a well-known statement by the late President Kennedy: 'Ask not what you can do for ethology; ask instead what it can do for you.' As a social psychologist who has been interested for some time in the study of the psychological aspects of social conflict, I have come to a conclusion which I might as well state as a point of departure for this paper: I believe that we can learn, and have learned a great deal from ethology in methods of observation; I also believe that ethological *theory* (or theoretical approach) has been largely irrelevant to our preoccupations.

As John Crook (1976) recently wrote: 'If we look at the gallant attempts of ethologists such as Lorenz (1966) and Morris (1967) to seek the heights of sociological relevance, the result is a great deal of sound and fury signifying very little' (p. 253). Although it is undoubtedly true that these earlier 'gallant attempts' are by now quite untypical of what most ethologists would be prepared to claim, their impact on our social and intellectual *Zeitgeist* has been substantial. Blurton Jones (1976) meant perhaps something of the same kind when, after complimenting the authors of 'the popular books on comparisons of men and animals' on their 'courage', he added:

Caution and modesty have held back too many good biologists from getting involved in the study of human behaviour. But courage needs to be allied to a

[1] Sections of this paper describing some aspects of the theoretical approach to problems of intergroup behaviour have appeared in Tajfel 1976 (in Italian) and in Tajfel 1978. My thanks are due to Il Mulino, Bologna and Academic Press, London for permission to use them here.

great deal of reading and discussion aimed at finding out what the issues are in established human behaviour research, and even more important, at finding out what the data are and what they are worth. Too many biologists remain either totally unaware of enormous areas of social science literature, or else treat it much less critically than do their social science colleagues.   (p. 427)

The fact remains that Blurton Jones' 'good biologists' cannot be too heavily blamed for their neglect of trustworthy 'social science data' in the social psychology of human intergroup conflict. We have learned a great deal about certain issues; for example, about individual patterns of pre-judice, about conditions and determinants of interindividual aggression, about cognitive processes leading to intergroup stereotyping. But all this together has never amounted to a consistent perspective upon the psychological aspects of large-scale social conflict. In order to get this, we must beware of direct extrapolations from interindividual to intergroup behaviour and we must adopt a definition of a 'social group' which would probably sound too phenomenal by far to a biologist. This definition needs to be based on the 'felt' membership of a group which *must* include a cognitive component in the sense of the awareness of membership and *may* include positive or negative value connotations and/or an emotional investment in the group. This phenomenal approach need not, however, remain empirically vacuous. Its antecedents and consequents, together with the relationships between the 'external' and the 'internal' criteria of group membership, can, and have been shown to, lead to reliable data and they can also be related to orderly theoretical predictions. This kind of definition is inescapable if we are prepared to come to terms with the fact that the behaviour towards each other of members of large-scale human groups in conflict cannot be analysed (although it can be *described*) in terms of face-to-face interactions either inside a group or between groups. As a matter of fact, this is probably the major theoretical differ-ence between, on the one hand, conflicts involving individuals or small face-to-face groups and, on the other hand, social conflicts involving large-scale human social 'categories'.

It is at this point that it becomes crucial to decide what level of theoreti-cal analysis of *behaviour* is likely to be the most useful for the construction of a consistent theoretical perspective on the social psychology of social conflict. I agree entirely with many sociologists, economists and biolo-gists who, from their different points of view, would argue that such an analysis cannot start from psychological processes. We cannot usefully start, again in Blurton Jones' terms, with the view that 'culture and ideology have their own life independent of economic, physical or bio-

398 Intra- and intergroup relationships in primates

logical factors' or with theories assuming that 'ideas are prime causes' of behaviour. It remains true, however, that at some point, which needs to be specified, certain ideas or views or ideologies or cognitive orientations shared by large masses of people do intervene in the observed uniformities of their behaviour towards others they perceive as members of the ingroup or of the outgroup, as 'us' or as 'them'.

The causal sequence must start, in my view, with a 'distal' analysis. I mean by this an analysis of the economic, biological and 'material' factors contributing to the creation of certain conditions which converge upon conflict between large-scale groups, be they national, racial, socioeconomic, religious, or other. An historical analysis is one example; another is provided by Blurton Jones in his proposal to combine the study of evolutionary selection pressures with the study of the physical and economic (and therefore also social) ecology of a social system. As he maintains, this can be done properly only if the 'etic' research option is adopted; i.e. the data cannot originate from categories of experience which are significant to those whose behaviour is being studied (the 'emic' approach), but from operational distinctions made independently on the basis of scientific observation.

The question which arises then concerns the nature of the links that can be established between these 'distal' forms of analysis and the observed intergroup uniformities of behaviour. Let me try two examples: one concerns the present conflict in Northern Ireland and the other the well-known field experiments of Sherif (e.g. 1966) on zero-sum conflicts between groups of boys in a holiday camp. The analysis of the Northern Irish situation must be made in terms of the social, economic and historical background to it which, together with the 'material' circumstances of the island, provide both the 'ecology' of the conflict and some understanding of its development. I am not concerned here with, nor would I be competent to judge, the relative merits of the various points of view which have been advanced; it is, however, important to assert that this kind of approach to a 'distal' analysis needs to be adopted, and that it would presumably not be very different from a systematic analysis of other conflicts of a similar nature. The question that I must ask as a social psychologist concerns the point of insertion of the study of concrete social behaviour into this causal spiral. Without its economic, historical, ecological and material background the conflict would not have been what it is – this is a truism. But the question is: what are the processes intervening between these underlying conditions and the classes of uniformities of social behaviour observed at present in Northern Ireland? An assumption which seems defensible (and can be proved useful in the study of these classes of behaviour) is that these intervening processes can be parsimoniously described in terms of the socially *shared* perception of the situation by those involved in it – in other words, the point at which Blurton Jones' 'emic' research option may come into its own. This does not imply that this research option can float in an ecological or 'material' vacuum; it does not, therefore, need to imply some form of a naive 'psychologizing' of large-scale conflicts. However, in any complex modern society the most important feature of the ecology of any social group consists of other social groups which stand in certain relations to it. This results in certain interactions between 'objective' conflicts of interest and their psychological concomitants, and the analysis of these interactions enables one to make sense of the relevant uniformities of social behaviour.

My second example is more rudimentary. For those who are not familiar with Sherif's studies on intergroup conflict, I shall provide a brief version. There have been several replications and modifications, but the general procedure has remained constant. Boys were brought to a holiday camp. A number of common activities were started during which various personal friendships and preferences were developed. At this point, the boys were divided into two groups, care being taken that those who had become friends found themselves in different groups. Several competitions between the groups were then arranged by the camp authorities, devised by the social psychologists who were pulling the strings; in each of these competitions one of the groups had to win and the other had to lose. As a result, Sherif and his collaborators were able to observe all the well-known and familiar behavioural effects of an acute intergroup conflict. One of the more interesting theoretical aspects of the data is the impact of an intergroup conflict on the previously existing interpersonal relationships between individuals who found themselves later in different competing groups.

Here again, a distinction can be made between a distal and a proximal analysis of the conflict. At one level, the conflict between the boys' groups is a good example of the old Roman *divide et impera*. The social psychologists on the site can be cast in the role of Roman province governors who fomented conflicts for their own purposes which had nothing to do with the welfare of those who were consequently and effectively set at each other's throats. Or, as Billig (1976) pointed out, intergroup behaviour of the boys in the camp can be considered as providing a textbook example, even if it is over-simplified, of the operation of 'false consciousness'. This is undoubtedly a valid level of analysis of the conflict. If the issues were more important and worth the effort, this distal analysis could take into account the historical, economic and material considerations which led the social psychologists to impose their odd designs upon an innocent holiday camp which would have undoubtedly functioned more happily without their *deus ex machina* intervention. But the intervention *was* there, and it *did* succeed in creating the conflict. The development of the conflict and the detail of the social behaviour of the participants in it can, and should, be simultaneously studied from two points of view. The 'etic' approach would take into account the conditions created *by* the social psychologists (and also perhaps the conditions which created the social psychologists) as they affected the nature of the social and the physical situation. The 'emic' approach would complement this by studying those aspects of the conflictive intergroup behaviour which were determined by the participants' social location in the situation and their perception of it. It is interesting to note at this point that although this approach is 'based on the categories of experience which are significant to those whose behaviour is being studied', the resulting data can be quite as 'hard' as any other. To be of some use, they need to fulfil two sets of criteria: the usual ones of the validity and replicability of the observations made; and a consistent relationship to a structure of a testable theory. In summary, I am putting forward two general statements: (i) the proximal analysis of human intergoup conflict needs to involve some 'emic' considerations; (ii) within the 'emic' approach, data of an 'etic' kind can be collected.

It would not be possible to provide within the brief of this paper a detailed example of such an analysis or a description of empirical studies related to it. I can, therefore, do no more here than outline very briefly the direction that this kind of work has recently been taking in the research of my colleagues and myself. (For detailed discussions and reports of research see Tajfel 1978.)

The research we have been doing is based on three converging sets of background considerations. The first of these is concerned with certain differences between interindividual and intergroup behaviour. The second relates to social psychological processes intervening in the uniformities of intergroup behaviour. The third attempts to specify how special features of intergroup behaviour are determined by the nature and characteristics of different kinds of relations between social groups. Each of these sets of considerations will be briefly summarized.

1. *Differences between interindividual and intergroup behaviour*

These differences can be described in terms of four interrelating theoretical continua.

1. The first of these continua can be characterized in terms of its two extremes: fully interpersonal behaviour at one end, and fully intergroup behaviour at the other. The former is defined as interaction between two or more individuals which is very largely determined by their individual characteristics and the nature of the personal relations between them. Examples of interactions approaching this end of the continuum would be those between wife and husband or between two old friends. It is, however, unlikely that these or any other examples would represent this extreme constantly in a 'pure' form. For instance, wife and husband (or two old friends) may find themselves in some situations in which much of their behaviour towards one another will be determined by the social significance and behavioural implications of the distinct social categories (or 'groups' in the sense defined earlier in this paper) to which they belong. In other words, the distance of the interaction from the 'interpersonal' end of the continuum is jointly determined by the nature of the enduring relationship between the individuals involved and the relevance to the social situation of their membership of the social categories to which they respectively belong. Thus, the interaction between a wife and husband or two old friends who are of different nationalities *may* be powerfully affected in the direction away from the interpersonal end when acute conflict develops between their national groups.

At the 'intergroup' end of this first continuum one finds interactions which are largely determined by group memberships of the participants, and very little – if at all – by their personal relations or individual characteristics. Soldiers fighting on the opposing sides of a battle or the 'selection' procedures in concentration camps during the last war provide extreme examples here. Most cases of intergroup conflict will lead to a variety of interactions between individuals in which their behaviour towards each other will be structured and directed by the nature of the relations between their respective groups, even when those same individuals share a history of a relationship which was located much nearer to the 'interpersonal' end. An example was mentioned earlier: in Sherif's field studies care was taken to place in opposing groups those boys who had become friends before the intergroup competitions started. Although previous friendships may have continued to manifest themselves in some of their encounters irrelevant to the intergroup conflict, this was not the case in most of the activities which were powerfully dominated by that conflict.

2. The second continuum concerns one of the fundamental features of the distinction between the interpersonal and the intergroup ends of the first continuum just discussed. It is a direct consequence of the location of a series of social encounters nearer one or the other end of the previous continuum. It can be described as moving from maximum variability to maximum uniformity of behaviour of members of an ingroup towards members of an outgroup. In other words, one of the major consequences of a social situation being located (and/or perceived as such) near the intergroup extreme is that the behaviour towards each other of individuals belonging to the distinct groups is structured and directed *in common* by the features of the intergroup relationship. This does not tell us anything, of course, about the *kind* of uniformities that will be displayed. Predictions concerning the nature of these uniformities can, however, be made with the help of other considerations, which include: (i) the location of a group in a multigroup structure; and (ii) the flexibility or rigidity of this structure. I shall briefly return to these issues later in this paper.

3. The second continuum just discussed concerned the movement from variability to uniformity in the behaviour of members of the ingroup towards members of the outgroup. The third is a parallel movement in the treatment and attitudes shown by any *one* individual of the ingroup towards members of the outgroup. This can be described as contained between, at one end, members of the outgroup being considered in their full variability *as* individuals and, at the other end, members of the outgroup being considered as undifferentiated items in a unified social category. In other words, the movement from interindividual to intergroup behaviour, as outlined in the description of the continuum (1) above, is reflected here in an increasing *interchangeability* for the individual of members of the outgroup. If 'black' immigrants in Britain find it more difficult than other people to obtain accommodation or employment, it is very often not because of their 'personal' characteristics, but because of their membership of a certain social category. This interchangeability is more or less co-terminous with what is often referred to as 'depersonalization'; the next step in the same direction is the dehumanization of entire selected outgroups.

4. The fourth continuum concerns the systems of beliefs about the nature of the multigroup system in which individuals live. It contains the movement between, at one end, beliefs that individual social mobility

governs the system and, at the other end, beliefs that the system is characterized by group or social change. This fourth continuum is assumed to have a causal function in relation to the first three. The belief system of social mobility is defined here as an individual's perception (most often shared with many others) that he can improve in important ways his position in a social situation, or more generally move from one social position to another, *as an individual*. The first direct implication of this is that the individual's system of beliefs about the society in which he lives contains the expectation that, in principle, he is able to leave his present social group or groups and move to other groups which suit him better. Social mobility in this sense consists therefore of a subjective structuring of a social system (however small or large the system may be) in which the basic assumption is that the system is flexible and permeable, that it permits a fairly free movement from one group to another of the individual particles of which it consists. It does not matter very much, from the point of view of the present discussion, whether the causation of free individual movement is perceived as being due to luck, merit, hard work, talent, ability or other attributes of individuals.

'Social change', as the term is used here, refers to the other extreme of the subjective modes of structuring the social system in which an individual lives. It refers basically to his belief that he is enclosed within the walls of the social group of which he is a member; that he cannot move out on his own into another group in order to improve or change his position or his conditions of life; and that therefore the only way for him to change these conditions (or, for that matter, to resist the change of these conditions if he happens to be satisfied with them) is together with his group as a whole, as a member of it rather than as someone who leaves it, or, who can act in a variety of relevant social situations as an individual independently of his group membership. It is the consideration of the 'variants' of social reality underlying the 'social change' system of beliefs and the relationships between these 'variants' and the belief system which provide a link between a distal and a proximal analysis of the uniformities of social behaviour in intergroup situations. I shall return to this issue later in this paper.

2. Social categorization, social identity and social comparison

The second support of the conceptual tripod consists of a sequence of social psychological processes which lead to forms of intergroup behaviour *common* to members of a group under some conditions of relations between the groups involved. The sequence starts from processes of social categorization and their role in the individuals' defining their place inside the social network in which they live. (For a more detailed discussion of intergroup social categorizations and their cognitive 'mechanics', see Tajfel 1959, 1963, 1969, 1972a, Eiser and Stroebe 1972, Doise 1976.) This is, in turn, related to the notion of 'social identity' which remains, however, a strictly limited concept. Its purpose is *not* to serve as a clarification of the vast and complex issues of self and 'identity'. Social identity is conceived in its limited sense as a background variable in *intergroup* behaviour. The notion only applies to those aspects of an individual's image of himself – positive or negative – which derive from his membership of groups that are salient to him. This is by no means a concept which can adequately account for the complexities of the notions of self and self-identity. The usefulness of this deliberate limitation resides in the possibility that it offers of formulating specific hypotheses specifically applying to intergroup behaviour. These hypotheses are based on the notion that 'negative' and 'positive' social identity (i.e. respectively, the unsatisfactory or the satisfactory contributions that the membership of a group makes to an individual's concept of himself) have different and specifiable effects on intergroup behaviour.

The notion of social comparison serves as the indispensable link between social categorization and social identity. The principal assumption is that the value connotations, positive or negative, of group membership can only be derived through comparisons with other relevant social groups. There are certain important differences between *intra*group *inter*individual social comparisons (as discussed in Festinger's theory of 1954) and intergroup social comparisons.

The major distinction between interindividual and intergroup social comparisons relates to conditions in which comparisons will be made with outgroups which may be highly *dissimilar* to the group which is making the comparisons. The assumption that a certain degree of interindividual similarity is needed for social comparisons to be made is central to Festinger's theory and to much of the subsequent work which derived from it. Intergroup situations may be characterized by drastic differences in power, dominance or status between two or more groups. These differences tend to make these groups highly dissimilar. The rigidity and firmness of social stratifications *may* prevent relevant comparisons being made in a social system conceived as fully legitimate and unchangeable – a case becoming increasingly rare in the contemporary world. Once the group differentials begin to be perceived as illegitimate, and/or capable of change, it is this perceived instability and/or illegitimacy of the system which provides a link between previous non-comparability and the development of new social comparisons. It is probable that a combination of perceived instability and illegitimacy of status and other differentials is the most powerful ingredient in the creation of these new perspectives for social comparisons (e.g. Turner and Brown 1978, Caddick 1977). 'Relative deprivation' is the major outcome of these new inter*group* comparisons; there is abundant evidence of its importance in present-day industrial and social conflicts.

The sequence of social categorization–social identity–social comparison leads, in specifiable conditions, to intergroup behaviour aiming at the creation or preservation of a group's distinctiveness from other groups. The function of this distinctiveness is to acquire, or preserve, the positive value connotations of group membership. This is as true of groups which need to acquire a new image of themselves as of those which need to work hard to ward off the threats to their present valued distinctiveness from others. In our complex societies a group is no more of an island than an individual can be. The positive or negative value connotations of the membership of a group and of its characteristics cannot be conceived to exist in a social vacuum. Other relevant groups are the most important feature of a social ecology of any one group. Value connotations attached to a group membership are generated in a matrix of intergroup comparisons and acquire most of their significance in the context of these comparisons. This is why when we try to look at the social psychological aspects of social change (which can be defined here, in a limited way, as change in relations between large-scale social groups) we must take into account the fundamental fact that we are dealing with a continuously changing dynamic system. The preservation, creation or erosion of 'differentials' (whatever they may be) of any one social group makes sense only in relation to what happens to other groups. The nature and direction of social comparisons which underlie these changes must be seen in the light of the social psychological effects of various forms of multigroup structures and of the *shared* conceptions of the social system which are generated by these structures.

3. *Group distinctiveness, multigroup structures and systems of beliefs*

The aim of this section of the paper is to sketch out very briefly (cf. Tajfel 1974, 1978, Turner 1975, for more detailed discussions) some of the social and psychological conditions which lead to certain forms of social comparison and social action relating to them. The first of these has to do with the continuum of systems of beliefs (see §I.1.4 above) contained between 'social mobility' and 'social change'. There is no doubt that these two systems (as previously described) are related (although by no means in a simple manner) to various forms of underlying social reality; these relationships will be discussed later. The important issue at this point is that, whatever may be their background and their validity in reflecting social reality, they determine the direction of social action that individuals undertake either *separately* or *in common*. Our interest in the concept of social identity, as defined earlier in this paper, is not in attempts to describe it for 'what it is' in a static sense – a daunting task which has baffled many social scientists of various persuasions and for which one lacks both optimism and temerity. Social identity is understood here as an intervening causal mechanism in situations of social change (cf. Tajfel 1972b) – observed, anticipated, feared, desired or prepared by the individuals involved; and the effects of these changes on their subsequent intergroup behaviour and attitudes. From this point of view, three categories of situations appear crucial:

The badly defined or marginal social situation of a group, which presents the individuals involved with difficulties as regards defining their place in a social system;

The groups socially defined and consensually accepted as 'superior' at a time when this definition is threatened either by occurring or impending social change, or by a conflict of values inherent in the 'superiority';

The groups socially defined and consensually accepted as 'inferior' at a time when – for whatever reason – either (a) members of a group have engaged in a shared *prise de conscience* of their inferior status; or (b) they have become aware of the feasibility of working towards alternatives to the existing situation; or a combination of (a) and (b), which may also imply (a) leading to (b), or (b) leading to (a).

The 'dynamic' approach to problems of social identity adopted in this discussion is based on several considerations. First, it is unlikely that there exist many examples of intergroup situations which are static in the sense that they consist of an unchanging set of social relationships between the groups. We are, however, less concerned here with social situations than with their psychological counterparts; these are bound to be even less static. This becomes quite clear when one considers briefly for the purpose at hand the focal problem of this paper: that of social identity understood as deriving in a comparative and 'relational' manner from an individual's group memberships.

For the purpose of our argument, one can distinguish between 'secure' and 'insecure' social identity. A completely secure social identity would imply a relationship between two (or more) groups in which a change in the texture of psychological distinctiveness between them is not *conceivable*. For an 'inferior' group this would imply the existence of a total consensus about the nature and the future of their inferiority; in other words, if we think of social 'reality' as being powerfully determined by dominant views about the 'natural' positions of various groups, there would have to exist a complete psychological 'objectification' of a social status quo with no cognitive alternatives of any kind available to challenge the existing social reality. It is possible that historians and social anthropologists could provide some relevant examples in completely stable and isolated societies; these examples could hardly, however, find their counterpart in most of the contemporary world.

A completely secure social identity for a group consensually superior is almost an empirical impossibility. The kind of psychological distinctiveness that ensures its unchallenged superiority must not only be attained; it must also be preserved. And it can be preserved only if social conditions of distinctiveness are carefully perpetuated, together with the signs and symbols of distinctive status without which the attitudes of complete consensus about superior distinctiveness are in danger of disintegrating. In this sense, therefore, even in the most rigid caste system (be it racial or any other), the social distinctions which may appear very stable are related to a continuously dynamic psychological situation in which a superior group can never stop working at the preservation of its distinctiveness. It is very difficult to think of cases of intergroup relations which would present exceptions to this statement, apart perhaps from infants and teachers in a nursery school. (This also happens to be the exception for which it is difficult to imagine the possibility of a sustained and socially shared pattern of intergroup discrimination based on hostility.)

A more serious example can probably be found in the notions about the 'nature' and the relative roles and positions of men and women prevailing in some cultures and some historical periods. In these cases, the massive acceptance by both sides of certain kinds of psychological intergroup distinctiveness prevents the occurrence of serious, socially shared identity problems. It is, however, interesting to see that as soon as these accepted notions are seriously challenged, the intergroup attitudes undergo certain changes which are in line with the present argument. The psychological differentiations of sexes, as long as they are highly consensual, are not accompanied by, or related to, attitudes of intergroup hostility; however, the new search by an active minority in the 'inferior' group of distinctiveness on an *equal* level creates, in some cases, explicit outgroup hostility on one side and equally hostile defensive reactions on the other (Doise and Weinberger 1972–3, Williams and Giles 1978). The impact of the implicit, socially shared problems of identity which are involved can perhaps be gauged from the extent of coverage given by various communication media to all kinds of scientific and pseudoscientific pronouncements about the 'nature' of psychological sex differences.

All these considerations lead to a schematic two-by-two table in which 'insecure social comparisons' are considered in terms of two criteria of division. The first distinguishes between 'conditions conducive to leaving one's group' and 'conditions conducive to staying in one's group'. The second is based on a distinction between 'consensually superior' and 'consensually inferior' groups. Predictions about the characteristics of intergroup behaviour to be found in each of the resulting four 'boxes' cannot be discussed here in any detail (cf. Tajfel 1974, 1976, 1978). It will be sufficient to say that the two boxes containing 'conditions conducive to staying in one's group' (i.e. those which correspond to the 'social change' systems of beliefs) are the most directly pertinent to a social psychology of common action in the contexts of intergroup behaviour.

Thus, it may be said that the 'social mobility' system of beliefs will be closely related to individual action; the 'social change' system to group action. The main concern of this discussion of human intergroup conflict is with the latter. And it is also the latter which requires a form of theory that goes beyond face-to-face interaction even if, in the last analysis, the data for its study must originate from observable encounters between two or more individuals.

II. Face-to-face interaction and social conflict

Sherif's field studies involved a great deal of face-to-face interaction within and between each of the (small) groups in conflict, although it is true that as the conflict proceeded the face-to-face interaction between members of the opposing groups was both severely curtailed and *directed* by the structure and the development of the conflict. In other words, one of the useful ways to start a theoretical analysis of Sherif's conflicts is to assume that the powerful intergroup context consistently dominated the interindividual features of the social behaviour which was observed. This is true *a fortiori* of social behaviour displayed in conflicts between large-scale human groups in which the analysis of face-to-face vagaries of mutual interaction provides indeed a rich source of data; but these data can only be understood when they are viewed as a function of a much wider and *consistent* system of social behaviour. If this is true, the inference must be that, with respect to the behavioural study of social conflict, any data obtained by ethological methods would have to be interpreted in terms of extra-ethological theories. As Michael Chance (1976) wrote:

Doubts are often expressed about the competence of ethology to study human society. If we take the whole complex phenomenon known as society, no single discipline could possibly claim sole relevance, though many of the arts claim to be concerned with an overall entity known as society. So let us see what can be said about the relevance of ethological method. It is concerned with the study of a quite specific part of social relations: namely, the face-to-face situations where observation is indeed possible and then it also becomes possible to note what human features, such as different forms of language, *are* associated with each form of social relation. Yet even here, care is needed to specify the exact way in which social relations take place and the exact composition of the group. In human social gatherings, size is a factor. Some groups are small enough to consist of the same individuals who come together at different times. This is what we encounter in Hell's Angels, street corner groups and Glasgow gangs (Whyte 1969, Patrick 1973).   (p. 226)

One could argue that, even in the case of the Hell's Angels or the Glasgow gangs, the kind of analysis suggested by Chance, although undoubtedly useful in many ways, would probably miss out some of the crucial *intergroup* aspects of their behaviour. For example, as Chance wrote: 'One other aspect of the Hell's Angels is their concern for badges and uniforms, which are also seen as extensions of an individual's person. Badges function as a simple method of identifying a group and those outside it as indeed uniforms do when they assist the definition of social roles. These fixed elements help to define social position' (p. 225). The references to the 'extensions of an individual's person' and the defining of social position are an excellent basis for asking some of the theoretical and empirical *questions* about the Hell's Angels' behaviour, but they provide no basis or theoretical structure for answers to these questions.

My colleagues and I have recently attempted to formulate a theoretical perspective which would help us to provide some of the answers and followed it up by a large number of studies, both in the laboratory and in 'natural' conditions (Tajfel 1978). In this paper, however, I am more directly concerned with the possible applications or extensions of ethological approaches to the study of social groups in conflict and of the part that can be played in this study by the analysis of face-to-face interactions.

Face-to-face behaviour is not confined to non-verbal behaviour. For example, in his paper on 'Organization of attention in groups', Chance (1976) included some interesting comments about Bernstein's restricted and elaborated codes stressing their dependence upon direct social experience of an individual. This, in turn, can be related to the analysis of the infrastructure of human relations in the individual's immediate social environment. We need, therefore, in this domain, a convergence of three levels of analysis: (i) the nature of codes used in verbal communication; (ii) the infrastructure of human relations in a small social sub-universe; (iii) the interaction between the features of this infrastructure and those of the wider social system from which the infrastructure derives. This is a very difficult task, but it is not impossible. Parts of it have been brilliantly attempted by various linguists, social psychologists and sociologists. There is no doubt that, in many of these attempts, ethological methods have been, or can be, used to great advantage.

We do, however, have a problem here relating to the interaction, just mentioned, between the face-to-face infrastructure and the wider social system. The distinction between the 'distal' and the 'proximal' levels of analysis can perhaps again be useful. Bernstein's earlier work on restricted and elaborated codes, important as it was, did not focus on one fairly crucial link in the social-linguistic situation: the link between the 'objective' social relations between groups of people using different idioms of verbal communication and the effects, in turn, of these objective relations on people's modes of communicating within the ingroup and with the outgroup. There is now a great deal of evidence (e.g. Fishman 1972, Giles 1973, 1977, Giles and Powesland 1975, Haugen 1966, Labov 1965, 1966, 1970) showing that identification with a social group (which can only be understood in terms of its perceived differentiation from other groups) will determine, to a large extent, what Giles called the 'divergence' or 'convergence' of modes of speech with people from one's own or other groups. To use a distinct 'internal' dialect, accent, language or vocabulary may become both an important symbol and an effective means of an ingroup's separate identity; to accentuate these forms of 'distinctiveness' in communication with members of relevant outgroups may serve the same functions, and sometimes also the simpler one of neutralizing an external threat. A theoretical structure which would enable us to formulate hypotheses about this kind of behaviour, and to understand it as a part of a wider social system, can only derive from a study of what the French call *représentations sociales* of intergroup relations by those who are involved in these relations, one example of which I attempted to provide in the previous section of this paper.

I still fail to see the distinct relevance of ethological *theory* to these issues. This is, therefore, my first question to the ethologists; and it is my hope that the answers may become relevant to my own research interests in the social psychology of social conflict. My second question is perhaps more contentious: can the analysis of the evolutionary background and the present forms of human face-to-face behaviour contribute more than a collection of fairly marginal curios to the study of those uniformities of social behaviour which are pertinent to the determinants and development of conflicts between large-scale human social groups or social 'categories'? For example, I would not find it difficult to agree with Roger Masters (1976) that 'the more isolated the leader, the more he must rely on bureaucratic or legal devices for assessing his dominance' (p. 221). From this, he draws the more specific inference that 'insofar as the non-verbal gestures and signs of dominance are not utilized by a human leader, increased reliance on purely cultural aspects of the power relationship would seem to be necessary' (p. 221). Perhaps so, although one suspects here a vast and ethno-TV-centric over-simplification of complex issues. The next inference is a little more breathtaking. Masters proposes that the above hypothesis 'suggests an explanation for different styles of politics within a given society – and perhaps even for differences in political regimes' (p. 221). This is, it seems to me, not a bad example of what I meant when I referred to the contribution of 'marginal curios' of face-to-face interaction to the study of large-scale uniformities of social and political behaviour.

III. The proximal analysis and the ethology of human intergroup conflict

In the final section of this paper I should like to return from a slightly different perspective to the issue of the usefulness of ethological theory for both the distal and the proximal analysis of human large-scale intergroup conflict. As will be clear from the previous sections of this paper, there is a certain parallel between these two kinds of analysis on the one hand, and the 'objective' versus 'subjective' aspects of conflict on the other. Let me state once again that the 'subjective' proximal aspects are amenable to treatment in terms of testable hypotheses and relatively 'hard' data. At the same time, none of the arguments outlined so far in this paper must be understood as implying that the social psychological or 'subjective' type of conflict is being considered here as having an equal priority or an equally important causal function in social reality as the 'objective' determinants of social conflict of which the basic analysis must be sought in the social, economic, political and historical structures of a society. The major aim of the present discussion is to determine what are the points of insertion of social psychological variables into the causal spiral; and its argument is that, just as the effects of these variables are determined by the previous social, economic and political processes, so they may also acquire in turn an *autonomous* function which enables them to deflect in one direction or another the subsequent functioning of these processes.

These points of insertion can be considered in relation to two analytic distinctions between types of conflict. One of them is concerned with differentiation between an 'objective' conflict and one which could be referred to, in terms of the present argument, as a conflict of comparative identities. The other attempts to differentiate between conflicts which are *explicit* and/or institutionalized in some form and those which are *implicit*.

The first of these distinctions has been succinctly made in a paper by John Turner (1975) from Bristol. As he wrote:

it is worth making an explicit distinction between four kinds of intergroup competition. This classification will be helpful from the standpoint of gauging how much of an explanatory burden social competition may be required to carry. Firstly, there is competition which is characterized primarily by the independent desires of various groups for a material reward which can be gained by only one group. 'Material' is not meant narrowly; it could, for example, encompass such things as control of a political or social institution. The theme of this competition is expressed by the notion of a 'conflict of interests'. At the other pole, there is what we have referred to as 'social competition' arising from the social comparative aspects of social identity as they interact with shared values. Its generally necessary conditions (their sufficiency is a larger problem) are the salience of the intergroup situation and the possibility of differentially valued actions relevant to the particular social categorization into 'groups'.

The third type of competition is defined by the overlap between the first two: where a material reward to some extent valued of itself serves as a token or symbol of a value differential associated with a possible social comparison between groups. It is an open question whether competition in this case has its own distinct behavioural repercussions or whether this kind of situation tends to collapse into one of the other two types, depending on, for instance, just how much independent value is possessed by the token or the degree of arbitrariness in the relation between symbol and that which is symbolized. This is also an important question because intuitively many workers tend to assume that the use of, for example, small monetary rewards produces a situation of conflict of interest, whereas in fact the results often seem more intelligible if one assumes that the reward had an especial effect only insofar as it helped to make salient the possibility of what we referred to as social competition.

A fourth type of competition or competitive situation is worth suggesting although it will not be discussed in any detail; it is the counterpart of the third type in that it is defined to some extent by an overlap between the first two and is presumably a form of transition between them. It differs in the direction of transition; here it is a social-competitive situation which gives rise to a conflict of interest. This might happen where comparison results in a stable and explicit inequity between two groups and thus the desire for positive self-evaluation leads to directly conflicting group interests with regard to the maintenance of the comparative situation as a whole. (p. 12)

It is nearly impossible in most natural social situations to distinguish between discriminatory intergroup behaviour based on real or perceived conflict of 'objective' interests between the groups and discrimination based on attempts to establish a positively valued 'distinctiveness' for one's own group. However, as has already been mentioned, the two can be distinguished to some extent theoretically since the goals of actions aimed at the achievement of a positively valued ingroup distinctiveness retain no value outside of the context of intergroup comparisons. An example would be a group which does not necessarily wish to increase the level of its salaries but is acting to prevent other groups getting nearer to this level so that differentials can be preserved. But the difficulty with this example – as with many other similar examples – is that, in this case, the preservation of salary differentials is probably associated with all kinds of other 'objective' advantages accruing to the group which cannot be defined in terms of money alone. In turn, *some* of these advantages will again make sense only in the comparative framework of intergroup competition. Despite this confusing network of mutual feedbacks and interactions, the distinction is important because it helps us to understand some aspects of intergroup behaviour which have often been neglected in the past.

The second distinction, between the 'explicit' and the 'implicit' intergroup conflicts, has to do with objectivity in a different way. A conflict can be 'objective' despite the fact that the goals the groups are aiming for have no value outside of the context of intergroup comparison. This is so when the conflict is institutionalized and legitimized by rules and norms, whatever their origin may be, which are accepted by both groups. This was the case in Sherif's studies in their phase of competition between the groups; and it also is the case in any football match and in countless other social activities. The behaviour towards outgroups in this kind of conflict can in turn be classified into two categories, one of which can be referred to as instrumental and the other as non-instrumental. The instrumental category consists of all those actions whose explicit aim can be shown to be directly aimed at causing the group to win the competition. The non-instrumental category could be referred to as 'gratuitous' discrimination against the outgroup, such as the creation of negative stereotypes and all other aspects of 'irrelevant' ingroup–outgroup differentiations so well described, for example, in Sherif's (e.g. 1966) studies. The first category of actions can be theoretically accounted for by assuming nothing more than the group's desire to win the competition (although this also poses some theoretical 'comparison' problems, such as those which were discussed earlier in this paper); the second category of action can be directly and parsimoniously accounted for in terms of the social comparison–social identity–positive ingroup distinctiveness sequence discussed in this paper.

The 'implicit' conflicts are those which can be shown to exist despite an absence of their explicit institutionalization or even of an informal normative acceptance of their existence by the groups involved. The proof of their existence is to be found in the large number of studies (and also everyday occurrences in 'real life') when differentiations of all kinds are made between groups by their members although, on the face of it, there are no 'reasons' for these differentiations to occur. A clear example can be found in some of the data of the experiments by Tajfel *et al.* (1971) and others in which the introduction by the subjects of various intergroup differentiations directly *decreases* the kind of 'objective' rewards that could have otherwise been gained by the ingroup; or even, as is the case in one of the conditions in the experiments by Turner (1975, 1978), when this discrimination diminishes the objective rewards that the individual could have gained for himself. Situations of this kind, which can be widely generalized to many natural social situations, including the 'non-instrumental' differentiations in many explicit conflicts, provide a clear example of the need to introduce social psychological variables of the kind discussed here into the complex spiral of social causation. We now have direct evidence that these 'non-instrumental' differentiations are by no means confined to the bare and Spartan settings of social psychological experiments. Brown (1978) reported a set of findings very similar to those obtained in the experiments from a study of groups of shop stewards in the development and production sections of a large factory.

The distinctions made above between the 'objective' and 'subjective' intergroup conflicts or between the 'objective' (i.e. instrumental) and 'subjective' aspects of any one intergroup conflict relate back to two preoccupations of this paper. One is the establishment of links between the 'distal' and the 'proximal' – in this case between features of social reality and the shared perspectives on the social world (such as those of 'social mobility' and 'social change' previously discussed) which are assumed here to be closely related to common group actions in intergroup contexts. The second concerns the part, if any, that ethological theory can play in this transition from a distal to a proximal analysis of social behaviour in human intergroup conflicts.

The first of these issues can be discussed, once again, in terms of the continuum of systems of beliefs moving between social mobility and social change (see §I.1.4 above). As we are mainly concerned here with common group actions, we shall only consider the 'variants' of social reality which may be conceived as underlying the social change system of belief. It appears that four such 'variants' can be distinguished.

1. The first of these, and perhaps the most obvious, consists of a rigid social stratification (such as, for example, a caste system based on any set of criteria) which makes it impossible or extremely difficult for an individual to move from one group to another. If and when this objective impossibility or difficulty of moving is reflected in the system of beliefs about the multigroup structure *and* the structure is losing its perceived legitimacy and/or is perceived as capable of change, group actions can be expected to occur. These group actions will originate both in the groups whose aim it is to change the structure and in those which aim to preserve (or enhance) the status quo. The detail of the 'objective' and 'subjective' aspects of these common actions is discussed elsewhere in publications previously mentioned and is not of direct concern to the present discussion.

2. The second 'variant' concerns individual differences. In most social systems there exist *some* individuals who, for whatever emotional reasons, *need* the crutch of clear-cut and dichotomous distinction between a group of which they are (or imagine themselves to be) members and related outgroups. In other words, *some* individuals will perceive *most* situations involving members of a particular outgroup as being relevant to an intergroup rather than an interindividual context of social encounters. As we know only too well, there are certain social situations (such as those of economic difficulties or national reversals) which provide excellent conditions for a rapid diffusion of these perspectives and actions relating to them. These individual patterns are the traditional domain of many psychological studies of prejudice. In terms of the present argument they represent, however, no more than one amongst several patterns of back-

ground conditions which lead to certain forms of intergroup behaviour.

3. A clear example of the third 'variant' can be found in the recent development and intensification of many national movements. The relationships between the social background of some of these movements and the social psychological processes which develop in them must be distinguished from situations where there is a close correspondence between the realities of a social stratification and the corresponding 'social change' system of beliefs. For example, the socio-economic and other crucial objective differences of status and mode of life between blacks and whites in South Africa are beyond dispute, and they can easily fit in with the 'social change' structure of beliefs as soon as these differences begin to lose their perceived legitimacy and stability. To a lesser extent, but also quite clearly, the same is true of any society in which birth, religion, social background, race, language or other cultural and social characteristics of a group of people are a crippling load they continue to carry with them in a large variety of social situations and social positions. But all this is not necessarily true of many situations in which the social assimilation of an individual from one group to another presents no special difficulties. A Welshman in Britain need hardly suffer *individually* as a *Welshman*, wherever he lives in the United Kingdom, and chooses to remember and demonstrate his Welshness in a variety of ways. Despite this, there is today a rapid development of national group awareness in Wales which is shown in a number of new linguistic, cultural, educational, economic and political initiatives. There is now an important and active group of people in Wales whose aim it is to foster the 'social change' structure of beliefs for which they use all the initiatives just mentioned. It is not within the competence of a social psychologist to describe or analyse in any detail the social, economic, and historical background for the development of this kind of social movement; but it is not difficult for him to ascertain its existence and to assume that its diffusion may have a lot to do with the operation of the processes of 'minority social influence' such as described, for example, by Moscovici (1976).

4. Finally, the fourth 'variant' of social conditions leading to the social change structure of beliefs need not be related at all to a stratification of the social system, if stratification is meant to imply consensually accepted status differentials between the groups. A sharp *division* into two or more groups may be sufficient for the purpose. A clear example is provided by two groups which are in direct conflict and which present no general status, power, domination or any other social differences – at least in the

initial stages of their interaction, but very often also in the later stages. Two football teams competing from season to season with varying fortunes are one case in point. Other cases are to be found in the competing teams of Sherif's field studies, in many other social psychological studies employing groups in competition, and in equivalent 'natural' situations. The point is that in most of these situations it is very difficult – if not impossible – for anyone to conceive that he could move individually from one group to the other. In an intense intergroup conflict of this kind the belief in the feasibility of individual social mobility is practically non-existent and the belief system of 'social change' – in the form of one's fate depending entirely upon the fortunes of one's group as they relate to the fortunes of the other group – is at a maximum. It is horrendous to imagine what could happen if, during a football match watched by tens of thousands of fans, one of the players suddenly decided to change teams; nor, one imagines, would life be very comfortable for a subject in Sherif's field studies who decided to leave his losing team in order to join the winning one. The social sanctions – both external and internal – for this kind of behaviour are extremely powerful in our cultures, although instances of 'betrayal' and decisions to become a 'renegade' do happen occasionally. The social psychological consequences of the interaction between groups which are in this kind of 'objective' competition or of sharp conflict of interests can once again be simply described in terms of the concepts previously used; a sharp social dichotomy is reflected in the predominance of the 'social change' system of beliefs which, in turn, leads to behaviour in terms of respective group membership of the participants (with a corresponding minimum of interpersonal behaviour) in a variety of situations whose nature will be determined by the nature of the conflict between the groups.

To sum up, we distinguished between four variants of the conditions which help to determine the development of the 'social change' structure of beliefs. The first relates to the reflection in these beliefs of an existing rigid system of social stratification – at the point when the perceived stability of the system begins to break down. The second finds its origins in certain individual needs for establishing clear-cut and impenetrable social dichotomies. This is the traditional area of most social psychological studies on intergroup prejudice. The third concerns the *creation* of a 'social change' system of beliefs in social conditions which do not necessarily prevent individual movement from one group to another. The fourth is a consequence of an intense and explicit conflict of interest between groups which is not related to a stable social stratification.

It will be obvious that the insertion of social psychological variables into the study of any one special instance of conflict would have to rely on a thorough preliminary analysis of the underlying social reality. It is only in this way that a theoretically meaningful relationship can be established between the three stages of a sequence: the 'variant' of the social reality; the variety of the shared structures of belief associated with it (and this association need not be, by any means, a simple one); and the consequent uniformities of intergroup behaviour. The 'distal' social analysis and the 'proximal' social psychological one can only be useful together if two conditions are fulfilled: the specification of the steps or links between the 'natural' social context and its psychological consequences; and a clear specification of the hypotheses linking these consequences to observable social behaviour.

The question then arises about the place and role of ethological theory and hypotheses deriving from it in this kind of a sequence. Is it 'distal' or is it 'proximal'? If it is distal, what are its links to the more direct determinants of social behaviour in natural social situations? If it is proximal, can it generate interesting hypotheses or, alternatively, plausible *post hoc* explanations which would give us more insight into various types of conflict? Does it use psychological assumptions, implicitly or explicitly? If so, are they based on independent and well-grounded research and systematic observation or are they no more than unacknowledged 'intuitions' which would be far removed from the hard-headed 'etic' stance rightly recommended by many ethologists?

I do not feel that I have enough information about the current ethological research on human intergroup conflict to answer any of these questions with any degree of certainty. At the same time, it is perhaps not inappropriate to voice the suspicion that, as distinct from programmatic statements and vast generalizations (of which ethologists would rightly beware in the study of animal social behaviour), there is not very much of this kind of human ethological research in evidence. Avoiding the 'sound and fury' to which John Crook (1976) referred, I can fall back perhaps on a paper which is, to my knowledge, the only one in this volume attempting to relate directly ethological theory (we all probably agree that ethological methods are useful and relevant) to human intergroup behaviour. In his discussion of spacing and competing in ritual and ritualization (chapter 1.1 above), Eibl-Eibesfeldt starts from a clear and useful distinction, which has been too often forgotten by social psychologists, between interindividual and intergroup behaviour. As he wrote, 'each level is distinguished by a number of characteristics'. Some of these distinctions have been discussed earlier in this paper and more extensively elsewhere (Tajfel 1972b, 1978).

The various statements of Eibl-Eibesfeldt about human intergroup behaviour fall into two classes which can be respectively characterized as: (i) statements of theory; and (ii) statements of psychological presuppositions. Examples in the first category would be: 'Many of the subcultures and groups with specific rituals which form part of the same culture will demarcate themselves from others, as if there were an urge to go new ways, to experiment in cultural pseudospeciation . . . It could well be that this urge to try new ways has been selected to speed up cultural evolution, to cause mutations, so to speak, on the cultural level.'

Differentiation between social groups is undoubtedly a universal phenomenon. There is little doubt, however, that the two remarks made by Eibl-Eibesfeldt about its causal aspects are of a 'distal' nature from which theoretical links would have to be established to observed behaviour. It is the second class of statements which I called 'psychological presuppositions' which seems to provide the links. For example: 'Human groups tend to define themselves as the only real human beings and to speak of their neighbors in derogatory terms. Neighbors are also not considered to be fully human and sometimes are even spoken of as if they were not people at all. The neighbor is thus dehumanized and *in this process of self-indoctrination man shuts himself off from those signals which release pity* . . . war tends to get ritualized into a sort of territorial display, to retain one's territory, *and confirm one's group identity* . . . In this way human languages and cultures evolved diversely, a process which Erikson terms "cultural pseudospeciation" *because to a certain degree cultures behave like species*' (my italics). The italicized parts of each of these statements (there are many other similar ones in the paper) provide the 'presuppositions' and presumably the links to observed social behaviour.

It could be argued that, in this kind of perspective, the background and the observable forms of ritualized behaviour provide the links between the assumed universal tendencies of the human species and the uniformities of behaviour in situations of conflict between social groups. There are, however, some serious difficulties in this assumption of a 'universal' sequence from 'distal' presuppositions to ritualizations to observed social behaviour. These difficulties are mainly due to considerable oversimplifications which characterize the assumed progression from the antecedents of collective behaviour to its manifestations. Two examples will perhaps be sufficient to make the point. The first concerns the behaviour of football crowds at matches in England. There have recently been attempts (e.g. Marsh 1975) to account for this behaviour in terms of its ritual patterns and the effects (such as outbreaks of violence) of the forcible disruption of these patterns. A recent study by Glynis Breakwell (1978), which is generally concerned with 'marginality' of group membership, reported on the attitudes and behaviour of two categories of 'fans': those who went to a large number of 'away' matches and those who never went to any, restricting themselves to the vicarious pleasures of television watching. There are some interesting differences, reported in the study, between these two categories. But there are also some fundamental similarities in their attitudes towards the ingroup and the outgroups (i.e. fans of other clubs), towards the role of violence, symbols of membership, etc. This is so despite the fact that the television-watching-fans-at-a-distance obviously had neither the opportunity nor perhaps the desire to find themselves in the middle of uncertain and unpredictable crowd situations. This failure to participate in the 'rituals' does not seem to have affected the nature of their group identifications and it has probably very little to do with whatever inner or outer pressures led them to identify with the group in the first place.

My second example takes a much longer time-span. In his recent book on *The nationalization of the masses*, the historian George Mosse (1975) provides an analysis and a description of the means whereby, from about the beginning of the nineteenth century, 'the new politics attempted to draw the people into active participation in the national mystique through rites and festivals, myths and symbols which give a concrete expression to the general will' (p. 2). As he wrote: 'The new politics provided an objectification of the general will: it transformed political action into a drama supposedly shared by the people themselves' (p. 2).

Mosse traces in his book various forms of this 'objectification' through a variety of means, each of which represents a ritualization of certain aspects of public life. He was thus able to describe the contributions to the 'nationalization of the masses' of such diverse elements as new styles of national monuments, public festivals, theatre, dance, symbols and rites of membership, military parades, popular forms of music, mass meetings, sports associations, etc. Each of these elements represented and developed its own full-blown forms of ritualization. There is no doubt that they all powerfully contributed to the creation of mass movements of a certain kind. But a historical account or a social psychological theory of these movements cannot take for their points of departure (and arrival) the rituals themselves and their effects. The rituals are no more than the stage props of a scenario which takes its plot from elsewhere. An accumulation of diverse rituals, such as those described by Mosse, quite obviously cannot be coherently understood or explained in terms of their own detailed characteristics. Their common meaning, historical or psychological, must be sought elsewhere.

It seems to me that each of the series of questions I asked earlier about the place and role of ethological theory and hypotheses in the study of the causal sequences in human intergroup behaviour finds its own answer in the approach to ritualization represented in Eibl-Eibesfeldt's paper. But rather than go back to these questions and answers in some form of a superfluous textual analysis, it may be more useful to provide yet another quotation, this time from a paper by another historian which, at a recent colloquium, formed the basis of a discussion on methods of historical research concerned with the mass murders committed during World War II:

The Holocaust, it is submitted, could be regarded as the result of the confluence of the following main factors: a very specific age-old hatred with an inherent capacity for extreme escalation; a technological potential for industrial mass destruction of human lives; a well-developed bureaucratic apparatus with drive, initiative and a motivation for the execution of murderous instructions; a dictatorship whose heads are ideologically motivated to act upon the age-old hatred; an economic system whose basic interests do not make the mass murder impossible of execution; and an economic, cultural, social and political crisis escalating into a war. Basic to all these was the removal of the victim from a category comparable in principle to that of the murderer: it was only when the development of antisemitism made it possible to remove the common bond between Jews and non-Jews by labelling the Jews as non-humans, that mass murder became feasible. Slavs and others were destined to become slaves in a future Nazi Reich, with their intelligentsia and clergy annihilated. The Jews as such ('überhaupt') were to disappear ('. . . *sollen eines Tages, den Wünschen des Führers entsprechend, die Juden verschwinden*'. Himmler in October 1942). (Bauer 1977)

There is a point of agreement here with Eibl-Eibesfeldt's statement about the dehumanization of the neighbour. But 'the removal of the victim from a category comparable in principle to that of the murderer' is not usefully explained if we rest content with the statement that, as humans, we have a 'tendency' to do this kind of thing or even when this tendency is then functionally ascribed to the needs for survival of a group or a culture. Nor is it likely that the Lorenzian *Kindchenschema* helped very much the uncounted numbers of children who were involved, or that the cutting-off 'from those signals which release pity' amounted to more than a wrinkle in the wave of horror. Bauer attempts to summarize the 'confluence of the . . . main factors'. It is the duty and the job of the social psychologist to attempt a useful analysis of the links between this confluence and the 'basic' phenomenon of 'the removal of the victim' from the category of humankind. This is a difficult job – and I apologize for having used such an extreme example for pointing out its difficulties. The problems are nearly as difficult in less extreme cases. A detailed description of face-to-face behaviour will only help us if it is seen against its cultural, social and psychological background. 'Identity' explains nothing by itself: in its social intergroup setting it is no more than one term of an equation whose antecedents and consequents *need* to be explained and related to each other. Otherwise we shall never go beyond the stage of generalizations which are as plausible as they are sweeping and which are likely to remain forever in their vacuum of splendid distal and untestable isolation.

Comments on papers by Kummer and Tajfel

Social relations and intergroup conflict

MARIO VON CRANACH

Both papers are relevant to the topic of this volume. However, neither of the authors enters the arena of human ethology; they both stay deliberately on their side of the fence. Kummer discusses primate ethology, Tajfel human social psychology from a cognitive viewpoint. The papers are also different in terms of the level of the problems they discuss: Kummer treats a problem of individual relations between partners, Tajfel deals with problems of intergroup relations. Thus, the two papers hardly meet, and I shall discuss them separately.

Hans Kummer tackles the general question of why primates are social. He decides to seek the answer in the outcome of individual investments and benefits and starts by concentrating on the question: what does a primate gain in establishing a social relationship? In order to reduce complexity he restricts his discussion to the case of the gains of one primate A in relation to one companion B; he discusses B's value for A and A's means to operate on B's value for him.

Social psychologists have used somewhat similar approaches for nearly thirty years: namely *exchange theory* and the concept of *group cohesiveness*. These concepts are relevant to our discussion, since they aim at the solution of problems Kummer also has to tackle: first to derive individual strategies from selfish needs, and second to get from the individual level to the group level. Although it is not possible here to

423

discuss these concepts in detail, nor to do justice to the different contributions different authors have achieved in these areas, it may be helpful to recall some of the strong and weak points of these approaches.

Exchange theory has been applied to many problems, but one of its central applications is in the field of interpersonal attraction, where it tries to predict the value of a person B for A from the profit A gets from B. Some of its basic concepts in this approach are *reward, cost* and *outcome* (= reward minus cost), the latter being positive (*profit*) or negative (*cost*). (The origin of these terms in economics is obvious.) In addition the theory assumes that these variables are mediated by cognitive instances, which are conceived as a *comparison level* (CL), the level of reward a person expects from experience in previous relationships and interactions (outcomes more positive than CL are gratifying), and as a *comparison level for alternatives* (CL alt.), which takes into account the comparison level a person could realize in the best available alternative relationship. It is generally assumed that a person acts to maximize the positive outcome of relations. On these prerequisites, hypotheses about interpersonal attraction have been developed. Thibaut and Kelley (1959) suggest (1) that the relation of outcomes actually received through CL determines the actor's *degree of attraction*, and (2) that the relation of outcome to CL alt. defines his *dependence on the relationship*. Furthermore, attempts have been made to establish repertoires of the behaviors of the actor and their values for the partners and to use these figures, by application of certain concepts and methods of game theory, to determine mutual *outcome control*. This then leads to a *theory of power*. Finally, the proponents of this approach consider it necessary to introduce a notion of a norm of *distributive justice* (Homans 1958, 1961), or *equity* (Walster, Berscheid and Walster 1976) to counterbalance the egocentric variables.

What could an ethologist learn from the developments in this research area that he doesn't already know? As far as I can see, the problems concern the attainment of outcome, the introduction of mediating constructs and the invention of counterbalancing forces. Let us have a short look at these points.

1. Attainment of outcome

A. Problems of assessment. Unfortunately, reward and cost of a behavior are not obvious. In detail, we find:
  (i) It is difficult to determine even the reward and cost of a specific behavior.

(ii) Investments, cost and reward may be located between the distant past and the distant future.
(iii) Many acts are based on many investments and have many consequences.
(iv) Many acts concern the relationships to different partners.
(v) Several behaviors of one person may occur simultaneously, which further complicates the matter.

B. Problems of computation. Even if assessment of investments, reward and cost is possible, the computation of outcome cannot be a simple arithmetic operation, but presupposes detailed knowledge of the organism's functioning.

2. Mediating constructs

In the study of any complicated behavior system (which I assume we find in all primates) it might be unavoidable to introduce mediating variables that function similarly to CL and CL alt. In the study of nonhuman primates, this may create considerable conceptual and methodological difficulties.

3. Counterbalancing forces

In order to account reasonably for observed behaviors, it seems necessary to introduce altruistic variables that counterbalance the 'egocentric' ones. On the individual level, these can be introduced as postulates or constructed from the egocentric variables, a complicated and often somewhat artificial proceeding. Or they can be introduced on the social level, which then interferes with the reductive simplicity of the approach.

In general it is my impression that the attractive simplicity of the exchange approach cannot be preserved if it is used as a tool to explain and predict behavior in natural situations. It may, however, fruitfully serve as an heuristic device to develop specific research questions; and that seems to be how Kummer uses his concepts.

Let us now very briefly turn to 'group cohesiveness'. This concept has been introduced to derive a property of the group, its coherence or capacity to bind its members to the social unit under varying circumstances, from tendencies of the individual members. The most popular definition has been proposed by Festinger, Schachter and Back

(1950:164–5): cohesiveness is the 'total field of forces which acts on members to remain in the group . . . and may be defined (operationally) as the average for all the members of the resultant force toward remaining in the group'. The deficiencies of this definition have been clearly summarized by Golembiewsky (1962:151–2):

1. The conceptualization is not unidimensional, for the total field of forces to remain in a group might include factors (such as a prison sentence) which would contradict this prediction assumed by cohesiveness theory: that the greater the forces acting upon individuals to remain in a group, the more attractive the group is to the individuals.
   2. It is impossible to measure the total field of forces directly, and each indirect operational definition is but a partial measure at best and, at the worst, may not be related to the 'total' measure.
   3. Both the conceptualization and the suggested operation neglect forces to leave the group (although it might be argued that the total field of forces is ambiguous enough to include forces toward leaving the group, those who formulated the concept used positive sociometric choices as their operational measure, which suggests that the interpretation here is correct).
   4. The total field of forces and the suggested operational definition are not obviously equivalent formulations.

After our discussion of difficulties in the application of exchange theories, these problems appear to be somewhat familiar. Of course in the area of group psychology other more useful concepts of cohesiveness have been proposed and fruitful empirical research has been conducted (Lott and Lott 1965). Still it remains the major task in research strategy to get from the interindividual to the group level. I would assume that success in this attempt depends on the identification of processes that integrate these levels. Here, we could begin to discuss Kummer's paper in detail and it might be useful to apply to each of his proposed problem areas, the question: how does the involved mechanism help us to get from the individual to the social relationship and from there to the group? It should be clear that I do consider Kummer's approach, centered as it is on the individual, interesting and useful. But I think it important to consider in advance the means of going beyond the individual level.

Henri Tajfel develops a research strategy for intergroup conflict. He distinguishes two levels of analysis, a distal and a proximal one. He points out that research should start from distal analysis, which concerns the historical, economical and biological basis of the conflict; on the proximal level, he assumes, the most salient social-psychological questions are of a cognitive nature (in fact, the elaboration of cognitive processes in intergroup conflict constitutes a major part of his propositions).

For this reason, he argues that human ethological theory, which mainly concerns noncognitive behavioral details of human conduct, cannot contribute to the important problems in the area of intergroup conflict.

I should like to say here that I am sympathetic with Tajfel's basic assumptions, although not with all the details and the conclusions he draws in relation to human ethology. To explain, let me start by hinting at a point of criticism: there is no reference in the paper to what kind of groups are discussed; according to the examples used, it could be anything from boys' groups in a summer camp to nations. By lack of definition it is also hard to determine where the borderline is between individual conflict, intragroup conflict, intergroup conflict, conflict between organizations, institutions etc. Detailed distinctions between kinds of groups should, however, already result from Tajfel's 'distal' variables, should we really take them seriously.

A second point I should like to mention is Tajfel's almost total neglect of emotional factors. Emotional disturbance is so conspicuous in intergroup conflict that I cannot persuade myself not to consider it. As a compromise I should like to suggest that emotion might be reflected in cognition in intergroup conflict.

But why stress so much cognition? (And here I completely agree with Tajfel's position.) Tajfel has worked out detailed arguments and propositions about cognitive processes in intergroup conflict which I cannot discuss since I am not sufficiently familiar with this research area. But let me state the problem in a more general way: Tajfel has to deal with various levels of analysis (for example, in his proposition of proximal within the framework of distal findings). The inherent logic of such a strategy is that of systems theory, and from the general experiences in the application of systems theory in many disciplines we have learned that the distinction of the systemic levels is not really fruitful unless we identify the mechanisms that mediate between these levels. And this is just the role of cognition in human affairs, of which intergroup conflict is only one example: cognition mediates between individual and social levels of organizations. Of course, it is the individual that processes cognition; but in social systems these cognitions are preserved, reorganized in a general form and handed back to the individual that enacts them; and it is in these individually enacted social cognitions that social structures become manifest. (This of course is an assumption, a preferred viewpoint in modern social sciences, not an established truth.) Tajfel's paper provides a detailed example of this hypothesized process, and that is why I consider it valuable; and referring to Kummer I may perhaps ask how he will proceed – if he ever decides to – from the individual to the social level without using cognitive constructs.

May I conclude with a few general apprehensions on trends in the development of the study of animal behavior, as seen by a social psychologist. (This does not directly refer to Kummer; I am just using an opportunity.) Ethologists have turned to the study of more complicated organisms, and finally of man. They seem to get fun and excitement out of this new venture, but this pleasure has its price: they are in danger of losing their innocence. Until recently a psychologist in discussion with an ethologist was often impressed by his partner's charming simplicity in handling behavioral 'facts'. A certain behavior or movement was considered to be just what it was, but in man (and in other primates too, I am afraid) a movement is never just a movement. At least partly, its identity emerges from its meaning. In dealing with meanings, ethologists will be in danger of losing their firm foothold in 'facts', the source of their strength, and of becoming like psychologists and other students of human behavior: miserable and full of doubts. Next there will be the temptation to seek comfort in the illusionary security of formal models. Let us hope that these dreadful visions never come true.

H. KUMMER: REPLY TO VON CRANACH'S COMMENTS

Drawing on his assessment of equity theory and of psychological modeling in general, von Cranach expresses concern with an array of problems that might hamper research following the lines of my heuristic scheme. I will not venture into any prophecies on whether my exercise will be useful. It is neither a model nor a plan of research. Ideas were included for the sake of completeness and consistency even if I could not see a way of testing them. It is good to know what parts of the picture are hidden in the dark while we explore its brighter areas. And brighter areas there are. If we know, for example, that high-ranking rhesus mothers bear more offspring than lower-ranking ones and that their infants more often survive the first year (Drickamer 1974), the benefit of high rank is demonstrated. If we could also establish that allies raise a primate's rank and that this primate can muster allies by social grooming – both hypotheses are testable by experiment – we would have, I think, a meaningful result along the lines of my scheme.

Parallels with equity theory can be misleading. As the above example illustrates, the biological currency of benefit and cost is fitness, i.e. roughly the number of an individual's offspring that reach maturity. It is not gratification (as suggested by von Cranach's sentence that 'outcomes more positive than CL are gratifying') or resources (as suggested by the propositions in Walster, Berscheid and Walster 1976). Gratifications and access to resources are goals that can affect a primate's choice of behavior through his monitoring of goal states. These goals, however, are coupled by natural selection with the more distant behavioral effects on fitness, and it is this ultimate 'function' that biologists mean when they talk of benefits and costs. In primate ethology, both 'goal benefits' or gratifications and 'fitness benefits' or functions are of interest, but they are very different things and require different methods of study. Von Cranach's concern about their measurement applies to both. One current procedure in behavioral biology is to assign an obviously beneficial act a constant value and to see how a subject distributes it among his partners (e.g. Kurland 1977).

Unlike equity theorists, primate ethologists do not assume that their subjects have a sense of equity or that they are guided by an accepted norm of distributive justice. My scheme simply suggests that a monkey is selected and conditioned to seek his fitness-related goals in a social landscape of conspecifics which to him are resources as well as impediments. I assume that he is not aware of any equity between himself and others. It is perhaps this difference of assumptions that caused von Cranach's question as to how one can 'get from the individual to the social relationship and from there to the group'. My answer is that the dyadic relationship is the interaction of two streams of goal-seeking strategies and the triad of three, and that our experiments begin to throw some light on the way they mesh. The social landscape will become increasingly complex, but aside from choice and competition among members I do not as yet see any *basic* difference creeping in as we move from dyads to larger groups.

It is apparent from this response that not all ethologists have lost their innocence. They may worry about unmanageable complexity, but they have the advantage of experimentation. They know that a movement is not just a movement, but also that the meaning of one movement does not vary beyond limits, at least in a macaque. There are even some ethologists who do not feel tempted into out-modeling what they have at least intuited and some who are wise enough to learn as much as possible from monkeys before they wish to tackle man. But one thing they cannot do: remain innocent merely as suitably simple subjects for despairing social psychologists.

References

Abegglen, J.-J. 1976. On socialization in hamadryas baboons. Unpublished Ph.D. thesis, University of Zurich.

Alexander, R. D. 1974. The evolution of social behavior. *Annual Review of Ecological Systems*, 5:325–83.

Altmann, S. A. 1965. Sociobiology of rhesus monkeys: II, stochastics of social communication. *Journal of Theoretical Biology*, 8(3):490–577.

1974. Baboons, space, time, and energy. *American Zoologist*, 14:221–48.

Altmann, S. A. and Altmann, J. 1970. *Baboon ecology*. Bibliotheca primatologica no. 12. Basel: Karger.

Bauer, Y. 1977. 'Unique and universal': Some problems arising out of Holocaust research. Paper presented at the Inter-university Seminar on the Systematic Study of Contemporary Jewish Civilization, Jerusalem, August 1977.

Billig, M. 1976. *Social psychology and intergroup relations*. European Monographs in Social Psychology. London: Academic Press.

Bischof, N. 1975. A systems approach toward the functional connections of attachment and fear. *Child Development*, 46:801–17.

Blurton Jones, N. G. 1976. Growing points in human ethology: another link between ethology and the social sciences? In P. P. G. Bateson and R. A. Hinde (eds.), *Growing points in ethology*. Cambridge: Cambridge University Press.

Breakwell, G. 1978. Some effects of marginal social identity. In Tajfel 1978.

Brown, R. 1978. Divided we fall: an analysis of relations between the sections of a factory workforce. In Tajfel 1978.

Caddick, B. 1977. Legitimacy and illegitimacy in intergroup behaviour. Unpublished manuscript, University of Bristol.

Chadwick-Jones, J. K. 1976. *Social exchange theory*. London: Academic Press.

Chance, M. 1976. The organization of attention in groups. In M. von Cranach (ed.), *Methods of inference from animal to human behaviour*. Chicago: Aldine/The Hague: Mouton.

Coulson, J. C. 1966. The influence of the pair-bond and age on the breeding biology of the Kittiwake gull *Rissa tridactyla*. *Journal of Animal Ecology*, 35:269–79.

430

Crook, J. H. 1970. The socio-ecology of primates. In *Social behaviour in birds and mammals*. London: Academic Press.

1976. Problems of inference in the comparison of animal and human social organizations. In M. von Cranach (ed.), *Methods of inference from animal to human behaviour*. Chicago: Aldine/The Hague: Mouton.

Deag, J. M. and Crook, J. H. 1971. Social behaviour and 'agonistic buffering' in the wild Barbary Macaque, *Macaca sylvana* L. *Folia primatologica*, 15:183–200.

Doise, W. 1976. *L'Articulation psychosociologique et les relations entre groupes*. Brussels: De Boeck.

Doise, W. and Weinberger, M. 1972–3. Représentations masculines dans différentes situations de rencontres mixtes. *Bulletin de psychologie*, 26:649–57.

Drickamer, L. C. 1974. A ten-year summary of reproductive data for free-ranging Macaca mulatta. *Folia primatologica*, 21:61–80.

Drickamer, L. C. and Vessey, S. H. 1973. Group changing in free-ranging male rhesus monkeys. *Primates*, 14:359–68.

Eiser, J. R. and Stroebe, W. 1972. *Categorization and social judgment*. European Monographs in Social Psychology. London: Academic Press.

Erwin, J., Maple, R. and Welles, J. F. 1975. Responses of rhesus monkeys to reunion. Evidence for exclusive and persistent bonds between peers. In S. Kondo, M. Kawai, A. Ehara (eds.), *Contemporary primatology*. Basel: Karger.

Festinger, L. 1954. *A theory of social comparison processes. Human Relations*, 7:117–40.

Festinger, L., Schachter, S. and Back, K. 1950. *Social pressures in informal groups*. New York: Harper.

Fishman, J. A. 1972. *Language and nationalism*. Rowley, Mass.: Newbury House.

Giles, H. 1973. Accent mobility: a model and some data. *Anthropological Linguistics*, 15:87–105.

(ed.) 1977. *Language, ethnicity and intergroup relations*. European Monographs in Social Psychology. London: Academic Press.

Giles, H. and Powesland, P. F. 1975. *Speech style and social evaluation*. European Monographs in Social Psychology. London: Academic Press.

Goldschmidt, W. 1959. *Man's way. A preface to the understanding of human society*. New York: Holt, Rinehart and Winston.

Golembiewsky, D. T. 1962. *The small group*. Chicago: University of Chicago Press.

Haugen, E. 1966. Dialect, language, nation. *American Anthropologist*, 68:922–35.

Hausfater, G. 1975. Dominance and reproduction in baboons (*P. cynocephalus*). *Contributions to Primatology*, vol. VII. Basel, Karger.

Hinde, R. A. 1975. Interactions, relationships and social structure in nonhuman primates. In S. Kondo, M. Kawai, A. Ehara, S. Kawamura (eds.), *Proceedings of the Symposium of the Vth Congress of the International Primatology Society*. Tokyo: Japan Science Press.

1976. On describing relationships. *Journal of Child Psychology and Psychiatry*, 17:1–19.

Homans, G. C. 1958. Human behavior as exchange. *American Journal of Sociology*, 63:597–606.

1961. *Social behavior – its elementary forms*. New York: Harcourt Brace.

Kummer, H. 1957. Soziales Verhalten einer Mantelpavian-Gruppe. *Beiheft Schweizerische Zeitschrift für Psychologie*, 33:1–91.

1967. Tripartite relations in hamadryas baboons. In S. A. Altmann (ed.), *Social communication among primates*. Chicago: Chicago University Press.

1968. *Social organization of hamadryas baboons. A field study.* Bibliotheca primatologica no. 6. Basel: Karger/Chicago: University of Chicago Press.

1971. *Primate societies.* Chicago: Aldine Atherton.

1975. Rules of dyad and group formation among captive gelada baboons (Theropithecus gelada). In S. Kondo, M. Kawai, A. Ehara, S. Kawamura (eds.), *Proceedings of the Symposium of the Vth Congress of the International Primatology Society.* Tokyo: Japan Science Press.

Kummer, H., Götz, W. and Angst, W. 1974. Triadic differentiation: An inhibitory process protecting pair bonds in baboons. *Behaviour, 49*:62–87.

Kurland, J. A. 1977. Kin selection in the Japanese Monkey. *Contributions to Primatology*, vol. XII. Basel: Karger.

Labov, W. 1965. On the mechanism of linguistic change. *Georgetown Monograph Series on Language and Linguistics, 18*:91–114.

1966. The effect of social mobility on linguistic behaviour. *Social Inquiry, 36*:186–203.

1970. Language in social context. *Studium Generale, 23*:30–87.

Lamprecht, J. 1973. Mechanismen des Paarzusammenhaltes beim Cichliden *Tilapia mariae* Boulanger 1899 (Cichlidae, Teleostei). *Zeitschrift für Tierpsychologie, 32*:10–61.

van Lawick-Goodall, J. 1971. *In the shadow of man.* Boston: Houghton Mifflin Co.

Lorenz, K. 1966. *On aggression.* London: Methuen.

Lott, A. L. and Lott, Bernice, 1965. Group cohesiveness as interpersonal attraction. *Psychological Bulletin, 64*(4):259–309.

McGrew, W. C. 1975. Patterns of plant food sharing by wild chimpanzees. In S. Kondo, M. Kawai, A. Ehara (eds.), *Contemporary primatology.* Basel: Karger.

Marsh, P. 1975. Understanding aggro. *New Society, 32*(652):7–9.

Mason, W. A. and Hollis, J. H. 1962. Communication between young rhesus monkeys. *Animal Behaviour, 10*:211–21.

Masters, R. 1976. The impact of ethology on political science. In A. Somit (ed.), *Biology and politics.* The Hague/Paris: Mouton.

Menzel, E. W. 1966. Responsiveness to objects in free-ranging Japanese monkeys. *Behaviour, 26*:130–49.

1971. Communication about the environment in a group of young chimpanzees. *Folia primatologica, 15*:220–32.

Morris, D. 1967. *The naked ape.* London: Jonathan Cape.

Moscovici, S. 1976. *Social influence and social change.* European Monographs in Social Psychology. London: Academic Press.

Mosse, G. L. 1975. *The nationalization of the masses.* New York: Meridian.

Nishida, T. and Kawanaka, K. 1972. Inter-unit-group relationships among wild chimpanzees of Mahali Mountains. *Kyoto University African Studies, 7*:131–69.

Patrick, J. 1973. *A Glasgow gang observed.* London: Eyre Methuen.

Rosenblum, L. A. and Lowe, A. 1971. The influence of familiarity during rearing on subsequent partner preferences in squirrel monkeys. *Psychonomic Science, 23*(1A):35–7.

Rowell, T. E. 1974. The concept of social dominance. *Behavioral Biology, 11*:131–54.

Sade, D. 1967. Determinants of dominance in a group of free-ranging rhesus monkeys. In S. A. Altmann (ed.), *Social communication among primates.* Chicago: University of Chicago Press.

Seyfarth, R. M. 1976. Social relationships among adult female baboons. *Animal Behaviour*, 24:917–38.

Sherif, M. 1966. *Group conflict and cooperation: their social psychology*. London: Routledge and Kegan Paul.

Stammbach, E. 1978. Social differentiation in female groups of hamadryas baboons. *Behaviour*, 67:322–38.

Strum, S. C. 1975. Primate predation: Interim report on the development of a tradition in a troop of olive baboons. *Science*, 187:755–7.

Tajfel, H. 1959. Quantitative judgment in social perception. *British Journal of Psychology*, 50:16–29.

1963. Stereotypes. *Race*, 5:3–14.

1969. Cognitive aspects of prejudice. *Journal of Social Issues*, 25(4), 79–97.

1972a. La catégorisation sociale. In S. Moscovici (ed.), *Introduction à la psychologie sociale*. Paris: Larousse.

1972b. Experiments in a vacuum. In J. Israel and H. Tajfel (eds.), *The context of social psychology: a critical assessment*. European Monographs in Social Psychology. London: Academic Press.

1974. Social identity and intergroup behaviour. *Social Science Information*, 13(2), 65–93.

1976. Psicologia sociale e processi sociali. In A. Palmonari (ed.), *Problemi attuali della psicologia sociale*. Bologna: Il Mulino.

(ed.) 1978. *Differentiation between social groups: Studies in the social psychology of intergroup relations*. European Monographs in Social Psychology. London: Academic Press.

Tajfel, H., Flament, C., Billig, M. and Bundy, R. P. 1971. Social categorization and intergroup behaviour. *European Journal of Social Psychology*, 1:149–78.

Teleki, G. 1975. Primate subsistence patterns: Collector-predators and hunter-gatherers. *Journal of Human Evolution*, 4:125–84.

Thibaut, J. W. and Kelley, H. H. 1959. *The social psychology of groups*. New York: Wiley.

Tinbergen, N. 1948. Social releasers and the experimental method required for their study. *Wilson Bulletin*, 60:6–53.

Turner, J. 1975. Social comparison and social identity: Some prospects for intergroup behaviour. *European Journal of Social Psychology*, 5:5–34.

1978. Social categorization and social discrimination in the minimal group paradigm. In Tajfel 1978.

Turner, J. and Brown, R. 1978. Social status, cognitive alternatives and intergroup relations. In Tajfel 1978.

Tutin, C. E. G. 1975. Exceptions to Promiscuity in a feral Chimpanzee community. In S. Kondo, M. Kawai and A. Ehara (eds.), *Contemporary primatology*, Basel: Karger.

Vaitl, E. In press. Nature and implications of the complexly organized social system in non-human primates.

Walster, E., Berscheid, E. and Walster, G. W. 1976. New directions in equity research. In L. Berkowitz and E. Walster (eds.), *Equity theory: Toward a general theory of social interaction*. Advances in experimental social psychology 9. New York: Academic Press.

Whyte, F. 1969. *Street corner society*. Chicago: University of Chicago Press.

Williams, J. and Giles, H. 1978. The changing status of women in society: an intergroup perspective. In Tajfel 1978.
Zajonc, R. B. 1971. Attraction, affiliation and attachment. In J. F. Eisenberg and W. S. Dillon (eds.), *Man and beast*. Smithsonian Annals 3. Washington: Smithsonian Institution Press.

Part III

Ontogeny of primate behaviour

7. Development of social interaction

7.1. Maternal attributes and primate cognitive development

WILLIAM A. MASON

Within the general theme of this volume the specific focus of this paper is on primate ontogeny. Although I will draw heavily on some recent findings my colleagues and I have obtained on rhesus monkeys, I ask you to consider them as a specific illustration of some general features of primate development that have a special relevance to human ethology and to the question of the human potential for adaptive modification. This potential, I am sure you will agree, is the central fact about human behavior that any biologically based theory must address.

The ontogenetic perspective is indispensable to any effort to deal with human behavior within an evolutionary framework for at least two reasons: first, the study of the ontogeny of a species is the primary means available to use for discovering the capacities, dispositions, special sensitivities, and the like, that provide the early structural basis for all subsequent behavioral development. This is nothing more than an assertion that development is an epigenetic process; it is a monumental platitude, I know, but one that bears repeating in the context of this volume because some of the most important clues as to what makes up our unique potential for culture, and constrains and conditions the kinds of cultural variations we may produce, will come out of a clearer understanding of the distinctive features of the earliest stages of human postnatal life. The second reason is closely related to the first, but emphasizes a comparative dimension. Comparing the ontogenies of several related species can provide insight into the ways that evolutionary change may have come about at the phenotypic level. Phylogeny is the succession across many generations of modified ontogenies. In other words, at the phenotypic level evolution proceeds through changes in the way the individual develops.

That is true of all evolutionary change. One kind of change, however, having a special significance for the understanding of human evolution, involves modification in the rates of development of different functional systems. The most interesting examples of such developmental hetero-chronies with respect to the primates in general and man in particular are the neotenic changes described by DeBeer (1958) and others, in which there is a relative retardation in the rate of development of the body as compared to the reproductive system. As a result, the individual retains into full reproductive maturity some of the traits of the immature organism, including its behavioral attributes. Although I cannot develop the argument here, let me assert that there is persuasive evidence that neoteny has played a very important role in primate evolution, and that man is in many respects the most neotenous of primates. Moreover, there is good reason to believe that the most important functional outcome of neoteny in the primates is an increase in adaptability through greater behavioral plasticity (Mason 1968; Mason, in press).

Adaptability means a broadening of the range of environmental conditions in which an individual may survive and reproduce. In ecological terms, adaptability is an extension of the fundamental niche; it may equally well be regarded as a move toward emancipation from the environment, a loosening of close dependence on specific 'presupposed' environmental structures and supports. As an evolutionary strategy it is not without its risks, for any generalized change in the direction of greater openness and behavioral plasticity brings with it a loss of phylogenetic 'wisdom'. As this heritage recedes in importance, there is inevitably an increased demand on the individual to create meaning out of its own history, to construct out of its personal experience the order and regularities of its individual world.

And where and how does this come about? As to the where, the usual answer, and I believe the correct one, is that much of it comes about during the early phases of development, the so-called formative period, the years of primary socialization. As to how it comes about, the usual answer is that it is the result of learning. No doubt this is also correct. Obviously, however, it is not a satisfactory answer since it says nothing about the forms of learning, their developmental consequences, or the conditions under which they occur. Indeed, its explanatory content is close to zero.

Knowing how and knowing that

We come then to the central problem of this essay: how is it that the individual comes to know about his world and what is the mother's role in this process? In approaching this problem it will be useful to distinguish between two different kinds of knowing. Consider these examples: I know how to ride a bicycle, eat with chopsticks, operate a typewriter without looking at the keys, and ask for a bottle of beer in Spanish; I also know that a bicycle is harder to pedal against the wind, chopsticks will not turn to limp pieces of spaghetti in my hand, a typewriter will not produce prose on its own initiative, and the beer will taste bitter. Examples of the first type of knowing refer to something I can do or claim to be able to do; at issue is a specific competence that can be inferred by assessing my actions against explicit criteria. Examples of the second type relate to something broader and more generic; they do not refer to particular skills or achievements, but to information I claim to have about certain aspects of the world in which I live. Gilbert Ryle expresses a similar idea in his distinction between knowing *how* and knowing *that* (Ryle 1949).

The difference between the two kinds of knowing is familiar to animal behaviorists. It is reflected, for example, in the use of such terms as 'habit' to refer to a learned tendency for a specific stimulus to elicit a certain response and 'expectancy' to refer to the anticipation that certain consequences are likely to follow the appearance of a particular stimulus or the performance of a particular response. Nevertheless, we are not entirely comfortable with the distinction and we often ignore it, particularly in research on the cognitive consequences of early social experience.

I believe that this is a mistake – at least when we are dealing with some species of nonhuman primates – and that if we are to reach an understanding of the role of social experience in the cognitive development of certain species it is essential to distinguish between the organism's competences, which are reflected in its specific achievements, and its generalized expectancies or coping strategies, which are reflected in its basic stance toward the environment (Lewis and Goldberg 1969). It is a distinction, if you will, between the individual's successes in dealing with problem-situations and its style in doing so. Although both kinds of knowledge are dependent on experience, I believe they have different developmental antecedents and carry quite different implications for behavioral adaptability. A primary concern in what follows is to illustrate what I mean by generalized expectancies or coping strategies, and to show that the kind of strategy that a developing individual acquires can be heavily influenced by its relationship with its mother or a comparable attachment figure.

I recognize that the attachment figure is only one of the many sources in the early environment that are likely to contribute to cognitive growth. Nevertheless, the peculiar features of the filial bond give the attachment figure a special status, and they suggest with unusual clarity the kinds of experiences that are involved in the acquisition of coping strategies and the developmental processes through which they operate.

Consider the nature of the filial bond. Anyone who has observed an infant rhesus monkey with its mother probably shares my impression that she is the most interesting, important and compelling object in its small world. Much of its early behavior is organized around her. She is its point of departure for forays into the surrounding environment and a haven to return to when things get out of hand. She is the focus of attention, a source of rewards and punishments. Her comings and goings, her actions on the environment, have a salience for the infant that no other object commands.

If this characterization is essentially correct, it appears that the attachment figure occupies a privileged and influential position, one particularly well-suited to shape the early development of behavior. Yet, in spite of the amount of attention that has been devoted to mother–infant relations in nonhuman primates, we have little systematic information on the cognitive implications of the maternal role.

I believe that one reason why our understanding of the mother's influence on the cognitive development of species other than man has not advanced farther is our reluctance to give credence to the distinction between competence and coping strategies. The source of this reluctance is easy to appreciate. We are comfortable with the concept of competence because it is easily translated into operational terms. It has a concreteness that lends itself readily to empirical demonstration. In contrast, coping strategies are more patently and persistently hypothetical. One can never hope to find a specific instance – a concrete example of a coping strategy. In order to draw an inference regarding its presence or nature in an individual, it is necessary to sample his behavior across many situations, to classify those situations in terms of a common pattern or theme, and to show that his reactions across the situations conform to a general plan that possesses potential biological utility for him, in the sense that it is likely to lead to an adaptive or 'life-preserving' outcome. With so many problematic features, can there be any wonder why we have been unwilling to make a place for such a concept in our thinking?

Wild-born and lab-raised monkeys

Speaking for myself, I did not set out with any particular convictions regarding the distinction between the two kinds of knowing, and only gradually came to appreciate its importance to problems of primate socialization and cognitive development. My first inkling that the distinction might be useful occurred about twenty years ago. I was engaged in a series of experiments comparing the behavior of wild-born rhesus monkeys with the behavior of monkeys raised from birth in individual cages. The results showed clearly that lab-raised monkeys were not socially competent. This was most evident in sexual performance, particularly by males. In interpreting these findings I emphasized that lab-raised monkeys lacked many elementary social skills (Mason 1960). I still believe that this interpretation is correct.

Nevertheless, certain observations and results coming out of this research were not readily explained on the basis of a simple lack of competence. For example, one test designed to measure the monkey's attraction to conspecifics required that the animals first learn to pull a simple latch-string. I used food to pre-train them for this task (Mason 1961). The lab-raised monkeys required much more time than the wild-born animals to learn to pull the string, and it was evident that their whole approach to the problem was qualitatively different. Wild-born monkeys gave every indication that they perceived the situation as a 'problem' in which some solution was possible. Some monkeys hit upon the latch-string straight off, but others in this group tried a variety of different responses until they discovered the correct one. In contrast, the lab-raised monkeys behaved as though they lacked any consistent strategy or plan. In order to train some of them to pull, I had to resort to various tricks, such as smearing banana on the string or giving personal 'demonstrations'. Although all monkeys eventually acquired the appropriate response and continued to perform efficiently once they had done so, the differences between groups in their initial approach to the problem made a lasting impression on me.

Another test in this series suggested even more clearly that something other than competence was involved in the differences between groups. The monkeys were observed while alone in a 12×14 foot room. As compared to lab-raised monkeys, those born in the wild more frequently engaged in gross motor activities (jumping, backward somersaults), had higher locomotion scores, defecated or urinated in more sessions, and more frequently touched the objects that were placed in the room. All these differences were statistically significant. They also vocalized more, although not reliably so (Mason and Green 1962). Clearly 'skill' was not an important factor in this situation. There was no 'problem' – at least from my point of view – inasmuch as I had set no task for the monkeys, had provided no visible goal that they could reach. Nothing they did changed the situation; it was simply a matter of the monkeys remaining in the room for the prescribed period, whereupon they were removed and returned to their living cages. Yet, even though it made no sense in this context to describe one group as more or less competent than the other, it was clear that the groups differed markedly in their styles of coping with confinement in a strange place.

Mobile and stationary artificial mothers

The problem of coping strategies was raised again a few years later, but this time in an experiment that pointed more directly to the potential importance of the attachment figure. The research involved two groups of lab-raised rhesus monkeys, both maternally separated at birth and placed with cloth artificial mothers that were identical in construction except that for one group the surrogates were stationary and for the other they moved up and down and around the cage on an irregular schedule throughout the day (Mason and Berkson 1975). The original purpose of the experiment was to test the hypothesis that the stereotyped body-rocking shown by most macaques raised alone or with inanimate surrogates was a response to the absence of maternal movement. This expectation was fully confirmed (Mason and Berkson 1975).

It soon became apparent, however, that the mobile artificial mother was doing a great deal more than just carrying the infant about the cage. We had unwittingly created a social substitute that was capable of simulating some of the generic attributes of social interaction. The movements of the surrogate were not completely predictable: it could withdraw from the infant without warning, or sneak up behind it and deliver a gentle rap on the head; its comings and goings demanded adjustments that were not required of the monkey raised with a stationary device. The mobile mother also stimulated and sustained interaction: it was withdrawn from, pursued, pounced on, and wrestled with. Rough-and-tumble play, for example, was about three times more frequent in monkeys raised with moving surrogates than in those raised with stationary devices.

To explore the nature and range of developmental effects that these unanticipated contrasts in the two types of artificial mothers might have produced, we observed the monkeys in many different situations. Where intergroup differences were found they suggested that animals raised with mobile mothers were more like wild-born monkeys than those raised with stationary devices. For example, when the monkeys were about nine months old they were tested in a novel room in a replication of Mason and Green's study comparing wild-born and maternally separated monkeys. Monkeys raised with mobile mothers more often entered the room without prompting than did those raised with stationary mothers; they also had higher scores for gross motor activities, contact with objects in the room, and for urination and defecation. The measures that differentiated monkeys raised with mobile and stationary surrogates and the direction of the differences were the same as those that differentiated wild-born and lab-raised monkeys in the original experiment (Mason and Berkson 1975).

When these monkeys were about two years old, more than a year after they were permanently separated from their artificial mothers, we measured their tendency to look at other monkeys. Various stimulus conditions were used, such as a mother with her infant, a juvenile male, and monkeys of another species. The data clearly demonstrated that the level of looking behavior was higher in monkeys raised with the mobile surrogates than in those raised with the stationary devices (Eastman and Mason 1975). Figure 1 presents the results by sessions, summed across viewing conditions, for the two lab-raised groups and a wild-born comparison group.

Tests of problem-solving and social behavior produced few dramatic intergroup differences, although the general pattern was consistent with that suggested by other results. For example, in the initial series of problem-solving tests, monkeys raised with mobile mothers made contact with significantly more problems, even though they were no more successful in solving them (Anastasiou 1970). The first social pairings (starting when the monkeys were about fourteen months old) indicated that animals raised with mobile surrogates approached other animals more and withdrew from them less, and made fewer threats and attacks (Mason and Berkson 1975). When the monkeys were four to five years of age they were tested for a second time in a social setting; once more we found that relations were less tempestuous in the mobile surrogate

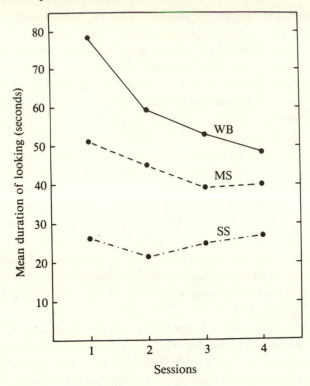

1. Duration of looking by wild-born monkeys (WB) and monkeys raised with mobile (MS) or stationary (SS) artificial mothers.

group. Moreover, the only females to brace their legs and support the males during mounting attempts, and the only male to show the complete mounting pattern, were raised with mobile mothers (Anderson, Kenney and Mason 1977).

I was convinced by the time this research was completed that we needed to look much more carefully at the attachment figure as a determinant of early cognitive development. It seemed obvious that a cloth-covered dummy, even a mobile one, was not the optimum vehicle for such a task. Another approach was required. We needed an attachment figure that was less mechanical, more truly social, and at the same time less 'specialized' than the natural mother.

Dogs as mother substitutes

With this end in view we did some preliminary research with dogs as mother substitutes (Mason and Kenney 1974). The monkeys formed strong attachments to the dogs and the dogs got along well with the monkeys. They played together, slept together, groomed each other. The dogs conformed completely to the popular stereotype of tolerant, accepting and highly social creatures. At the same time, however, there was no indication that the dogs (all female) responded maternally to the monkeys. Our hope was that such a 'generalized' companion would as surrogate mother throw more light on the broader cognitive consequences of early social relationships than a natural mother, whose behavior has been shaped by evolution to complement, support and direct the development of her offspring along species-typical paths. It was also convenient to have a 'mother' who was not undergoing developmental changes concurrently with those in the infant, and who would not object violently when we removed the infant for brief periods in order to test it.

Our current project includes monkeys separated from the mother at birth and raised with either inanimate surrogates or with dogs. The inanimate surrogates are plastic hobby horses mounted on wheels and they are covered with an acrylic fur saddle; the dogs are female mongrels. All monkeys are housed outdoors with their surrogates in kennels that afford them frequent visual contact with people, dogs, other monkeys, and a variety of other frequent or occasional events. Moreover, from the third to the fifteenth month of life every monkey was routinely allowed to roam in several different complex outdoor enclosures containing a variety of playthings, puzzles, barriers, and climbing devices. Our aim was to provide each monkey with a varied and stimulating environment, and I am confident that their general experience was more diversified and 'enriched' than that of the typical mother-raised laboratory macaque, to say nothing of the maternally separated infant raised in a nursery. We hoped in this way to obviate some of the confounding produced by the general environmental restriction present in most primate rearing studies and to gain a clearer view of the way in which interaction with an attachment figure contributed to cognitive growth.

Six monkeys were assigned to inanimate surrogates and six monkeys to each of two dog groups. The dog-raised monkeys differed in that in one group, the Free-dog group, dog and monkey could roam together in the complex environments, whereas in the other, the Restricted-dog group, the dog was confined to a small region in the exposure environment that was visually isolated from the whole. Monkeys raised with hobby horses were exposed to the complex environments precisely in the same way as the monkeys in the Restricted-dog group. The project is now in its fourth year and is continuing. Sufficient data have been collected, however, to establish differences between all groups. The most pervasive and abiding contrasts are between the dog-raised monkeys and those raised with inanimate surrogates and I will limit myself here to such comparisons.

These data provide the strongest suggestion that we have obtained thus far that the monkey's basic stance toward the environment, its 'generalized expectancies', or characteristic 'coping strategies', are heavily influenced by the kind of attachment figure with which it has been raised. Our results indicate that monkeys raised with dogs are more attentive to the environment, more responsive, less likely to be indifferent when confronted with change, and more likely to achieve an adaptive outcome by acting on the environment than are monkeys raised with hobby horses. To document this interpretation I will draw upon the results of many different tests, and present the findings within broad functional categories. Although results are shown in longitudinal format, this is done in order to convey the consistency of group differences over time; no significance can be attached to suggested 'developmental trends' inasmuch as the details of setting and procedures (e.g. number of exposures, duration of exposure periods) varied across tests.

A number of tests have been completed in which the monkeys were observed while alone in novel surroundings. The first observations were made when the animals were less than two months old and the most recent were completed when they were in their fourth year of life. Measures were routinely made of heart rate and distress vocalizations. Results for heart rate, presented in figure 2, indicate a higher level for dog-raised monkeys than for monkeys raised with inanimate surrogates on every occasion. Overall differences between groups are significant beyond the 0.01 level. The picture is similar for distress vocalizations, except for the two most recent tests, and overall differences are also significant ($p<0.01$; figure 3). On a few occasions we have also assayed plasma cortisol to provide an additional measure of responsiveness. The results, presented in figure 4, show higher levels in the dog-raised group on three of the four tests. For the combined tests the difference between groups is significant at the 0.05 level.

Do these results indicate that monkeys raised with hobby horses are simply calmer or less susceptible to stress than those raised with dogs? If this were the whole story, one might expect that in problem-solving situations, the monkeys raised with inanimate surrogates, being less agitated, would enjoy some advantage over monkeys raised with dogs. In fact, just the reverse seems to be the case.

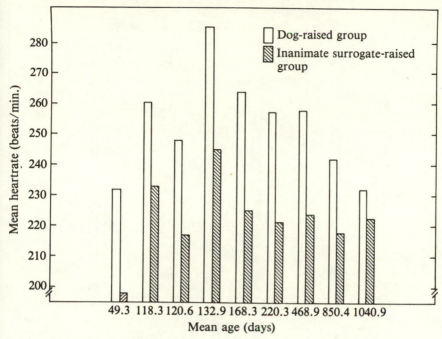

2. Mean heart rate of monkeys raised with canine and inanimate mother substitutes.

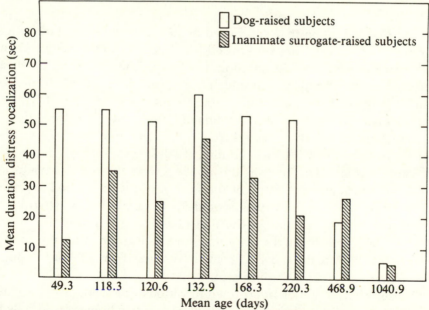

3. Mean distress vocalizations (coo, scream) of monkeys raised with canine and inanimate mother substitutes.

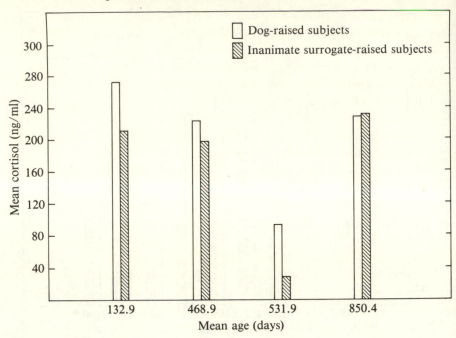

4. Mean levels of plasma cortisol in monkeys raised with canine and inanimate mother substitutes.

Our first indication that dog-raised monkeys were likely to be better problem-solvers than monkeys raised with hobby horses occurred when the animals were about four months of age. They were tested in a delayed-response situation in which the reward for a correct response was contact with the substitute mother. As the monkey watched, a handler led the surrogate through one of four differently colored doorways whereupon it disappeared from view. The disappearance of the surrogate coincided with the beginning of a delay period ranging up to 45 seconds. At the end of the delay the monkeys were allowed 30 seconds in which to select and enter one of the goal boxes; if they failed to enter within this period a 'balk' was scored for the trial. The most striking difference between groups in the first phase of testing was the much higher level of balking in the inanimate surrogate group. They refused to respond to 46% of the trials, as compared to less than 2% for the dog-raised monkeys ($p<0.001$; figure 5).

These results might be interpreted in various ways. For example, the high level of balking by monkeys raised with hobby horses could reflect the fact that these animals had had no opportunity to learn to follow their substitute mothers before they were tested. In contrast, even the monkeys raised with restricted dogs could have learned to follow their companions in the kennels. Another possibility is that the strength of attachment was less in the inanimate surrogate group, that their motivation to regain contact with the surrogate was low. Actually, we have a great deal of information to the contrary. Although I cannot claim that the strength of attachment to the surrogate is equal in monkeys raised with hobby horses and with dogs, there is no question that the hobby horse was a powerful incentive and an effective security object.

Fortunately, there is no need to resolve these interpretive difficulties here, for we have other data showing striking contrasts between groups in problem-solving situations in which the attachment figure played no direct role. Although it was present during testing (to eliminate the potentially disruptive effects of separation), the situations were designed so that it could not contribute to successful performances.

The problems were for the most part relatively unstructured. We were not interested in controlling performance, or training the animals on a particular task, or measuring their specific problem-solving skills. Our aim was to place them in settings in which they could achieve some

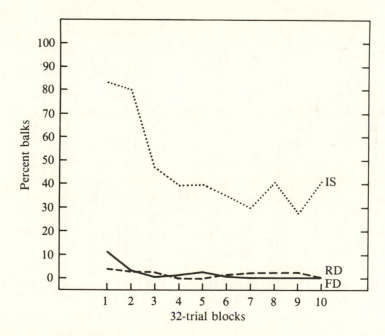

5. Percentage of trials in which monkeys raised with canine and inanimate mother substitutes failed to respond.

appropriate reward – typically a bit of preferred food – by interacting with the situation, attending to its relevant features, and performing some simple instrumental response, such as pulling, climbing, or pushing, which was within their normal repertoire. Furthermore, we made no attempt to maximize motivation. Although the monkeys were tested before the daily feed, scraps of food were generally lying about from the previous day's ration, even though they were not as highly preferred as the fruits, nuts and candies that were presented in the tests. Such a relaxed approach to the testing of problem-solving behavior is bound to encourage individual variability, and we have had our share of it. Nevertheless, the general pattern of results is remarkably consistent over more than a year of measuring performance on such tasks. The percentage of trials in which problems were touched is presented for eleven different situations in figure 6. This measure is consistently higher in the dog-raised group ($p<0.05$); figure 7 shows that successful performance is also substantially higher in this group ($p<0.02$).

We have examined another aspect of behavioral adaptability and the results are completely congruent with the findings on problem-solving behavior. For the nonhuman primates, as for man, keeping in touch with

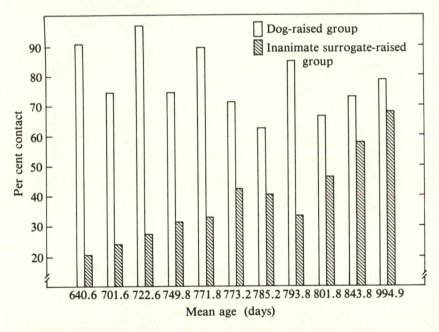

6. Percentage of trials in which problems were touched by monkeys raised with canine and inanimate mother substitutes.

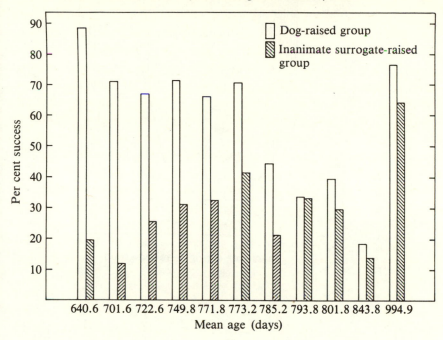

7. Percentage of problems solved by monkeys raised with canine and inanimate mother substitutes.

the world is very much a visual affair. It will be recalled that the Eastman and Mason experiment indicated that the tendency to look at novel social stimuli was substantially stronger in monkeys raised with mobile artificial mothers than in those raised with stationary surrogates. We were interested in whether similar contrasts would be found between monkeys raised with dogs and hobby horses in an environment that provided a much richer visual world to both groups than was available to the monkeys in the original study. The apparatus was similar to the one used by Eastman and Mason. Essentially, the animals were placed in an enclosed chamber containing peepholes, through which they could look at projected color transparencies. In the first test series we presented a single slide (e.g. landscape, interior of a room, etc.) for nine trials, and on the tenth trial introduced a new picture. The results are presented in figure 8. It is evident that monkeys raised with dogs demonstrated a much higher level of looking behavior in this situation than did monkeys raised with hobby horses. Moreover, should there be any question that the dog-raised monkeys were actually looking at the projected pictures, their

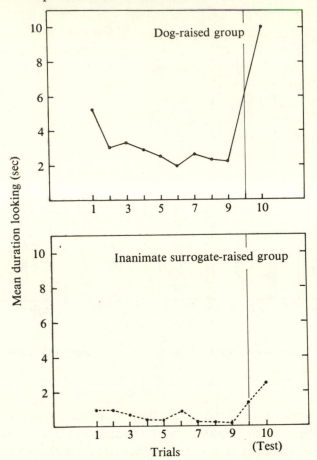

8. Duration of looking at projected color slides by monkeys raised with canine and inanimate mother substitutes. The same slide was presented on trials 1–9 and on trial 10 a novel slide was introduced.

performance on the tenth trial presenting the novel picture removes all doubt. They not only showed a sharp increase in duration of looking, as compared to the immediately preceding trial, but evidenced a strong positive contrast effect: the duration of looking at the test slide was nearly twice that elicited by the repeated stimulus even on its first presentation, even though it was also completely novel on that trial.

Partly to confirm this incidental finding, and partly to determine whether or not additional experience with the situation would lead to increased looking behavior in the inanimate surrogate group, a second experiment was completed in which on half the sessions a different picture was presented on each of the ten trials (variable series) and on half the sessions the same stimulus was repeated for nine trials, with a novel stimulus on trial ten, as in the first experiment (constant series). The results, presented in figure 9, confirm the contrast effect, show that a variable series produced essentially no intrasession decrement in looking behavior, and provide no evidence that the additional experience in the test situation had any strong positive effect on the behavior of the monkeys raised with hobby horses. The final test of looking behavior was completed about one year after the start of the first test. Transparencies were again used, but pictures were scaled to represent three levels of

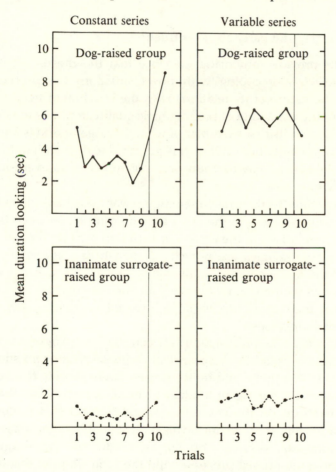

9. Duration of looking at projected color slides by monkeys raised with canine and inanimate mother substitutes. Constant series: The same slide was presented on trials 1–9 and on trial 10 a novel slide was introduced. Variable series: A different slide was presented on each trial.

complexity. Although duration of looking increased somewhat in the monkeys raised with hobby horses, the level was less than half that of the dog-raised groups. Furthermore, in contrast to dog-raised monkeys, they failed to differentiate reliably between the three levels of stimulus complexity. As a check against the possibility that looking was suppressed in monkeys raised with hobby horses because they were excessively stressed by the situation, measures were obtained of distress vocalizations, plasma cortisol and heart rate. The only reliable difference between groups was in heart rate, and it was significantly lower in the inanimate surrogate group.

Coping strategies and early social influences

These results provide convincing evidence that the rhesus monkey's characteristic ways of coping with novel situations are profoundly affected by the nature of its relations with the attachment figure. This figure apparently has a kind of paradigmatic quality; it serves the developing individual as its first exemplar of what the larger world is like and exerts a powerful influence on how it is prepared to deal with it. Merely 'enriching' the general environment was not sufficient to override this paradigmatic influence.

The fact that the effective attachment figure was a mechanical device in one experiment and a dog in the other is significant, for it suggests that the relevant dimensions of the early social environment for the development of coping strategies are not closely tied to the species-specific structure of the mother–infant relationship. This is not to say that the particularities of the natural relationship are inconsequential, of course, but only that they appear to be superimposed on more generalized developmental processes.

I believe that the critical distinction between attachment figures in these experiments is the presence or absence of response-contingent stimulation. Stationary surrogates and hobby horses surely provide few opportunities for the developing individual to experience the fact that his behavior has effects on the environment and to learn that the events going on around him are amenable to his control. Inert mother substitutes make no demands, occasion no surprises, do not encourage the development of attentional processes and the acquisition of the simple instrumental behaviors that are the fabric of social interaction.

The importance of response-contingent stimulation in human perceptual-cognitive development is illustrated by the research of J. S. Watson

(Watson 1971, Watson and Ramey 1972). Watson demonstrated that infants will learn to control a mobile suspended above their cribs, and respond to its movements with smiling and cooing. Of greater interest in the present context is his finding that infants whose mobiles moved on a fixed schedule independent of their behavior learned that they could not control the device; moreover its movements did not produce smiling and cooing. Later, when both groups were tested in the laboratory with a different mobile that all infants could activate, only those having previously experienced response-contingent stimulation with mobiles learned to control it. Watson concludes: 'the ability to learn that something is *uncontrollable* is probably nearly as adaptive a capacity as the ability to learn to control those things which can be controlled' (Watson 1971:149, italics mine). The fundamental importance of response-contingent stimulation is also emphasized by Seligman (1975) in his discussion of learned helplessness.

That monkey mothers can be an important source of response-contingent stimulation for their offspring hardly requires comment. However, the implications of this fact for perceptual-cognitive development of the infant macaque are not intuitively obvious. The results presented here are quite consistent with Lewis and Goldberg's suggestion for the human child that

contingency is important, not only because it shapes acquisition of specific behaviors, but because it enables the child to develop a motive which is the basis for all future learning. The main characteristic of this motive is the infant's belief that his actions affect his environment . . . the mother is important because it is the contingency between the infant's behavior and her responses that enables the infant to learn that his behavior does have consequences.

(Lewis and Goldberg 1969:81)

7.2. Early ontogeny of human social interaction: its biological roots and social dimensions[1]

HANUŠ PAPOUŠEK AND
MECHTHILD PAPOUŠEK

Introduction

The genetic principle has already been proven in both animal and human research so that advocating it would be redundant. One of its consequences in human studies is the multidisciplinary approach to early behavioral development, which is so crucially important for all those who are striving for a generally valid synthesis of observational experience and experimental data in this field. Even individual students increasingly combine concepts and methods from different disciplines and regroup themselves in new biosocial, biopsychological or psychobiological subdisciplines. This enables interactionistic or dialectic conceptual rapprochement even between views formerly separated by a sharp dividing line, such as the genetic and environmentalist ones. Rapprochement between such views leads to a better understanding and greater appreciation of individual variability.

One of the factors that brought together the psychological and sociological approaches was the experience that the beginning of postnatal mental development cannot be fully understood unless the infant is viewed in the context of his social environment. Therefore, much attention has recently been concentrated on the study of infant–adult inter-

[1] The preparation of this paper was kindly facilitated by grants from the Deutsche Forschungsgemeinschaft (Pa 208/I) and from the Stifterverband für die Deutsche Wissenschaft to the Max Planck Institute for Psychiatry in Munich.

action. One of the major problems of both the psychological and socio-logical approaches is the question of early educational interventions. Whereas some researchers view infancy as a particularly formative period, suitable for various educational interventions, others stress its vulnerability and warn against any premature intervention. This ques-tion even has topical ideological and political aspects: the way it is ans-wered has a bearing on woman's emancipation and also on the impor-tance accorded to parenthood by the administrative institutions at a time when human society should pay more attention to the qualitative rather than quantitative growth of population.

Our own interest in infant–adult interaction resulted from our studies of the early development of learning and cognitive abilities and from the observation that play and social interaction represent *the* chance for learning and cognition in the infant's everyday life. Since we already had applied certain principles of comparative biology in our experimental studies of learning, we tried to do the same in respect of the analysis of early social interaction. However, we soon realized that not enough was known about the biological aspects of human parenthood at the earliest postpartum stage of childrearing.

In fact, we felt very much like biologists observing a new species when we turned our attention to the parent and began looking for a set of adaptive behaviors characteristic of parental interaction with newborns and infants. We also had to develop methods allowing us both field studies and microanalyses of infant–adult interaction under natural ecological conditions. The only obvious category of parental behavior concerned the fundamental protection of the fragile infantile organism against excessive fluctuations in environmental conditions. Less evident were the forms of emotional attachment considered responsible for the further healthy development of the infant both in somatic and mental terms. And there was nearly no evidence of a category of parental responses that might directly support the infant's learning and cognitive capacities.

If we attempt now to summarize our present view of infant–adult interaction from the psychobiological position taken in this paper, we shall have to introduce a hypothetical model only partially supported by empirical evidence; moreover, this model may be biased by our primary interest in cognitive development. Nevertheless, we want to draw more of the attention of our colleagues, of human ethologists in particular, to problems which have not been accorded the study due to them consider-ing their scientific and social relevance.

Some methodological aspects

The rapid development of modern film and television techniques has made it possible to reproduce audiovisually what has been observed either in field studies or in laboratory experiments. This in turn has broadened the possibilities for the analysis of observations to include microanalysis, analyses by more independent observers, consecutive analyses forced by a larger number of parameters or stimulated by application of new views. Certain methods of observation have become feasible where before the presence of an observer or lack of illumination have imposed serious obstacles. Slow-motion technique facilitates the analysis of very brief events, whereas time-lapse records allow economical reproduction of long lasting observations. Split-screen techniques in television combine pictures from several cameras on one screen or a picture of overt behavior with relevant polygraphic curves.

For our purposes, it was also important to find that a televised record may be substituted for reality and serve as a standardized stimulation in experiments with infants. At the age of four months, infants were able to discriminate between visual contact and contingent behavior in televised movies of social partners (Papoušek and Papoušek 1974).

Thus, a description of some of the apparatuses we developed for the purpose of better analysis of infant–adult interaction may be of interest (Papoušek, 1978). Filming and video-taping techniques each have specific advantages and disadvantages and, therefore, neither serves as a complete substitute for the other. Filming still provides a higher quality reproduction for publication in print. The use of color films where color reproduction is necessary is less expensive and less elaborate technically than color television. On the other hand, conversion of an optical picture into an electromagnetic record allows immediate electronic operations with such a record, which is not possible with photochemical processing.

When filming we have mainly utilized the advantages of the time-lapse technique since the majority of responses involved in infant–adult interaction last more than 0.5 sec. A built-in adjustment for slow speed filming is now available even in some S-8 movie cameras, e.g. allowing speeds from six frames per second to one frame per minute in the Nizo-Braun cameras which we use. For the purpose of synchronizing up to four cameras we constructed an adjustable synchronizer for triggering at speeds of exactly 1, 2, 5, 10, 20, 50, and 100 frames per minute. A synchronous noiseless light counter displaying numbers from 00 to 99 in the visual field of the cameras is used to label every frame and also serves as an optical event marker with two additional spotlight signals. An on-line signal is sent to a tape recorder with every tenth frame to enable matching of the films with audio-taped vocalization or comments. Four professional S-8 projectors housed in pairs in two twin cases (figure 1) allow easy analysis of up to four synchronized films at once. Both single-frame steps and continuous projection in either direction at different speeds can be operated with a single button. Each projector has its own frame-counter and can be used separately.

When video-taping we use four IVC video-recorders simultaneously (figure 2), allowing us to use some of them for displaying one or two kinds of playback (e.g. as a stimulation in preferential designs) and, at the same time, the others for recording responses to such stimulation. We chose one-inch recorders in order to be able to utilize additional available equipment for analysis to the full extent. An electronic quartz timer generates data for labelling each of fifty half-pictures per second and time measurement with an accuracy of 0.02 sec. A built-in system of IVC-471 recorders produces seven different speeds for time-lapse recording so that observations of up to seventy-two hours can be recorded on a one-hour videotape. An additional memory system can store individual pictures for several weeks, convert them into negatives, blow them up ten times and scan for details. All parts of the set-up, including cameras with bi-directional remote control, can be turned on or off with a single button.

Such equipment, of course, requires a special studio and is designed for special laboratory purposes. However, with the help of appropriate mixers, records from small portable video-recorders can be displayed or re-taped here, too, and thus also analyzed in a way comparable to that described above.[2]

Prenatal and perinatal aspects of parent–infant interaction

Nature allotted very different roles to the two parents in respect of the prenatal care of progeny. For obvious reasons the maternal role has attracted much more attention in both animal and human studies.

From systematic studies of determinants of maternal behavior in the rat we know that nursing, retrieving, nest-building, and licking the pups to stimulate elimination are regulated by different kinds of processes during

[2] The laboratory equipment concerned here was established at the Science Centre in Bonn-Bad Godesberg, Ahrstrasse 45, from the financial support provided by Stifterverband für die Deutsche Wissenschaft, whose help we wish to acknowledge.

1. A synchronized double film-viewer (S–8 mm) (Schmidt Co., Straubing, West Germany).

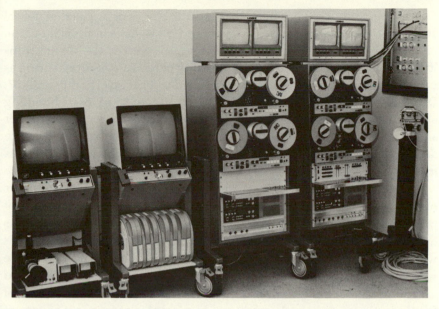

2. The television studio in our laboratory at the Science Centre in Bonn – Bad Godesberg.

different phases of the material behavior cycle (Rosenblatt 1975). Non-pregnant females can be stimulated to show maternal behavior if exposed to pups continuously for four to seven days (Rosenblatt 1967). They obviously dislike the smell of the pups because initially they try to avoid them. If olfaction is reduced or eliminated in the adult rats, they exhibit maternal behavior within twenty-four hours of their exposure to the pups. This sensitization is not determined hormonally, because cross-transfusion of their blood to non-sensitized virgin females does not shorten the time that exposure to pups is necessary for eliciting maternal behavior.

During pregnancy, complex hormone changes take place, leading to the onset of maternal behavior, which appears about twenty-four hours prepartum under normal conditions. If virgin females are cross-transfused with newly parturient mothers, they also show maternal behavior. However, if mothers are not permitted contact with pups for 1.5 days after the onset of maternal behavior, their readiness for maternal behavior decreases dramatically. After parturition, maternal behavior appears to be regulated chiefly by stimuli from the pups. During the transition from hormonal to non-hormonal regulation, the mother–young interaction can easily be disrupted by externally induced stress.

A series of other studies in rats reveals the effects of prenatal maternal stress on the intrauterine development and postnatal emotionality of the offspring. Conditioned anxiety-evoking signals with denial of opportunity to reduce anxiety increased emotionality or fearfulness in offspring as measured with open-field activity levels and defecation (Thompson 1957, Doyle and Yule 1959, Hockman 1961). On the other hand, extra handling of pregnant rats decreased emotionality or fearfulness in offspring (Ader and Conklin 1963). Moreover, Denenberg and Whimbey (1963) have demonstrated decreased emotionality in the offspring of female rats treated with extra handling during their own infancy.

These few examples help us to understand the biological determinants of maternal behavior in the rat on the one hand, and the influence of prepartum maternal experience on the young on the other. It is obvious how relevant comparable knowledge of maternal behavior in humans would be, where social aspects, e.g. the marital state or the socioeconomic circumstances, give the pregnancy new dimensions and may increase the danger of stress. An unwanted pregnancy or a fear of failure in the maternal role are just two examples of frequent causes of prepartum maternal stress. Not only obvious ethical reasons but also a lack of measurable parameters of motherhood are responsible for the scarcity of human studies on human maternal behavior in general and its prepartum development in particular.

Sontag (1941) was among the first to warn that maternal emotional stress may have adverse effects on fetal behavior and development. According to Wallin and Riley (1950), early and prolonged stress is more dangerous than stress occurring later in pregnancy. Maternal stress causes an increased frequency of clinically reported behavioral disorders in infants, such as the 'colicky syndrome' (Stewart *et al.* 1954, Lakin 1957), but it is still difficult to say whether stress plays a primary role. Increased fetal losses, fetal dystrophy, and perinatal mortality and morbidity in illegitimate children are other indirect clinical indices drawing attention to the prepartum development of maternal behavior, a better understanding of which might help to solve important medical and social problems.

When we started our studies on neonatal learning twenty years ago, there was still very little known about the mental capacities of the infant, compared to the rich literature on his somatic development, nutritional needs, and diseases. It was difficult to imagine how the newborn could benefit from interaction with his parent. However, it was even more difficult to say what might be typical parameters of parental behavior. Only a few authors (e.g. Rheingold, Gewirtz and Ross 1959, Rheingold

1960, Gewirtz 1961) attempted to analyze maternal behavior in man in relation to the infant's social learning.

One category of maternal behavior was, of course, known to compensate for the newborn's insufficient capacity to ensure his metabolic needs, maintain thermoregulation and escape from dangerous situations. But behaviors facilitating nursing, such as massaging of the breasts, stimulation of nipple erection before breast-feeding, and holding the newborn in an appropriate position, probably did not seem interesting enough to warrant scientific investigation. Typical tendencies to touch the newborn with open palms, to direct breath toward him, and to give him maximum bodily proximity were difficult to interpret unambiguously. They might be relics of the basic biological protection from earlier periods of phylogeny as well as signs of communicative or emotional behavior, but they hardly represented desirable parameters for explicit quantification of maternal behavior.

To a large extent these basic needs of the newborn can now be met by technology without major difficulties. It was known, of course, that even perfect physical conditions could not prevent adverse effects if there was parental deprivation. However, attempts to explain *how* parental love may influence learning or cognitive development failed to convince students of social interaction.

Our own interests led us to start by analyzing the beginning of postnatal learning in the newborn. At that time the behavioral sciences offered only a narrow interpretation of adaptive processes in terms of conditioning. However, studies of conditioning in infants were scarce and did not lead to convincing conclusions on learning abilities in the newborn.

After looking for a convenient motor response which could be used in experimental designs for both conditioning and concept formation, we settled on head movements. Left and right head turns are movements simple enough to be recorded polygraphically and analyzed in terms of latency and intensity (Papoušek 1961). As a model of adaptive behavior, head turns can be varied either in the sense of classical associative conditioning or as an instrumental act for obtaining food, switching on visual displays (Papoušek and Bernstein 1969) or avoiding unpleasant stimulation (Papoušek 1967a). Together with eye movements, head turns represent a fundamental orienting behavior which the infant adaptively uses either to facilitate information input in novel situations or to limit and avoid such input in distressing situations (Papoušek and Papoušek 1975).

Since our main concern was the question of *how* the newborn learns, we did not use traditional trial blocks in a single experimental session. Rather, we ran ten conditioning trials a day for as many days (five times a week) as necessary to reach a criterion of relatively stable performance. Thus, next to the course of learning, we could also pay attention to concurrent social, emotional, and autonomic behaviors. We learned much of interest about social behavior even though the newborn was isolated from his usual social environment during experimental conditioning. We could demonstrate that some elements of social communication and emotional behavior were determined by the process of learning itself and independently of any social stimulation (Papoušek 1967a, b).

The fact that we successfully demonstrated instrumental conditioning in the newborn (Papoušek 1961), in whom associative conditioning had not previously been shown convincingly, proved at the same time that the newborn can readily detect and learn to control contingent stimulation. This was the earliest evidence that his fundamental adaptive behavior depends not only on the physical parameters of external stimulation but also on related intrinsic invariants resulting from his prior experience with that external stimulation. Another similar intrinsic invariant effectively influencing the newborn's adaptive behavior is the degree of familiarity of environmental events.

Our studies also brought the first evidence that memory functions in the newborn during the first week of life, since the percentage of correct responses gradually increased in spite of intervals of twenty-four to seventy-two hours between experiments. Other studies confirmed the newborn's capacity to process the temporal parameters of environmental events and to reveal temporal conditioning (Marquis 1941, Bystroletova 1954, Krachkovskaia 1959, Brackbill, Fitzgerald and Lintz 1967). The ability to habituate protective responses to a regular sequence of external stimuli was demonstrated even during non-REM sleep in the newborn (Martinius and Papoušek 1970). Recently, N. Solkoff and C. Cotton (1975) reported a contingency awareness and resulting instrumental learning in premature infants at the mean gestational age of thirty-one weeks.

With the increasing evidence of the newborn's adaptive competence, we also became aware of conditions important for his optimal learning: (1) a relatively large number of trials; (2) optimal waking state. The newborn needs four times as many trials as a three-month-old infant and six times as many as a five-month-old infant to reach the same criterion of learning (Papoušek 1967a). There are as striking individual differences in the course of learning and response parameters among newborns as among older infants within the first five months of life. Correct responses occur most frequently and latency is shortest in the waking state characterized by well coordinated gross movements and/or quiet vocalization (Papoušek 1969).

The interrelation between behavioral state and learning however, was found to be bi-directional, i.e. the course of learning also influenced the subsequent behavioral state (Papoušek 1969). This influence was much more striking in the newborn than in older infants and ranged from exaggerated activation of motor, autonomic, and emotional behaviors to a catatonic sleeplike state with gazing eyes.

As we were gaining a better understanding of the learning process, we were also finding interesting evidence of a very fundamental regulatory mechanism through which orienting and exploratory responses with concurrent autonomic, emotional, and communicative responses were either activated or inhibited in relation to the course of learning or cognition (Papoušek and Papoušek 1975). Signs of displeasure accompanying unsuccessful attempts to organize appropriate responses and signs of pleasure upon success indicated intrinsic motivation connected with these fundamental adaptive processes.

With this view of the newborn's competence, we then turned our attention to the adult caretaker and looked particularly for those behaviors that might influence the course of learning or elementary cognition in the newborn. Here, the microanalysis of observable behaviors with the help of films and video-recordings revealed an unexpected parallel between behavioral changes in the adult exposed to newborns and the prerequisites of neonatal learning mentioned above. At the same time it became obvious why such parental responses have escaped attention: they are short, frequent, and usually made without conscious control. Therefore, they can hardly be derived from parental responses to questionnaires or from restrictive observation of items selected *a priori* (Papoušek and Papoušek 1977a).

At least two behavioral tendencies in the adult correspond to the first requirement of many repetitions of trials for successful learning in the infant. First, the adult tends to modify his speech, facial expressions, movements, and various other behaviors into simple and repetitive patterns (Papoušek and Papoušek 1975). Second, some conspicuous responses to neonatal behaviors are carried out as consistently, albeit unconsciously, by the adult as unconditioned responses elicited by specific stimuli. Thus, they belong to the first natural contingencies offering the newborn chances for controlling parental behavior through instrumental learning.

Other behavioral tendencies in the adult seem to be addressed to behavioral states whose evaluation and prediction are particularly difficult. The amount of attention adult caretakers pay to the level of waking in newborns is evident from frequent comments on it included in their babytalk. Moreover, maternal behavior includes elements reminiscent of tests of muscle tone typically used by researchers studying behavioral states.

Let us now take a closer look at some of the behavioral changes we have just mentioned.

Modifications in adult speech during interaction with infants – usually referred to as 'babytalk' or 'motherese' – have already been viewed by some linguists as an adjustment to the baby's limited cognitive capacities and to aid in language acquisition (Shipley, Smith and Gleitman 1969). Rather generally, infant-directed speech is slower and adjusted for intelligibility (Broen 1972), its vocabulary is restricted and concrete (Phillips 1970, Remick 1971), its pitch higher and more variable than in adult-to-adult dialogues. Typical features of babytalk are also used toward newborns.[3] It is astonishing how quickly a mother may alternate two strikingly different forms of speech when talking alternately to her baby and to another adult (Papoušek and Papoušek 1977b). A similar kind of babytalk is used with infants even by non-parents (Snow 1972), aged men (Papoušek and Papoušek 1977b), and three- and four-year-old children (Slobin, 1968).

The balance between repetition and modification in speech, movement or any other stimulation directed toward the newborn is an important factor affecting his attention. McCall and Kagan (1967) showed that in infants maximum attention can be generated by repeated and only slightly modified stimulation. Similarly, Lewis and Goldberg (1969) stressed this balance in their 'response decrement' theory of early social interactions. A certain continuity and consistency in the adult's behavior is important to help the slowly learning newborn to discover essential and stable components of stimulation generated by a very complex and unknown environment. On the other hand, the variable components keep his attention aroused (Papoušek and Papoušek 1975).

Among adult behaviors mentioned above as probably being the first consistent reinforcement contingent on the newborn's behavior, two

[3] Paper on 'The mother's speech to the newborn' delivered by Fernald at the Max Planck Institute for Psychiatry, Munich, on 10 November 1976. This paper is in preparation for publication.

examples deserve special attention: behavior supporting visual contact and imitative behavior.

Visual contact obviously plays a multiple role in adult–infant interaction. If accompanying other kinds of behavior, it increases their effectiveness. The attainment of visual contact is a crucial condition for sending the infant other than acoustic messages. Moreover, all our evidence indicates that the infant's visual contact is important feedback information telling the adult caretakers how much attention they attract, what the infant is interested in and what he prefers to avoid.

The parent tries very hard to stay centered in the newborn's visual field and at a distance of 20 to 25 cm, independent of his own optimal reading distance or belief that newborns can or cannot see him at all (Schoetzau and Papoušek 1977). For every visual contact, the parents, mothers in particular, reward the newborn with a typical greeting response beginning with a slight retroflexion of the head, raised eyebrows, widely opened eyes, and slightly opened mouth, followed by a verbal greeting and/or smile (Papoušek and Papoušek 1977a). This response, too, is made even by parents who do not expect the newborn to be capable of seeing at all. To analyze the relation between greeting response and visual contact we filmed the mirror image of this response on the neonate's cornea (figure 3).

The importance of visual contact for the infant becomes evident if the mother closes her eyes for two minutes while talking to the infant as in one of our tests (figure 4).

Another similarly consistent contingent behavior in the adult is his imitative behavior. The parent tends to imitate the newborn from the very beginning and shows a definite preference for imitating facial expressions and vocalizations. Often he exaggerates while imitating, as if to demonstrate that he is providing the desired response to the newborn's behavior. He also tends to imitate more whenever new behavioral patterns develop in the newborn (Papoušek and Papoušek 1977a).

We call this imitation a 'biological mirror' and consider it not only a display of contingent events stimulating for instrumental learning but also an important step in the development of imitation and self-awareness in the infant. The interrelationship between imitation, play, and intelligence in the child was stressed by Piaget (1951).

Initially, the newborn only learns how to manipulate parental behavior through operant conditioning, without realizing the similarity in the imitative behavior. Later, when producing vocal sounds or hand movements which his caretaker imitates, he may begin to discover similarity,

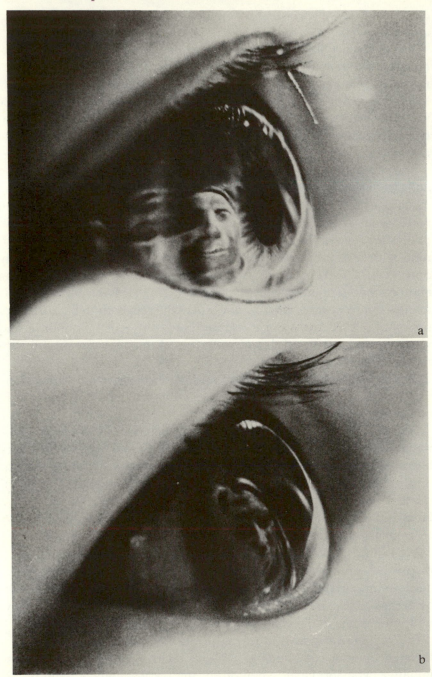

3. Mother's 'greeting response' to the visual contact with the neonate as observed in the corneal reflection. (a) and (b) maternal face out of the neonate's sight; (c) a visual contact between mother and neonate; (d) mother's 'greeting response' following the achievement of visual contact.

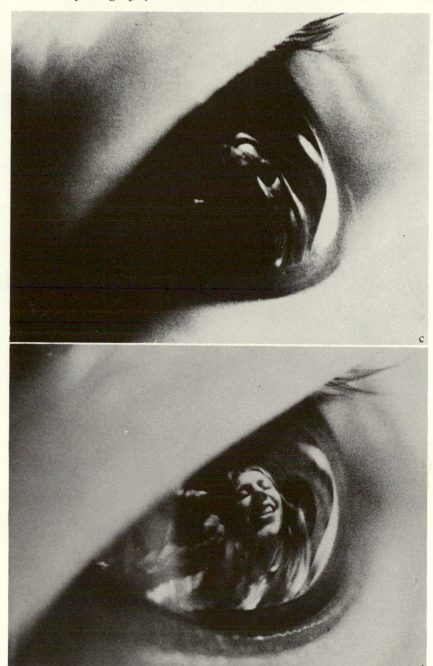

c

d

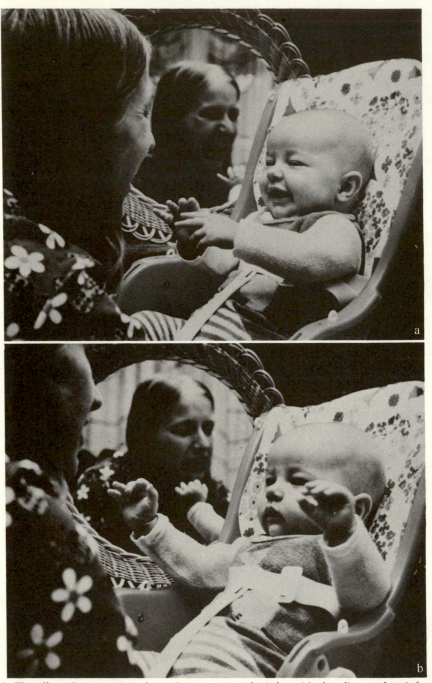

4. The effect of interruption of visual contact upon the infant. (a) a baseline mother–infant interaction; (b) to (e) gradual changes in the infant's behavior while his mother closed eyes for a period of two minutes.

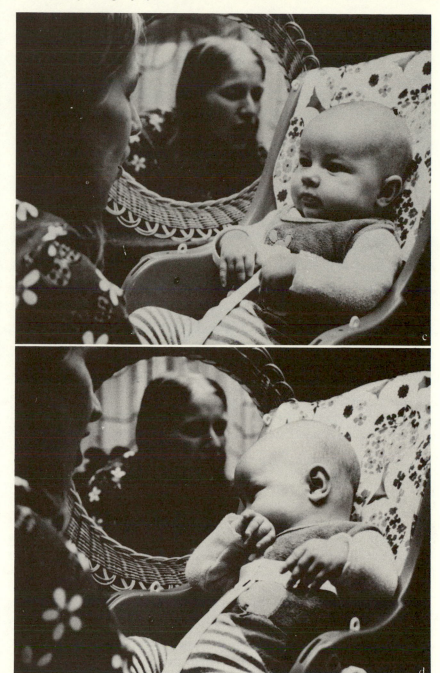

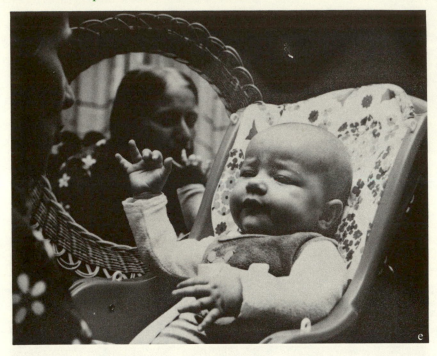

4. *Continued*

another important step in the development of his own ability to imitate. No matter how similar the vocal sounds of both partners may be, their temporal relation to particular movements which the newborn makes helps the baby to differentiate his own products from those of his environment. Gradually, he may also associate the other person's sounds with typical, say facial, movements, and then this complex scheme with the scheme of the production of a similar sound on his part. Needless to say, such cognitive processes are important prerequisites for acquisition of language through imitation on the one hand and of self-awareness on the other. In some cases, an imitative act may have the character of an instruction, e.g. mouth opening in the mother feeding her infant (figure 5).

Since correct evaluation of the newborn's general behavioral state is a crucial condition for the application of learning trials, we found it interesting how often parents touch and try to open the newborn's mouth (figure 6) or hands (figure 7) when unsure about his state of wakefulness. This activity is reminiscent of testing muscle tone, a standard procedure for students of behavioral states, and does elicit different responses depen-

5. Instructive imitation. (a) mother opens her mouth while bringing a spoon to the mouth of her baby; (b) similar behavior in the baby at the age of eight months.

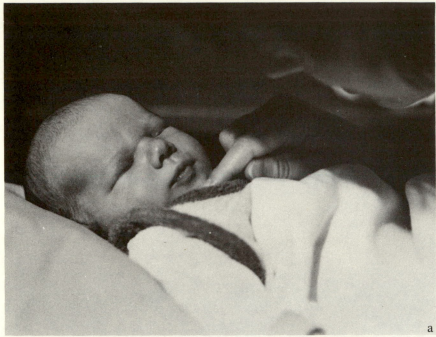

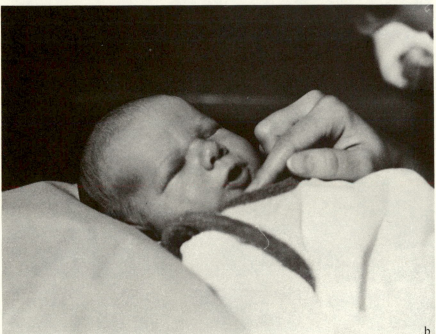

6. Mother testing the muscle tone of jaw muscles in the neonate.

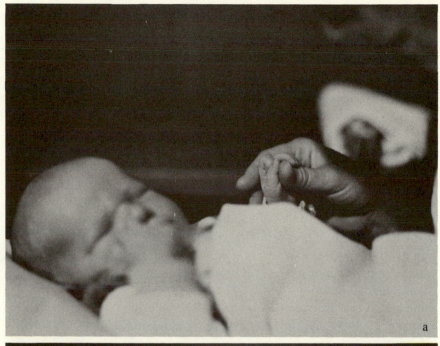

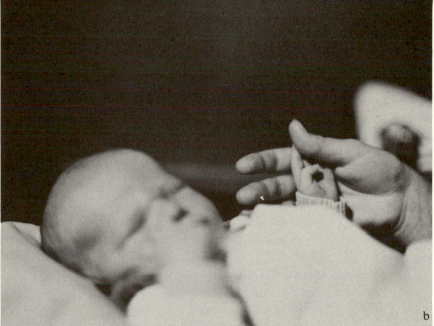

7. Mother testing the muscle tone of fingers in the neonate.

dent on the level of waking. In a drowsy state or when sleeping the newborn offers no resistance and carries out no response. With increasing hunger, he responds with sucking movements, mouth opening and, finally, vigorous rooting reflexes if we touch his oral area. In contrast, firmer lip protrusion and an avoiding head movement indicate full satiation of his hunger.

Similarly, the position of the hands, their muscle tone, readiness to grasp, open or closed fists and firmness of grip inform us about different levels of wakefulness ranging from drowsiness to motor upset and distress.

Mothers substantiate our interpretation of their behavior through their frequent comments on the state of wakefulness when they talk to babies. They also intentionally try to manipulate behavioral states in newborns by increasing stimulation and lifting the babies into an upright position if they want them to stay awake for more feeding. If they want them to take a nap they put them into a horizontal position and quiet them with a lullaby-like babytalk.

In animal studies, Hopf (1972) reported a tendency in squirrel monkeys to make contact with infants which was dependent on the infant's behavioral state.

The degree to which a seemingly chaotic and certainly complex situation represented by adult–newborn interaction may appear harmoniously organized in the microanalysis of its individual behavioral units is suggested by studies of entrainment, i.e. synchronization of body movements with speech.

The speaker's speech structure is not only hierarchically synchronized with his own non-verbal motor behavior. A similar synchrony was described between the speaker's speech and the listener's motor behavior during social interaction. Such an entrainment has been reported even in newborns (Condon and Sander 1974, Condon 1977).

The analysis of temporal relations between vocal and kinesic sequences observable in infant–adult interaction also supports the conclusion that individual sequences are well synchronized and their structure adjusted by the adult to the newborn's capacity to process informational input (Stern *et al.* 1977, Fogel 1977, Schaffer, Collis and Parsons 1977).

The list of capacities with which the newborn infant is equipped is certainly still incomplete, and yet, during the past two decades, much more autonomy and competence have been attributed to the newborn than ever before. In spite of this, all his adaptive capacities must still develop intensively to allow him a good utilization of social interactions for desirable social and cultural adjustment. At the beginning, it is his caretaker who must adapt to facilitate the newborn's cognitive start and to arrange appropriate learning situations for him. Parental behavior appears to include behaviors appropriate for this purpose, and the discovery of the parents' competence is another important achievement of human research.

In general, the tendencies in adult behavior mentioned above fulfill conditions under which the infant is offered opportunities to practice elementary steps in the cognitive integration of his novel experience. First of all, the adult caretaker makes himself familiar to the newborn. She or he does a lot to be seen, heard, smelt and felt, in short, perceived in all perceptual modalities. Second, the caretaker makes himself predictable, so much so that he makes his behavior contingent on the infant.

To become familiar with the adult, the newborn has to learn to discover the more stable or more frequent elements in his total information input and store them in his memory in order to compare their engrams with the elements of the next inputs. A certain temporal or spatial regularity with which familiar elements re-appear allows the infant to predict their re-appearance, and, if necessary, to learn how to adjust his behavior in advance. To discover contingency requires associative processes for matching relevant informational inputs with engrams of preceding movements, for developing and testing hypotheses on the relation between movements in question and relevant events, and for comparing the real achievement with the expected one.

The fact that these capacities already exist in the newborn, albeit in elementary forms, may seem surprising; however, we must not forget that they may function before birth and process simpler regularities under rather monotonous conditions first.

The nature of newborn–adult interaction facilitates the transition from intrauterine to extrauterine circumstances in different ways from different aspects. The cognitive aspects have not been neglected by nature herself even if they have been escaping behavioristic attention for such a long time. In fact, the set of adaptive parental behaviors we have tried to consider in regard to cognitive development in this paper may well be the first natural model of educational activities to which the child is exposed after birth.

The most important educational principles, i.e. to deliver knowledge in an appropriate amount at appropriate times through multiple sensory modalities repeatedly and with respect to the recipient's capacity to

478   Development of social interaction

process them, seem to be perfectly guaranteed in this primary educational situation. In this sense, the first postnatal infant–adult interactions may gain another social dimension, which in this case may be of more interest to educational scientists and give them a starting point for the development of educational biology.

Comments on papers by Mason and the Papoušeks

Toward a unified science of development

HARRIET L. RHEINGOLD[1]

With the papers prepared by the Papoušeks and Mason we enter a new arena of research. We leave the study of groups and societies, of conflicts and aggression. We consider, instead, two-person systems, one of whom is very young but fast developing, the other being the caretaker, at least nominally as we shall see. The two papers, despite their large differences, nevertheless lend themselves to a coherent discussion. They are united by a major principle of development, namely, that the development of cognitive behavior is supported by the social environment, that is, by interacting with other living organisms. The subjects of the Papoušeks' paper are human infants and their parents; those of Mason's paper are rhesus monkeys and their canine companions. The Papoušeks' presentation stems from Hanuš Papoušek's pioneering conditioning studies of newborn human infants; Mason's, from his early collaboration on the Wisconsin studies of the social development of rhesus monkeys. The method of the Papoušeks' paper is descriptive, while Mason's is experimental. Where one provides details, the other does not; yet as I shall show, each complements the other.

At the outset, the point should be made that for none of these investigators is cognition a purely mentalistic term, that is, considered in terms

[1] Work on this paper was supported in part by NIH Career Award number HD23620 from the National Institute of Child Health and Human Development.

of a formal logico-mathematical system of mental structures and stages. For none also is learning a concept to be shunned. Rather, the terms *cognition* and *learning* are used almost synonymously. The Papoušeks, especially, spell out the mental processes underlying learning (more exactly, instrumental conditioning); these include memory and the ability to differentiate between the familiar and the novel. Their statement makes explicit what is now obvious but has gone too long unrecognized: that conditioning produces changes in cognitive processes as well as in motor processes. Both Mason and the Papoušeks show by their research that one can talk of cognition *and* study behavior. Of course, one cannot inquire of newborn human infants and juvenile macaques the reasons for their behavior or inquire into their mental events, yet their behavior does reveal the operations of cognitive processes. In different ways, then, both papers counteract the current tendency of some cognitivists in their rediscovery of mental processes to shun both behavior and learning.

I would now like to consider each paper separately, then return to the common themes, show how they reinforce each other, and at the end present some thoughts on human ethology as a discipline.

From the nigh perfect conditioning studies of newborn infants executed by Hanuš Papoušek during the 1960s, the Papoušeks have abstracted a set of developmental principles. The first is that the newborn's behavior can be modified by contingent stimulation. Second, the ability to remember is shown in the increase of correct responses from session to session. Third, the perceptual ability to recognize the familiar elements within a situation must underlie successful conditioning, that is, a main effect of prior experience is its providing a standard of familiarity against which the novel can be compared. Then, in addition to spelling out the cognitive processes that occurred during conditioning sessions, the studies also showed that emotional responses accompanied the increase in learning. Furthermore, not only did learning occur faster when the infant was quiet and alert, but success or failure during conditioning trials enhanced or dissipated that 'state'.

In the natural course of events, newborn infants are not subjects of laboratory experiments. In what ways, then, do their natural environments present stimuli and responses to them that provide occasions for learning? Here the Papoušeks found that typical parental responses, conscious or unconscious, contain some elements concordant with the procedures of the laboratory studies. Parents, when faced by a newborn, simplify their responses. Parents repeat their own responses and thus provide familiarity. They, however, provide more varied stimuli and responses than the conditioning procedures of the laboratory. As the Papoušeks point out, the parent pays attention to behavioral state, the parent imitates, the parent responds differentially to visual contact with the infant's eyes. And, if they respond similarly to certain behaviors of the infant, the infant learns how to produce that particular response once again; the infant thereby controls the behavior of his partner. Thus, as the newborn infant responds to social stimuli and as his behavior is modified, so too do adults respond to the infant's behavior, and so too is *their* behavior modified.

The sensitive portrayal of the subtle interactions between infant and caretaker presented by the Papoušeks provides a conceptual synthesis, on the one hand, of cognition and learning, and on the other, of the motor, social, affective, and cognitive abilities of the infant. Both these syntheses qualify as substantive contributions to knowledge.

The Papoušeks' efforts to work out the precise nature of the interaction between infant and parent I place in the mainstream of current research on infancy. The nature of the interaction between parent and child is exactly the focus of much work today. Their contribution adds exquisite details of the interaction as revealed by the use of special filming. They must now, however, show how regular the events are. Although there is no substitute for the discerning eye, stunningly portrayed in their illustrations, and for imaginative conceptualizing, one would still like to ask for information on probability of occurrence, and on variability and regularity within a parent and across parents.

I do not ask for evidence of the consequences in either the infant or the parent of variations in the interaction. This important question need not be their concern; the value of their findings does not require such support. Yet by their references to the effects of stress on the interaction (here enough data support the effects in humans to obviate their recourse to rats) and to the child's education, they do show just such concerns. The dangers here are considerable. It has proved all too easy for investigators to ascribe present or subsequent differences in the behaviors of infants to differences in parental behavior without acknowledging the contributions of the infant to parental behavior.

Then, visual contact between infant and adult, long a subject of great interest, may by its very charm serve to distract our attention from the importance of auditory contact for the development of social behavior. Recently I collected evidence that even hospital personnel talk a great deal to newborns from the first day of life. Given that the infant's auditory system is better developed at birth than his visual system and given the ubiquity of speech, auditory contact deserves more attention as an important avenue of communication between infant and caretaker.

The two references the Papoušeks do make to adult speech, however, occasion further comment. First, Condon's findings on the differential motor responses of newborns to different spoken words remain at this time only suggestive until they are replicated by others. Also, although adult speech to children is in general shorter and simplified, the evidence suggests that its greatest reduction may occur not at birth but at the time children themselves are beginning to use words.

Mason's paper takes us to quite another theater of research. Not only are the subjects now monkeys, but they are also older than the Papoušeks' newborns, and furthermore they were raised without their mothers. Here Mason draws contrasts in the behavior of monkeys living with dogs and those living with replicas of dogs, all raised in complex 'enriched' environments. Despite the differences in species, age, and rearing conditions between the reports by Mason and the Papoušeks, the purpose is similar in that each seeks to assess the effect of social agents on cognitive abilities. A variety of measures taken by Mason during the course of four years showed that monkeys raised with dogs were more active in novel settings, more ready to try new problems, more proficient in solving them, and more attentive to novel visual stimuli. These differences Mason attributes to the response-contingent stimulation offered by an animate rather than an inanimate companion'. Mason characterizes the monkeys' behaviors as cognitive, and concludes that the live dogs provided the social stimulation necessary for the development of the behaviors.

A distinguishing feature of Mason's research is the attempt to understand the nature of the maternal role in the development of an organism by the use of models: the dog for the monkey's own mother, and the inanimate hobby horse for the live dog. Models provide control and confer great power. But we must ask what they control for. The dogs provided some subset of the stimuli and responses a monkey mother would: the monkeys and the dogs played together, slept together, and groomed each other. The stimulus–response contingencies between them in even this partial set would be many and varied. Here knowledge of the exact nature of the contingencies would be useful, difficult to chart as they would be. It is just here that for a more limited period of time in the organism's life the Papoušeks present explicit details.

Mason then supplies the evidence that these rearing experiences had effects over the years of observation. He thus provides the evidence that the Papoušeks' line of investigation may one day be expected to supply. Mason's tests are varied and interesting, and one would like to know the rationale for the use of these particular ones. Are they the most appropriate for measuring such concepts as 'coping strategies' and 'generalized expectancies'? Popular though these concepts are, they could profit by more precise definitions.

Together these papers lend themselves to some response contingencies of my own. Both are laboratory studies, searching for the events that affect cognitive behavior, both trying to discover what goes on in real life, the Papoušeks with a minimum of intervention, Mason by a major intervention. In both papers we note the absence of any consideration of the caretaker as a satisfier of the infant's primary needs. Reasonable as that seems today, not too many years ago such an omission would have been unthinkable. Nor does either talk of attachment or the bond. It is assumed that we are now ready to examine the underlying processes. Furthermore, instead of thinking that enriching the physical environment is the sine qua non for cognitive development, the investigators point to social interaction by itself as the important experience for cognitive development. But let me note in passing that interaction with the inanimate environment can teach a great deal. It too can be responsive and can offer contingent stimulation (e.g., the infant reaching for a mobile), but at least in the case of human infants, much of the inanimate environment also comes to them at human hands.

Both papers, I note, concentrate on the maternal figure as the dispenser of social stimulation. The term *mother* can of course be used in its generic sense, yet current research is extending our horizons to other members of the infant's social group. Mammalian mothers, both human and non-human, usually do interact more often with the infant than fathers, aunts, siblings, and peers (I recognize of course that the age and sex of the members of the group, other than the mother, vary with the species). But no evidence exists to show that the *amount* of interaction qualifies as the crucial variable in determining present or later behavior. It is probably not sheer amount, but rather the nature of the interaction, that is, the nature of the stimulus–response contingency. Thus, an infrequent interaction, if only by its very novelty, may have a greater effect than a familiar one. At least in the human infant research of today, the behavior of the father receives increased attention. The role of siblings in the development of social and cognitive skills still remains to be explored. Divorced from the routine care usually administered by the mother, the interaction of father, sibling, and so on *may* by its playfulness be the more salient and effective.

Finally, both papers, in stressing the importance of the social interaction provided by a partner's behavior, scant the contribution of the infant to the interaction. It is true that infants in general evoke parental behaviors in general. But infants vary as much as their caretakers. Although we are making some progress in human research in beginning to specify the nature of differences in infants – for example, in activity level, soothability, sensitivity to stimulation – I do not know of similar studies among nonhuman infants. Here I am not calling for studies of individual differences but for explication of the relation between, on the one hand, the interaction between infants and others and, on the other, the infants' cognitive, emotional, and social development.

Here I change topics and ask how I can relate these papers to the theme of the conference, the claims and limitations of human ethology?

My reading tells me that the hallmarks of ethology are concerns with the ontogeny, causes, functions, and evolution of behavior. Both papers exhibit one or more of these concerns. My reading also tells me that yet another hallmark of ethology specifies the importance of describing an animal's behavior in its natural environment. Here neither paper fits, for even the Papoušeks bring the infant and mother into the laboratory. Neither paper, unless I have overlooked it, states a position on the claims or limitations of ethology. Mason, however, proposes that his studies of primate development have 'a special relevance to human ethology'. On the available evidence I conclude, therefore, that in the absence of disclaimers, both papers accept human ethology as a new discipline, the other part and almost invisible implication of this volume's title.

It is this implication that I now venture to question, that is, the need for human ethology as a new discipline. I do so with a measure of diffidence because my remarks are somewhat special to my discipline, that of developmental psychology.

Ethologists often claim that psychology must now obtain the descriptive data it ignored by moving too quickly to the experimental testing of hypotheses. Although psychologists have not described all the behaviors of all the species in all environments, and although new behaviors come to our attention every day, the careful reader can easily find a steady stream of observational studies. Limiting my account to the human infant and young child, I can start with Tiedemann in 1787, and in more recent times continue through the Bühlers, William Stern, Valentine, Guillaume, Gesell, Piaget, Shirley, Bridges, Blatt, to mention only the most outstanding. To these I add countless observational studies in nursery schools, preschools, playgrounds, and homes. Today, observational studies in all these settings continue to flourish. On the topic of parent–child relations, observational studies are more the rule than the exception, and are more often conducted in homes than in laboratories. To attribute recent observational studies in natural environments to the influence of ethology, however, shows only a short reading of the literature.

The term *natural environment* also deserves examination. For human children, the natural environment obtains wherever they happen to be. Laboratory settings usually are no more than rooms, and with these they have had much experience. The human infant or child in a laboratory setting ought not to be equated with a wild animal in one. Even infants have much experience with diverse environments. In modern societies they are routinely wheeled down streets, taken into stores full of people and new objects, and driven about in automobiles. For infants and young children the dichotomy between laboratory and natural environments breaks down; the dichotomy may well be a distinction more salient for the experimenter than for the child. In the last analysis, not the environments but the questions asked should determine the value of studies.

In another vein, students of behavior may indeed welcome one of the implications of the term *human ethology*: that students of nonhuman animals of the ethological persuasion are now turning their attention to man. In studying the human infant I often turned to infants of other species to look for similarities and differences, and to clear my eye and sharpen my perspective. And I was not alone, but following a tradition established by Preyer in 1898. Indeed, in a chapter entitled 'A comparative psychology of development' (Stevenson, Hess and Rheingold 1967), I called for a unified science of development to include the study of man's behavior as one among the animals. Although the literature of psychology through every period of its history has always contained studies of both human and nonhuman species, for all the many years I have read the journal *Animal Behaviour* I have rarely found a study of humans (none of ninety-two articles in 1974, one of eighty-five articles in 1975, and two of ninety-seven articles in 1976), while in the *Journal of Mammalogy* I have yet to see a single study.

As for the ontogeny and causes of behavior, these do indeed constitute the primary concerns of developmental psychology, and therefore no more need be said about them. The concerns of survival function, in the biologist's sense, and of evolution emphasize concerns that in the past have been slighted or ignored. Here developmental psychology can benefit by an infusion of evolutionary theory. Yet the work of many noted developmental psychologists incorporated just such concerns, among them G. Stanley Hall, J. M. Baldwin, and Arnold Gesell. More recently, the relation of ontogeny to phylogeny has been pondered by, among others, B. F. Skinner and R. B. Cairns. There is no doubt in my mind that psychology in general and developmental psychology in particular will increasingly incorporate analyses concerned with the function of behaviors as well as their evolution. Sciences do not have rigid boundaries, but are always in flux. Like the people who engage in the scientific enterprise, sciences too are flexible and capable of incorporating new ways of thinking. Today psychologists do not contemplate the demise predicted for them by Wilson (1975). Instead, as they will profit by the insights of sociobiology, so too they will profit by those proposed for *human* ethology.

For myself, I find my thinking about the young child's social development enriched by evolutionary theory. But I must guard against selecting whatever of the theory fits my own biases. Similarly I feel constrained to caution others also to guard against selecting from developmental psychology whatever fits their own theories. In my own area of research, infant behavior, there have been numerous instances of late where unverified or disputed findings have been accepted as fact by ethological theorists. With no modesty at all, I suggest that investigators of animal behavior and students of evolution have much to learn from studies of human children; it behooves them to pay as much attention to that body of literature as developmental psychologists should to the ethological literature. It may even be the case that the principles and findings that have been derived from the study of child development will provide guides for the reevaluation and solution of the problems of animal behavior.

References

Ader, R., and Conklin, P. M. 1963. Handling of pregnant rats: effects on emotion-ality of their offspring. *Science*, *142*:411–12.

Anastasiou, P. J. 1970. Problem solving ability of differentially reared rhesus monkeys. Unpublished Ph.D. thesis, Tulane University.

Anderson, C. O., Kenney, A. McM. and Mason, W. A. 1977. Effects of maternal mobility, partner, and endocrine state on social responsiveness of adolescent rhesus monkeys. *Developmental Psychobiology*, *10*:421–34.

Brackbill, Y., Fitzgerald, H. E. and Lintz, L. M. 1967. A developmental study of classical conditioning. *Monographs on Social Research in Child Development*, *38*(116).

Broen, P. A. 1972. The verbal environment of the language-learning child. *ASHA Monographs*, *17*.

Bystroletova, G. N. 1954. Obrazovanie i novorozhdennykh detei uslovnogo refleksa na vremia v sviazi s utochnym ritmom kormleniia (The formation in neonates of a conditioned reflex to time in connection with daily feeding rhythm). *Zhurnal Vyssheĭ Nervnoĭ Deyatel'nosti*, *4*:601–9.

Condon, W. S. 1977. A primary phase in the organization of infant responding behaviour. In H. R. Schaffer (ed.), *Studies in mother–infant interaction*. London: Academic Press.

Condon, W. S. and Sander, L. W. 1974. Neonate movement is synchronized with adult speech: Interactional participation and language acquisition. *Science*, *183*:99–101.

DeBeer, G. 1958. *Embryos and ancestors*. 3rd edn. London: Oxford University Press.

Denenberg, V. H. and Whimbey, A. E. 1963. Behavior of adult rats is modified by the experiences their mothers had as infants. *Science*, *142*:1192–3.

Doyle, G. A. and Yule, E. P. 1959. Early experience and emotionality: the effects of prenatal maternal anxiety on the emotionality of albino rats. *Journal of Social Research, Pretoria*, *10*:57–66.

Eastman, R. F. and Mason, W. A. 1975. Looking behavior in monkeys raised with mobile and stationary artificial mothers. *Developmental Psychobiology*, *8*:213–22.

Fogel, A. 1977. Temporal organization in mother–infant face-to-face interaction. In H. R. Schaffer (ed.), *Studies in mother–infant interaction*. London: Academic Press.

Gewirtz, J. L. 1961. A learning analysis of the effects of normal stimulation, privation and deprivation on the acquisition of social motivation and attachment. In B. M. Foss (ed.), *Determinants of infant behavior*. London: Methuen.

Hardy, A. C. 1963. Escape from specialization. In J. Huxley, A. C. Hardy and E. B. Ford (eds.), *Evolution as a process*. New York: Collier Books.

Hockman, C. H. 1961. Prenatal maternal stress in the rat: its effects on emotional behavior in the offspring. *Journal of Comparative and Physiological Psychology*, 54:679–84.

Hopf, S. 1972. Sozialpsychologische Untersuchungen zur Verhaltensentwicklung des Totenkopfaffen. Unpublished Ph.D. thesis, University of Marburg.

Krachkovskaia, M. V. 1959. Reflex changes in the leukocyte count of newborn infants in relation to food intake. *Zhurnal Vysshei Nervnoi Deyatel'nosti*, 9:193–9 (in Russian).

Lakin, M. 1957. Personality factors in mothers of excessively crying (colicky) infants. *Monographs on Social Research in Child Development*, 22(64).

Lewis, M. and Goldberg, S. 1969. Perceptual–cognitive development in infancy: A generalized expectancy model as a function of mother–infant interaction. *Merrill-Palmer Quarterly*, 15:81–100.

McCall, R. B. and Kagan, J. 1967. Attention in the infant: effects of complexity, contour, perimeter, and familiarity. *Child Development*, 38:939–52.

Marquis, D. P. 1941. Learning in the neonate: the modification of behavior under three feeding schedules. *Journal of Experimental Psychology*, 29:263–82.

Martinius, J. W. and Papoušek, H. 1970. Response to optic and exteroceptive stimuli in relation to state in the human newborn: Habituation of the blink reflex. *Neuropädiatrie*, 1:452–60.

Mason, W. A. 1960. The effects of social restriction on the behavior of rhesus monkeys: I. Free social behavior. *Journal of Comparative and Physiological Psychology*, 53:582–9.

1961. The effect of social restriction on the behavior of rhesus monkeys: II. Tests of gregariousness. *Journal of Comparative and Physiological Psychology*, 54:287–90.

1968. Scope and potential of primate research. *Scientific Psychoanalysis*, 12:101–18.

In press. Social ontogeny. In J. G. Vandenberg and P. Marler (eds.), *Social behavior and communication*. New York: Plenum.

Mason, W. A. and Berkson, G. 1975. Effects of maternal mobility on the development of rocking and other behaviors in rhesus monkeys: a study with artificial mothers. *Developmental Psychobiology*, 8:197–211.

Mason, W. A. and Green, P. H. 1962. The effects of social restriction on the behavior of rhesus monkeys: IV. Responses to a novel environment and to an alien species. *Journal of Comparative and Physiological Psychology*, 55:363–8.

Mason, W. A. and Kenney, M. D. 1974. Redirection of filial attachments in rhesus monkeys: dogs as mother surrogates. *Science*, 183:1209–11.

Newport, E. L. 1977. Motherese: the speech of mothers to young children. In N. J. Castellan, Jr, D. B. Pisoni and G. R. Potts (eds.), *Cognitive theory*, vol. II. Hillsdale, New York: Erlbaum.

Papoušek, H. 1961. Conditioned head rotation reflexes in infants in the first months of life. *Acta paediatrica*, 50:565–76.

1967a. Experimental studies of appetitional behavior in human newborns and infants. In Stevenson, Hess and Rheingold 1967:249–77.

1967b. Conditioning during early post-natal development. In Y. Brackbill and G. G. Thompson (eds.), *Behavior in infancy and early childhood*. New York: Free Press.

1969. Individual variability in learned responses in human infants. In R. J. Robinson (ed.), *Brain and early behavior*. New York: Academic Press.

1978. Zur objektiven Analyse und Mikroanalyse des Verhaltens: Audiovisuelle Versuchsreproduktion mit Hilfe von Film- und Fernsehtechnik. In H. Remschmidt and M. H. Schmidt (eds.), *Neuropsychologie des Kindesalters*, vol. I. Stuttgart: Enke Verlag.

Papoušek, H. and Bernstein, P. 1969. The functions of conditioning stimulation in human neonates and infants. In A. Ambrose (ed.), *Stimulation in early infancy*. London: Academic Press.

Papoušek, H. and Papoušek, M. 1974. Mirror image and self-recognition in young human infants: A new method of experimental analysis. *Developmental Psychobiology*, 7:149–57.

1975. Cognitive aspects of preverbal social interaction between human infants and adults. In M. O'Connor (ed.), *Parent–infant interaction*. Amsterdam: Elsevier.

1977a. Mothering and cognitive headstart: Psychobiological considerations. In H. R. Schaffer (ed.), *Studies in mother–infant interaction*. London: Academic Press.

1977b. Die ersten musikalischen Erfahrungen des Kindes und ihre biologische und psychologische Bedeutung. Paper presented at the Symposium of the Herbert-von-Karajan-Stiftung, Salzburg, April 1977.

Phillips, J. R. 1970. Formal characteristics of speech which mothers address to their young children. Unpublished Ph.D. thesis, Johns Hopkins University. Reference in Newport 1977.

Piaget, J. 1951. *Play, dreams and imitation in children*. London: Heinemann.

Remick, H. 1971. The maternal environment of linguistic development. Unpublished Ph.D. thesis, University of California, Davis. Reference in Newport 1977.

Rheingold, H. L. 1960. The measurement of maternal care. *Child Development*, 31:565–75.

Rheingold, H. L., Gewirtz, J. L. and Ross, H. W. 1959. Social conditioning of vocalization in the infant. *Journal of Comparative and Physiological Psychology*, 52:68–73.

Rosenblatt, J. S. 1967. Nonhormonal basis of maternal behavior in the rat. *Science*, 156:1512–14.

1975. Prepartum and postpartum regulation of maternal behavior in the rat. In M. O'Connor (ed.), *Parent–infant interaction*. Amsterdam: Elsevier.

Ryle, G. 1949. *The concept of mind*. London: Hutchinson and Co. Reprinted New York: Barnes and Noble, 1971.

Schaffer, H. R., Collis, G. M. and Parsons, G. 1977. Vocal interchange and visual regard in verbal and pre-verbal children. In H. R. Schaffer (ed.), *Studies in mother–infant interaction*. London: Academic Press.

Schoetzau A. and Papoušek, H. 1977. Mütterliches Verhalten bei der Aufnahme von Blickkontakt mit dem Neugeborenen. *Zeitschrift für Entwicklungspsychologie und Pädagogik*, 9:231–9.

Seligman, M. E. P. 1975. *Helplessness: on depression, development, and death*. San Francisco: W. H. Freeman and Company.

Shipley, E. S., Smith, C. S. and Gleitman, L. R. 1969. A study in the acquisition of language: free responses to commands. *Language*, 45:322–42.

Slobin, D. I. 1968. Question of language development in cross-cultural perspective. Reference in (1968a) Newport 1977.

Snow, C. E. 1972. Mothers' speech to children learning language. *Child Development*, 43:549–65.

Solkoff, N. and Cotton, C. 1975. Contingency awareness in premature infants. *Perceptual and Motor Skills*, 41:709–10.

Sontag, L. W. 1941. The significance of fetal environmental differences. *American Journal of Obstetrics and Gynecology*, 42:996–1003.

Stern, D. N., Beebe, B., Jaffe, J. and Bennett, S. L. 1977. The infant's stimulus world during social interaction: A study of caregiver behaviours with particular reference to repetition and timing. In H. R. Schaffer (ed.), *Studies in mother–infant interaction*. London: Academic Press.

Stevenson, H. W., Hess, E. H. and Rheingold, H. L. (eds.) 1967. *Early behavior: comparative and developmental approaches*. New York: Wiley.

Stewart, A. H., Weiland, I. H., Leider, A. R., Maugham, C. A., Holmes, T. H. and Ripley, H. S. 1954. Excessive infant crying (colic) in relation to parent behavior. *American Journal of Psychiatry*, 110:687–94.

Thompson, W. R. 1957. Influence of prenatal maternal anxiety on emotionality in young rats. *Science*, 125:698–9.

Wallin, R. and Riley, R. 1950. Reactions of mothers to pregnancy and adjustment of offspring in infancy. *American Journal of Orthopsychiatry*, 20:616–22.

Watson, J. S. 1971. Cognitive-perceptual development in infancy: setting for the seventies. *Merrill-Palmer Quarterly*, 17:139–52.

Watson, J. A. and Ramey, C. T. 1972. Reactions to response-contingent stimulation in early infancy. *Merrill-Palmer Quarterly*, 18:219–27.

Wilson, E. O. 1975. *Sociobiology: the new synthesis*. Cambridge, Mass.: Belknap Press.

8. Cognitive development

8.1. Ethology: understanding the other half of intelligence[1]

WILLIAM R. CHARLESWORTH

Introduction

It is the main thesis of this paper that researchers working in the area of human and animal intelligence over the past one hundred years have dealt primarily with 'one half' of intelligence, namely, with intelligence conceived of as a disposition – that is, as a trait or ability which can be measured by means of tests and manipulated to some extent in experimental settings. On the whole, such researchers have shown little interest in studying the function and ecological significance of intelligence; using my terminology, they have not dealt conceptually or empirically with the 'other half' of intelligence. Studying the other half requires observing the animal in its natural habitat and documenting its behavioral interactions with the problematic part of its environment – that part which demands intelligent behavior for optimal adaptation and survival. The position taken here is that, while ethology has no tradition of studying intelligent behavior, there is nothing intrinsic in ethology, as a discipline, that prevents researchers from applying its theoretical orientation and methodology to the study of intelligence. For reasons which will, I

[1] Preparation of this paper was made possible by sabbatical support from the Max Planck Institute for Psychiatry, Munich and the University of Minnesota. Support for the empirical portion of this paper was provided by Program Project Grant 1 PO1 HD 05027 from the National Institute of Child Health and Human Development and OE Grant 300–76–0036 from the Bureau of the Education for the Handicapped. Special thanks go to Professor Dr Detlev Ploog, Director of the Max Planck Institute for Psychiatry, for his generous support and friendly criticism while this paper was being written. Thanks also go to Ms Maria Craig, Bernhard Eble, and Donna Williams for gracious last minute assistance and correction.

An earlier version of this paper appeared as Charlesworth 1978b.

hope, become clear below, ethology is therefore viewed as the most appropriate discipline to study the other half of intelligence.

The first part of this paper provides historical information on research on the first half of intelligence and reasons why the position described above is taken in regard to the second half. The remaining parts of the paper describe an attempt to develop a method for studying intelligent behavior in humans (and possibly in some other primates) from an ethological perspective. This attempt includes a conceptualization of intelligent behavior (loosely derived from evolutionary theory as well as from cognitive psychology) that makes it amenable to observation and ultimately to quantitative analysis. Intelligent behavior is defined briefly as cognitively guided behavior employed to deal with problems. More will be said on this definition below as well as on the attempt to operationalize the elements within it for observational purposes.

Given space restrictions, only the essentials of this approach to intelligence will be touched on here. It is hoped, however, that these essentials will serve as material for a fruitful discussion of more general problems that deal with the claims and limits of human ethology.

Historical sketch

The following sketch is built around the two ways of dealing with intelligence already mentioned: (1) dealing with it as a disposition or potential to behave intelligently when presented with a test or problem-solving task, and (2) dealing with it as intelligent behavior which is elicited (and strengthened or weakened) by natural, everyday events and conditions. Both ways are, of course, not independent of one another and both are important for understanding intelligence. In my opinion, however, the latter (the other half) has been neglected in research for various reasons and consequently has the greater potential at present for adding something new to our current understanding of intelligence.

The one half

As far as rigorous empirical work is concerned, dealing with intelligence as a disposition has historically been by far the most popular way researchers have approached intelligence. The first systematic attempts by Sir Francis Galton (1869) at mental testing (as well as testing for other psychological traits such as personality and temperament) became, within a short period of time, the major occupation of a large segment of the newly born science of psychology (Guilford 1967, Butcher 1968). Not only did test results lead to improved knowledge of mental structure and functioning, but as Binet and Simon (1905) demonstrated, testing for intelligence levels in children had significant diagnostic value in placing children in school and establishing relevant, age-appropriate school curricula. During the decades following Binet and Simon, intelligence tests proliferated at a rapid rate, both in response to practical needs to predict performance (mostly in school and on the job) and to satisfy the curiosity for knowledge of the nature and functioning of the human mind. As a result of this proliferation, different kinds of tests multiplied greatly along with opinions on the nature of intelligence itself. Guilford (1967), for example, maintained that some 120 independent measurable abilities were necessary to describe adequately human intelligence, whereas earlier, Spearman (1927) argued that a single factor (general intelligence) plus some minor factors were sufficient to account for most of human performance on intelligence tests. Others maintained that the number is somewhere between those of Guilford and Spearman. Others made more qualitative claims (Piaget 1947, for example) and argued that intelligence is something more dynamic than that which is tapped by conventional psychometric methods and has to be studied longitudinally with a totally different measurement procedure.

This state of affairs, plus the fact that omnibus intelligence tests (those testing as many sub-abilities as possible) do not account for more than 30 to 40% (correlations of 0.60 are common) of the variance on academic achievement (Buss and Poley 1976) and even less variance on life or job success (Jencks *et al.* 1972), raises the question of whether the first half approach to intelligence should be continued. The question of the value of tests for shedding more light on intelligence is also raised with regard to the vast amount of effort and resources put into them. Despite such shortcomings, intelligence testing still, of course, produces results with important practical value.

If we look at the dynamic theories of intelligence, that is at those which do not attribute the degree of stability to intellectual abilities which is generally attributed by psychometricians, we find that most of them, nevertheless, view intelligence as dispositional properties of organisms which can be measured with appropriate tests. Piaget's (1947, 1952) theory is a good example. Responding to what he felt was a static view of intelligence shared by most psychometricians, Piaget developed a theory of intelligence that reflected various changes in children's intellectual performance during the first fifteen or so years of development. His theory also takes into account the role of environmental factors in aiding the construction of intelligence over ontogenesis. Nevertheless, despite such a dynamic emphasis, intelligence is still viewed as a disposition by Piaget and the methodological foundation of his research is basically psychometric. Cognitive operations or abilities are tested for in standard, predetermined settings, many of which appear to have little or no representation in the everyday life of the individual and hence little direct behavioral relevance. What is meant by the latter will be discussed in more detail below.

If we turn to human problem-solving research aimed at exploring the causal conditions governing cognitive processes, we discover that it, too, follows the same conceptual and methodological paradigm as that of mental testing (see Bourne, Ekstrand and Dominowski 1971 for a treatment of this topic under the heading of thinking). Problem situations are posed to subjects – occasionally preceded by various experimental conditions chosen to influence information processing, retrieval, etc. – and behavior is subsequently observed, recorded and measured. Problem-solving behavior as it is elicited and controlled by everyday (non-laboratory) environmental conditions has generally not been studied. While the cognitive processes tapped by standard problem-solving research may not be as stable as those measured by intelligence tests, they are still conceived of as being backed in some way by cognitive dispositions (short- or long-term) to act in a predictable way when presented with a certain problematic situation. In short, the psychometric tradition still holds. Processes (or abilities) are postulated, particular stimulus conditions assumed to tap these processes are carefully chosen and administered, and responses are recorded and evaluated.

If we turn to the vast majority of animal research on intelligence, we discover that the major research paradigm is very much like that of intelligence research with humans. From Thorndike (1911), through Köhler (1921), Hebb (1949), Bitterman (1965a), Harlow *et al.* (1971), and Rensch (1973), subjects are presented with problematic stimulus conditions that require solution. On occasion, experimental variables, such as early stimulus deprivation or enrichment, are included to measure their effects on such behavior. Responses to such tests are measured and evaluated in terms of predetermined criteria as to how intelligent or unintelligent such responses are, whether they reflect simple habituation phenomena, associative functions that occur 'higher up' in the central nervous system, or complex processes such as abstraction, deduction, or hypothesis formation that involve the frontal lobes. Frequently, comparisons are made between various animal species and between animals and humans. In most such research emphasis is usually upon what the animals can do under optimal or suboptimal testing conditions. What the animal normally does do or must do in its natural habitat to survive has been seldom investigated by comparative psychologists. The question is more frequently asked by those with biological training, as in the tool-using observations, for example, of Eibl-Eibesfeldt and Sielmann (1962), Goodall (1965), and Kortlandt (1968). Thorndike (1898), the pioneer of much comparative research, was in contrast convinced that observations (and anecdotes) of animal behavior in the wild had to be replaced by experimental findings. If there was any interest on the part of comparative psychologists in the animal's extra-laboratory, extra-test situation behavior, it was usually related to or based upon little scientific data. Furthermore, the choice of stimuli or tasks or experimental conditions in most experiments appears to be based on intuition, tradition, or shrewd guesses. As far as I can determine, it was seldom based upon field data. As a result, generalizations to behavior outside of the laboratory or test situation to the animal in its natural habitat were either non-existent or simply tenuous because there were little or no relevant data on the animal in its natural habitat.

Much of what has just been said also appears to be true for research involved with the neurological and physiological causal mechanisms underlying intelligent behavior (for coverage of this research, see Jerison 1973 and Bindra 1976). In summary, then, the vast majority of researchers interested in animal intelligence have employed (and still are employing) the same general approach to intelligence as their colleagues studying humans. Their primary orientation has been between understanding the structure of intelligence and some of the factors that influence its expression. It is true, though, that the function of intelligence (as already noted), or the bigger question as to why the mechanisms for such behavior evolved, was of interest to many of these researchers, but they did little or no empirical research into it.

The other half

Those who approach intelligence primarily as behavior realize, of course, that behind every intelligent act there is a disposition to act intelligently: a child solving a mathematical problem must certainly possess some mathematical ability before working on the problem which he will still have after he solves it. 'Other half' researchers, however, are less interested in abilities and more interested in what intelligence actually does for the individual when it is expressed in everyday behavior. Such researchers feel obliged to observe and record behavior as it is released from the animal by problems in everyday situations. Only then is it possible, they argue, to get a picture of what function the behavior serves and hence some vague idea of how it may have served the species during phylogenesis. The other half researcher approaches intelligent behavior as something the environment forces out of the animal and not as something a researcher should feel obliged to force out. The latter should be done in the second phase of research, that is, after more is known about what the animal normally does in everyday life when the environment puts it under pressure to act intelligently.

To simplify matters, we can divide the other half researchers historically into two groups, keeping in mind that they never progressed with their research to the extent that the one half did. The two groups include the naturalists who observed intelligent behavior as it occurred in animals in the wild, and the evolutionists–functionalists who theorized about intelligence and seldom if ever observed it. We can speculate that the naturalist group is a very old one, going back to early hunters who needed to know the habits of their prey as well as how clever they were in novel situations. With hunting and later animal domestication, accumulating information on animal intelligence was probably exclusively a practical undertaking. By Aristotle's time, accumulating knowledge about animal behavior became a non-practical or purely epistemic undertaking: it became valuable in itself. It was a part of man's knowledge of his universe. Since the Greeks, the epistemic approach to animals gradually picked up impetus over the centuries and began reaching its climax in the nineteenth century, a period when professional naturalists began appearing on the scene.

A prototype example of a nineteenth-century observer of intelligent behavior in animals was Wesley Mills. In his *The nature and development of animal intelligence*, Mills (1898) insisted that naturalistic observation of behavior was of immense importance for laying the foundation of psychology and that 'mere closet psychology is of little value in advancing the subject as applied to animals' (p. vii). In Mills' mind it was clear who was in the closet – the laboratory researchers and test psychologists who were rapidly taking over the field. Mills went further and also insisted that observation take place in the context of longitudinal research. Individual animals were to be studied over their life span, if possible. Then, and only then, he argued, would everyone see how plastic intelligent behavior was and how tightly connected it was to environmental conditions. To top off his argument, Mills, in reply to comments from a well-known evolutionary theorist, noted, 'I fail to see that a single safe step can be taken in explaining evolution either in biology or psychology, if the effects of the environment and of use [presumably the use by the animal of built-in behavior mechanisms] be ignored' (p. 286). Mills could not have anticipated more accurately the task of modern ethology or Tinbergen's (1972) controversial remark that psychology was still not yet a science because it lacked a foundation of descriptive research.

Mills was not taken very seriously, however. As defenders of naturalistic observation and ecological psychology point out, naturalistic observation played a relatively minor role in psychology's first hundred years (Barker 1968, Willems and Rausch 1969). Apart from baby diaries which helped greatly in launching the scientific study of children, more convenient ways of studying human and animal behavior quickly took over psychology, once it was clear that psychology could be a scientific discipline independent of philosophy. The impact of Wundt's successful attempt to harden psychology quickly (with brass instrument laboratories), combined with Galton's efforts at trait measurement, set the modus operandi for psychologists at a respectful scientific level. Anecdotal reports, casual observations, common sense, speculations about human and animal mind and behavior were definitely out, rigor and control were in. Naturalistic observation became somewhat quaint.

It never totally perished, though. In child psychology, for example, as Wright (1960) pointed out, a small, persistent, and scientifically respectful cadre of child observers continued their labors down through the decades, especially in the 1930s. This trend notwithstanding, it has been only fairly recently that the work of ecological psychologists, chiefly Barker, Wright, Gump, Schoggen, Willems, and others of the Kansas school, plus a new breed of human psychologists (Blurton Jones 1972, McGrew 1972), helped establish a respectable foothold for field observation. This foothold, though, has been almost exclusively in the area of social behavior. In the psychology of intelligent behavior it established virtually no foothold whatsoever.

In addition to naturalistic observers, the nineteenth century also produced a vast number of evolutionists, many of whom, unfortunately, were much less empirically inclined than Darwin and hardly came close to his commitment to the observational method. Darwin's last book in 1881 on vegetable mould and earthworms (aimed at demonstrating that earthworms manifested a very early stage of intelligence) was based on over forty years of steady terranean and subterranean observation. Needless to say, his intellectual descendants, for the most part, did not repeat him. The armchair was never used more vigorously and with more verbosity in the service of evolutionary theory (despite his good example) than during the fifty odd years after the publication of the *Origin of species*. This was especially true when the origin and descent of *Homo sapiens* was being scrutinized. Beginning as early as Spencer (1855) who viewed mind (including intelligence and instinct) as a product of evolution (actually the notion goes back further but Spencer made the most of it), the notion that intelligence was implicated in evolution picked up tremendous impetus. The impetus, though, materialized in words, rather than in data. No one, apparently, knew how (or even, in some cases, why) data should be collected. There were attempts, though, to find indirect support for the evolution of mind in comparative studies. Romanes (1884, 1889), for example, lent support to Darwin's (1872) argument that if morphological traits were subject to evolution, so, most probably, were behavior and psychological traits. Romanes' support came in the form of two large volumes on mental evolution in animals and man, both filled with theory and speculation as well as many anecdotal accounts of how animals shared clever cognitive traits with humans. The notion of mental continuity between so-called lower species and higher ones was an evolutionary principle vigorously defended. Speculating about mental evolution was very popular. Even Thorndike (1898, 1911), who preferred the clean confines of the laboratory and studied the cleaner laws of exercise and effect, felt compelled to comment on the evolution of intelligence. But most of the defenders, such as Hobhouse (1901) and James Mark Baldwin (1895, 1902), eschewed empirical work and preferred to develop doctrine rather than collect facts.

While much mental energy was put into arguing that mind had evolved just as body did, a few evolutionists thought otherwise, or did not argue at all. One of the few that thought otherwise was Alfred Russel Wallace (1870), the co-founder of evolutionary theory. For modest scientific reasons and perhaps also with some religious reservations, Wallace declined to argue for the evolution of mind and gave reasons why. But he was in the minority amongst scientists. Aside from the Lamarckians, such as Spencer, who lost virtually every argument in the end, the most promising arguments came from those who argued that mind, human or animal, became what it is because the environment over the millennia of its evolution required it. The most modern representative of this view is Lorenz (1973) who, in his *Die Rückseite des Spiegels*, argues that cognitive operations have come to reflect environmental invariants characterizing the species' evolutionary trek over millions of years. By reflecting such invariants, mind came to serve an important biological function, namely, improved interactions with the environment.

With such notions, then, functionalism was born, as a large, less biologically educated subclass of evolutionists. Anticipations of functionalism appeared in Goethe and later Spencer, then blossomed in full form in the work of William James (1910), an enthusiastic Darwinist (amongst many other things). James was accompanied by his student, G. Stanley Hall, and Hall in turn by his student John Dewey. All three helped to set functionalism going in a very determined way. Following or accompanying these three pioneers were Angell, Judd, Woodworth, Yerkes, Carr, Robinson and others (see Boring 1922), all American, all interested in the pragmatics of behavior, and all psychologists. The idea was also expressed forcefully in philosophy by Alfred North Whitehead (1929) in The function of reason, where he eloquently argues that reason exists in order to 'promote the art of life', not only to help man live, but to help him live better. Today the function of intelligence is still being questioned but this time by those with more specific biological interests such as Humphrey (1976), who entertains the hypothesis that biological fitness is served by intelligence which has major origins in social behavior.

Before long it became clear that the functionalism of James and the rest had to pay the price of being an 'ism'. It was good on argument, was almost logical, had metaphysical appeal, and even made some plain sense, but it lacked an operational method and a strong desire to test itself. As Humphrey (1977) points out, the trouble with functional psychology was not that it was wrong but that it had no way of knowing that it could be wrong. Apart from Thorndike, who had a method with his cats-in-boxes trial and error paradigm, there was no attempt to develop a way of rigorously testing behavior for its biological function. Small wonder, then, that the test and laboratory workers, inspired by the achievements of Galton and Wundt, forged an impressive array of methods for prying open the empirical secrets of the structural nature of intelligence and the conditions affecting its expression. There was little competition to tempt them to do otherwise.

Laboratory and test methods are, of course, analytic. They require the setting up of ideal conditions for isolating variables. This frequently means creating highly artificial situations far removed from what the species under investigation are accustomed to. Instead of viewing animals as organisms adapting to environments, early psychologists began viewing them as manageable bundles of interesting secrets which, if approached correctly, would reveal general laws of the mind and behavior and how they were acquired.

For many years functionalists, mostly, psychologists, only went as far as insuring that the animal functioned in the laboratory or the human in front of a paper–pencil test. The function, or more correctly, the malfunction, of everyday behavior in humans was left up to psychiatrists, clinicians, school teachers, and workers with the retarded and handicapped. The important problem of intelligent human adaptation was, in other words, ignored by trained scientists and left up to practitioners who worked in clinics, schools, industrial settings, all far from the broad and interesting theories that were attempting to connect evolutionary theory (and much of biology, for that matter) to behavioral research (see Charlesworth 1973 for a discussion of ethology's role in bridging the gap between the latter and the former). The relationship between the human or animal and the natural environment was studied by a few splinter groups. But these groups were not totally dissociated from the gentle stigma attached to bird lovers or overly impressed parents who fondly observe their children and amass notebooks of information on them which, alas, no one reads. According to the rigorous, the content of such notebooks could never be considered scientific fact. Facts came from controlled settings and from the numbers that ultimately ensued from them. This was the case until only a few decades ago. Today, the scene has changed somewhat, though not radically. An untrained school teacher, physician, or parent is still not considered on a par with a trained observer when it comes to observing and recording behavior.

Forerunners

Fortunately, the reality of such a century of intelligence testing and speculation was not as one-sided as may appear from the above. Ever since testing and experimenting with intelligence got under way there were general concerns about whether scientific psychology had prematurely attempted to become like its very distant relatives, physics and chemistry, and not enough like its brother science, biology. As the intelligence testing movement itself got under way, concern began to develop about the appropriateness of using test situations in which predefined test items were used to diagnose level of intellectual functioning. One of the most concerned was William Stern (1920), a child psychologist of wide interests and great conceptual and methodological ability. Critically analyzing the concepts of intelligence current at the time, Stern concluded (as the functionalists and evolutionists had) that most such concepts ignored or minimized what he felt was the most distinctive feature of intelligence, namely, that it functioned to aid the individual to adjust to the problematic nature of his environment. In reality, Stern argued, intelligent behavior was frequently spontaneous, not only reactive as defined by test makers. Such behavior was also highly variable. Something in testing had to be done to allow such behavior to occur. However, if spontaneity were allowed, it would create serious scoring problems. Realizing this, Stern suggested an alternative, while not dropping testing completely. He suggested that the individual whose intelligence was being evaluated be observed by those around him in his everyday environment where spontaneous as well as reactive acts of intelligence occurred. Parents, teachers, caretakers, physicians – anyone around the child – would be trained in observing and recording or rating the child's intelligent behavior. As far as I am aware, this was a novel suggestion at the time and one which was never followed up in any serious way. Stern also differentiated between practical and theoretical intelligence, the former being much closer to, or identical with, the kinds of intellectual activities one engaged in while in daily interaction with the world. This distinction (also made by others) was tested out under the rubric of natural intelligence by Lipmann (1918) and Erich Stern (1919).

A second impulse that challenged existing research paradigms in psychology related to intelligence (and also to perception and learning) came in the work of Edward C. Tolman (1932). Tolman, classified by historians as a proponent of purpose behaviorism, tried to keep cognitive processes, means–ends (purposive) behavior, individual differences in learning capacities (intelligence), and in general, functional molar behaviors actively alive in the face of the great elementist, associationist orthodoxy of learning theory at the time. Tolman's relevance for an ethological approach to intelligent behavior is expressed in his notion of cognitive maps that animals have to construct in order to get important survival jobs done. These jobs were done by means of the maps and goal-direct behavior, both being directly responsible for the animal maintaining its equilibrium with its environment.

While not a direct intellectual descendant of Tolman, Egon Brunswik (1956) picked up on the concept of molar and purposive behavior and saw the main task of every animal as struggling for survival in a means–end way with its environment. In this respect Brunswik's approach had a distinct Darwinian flavor. The environment, though, was not as predictable or as stable as that in laboratories. It was a highly probabilistic one. Brunswik thus went one step farther than most Darwinian psychologists of his time by insisting that precise observations and measurements of the probabilistic environment be included in analyses of behavior and its determinants. Furthermore, he insisted that when the decision was made to do this, a 'representative design' acknowledging the probabilistic nature of the environment be employed ('representative design . . . is geared to the way in which situations occur in life', p. 139). In effect, Brunswik was asking researchers in learning, perception, and cognition to go out and laboriously collect representative samples of the animal's ecological situation – a big order, to say the least, but very necessary. In Brunswik's words: 'Needs toward ecological representativeness are so urgent, past neglect so drastic, and the inhibitions of tradition so powerful that our methodological watchword should be kept as sharply focused' (p. 139).

By insisting on adding purpose, cognitive maps and ecological representativeness to research designs – all of which can complicate research efforts – Tolman and Brunswik were bent upon keeping psychology in contact with the realm of everyday behavior. Whether they were right in feeling that the elementist, associationist trend in experimental psychology at the time was overdone and approaching the point of being counterproductive can be debated. Their effect on psychology was varied and in my estimation hardly commensurate with their promise, especially in the case of Brunswik.

A third trend that directly or indirectly called into question the deficiencies of conventional views of intelligence is represented by an unlikely cluster of two unrelated research approaches. The first of these is called the 'naive theory' approach represented by Fritz Heider (1958, see also Baldwin 1967). Heider claims that all humans have tacit theories about human behavior which they employ in everyday social interaction. These theories are built up on common-sense knowledge acquired from everyday personal experience, from imitating others, following the dictates of tradition as taught by parents, friends, teachers, figuring things out on one's own, etc. Such theories may be situation-specific and non-verbalizable, or quite general and expressable in such basic terms as 'want', 'can', 'benefit other', 'harm other' and so on. Common sense is very functional since it plays a major role in regulating social intercourse and dealing with everyday social problems.

The second approach is anthropological. It consists of collecting information on the social and practical behavior and achievements of different cultures. From this information it has become clear that man, wherever he is found, is more or less successful in adapting to his environment and part of this adaptation is achieved by the employment of cognitive skills in daily problem-solving situations. A good example of research into these skills can be found in Mason's (1966) account of the origins of invention in primitive peoples where a wide array of material evidence, eye witness accounts, and oral histories reveal the ingenuity of pre-industrial man in mastering his physical and social environment. An up-to-date account of intelligence in daily action can be found in Gladwin's *East is a big bird: navigation and logic on Puluwat Atoll* (1970), a detailed account of the skills and knowledge employed by the Puluwat people in building and navigating their great canoes in a very successful manner.

The common-sense and the anthropological approach have elements in common: both focus on intelligence in everyday action, both include reference to actual everyday situations or problems which elicit intelligent behavior, and both reveal the wealth of untutored intelligent acts that help man make his way through life. The approaches also differ in a number of ways – the common-sense approach is much more cognitively oriented and deals almost exclusively with social interaction; the latter is behaviorally and cognitively oriented and deals with physical and social problems, as well as with physical products of behavior.

Accompanying this trend there has also been a recent growing insistence amongst behavioral scientists that behavior has to be studied in natural contexts along with the ecological factors that affect it. While hardly a new idea, given the work of naturalist and ecological psychologists, the notion that behavior is the principal means whereby the animal regulates its interaction with its environment and is thereby involved in evolution needs constant repetition (Mayr 1970, Mason and Lott 1976, McGurk 1977). While this trend is present in human and animal psychology, it appears that, as far as intelligent behavior itself is concerned, emphasis on connections between intelligence and environmental factors is greater amongst those working with animals than with humans. Moynihan (1976), for example, discusses differences in intelligence between various primate species and how these differences appear to be related to variations in the species' habitat. Researchers working with humans who also recognize how behavior is connected to environmental demands usually come from anthropology or related disciplines. Klein (1973), in his *Ice-age hunters of the Ukraine*, for example, makes a very interesting interdisciplinary attempt to synthesize environmental (terrain, flora, fauna), climatic, and cultural factors to account for differences in adaptation between the Neanderthals and the *Homo sapiens* who eventually displaced them. Intelligence or intelligent behavior is inferred by Klein from differences in artifacts, dwellings, hunting patterns, etc.

Critique

To sum up, then, a century of intelligence research has been devoted to testing, experimental manipulation, some unsystematic observation, and much speculation about intelligence and its function in evolution. Unlike the extensive field observation research done in the area of social behavior by both psychologists and those working with animals, very little analogous work has been done in the area of intelligence. Why this has been the case is open to speculation. It could be historical accident that testing and laboratory investigation got under way so quickly in psychology – in light of the early success of physics, psychologists were anxious to prove that they, too, could deal with complex phenomena in a rigorous scientific fashion. Or it could be that the practical problems in observing and recording cognitive behavior in everyday action were intuitively recognized by early psychologists. Unless one knows something of a subject's history and the context variables that surround a particular cognitive act, most cognitive behavior is difficult to identify and interpret. Also, establishing the functional or adaptive significance of the behavior is even more difficult. Finally, it could be that cognitive behavior is such a common phenomenon in humans that it attracted no attention from psychologists, and is such an uncommon phenomenon amongst animal species that it was not considered worthwhile for special systematic investigation.

Whatever the case, the past century, as already noted, has produced only a partial picture of intelligence. The research approaches responsible for this partial picture have, in my opinion, run their course – at least temporarily. Most behavioral scientists, it appears, still do not heed Uexküll's (1957) argument that the cognitive accompaniment of behavior can be viewed functionally, that is as an important element in the behavior the animal uses to regulate interactions with its environment. In a review of Razran's *Mind in evolution* (1971), which deals with intelligence almost exclusively in terms of the first half approach, Thompson (1973) notes that 'Only when psychologists begin to apply mentalistic models in a functional context will we be able to truthfully entitle a book *Mind in Evolution*' (p. 405).

What is difficult to understand is that the testing approach still continues even though tests have proliferated beyond practical, as well as theoretical, control. As Horn (1976) in a recent review of the field points out, the major issue in the area of mental abilities continues to be one of specifying basic cognitive processes, even though these processes reflect intellectual capacities that are 'immensely varied', and 'the sheer complexity' of their variety is overwhelming. It should be clear by now that there most probably is no limit to what the human subject's brain can do in front of a test and that continued testing will just require increasingly more complicated statistical techniques for extracting order from test performance. What is feared is that such order may become increasingly remote from psychology's lexicon of working concepts as well as from behavior itself. The human brain is a very extravagant organ. It seems capable of responding to anything, sometimes very predictably, sometimes very unpredictably (if the stimulus is interesting enough), and it can put itself into the service of virtually anything that demands it to function – from creating personal illusional systems to building practical models of physical phenomena, constructing theories to justify political action, or satisfying test psychologists.

That the laboratory approach to animal behavior has continued in the old paradigm for so long without having relevance for understanding animal behavior in the natural habitat (Klopfer and Hailman 1967) is also difficult to understand. In a controversial article on the 'fall of comparative psychology', Lockhard (1971) challenges the comparative psychologists' laboratory approach on a number of points. Two are relevant here: first, comparative psychologists ignored evolution and genetics in their actual empirical work, and second, they established the laboratory as the only appropriate way to study animal behavior rigorously. The net result, Lockhard concluded, is a 'confused scatter of views of nature, problems, and methods'. While some may debate this conclusion, one certainly cannot argue that all is well in comparative laboratory research with animals. That things were not turning out well was anticipated about thirty years ago by Lashley (1949), who began seeing the weaknesses of conventional animal training studies. He noted that: 'Unless the experimenter has wide experience with the animals that he studies and adapts his questions to their modes of behavior, the results give little information about their true capacities. There are remarkably few comparative studies which are really significant for the evolution of behavior' (p. 28). Lashley was not asking for the abolition of the laboratory approach – that would be senseless. He was asking for pre-laboratory research that would give laboratory research more meaning and be less wasteful of time and resources.

In conferences held in 1955 and 1956 on the theme of behavior and evolution (see Roe and Simpson 1958), it became clear that there were two separate approaches to the study of animal behavior and there was no sign that they were converging. While discussing difficulties involved in using behavioral characteristics in systematics, Hinde and Tinbergen (1958) made it clear that 'the importance of a knowledge of the natural history of the animal and of the causation and function of the behavior cannot be overemphasized' (p. 265). At the same conference Harlow (1958), representing the laboratory–learning position, demonstrated little feeling for natural animal intelligence (that which is expressed in the natural habitat) and the need to know what it was before subjecting a particular species to laboratory tests of learning ability. In establishing a scale of tasks for cross-species comparisons, Harlow used as criteria of difficulty both logic and information based on the 'ontogenetic development in the higher animals'. He apparently took no cues from naturalists or ethologists as to what constitutes a problem for a specific species in the wild. If he had, he would have immediately discarded the notion of a common scale. The position of the animal in the phyletic scale, he felt, was related to the complexity of the problems it could solve, not realizing, apparently, that scaling species in terms of ability without taking into account their particular environmental adaptations makes little sense, as Hodos and Campbell (1969) convincingly point out. Furthermore, Harlow was 'puzzled by the fact that the study of animals under laboratory conditions reveals many learning capabilities whose existence is hard to understand in terms of survival value' (p. 273). While this is a very interesting puzzle, and one that much earlier had bothered Wallace (1870; he maintained that the brain is programmed with abilities far out of proportion to what selection pressures could ever have demanded), it is just as interesting that Harlow did not call into question the utility of the laboratory approach given the state of the field at the time. He, himself, pointed out that 'It is a common error to fail to differentiate between capability and achievement' (p. 278). He needed to go only one step further to perceive that the laboratory study of mammals, especially primates (because of their happy superabundance of cortical matter), is bound to demonstrate just how extravagant the brain can be in demonstrating its capabilities. If comparative psychologists had heeded the Hinde and Tinbergen message, the field would be quite different today. The same can be said for intelligence testing in humans.

In discussing the function of reasoning, Whitehead (1929) noted that 'The main evidence that a methodology is worn out comes when progress within it no longer deals with main issues. There is a final epoch of endless wrangling over minor questions' (p. 18). This, in my estimation, describes the current state of our knowledge of intelligence. A new epoch is on the way or should be on the way. What is needed in intelligence research is a daring act of parsimony – one that would provide a relatively simple but powerful theory which would help to structure research conceptually with a minimum of confusion and abstraction, as well as provide a few simple methodological guidelines.

Ethology to the rescue

Ethology for some of us may no longer be definable as a particularly distinctive research approach to the study of behavior. So many diverse researchers today are labeling their work ethological that the field seems to have lost the boundaries it had twenty or forty years ago. Nevertheless, from the undifferentiated view granted to a newcomer, ethological research still has at least two distinctive features which in combination set it off from other behavioral and social sciences. The first feature is ethology's commitment to the synthetic theory of evolution as being the most reasonable way to organize our thinking about the historical origins and evolution of behavior, as well as helping to structure research into the nature, function, and development of current behavior. The second feature is ethology's commitment to account for animal behavior as it occurs and develops in the natural habitat. This commitment requires that naturalistic observation and description be the predominant methodology during the early phases of research, especially when the animal's behavioral repertoire and environment are not well known. Laboratory studies, of course, would be predominant in later phases.

Evolutionary theory

The commitment to evolutionary theory requires that we put all behavior, including that controlled by cognitive processes, into a single very large picture containing all conceivable elements of behavior and their determinants. In this sense the theory is truly synoptic. This picture, ideally, includes information on the animal's ancestors and living relatives and their environment, the current environmental and stimulus conditions that release and regulate the behavior, the various maturational and experiential factors that account for its ontogenesis, the neurophysiological mechanisms underlying it, and the genetic factors that condition it. All these elements are necessary to complete the picture and all are logically interlocked with one another in the sense that information on any one element should not contradict information on any other element. If contradiction occurs, it is assumed that there is a logical or methodological error somewhere – an error in reasoning, inadequate sampling of subjects or stimulus conditions, a failure to obtain adequate observer reliability, ambiguous protocol terminology, etc. The error is not in the animal and its environment; they do not contradict themselves or each other, only researchers do.

Such a super theory has many strengths and weaknesses which cannot be gone into here. Two of the former, though, will be mentioned briefly because they have been relevant in the construction of the present approach to intelligence. The first strength of the theory is that it provides the researcher with a set of general concepts – e.g. selection pressure, adaptation, survival, and reproductive success – which, as simple, general, and imprecise as they may be, are excellent conceptual tools for generating assumptions and hypotheses for empirical test. These concepts are not just operable within natural sciences domains. They are also useful, as Toulmin (1972), for example, has demonstrated, in dealing with such complex symbolic phenomena as conceptual change in the history of science. When projected upon a behavioral domain such as intelligence these concepts have a profound liberating effect. In the case of intelligence research, they expose the full meaning of the term intelligence, which came to be concealed over the years by a dominant research paradigm. It is noteworthy in this respect that Piaget's liberating impact on the study of intelligence was partly due to his use of the concept adaptation which he imported from his background in biology.

The second strength of the theory is its tacit insistence upon keeping interactions between the animal and its environment as the primary focus of research. This may sound like an odd virtue to ethologists trained in biology. But for most psychologists, subject–environment interaction, while routinely acknowledged as important, has not been a serious object of empirical research. This brings us to ethology's second commitment.

Naturalistic observation

Ethology's second commitment, to naturalistic observation, rests on a deeper commitment to the epistemological position ('critical realism' for want of a better term) that acknowledges that there is a real world outside of us and that as clever humans we can acquire reliable knowledge of this world, providing we are careful, systematic, and flexible in our observation of it. This knowledge, while always incomplete and potentially erroneous, nevertheless allows us as scientists to make better-than-chance predictions in the long run and also provides great satisfaction. This commitment implies that it is by description, as detailed, perfect, and comprehensive as ethologists can make it to suit their needs, that ethology stands or falls as an empirical science.

It is true that in the minds of many modern philosophers realism, as an epistemological position, has been obliterated by the latest thinking and all but buried. Many philosophers are convinced that scientific objectivity is a self-deception (it lives off the 'myth of the given'), that man constructs his knowledge rather than discovers it, and that the idea of mapping the real world on the basis of observation is naively erroneous because there can never be consensus on what is real (see Gunnell 1975 for a good discussion of this). These and similar claims have been made with great industry over past decades and have succeeded in annihilating, in some minds, the whole observational foundation upon which logical empiricism and behaviorism rest. Most practicing scientists, however, are not aware of this annihilation. They blindly and gradually go about cracking open nature's secrets one after the other and, apparently, are having a good time doing it.

There is a Chinese proverb which claims: 'It is easier to draw a goblin than a horse.' This proverb says much, especially about some areas in the behavioral and social sciences. Drawing horses is a tough business, maybe because everyone knows what a good horse looks like, or thinks they do. Drawing a goblin – well, anyone's goblin is about as good as anyone else's, although it is probably true that there is some weak consensus that prescribes what a good goblin should look like. Depicting the everyday behavior of a horse is even more difficult than drawing a horse. But it has to be done. Ethograms have to be written, otherwise animal behavior does not exist scientifically. That there are language problems with writing ethograms, and problems of obtaining inter-observer reliability is hardly to be denied. But muddling through with them is better than not writing ethograms at all.

Ethology, then, comes to the rescue by making these two offerings to the study of human behavior – evolutionary theory as a conceptual framework and naturalistic observation and description as the main methodological approach, propaedeutic to (not replacing) testing and experimenting. In this manner ethology can help prepare the new epoch mentioned above for the study of human intelligence in particular and human behavior in general. The act of parsimony required to cut through the 'wrangling over minor questions', noted by Whitehead when he discussed worn-out methods in science, can now be carried out by those who feel that evolutionary theory is simple, broad, and flexible enough to be tried out on all aspects of animal and human behavior.

Ethology and intelligent behavior

Before going into a specific empirical study involving the application of ethology to the investigation of human intelligence, a few words must be said in transition. The study is based on the assumption that most behavior serves various survival functions directly or indirectly. Intelligent behavior is no exception. Such behavior can be defined tentatively as problem-directed behavior which an observer has reason to believe is guided by cognitive processes. Problems can be defined as external or internal barriers to behavior. Both definitions will be expanded upon below. Whether every intelligent behavior functions to serve survival and is successful at doing it is not crucial for the definition. We assume (somewhat circularly) that intelligent behavior did aid survival over evolution – that the gene complexes responsible for the brain mechanisms generating such behavior were selected for positively by certain environmental factors during evolution because the behavior itself contributed to reproductive success.

It should be quickly pointed out that defining intelligent behavior as problem-directed behavior is a standard one in psychology and does not flow from ethology. The ethological twist to it comes in exploiting the implications of the term 'problem' in the definition. Its presence moves the ethologist to raise a number of interesting questions: what actually constitutes specific survival problems for an animal that require intelligent behavior rather than some other kind of behavior, and how can such problems be identified, recorded, and classified? How exactly does a problem threaten individual survival, development, and reproductive success? How frequently do problems arise in the life of the animal? What are problems associated with in the animal's social and physical environment? These questions move intelligence from the cage into the animal's natural habitat; they shift the focus from intelligence as a disposition to intelligence as a behavior. They also challenge those who speculate that intelligence is an evolutionary product by asking them for evidence of the environmental conditions that specifically put selection pressure on animal species to be more intelligent. Claiming, for example, that the Pleistocene climate contributed greatly to the rapid evolution of human intelligence is an interesting hypothesis, but not based on empirical evidence that demonstrates exactly what selective pressures were involved and what the specific behaviors were that such pressures elicited.

In short, there are many new questions and some old unanswered questions that are raised once intelligence is viewed as a behavioral phenomenon serving the animal in its everyday environment (an idea which is hardly new). As noted above, naturalists, evolutionists, and functionalists were all well aware of this and at least the first two had influence on the development of ethological thinking. None of them, though, had all the elements put together into what I would like to claim is the ethological approach with a bit of cognitive psychology thrown in.

An observational study

The study to be reported below is the first of what I hope will be a series of studies of intelligent behavior in natural settings. Part of the general strategy guiding this series will be briefly mentioned here.

General strategy

At a very general level this strategy is similar to Lorenz's (1971) method of 'analysis on a broad front'. Using the analogy of a Martian trying to understand a moving automobile, Lorenz proposes that the most effective strategy is to obtain a picture of each of the major parts and how they function with each other, a process which requires that the observer attempt to get a broad view of the whole system before going into a detailed analysis of each part and its function. Such an attempt may at first be disorderly and unsystematic and hence reveal only provisional ideas of what the significant parts are and how they function. Over time, though, a more accurate and detailed picture is built up and the system becomes more intelligible. Only then would a detailed analysis of the parts and their functioning principles be meaningful. If Lorenz's strategy had been applied to intelligence research forty odd years ago, when modern ethology was just getting under way, chances are very great that our understanding of intelligence would be much further advanced today.

This approach also proceeds on a broad and general front. Using a highly general definition of intelligence, it requires going out into the field and getting a broad picture (with individual details) of intelligence in action. To structure this rather undiscriminating inductive approach, a set of general rules has been developed.

Briefly these rules are as follows. (1) Focus on observing individuals in their natural habitats. As Paul Weiss (1949) once said: 'The only scientific way to deal with adaptation is to get the facts for each case.' (2) Obtain as varied a sample as possible of the individual's activities, and the settings in which they take place, and observe a sufficient number of different individuals of a predefined population until the findings become redundant – at a general level, at least. (3) Observe each individual longitudinally – before, during, and after transitional periods of development, if a child – or over an 'extended' period of time, if an adult. (4) Record the environmental conditions antecedent and consequent to the target behavior (intelligent behavior) with no less enthusiasm than that given to the target behavior itself. (5) Establish behavior and environmental observation units that are theoretically relevant as well as methodologically feasible. (6) Be prepared to add, subtract, or modify observation units if the facts call for it. (7) Do not attempt to establish criteria of success or failure for intelligent behavior until all behaviors, or classes of them (for a particular population of subjects), are correlated with established criteria of successful adaptation such as survival, normal developmental progress, good health, success in school, on the job and in the community, personal happiness, reproductive success and professional productivity.

Let us turn now to the first study.

Definitions

The target of this study is intelligent behavior as already defined – problem-directed behavior (for a more detailed report of this study, see Charlesworth *et al.* 1976). The crux of the definition centers on what is meant by a problem. There is no need to go into depth to demonstrate that problems range across common everyday phenomena – from dealing with social interruptions, planning one's life goals, opening a bottle without an opener available, forgetting someone's name, controlling impulses, trying to express one's thoughts in a letter. In all instances, ongoing behavior is disrupted by someone or something, or there is a deficit, a need or want for something that is not available.

On the basis of narrative records of approximately a thousand problem situations observed in seven preschool children, it was possible to give dimensions to the problem universe in two ways: (1) in terms of observed instances of impositions on the individual or resistance to the individual's behavior versus observed–inferred instances of needs or wants on the part of the individual due to the absence of something or some person, and (2) in terms of the content of the impositions or needs, content being divided into social, physical, and cognitive. These dimensions yield, then, six separate categories as indicated in figure 1. These categories are useful in helping us organize our thinking about the problem universe in general. All instances of problems involve a block of the individual's ongoing behavior – the mother tells the child to stay seated (an observed social imposition on the individual); the juice glass is out of reach and the child wants juice (an inferred physical need and the observed gap between the child and the juice); someone seeks information from the child (an observed request for information, hence for a cognitive response). In all instances problems define a relationship between the subject and the environment, either being resistant to or deficient for the other, thus creating an imbalance between them. This relationship results in a block to ongoing behavior. For this reason we emphasize the block in our expanded definition of behavior – a problem is essentially a block which disrupts ongoing behavior. After we formulated this definition, we discovered that Fawl (1963), from the Kansas ecological psychology team of Barker and Wright *et al.*, collected instances (from day-long specimen records) involving unpleasant disruptions of ongoing experiences. This is very similar to our approach, but we include all disruptions, not only those which strike the observer as unpleasant. Block-directed behavior in the present scheme, therefore, is what is normally called problem-solving behavior. We felt that block-directed was more accurate, to emphasize the notion of a block and to avoid the term 'solving' because in many instances no problem solving takes place.

Given these definitions, it was possible for us to construct a model of a problem and the problem-solving process which helps us organize data for statistical analysis. This model, as can be seen in figure 2, contains five major elements (in rectangles) with repetitions of two elements, along with external interventions (circles). These five major elements (plus the others when appropriate) are recorded on the spot by the observer or derived afterward from the observer's narrative record of the problem. So far the model accounts for over 800 problems or over 2000 blocks, the former being defined as one block or an aggregate of two or more blocks having a common theme.

Intelligent behavior, as already noted, is defined here as problem-solving behavior with cognition behind it. This was originally done to

	Social	Physical	Cognitive
Observed (imposition, resistance)	**1** Mother tells child to stay seated (B); child says: 'No!' (R) Granting agency rejects grant applications (B); scientist writes another application (R)	**2** Child tries to open jar, fails (B); persists in trying to turn jar cap (R), cries (R), calls mother (R) Begins to rain while recording field observations (B); scientist curses (R), leaves field (R)	**3** Sister asks child where she put crayons (B); child says: 'Under the pillow' (R) Animal under observation makes unusual response to ordinary stimulus (B); scientist puzzles for two weeks (R)
Observed/ Inferred (need, want)	**4** Child and mother looking at book (B); child asks mother to turn pages (R) Scientist finishes first draft of paper (B); asks colleague to read it (R)	**5** Child in highchair; juice glass on counter out of reach (B); child reaches for glass and fails (R), calls for mother (R) Scientist lacks protocol forms for field observation (B); calls assistant, asks him to bring them (R)	**6** Mother and child looking at animal cards (B); child asks mother name of animal pictured (R) Scientist forgets technical term (B); consults dictionary (R)

1. Categories and examples of blocks (B) and block-related responses (R) observed in a real two-year-old child and fantasized in an unreal scientist.

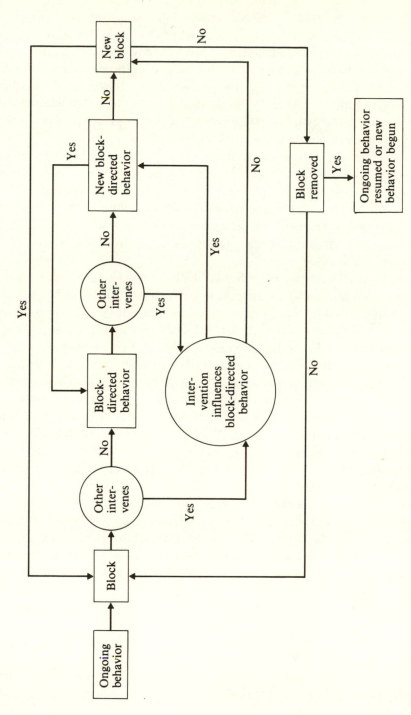

2. Model of the problem-solving process.

exclude the standard list of 'automatic' behaviors (reflexes, tropisms, fixed action patterns) which do not appear to be learned or under cognitive control and are usually listed as instinctive in contrast to intelligent. Early in the study we found it difficult to infer cognition in many instances and hence settled for any responses directed toward the block. We then gradually shifted to using the block itself as the criterion of whether we would record the event or not. Settling on how cognitive the responses were, we reasoned, could be done afterward.

In the pilot studies we noticed that what appeared to be cognitive at one age for a child was not at a later age. At the early age the child seemed to struggle and show signs of delay and cognitive involvement with a response which later became spontaneous and quite routine. If this is truly the case, then we may have a standard way of tracing the growth of intelligence over ontogenesis, and possibly even across some other species of animals.

In the actual study we recorded all block-directed responses (and even those which did not seem immediately directed towards the block, such as ignoring it). This strategy then forced us to rest our whole approach on the observer's ability to detect blocks. What exactly a block was had to be made clear – any disruption of ongoing behavior? This would encompass a good chunk of the behavioral universe. It would include simple visual or auditory distraction, sneezing, falling, an itching sensation in the scalp. We asked ourselves whether these were problems, and the answer was that it depends on the circumstances. If one's nose itches and one's hands happen to be filled with a tray of dishes it could be a problem. This is a weakness of the method, but we decided to stay in the field and see how many of these instances occurred. The flexible inductive approach has its comfortable compensations.

A second weakness of our scheme was in dealing with purely cognitive problems. An individual could have such a problem, sit quietly with his eyes closed for a few minutes, and solve it, and the observer would never have an inkling of what happened. We decided that when the observer believed that this was the case, the individual could be asked afterward. The human ethologist always accommodates to the properties of the species under investigation.

Method

This study was preceded by a pilot study during which the observational methods were tested and a preliminary short-term longitudinal study conducted involving 180 observation hours of four normal, white middle class children while they were between twenty months and four years of age.[2] Children of this age were chosen because they are less complicated than older children but are still capable of relatively unambiguous instrumental behavior compared to younger children. The problem category scheme and the problem-solving model, plus the development of protocol sheets and the training of new observers, were carried out on these four children. Percentages of inter-observer agreement as to the occurrence and nature of problems were calculated for observers across seventy hours of actual data-gathering observation (one pair at a time). Inter-observer agreement for the four pairs was 75%, 81%, 83%, and 86% with an overall mean of 81%.

The subjects in the study itself were two white, middle class girls, a Down's Syndrome girl, twenty-two months old, with a Bayley Score of 75, and a normal girl of the same age with a Bayley Score of 132 (Bayley Scores are derived from the Bayley Scales of Infant Development designed to measure motor and mental developmental progress during the first two years – see Bayley 1969). The choice of two children differing widely in intellectual performance was deliberate for a number of reasons. Each child was observed by two of the trained observers for sixteen hours, sampling each waking hour at least once, on seven separate days across an approximately two week period during the winter months. Simultaneous observations were made by two observers for six of the sixteen hours. The two observers agreed on 274 out of 331 problems (83% agreement) which means that both observers recorded the same block in the same period and the same block-related response. The actual data-gathering observation period was preceded by three to four hours during which the family and the observer became acquainted and the child learned to refrain from relating to the observer.

In addition to recording in narrative form all instances in which a problem occurred (event-sampling), on-the-minute checks were made of whether the child was engaged in non-problem behavior (time-sampling). The latter included twelve categories: playing, interacting socially, locomoting toward a goal, looking intently (excluding casual, 'normal looking'), caring for body, dressing, attempting to acquire an object, self-stimulating, toileting, eating, doing nothing (including aimless activity), and unknown. Inter-observer agreement on these categories ranged from 84% to 89%.

---

[2] Versions of this study and some of its findings can also be found in Charlesworth 1978a.

Results

The everyday problems of the two children constituted 8% of the total observation time of the Down's child and 16% of the normal child's time (table 1). The former experienced 814 blocks, or one block on the average every 1.2 min.; the latter experienced 1350 blocks or one block on the average every 0.7 min. Average time spent on a single problem was 14 sec. for the Down's child and 18 sec. for the normal child. This gives some idea of what a child is up against when trying to get through a normal day.

Table 1. *Frequencies of problems and blocks and time spent on problems for the Down's Syndrome (DS) child and normal control child (N)*

	DS	N
I. *Problems and blocks*		
Frequency of problems	328	535
frequency of blocks (one problem can include more than one block)	814	1350
ratio of problems to blocks	0.40	0.40
II. *Time spent on problems*		
Total of observation time (960 min.) spent on problems	77 min.	155 min.
% of total observation time spent on problems	8	16
Average time spent on a single problem	14 sec.	18 sec.
Range of time spent on problems	2 sec. to 6½ min.	2 sec. to 4 min. 6 sec.
One problem occurs on the average every	2.9 min.	1.8 min.
One block occurs on the average every	1.2 min.	0.7 min.

Table 2 gives us an idea of what kinds of problems or blocks the child faces. The overwhelming majority of blocks were social (86% and 89% for Down's and normal child, respectively). Over 99% of these were impositions made on the child by someone else, usually the mother. In less than 1% did the child want the other to do something.

Physical blocks occurred infrequently – 2% in the case of the Down's child, 6% in the case of the normal. Unlike the social blocks, the majority of physical blocks were needs or wants involving unavailable objects or failing to deal adequately with gravity.

Table 2. *Frequencies and percentage of classes of blocks*

	DS		N	
	f	%	f	%
I. *Three major classes of blocks*				
Social	702	86	1208	89
Physical	13	2	80	6
Cognitive	89	11	51	4
Unknown (child cries, screams for unknown reason)	10	1	11	1
TOTAL	814		1350	
II. *Subclasses of social blocks*				
Observed (imposition)				
Other makes prohibitive demands	176	25	355	29
Other demands that child does something	220	31	345	28
Other asks child to do something	18	2	41	3
Other non-verbally blocks child (physical threat, force, takes away object, disrupts child's activity)	210	30	245	20
Other makes an ambiguous statement which could be considered as a blocking condition ('You should play outside.' 'Wait just a minute.')	71	10	173	14
Other asks child rhetorical question ('Why did you do that?')	4	<1	16	1
Other scolds or spanks child	2	<1	4	<1
Other refuses to do something for child	0	0	18	1
Inferred (need)				
Child wants other to do something	1	<1	11	1
TOTAL	702		1208	
III. *Subclasses of physical blocks*				
Observed (imposition)				
Object blocks gross movement	1	—	5	6
Object cannot be manipulated, handled, etc.	4	—	6	7
Inferred (need)				
Object unavailable or prohibited	5	—	55	69
Instances of child slipping, falling, dropping objects, etc.	3	—	14	18
TOTAL	13		80	
IV. *Subclasses of cognitive blocks*				
Observed (imposition)				
Other demands child to say something	14	16	13	25
Other asks child to say something	8	9	3	6
Other asks child to identify something	48	54	1	2
Other seeks information from child	19	21	31	60
Inferred (need)				
Child seeks information	0	0	3	6
TOTAL	89		51	

Cognitive blocks constitute 11% of the Down's child's total blocks and 4% of the normal child's. The vast majority of these blocks for both children consisted of the mother demanding or asking the child to say or identify something, or seeking information from the child. That the Down's child had almost three times more cognitive blocks than the normal was due to a training program undertaken by the mother to help the child learn.

The child's responses to the blocks can be found in table 3. As expected, the overwhelming majority of the child's block-directed responses are social. Of these, over a third involve complying (partially or completely) with impositions. Ignoring the impositions is the second most frequent response for both children.

Physical responses constitute a very small percentage of the total, and cognitive responses even smaller. The undefined category of 'other responses', most of which appear to be non-instrumental, occur more frequently than the physical or cognitive.

It was not possible at the time of writing this paper to connect block-directed behavior with results. However, it was possible to calculate overall percentages of instances in which blocks were removed. Table 4 reveals that the Down's child was successful 36% of the time in removing the block and the normal child 41% of the time. In many cases this meant that the child did not comply with the imposition either by ignoring it, or by engaging in another activity, all of which resulted in the imposition no longer being repeated. Most of the time, though, the block was not removed. The child complied.

Problem outcomes revealed that only a little less than a third of the time did the children resume doing what they were doing before the interruption occurred. Others intervening in the problem-solving episode occurred in 6% of the episodes for the Down's child and 11% for the normal child.

Discussion

These, then, are the results from our first attempt to apply the ethological approach to the study of early intelligent behavior in two humans. Whether this attempt can be classed as a true member of research *Ethologus humanus* probably will have to be left up to some journal editor. Many traditions are reflected in it – the naturalist, the functionalist, the evolutionist, the cognitive psychologist and a bit of the ecological

Table 3. *Frequencies and percentages of block-related responses*

		DS		N	
		f	%*	f	%
I.	*Four major classes of responses*				
	Social	428	83	965	79
	Physical	15	3	42	4
	Cognitive	1	—	31	2
	Other	67	13	174	14
	TOTAL	511	99	1212	99
II.	*Social responses*				
	Verbal attempts to get other to respond	0	—	82	7
	Non-verbal attempts to get other to respond	29	6	33	3
	Ignores other, continues own activity	79	15	216	18
	Ignores other, changes own behavior	20	4	69	6
	Ignores other, does nothing	72	14	83	9
	Refuses to comply	0	—	23	2
	Complies	214	42	430	35
	Partially complies	14	3	29	2
	TOTAL	428	84	965	82
III.	*Physical responses*				
	Uses force	0	—	2	—
	Uses tool	0	—	—	—
	Uses whole body	1	—	2	—
	Uses arms	6	1	15	1
	Accidental movement or observer uncertain	8	2	23	2
	TOTAL	15	3	42	3
IV.	*Cognitive responses*				
	Asks for information	0	—	1	—
	Answers question	1	—	27	2
	Searches for object	0	—	3	—
	TOTAL	1	—	31	2
V.	*Other responses*				
	Irrelevant behavior	10	2	76	6
	Aimless activity	0	—	2	—
	Positive emotion	3	—	2	—
	Negative emotion	46	9	72	6
	Ceases to cry or babble	8	2	22	2
	TOTAL	67	13	174	14

* Percentages approximate due to rounding off

psychologist. Nevertheless, I would never have made such an attempt if I had not become interested in ethology.

Whether this attempt can be defended as having anything to do with intelligence can probably also be challenged. The children's problems, for the most part, seem a long way from intelligence test items; the same can

Table 4. *Results, outcome, and other-intervention (in percentages)*

	DS	N
Result		
Percentage of total number of blocks removed	36	41
Outcome		
Percentage of episodes in which behavior prior to block was resumed	31	28
Other-intervention		
Approximate percentage of episodes in which other intervened in the problem-solving process	6	11

be said for their responses. Here again it may be more of a question of expanding or contracting definitions. It seems reasonable to expand the definition to include the child's everyday problem-solving behavior, whether the behavior reflects complex cognitive processes or not. Surely such behavior is not unrelated to general intelligence as we commonly understand it. In the three-year-old children we observed we discovered recognizable examples of complex problem solving that lasted minutes and others that lasted seconds. The method, in other words, detects the long, interesting problems as well as the short ones. Unlike most tests, which throw out a small net with a small mesh, the present method throws out a big net with a small mesh and thereby catches many small fish. Herein, of course, lies a big problem of effort and cost. The net gets awfully heavy very quickly.

One could argue that the method has a built-in sampling bias because it only obtains data when the individual and the environment are not in harmony: the more harmony between the two, the less data. To put it briefly, the method would not work in paradise. The problem of cross-individual comparisons when problem sample sizes vary considerably has not been grappled with yet.

With the present two children it is interesting, nevertheless, to get a view of how problematic the world is for both of them and how they react to it. What is surprising is that so many of the problems for both of them are social and so few physical and cognitive. Preliminary analysis of data from other children reveals the same results. If one discounts most of the social problems (e.g. a parent demanding the child to stop doing something) as legitimate challenges to intelligence, then the number of problems that appear to be intellectually challenging drops to a very small percentage. This is interesting when one considers intellectual growth at this age. Earlier data collected on similar age children when faced with different tool-using tasks, some fairly complicated, revealed that the children were able to solve many of the tasks even though it appears that the average child has very few opportunities to do so at home. A straight reinforcement theory would have trouble with these data.

The fact that both children remove a little more than one third of all the blocks that come their way is interesting, along with the fact that blocks bring to a more or less permanent halt over two thirds of ongoing behavior. Furthermore, it is interesting that while the two children differ in the total number of problems they experience, the kinds of blocks they experience are quite similar. The same can be said for most of their responses to the blocks. At this age significant differences between the two children in the bulk of their behavior appear to be almost non-existent. A content analysis of the responses in terms of various criteria – complexity, ingenuity, etc. – still has to be made. Conclusions about early differences or similarities between Down's Syndrome children and normal children obviously cannot be reached. The N is too small, the children may not have been equally matched on all variables (except, of course, IQ), etc.

It was not possible by the time this was written to follow up both children longitudinally as Rule 3 of the strategy requires. Such a follow-up will be valuable for a number of obvious reasons. With longitudinal data it will be possible, given adequate sampling, to trace changes in the child's problem-solving behavior in reference to particular kinds of problems. A tentative scheme for working this out has been drawn up. Secondly, it will be possible to connect such changes to standard indices of adaptational success. Thirdly, and perhaps most importantly, it will be possible to shed a bit more light on the role of experience in the development of intelligence. This role has been championed vigorously by James McVicker Hunt (1961) in *Intelligence and experience*, but no convincing concrete evidence is available that shows specifically how environmental influences are directly implicated in the growth of intelligence. Most data are correlational and based on gross categories. The present data would not, in my opinion, shed any new light on the nature–nurture issue in intelligence that primarily interests Hunt.

Substantive questions can be raised as to what the findings of such a study would be like with older children or children in a school setting (many more cognitive blocks and cognitive responses?), with children living in a slum, rural setting, or preliterate society (many more physical problems?).

'Validations and extensions'

A number of attempts have been undertaken to validate the present problem-solving model as a method of analyzing both other types of protocols, and other samples of children observed in other situations besides the home. Spiker (1977) conducted a study similar to that above with six three- to four-year-old children in a preschool setting and found it possible to use the present method to observe and record problem episodes. A pilot study conducted in collaboration with a student mother of two gifted children concentrated on the former recording the latter's day-to-day questioning and information-seeking behavior (mostly category 6, some category 3). Results show that it is possible to have parents unobtrusively observe and record at least two categories of their children's problems and problem-solving behavior. Inter-observer reliability in this study, however, could not be obtained.

In a third pilot study, parents with disturbed children attended a clinic and between clinic visits observed and recorded their children's problematic behavior (for the parents, mostly at home). Results show that the method is operationally feasible, but here again no inter-observer agreement could be reliably obtained.

As part of a workshop on observational methods conducted at the Child Psychiatry Department of the Max Planck Institute for Psychiatry in Munich, a number of attempts were made to apply the present method to video records of children in problematic situations and to protocol information collected by others. A video tape of a child working with his mother on school homework was analyzed independently of, and compared with, an analysis using procedures from *Das Münchner Training-modell* (Innerhofer 1977). Results revealed a high degree of overlap in the ability of both methods to detect and describe specific problem situations in the stream of behavior interaction between child and parent. A comparative analysis of a 'Practice Scenario' (from Wahler, House and Stambaugh 1976) used to train observers to carry out an ecological assessment of child problem behavior in home, school, and institutional settings, also revealed a high degree of overlap between both methods in detecting and describing problems in children. A reverse analysis – using Wahler *et al.*'s method on a protocol obtained using the present method – revealed the same degree of overlap. However, the present method, because of its breadth, detected additional problems not detected by Innerhofer and Wahler *et al.*

General implications

In a number of other papers I have attempted to apply this approach to the study of the educational process and assessment (Charlesworth 1972, Charlesworth and Spiker 1975, Charlesworth and Bart 1976). However, in making such an attempt it became clear that the concept of intelligent behavior as a mode of adaptation and the present method for putting this concept into operation also have general relevance for practice and research. The concept can conceivably be applied to such areas as psychiatry, clinical psychology, work with the retarded, etc., where cognitively guided adaptive behavior is a goal, but where few, if any, adequate theories and methods exist for conceptually and procedurally hardening the treatment and training process. Apart from behavior modification (the present approach can incorporate it) which has a very powerful methodology but limited theoretical basis, there are few paradigms available to bridge theory and practice. For example, in discussing human coping (adaptive) behavior, Lazarus, Averill and Opton (1974) note that 'Progress in the development of an adequate psychology of coping is unlikely to be rapid until a theoretically based system of classification for coping acts has been evolved, linked to more general psychology theory, and tied to observable antecedents and consequences' (p. 259). The present approach, with its diffuse grounding in evolutionary theory – a much more general theory than any found in psychology – can, nevertheless, contribute concretely toward an operational definition of coping acts and their classification. In short, evolutionary theory can connect with everyday human behavior in a very relevant way. The applied setting, actually, is the only setting where theoretically guided naturalistic observation and experimentation by direct intervention can ethically be carried out with humans. In other words, ethology may well find its ultimate experimental test in medical and educational institutions. Actually, on a more general level, it can be argued that ethology's joint commitment to field research on one hand and to controlled laboratory research on the other makes it a perfect linking discipline between pure and applied behavioral sciences (Charlesworth 1973).

Weaknesses and limits

It is difficult to get a full perspective of the weaknesses and limits of one's own approach. This perspective is best gained from others at conferences. From my perspective, there are at least two major categories of weaknesses and limits – one conceptual, one methodological. As for the former, this approach may well have problems, but they are difficult to see at present. A conceptual limit is best tested empirically while a conceptual weakness based on lack of facts or a distorted view of them or of alternate conceptual schemes can best be demonstrated by others.

The methodological weaknesses of the present approach are more obvious. One weakness is in identifying problems or blocks reliably. As already noted, an interruption of behavior constitutes a block, but what constitutes an interruption? Is it possible that an interruption under one circumstance qualifies as a block and under another circumstance does not? The answer is yes, and in some such circumstances the response to the interruption is used to make a distinction between the two. But there are troubles with this. Sometimes responses are neither quick and smoothly automatic nor long and halting. They are intermediate, in a gray area which observers find troublesome. For example, a child sees a juice glass on the counter, begins reaching for it, perceives that he will not get it unless he makes a postural change. He makes the change immediately, continues his reach, and succeeds in getting the glass. Is this a problem? In a way it is, since his ongoing behavior was blocked (we assume by his perception that the distance to the glass was too great) and his response to alter his posture was the block-directed response. His change in behavior suggested he had a problem. But the change happened very quickly, almost imperceptibly, and with almost no difficulty on the part of the child. He demonstrated a routine way of handling such a problem, a way which may not have been routine earlier. He had to learn it. Such instances have caused our observers much trouble and hence lowered inter-observer agreement.

A second methodological weakness deals with sampling. Is it possible to get a representative sample of subjects and subjects' behavior when the observer has to be present in the subjects' everyday setting? Usually not; it depends on the subject. Young children do not seem to be affected by the observer. Our experience is that a rather small percentage of parents are willing to participate in such research under such conditions. We have no idea about observing adults. Much, though, depends on the setting. If the observations are made in the home, there are bigger problems of getting a representative sample than if they are made in the school, in the work setting, or in other public places. But even in public settings obtaining consent to participate in research is rapidly becoming necessary for researchers, at least in the US. Getting consent touches on the issue of whether being aware of the researcher will bias behavior. Current feeling is that human ethology can only be carried out with infants, young children, who usually lose their self-consciousness quickly, or individuals who do not know they are being filmed or observed. Eibl-Eibesfeldt's angle-lens camera was built to handle this problem (Eibl-Eibesfeldt and Hass 1966). There are ways, of course, to reduce the effects of this bias – for example, by participant observation – but this technique also has its problems.

A third problem is one involving the great deal of effort and time that goes into such field research. Is it worth it? Is not observing intelligent behavior in the natural setting similar to using an elephant to crack a walnut? As training our observers has shown, just getting the elephant to stand over the walnut with an educated foot is a big problem. From an intelligent tester's point of view, it is also a very legitimate problem. We can argue, though, that the testers' goals are very different from ours. Usually, testers want to elucidate the structure of intellect or predict subsequent or adjacent performance. The goal of our approach is to get a picture of intelligence in action. One could use parts of this picture afterward to help generate items for intelligence tests if desired. This may not however, justify the cost of the effort in light of the first two problems.

A final criticism may be that the whole approach is too behavioristic and actually ignores the basic ingredient of intelligence – namely cognitive processes. It never gets to them, only to their manifestations. This criticism is justified up to a point. It is true that by not intervening experimentally in the behavior stream the ethologist never knows what is going on in the subject's head. It should be recalled, though, that this approach is propaedeutic to, not substitutive of, test and experimental research aimed at getting inside the head. Also it is just as possible to infer cognitive processes from behavior elicited by natural circumstances as it is from behavior elicited artifically. But one can argue that this is still not enough because one could write hundreds of fine intelligent-behavior protocols on very cognitively interesting subjects and still not produce the kinds of interesting stimuli, settings, and behavior one can conjure up artifically in the laboratory. In short, there is no substitute for experimental laboratory research (in any phase of research) that ignores the real world and follows a problem wherever the events take it.

The final criticism touches on an issue involving the application of ethology to human behavior in general. Is the latter, because it is so cognitive, so permeated with personal symbols, collective concepts and language, on a distinctly different plane than animal behavior? If so, is it not better to interview and interact with humans to grasp the nature of this plane, rather than to observe them coldly at a distance? The answer to this is simple: interviewing and interacting with subjects exposes one plane of the human, observing explores another, and there seems to be no reason why an ethologist cannot do both, providing that the two approaches do not interfere with each other. After all, ethologists have to be true to their discipline and accept the properties of the species under investigation, no matter how strange they are. When they do this they will discover they have much to learn from psychologists and other social scientists.

Concluding remarks

To address the theme of this volume more directly, one can argue that ethologists have a right to invade the domain of human behavior in general, and the areas of intelligence or higher cognitive functioning in specific, just as psychologists had the right to invade the domain of animal behavior a hundred years ago. Actually, at the present stage of the behavioral sciences any approach to any domain seems to be the best initial strategy for research. As for ethologists, in particular, they should continue doing what they are good at doing, namely, observing and describing behavior, searching for its underlying neurophysiological mechanisms, trying to understand the relationship between the animal and its living relatives, as well as its ancestors, and above all the relationship between the animal and its environment. They should not deal with phenomena outside their competence if it forces them to reduce the phenomena to elements only their methodology can handle but no one outside of ethology finds relevant.

As for the term 'human ethology', somewhat misleading as it may appear ('ethology of human behavior' is more accurate), it seems no worse than the term 'human biology', which presumably is used merely to inform the reader that attention is being focused on a particular species. Combining 'human' with 'ethology' does this job of focusing and also signals the special tension that exists when a biological discipline is applied to the whole of human behavior. This tension makes the discipline interesting. The added tension that may come between ethologists and psychologists because of differences in background can be remedied by the latter taking time to learn what ethology is actually about.

8.2. Instincts for human understanding and for cultural cooperation: their development in infancy[1]

COLWYN TREVARTHEN

Introduction

In this paper I claim evidence that human infants are *intentional*, *conscious* and *personal*; that above all they have a faculty of *intersubjectivity* which is in embryonic condition in the neonate and rapidly developing active control over experience after that, and which soon becomes the central motivator and regulator for human mental growth. I believe that each of the words italicized above may be defined clearly and defended scientifically by reference to how infants behave. Infants are intentional because they are capable of formulating forms of actions that are measurably aimed at specific external goals, these goals being not immediately present to cause the actions reflexly. They are conscious because they carry images of external goals through perception within a complex space that is full of many events, selecting objects of adaptive value. They are personal because they are appealing to, conscious of and expressive to other human agents and the intentions of these agents. The intersubjectivity of infants endows them with both recognition and control of cooperative intentions and joint patterns of awareness.

The above definitions seem unsound only when viewed from a reductionist position which I reject on the evidence from nature. The virtue of

[1] Grateful acknowledgement is given to the Social Science Research Council of the United Kingdom for support of research on mother–infant communication discussed in this paper.

Thanks are also given to Mrs Marty Friedlander of Auckland, New Zealand for permission to use her beautiful photographs for figure 6, and to my colleagues Mrs Lynne Murray, for figure 4, and Mrs Penelope Hubley, for figures 8, 9, 10, 11 and 12.

objectivity is often claimed for simpler explanations. But nature is not simple and in considering psychological processes, which undoubtedly do exist, the kinds of explanation offered from a reduction to genetics or physiology are at best an insufficient guide to a more general understanding of the human mind, and at worst absurd. Developmental psychologists have believed explanations for mental growth that would not be accepted by any embryologist to explain morphogenesis of an organism. They have been too reluctant to accept that the self-regulating structures of intelligence, being products of natural selection, must anticipate information from experience. Surely we may choose to see other facts about human behaviour that measure up better with what we are trying to understand in this volume?

If there is an intersubjectivity or understanding of other persons that regulates personal relations and that impels humans to cooperation in awareness and purpose, then we must consider the possibility that humans are born with a mechanism for generating culture. This implies that the process of education, by which the symbols, values and constructions of any particular culture are discovered and passed on from generation to generation, is also regulated in the minds of children. I conclude from my research that inherent and developing attributes of intelligence of young children have a powerful control function in creating educative relations with adults or peers and, therefore, in transmission of culture. I think these intellectual habits of children also play a central part, in collaboration with the impulses of older persons, in the maintenance of the human social order.

Some kind of cause of instruction inside the child seems to undergo controlled changes with growth of the child's brain, as if the latter is working to further its own developmental programme. If there is any truth in this idea, then we shall have to gain knowledge of these generative functions and their intrinsic life history before we can understand the highly specialized adaptations of parents and teachers to the role of educator, a role which has to change to meet the needs of children of different ages. I hope I can convincingly show that the first steps in the life history of all forms of cooperative understanding are indeed to be seen in the first year of infancy.

The intersubjectivity to be seen in the infant is evidently not a self-sufficient, genetically specified faculty. Though robust, it depends on complementary functions of other humans. There is abundant evidence now from Head Start research and follow-up studies of older children that the ability to learn is created out of intimate sharing of experience with others. But the effects on mental growth of different opportunities for parental support and cooperation with teachers in early childhood can only be understood with reference to the intrinsic processes of children, processes that struggle to make cooperation occur. We need to know what it is in persons that sets the minimum human requirement for affection and companionship from others. Learning, the alchemical principle of modern behaviourist psychology, is, in humans, an abstraction of natural activity. Improvement in knowledge or skill depends, in the real world, on elaborate self-regulating mental functions of demand and response between pairs of persons who cooperate as pupil and teacher. The completeness of the isolated learner is a laboratory illusion, a fiction of psychological literature.

It is likely that, in all human societies, an intense competition is created when individuals of different ages work together in the regulation and development patterns of cooperation. In this case every individual may achieve only a particular form of success in relation to others, and some may develop their potential less than others. To speak accurately about such things, which are matters of passionate importance in any society, humanitarian or not, we need to know the goals and regulations that are common to the development of all individuals and that generate certain kinds of adaptive variations between individuals. It is important to know that these regulations may be seen in infancy, perhaps in prefunctional form for the most part, but unmistakeable.

In considering the wider implications of infant intersubjectivity I shall draw on other psychological evidence that supports the view that the human mind is elaborately adapted to a cooperative mental life. The human brain has extraordinary power for functioning in societies that vary in size from a handful of individuals to hundreds of millions and that can employ technologies requiring planned effort of one individual in confrontation with raw nature, or the joint action of thousands in an interlocking set of hundreds of industries and institutions. Through all the activities of man runs a thread that is spun in the fetus before birth and that begins its weaving in the family before a baby can walk or speak.

Some autobiographical explanations and theory

My research with infants began from a particular philosophy which I owe to my excellent teachers in biology, to unique opportunities for observing nature in New Zealand where I was born, and particularly to my apprenticeship at the California Institute of Technology with Roger Sperry. He is

a developmental biologist who has spent most of his scientific life studying the embryology of the brain and the functional morphology of the
adult brain (Sperry 1975). His psychobiology is nativistic. He considers
the brain to grow structural determinants for conscious intended action
and social life. He has always been sympathetic to the evolutionary
theory of ethology and always sceptical of the out-and-about empiricists
or social pragmatists in American psychology.

In developmental biology the primary facts are patterns of change in
morphology and the creation of life histories of organisms adapted to
ways of exploiting an environment that complements their activities. The
life forms and metamorphoses of plants and animals were known before
genes or conditioned reflexes were discovered. Generation after generation, life histories repeat the transition from egg to adult, but, as von
Uexküll explained, every organism depends on a delicate adjustment to
and regulation of a specified habitat that changes in the course of
development, sometimes radically. Life histories which reflect complex
cooperative activity among living elements are neither linear nor rigid.
Furthermore, all life histories or habits of life involve intricate preplanned
cooperation within and between species because organisms have evolved
in communities where each form may become part of the environment of
another.

A biologist has no reason to believe that higher psychological functions
are different in principle from other processes in organic systems. These
develop by mutual regulation of cells in the body and by mutual regulation of individuals in a common environment. Indeed all we know about
behaviour makes it seem the epitome of a regulated relationship of
interacting organismic elements.

Genes were discovered by carefully controlled breeding experiments in
an attempt to explain life histories and their transmission with lawful
variation from generation to generation. Geneticists have never been
happy with problems of interaction of living matter with the environment
in the development of an individual. They are puzzled that many
phenotypical variations that arise in ontogeny are adaptive. The genes
must regulate a set of dynamic alternatives of adaptation to an ecological
range. Modern molecular biologists with the 'code of life' in their hands
felt a great confidence fifteen years ago that embryology would succumb
to analysis in terms of the DNA and RNA molecules they had learned to
isolate in viruses and bacteria and from chromosomes of higher forms.
Their hope was high because embryology and development have always
made the more analytical of geneticists and biochemists feel miserable. It

is clear now that the wonderful increase of knowledge of gene transcription and its regulation within the cell of bigger-than-gene structures does not and can never on its own explain how an embryo develops its various kinds of cell in the right places. Old ideas of epigenetic processes, of differentiations and reintegration in fields of inductive interactions among many cells, are strong again. Genes drop back into place within a larger picture.

At the other end of the systems of life, adaptation of brains to the environment became part of physiology with Pavlov's simplification of habit formation in terms of conditioned reflexes. S-R learning theory is a magnified view of one aspect of the life history, the non-genetical aspect that lets a development adjust to control of circumstances on which it has dependency or for which it has a prescribed need. Pavlov doubted that humans, with language, learn by conditioning of reflexes. Now we know that natural learning is never as passive or reflex as the learning of Pavlov's dogs seemed to be (Sperry 1955). It is regulated by innate developmental processes such as motivation and curiosity. As memories consolidate they gain new integrative properties. Creativity in understanding and in action cannot be explained by conditioning of rudimentary sensory-motor reflex arcs.

I do not believe we need an interactionist or dialectical view in psychobiology. All we need to do is to remember that nature and nurture, gene and environment and innate and learned are artificial analytical abstractions to explain essential facets of development in organisms. If we are in trouble with either extreme we would do best to disengage our behinds from the horns of the dilemma and step to a more balanced view of the patterns of development, trying to see the regulations that cause them. Interactionism does not state this tactic boldly enough.

In every case where structures of behaviour have been studied developmentally, evidence has been obtained for powerful innate preadaptive regulations and for their prescribed response to environmental information (e.g. Gottlieb 1971, Hubel, Wiesel and Le Vay 1977).

We should remember where human beings stand in evolution. They are animals coordinated by an elaborate nervous system capable of integrating actions with experiences. They have, like all active animals, a prewired impression in their brains of the field in which their body may act. Like all birds and mammals they live through an inert fetal period in which new cerebellar and cerebral structures grow in the brain. Indeed there is no animal which generates a more elaborate brain structure before birth, and yet none which has more intricate postnatal differentiations in that brain after birth. The exceptional motor agility of humans and an unequalled capacity for acquiring athletic and manipulatory skills are combined with powers of perceiving the useful layout and objects of the world more completely than any other species. Mankind shares with birds and mammals highly regulated social structures and complex co-operations, but humans cooperate much more effectively than any other species. Human children are soon alert to the world but they are unable to fend for themselves for years and they live long in dependence on others with whom they form close friendships and common interests. They learn from their elders and by play with their peers to belong to a culture in which objects are used cooperatively and language is used to transmit understanding and to regulate many forms of cooperation.

Ethology has paid attention to the development of some kinds of animal cooperation with obvious biological benefit and neglected others with more significance to the development of specifically human intelligence. I believe we need a change of interest to direct study towards the development of understanding in all species that learn by example, that practise interaction in play and that develop highly cooperative use of knowledge of their worlds. The secret weapon in this kind of development and in its evolution seems to be an ability *to perceive intention in others* and to act to communicate with that intention *to control and be controlled by it*. Neither the theory of instinctive, gene-governed motor patterns nor social learning theory will explain this, either for humans or for the animals in evolutionary relation to humans.

I have for the past ten years been studying the patterns in behaviours of infants during the first year of life after birth, and changes in these patterns. My interest started when I watched the movements of our first child carefully from the moment he was born in a clinic at Marseille. Soon afterwards I gave up research with split-brain monkeys and began, at Harvard, to use film and TV to record samples of infant behaviour. I felt like a beginner, but when I looked at what ethologists, clinicians or experimental psychologists said about infants I did not feel much wiser. So I left these approaches to one side and collected my descriptions. Luckily I was working under the patronage of Jerome Bruner whose extraordinary imagination and enthusiasm had been caught by the idea that infants might hold important information for his long pursued project of understanding how children became educated (Bruner 1968).

Bruner and I felt very similar enthusiasm for physiological evidence, brought to my attention by Jacques Paillard, that intentions might be outlined in the acts of infants (Trevarthen 1974a, 1977). We were both also influenced by Bower's evidence on infant perception of objects in space. We were ready to see elaborate design in the acts of even very young babies. Finally, at this early stage of my work I was encouraged to a particular kind of humanist approach by collaboration with Dr Berry Brazelton, who is an extremely sensitive pediatrician, and with Martin Richards, then an expert on the ethology of nestling rodents, now a campaigner for humane treatment of mothers and infants in a technological world.

Methods[2]

My observations of infants with their mothers or with objects are made with TV and 16 mm cine film. Most of the general observations are made from TV which has sound. The films are analysed with a multispeed projector, the image being reflected upwards to the underside of tracing paper on a glass table top. Drawings can be made to plot movements of object, infant and mother frame-by-frame. Some infants less than four weeks of age have been filmed on the mother's lap or lying on a mattress, but usually the baby is supported with back nearly vertical in a seat designed to permit free movement of all limbs. A vertical mirror permits one cine camera to record both the mother and the baby near full face. We can study the face expressions, gestures, etc., of each of them separately.

In observing what babies do in response to suspended objects and their mothers my aim has not been to study events such as might be expected commonly in the home, but to probe the babies' abilities and to observe their variety when solicited optimally. On the other hand, I take care to have no fixed formulae of 'stimulation' but to allow a maximum flexibility of 'response' to object or mother to encourage the highest levels of coordinated action in the infant and the highest degree of cooperation. Luckily, infants can be happy and alert anywhere, as long as they are with friends.

Our staged encounters between mothers and infants are also an excellent source of information about the adaptations of mothers to the infants' expressive behaviour. We transcribe the mother's speech and compare it to her gestures and expressions. The techniques are also easily adapted for older infants to the study of joint enterprise with objects.

Finally we have explored some artificial regulations of the interchange. Recently Lynne Murray and I have transformed its potentialities by interposing double closed circuit television between the mother and

[2] Trevarthen 1974c, Trevarthen, Hubley and Sheeran 1975, Trevarthen 1977.

baby. This gives us greatly increased possibilities of recording and controlling communication between them.

I have avoided quantitative analyses until the patterns of action become clear. They are difficult to capture. In studying movements of the infant, for example in prespeech, we have been aided by using a 35 mm camera motor-driven at 4 frames/second. This gives us excellent pictures of fleeting events.

The neonate: a state of latent sociability and intentionality

As Papoušek has described (chapter 7.2 above) we now know that the responsiveness of a newborn to the immediate presence of the mother is subtle and refined, and that specific patterns of response to the individual mother are rapidly learned. The mother too has elaborate hormonally regulated adaptations in her behaviour to the baby. These nourish and support both the physiological and psychological functions of the infant.

As with other newborn mammals, human newborns are attuned to signals of their mother's presence in several modalities. They become imprinted quickly to the taste and odour of her body. They have a differentiated alertness for her voice and for the rhythms of her movements. They adapt to being held and adjust their body to the contacts and displacements transmitted to them from the mother. Of course, they show special aptitude for finding the breast and for sucking.

At the same time, alertness to the distant visible and audible world and reaction to the faces of people speaking to them, fragments of which responses can be seen already formed immediately after delivery, weaken in the next two weeks. The neonate generally sleeps when not feeding, avoiding ex-afference.

The neonate is elaborately preadapted for maternal care and fitted to complement the sensitivity and specialized care behaviour of the mother. Feeding and holding are soon highly cooperative, both baby and mother rapidly becoming better at anticipating the signals or acts of the other. There is evidence that this 'bond' or 'relationship' has importance for later development of more complex behaviour. But neonatal communication has severe limitations. Both active exploration of surroundings remote from the body and the capacity to enter into reactive face-to-face encounter are weak and unpredictable in the newborn.

A change of alertness to the world outside at five to six weeks is generally taken to indicate the end of the neonate period. Anbara aborigines in Australia also traditionally classify the newborn apart from children, with the fetus. It is a fetus 'outside' instead of 'inside'. No distinction of gender is made. At six weeks when the baby starts to smile it gains humanity by showing a capacity for interacting with others. Only then is it a male or female 'small one' (Hamilton 1970).

It is significant that neonates may show active avoidance of face-to-face, conversation-like interaction. While alert to the mother's voice and the proximity of her body, they evade her eyes and curl over when held upright to regain a cuddling or lying down position. They also show evasive mannerisms like autistic children, and make athetoid retractions of the hands after the tentative movements for prehension of objects that may be triggered by touch or by sight.

These avoidances or withdrawals may be compared to light avoidance in nestling kittens at a time when Cragg (1975) has found synapses are proliferating in the visual cortex. He has suggested that the visual circuits must be protected from excitation by light as they form contacts according to prescribed morphogenetic principles, before being validated and refined under patterned excitation in a 'critical' period. There is indeed evidence that circuits for human pattern vision, which as in other primates are relatively mature at birth, are exercised at a critical stage by edge-seeking, conjugate eye movements (Haith 1977). The conjugate eye movements are present at birth (Trevarthen 1974c), but they are not often exercised against stimuli in the first weeks.

The developments in active vision may be taken as illustrative of general principles by which cerebral systems for awareness are differentiated within a specification that is independent of patterns of stimuli until a critical stage (Blakemore 1974, Barlow 1975, Hubel, Wiesel and Le Vay 1977, Trevarthen 1978a). We may regard the neonate, who also shows movements adapted to face-to-face communication in weak open-loop forms, as a predialogical or preconversational being as well as a pre-object-seeking one. It has embryonic cerebral structures for social interactions and is protective of these when they are differentiating rapidly, seeking humans for comfort and care, but not socializing. A sensitive mother may make extremely subtle adaptations of her behaviour to changes in her newborn's attention and alertness. The baby may respond positively to this care and it could be important in development, but most communication appears systematically limited by avoiding acts of the neonate. The baby is unresponsive but not insensitive to the mother and is capable of learning. Avoidance of eye-to-eye contact reported by Maurer and Salapatek (1976) for babies less than six or seven weeks of age, an avoidance that under experimental conditions is more marked for the mother, must be due to some structure that can identify her particular face alone or in combination with other signals that identify her. Presumably this recognition is learned postnatally.

Complex motor patterns preadapted to visual exploration, manual prehension, walking and social interaction are generated spontaneously by neonates in light sleep (Jouvet 1975). We have observed gesture-like movements of the hands accompanying a great variety of face expressions (figure 1). Both the reaching movements and the social gestures and expressions can be excited in a quiet alert waking subject but they are very poorly integrated with perception of objects or persons at this stage. This weakness of perception does not mean that the structures that reveal themselves in intricate motor patterns are not associated with latent, subthreshold systems for perception. Subsequent developments indicate that there are indeed highly elaborate structures for awareness in the newborn brain.

Oster's analysis of the face movements of neonates and premature newborns reveals that most of the muscles of the human face are present and differentially governed by patterned efferent commands from the brain (Oster and Ekman 1977). Rudiments of the integrated movements of face expression, gesture, prehension and walking may be seen in Hooker's films of fetuses of the fourth and fifth month, though these were interpreted by Humphrey as appetitive or defensive 'reflexes' (Humphrey 1969).

Further evidence that the structures serving interpersonal communication are present in latent condition in the neonate, even though they are protected from visual and auditory excitation, comes from observations of patterns of response when the baby is in a state of optimal alertness. Neonates react to being called gently from one side with orientation of head and eyes in the direction of the voice, and then mouth-aiming, hand movements, and sometimes vocalization (Alegria and Noirot 1977).

An even more revealing response of infants about the end of the first month, if not before, indicating that they have a rudimentary person-perceiving template, is a reflex-like or 'magnetic' imitation of tongue protrusion, vocalization and hand movement (Maratos 1973, Meltzoff and Moore 1977). These imitations prove the neonate to have a discriminating image of the visible and audible expressive movements of a nearby person's face or hands, and that this image is integrated with the mechanism for patterning matching movements. That this readiness to imitate declines at six to seven weeks when well-oriented greetings and complementary utterances are made to the mother (Maratos 1973) sug-

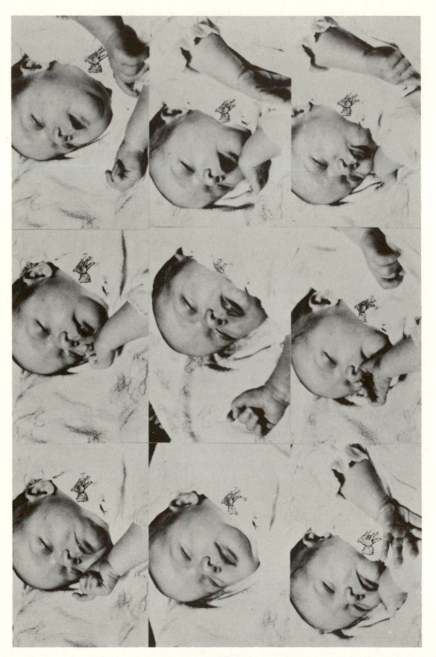

1. Expressions and gestures of a three-week-old girl in sleep.

gests that the imitative behaviour reflects a temporary state of hyper-excitability of a person-mirroring mechanism that is at a critical stage of developing into a system for guiding productive communication. It may be analogous to the compulsive scanning of light patterns at the same age (Haith 1977). However, neonatal imitation has been little studied yet and its dynamics and control have not been described.

It is possible to evoke brief episodes of oriented prereaching with a baby under one month of age. Bower (1974) claims that the movements include orienting of the hand and adjustment of wrist orientation and finger opening to the size and form of an object before contact. If he is correct, then we may suggest that a number of mechanisms predicting associations between modalities of perception emerge at the same time in rudimentary automatic formulae of actions. Visual perception of an object as a solid form to be grasped by hand before reaching can be modulated effectively is analogous to perception of another as model for a matching but unmonitored act of expression by oneself before communication is organized. Both responses could be called proto-intentional because they contain prediction of phenomenal aspects of the goal (graspability and communicative equivalence) for which there is no immediate evidence in stimuli.

With such precocity of motor patterning over guidance of the movements by perception of appropriate forms of experience, the evasive or defensive neonate, while clearly able to be excited by nearby objects or people and their distinctive forms and motions to some degree, looks like a puzzling store of rudimentary actions. The mother receives an impression of dreamlike purposiveness that defines goals without completing acts. She reflects this in her speech which attributes changes of feeling, interest and intention to the baby. Her uncertainty is shown in the questioning and wondering of her speech while she watches these movements. Unfortunately, she can easily be persuaded by a scientifically qualified authority or by an elder that her baby has no awareness whatsoever of the outside world.

The primary intersubjectivity of two- and three-month-olds

The behaviour of a two-month-old with the mother is quite different from that of a one-month-old (Trevarthen 1974b, 1978b). A rich repertoire of expressive behaviours is combined with ready orientation of the gaze to or away from the mother's face and immediate response to her signs of interest and her talking (Wolff 1963). These responses show the baby to be adapted to mutual perception of others and conversational interaction. This is confirmed by both descriptive and experimental studies.

Visual focalization matures rapidly in the second month. This is shown in scanning of stationary arrays and in tracking of moving objects. This enables observers to perceive babies as alert and interested in phenomena of the outside world. When persons are looked at the gaze is aimed at the eyes and there is a marked change in willingness to look at the eyes of the mother who is recognized and preferred to other persons (Stern 1974, Maurer and Salapatek 1976). Watchfulness of the infant is contingent on a friendly approach and encouraging baby talk as well as the familiarity of a face. Many discrimination tests show the baby to have a complex awareness of what the mother sounds and looks like. The baby can track her animated movements of greeting, utterance, reply and withdrawal, showing undifferentiated but appropriate reactions. Artificial modification of the baby's view of the mother (Brazelton, Koslowski and Main 1974, Murray 1978, Papoušek and Papoušek 1975) as well as comparisons of communications with mothers of different degrees of expressiveness or affectionateness (e.g. Blehar, Lieberman and Ainsworth 1977) show that the baby is sensitive and moved to an appearance of unhappiness by unfriendly, uncontingent, unresponsive or destructured forms of the mother's communication (figure 4).

Added significance is given to this evidence of powers to perceive persons for the claims of a well-formed personality in the baby by the range of expressive movements and the subtlety of their control. There are face expressions resembling those adults make to show a wide range of moods and emotions, prespeech and gestures obviously preformed for conversational communication and various degrees of animated signalling for the attention of others (Trevarthen 1974b, 1974c, 1977, 1978b). The expressions of two- to three-month-olds are organized in episodes of a few seconds in length that resemble sentences (figure 2). They are interpreted by mothers as 'speaking' (Sylvester-Bradley and Trevarthen 1978). Although frequently not vocalized and never with articulated sounds resembling words, these utterance-like behaviours are of about the same length as the time taken by an adult for controlling a short utterance motivated with one expiration of the lungs.

At this age vocalizations, excluding distress sounds and crying, are rudimentary. Apart from crying, they take the form of brief clucks and coos. Nevertheless, subtle coupling of the infant's sound-making to the mother's speech is shown in recordings where infant vocalizations may accurately 'reply' to rhythmical bursts of the mother's baby talk (Trevar-

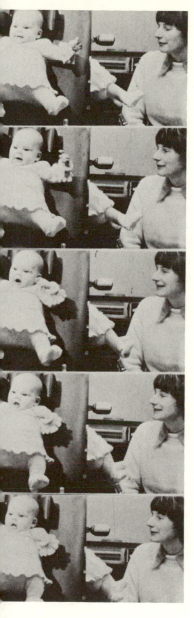 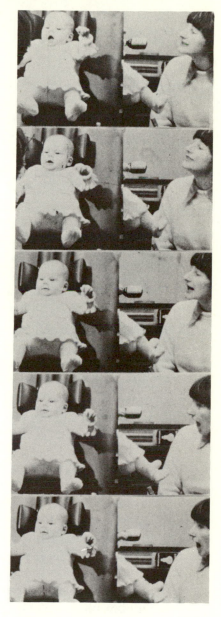

2. An eight-week-old girl interacting with her mother, waves her left arm and vocalizes while her mother watches (*left*). She watches while her mother gives a mocking reply. Time between pictures = ¼ second. Read from top to bottom.

then 1977). This suggests that the functions of sing-song baby talk and other rhythmical signals that mothers give the babies is to engage the infant in prediction of their occurrence and thus in regulation of reciprocal or synchronous action.

The control properties of infant expressions are clearly reflected in the mother's actions and comments which at this stage 'identify' with or 'mirror' strongly the infant's apparent feelings and state of intention (Sylvester-Bradley and Trevarthen 1978) (figure 3). When the mother does not support or complement the baby's expressions, the latter's actions change towards forms of behaviour indicative of withdrawal, concern or distress. This is evident when the mother is told to withhold her replies or when she is artificially cut off from her infant and acting without relationship to what the baby does (Brazelton *et al.* 1975, Trevarthen 1974b, Murray 1978). The baby's responses to this break of communication may be compelling solicitations for help including distressful grimaces, shouts, large flailing movements and crying. A watching mother can resist these only with difficulty. The reactions of the mother in an experiment of Lynne Murray where the mother was asked to keep her face still proved that the infant may be seen by her to be in a state of extreme distress. When the mother attempts to talk to her baby after such an interval of withholding her natural responses, the baby may show withdrawal and avoidance (figure 4). This the mother interprets as unhappiness and resentment. This simple experiment, lasting two minutes, shows that an emotional attachment is in effect, at least while the mother is actually present, at the end of the second month (Murray 1978).

The true character of the infant's communication behaviour is only clear when the acts of both mother and baby in a well-organized mutually absorbing interaction are observed in fine detail. Experimental procedures and methods of analysis that direct attention to the infant's powers of discrimination or to the actions of the mother alone give a misleading picture. It emerges from complete descriptions that both partners exercise control. The balance of expressive initiative may be assessed for each separately and their constantly adjusting, complementary but unequal contributions then become clear. It also emerges that dialogue-like behaviour occupies a place of balance where turn taking is negotiated in mutual attention. Outside this condition one or other partner assumes a more assertive or dominant role (figure 5). When assertion is moderate there may be smiling or laughter, the two often expressing excitement or amusement in unison. If one partner becomes strongly

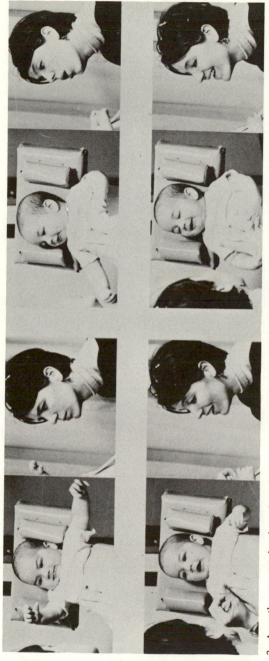

3. A mother reacts closely to her eleven-week-old boy, 'mirroring' his mood.

546

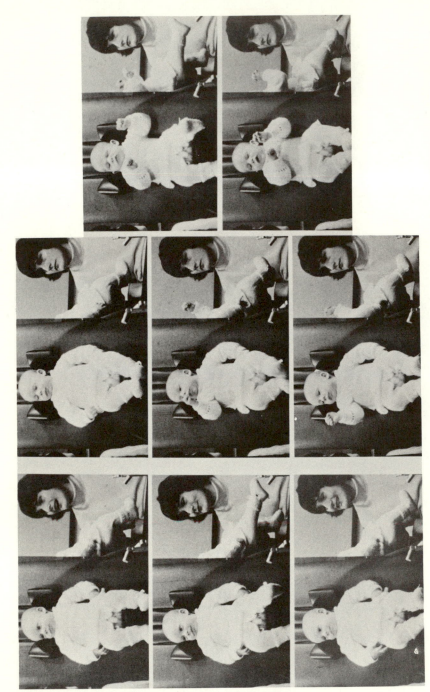

4. *Left*: An eight-week-old boy smiles and moves as if speaking while his mother speaks. *Right*: On instruction she immobilizes her face. Immediately her son looks down, stares at his hand, and grimaces and gesticulates as if distressed.

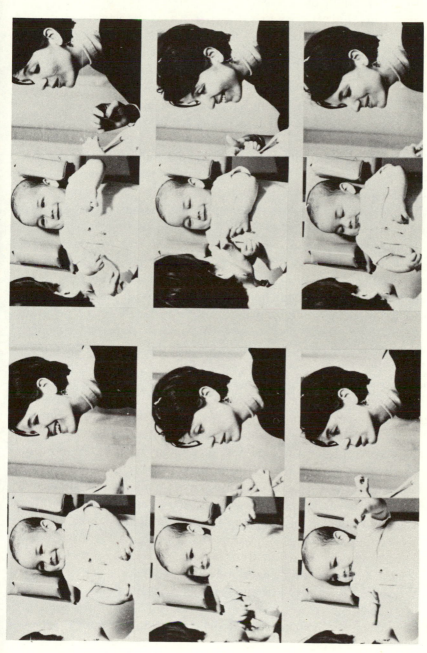

5. Shifting balance of initiative in mother–infant interaction. Eleven-week-old boy. *Left*: Both smile. The infant stares, clamps his jaws and knits his brows. The mother expresses pleasure, then surprise or dismay. *Right*: When she pokes and teases, he smiles then looks down and withdraws.

assertive the other becomes dismayed or intimidated, and the balance of communicative motivation is broken.

I believe this kind of analysis shows a pattern of interaction which could be used as a basis for a natural classification of emotional expressions, and conclude that emotional states should be defined within personal interaction rather than as supposed moods of an isolated individual. Analysis of unself-conscious behaviours of an adult with a young baby and of the baby as well may also lead to understanding of the variability of expressions for moods in individuals of different 'temperament' or 'personality' as well as in different societies, where human cooperation is cultivated with different values. Differentiated states of mind like sadness, fear, anger, etc., may be difficult to classify because they are more artificial or arbitrary than mutual states of action and reaction or balance of assertion and animation in direct face-to-face confrontation or in cooperative interaction – states such as jealousy, love, disdain, teasing or hating. It is interesting that the 'blend' expressions of Ekman and Friesen (1975) are nearly all taken to signify qualities of intersubjective relationship.

The simplest form of person-to-person display is probably this one that we see between a mother and her two- or three-month-old. Comparisons can easily be made to children and adults in face-to-face encounters (figure 6), even though both mother and infant are displaying special forms of behaviour adapted to bridge the large differences in their maturity.

In primary intersubjectivity the infant exhibits a number of preadaptations to language in which speech and gesture express acts of communication in address and reply with another. The infant's acts of expression constitute a 'fate map' of rudimentary acts of declaration, instruction, doubt, surprise, annoyance, denial, agreement, enjoyment, indication (deixis), teasing, etc., relative to the mother. There is no discernible topic contained in these 'messages' apart from their quality of intersubjectivity within the dyad of mutual interests, and the infantile communications must be regarded as very crude in linguistic differentiation. Most are unvocalized. Nevertheless it is not a great act of interpretation to attribute a presumptive language function to the remarkable associations of movement of head or body, of aims of gestures of hands, of expression of mood on the face, and of lips and tongue in articulations of prespeech (figures 6 and 7).

I do not yet understand persistent associations I observe between gesture and face expression or vocalization, but they are certainly relevant to 'theatricalities' of adult face-to-face encounter that closely parallel

6. Exchanges. *Above*: Showing, watching and sharing. *Centre*: A grandmother tells a story, a prime minister speaks, an author talks of his work and a carpenter discusses a job. *Below*: Telling a joke and enjoying it. (Photographs by Marty Friedlander, New Zealand.)

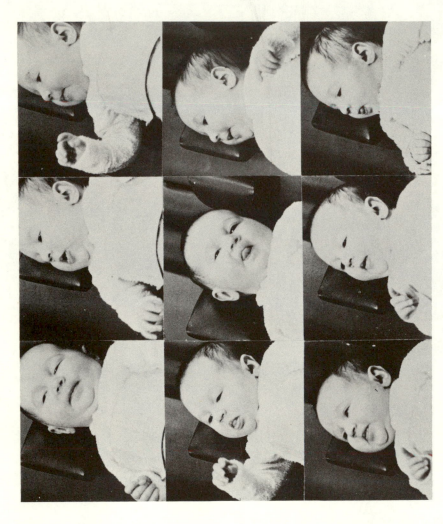

7. Face and hands of a seven-week-old girl. Tonguing of prespeech, with gestures.

interpersonal meaning in speech acts and other semiotics. In adults such paralinguistic signals become stronger when verbal comprehension is in doubt. They appear to be superlatively rich in the utterances of two-month-olds who have no real speech. It was Darwin's belief that posturings and mannerisms of the theatre were related to innate ways of expression (Darwin 1872). I think the movements of infants give considerable support to this belief.

The mother of a two-month-old interprets the infant as having an assertive, comical, fierce, interested, eager-to-tell kind of mind. This may be brought to objective analysis by study of the unconscious richesse of her speech to the baby (Snow 1972, Sylvester-Bradley 1977). One could call the mother's speech conversational. It sounds like half a telephone conversation, except that it obviously reacts to a visual message. It is closer to half a communication by telephone with televised image, but this is not yet part of everyday life. Perhaps we can model it closely by having a person talk to another through a double glazed window while being heard but hearing nothing themselves. By use of the television intercom we have developed we hope soon to know much more about the control of mother–infant interactions (Murray 1978).

The expressive actions of neonates are undoubtedly subject to reinforcement and to effects of exercise, as has been shown experimentally for the smile. But it is uncertain that such learning effects are important in the long term. The speed with which the expressive movements develop, their richness, the fact that they do not follow acts of the model imitatively and that most of them never appear in the acts of the mother to the baby, all point to their innate formulation and regulated growth within the infant. They differ between individual babies (of the same age) and there appear to be characteristic differences between the sexes, with males being more vigorous and assertive and females being more observant of the mother and making more prespeech and more delicate gestures. These impressions are still to be supported by systematic recording and analysis. I do not know how differences between individual babies observed at two or three months relate to differences seen later in life, but films I have made of my own children show that some features of their infant personalities persist long into childhood.

A mother is highly imitative of her baby, often accepting the baby's acts as models for reproduction in a sometimes ironic or exaggerated form (Trevarthen 1974c, 1977) (figures 2 and 3). We have evidence that the mother is usually unconscious of what she is doing. She may be unconscious of what the baby has done after imitating or replying to it both appropriately and vigorously. Analyses from verbal reports of communication by mothers after the fact are therefore much less informative than the actual patterns of her speech and expressive behaviour when she is with the baby.

Stern *et al.* (1975) distinguish between concerted and alternated action of the mother and infant. Overlapping actions (coactions) tend to be more animated and emotional in character. They appear to serve in the mutual regulation of moods or states of excitement. I doubt that it helps to consider these regulations within the confines of physiological arousal theory, as Stern does, because the form as well as intensity of animation is surely important to both partners as a quality of personal expression. It is a person that is aroused or calmed, not a reticular formation. More subdued acts of speaking tend to alternate between the partners. The infant frequently looks away from the mother at the start of an utterance and stops smiling. This appears to cause the mother to watch and wait until the utterance is finished. Likewise when the mother is talking carefully and softly to her infant the latter may remain still and closely watching what she does for several seconds.

Much attention is being given now to the idea that synchrony and 'turn taking' in interaction of baby and mother is due to simple automatic mechanisms of mirroring or inhibition in the infant coupled to a sensitivity of the infant brain to temporally contingent events that signal response of a reactive agent to what the baby does (Schaffer 1977, Kaye 1977, Stern 1974). Undoubtedly the rhythmical and contingently reinforcing acts of the mother have special salience for the infant due in some way to their regular rhythms and precise delay of response. However, there is evidence that the infant understands much more of interpersonal activity than this. Assuming the social signals (vocalizations, smiles, etc.) of a two-month-old playing with a reactive toy like a mobile (Watson 1973) are the same as signals to a person, this is no proof that the mother is not perceived as different from such a mechanism. Evidence from play behaviour indicates that infants have a general ability to express excitement from effects of their actions in a form that communicates to observers. Imitation of her expressions and subtle modification of reply to the form of her actions prove the baby can perceive the mother's unique person-like attributes. Hamlyn (1974) is justified in his criticism of the mechanistic conditioning approach to this behaviour of the baby; his thesis that to perceive a person the infant must be a person is supported by the complexity of what infants do early in life.

The mechanistic analyses of turn taking assume, first, that strict alternation of roles is essential to normal adult dialogue, which it is not, and secondly that the infant cannot be capable of the perceptions and plans for action needed to understand statement and reply. Most of the experiments undertaken to support this position are one-sided. They seek to show that what the mother does could support turn taking with a mindless infant prone to make acts in bursts and sensitive to inhibition of action by an interrupting stimulus. The self-regulated form of infant utterances is not adequately considered, nor is the subtlety with which this form changes depending on the mood of the mother's expressions.

It is confusing to compare, as Kaye (1977) has done, the turn taking in suckling, in which neonate and mother cooperate by direct touch stimulation (sucking or jiggling), with conversational interaction where many forms of sound-making and visible expression are regulated in combinations. Indeed it is not turn taking but *complementation* of the utterances that transmit information in an interpersonal situation which is important in dialogue. The interpersonal control and the effort at informative speech exist in rudimentary form in primary intersubjectivity.

When the mother is confronted with a replayed televised image of her baby talking to her she may not be conscious of what has been done, but she reveals by what she says to the TV image that she perceives the baby in it to be unaware of what she is now doing (Murray 1978). This proves that she normally sees the real baby to be perceiving her communications and reacting appropriately. She cannot communicate normally with an unreal baby who is not responding to her.

The epoch of games: months four to eight

The primary form of human dialogue seems to break up at about the middle of the fourth month. I do not know why, but there is a clear change in the infant's willingness to engage in purely dyadic face-to-face play with the mother. Eye-to-eye contact, smiling, prespeech and the primitive gestures all decline and the mother's behaviour also changes (Sylvester-Bradley and Trevarthen 1978, Trevarthen 1978c). I believe the change may be connected, in part, with marked developments in cerebral control of the complex proximal motor system, the system of joints and muscles that governs looking and listening widely in space with head rotations, and reaching with tracking of the inertia of the arm as it moves vigorously to specified loci for prehension of objects. The changes in movements of neck, trunk and limbs accompany developments in awareness of objects and of space (Trevarthen 1974a, 1974c, 1978c, Trevarthen, Hubley and Sheeran 1975). As effective reach and grasp emerges at the end of the fourth month, the infant also becomes more enigmatic in recognition of persons. There is a subtle change in humorousness and a more conspiratorial behaviour with other persons which appears to be closely related to adjusting the developing private intention to know or do against public sharing of one's increasingly vigorous intentions and aims. This relates to Piaget's 'pleasure in mastery', i.e. manifest enjoyment of the power of exercising control over perceptions in play with a familiar object (Piaget 1936, 1962). Expressions of pleasure for recognition or successful prediction have been reported for one- and two-month-olds by Papoušek (1967, 1969) and Wolff (1963, 1969).

In the thought-emphasizing perspective of Piaget the interpersonal importance of signs of affect is overlooked. Nevertheless, expressions of 'joy', 'serious intent', 'surprise' or 'dismay' may be observed closely by a person who is with the baby and reacted to by this person immediately. Correlated with rapid developments in exploratory abilities and a need to accommodate continuously to unexpected events, four- and five-month-olds exhibit an increase of 'serious intent' and this tends to close partners out to a peripheral observing role while objects absorb the baby's interest and attention (figure 10).

Penelope Hubley and I have made a case study of a baby girl in an attempt to understand what happens to interpersonal communication beyond this point (Trevarthen and Hubley 1978). We have compared the findings with films taken of other infants in the US and Scotland.

A five-month-old is frequently engrossed in grasping, handling and mouthing objects. At this age babies often refuse to respond to invitations to look at a person's face and 'talk' though they may vocalize 'about' what they do (figure 10). Avoidance of face-to-face interaction is often much more marked for the mother than for other friendly persons. We have recorded sessions in which the mother is hurt and confused by her baby singling her out for rude refusal of direct person-to-person play. Other forms of cooperative behaviour, such as feeding, may also suffer interference at about twenty weeks.

Adults who seek to interact with a baby at this age usually adopt playful teasing tactics that amuse the infant (figure 8). Four- and five-month-olds, while avoiding prolonged eye-to-eye regard, like to reach for and touch the face. They touch the eyes, and attempt to grasp the nose or mouth and they laugh when they feel the mouth move. This kind of interaction illustrates how the essence of a 'joke' lies in the sharing of a climax or paradox in mutual intentionality (Trevarthen and Hubley 1978).

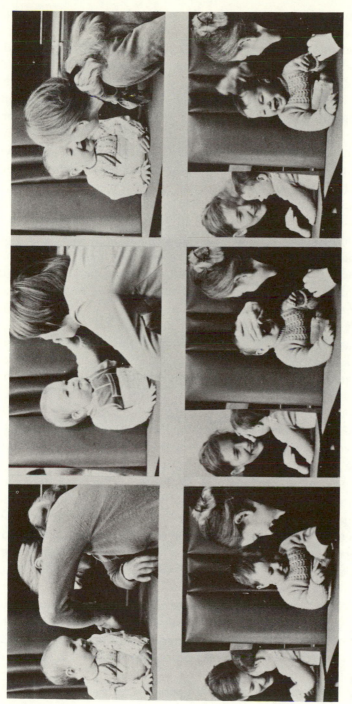

8. Games of the person. Tickling, poking, touching noses. Touching fingers. Peek-a-boo.

The behaviour of the baby playing with a mother's face has an expressive social aspect lacking in exploration of inanimate objects.

Mothers and other familiar companions join in a wide variety of *games of the person* that appear to bring in the infant's curiosity about face or hands. In spite of differences in how animation by the mother is made to interact with the baby's looking, reaching to touch, kicking, bouncing and, hopefully, smiling and laughter, these games have in common a remarkably restricted set of rules for pace, repetition and emphasis. Game after game fills a pattern of clustered impulses, three to four moves per cluster, with an accentuated climax. Pauses and changes in rate or emphasis are employed to regulate the infant's interest and to control the amusement. The regularities must reflect, and be adaptations to, control features of the infant's mind.

A six-month-old may imitate vocalizations, face movements, mannerisms or hand movements made by the mother in play demonstrations. The imitation is studied; it is part of a deliberate controlled interest in the other. It is different from the 'magnetic' imitation of one-month-olds when they are offered models based on their own spontaneous forms of expression (Trevarthen 1974d, 1978c). I have called the more elaborate imitation 'discretionary', but it could be called playful or even mocking. Imitation assists mother and infant to create together standardized routines of joke or game that strengthen their affectionate attachment. Indeed I believe one may see the full significance of attachment between a six-month-old and the principal companion (usually the mother) in these unconscious explorations of cooperative action that lead eventually to a special form of learning (cf. Stayton, Hogan and Ainsworth 1971). Imitations form a special subset of acts of mutual understanding.

A playing six-month-old may become highly excited and continue to participate for several minutes, but the baby may also terminate the game or refuse to play. Throughout the play it is clear that the intentions of the infant have to be carefully matched. The rules of play are evidently not imparted by the mother although they may be cultivated and ritualized as in 'pat-a-cake' or 'peek-a-boo'. They all derive from rules of the infant's motivation which we are only beginning to discern.

Babies become highly vocal at this age and they join in noise-making games with an imitating partner out-of-sight. They also practise babbling on their own. We believe that the mother's use of nonsense sounds in play follows the lead of the baby who now illuminates intentions with voice sounds.

We have recorded many games in which the mother of a four- to six-month-old moves hands, face or head in sequences of tracking and looming, appearance and disappearance for the baby's interest and amusement, and others in which she displaces part or all of the baby in repeated rhythmical bursts of patting, poking, jiggling or bouncing (figure 8). Usually she dubs in nonsense sounds, singing or rhymes that match the pattern of movement and emphasize the climaxes. There is an obvious relationship between these games where the mother uses herself or the baby as play object and play of the infant with objects and with effects self-created by moving them (secondary circular reactions). They are also undoubtedly related to babies' heightened awareness of their own mouth or hand. Both mouthings of the hand and hand regard are common at this age.

Games with objects, things that baby and mother may manipulate, begin about the fifth month, one or two months after games of the person may be familiar. The mother increasingly incorporates a toy of interest to the baby in her attempts at play (figure 9). At this age a baby will take an object held out on the hand. From this point the mother can easily tease the baby into reaching for an object moved just out of reach. She can make an object suddenly approach and touch the baby, adding sound effects with her voice. She can hide an object and make it reappear. Games with objects, like games with persons, exercise a bridge or coupling between the will of the mother and the exploratory or praxic intentions of her baby. The baby makes these coactions and interactions social by smiling, laughing, vocalizing, by expressing curiosity, puzzlement, fear or sadness and by gestures and attitudes of the hands, the feet or the whole body.

In spite of this adaptation to sharing of mood and motivations, the infant does not show at this stage any ability to turn an object into the *topic* of a comment passed spontaneously to the other. At the same time the baby resolutely fails to *give* an object to a person when it is asked for with open hand (figure 11). Usually objects are dropped, thrown or pushed away to the floor when they are requested. Nothing that the baby does has a deliberate message-carrying quality. There are no *acts of differentiated meaning* in a linguistic sense. The eager 'utterances' of prespeech combined with gesture have given way to a self-absorbed tolerance of others as caretaker observers (figure 10), or a willingness to become part of an experience built by a partner into a joke or game (figure 9).

Close observation of the behaviour of the mother in her spontaneous adaptation to the infant's changing consciousness of objects, and powers to use them for explorations in this consciousness, shows that she is

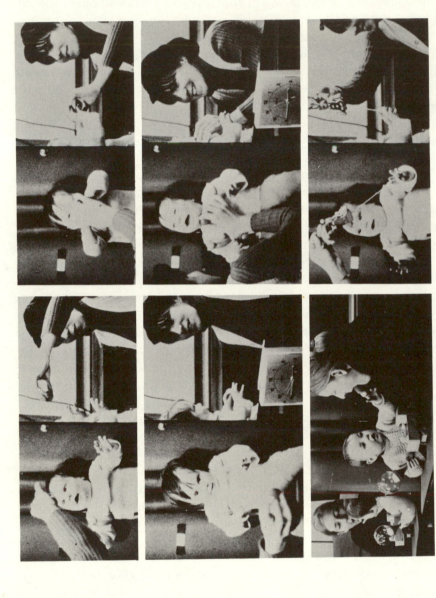

9. Games with objects. *Top:* Mother brings a ball in for her waiting six-month-old to grasp. *Middle:* She pokes it under her daughter's chin. *Bottom:* Making a doll, mother hits a doll, watching her face while moving a puppet.

making something social out of interests that could well not be social. The baby, though hating to be alone, could amuse himself. Often the infant prefers the mother just watching or listening, or even just being there as a companion. Reports of babies in the home, and in other cultures where mothers have much work to do, lead to the conclusion that deliberate time off to play with the baby, while it reveals what infants are capable of sharing, may not be essential to further development. Of course, siblings or aunts can stand in for the mother. But this has, I believe, not been studied with adequate attention. We just do not know enough about it.

At this stage of development, even the artificially facilitated cooperations we observe are one-sided, the mother adapting to a self-centred infant. Nevertheless, it is significant that after six months the baby will accept a toy animated by the mother both as mediator of what the mother intends and as a focus for the baby's interest for looking, tracking, manipulation, etc. This must involve a mechanism of sharing in the infant (figure 9). It actualizes a significant development in the capacity for cooperation and makes possible a form of joint action in which the baby is actor or motivator and the mother a secondary participant in the action. The baby either lets the mother move the toy and accepts it as a focus of interest inside her intentions (Object Game I), or the baby moves the toy and, instead of watching the effect directly, looks at the mother's face or listens to her voice and observes with amusement the effect on the mother

10. Mother watches her thirty-four-week-old 'working' with a toy and 'talking'. The baby does not look at her mother.

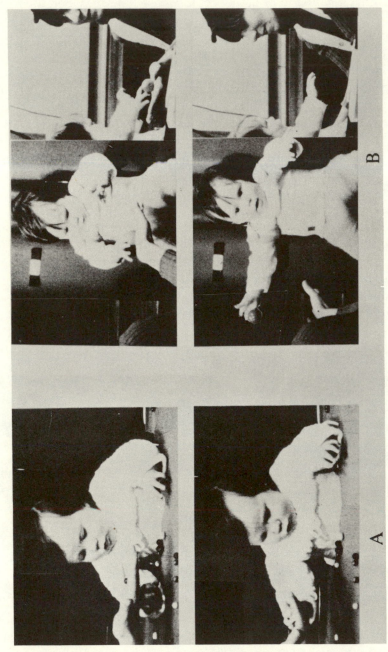

11. A determined six-month-old pushes away an offered bead (A), and takes a ball, then drops it on the floor when asked to give it back (B).

who is deliberately tracking or accommodating to the movement of the toy (Object Game II) (figure 9). Such games arise out of cultivation, by an observant mother, of the baby's sociable initiatives. The games grow with the baby's developing intentions and the openness of their motivation to the mother's sharing. In step with her following, the mother's speech to the infant in these games is questioning and entertaining. She does not instruct. In Object Game II an important change has occurred in that the mother's response to what the baby does has become of central interest to the baby. This change appears linked to more complex experiments of the infant with objects, and to generalization of experiences between objects as described by Piaget (1936), but I see no reason to believe that the mother is ever confused by the infant with impersonal objects as most cognitive psychologists believe.

At eight or nine months more complex patterns of sharing of interest in surroundings with conspiratorial exchange of glances show that an infant is developing a new awareness of the possibilities of shared experience. This is the beginning of genuine acts of meaning in the child and of a true process of education in which the child is actively seeking help and amplification of understanding and anticipating the getting of new information from another who is willing to help and teach.

Secondary intersubjectivity: manifestations of the fundamental instincts for cooperative understanding

We have observed several nine-month-olds on the threshold of a large change in awareness and in personality (Trevarthen and Hubley 1978). They have become more confiding and more confident and altogether more aware of their sharing the world of experiences with others. Scanning the literature we discover that an impressive list of new achievements, as well as a new kind of anxiety, is recorded for babies of this age or a little older (table 1). Before the first year is out something happens to transform the infant's mind, and, quite apart from development of object perception, a uniquely human sharing of experience begins. This is exemplified by mastery of giving.

In the spontaneous play of mother and an infant between six and eight months of age, we see objects become toys, both by the playing of the child and by extensions of this by an observant mother, as described above. The child has not lost the awareness of the second and third month that the mother is a person who can be communicated with, but now this awareness is used less directly in appreciation of the mother's initiatives

Table 1. *Line-up description of infant development*

| | The nine to ten month change | |
	Before	After
A. *Emotional, affectional*		
Psychoanalysts generally	Infant narcissistic, egocentric	Self–other relation (object relation) develops
Klein	Not capable of distinguishing own impulses from those of other	Capable of remorse for causing pain to other. Anxious 'depressive position' in neurosis
Mahler	Symbiotic community between infant and mother	Separation–individuation of infant
		Fear of isolation brought on by increased mobility
Winnicott	Baby develops unit status 'living with' mother	'Fierce and terrible' attachment to mother–object, 'objectively perceived'
		Communicating and non-communicating self distinguished
		First reciprocal communication
Spitz, Bowlby, Rutter, Ainsworth	Development of attachment to mother or other main companion	Strong attachment, usually to mother. Separation effects severe. Good attachments lead to greater confidence
B. *Cognitive*		
Piaget	No representation of an object outside sensory-motor relations	Schema of object
		Secondary circular reactions combined, uses objects against other objects as instruments
	Practises secondary circular reactions in manipulation of objects	
	Explores predictions of effects of object use	
Kagan	Thoughtless	Thinking
		Increased attentional differentiations shown in orienting
C. *Language*		
Halliday	No grammatical utterances (or only a weak prelude)	Vocal 'acts of meaning' in a 'protolanguage'
D. *Performative in communication, socialization*		
Piaget		Imitates, invokes help with an object, points for others' attention, pretends in play (all treated as cognitive)
Bruner *et al*.		Controls screen in game of peek-a-boo, holds cup to doll's mouth, looks where another is pointing or looking, points to

Table 1. *Line-up description of infant development (continued)*

| | The nine to ten month change | |
	Before	After
Griffiths		remote objects and to items in pictures. Give and take games develop. Takes turns in play (treated as protolinguistic) Points to show, returns embrace, waves 'bye bye', obeys simple spoken requests, marks paper with pencil and watches effect, invites personal attention
Bates *et al.*	Perlocutionary acts of communication not intend-ing (controlling) the effect on the listener	Illocutionary acts, imperatives and declarations taking account of effect on listener (based on cognitive 'means–ends schemes')
E. *Self-image* Amsterdam Lewis and Brooks		Self conscious in front of mirror Age, gender and familiarity distinguished in perception of others. Prefers pictures of own age and gender, of self and of mother
F. *Maturation of behaviour* *Motor development* Gesell *et al.*	Looks at objects and grasps and manipulates. Touches mother's face	Pokes with index finger. Plays with small objects. Puts objects together. Puts in and takes out. Looks into details. Examines parts of objects. Hand dominance becomes clear
McGraw	Development of sitting, standing; start of crawling	Crawls, walks while holding on

and how they relate to the baby's own. Often the mother gives an object to the child and it is increasingly taken with a conspiratorial look of acknowledgement. But the child never freely gives an object to the mother for her to do with what she will, marking by expression that it has become hers. Giving up an object when it is taken is not the same. Without free giving there is no reciprocal play, no giving and taking of turns, no swapping the role of possessor before the eighth month. The mother may ask but the baby refuses (figure 11). The mother must take. The refusal is not so much uncomprehending as actively rejecting. Indeed requests for an object to be handed over may provoke holding of the object away from the mother, without looking, and dropping of it on the floor. The object is put away with a precocious, Spitzian 'No!'

Then, inside a couple of weeks, the baby may begin to look for interest in the mother and to wait for a chance to follow her ideas. Quickly, give and take games become routine, and the baby begins to look about for the mother, to comment on things vocally as well as to hand toys over to her with a look to her eyes and a smile of recognition and agreement. Often both mother and child call and posture triumph at the coincidence of their intentions and mutual recognition.

This change is a fundamental one, not a new trick with prehension or perception of object permanence taught by the mother. It is coincident, or closely involved with, superficially quite different acts all of which contain at their core a heightened recognition by the baby of the mother's meaning, or her possession, or her need, or her understanding. For example, this is when a baby vocalizes clear intersubjective statements to familiars in Halliday's protolanguage (Halliday 1975) or Bates' declarations and imperatives (Bates, Camaioni and Volterra 1975), and when the names of familiar things are easily learned and remembered. Games of showing pictures or naming and finding are picked up for the first time (Ninio and Bruner 1978). Tasks that are too difficult for the baby are cause for a demand for help from another person (Piaget 1936, Bates, Camaioni and Volterra 1975).

Other performances which are carried out 'alone' seem unrelated. For example, pretending to use a pillow, a cup, a toy telephone, or clothes in their proper, customary way. But these are imitations or acts of imagining that require the baby to step into the shoes of another who is given the role of either actor or observer.

Probably the most significant achievement, perhaps the central one for which the mental developments we infer have evolved, is the ability to be shown a new skill and to practise its potentialities under the guidance of another. This involves bringing an object freely into relations in a triadic person–person–object network – one in which each of the two persons shifts in awareness between the common object and the other. For minute after minute our mothers and their ten-month-olds are absorbed in showing and doing with an object or a set of objects (figure 12). The child quickly masters new gains in technique, new ways of motivating and combining objects. He has now, among other virtues, the graciousness to be an excellent, if often deceived, subject of a test of cognition, with objects that disappear, arrange themselves or combine in unfamiliar ways under the agency of a tester who withholds important items of normal

12. A one-year-old takes an offered doll, looks at it while her mother repeats a request to put it in the truck, then puts it in herself.

intercourse. I prefer the point of view that sees the child in such tests as acting to teach cognitive psychology to the psychologists by generous participation in these games that reveal a newly developed imagery of an object so that the object persists in the mind when it is concealed in various ways. Of course the tests deceive the child because they are not designed to assist or share with the child. Rather are they designed to help the psychologist vis-à-vis his colleagues at another time and place. How unfair it is to attribute egocentricity to the child in these situations! Here I share misgivings that Donaldson has expressed about the concept of egocentricity in infants (Donaldson 1977).

In our study of one child at play with her mother in months ten to twelve (Trevarthen and Hubley 1978) we have many examples of co-operation in a joint task. The baby looks to the mother to obtain suggestions about which game to play, which object to select, how to put objects together, and the mother instructs. Transcripts of the mother's talk are completely different from those of two or three months previously. Now she does not question or request, she names and instructs. Clearly she has adapted to the fact that the baby is willing and able to do what she says. She has become a teacher and has done so because the baby has marked characteristics of a good pupil soliciting instruction. The baby does not use words in language but does vocalize with language-like intent, with support of appropriate gestures and expressions, and does understand many words. They are understood 'in context' because the baby and the mother are not only aware of surroundings, but practised in being aware of each other's usual forms of awareness. They share understanding of many tricks of communication as well as a common and familiar environment.

The psycholinguists raised the problem of how children acquire language and it has been found that there is a great deal of communication of intentions before language is learned (Bruner 1976). It is often said that the social environment 'provided for' the infant can define meanings and goals as well as create social abilities and roles in the child's mind. According to the sociological theories of Becker (1972), Berger and Luckmann (1966) and Mead (1934), the child is conditioned in the social situation and learns how to think and know in proper conventional terms. One learns what it is to be a self, which gender he or she has and a host of roles in a plot written by the society. Speech, invented by culture, is taught as a tool for communication and for thought. The mother, especially, can cultivate an infant's or toddler's awareness of language and other forms of cooperative understanding by reading into imitative intentions possible meanings and symbolizing them. Conceptualization, language and conscious understanding are thought to depend on socially defined meanings and to be picked up by a highly plastic intelligence.

There is in the many presentations of this view no justification for the customary assumption that the mother adds all to an unsocial, uncooperative intelligence in the infant. The facts of developing cooperation between infant and mother suggest otherwise. What is learned and how it is learned are limited, regulated and organized by specific forms of readiness of the infant for social interaction and for cooperative understanding, from the start of life with others. The infant as well as the social environment cause the developments.

Mead (1934) states that gestures and acts of the self for communication with others have no meaning except that achieved through active negotiation with others who are sensitive to these acts and who understand them for what they are. The self arises through acts in control of experience that become gestures perceived by others. The way they are perceived by others becomes known and that defines the self.

All the functions needed for this process of 'self awareness' and negotiated understanding of meanings and symbols are achieved in rudimentary form by the ten-month-olds I have described. The way they are achieved indicates that they are already present as structures in the baby's mind and visible in behaviour before they are used with even this level of control. These structures 'learn' particular applications and they greatly aid learning of new instances with other persons, but they themselves are not learned.

Conclusions with regard to human ethology

To further understanding of the predispositions of infants to be human and to develop in a human way we must, I believe, accept an ethologist's dedication to observation and description. We also need his general concept of inherent adaptive constraints on forms of behaviour and perception. But it is doubtful if the theory of ethology, which has rather rigid categories of action, motivation, signal and interaction, will, without extension, embrace the mental functions of man or their antecedents in the more intelligent, more socially cooperative, animals.

The conscious, voluntary and interpersonal qualities essential to human existence and their peculiar process of development may be beyond ethology. The acts that express and regulate them, and the cognizance implied by the predictions made in using these acts, cannot be recorded in an ordinary ethogram. Without a psychological theory adequate to these, no amount of description will make sense. Nor can we expect much help from studies of animals which transfer to them an idea of humans as inherently neither aware nor intending but gene machines with a great capacity for learning in society how to be aware and how to intend. (Speaking of 'gene machines', we need to remember that even if rituals of mating and rules of kinship do affect gene flow significantly and adaptively in human societies as they do for animals, these rituals and rules also serve the mental cooperations on which human existence depends. They have vital epigenetic applications in human social life.)

If ethology aspires to study all forms of natural spontaneous behaviour, it can only illuminate the human case by observing appropriately complex aspects of behaviour. The human mechanisms of intelligence have to be observed developmentally in an epigenetic perspective if they are to be understood. We have constantly to ask what developmental constructive purpose, for the individual and for the society, is served by them. Thus, the acts of babies look far ahead to kinds of cooperative behaviour beyond them – not only to talking with words, but to achieving powerful structures and institutions of joint enterprise and knowledge-sharing with others. No other animal comes near to having such ambitions.

Nevertheless there are some remarkable discoveries in recent work with animals, especially carnivores and primates, that show that the evolutionary perspective is as exciting as ever it was. We obviously have a lot to learn to catch up with Darwin's view of mental evolution expressed, for example, when he concluded that it was not forms of expression that evolved or were inherent but motives (Darwin's notebooks, Gruber and Barrett 1974). To understand the evolution by natural selection of human intersubjectivity, that is, the knowing of persons and oneself in relation to others, I believe we need more investigations of the controlled interest of highly cooperative animals when they are just watching and interpreting one another without using highly differentiated signals or obeying fixed rituals of action. Face-to-face observation is obviously an ancient mammalian skill. Why do kittens, wolves and young monkeys attend so strongly to their mothers' faces? How much do they see beyond the eye-brows, teeth, coloured skin and spots or the signal movements? How much do animals imitate the spirit and intensity of attitudes, gestures and expressions? The case of macaques and chimps transferring tricks of sweet-potato washing and termite-catching indicates they see each other as manipulators like themselves. What perception of intentions do they need to learn that? To what degree do primates play together with objects using their properties cooperatively? I know they steal and exchange, but do they ever show? When they greet or give, is it always appeasement? Menzel's (1971) demonstrations of communication about surroundings excites the imagination because it proves that his young chimpanzees have an integrated awareness of signs of interest and mood in application to the shared space. Asking and offering help covertly or overtly is not just altruistic, it implies an identification with the situation and experiences of the other as well as perception of oneself in relation to them, and vice versa. Hinde (1976) has found by detailed analysis of transactions between young monkeys and their mothers and peers that 'relationships' are built up which serve the integration of the larger group and generate a network of mutual understandings that last and predict. These relationships must aid the awareness and cooperative effectiveness of most individuals in a group. Barnett (1973) suggests that only humans have an 'instinct to teach'. I am sure that a human infant instinctively provokes being taught. A human toddler living with wolves or gazelles may well change the whole balance of understanding by getting them to teach him how to be like them. At least the possibility makes a wonderful story (Armen 1974). Such a child would be in a quite different situation from a puppy in a human family.

Until the building up of mutual awareness of each other and of the environment and the extending of this awareness cooperatively or competitively have been put into a proper order for animal societies, we can have no perspective on the natural selection of human cognition and of the power of humans to form societies based on the transmission of language, culture and technology.

Developmental psychologists have, in accepting the leadership of Piaget, firmly established that man has a cognitive endowment for conceiving objects in relation to his purposes. We still do not know how the concept of the object develops, but that thought represents objects of acts of cognizance is accepted. *This leaves the social character of man unexplained.* I believe that when it is explained the cognitive functions will appear a part of it, more important in joint or simultaneous awareness than in the thinking of an isolated individual discovering a representation of a permanent reality on his own. I believe that is why educators are finding so much evidence that it is the effective community of the child that determines how its mind will develop.

I cannot think of one cultural achievement of humans, or one cognitive achievement for that matter, that does not depend upon a voluntary transmitting and receiving of knowledge, symbols and techniques. The psychological basis of this transmitting and receiving is not in the knowledge, symbols, techniques, concepts, or in the constructions that are made of them. It is in the motives of humans to see what another is aware of or what another intends, and there is a matching ability to see how these awarenesses and intentions may be taken for oneself, and to see how more than one person may work with one to a common goal. The way infants enter into mutual recognition with other persons and the way they develop an ability to join in a cooperative experience proves to me that the required mechanism is active in them and is regulating its own growth by seeking stimuli in relation to a world in which the essences of physical objects and of persons are totally different.

If we accept that man has a special instinct to be a person and know persons, we can go one step further. The emotional quality of an infant's relations with significant other persons who, all being well, become affectionate and loyal companions in development of understanding well into childhood, is sufficient to indicate how the powerful value systems that permeate all human cultures may have come about. Like the practical achievements of technology, the spiritual and moral beliefs of humans, and their art, are products of their inborn response to and need of other persons. It is not necessary to restrict ideas of instincts to the more competitive violent and unimaginative acts of human beings.

Psychobiological postscript

If misgivings remain about an account of human infants that is nativistic but based on a mentalistic interpretation of behaviour and no more direct evidence, I believe I can offer assurance that it is not all illusion by reference to certain relevant facts about brain growth (Trevarthen 1978a).

The human brain develops the main layout of its cells and its primary intercellular connections in the fetus. It does not grow much in size after birth. However, some large psychologically important regions undergo synaptogenesis and synaptic validation (selective opening and closing of intercellular transmission points) for long after birth in a well-regulated pattern. Different integrative contingents of cells, different lines of communication, are developed at different rates in a life-long schedule. The plan of the human cerebral hemispheres laid down in the fetus includes prefunctional generation of structures that mature in childhood into the main mechanisms for regulation of speech and language. At least part of Wernicke's area, the tissue for understanding of speech, is not only localizable in the adult. Its rudiments are contained in structural differences between the hemispheres that are visible in the fetus.

If an adult brain is divided by commissurotomy, two different kinds of consciousness are separated. The left and right hemispheres are aware of different worlds. The nature of the difference cuts to the basis of individual differences in mentality, such as ability to handle spatial concepts or fluency with logico-verbal argument, and elucidates the different cognitive approaches that one individual may make to problem solving. Both hemispheres see persons and grasp their meaning deeply, but only one can communicate with them by speaking, and that is the one that regulates gestural communication by acts of the hands moving away from the body. The speaking hemisphere usually has a more precise visual regulation of acts by a 'dominant' hand.

These inborn categories and processes of mind activity that are segregated between the cerebral hemispheres take about one and a half decades to mature and all of them are highly sensitive to experience and education; that is, *all of them develop in adaptation to the cultural situation*. They do not stop developing in adolescence, but less is known about the later stages.

With this kind of evidence from brain research, incomplete but supported as far as it goes by a great amount of surprisingly clear data, it is not difficult to believe that human minds and their motivations and values have a prescribed but long developing shape that is adapted to regulate social life. Sperry (1976) concludes this is the case. The life cycle of the brain looks like a cycle of mental growth with an enormous degree of prefunctional morphogenesis of main structures as well as great plasticity. It could well contain the specifications for a self-aware creature, with cooperative tendencies sufficient to generate cultures like those we know.

Comments on papers by Charlesworth and Trevarthen

Ethology, psychology, and the study of human intelligence

DALBIR BINDRA

The papers of Charlesworth and Trevarthen are concerned, in different ways, with defining the behavioral capacities that make the human species supreme in intelligence. Their approach is developmental and observational. The empirical work they report is engagingly simple, yet provocative and promising for understanding the cognitive processes involved in the production of intelligent actions of the highest order. However, their methodological and theoretical message is, I think, misleading. I shall here deal with only a few of the issues raised in their papers.

The problem of species comparisons

Charlesworth gives us a relevant and perceptive historical account of the various approaches to the study of animal and human intelligence. He notes that the early laboratory studies of species differences in intelligence did not materially advance our understanding of the nature of intelligence as a biological capacity. He then attributes this lack of success to the use of laboratory tests that were in some sense 'artificial', not representing the 'natural settings' in which each species lives. My reading brings me to believe that the reason for the lack of success of the early studies can now be identified much more precisely. It lay in the failure of

572

the investigators to adapt the test tasks to the sensory and motor capacities of the species (see Hodos 1970, Hodos and Campbell 1969). Without adequate control for the confounding factor of sensory and motor capacities, it is of course impossible to say what the observed performance differences between any two species might indicate about their relative intellectual capacities. The issue of artificial versus natural setting may thus have little bearing on why those particular studies failed. Indeed, with greater attention to tailoring the tasks to the sensory and motor capacities of the species (Bitterman 1965b), as well as by the adoption of the 'learning set' or transfer (Harlow 1959) paradigm, significant advances have recently been made in species comparisons of intelligence (see Hodos 1970), and this has happened without any shift in the location of studies from the laboratory to natural settings. Perhaps we all have been guilty of accepting too readily rather vague and general methodological dicta instead of clearly defining specific reasons relevant to each investigation. It now appears that a concern with pinpointing the specific factors that make for success or failure in studies of species comparisons would advance our understanding of animal intelligence more than preoccupation with the artificial laboratory versus natural setting issue.

The issue of ecological representativeness

Charlesworth and Trevarthen remind us that the understanding of behavior is promoted by background information about the species – its phylogenetic history, the ecology of its normal habitat, its life cycle, and the functional significance of its typical action patterns for species survival. And they make the plea that it is important to have the environment in which a species is studied ecologically representative of the natural habitat of that species. With all this there can be little disagreement (cf. Miller 1977). But, pertinent though this point is, we should not forget the importance of its obverse. That is, an understanding of the processes involved in the production of intelligent actions may also be promoted by interventions that deliberately distort the natural conditions under which those actions normally occur. For one way to determine the role of ecology in the production of a particular type of behavior is to try to see how that behavior is modified by ecological distortions, as well as how that behavior may be 'artificially' produced (in species in which it does not normally occur) by arranging abnormal ecological and organismic conditions. Many years ago, when I was concerned with the problem of hoarding – food storing – in the rat, I had certain ideas about the conditions required for the emergence of hoarding behavior. I was successful in applying the ideas to make nonhoarding rats into hoarders and hoarders into nonhoarders (Bindra 1948). Similarly, I believe that creating conditions under which chimpanzees would use a symbolic language for communication is important precisely because such language is not natural to the chimpanzee and requires a foreign ecology and artificial methods of training. In almost every discipline, the study of abnormal conditions and abnormal outcomes contributes a great deal to the understanding of normal processes, and the study of intelligent actions is no exception.

I don't want to overstate the case. My point is simply that emphasis on what can be learned by studying behavior under ecologically representative conditions should not be allowed to overshadow what can be learned by studying behavior under abnormal conditions or studying abnormal behavior under normal conditions. More broadly, I may say that useful ideas for the analysis and interpretation of adaptive behavior have been suggested by findings, theories, and analogies of diverse kinds, now by some neural, biochemical, or pharmacological consideration and now by some evolutionary, functional, or anthropological consideration. The fact is that good ideas in science come from many sources and it is pointless to single out any one source – considerations of natural ecology, evolutionary history, life cycles, etc. – as either necessary or more important than the other sources.

Defining cognitive abilities

An important point made by Charlesworth is that many traditional assessments of both animal and human intelligence were based on the unwarranted suppositions about what success or failure at a given test task means in terms of underlying cognitive abilities. You will recall that Lashley (1949:28) observed that one of his monkeys failed on a string-pulling discrimination task but only because it had found a way of pulling both strings – the correct and the incorrect – on each trial, thereby displaying more intelligence than the experimenter had allowed for. The problem here is that unsuccessful or successful performance, whether in the laboratory or in the natural environment, does not by itself tell us whether the subject's behavior involved the simpler processes of habituation, persistence, and association or the more complex cognitive processes of prediction, deduction, abstraction, and extrapolation. Clearly, this problem calls for careful experimental studies designed to analyze and isolate the abilities required or involved in the successful performance of various test tasks under given conditions. However, both Charlesworth and Trevarthen seem to come out against experimental analysis and in favor of observational study of spontaneous behavior. It is not clear to me how the observation of spontaneous intellectual feats would lead to the isolation and clear definition of the cognitive processes that contribute to the production of different types of intelligent actions.

Observations of spontaneous behavior undoubtedly provide fascinating instances of the intellectual feats of which an animal is capable, and the documentation of these feats by ethologists has opened the eyes of other behavior scientists to the richness of the behavior that awaits understanding. But field observations provide no basis for deciding with certainty which type of underlying processes, sensory salience, conditioned expectancy, discrepancy or novelty, associations (form, spatial, or temporal), conceptual principle, abstraction, extrapolation, etc., or what combination of these processes, may have been involved in a given intellectual feat. Indeed what little progress has been made in specifying cognitive abilities and understanding their underlying processes is due largely to analytic studies (experimental or statistical) of the responses of subjects in highly contrived tests. So far as the work with animals is concerned, there is a long tradition of careful experimental analysis of cognitive abilities, which started with Hunter (1913, 1929) and Lashley (1929), and has been nurtured over the years by Krechevsky (1937), Hebb (1946), and Nissen (1951), and more recently by Menzel (1973), Premack (1976) and others (see Warren 1973, Riopelle and Hill 1973). We must look to this tradition more than to field studies for the final step that is required for delineating and classifying cognitive abilities and understanding the underlying processes.

Communication and intentionality

Trevarthen, in his paper, has treated us to a thoughtful study of human development within a broad perspective that ranges from the neurobiological to the psychological and societal. He tells us about the development of communicative acts in the infant – about how they are shaped from the rather disjointed and chance 'biological expressions', involving arms, hands, face, mouth, eyes, and diverse vocalizations (gurgles, shouts, and calls), to the more coherent and purposeful culturally shaped communicative actions which express interests, needs, and commands. And he has neatly documented how this development is normally tied to mother–infant interactions, interactions that not only facilitate the occurrence of communicative episodes and hence the development of communicative skills, but also nurture the type of 'intersubjective understanding' on which human societal organization largely rests. Studies like these certainly make an important contribution to the understanding of the nature and function of language and other forms of communication and of their role in the intellectual, emotional, and social life of man.

Trevarthen notes that many expressions, responses, or gestures of the infant are 'understood' by the mother or an onlooker as signifying something about the current state or wishes of the infant, and suggests that such communicative acts are intentional. But there are difficulties with this interpretation. The mere fact that the *investigator* knows that intentional communication is typical of adult social interactions is not sufficient grounds for asserting that the infant's behavior in relation to the mother is intentional. Whether such acts are to be considered intentional must be determined by careful experimental analysis designed to separate what we might reasonably call intentional action from action that is merely an expression of a motivational state or a response to a certain stimulus configuration. Otherwise the use of the term intention will remain ad hoc and vague, telling us more about the biases of the investigator than about the processes underlying the behavior being observed. I believe that intentionality is an important aspect of primate intelligence, but that in order to understand the underlying processes and their ontogenetic development we must first try to define intentional action in terms of experimental criteria that clearly separate it from behavior that can be explained in terms of preference, discrimination, choice, and decision. Elsewhere I have indicated in rough terms how choice differs from discrimination, and how decision differs from choice, and have speculated about the additional factors that might be involved in intention (Bindra 1976). For the present discussion, it may be useful if Trevarthen were to tell us what his criteria are for distinguishing between these different determinants of adaptive behavior, and how he would proceed to demonstrate intentionality.

Psychobiology of man

Trevarthen suggests that the development of human communicative skills involves mental accomplishments that lie outside the concerns, or at least the practices, of both ethology and psychology. In trying to make this point appear plausible, Trevarthen is, of course, led to caricature ethology as the study of taxonomy and phylogeny of innate patterns of actions, and to caricature psychology as the application of certain simple-minded learning principles of the 1940s to the complex problems of intelligent actions. He then says that neither a too simple nativism (ethology) nor an unbridled empiricism (psychology) can deal with the intersubjective understanding and intentional actions that uniquely characterize human beings. He goes on to suggest that intentional actions are the outcomes of conscious understanding of the environment that only (human) mental processes can generate, and he recommends the study of these mental processes as the true study of human nature – 'a true psychobiology of man'.

Trevarthen does not make clear why he thinks that intersubjective understanding is a peculiarly human capability. It is obvious that coherent and stable patterns of group life emerge at least in some carnivores and primates, and it is unlikely that such coherent social organizations could develop or be sustained without some degree of intersubjective understanding and a network of interindividual emotional commitments. Mother–infant understanding is required not only for human language development but also for nursing and protection from predators and molesters in many species. Nor does Trevarthen explain why he considers intentional actions to be beyond the capabilities of an adult chimpanzee but not of an infant human.

The problems of intentionality, intersubjective understanding, and communicative action that Trevarthen so cogently raises seem to me to lie within the current concerns of many investigators of the psychobiology of adaptive behavior in animals and man. We do not need yet another discipline, called 'psychobiology of man', that would prompt young people into designating themselves as 'true human psychobiologists'! We have seen such self designations and ingroup, separatist, attitudes appear in connection with what have been thought to be new and promising disciplines, such as behaviorism, learning theory, ethology, cognitive psychology, psycholinguistics, and now sociobiology. They create all the excitement of new fashion for a brief period, but it is not clear that the excitement contributes to advanced understanding. It is doubtful that a new 'psychobiology of man' will fare differently.

The truth of the matter is that there are already several recognized disciplines that are concerned with understanding adaptive behavior; these include comparative psychology, neuropsychology, neurobiology, psychogenetics, learning theory, cognition, physiological psychology, psychopharmacology, primatology, ethology, anthropology, and so on. Being vital scientific disciplines, the objectives, methods, and interpretive concepts of these disciplines have continued to change over the years. Certainly neither ethology nor psychology today is what it was twenty-five, fifty, or seventy-five years ago. Today I see no overriding methodological or theoretical issues that separate those two or any other of the above disciplines; whether a person calls himself an ethologist or psychologist or neurobiologist or primatologist, his work – if it is good – is read by the others who are interested in the same phenomenon at the same level of analysis. All these disciplines share the common objective of understanding adaptive behavior, and their methods and interpretive concepts continue to converge. If we identified ourselves simply in terms of our common objectives of understanding adaptive behavior, we could save all the time that we now spend in arguing about whether one discipline is more limited or more promising than the others. Names of disciplines and chauvinistic self-designations are clearly not important. What is important is how rapidly we collectively progress toward achieving our common and important objective. It is my hope that we can learn to discard our parochial designations and become students devoted to the task of describing, analyzing, and interpreting the fascinating phenomena of adaptive behavior in all forms of animal life. We are all in this together, and we have a long way to go.

W. R. CHARLESWORTH: REPLY TO BINDRA'S COMMENTS

I agree with Professor Bindra's comment that the failure of early studies to advance our understanding of the nature of intelligence was the failure of investigators to adapt test tasks to the sensory–motor capacities of the species. This actually supports my point. Such failure was part of the overall failure to know the animal well enough before going into the laboratory and manipulating variables. Getting to know the animal well enough, as I point out in my paper, obviously means long hours of observing the animal in its natural habitat. Emphasizing this does not necessarily mean that I am against experimentation. Experimentation, obviously, has to be done to get a better understanding of behavior mechanisms. But it is where experimentation is done in the overall research sequence that makes the big difference. This is especially true when dealing with complicated organisms capable of generating responses to almost any conceivable stimulus situation. Man is the prime example. If we feel that everyday behavior is worth understanding, then we have to use it as the starting point of our research rather than laboratory or test behavior simply because we have no idea whether laboratory or test behavior really represents everyday behavior. For the human subject the laboratory is just another place to do something. If the laboratory is perceived differently from the everyday situation then the subject most probably is going to do something different. Not recognizing such profound disregard for problems of laboratory-to-nature generalizations on the part of his subjects, the scientist may labor a lifetime on a behavior that has validity only in his own laboratory. In order to minimize this, the research setting can be made to mimic the everyday situation as closely as possible. Then the manipulation of experimental variables can begin with some hope of producing results relevant to behavior outside the laboratory. Tinbergen's work on eggshell removal in the blackheaded gull as an antipredator device, or the observations by Lorenz, Tinbergen and others of fear responses in ducks and geese to overhead flying hawk shapes, which later led to the refined experiments of Melzack *et al.*, are good examples of field observations leading to experiments which resulted in exciting insights into everyday animal behavior and its function.

As for deliberate distortions of conditions in the laboratory in order to produce abnormal outcomes with the aim of shedding light on normal outcomes and their underlying mechanisms, there is no question that this approach can be helpful. There are two things to keep in mind, though, when doing this. First, phenotypes and ecological conditions vary widely for most mammal species. In man especially there is no dearth of the 'abnormal' which Professor Bindra refers to, both in behavior and in environment. Our study reported here with the normal and Down's Syndrome children manifests the importance we attach to studying individuals with diverse adaptations or diverse capacities for adaptation. ('Diverse' is, we feel, a more accurate way of describing differences between the two children than the term 'abnormal'.) The second thing to keep in mind is that there are usually very many ways to create normal or abnormal behavior (here I refer to Professor Bindra's hoarding studies). The natural environment of animals is doing it in different ways all the time. The question is whether a scientist's experimental way of creating behavior is at all like the environment's way. This is one of the problems I have in understanding Skinner. If the world conformed to all his contingency programs (laboriously wrung out of laboratory research), then scientists would really understand natural, everyday behavior. But I doubt this could even happen. The world and mankind have a way of eluding us with their unexpected novelties, defying our methodological power plays, or coercing us to recognize their truths even when we find it unpalatable or destructive of our most favorite theory.

I agree that good ideas come from many sources, but I am not convinced that different sources have the same scientific potential. Ideas completely devoid of empirical content are useless for most science (unless perhaps one is in mathematics and capable of Einstein's achievements). Ideas with empirical content acquired intuitively or through everyday observation and common sense are more useful, but not as useful as ideas coerced into being by the results of systematic observation of empirical phenomena. In this sense I am arguing that for most of us the inductive Baconian approach to generating good ideas is more productive than the Einsteinian approach with its reliance upon very abstract terms and deductive inferences.

I admit that the observation of spontaneous intellectual feats will not tell us much about their underlying cognitive processes. At the moment this does not bother me though, since I think it is more important to put the emphasis on intelligent behavior rather than the processes or dispositions that underly it. Evolution and everyday selection pressures operate on behavior, not on cognitive processes *per se*. I think it is important that we identify such behavior, plot its frequency and the conditions under which it occurs, and its overall effect on the individual, before we start thinking about processes. These processes, by the way, are largely hypothetical constructs or intervening variables, most of which have no representation in data from neurophysiological research. It is conceivable, therefore, that traditional concern with these processes may not lead us to the 'final step' that Professor Bindra mentions.

The need for a new discipline such as the psychobiology of man is being debated in many places, but the debates (interestingly enough) are not stopping the current formation of a human ethology society (or whatever name it finally acquires), the teaching of courses on human ethology, or the many queries from publishers and journal editors about the possibility of establishing human ethology or sociobiology journals. What is happening is that two major disciplines – human behavioral sciences such as psychology, sociology, anthropology, and the animal science of ethology – long separated by a big wall, are coming together now and human ethologists, or whatever one wants to call them, are standing on both sides of this wall. Whether their efforts will lead to a permanent fractionation of the field remains to be seen. I feel Professor Bindra's concerns very strongly and hope that his doubts will not be confirmed. I do not feel as he does, though, that existing disciplines, as they are now constituted both conceptually and institutionally, are capable of doing what a human ethology can potentially do. I can only offer as a defense for this feeling our work on studying intelligent behavior and how it came into being. It was a result of joining ethology to psychology in a very conscious way. A discipline that does not pay attention to environmental and developmental factors in its approach to intelligence is more limited and less promising in my mind than one that does, because there is sufficient evidence on hand to show that the two major factors of environment and development are indeed implicated in the construction of intelligence. The ethological approach to intelligent behavior presented here came into being as an attempt to overcome this limit by working out a conceptual scheme and method to incorporate these two factors into our definition of intelligence. This approach is by necessity interdisciplinary, thereby avoiding the problems and limitations of single-method approaches to intelligence. I admit, though, that our approach is single-mindedly observational at the moment, but this is a strategic move, rather than a permanent policy. Alfred North Whitehead in *The function of reason* (1929) noted that: 'Some of the major disasters of mankind have been produced by the narrowness of men with a good methodology.' This is, I feel, what happened (in not so drastic a way, of course) with psychology and its overemphasis upon testing and laboratory work.

I have another version of this quote – also by Whitehead: 'Ulysses has no use for Plato and the bones of his companions are strewn on many a reef and many an isle.' This quote refers to more than just methodological fixations; it also refers to the material, mechanistic, practical considerations that underlie much of biological research and the threat they pose research into that very mental, non-mechanistic, impractical phenomenon of man and culture.

C. TREVARTHEN: REPLY TO BINDRA'S COMMENTS

I am grateful to Dalbir Bindra for his comments, which should certainly help me clarify my argument. In replying, I wish to explain that some of the things I evidently appeared to say I do not intend to say, and to emphasize that there are observations which I thought were central to my case which he has overlooked. If I have expressed opinions that are overzealous, it is because I believe we are worrying at a doubt felt by many about the competence of human ethology. There is a problem. In my opinion it is not an insoluble one. Denying that there is a problem may get us deeper into the kind of trouble some of us, at least, feel we are in.

I would certainly not be much of a scientist if I did not believe in experimental studies. Of course, understanding of processes of intelligence (or any other natural activity of organisms) may be promoted by interventions that distort natural conditions. Indeed, usually I am at pains to say in my lectures on our research that we do not care about having an untampered with, 'ecological' (awful misuse of the word!) situation. We contrive a most bizarre studio situation in order to see the communication we seek as if it were in a test tube. The babies and mothers cope with the oddness of these surroundings, quickly ignore it, and produce intricate patterns for us to observe because it is in them to do so anywhere reasonably quiet, friendly and familiar. We do not experiment in the narrow stimulus-controlling, response-counting sense because we believe that would evade or destroy the kind of self-regulating process which we want to study. We, along with a number of workers who have published extremely interesting new data on mother–infant communication in the last two or three years, emphasize this descriptive side of the work to communicate with (or against) ardent infant experimenters (of which there are many hundreds very ardent, notably to the west of the Atlantic Ocean). We observe and record like Darwin on Galapagos Island (a favourable 'laboratory of evolution'), rather than test-stimulate and response-record. If I come out against experimental analysing in favour of observational study of spontaneous behaviour, I do so for strategic rather than doctrinaire reasons. I do not want to look for delicate interpersonal communication, mutually controlled, in conditions that devitalize it, just as one would not try to study genetics of fruitflies in a particle accelerator or with a pair of scissors.

Like Bindra I do not think that good ideas come from one or a few points of view. Fruitful ideas usually change emphasis, or change the kinds of facts taken into consideration. Of course we need everyone's skills. The powerful controls, quantitative methods and concepts of experimental psychology are 'in' us as are the well-tested tenets of evolutionary biology. The point is that, even with the most up to date versions of these, something is lacking. This lack is being filled in the studies just referred to by application of slightly different methods, largely benefiting from entirely new possibilities of data collection and analysis brought about by the availability of less expensive cine photography and television recording. There is a feeling of promise and discovery which we would be dull and misguided to pass by.

If I may encroach a bit on comments addressed more to Charlesworth, this word 'cognitive' begins to assume a rather pompous self-gratified air. Cognitive abilities, made comprehensible in developmental psychology largely by the success of Piaget's single-minded indifference to the once established views of experimental psychology in the US, are now given great explanatory power. They correct the unsatisfactory category of 'mediating variables' in learning theory. But one cannot claim that cognitive psychology knows all the answers, can one? In particular, I do not see the advantage in collapsing the babies' ability to communicate to persons with the object concept, to explain the former in terms of the latter, adding hypotheses of a few special sign stimuli like the face configuration or the smile to gain enough adaptive specificity. Cognition will soon become so big a word that it will be as hard to handle as 'intelligence'.

I am afraid that I do not feel in happy agreement with Dr Bindra's claim that 'what little progress has been made in specifying cognitive abilities . . . is due largely to analytic studies (experimental or statistical) of the responses of subjects in highly contrived tests', mainly because I feel unsure about the contrivances he has in mind. I thought we had gained most in the past ten years by relaxing our contrivances in testing infants, increasing their variety, giving the subject more of a say, as Piaget advocates.

More vital to my paper is the representation by Dr Bindra of the infant's behaviour as developing from 'rather disjointed and chance "biological expressions" . . . and diverse vocalizations (gurgles, shouts and calls), to the more coherent and purposeful culturally shaped communicative actions which express interests, needs and commands'. But I do not see his evidence for these sweeping claims. The larger part of my paper is a factual account of behaviours which are coherent, certainly not chance, and which I feel sure, as a result of my detailed and analytical photographic studies, bear direct morphological resemblance to culturally shaped communicative actions of adults in all human societies. The findings of preadaptive structure and process are so promising, even if startling, that I am planning to expose them to even closer examination and even more elaborate analysis. I am certain that if the interactions with the mother may, certainly do, facilitate occurrence of communicative episodes (it is easier to communicate with someone than with no one) and hence nurture the development of communicative skills, these skills do not *originate* by this means. The details of infant behaviour show that both infant and mother contribute to both perception and production of acts of communication. In the infant's case these acts are preadaptive to gestures that become ritualized and to grammatically formed patterns of speech acts that develop into the articulate words of a particular language. I propose and attempt to support the idea that intersubjective understanding is not acquired by a random, structureless gurgling infant by importation from the mother. It is not synthesized from language or social existence. The complexity of the loose relationship and interaction between mother and infant from early days makes this interpretation untenable. What the baby does has an innate foundation which one can see. The evidence for this conclusion is objective, if about subjective events for which we humans have strong and very useful powers of perception and understanding, would we only use them.

May I ask what is the 'mere' expression of a motivational state which leads to the *form* of a reach and grasp movement in a one-month-old? Does motivational state include formulation of the movements of a smile, a look of puzzlement or any one of a hundred other patterns of expression on the face of a two-month-old responding face-to-face? If so, is not motivation a more elaborate, more essential attribute of the brain than any unit of response recognized by the observer's selective vision?

Intention is a difficult term, but it has an established often-used place in common language, in which it has a meaning allied to 'motive'. I have explained my use of 'intention' to designate properties of infant movements elsewhere (Trevarthen 1974c, 1977, 1978b). What 'intention' means in common speech is what I mean when I say the patterns of action of the baby have an intentionality that cannot be explained by reference to basic body-serving motive states, arousals, excitements, drives, added to any number of conditioned responses. I am not able to understand what it means to define intentional action in terms of experimental criteria that clearly separate it from preference, discrimination, choice and decision. These I believe remain inseparable from intentional control in all its forms, except that they are more directly linked to measurement of effects of intentional control. I shall certainly read Bindra's book on how these factors or processes can be separated procedurally. Perhaps he is using all these words in a special technical sense.

I think I have said enough in my paper to indicate how I use the word intention to describe the goal-directed property of infant acts. I must, however, stress that I have nowhere stated that this form of image-based or model-based predictivity is fully fledged in a young infant. Nothing is easier than demonstrating that young infants have less aware, less elaborate, less defined, less differentiated and very much less effective intentions than an adult, or, for that matter, than the same infant will have a few months later. If intentions must be articulate and self-conscious in the sense that is required for legal responsibility then infants do not have intentions. But then neither do any animals or many adult humans have intentions. Ordinary lapses of this kind of intention must be common in all of us. Tracing the life history and cultivation of the elaboration of purposive control offers endless interesting prospects for human ethology and all the other disciplines called to battle by Professor Bindra at the end of his paper. But, it is important to all of these established fields if rudiments of intention, preformed acts of predictive mastery that are oriented to potentially elaborate perceptual monitoring, already exist just after birth. If, further, in their limited state, these rudiments can already enter into control of interpersonal interactions before they can mechanically explore or use any 'objects' of praxis, this is even more important. As it happens the evidence shows that the cognitive powers of infants are lop-sided at the start so as to seek out cognizant persons as cooperators. That is how we humans start in the task of developing a conscious responsibility for intention.

I am very sorry if I gave the impression that I believe conscious understanding is unique to human mental processes. Unlike Descartes, I certainly would attribute some manner of consciousness and intentionality to some animals, though the evolutionary elaboration of these processes is at present poorly understood. Intentional actions, as I see them, are certainly not beyond an adult chimpanzee. However, I do believe, and did say, that the *quality* of human understanding and purposes is unique. I think this uniqueness, when we know it better, will explain the achievements of individual learning in culture, not the other way about. Culture doesn't make man unique. Man uniquely needs culture.

Please do not think of me as a rouser of young people's irresponsible urges. I am not so young as to take that risk. Nor would I be responsible for misinterpretation of what I say by the politically overcharged. But I do wish to suggest that the notion of psychobiology, of an evolutionary mechanistic mentalism fitted to understanding of man's estate in any ways that are promising, by brain science, introspection, analysis (statistical or experimental), anything that works, may defend us from the 'self designations and ingroup, separatist, attitudes' of the *other* psychologists. Finally, I'd hate to create the excitement of new fashion for anything less than a long period.

References

Ainsworth, M. D. S. 1973. The development of infant–mother attachment. In B. M. Caldwell and H. N. Ricciuti (eds.), *Review of child development research*, vol. III. Chicago: University of Chicago Press.

Alegria, J. and Noirot, E. 1977. Auditory localization in neonates. Paper presented to the International Neuropsychological Symposium, Frascati, June 1977.

Amsterdam, B. 1972. Mirror self-image reactions before age two. *Developmental psychobiology*, 5:297–305.

Armen, J.-C. 1974. *Gazelle-boy*. London: Bodley Head (*L'Enfant sauvage du grand desert*). Neuchatel: Delachaux et Niestlé, 1976).

Baldwin, A. 1967. *Theories of child development*. New York: Wiley.

Baldwin, J. M. 1895. *Mental development in the child and the race*. New York: Macmillan.

1902. *Development and evolution*. New York: Macmillan.

Barker, R. G. 1968. *Ecological psychology: concepts and methods for studying the environment of human behavior*. Stanford: Stanford University Press.

Barlow, H. B. 1975. Visual experience and cortical development. *Nature*, 258:199–204.

Barnett, S. A. 1973. Homo docens. *Journal of Biosocial Science*, 5:393–403.

Bates, E., Camaioni, L. and Volterra, V. 1975. The acquisition of performatives prior to speech. *Merrill-Palmer Quarterly*, 21:205–6.

Bayley, N. 1969. *Manual for the Bayley scales of infant development*. New York: Psychological Corporation.

Becker, E. 1972. *The birth and death of meaning*. 2nd edn. Harmondsworth: Penguin.

Berger, P. L. and Luckmann, T. 1966. *The social construction of reality*. New York: Doubleday.

Bindra, D. 1948. What makes rats hoard? *Journal of Comparative and Physiological Psychology*, 41:397–402.

1976. *A theory of intelligent behavior*. New York: John Wiley.

Binet, A. and Simon, T. 1905. Méthodes nouvelles pour le diagnostic du niveau intellectuel des anormaux. *Année psychologique*, 11:191–244.

Bitterman, M. E. 1965a. The evolution of intelligence. *Scientific American*, 212(1):92–100.

1965b. Phyletic differences in learning. *American Psychologist*, 20:396–410.

Blakemore, C. 1974. Development of functional connexions in the mammalian visual system. *British Medical Bulletin*, 30:152–7.

Blehar, M. C., Lieberman, A. F. and Ainsworth, M. D. S. 1977. Early face-to-face interaction and its relation to later mother–infant attachment. *Child Development*, 48:182–94.

Blurton Jones, N. (ed.) 1972. *Ethological studies of child behaviour*. Cambridge: Cambridge University Press.

Boring, E. G. 1922. *A history of experimental psychology*. 2nd edn 1957. New York: Appleton-Century-Crofts.

Bourne, L. E., Jr, Ekstrand, B. R. and Dominowski, R. L. 1971. *The psychology of thinking*. Englewood Cliffs, New Jersey: Prentice Hall.

Bower, T. G. R. 1974. *Development in infancy*. San Francisco: Freeman.

Bowlby, J. 1969. *Attachment and Loss*, vol. I. New York: Basic Books.

Brazelton, T. B., Koslowski, B. and Main, M. 1974. The origins of reciprocity: the early mother–infant interaction. In M. Lewis and L. A. Rosenblum (eds.), *Origins of behavior*, vol. I, *The effect of the infant on its caregiver*. New York: Wiley.

Brazelton, T. B., Tronick, E., Adamson, L., Als, H. and Wise, S. 1975. Early mother–infant reciprocity. In M. O'Connor (ed.), *Parent–infant interaction*. Amsterdam: Elsevier.

Bruner, J. S. 1968. *Processes of cognitive growth: infancy*. Worcester, Mass.: Clark University Press.

1976. From communication to language – a psychological perspective. *Cognition*, 3:255–87.

Brunswik, E. 1956. *Perception and the representative design of psychological experiments*. Berkeley: University of California Press.

Buss, A. R. and Poley, W. 1976. *Individual differences: traits and factors*. New York: Gardner Press.

Butcher, H. J. 1968. *Human intelligence: its nature and assessment*. London: Methuen.

Charlesworth, W. R. 1972. Ethology's modest contribution to the assessment of education. In C. D. Smock and R. R. Cocking (eds.), *New perspectives in development assessment*. Mathemagenic Activities Program Report. Athens: University of Georgia.

1973. Ethology's contribution to a framework for relevant research. In J. H. Turnure *et al.*, *American Psychological Association Symposium Paper*. Research, Development and Demonstration Center Occasional Paper no. 24. Minneapolis: University of Minnesota.

1978a. Ethology: its relevance for observational studies of human adaptation. In Gene P. Sackett (ed.), *Observing behavior: theory and applications in mental retardation*. Baltimore: University Park Press.

1978b. Ethology: understanding the other half of intelligence. *Social Science Information*, 17(2):231–77.

Charlesworth, W. R. and Bart, W. 1976. Some contributions of ethology for education. *Educational Studies*, 7(3):258–72.

Charlesworth, W. R., Kjergaard, L., Fausch, D., Daniels, S., Binger, K. and

Spiker, D. 1976. *A method for studying adaptive behavior in life situations: A study of every day problem solving in a normal and Down's Syndrome child.* Research, Development and Demonstration Center in Education of Handicapped Children Development Report no. 6. Minneapolis: University of Minnesota.

Charlesworth, W. R. and Spiker, D. 1975. An ethological approach to observation in learning settings. In R. Weinberg and F. Wood (eds.), *Observation of pupils and teachers in mainstream and special education settings: alternative strategies.* Reston, Virginia: Council for Exceptional Children.

Cragg. B. G. 1975. The development of synapses in the visual system of the cat. *Journal of Comparative Neurology*, 160:147–66.

Darwin, C. 1872. *The expression of emotion in man and animals.* London: Methuen.
    1881. *The formation of vegetable mould through the action of worms with observations on their habits.* London: John Murray.

Donaldson, M. 1977. Development of conceptualization. In M. Vernon and V. Hamilton (eds.), *Development of cognitive processes.* New York and London: Academic Press.

Eibl-Eibesfeldt, I. and Hass. H. 1966. Zum Projekt einer ethologisch-orientierten Untersuchung menschlichen Verhaltens. *Mitteilung der Max-Planck-Gesellschaft*, 6:383–96.

Eibl-Eibesfeldt, I., and Sielmann, H. 1962. Beobachtungen am Spechtfinken Cactospiza pallida (Fringillidae), *Journal für Ornithologie*, 103:92–101.

Ekman, P. and Friesen, W. V. 1975. *Unmasking the face.* Englewood Cliffs, New Jersey: Prentice-Hall.

Fawl, C. L. 1963. Disturbances experienced by children in their natural habitats. In R. G. Barker (ed.), *The stream of behavior.* New York: Appleton-Century-Crofts.

Galton, F. 1869. *Hereditary genius: an inquiry into its laws and consequences.* London: Macmillan.

Gesell, A. and Amatruda, C. S. 1962. *Developmental diagnosis: normal and abnormal child development, clinical methods and practical applications.* New York: Harper.

Gladwin, T. 1970. *East is a big bird: navigation and logic on Puluwat Atoll.* Cambridge, Mass.: Harvard University Press.

Goodall, J. 1965. Chimpanzees of the Gombe Stream Reserve. In I. DeVore (ed.), *Primate behavior.* New York: Holt, Rinehart & Winston.

Gottlieb, G. 1971. *The development of species identification in birds.* Chicago: University of Chicago Press.

Griffiths, R. 1954. *The abilities of babies.* London: University of London Press.

Gruber, H. E. and Barrett, P. H. 1974. *Darwin on man.* London: Wildwood House.

Guilford, J. P. 1967. *The nature of human intelligence.* New York: McGraw-Hill.

Gunnell, J. G. 1975. *Philosophy, science, and political inquiry.* Morristown, New Jersey: General Learning Press.

Haith, M. 1977. Visual competence in early infancy. In R. Held, H. Leibowitz and H.-L. Teuber (eds.), *Handbook of sensory physiology*, vol. VIII. Berlin: Springer.

Halliday, M. A. K. 1975. *Learning how to mean.* London: Arnold.

Hamilton, A. 1970. Nature and nurture: child rearing in North-Central Arnheim Land. Unpublished M.A. thesis, University of Sydney.

Hamlyn, D. W. 1974. Person-perception and understanding of others. In T. Mischel (ed.), *Understanding other persons.* Oxford: Blackwell.

Harlow, H. F. 1958. The evolution of learning. In Roe and Simpson.

1959. Learning set and error factor theory. In S. Koch (ed.), *Psychology: a study of a science*, vol. II. New York: McGraw-Hill.

Harlow, H. F. Harlow, M. K., Schiltz, K. A. and Mohr, D. J. 1971. The effect of early adverse and enriched environments, in the learning ability of Rhesus monkeys. In Leonard Jarrad (ed.), *Cognitive processes in non-human primates*. New York: Academic Press.

Hebb, D. O. 1946. Emotion in man and animal: an analysis of the intuitive processes of recognition. *Psychological Review*, 53:88–106.

1949. *The organization of behavior*. New York: Wiley.

Heider, F. 1958. *The psychology of interpersonal relations*. New York: Wiley.

Hinde, R. A. 1976. On describing relationships. *Journal of Child Psychology and Psychiatry*, 17:1–19.

Hinde, R. A. and Tinbergen, N. 1958. The comparative study of species-specific behavior. In Roe and Simpson 1958.

Hobhouse, L. T. 1901. *Mind in evolution*. New York: Macmillan.

Hodos, W. 1970. Evolutionary interpretation of neural and behavioral studies of living vertebrates. In F. O. Schmitt (ed.), *The neurosciences: second program*. New York: Rockefeller University Press.

Hodos, W. and Campbell, C. B. G. 1969. Scala naturae: why there is no theory in comparative psychology. *Psychological Review*, 76:337–50.

Horn, J. L. 1976. Human abilities: a review of research and theory in the early 1970's. *Annual Review of Psychology*, 27:437–85.

Hubel, D. H., Wiesel, T. N. and Le Vay, S. 1977. Plasticity of ocular dominance columns in monkey striate cortex. *Philosophical Transactions of the Royal Society of London, Series B*, 278:131–63.

Humphrey, N. K. 1976. The social function of intellect. In P. Bateson and R. Hinde (eds.), *Growing points in ethology*. Cambridge: Cambridge University Press.

1977. Review of D. R. Griffin's *The question of animal awareness: evolutionary continuity of mental experience*. *Animal Behavior*, 2:521–2.

Humphrey, T. 1969. Postnatal repetition of human prenatal activity sequences with some suggestions of their neuroanatomical basis. In R. J. Robinson (ed.), *Brain and early behavior: development in the fetus and infant*. New York: Academic Press.

Hunt, J. McV. 1961. *Intelligence and experience*. New York: Ronald Press Co.

Hunter, W. S. 1913. The delayed reaction in animals and children. *Behavior Monographs*, 2(6).

1929. Experimental studies of learning. In C. Murchison (ed.), *Foundations of experimental psychology*. Worcester, Mass.: Clark University Press.

Innerhofer, P. 1977. *Das Münchner Trainingmodell: Beobachtung-Analyse-Verhaltensänderung*. Heidelberg/Berlin: Springer Verlag.

James, W. 1910. *Principles of psychology*. New York: Holt, Rinehart and Winston.

Jencks, C., Smith, M., Acland, H., Bane, M., Cohen, D., Gintis, H., Heyus, B. and Michelson, S. 1972. *Inequality: a reassessment of the effect of family and schooling in America*. New York: Macmillan.

Jerison, H. J. 1973. *Evolution of the brain and intelligence*. New York: Academic Press.

Jouvet, M. 1975. The function of dreaming: a neurophysiologist's point of view. In M. S. Gazzaniga and C. Blakemore (eds.), *Handbook of psychobiology*. New York: Academic Press.

Kagan, J. 1971. *Change and continuity in infancy*. New York: Wiley.

Kaye, K. 1977. Toward the origin of dialogue. In H. R. Schaffer (ed.), *Studies in mother–infant interaction*. London/New York: Academic Press.

Klein, R. G. 1973. *Ice-age hunters of the Ukraine*. Chicago: University of Chicago Press.

Klopfer, P. and Hailman, J. P. 1967. *An introduction to animal behavior: ethology's first century*. Englewood Cliffs, New Jersey: Prentice Hall.

Köhler, W. 1921. *The mentality of apes*. London: Harcourt Brace.

Kortlandt, A. 1968. Handgebrauch bei freilebenden Schimpansen. In B. Rensch (ed.), *Handgebrauch und Verständigung bei Affen und Frühmenschen*. Bern/Stuttgart: Hans Huber.

Krechevsky, I. 1937. A note concerning 'The nature of discrimination learning in animals'. *Psychological Review*, 44:97–103.

Lashley, K. S. 1929. *Brain mechanisms and intelligence: a quantitative study of injuries to the brain*. Chicago: University of Chicago Press.

1949. Persistent problems in the evolution of mind. *Quarterly Review of Biology*, 24:28–42.

Lazarus, R. S., Averill, J. R. and Opton, E. M., Jr. 1974. The psychology of coping: issues of research and assessment. In G. V. Coelho, D. A. Hamburg and J. E. Adams (eds.), *Coping and adaptation*. New York: Basic Books.

Lewis, M. and Brooks, J. 1975. Infants' social perception: a constructivist view. In L. B. Cohen and P. Salapatek (eds.), *Infant perception: from sensation to cognition*, vol. II. New York: Academic Press.

Lipmann, O. 1918. Uber Begriff und Erforschung der natürlichen Intelligenz. *Zeitschrift für angewandte Psychologie*, 13:192–201.

Lockhard, R. B. 1971. Reflections on the fall of comparative psychology: is there a message for us all? *American Psychologist*, 26:168–79.

Lorenz, K. 1971. Methods of approach to the problems of behavior. In *Studies in animal and human behavior*, vol. II. Cambridge, Mass: Harvard University Press.

1973. *Die Rückseite des Spiegels*. Munich: Piper Verlag. English version, *Behind the mirror: a search for a natural history of human knowledge*. New York: Harcourt Brace Jovanovich, 1977.

McGraw, M. B. 1943. *The neuromuscular maturation of the human infant*. New York: Columbia University Press.

McGrew, W. C. 1972. *An ethological study of children's behavior*. New York: Academic Press.

McGurk, H. (ed.) 1977. *Ecological factors in human development*. Amsterdam: North-Holland Pub. Co.

Mahler, M. 1963. Thoughts about development and individuation. *Psychoanalytic Development of the Child*, 18:307–23.

Maratos, O. 1973. The origin and development of imitation in the first six months of life. Unpublished Ph.D. thesis, University of Geneva.

Mason, O. T. 1966. *The origins of invention*. First published 1895. Cambridge, Mass.: MIT Press.

Mason, W. A. and Lott, D. F. 1976. Ethology and comparative psychology. *Annual Review of Psychology*, 27:129–54.

Maurer, D. and Salapatek, P. 1976. Developmental changes in the scanning of faces by infants. *Child Development*, 47:523–7.

Mayr, E. 1970. *Populations, species, and evolution*. Cambridge, Mass.: Harvard University Press.

Mead, G. H. 1934. *Mind, self and society*. Chicago: University of Chicago Press.

Meltzoff, A. N. and Moore, M. K. 1977. Imitation of facial and manual gestures by human neonates. *Science*, 198:75–8.

Menzel, E. W. 1971. Communication about the environment in a group of young chimpanzees. *Folia Primatologica*, 15:220–32.

  1973. Chimpanzee spatial memory organization. *Science*, 182:943–5.

Miller, D. B. 1977. Role of naturalistic observation in comparative psychology. *American Psychologist*, 32:211–19.

Mills, W. 1898. *The nature and development of animal intelligence*. London: T. Fisher Unwin.

Moynihan, M. 1976. *The new world primates*. Princeton: Princeton University Press.

Murray, L. 1978 (in preparation). Infants' capacities for regulating interactions with their mothers and the function of emotions. Unpublished Ph.D. thesis, University of Edinburgh.

Ninio, A. and Bruner, J. S. 1978. The achievement and antecedents of labelling. *Journal of Child Language*, 5:1–15.

Nissen, H. W. 1951. Analysis of a complex conditional reaction in chimpanzee. *Journal of Comparative and Physiological Psychology*, 44:9–16.

Oster, H. and Ekman, P. 1977. Facial behavior in child development. In A. Collins (ed.), *Minnesota Symposium on Child Development*. New York: Thomas A. Crowell.

Papoušek, H. 1967. Experimental studies of appetitional behaviour in human newborns and infants. In H. W. Stevenson, E. H. Hess and H. L. Rheingold (eds.), *Early behavior: comparative and developmental approaches*. New York: Wiley.

  1969. Individual variability in learned responses in human infants. In R. J. Robinson (ed.), *Brain and early behavior: development in fetus and infant*. New York: Academic Press.

Papoušek, H. and Papoušek, M. 1975. Cognitive aspects of preverbal social interaction between human infants and adults. In M. O'Connor (ed.), *Parent–infant interaction*. Amsterdam: Elsevier.

Piaget, J. 1936. *La Naissance de l'intelligence chez l'enfant*. Neuchatel: Delachaux and Niestlé.

  1947. *The psychology of intelligence*. London: Routledge and Kegan Paul.

  1952. *The origins of intelligence in children*. New York: International University Press.

  1962. *Play, dreams and imitation in childhood*. New York: Norton.

Premack, D. 1976. *Intelligence in ape and man*. Hillsdale, New Jersey: Erlbaum.

Razran, G. 1971. *Mind in evolution: an East–West synthesis of learned behavior and cognition*. Boston: Houghton-Mifflin.

Rensch, B. 1973. *Gedächtnis, Begriffsbildung und Planhandlung bei Tieren*. Berlin: Verlag Paul Parey.

Riopelle, A. J. and Hill, C. W. 1973. Complex processes. In D. A. Dewsbury and D. A. Rethlingshafer (eds.), *Comparative psychology: a modern survey*. New York: McGraw-Hill.

Roe, A. and Simpson, G. G. (eds.) 1958. *Behavior in evolution*. New Haven: Yale University Press.

Romanes, G. J. 1884. *Mental evolution in animals*. New York: AMS Press.

  1889. *Mental evolution in man: origin of human faculty*. New York: Appleton.

Rutter, M. 1972. *Maternal deprivation reassessed*. Harmondsworth: Penguin.

Schaffer, H. R. 1977. Early interactive development. In *Studies in mother–infant interaction*. New York/London: Academic Press.

Segal, H. 1964. *Introduction to the work of Melanie Klein*. London: Hogarth Press.

Snow, C. E. 1972. Mothers' speech to children learning language. *Child Development*, 43:549–65.

Spearman, C. 1927. *The abilities of man*. New York: Macmillan.

Spencer, H. 1855. *Principles of psychology*. London: Longman, Brown, Green, and Longmans.

Sperry, R. W. 1955. On the neural basis of the conditioned response. *British Journal of Animal Behaviour*, 3:41–4.

  1975. In search of Psyche. In F. G. Worden, J. P. Swazey and G. Adelman (eds.), *The neurosciences: Paths of discovery*. Cambridge, Mass.: MIT Press.

  1976. Mental phenomena as causal determinants in brain function. In G. G. Globus *et al.* (eds.), *Consciousness and the Brain*. New York and London: Plenum.

Spiker, D. 1977. An observational study of problem solving in six preschoolers. Paper presented at the Society for Research in Child Development, New Orleans, March 1977.

Spitz, R. A. 1965. *The first year of life*. New York: International Universities Press.

Stayton, D. J., Hogan, R. and Ainsworth, M. D. S. 1971. Infant obedience and maternal behaviour: the origins of socialization considered. *Child Development*, 42:1057–69.

Stern, D. N. 1974. Mother and infant at play: the dyadic interaction involving facial, vocal and gaze behaviours. In M. Lewis and L. Rosenblum (eds.), *Origins of behavior*, vol. I, *The effect of the infant on its caregiver*. New York/London: Wiley.

Stern, D. N., Jaffe, J., Beebe, B. and Bennett, S. L. 1975. Vocalizing in unison and alternation: two modes of communication within the mother–infant dyad. *Annals of the New York Academy of Sciences*, 263:89–100.

Stern, E. 1919. Der Begriff und die Untersuchung der natürlichen Intelligenz, *Monatsschrift für Psychiatrie und Neurologie*, 46:181–205.

Stern, W. 1920. *Die Intelligenz der Kinder und Jugendlichen*. Leipzig: Johann Ambrosius Barth.

Sylvester-Bradley, B. 1977. The study of mother–infant relationships in the first six months of life. Unpublished Ph.D. thesis, University of Edinburgh.

Sylvester-Bradley, B. and Trevarthen, C. 1978 (in press). Baby talk as an adaptation to the infant's communication. In N. Waterson and C. Snow (eds.), *Development of communication: social and pragmatic factors in language acquisition*. London: Wiley.

Thompson, N. 1973. Book review of Razran's *Mind in Evolution*. *Animal Behavior*, 21:402–5.

Thorndike, E. L. 1898. Animal intelligence: an experimental study of the associative processes in animals. *Psychological Review Monograph*. Supplement 2. 1911. *Animal intelligence*. New York: Macmillan.

Tinbergen, N. 1972. Foreword. In N. Blurton Jones 1972, vii–ix.

Tolman, E. C. 1932. *Purposive behavior in animals and men*. New York: Appleton-Century-Crofts.

Toulmin, S. 1972. *Human understanding*. Princeton, New Jersey: Princeton University Press.

Trevarthen, C. 1974a. L'action dans l'espace et la perception de l'espace: méchanismes cérébraux de base. In F. Bresson *et al.* (eds.), *De l'éspace corporel a l'éspace écologique*. Paris: Presses Universitaires de France.
1974b. Conversations with a two-month-old. *New Scientist* (2 May): 230–5.
1974c. The psychobiology of speech development. In E. Lenneberg (ed.), *Language and brain: developmental aspects*. Neurosciences Research Program Bulletin no. 12, 570–85.
1974d. Intersubjectivity and imitation in infants. *Proceedings of the Annual Conference of the British Psychological Society, April 1974. Bangor, N. Wales.* London: British Psychological Society.
1977. Descriptive analyses of infant communicative behaviour. In H. R. Schaffer (ed.), *Studies in mother–infant interaction*. London: Academic Press.
1978a (in press). Neuroembryology and the development of perception. In F. Falkner and J. Tanner (eds.), *Human Growth*, vol. III. New York: Plenum.
1978b (in press). Communication and cooperation in early infancy. A description of primary intersubjectivity. In M. Bullowa (ed.), *Before speech: the beginnings of human communication*. Cambridge: Cambridge University Press.
1978c (in press). Basic patterns of psychogenetic change in infancy. In H. Nathan (ed.), *Proceedings of the O.E.C.D. Conference on dips in learning*. Paris: OECD.

Trevarthen, C. and Hubley, P. 1978 (in press). Secondary intersubjectivity: confidence, confiding and acts of meaning in the first year. In A. Lock (ed.), *Action, gesture and symbol: The emergence of language*. London: Academic Press.

Trevarthen, C., Hubley, P. and Sheeran, L. 1975. Les activités innées du nourrisson. *La Recherche*, 6:447–58.

von Uexküll, J. 1957. A stroll through the world of animals and men. In C. H. Schuller (ed.), *Instructive behavior*. First published 1938. New York: International Universities Press.

Wahler, R. G., House, A. E. and Stambaugh, E. E. 1976. *Ecological assessment of child problem behavior*. Elmsford, New York: Pergamon Press.

Wallace, A. R. 1870. *Contributions to the theory of natural selection: a series of essays*. London: Macmillan.

Warren, J. M. 1973. Learning in vertebrates. In D. A. Dewsbury and D. A. Rethlingshafer (eds.), *Comparative psychology: a modern survey*. New York: McGraw-Hill.

Watson, J. S. 1973. Smiling, cooing and 'the game'. *Merrill-Palmer Quarterly*, 18:323–39.

Weiss, P. 1949. The biological basis of adaptation. In J. Romano (ed.), *Adaptation*. Ithaca: Cornell University Press.

Whitehead, A. N. 1929. *The function of reason*. Boston: Beacon Press.

Willems, E. P. and Rausch, H. L. (eds.) 1969. *Naturalistic viewpoints in psychological research*. New York: Holt, Rinehart and Winston.

Winnicott, D. W. 1965. *The maturational process and the facilitating environment, studies in the theory of emotional development*. London: Hogarth Press and the Institute of Psychoanalysis.

Wolff, P. 1963. Observations on the early development of smiling. In B. M. Foss (ed.), *Determinants of infant behaviour*, vol. II. London: Methuen.

1969. The natural history of crying and other vocalizations in early infancy. In B. M. Foss (ed.), *Determinants of infant behaviour*, vol. IV. London: Methuen.

Wright, H. F. 1960. Observational child study. In Paul Mussen (ed.), *Handbook of research methods in child development*. New York: Wiley.

9. Consequences of early experience

9.1. Social attachment and a sense of security

ERIC A. SALZEN

I. Early experience, sensory homeostasis, and appetitive orientation

One of the most important consequences of early experience in man and the primates is the acquisition of a familiar environment and a social partner, i.e. attachment. The evidences of such consequences are well documented and have been reviewed by Ainsworth (1962), Ainsworth and Wittig (1969), Bowlby (1969, 1973), Bronfenbrenner (1968), Hoppe, Milton and Simmel (1970), Mitchell (1968, 1970), Rosenblum (1971), Rutter (1972) and Schaffer (1971). There is some agreement that the short-term consequences of early experience include a tendency to maintain proximity to the parent and to show particular patterns of behaviour, so-called attachment behaviours, if this proximity is altered or broken, e.g. Ainsworth (1962), Ainsworth and Wittig (1969), Schaffer and Emerson (1964), Schaffer (1971). Where sexual and other adult behaviours are affected the effects are probably of a more general nature (cf. Money, Hampson and Hampson 1957, Jensen 1975).

Simple consideration would suggest three ways in which early experience might operate in the long-term and affect other behaviours.

(i) It may establish proximity relationships which will persist and, with generalization, will result in proximal contact-type consummatory behaviours being most likely to be elicited by appropriate species partners, i.e. will ensure appropriate associations for normal social interactions, e.g. grooming, maternal care.

(ii) It may establish an affective (emotional) state associated with proximity of the appropriate species partner which affects the nature of subsequent interactions. This is a sense of security which permits other tendencies to operate freely, e.g. exploration, sexual behaviour.

(iii) It is possible that the early proximity-maintaining behaviour simply directs and facilitates social interactions during early development but that these social interactions then proceed to self-differentiate.

The differentiation of interaction patterns can be visualized through the epigenetic landscape metaphor (figure 1) conceived by Waddington (1956), and which I used (Salzen 1968) to illustrate the long-term consequences of imprinting. Such an interactionist approach is comparable with that of Rosenblatt, Turkewitz and Schneirla's (1961) analysis of developing mother–infant interactions in cats. Early experiences are critical at nodal points in pathways where alternative reciprocal interactions are determined and are especially significant because of their early point in the expanding epigenetic landscape. Murphy's (1947) canalization hypothesis may be included to show how early interactions can become firmly established. It should be noted that in all three of the above processes something like Tomkins' (1963) concept of snowballing could lead to profound later effects from small initial ones. There is no doubt that the third of the above processes must operate in development. It is not clear to what extent the first two processes contribute directly to later behaviour. The part they play in early interactions is clearly of some interest. These two processes will be examined in what follows.

1. The epigenetic landscape and developmental canalization. The biased balls represent initial developmental states, the channels represent developmental pathways terminating in alternative behavioural mechanisms. 'Epigenetic crises' are points where the balls may enter alternative channels. Early choice points are fundamental, especially where channels become deep, i.e. strongly canalized, and resistant to environmental forces for inter-channel transfer. (Modified from Waddington 1956.)

Bowlby's (1969) proximity-maintaining goal-steered system for attachment, my own neuronal model orientation system for imprinting (1962) and for environmental learning (1970), and Hunt's (1965) theory of intrinsic motivation can be regarded as versions of a basic orientation system which maintains the animal in a secure and safe environment and which has evolved for this function. In fact this behaviour system can be seen as one of three basically different systems operating in vertebrates. Scott (1958) has categorized behaviour into nine elements, as follows: investigative, shelter-seeking, ingestive, eliminative, sexual, epimeletic or care-giving, et-epimeletic or care-soliciting, agonistic, and allelomimetic behaviour. These can be grouped into three classes (figure 2) that correspond with the three behaviour systems proposed above. The first, and most obvious, includes sexual, care-giving (parental), and agonistic.

CLASSES OF BEHAVIOUR	ASSOCIATED EMOTIONAL CLASSES
Physiological homeostasis	
Ingestion/rejection	Comfort—Discomfort
Elimination	Hedonism—Asceticism
Respiration	Appetites—Aversions
Thermoregulation	
Sensory homeostasis	
Orientation	Attachment—Loss
Protection	Security—Insecurity
Shelter-seeking	Social—Antisocial
Investigation	Boredom—Interest
	Shyness—Confidence
Reproductive mechanisms	
Agonistic	Love—Hate—Envy
Sexual	Pride—Shame—Anger
Parental	Dominance—Submission

2. Classes of behaviour in higher vertebrates and the associated emotions in man. The classes of behaviour form three distinct groups of different mechanism, instigation, and function. Physiological homeostatic behaviours are concerned with maintaining the normal internal physiological state of the individual and are instigated by imbalances in physiological homeostasis. Sensory homeostatic behaviours are concerned with maintaining the individual in its existing satisfactory and secure environment and are instigated by changes in the environment. Reproductive behaviours are concerned with maintaining the species (or the individual's genes) and are instigated by specific hormonal balances. The emotional classes are the major psychological classes of emotion which are associated with these three types of behavioural system. Specific affective states and emotions are easily assigned to these larger classes of emotion.

These are associated behaviours which depend on hormonal states and which are concerned with maintaining the species; they form the class of *reproductive behaviour*. The second class includes ingestive, eliminative, and perhaps part of care-soliciting behaviour, and in addition we might add respiration, thermoregulation and skin-care. These are all concerned with maintaining the physiological state of the individual and arise from imbalances in physiological homeostatis. We can call this *physiological homeostatic behaviour*. The remaining elements of behaviour – shelter-seeking, care-soliciting (in part), allelomimetic (protective) and investigative all depend on changes in the environment for their occurrence, and serve to maintain the individual in its safe environment by restoring the familiar environment, since any change is potentially to the organism's detriment if the familiar existing environment is supporting normal bodily functions. We can call this class *sensory homeostatic behaviour*. It is the basic security motivation system and it takes precedence over the others which will only operate if the security system is in a set steady state.

The basis of the sensory homeostatic system is perhaps found in the simple reflex responses to contact stimulation described by Sherrington (1906). In principle, gentle contact stimulation will elicit extensor reflexes giving adient movements, while strong or repeated stimulation will elicit flexor responses giving abient movements which ultimately take the whole body away from the stimulus source. Carmichael (1970) cites evidences of these responses in mammalian embryos. Such extensor–flexor systems can develop into approach–withdrawal behaviours in the way Schneirla has detailed in his biphasic response theory (1959, 1965). Using Sherrington's (1906) notion that distance receptor stimulation gives 'precurrent actions' which bring about (or avoid) contact or proximal receptor stimulation, we can see that these actions are orientation movements. Orientation movements also serve the other two behaviour systems (*reproductive* and *physiological homeostatic*) and in the same way bring about the required proximal stimulation. They all constitute Craig's (1918) 'appetitive behaviour'.

II. Sensory homeostasis, orientation and attachment

At hatching or birth the infant vertebrate has an established sensory world – mainly contact, proprioception, thermal and kinaesthetic. The new environment represents a drastic change and gives massive alternating extensor and flexor activity – struggling with crying – representing orientation behaviour that may bring about the familiar contact stimulation. Struggling ceases when such stimulation is applied, cf. Salzen (1963, 1967) for chicks and monkey studies; Harlow (1960) and Harlow and Harlow (1965) for rhesus monkey; Mason and Berkson (1962) for chimpanzee; Birns, Blank and Bridger (1969) for the human infant. If contact stimulation is restricted in space and degree then local responses will be directed and will give the typical adjustive movements made by the infant in relation to parental movement and contact. Such movements have been described in general for the human neonate (Robinson and Tizard 1966), but there is need for further studies of the kind made by Prechtl (1958) of directed head-turning and rooting behaviour. Such movements also include the clinging and climbing reflexes of rhesus monkey infants described by Mowbray and Cadell (1962). If local stimulation is intense, the flexor responses will withdraw the affected area and may spread to produce distress struggling again. If the infant is mobile total body withdrawal may occur; thus Harlow, Gluck and Suomi (1972) describe how an ice-cold mother surrogate caused an infant rhesus to flee screaming never to return to it. Inevitably the full pattern of embryonic contact stimulation cannot be restored and the infant adapts to a new pattern, e.g. ventral clasping contact in primates. Change in this pattern again leads to adjustive behaviour.

In the case of the distance stimulus receptors (vision, hearing and smell), the genetically programmed perceptual models must be unstructured to allow adaptation to the wide range of environments into which the infant may arrive (Salzen 1970). Schneirla (1965) has marshalled the evidence indicating that moderately intense and regular stimuli give approach, and intense and irregular stimuli give withdrawal, in many neonates. Turkewitz *et al.* (1966) attempted to test this claim in human neonates and found that lateral eye movements were related to sound intensity in this way. The evidence for the human infant suggests that, initially, visual attention-getting stimuli include contrasting edges, discs, and motion (Sackett 1963, Salzen 1963). The human face is a rich source of such stimulation and the infant soon comes to respond preferentially to it as a complex (Gibson 1969, Kagan 1970, Wolff 1963). Even earlier there is preferential responding to the sounds produced by the face (Eimas *et al.* 1971, Condon and Sander 1974). Similar elemental stimuli would seem initially to be the effective positive orientation stimuli for other primates (Frantz 1967). However, Sackett (1966) has claimed that pictures of rhesus infants and of threatening adults had a prepotent activating effect on isolated rhesus infants and that the threat pictures released a developmentally timed fear response at two and a half to four months of age.

More recently Sackett (1973) has shown that rhesus infants reared in isolation from adult vocalizations were nonetheless differentially responsive (active) when thirty days old to pure tones of two frequencies which lay within the two fundamental frequency ranges of maximal energy of many adult rhesus vocalizations. This corresponds with the finding that electromyographic responses of three to eight day human infants were maximal to sounds within the fundamental frequencies in the speech range (Hutt *et al.* 1968).

Positive orientation behaviour to such forms of distance stimulation will result in perceptual learning so that a sensory or perceptual model of the source will become increasingly defined. This will give increasing intolerance of changes in the source and so 'locks' the infant on to its attachment figure (Salzen 1962). It is possible then that the details of the mother-figure are acquired by perceptual learning (Sluckin and Salzen 1961) or exposure learning (Sluckin 1965). I have used Sokolov's (1960) concept of a neuronal modelling system for this learning (Salzen 1962) and Bowlby (1969) and Hunt (1965) have both employed the modelling concept of Miller, Galanter and Pribram (1960). All three systems when applied to attachment orientation behaviour involve two principles:
 (i) that adjustment or orientation is proportional to the degree of sensory or perceptual incongruity with the model,
(ii) that the intrinsic sensory or perceptual model adapts to persistent discrepant or incongruous input.

The question of possible reinforcement in this learning does arise because normally approach to a distance stimulus will have contact consequences. Obviously if the contact requirement is not satisfied then orientation behaviour will be likely to occur again to distance stimulation, and this will determine which sources become the persistent input for modelling. It is not clear from the experimental evidence whether at least some contact stimulation is essential for definition of distance models to occur, and I have discussed this question previously in relation to imprinting (Salzen 1970). In the case of primate attachment the surrogate studies of Harlow and Zimmerman (1959), Harlow (1960) and Harlow and Harlow (1965) suggest that contact is at least an important influence. When reared without surrogate objects infant rhesus showed all the usual signs of attachment to their diapers including distress on their removal and contact behaviour with strong positive affect on their return (Harlow 1960). Passman (1975) has also reported that in blanket attached human infants (32.5 months) the blanket provided security and facilitated exploration in a test situation just as effectively as did the presence of the mother, while a favourite toy did not serve this function. In a more disturbing situation of low illumination and intermittent noise (Passman 1976) the blanket was not as effective as the mother who is obviously a superior source of contact comfort. Studies with dogs have suggested that minimal contact with humans can reinforce the approach behaviour of puppies (Stanley and Elliot 1962, Stanley 1965). Lynch (1970) has shown that human tactual contact with dogs reduces both their behavioural and physiological fear responses, and he has emphasized the importance of reciprocal feedback for attachment to be a social attachment – a similar distinction to that which I have made (1967, 1970) but which could not be demonstrated in the case of chick imprinting (Salzen 1969). Of course, contact may be a powerful but not an absolute or exclusive reinforcing input for social attachment learning. Conventional physiological need reinforcers may be contributors, for Igel and Calvin (1960) demonstrated that lactation as well as contact comfort affected attachment in puppies reared with cloth and wire mother-surrogates. The comparable evidence of Harlow (1959), M. K. Harlow and Harlow (1966) and Mason (1965, 1967) shows that in the case of primates satisfaction of the infant's contact requirements would seem to be paramount. Further evidence of the significance of contact for attachment has been described by Sackett, Porter and Holmes (1965) and Sackett (1970). Despite extensive visual and auditory experience of other monkeys, partial isolates are grossly impaired in social interactions and attraction (Cross and Harlow 1965, Mitchell 1968), and early physical contact interaction seems necessary for permanent attachment formation. Whether contact stimulation results in some neural reinforcement of the pertaining neuronal models of the contact-providing attachment object, or whether lack of contact simply results in further orientation behaviour which will hinder the formation of restricted neuronal models of objects that fail to provide contact stimulation, is still not clear.

Whatever the neural mechanism may be, there is no doubt that the initial attachment orientation behaviour of primates is trapped by sources of contact stimulation and that such sources are essential for normal behaviour. Monkeys reared in total isolation without adequate sources of contact stimulation develop self-orality and self-clutching as though attempting to provide their own contact stimulation. Such monkeys also develop stereotyped behaviours including rocking, locomotory and other motor stereotypies. This isolation syndrome has been recorded and described in rhesus monkeys by Harlow and Harlow (1962, 1965) and Harlow, Dodsworth and Harlow (1965). Mitchell (1968, 1970) has reviewed the studies of isolate-reared rhesus and it is clear that self-stimulation and motor stereotypies are typical of the isolation syndrome. Similar abnormal behaviours have been described for isolate-reared chimpanzees by Davenport and Menzel (1963) and Davenport, Menzel and Rogers (1966). These behaviours seem to appear at about the time when fear behaviours would normally become recognizable (sixty to eighty days in rhesus) according to Suomi (1977). In the crab-eating macaque they are more severe the earlier the start of isolation (Berkson 1968). Just as in the case of normal fear behaviours, these abnormal behaviours are precipitated by unfamiliar stimuli and situations, e.g. Berkson, Mason and Saxon (1963), Harlow (1960), Harlow and Harlow (1962, 1965). It is significant that in the undisturbed environment these abnormal behaviours are not usually evident (Berkson 1968). Davenport and Menzel (1963) have suggested that stereotypies are substitutes for stimulation the infant normally receives from its mother (i.e. kinaesthetic stimulation from rocking), while Mason and Green (1962) suggest they are self-directed responses which normally are directed to the mother and which include sucking and clasping. Such responses and their associated stimulation are typical terminal acts and consequences of the normal patterns of attachment orientation which are activated by disturbances in the environment. The stereotyped locomotory behaviours could then be the locomotory element of orientation behaviour leading to self-stimulating kinaesthesis. Mason and Berkson (1975) have shown that infant rhesus reared with moving cloth-mother-surrogates do not show the stereotypies that develop with static surrogates – perhaps because the moving surrogate provides both kinaesthetic stimulation as well as contact.

The proposal then is that the mobile social partner will trap the first orientation approach behaviours and bring the infant to rest with adequate contact stimulation. Movements by the social partner that result in physical separation will give contact discrepancy, and orientation to restore distance and contact models to their steady state will follow. In the steady state the less salient distance stimulus foci and fields will impinge on the infant and be modelled (environmental imprinting or learning, Salzen 1970) so that subsequently focal disturbances may elicit orientation behaviour which readjusts or remodels these changes. It is this further orientation and modelling of secondary sources of stimulation that is the exploratory behaviour which appears after the principal attachment figure is established. Finally it is worth emphasizing that the term orientation is being used to include all adjustments that effectively alter the body and its receptors in relation to the external stimulus. The orienting reflex is a special reflex pattern which centres the distance receptors on to a focal distant stimulus and precedes the discrepancy detecting system that instigates subsequent orientation behaviour. Thus the hypothesis adopts Sokolov's modelling and instigating system but extends the instigated behaviour beyond the initial orienting reflex to the consequent adient or abient behaviours. The next section will consider the further development and differentiation of the orientation system in attachment behaviour.

III. Attachment and attachment behaviour

As motor development proceeds, so orientation behaviour becomes differentiated from early struggling movements into the complex patterns described as 'attachment behaviour', e.g. Ainsworth (1964) and Bowlby (1969). According to Ainsworth and Bell (1970), 'Attachment behaviours are behaviours which promote proximity or contact. In the human infant these include active proximity- and contact-seeking behaviours such as approaching, following, and clinging, and signalling behaviours such as smiling, crying, and calling.' I shall consider the signalling behaviours in §IV. The direct orientation behaviours could, in theory, develop as follows. Sources of high sensory–perceptual discrepancy will elicit the high threshold flexor responses to give eye and head aversion followed by total body turning and locomotion (if sufficient motor development has occurred). Sources of low discrepancy in sensory–perceptual familiarity, e.g. of insufficient proximity, will elicit the low threshold extensor responses and locomotory approach responses. At any one stage of definition of the infant's sensory–perceptual models there will be a level of discrepancy which gives a balance of flexor–extensor or approach–withdrawal tendencies so that the infant will stay still, inhibited and quietly looking. This kind of response has given rise to reports of recognition without 'fear' in young infants, e.g. Schaffer (1971). Bowlby (1969:390) has written, 'there is abundant evidence that an infant can discriminate familiar from unfamiliar long before he shows overt fear of strangers'. For this reason Bowlby accepts that 'separation anxiety' and 'fear of strangers' are distinct behaviours. Similarly Schaffer (1971) has rejected the neuronal model explanation of the development of fear of the unfamiliar through increasing familiarity (i.e. modelling) of the environment because recognition behaviour appears in development before fear behaviour. However the point is that withdrawal behaviour (i.e. recognizable fear) is simply a higher degree of orientation behaviour while recognition behaviours – cessation of reaching and wary staring – are lower level orientation responses. Precisely the same point is made by Bretherton and Ainsworth (1974) who include a range of orientation behaviours in a continuum with 'wariness' as the less intense and 'fear' as the more intense portions. Thus their continuum includes the 'wariness' pattern of Schaffer, Greenwood and Parry (1972). Yarrow (1972) also recognizes levels of discrimination of the mother and stranger, with behaviour ranging from passive visual fixation to the typical 'fear' responses, and he regards visual fixation as a precursor of stranger anxiety. Interestingly, Zegans and Zegans (1972) suggest that the earlier 'wariness' or attention response is in fact the orienting reflex of Sokolov (1960) and which they suggest may mature before the incongruity response and so permit incongruity detection. I have already suggested that the orienting response may be the initial reflex for mediating the subsequent orienta- tion behaviour.

The important point about orientation behaviour is that it is polarized; and in orienting *away* from a source there must be orienting *to* another source or at least down a gradient of perceptual incongruity. As incon- gruity elicits flexor turning responses so the degree of incongruity will change. If it falls then the turning tendency will decline and locomotion will produce movement in the direction of at least the relatively more familiar distance stimulation. If the turning movement produces an increase in incongruity it will be reversed in direction and so the locomot- ory movement will become directed to the focus or 'valley' of maximum congruity and away from the focus or 'hill' of maximim incongruity. Thus orientation behaviour should be analysed in terms of interacting fields of incongruity with gradients along which the organism is driven. In a totally and uniformly strange environment one would expect initially inhibition and freezing because there is no gradient down which to move. Then as the frontal visual field becomes less strange through adaptation of the sensory–perceptual models for the environment, so movement will develop, with a tendency to turn as the advance brings more distant, and hence less adapted and more incongruous, regions of stimulation. Thus typical 'searching' behaviour in a strange environment can be generated. Where a familiar focal object is present the fields of force will be polarized and movement will be maximally directed to the familiar focus. In a familiar environment polarization would be slight and the infant free to move independently of the attachment figure, or at least out into the field whose negative force increases with distance – hence the attachment figure provides a 'secure base' for exploration of mildly novel foci, as noted in so many studies of both monkey and man, e.g. Harlow (1960), Ainsworth (1964) and Ainsworth and Wittig (1969), but less frequently experimentally studied, e.g. Rheingold and Eckerman (1970). The same range of behaviours from 'wary looking' to 'withdrawal' can be expected. If looking persists, incongruity should decrease through adaptation and approach and contact exploration can follow. The present proposal is that exploratory behaviour, at least the class of exploration which Berlyne (1960) has called 'specific exploration', is part of the security–fear orientation behaviour which arises from environmental learning or modelling. 'Diversive exploration' (cf. Hutt 1966) appears to arise endogenously and if not instigated as appetitive behaviour by physiological or reproductive needs could occur if the sensory homeostatic system had a set state or steady state of moderately varying input. It is most likely that in a normal varying environment the environmental models will include a range of variation so that too invariant a sensory input would also give rise to orientation behaviour.

There are, as Smith (1974) has noted, too few situations in which ethological methods have been used in human ethology outside the home, hospital and nursery school. This is true of attachment studies (but see Anderson 1972 and Rheingold and Eckerman 1970), and many still concentrate on contrived experimental situations, e.g. Bretherton and Ainsworth (1974), Ainsworth and Bell (1970) and Ainsworth and Wittig (1969). Furthermore the interaction of the environment, as well as the attachment and stranger figures, is rarely adequately considered in attachment behaviour studies. Rheingold (1969) has made a preliminary study of the effects of a strange room as well as a strange person on the behaviour of ten-month-old infants and has noted an interaction effect. The Bretherton and Ainsworth (1974) study might be more interestingly analysed in terms of field gradients of incongruity or strangeness. But in any event it is clear that the kind and intensity of orientation behaviour (i.e. 'attachment behaviour', 'fear behaviour', and 'exploratory behaviour') will depend on the nature of the field of incongruity, i.e. on the nature of the infant's environmental and social models in comparison with the current sensory input.

Further consideration of this analysis can help in the distinction between attachment and attachment behaviour. Ainsworth has consistently recognized that attachment is not the same as attachment behaviour, and she accepts that there is an underlying property in the infant which is invariant, although its expression in the form of attachment behaviour does vary, e.g. Ainsworth (1972) and Ainsworth, Bell and Stayton (1974). Bernal (1974) has noted, as indeed Ainsworth and Wittig (1969) recognized and emphasized, that distress at separation can be shown by children who, on other evidence, may be securely attached, and equally by ones who are similarly known to be insecurely attached. Similarly, absence of protest has been noted in a 'strongly' attached infant as well as in 'non-attached' ones. A child may explore freely from the mother either because it is confident, i.e. securely attached, or because it has no attachment to her. Bernal favours Schaffer's (1971) position, namely that attachment is present only when the infant rejects a stranger, i.e. can recall the memory of the mother. This would make the internal model (or memory) of the mother the correlate of attachment. If internal models *are* postulated, then it is clear that 'strength of attachment' is a function of the specificity of the model of the attachment figure. Cohen (1974) has also pointed out that specificity is central to the concept of attachment and that attachment behaviours must be tested for their *selective* direction to the attachment figure. Selective direction of course will be a resultant of the complex gradient fields of incongruity of the test situation. Hence it is not surprising that simple 'measures' of attachment behaviours often fail to correlate across situations, studies and times, e.g. Masters and Wellman (1974) and Coates, Anderson and Hartup (1972). Consequently, there has been a series of papers on what constitutes attachment behaviour, cf. Ainsworth (1964, 1972), and attachment indices, cf. Corter (1977) and Gewirtz (1972). It is hoped that the present analysis of attachment behaviour and attachment will provide a fresh and sounder biological approach to these problems.

If attachment is a function of the definition or specificity of the internal models, then the tolerance of the infant to variations in people and objects will be greater if the models are poorly developed (i.e. early in development), will decrease as the attachment figure and immediate environment are established, and will increase again as more generalized models accommodate a wider range of experience. So stranger fear should peak and decline (cf. Schaffer and Emerson 1964). The literature on stranger reaction or fear development is confused by the same varied use of different behaviours and measures as is attachment. According to the sensory homeostatic orientation hypothesis it is the same behaviour continuum, and the early review by Bronson (1968) is compatible with this, as is the view of Freedman (1961) that the behaviour is essentially a flight response. The incongruity hypothesis has also been used in many studies (cf. Schaffer 1971), and Kagan (1974) has described a sequence of alerting and inhibition followed either by acceptance behaviour or by rejection or avoidance responses, i.e. smiling or crying respectively (see also Schaffer, Greenwood and Parry 1972). More recently attention has been given to the contribution of the test situation, the stranger's behaviour, and the child's prior experience, in determining the precise responses shown at different ages, e.g. Bronson (1972), Décarie (1974) and Rheingold and Eckerman (1973).

If the infant is reared in a restricted and invariant environment then it should be intolerant of, i.e. show exaggerated orientation behaviour in response to, novel stimulation. This is the case for monkeys and chimpanzees reared in isolation, e.g. Suomi (1977), Mason, Davenport and Menzel (1968) and Harlow and Harlow (1969). Sackett and Ruppenthal (1973) cite rhesus monkey studies showing that the willingness to enter a novel environment, exploration of patterns of different complexity and of moving objects, were all proportionate to the degree of restriction of rearing one to four years earlier. The rearing experiences included total and partial isolation, surrogate rearing, mother-peer rearing and feral. Clearly different 'styles of mothering' will also affect the amount and kind of interaction the infant gets with its social and physical environment. Harlow's (1969) account of rhesus infants raised in pairs shows how they restrict each other's experience. They trap each other's orientation behaviour and satisfy each other's contact requirements. Neither has need to re-orientate and, since there is no other source of focal moving stimulus in their environment, they develop in a restricted way and subsequently show little play with others.

Experience of the environment can be restricted by the actions of the mother, either through 'overprotection' by preventing its departure from her proximity, or by punitive or unresponsive mothering which will elicit strong and chronic orientation behaviour to her (cf. Cross and Harlow 1965). In a normal mother–infant pairing the mother's personal requirements will cause her to vary the infant's experience of the environment, cf. Hinde and White (1974), and there is evidence that a mother may actively instigate independence by separating herself from the infant by graded steps, cf. Jensen, Bobbitt and Gordon (1973) and Hinde (1971). Rosenblum (1973) describes how pig-tailed macaque mothers spatially separate themselves from the group and restrict their infants at first, but from the fourth to tenth weeks they actively reject and wean them. Both procedures are calculated to form specific models and strong orientation behaviour. Rosenblum reports that the infants do develop more selective and intense and enduring attachments, judged by separation tests, than do Bonnet macaques where the infants interact with a number of adult females. Rosenblum (1973) has also noted that pig-tailed macaques are also unlike Bonnets in that they interact in uterine-kin or 'family-clans' within which there may be physical contact. Suomi *et al.* (1973) have found that when laboratory rhesus are reared in a nuclear family environment with limited access to others there are graded preferences for mother and father compared with other females and males respectively. This is reminiscent of Bowlby's (1969) suspicion that 'monotropy' is a characteristic of a modelling attachment process. Certainly the human family presents a picture of graded attachment figures, e.g. Schaffer and Emerson (1964). Normally the most constant attendant will trap the orientation behaviour and become the prime attachment figure, but if another figure offers more attractive distance stimulation with adequate contact consequences it will become the prime attachment figure. Bowlby (1969) has reviewed some of the reports on infants reared in kibbutzim where prime attachments still seem to occur. If figures offer equal attachment properties then the infant should be indiscriminate in its attachment orientation. Sackett (1970) reports that rhesus infants given a succession of mothers were subsequently indiscriminate in a choice test with the biological mother and another female; the strongest orientation preferences were of course shown by infants with rejecting mothers. Harlow's (1969) peer-raised rhesus would also seem to have multiple or indiscriminate attachments, and in man the children described by Freud and Dann (1951) appeared to be equally attached to one another. Dunn (1976) has noted that there is evidence that although children who received day-care in infancy may appear normally attached at two years, when in nursery school at a later age they tend to interact closely in groups and are less amenable to the adult teachers. Johnston and Deisher (1973) have reviewed the evidence on children who are reared in communal groups and they believe that there are a few instances of healthy social development, presumably without 'monotropy'.

In summary, then, modelling of the social and physical environment for sensory homeostasis cannot be stopped by early privation, for this will simply give set goals (steady states or models) that are utterly inappropriate for the normal world, and entry to this world will be marked by exaggerated and chronic orientation behaviour to remove the new stimulation and return to the old. Once models (or attachments) have formed, loss or separation from the attached figure or environment again instigates the orientation behaviour – the protest of separation (cf. Bowlby 1969). Impoverished or stunted attachments due to privation, when operating in normal environments, will give chronic orientation behaviours. Well-differentiated attachments disrupted by separation will also give chronic orientation behaviour. The two syndromes are different, as Bronfenbrenner (1968) has emphasized, and they have not always been clearly separated in earlier reviews, cf. O'Connor and Franks (1961). Howells (1970) has also commented on the fallacy that 'separation' is synonymous with 'privation'.

IV. Attachment and emotion

It is clear from the foregoing account of the orientation behaviour shown in attachment that when it has the form of intense withdrawal (or struggling and crying) it is recognized and labelled as 'fear' behaviour, and we assume it to be accompanied by the affect or emotion of fear. Previously (Salzen 1970) I have proposed that the responses of domestic chicks to strange or unfamiliar stimulation form a simple continuum (figure 3) of orientation behaviour increasing from arrest and orienting, through approach, changing to withdrawal, and culminating in flight. This rising continuum may be accompanied by increasing sympathetic dominance and, following Andrew (1964), by a continuum of vocalization of increasing intensity. These vocalizations have been commonly labelled 'pleasure' or 'contentment' at the low end of the continuum, and 'distress' or 'fear' calls at the higher end. Hence I proposed a single continuum of affect with 'fear behaviour' as the orientation produced by a sensory homeostatic system and 'fear' as the feelings associated with this system. Furthermore, the so-called 'pleasure' or 'contentment' calls and feelings must be low level or decreasing orientation responses representing the final rapid changeover from sympathetic to parasympathetic dominance. This changeover was postulated to occur when the sensory input is restored to the familiar established or 'modelled' input. At first the restoration of contact stimulus patterns gives the changeover, but subsequently anticipatory changes will occur during orientation behaviour when the distance receptor input is restored to patterns that normally precede adequate contact stimulus patterns. Thus pleasure responses will occur at the sight of the familiar object (and this occurs in chicks). Thus so-called pleasure responses will occur at low levels of incongruity, i.e. to mild novelty, while silence is characteristic of the chick in its fully restored familiar world.

It is interesting that some of the vocalizations of the squirrel monkey can be arranged in a similar continuum since it curiously happens that

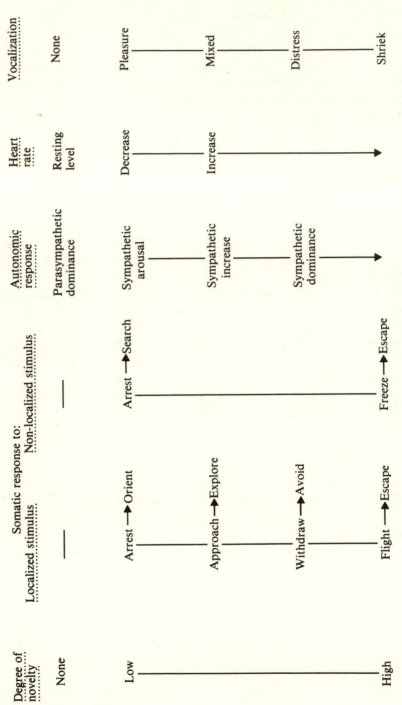

Sensory homeostasis — autonomic and somatic responses to novel stimulation

Degree of novelty	Somatic response to: Localized stimulus	Non-localized stimulus	Autonomic response	Heart rate	Vocalization
None	——	—	Parasympathetic dominance	Resting level	None
Low	Arrest → Orient	Arrest → Search	Sympathetic arousal	Decrease	Pleasure
	Approach → Explore		Sympathetic increase	Increase	Mixed
	Withdraw → Avoid		Sympathetic dominance		Distress
High	Flight → Escape	Freeze → Escape			Shriek

3. The parallel continua of orientation behaviour and its accompanying vocalizations and autonomic responses and states. These parallel the degree of strangeness of the instigating environmental disturbance. The scheme is based on the behaviour of the domestic chick but applies to a wide range of vertebrates. The autonomic responses and heart rates are based on general findings of studies of orienting responses. Patterning of orientation responses complicates the behavioural continua, but in general the patterns can be related

they are surprisingly like chick calls – as is apparent in sound spectrographs (figure 4). In both species the calls become longer, with more vigorous 'attack' at higher intensity, and the continuum parallels the behavioural identification and labelling, from contact calls when close to a social partner to distance calls when isolated. If this view of fear and pleasure in sensory homeostasis in general and in attachment in particular is adopted then it is clear that early experience will establish profound affective responses to specific social objects and environmental situations, with fear and anxiety in their absence and a pleasurable sense of security in their restoration (cf. Bowlby 1969).

Where adjustment to disturbances of the familiar environment is rapid and effective, well practised, and perhaps, in Bowlby's usage, with 'competent working models', the orientation behaviour is usually silent and effective. Orientation behaviour becomes most obviously vocal and emotional when it is ineffective and persists. In such cases the behaviour may be said to be thwarted either by physical obstruction or by conflict with other behaviour tendencies. Morris (1956) has provided an excellent analysis of the consequences of thwarting based on the feather postures of birds, and he has indicated how these consequences can give rise to social signalling. Figure 5 is based on Morris' analysis and I suggest that it is a ready-made analysis of emotional behaviour. The types of behaviour that may follow thwarted responses are often distinctive to the thwarted tendency or tendencies (in conflict) because they may include elements of intention movements of these responses. In addition they may have orientation elements (appetitive behaviour) which will be related to the arousing situation. Thus these thwarting responses may have considerable signalling value which can be and has been developed in evolution. Thus I believe that emotional behaviour is simply and solely the signalling of thwarted behaviour which serves to induce the social partner to remove the source of the thwarting or conflict – either by assistance with the obstruction or by changing its own behaviour if thwarting is due to its own inappropriate responses. The study and understanding of emotion would be facilitated if this was accepted and if it was recognized that the variously imputed functions of energizing, disorganizing, preparing, motivating or reinforcing behaviour are not the functions or evolutionary origins of emotional behaviour (cf. Arnold 1970, Strongman 1973 and Young 1973). If the present concept is accepted then ethological analyses of social signalling and conflict behaviour already provide the best understanding of emotion – or at least of the negative emotions. The pleasant emotions can be understood according to the present suggestion made

Graded calls and emotions

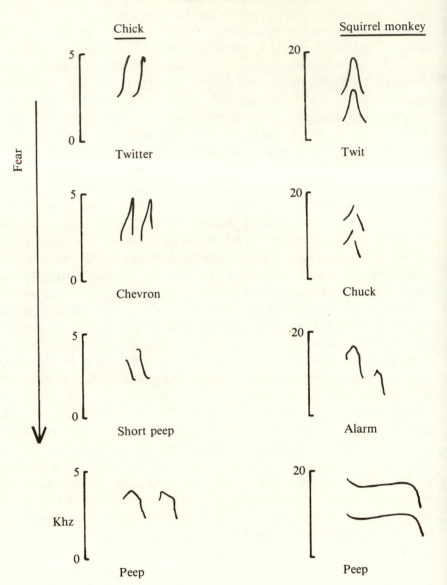

4. Sound-spectrographic patterns of isolation and contact calls of the domestic chick and the squirrel monkey. Records for the chick were taken from Andrew (1964) and those for the squirrel monkey are derived from Winter, Ploog and Latta (1966). They are arranged in a continuum corresponding with the degree of fear imputed from the situational and behavioural patterns and context. It can be seen that there is a continuum of vocalization and that with increasing fear the calls become extended in time and lose their initial rising frequency as the stronger 'attack' starts the call at its top frequency.

I   Absence of indispensible stimuli following intense arousal

II   Simple physical obstruction of aroused activity

III Simultaneous arousal of two or more incompatible tendencies

Primary responses to thwarting

Somatic

1 Perseverance – persistent approach and adjustment (I,II)

2 Snap decision – capricious choice of response (III)

3 Threshold intention movements – initial element of response (I,II)

4 Ambivalent posturing – elements of both responses (III)

5 Alternating intention movements – successive incipient responses (III)

Autonomic

1 Alimentary – salivation increase or decrease, urination, defaecation

2 Circulatory – pallor, flushing, genital vasodilation, fainting

3 Respiratory – changes in breathing rate and amplitude, gasping, sighing, panting

4 Thermoregulatory – sweating, pilomotor activity

5 Lacrimatory – weeping

Secondary responses to thwarting

1 Displacement activities — irrelevant behaviour

2 Redirection activities — response to another stimulus

3 Regressive activities — immature responses

4 Neurotic inactivity — loss of responsiveness

5 Aggressive behaviour — intense approach and adjustment

5. An analysis of the responses to thwarting and conflict based on a classification given by Morris (1956) and only slightly modified. Morris proposed this classification as the basis of social signalling since any of these thwarting responses can be developed as signals through evolutionary selective processes if they influence the social partner to assist in removing the source or cause of the thwarting. The scheme is used here as a classification of emotional behaviours and it is proposed that emotion and emotional behaviour are simply the social signalling of thwarting and conflict. The pleasant emotions can be seen as the signalling of the cessation of thwarting. This view provides a rational and biological definition of emotion. A practical application of the scheme is given in relation to attachment in primates and man.

for the 'pleasant' affect associated with the achievement of the security of the attachment figure and familiar environment. Thus the pleasant emotions are the behaviours and feelings (states) that occur at the cessation of thwarting and represent the rapid decline of the thwarting responses and the changeover to the performance of the previously thwarted consummatory behaviour. Thus there will be distinctive patterns of behaviour and internal state associated with the specific external situation which removed the thwarting or immediately preceded its removal, and so again these patterns have signal value and can be selected and developed during evolution to produce 'pleasure' signals.

This view of emotion is a logical development of Darwin's (1872) approach and can be shown to be consistent with a wide range of emotional phenomena. It applies to thwarting of any of the three types of behavioural system previously distinguished (cf. figure 2), and each system is associated with particular psychological qualities or types of emotion as shown in figure 2. (It is interesting that Scott (1969) has given a list of his nine behaviour elements and the emotions which are associated with them. His list is not incompatible with the present one although derived in a different manner.) The distinctive qualities of the emotions are due to the contributions of the different types of consummatory behaviours and associated internal states that are involved and that contribute to the overall pattern in each emotional circumstance or type of circumstance. In this way distinctive emotional 'states' of mind as well as appearance must result. Furthermore, as the motor patterns of consummatory and appetitive behaviour develop and differentiate, so the patterns and kinds of emotions will differentiate, and this accounts for the development of emotion which Bridges (1932) has described in the human infant. Also during development learned expectations will result in anticipatory thwarting responses or release of thwarting responses in response to distance stimulation.

The analysis of thwarting responses shown in figure 5 can be applied to the behaviour associated with attachment. If orientation away from strange stimulation and toward the familiar attachment figure is not immediately successful, i.e. aroused contact responses are thwarted, then the appetitive orientation behaviour persists and intensifies – this is the category of *perseverance* in Morris' scheme of *primary responses to thwarting*. An instance of intensified and persistent clinging as a thwarting or conflict response is that of the infant rhesus with a mother-surrogate equipped with air nozzles in the body which intermittently blasted the infant (Rosenblum and Harlow 1963). Here the surrogate was a common source of positive and negative orientation stimulation. Along with the struggling or searching movements of an infant without adequate contact stimulation there are vocalizations – cries and distress calls. These belong to the category of *autonomic* thwarting responses since they are derived from *respiratory* changes. Thus the pattern of separation protest (Bowlby 1969) can be seen as *perseverance* of attachment orientation responses. In older children learned anticipations of thwarted separation ('working models of the mother') might be expected to give thwarting responses such as persistent attachment orientations of approach and clinging (*perseverance*) or at least 'glancing looks' (*intention movements*) – behaviours common in 'anxious attachment' (cf. Bowlby 1973).

This analysis of emotional responses must, of course, be applied to smiling as well as to crying. Smiling can be understood as an *intention movement* for the 'protective face' given at less than full intensity, because it is blended with or followed by a relaxation to the normal 'resting face', giving an *ambivalent* expression more comparable with the 'grin face' commonly given in response to a dominant social partner in catarrhine monkeys (cf. van Hooff 1962). Ambrose (1961) has suggested that smiling is an indication of mounting fear followed by recognition relief and relaxation. Despite further consideration and differentiation of analyses of smiling, e.g. Wolff (1963) and van Hooff (1972), its essential character in early infancy as a fear–relief response involving intention or ambivalent facial movements appropriate to these states remains (Salzen 1967).

Persistent thwarting of attachment orientation is clearly the key element in 'separation studies', and experimental data are abundant for primates, e.g. Seay, Hansen and Harlow (1962), Seay and Harlow (1965), Bowlby (1973) and Kaufman (1973). Singh (1975) has reported the same 'separation' responses in feral rhesus in field experiments. In general, the picture is that described by Bowlby (1969, 1973), a 'protest' stage of active orientation, searching and distress calling is followed, if no substitute mother is available and separation continues, by 'temper tantrums' and aggressiveness alternating with or followed by a 'despair' stage of cessation of activity with depression (cf. Scott and Senay 1973, Kaufman 1973). These responses belong to the category of *secondary responses to thwarting* which follow when the *primary responses* fail to end the thwarting or conflict. Temper tantrums could be an instance of *regressive activities* as a regression to the undifferentiated neonatal struggling orientation behaviour. Inactivity and depression would seem to fit the category of *neurotic inactivity*. Children also show these secondary thwarting responses during separation – including *redirection* of clinging to a toy which may alternate with phases of rejection and aggression (*aggressive behaviour* may perhaps also be classed as a secondary thwarting response). Such children also show self-stimulation and self-contacting which can be seen as *redirection activities* of attachment orientation behaviour, and it is interesting that these behaviours form much of the list of children's behaviours which Kehrer and Tente (1969) have considered to be *displacement activities* (cf. figure 5, *Secondary responses to thwarting*). Regression of sphincter control may also occur and chronically separated children may show the apathy and depression of *neurotic inactivity* (cf. Bowlby 1969, 1973, Rutter 1972).

If reunion with the attachment figure takes place, there is usually an enhancement of attachment orientation behaviour, at least for a time, both in human and monkey. These patterns of separation and reunion have been well established by Hinde and Spencer-Booth (1971), who have also shown that reunion enhancement is greater and more pro-longed for infants who showed more attachment orientation before sep-aration – as though their tendency to 'anxious attachment' (Bowlby 1973) was enhanced. The 'detached' stage has been described by Bowlby (1969, 1973) as one in which, on reunion, the child shows no recognition or turns away, cries or becomes apathetic. The only comparable case for monkeys was reported by Mitchell (1970), where after rhesus infants were sep-arated for two days, one quarter ran away from their mothers, while after a further two days, one half ran away. In children the 'detached' behaviour may alternate with clinging and with hostile and aggressive approach – these are clearly *ambivalent* and *alternating intention movements* and are signs of conflict or thwarting. The mechanism of this conflict is not clear. It is possible that the attachment figure reactivates the original approach orientation along with the more recently associated thwarting responses. The latter are, of course, high level orientation tendencies – flight, searching or inhibition established at a high level in the separation phase. The occurrence of hostility and aggression in reunion may also be the result of conflict. *Aggression* (figure 5) is commonly agreed to be one consequence of thwarting, especially thwarted flight (defensive aggres-sion). Aggressiveness to strangers or to strange objects can thus be seen as thwarting or conflict of orientation tendencies – approach and retreat. It is not clear whether aggression of this kind is simply high level *persever-ance* of appetitive orientation, i.e. behaviour which changes the spatial relations of the actor and object – which aggression effectively does – or whether it should be regarded as a new category of *secondary responses to thwarting* with some possible relationship to *regression*. I have included it (figure 5) as an extra category to Morris' (1956) original classification. In either event its occurrence as a conflict response is clear in 'reunion' behaviour. Other signs of conflict in 'reunion' are *alternating intention movements* of blank expression or looking away before approaching. Another application of the concept of aggression as a thwarting response in attachment orientation might be the self-aggression shown by isolate-reared animals to their body parts, especially limbs, e.g. Harlow (1969) for rhesus and Mason, Davenport and Menzel (1968) for chimpanzees (see also Kruijt 1962a for chickens). Such self-aggression is precipitated when withdrawal orientation behaviour is elicited, e.g. by a strange stimulus. It is as though the body parts fail to give adequate contact security and so the orientation is thwarted.

The classification and use of thwarting and conflict behaviours in this way and its relevance to human behaviour has been suggested before (e.g. Kaufman 1960). Provided it is recognized that elements of conflicting behaviours may form mosaics, its use in analysing social communication is valuable (cf. Andrew 1963). Recently, Baerends (1975) has evaluated its use and made a tentative model for the causation of neurosis (1976) which uses control theory feedback, a discrepancy model of reafferance, and the effects of conflict and thwarting on appetitive behaviour. The system being described here obviously has many parallels. It can be used to consider the direct and indirect consequences of early experience on later behaviour, i.e. the long-term effects.

V. The long-term consequences of attachment

There is a considerable literature claiming evidence of the long-term effects of early life-experiences on later behaviour, and as much challenging the validity of this evidence, cf. Roberts (1974) and Rutter (1972). It is clear from the survey by Yarrow (1961) that any effects will appear as tendencies and be subject to individual differences. Lewis (1954) had to concede that separation from the mother beginning before the age of two years resulted in a significant number of long-term neurotic or delinquent effects. Bowlby (1965) and Ainsworth (1962) have reviewed the evidence and indicate possible long-term consequences. Conclusions which Rutter (1972) feels are acceptable include the existence of an association between delinquency and broken homes, and the fact that affectionless psychopathy sometimes follows multiple separation experiences and institutional care in early childhood. The studies of large samples of children by Douglas (1975) and Quinton and Rutter (1976) seem to have established that children who have spent more than one week or have had repeated periods in hospital before the age of five are significantly more likely to show emotional and behavioural disturbances in adolescence. Heinicke (1973) has also given strong evidence that parent deprivation or loss in infancy and childhood may be predisposing to depression responses in later life. There is also evidence of non-pathological long-term consequences of early experience of different styles of mothering (Moore 1975). With such ill-defined and largely correlational effects it is difficult to apply the attachment model previously described to human data, unless we have recourse to individual psycho-analytic case studies. We must turn, therefore, to the non-human primates.

The evidence is that early experience may set the attachment orientation system both in the level and type of orientation behaviour, an effect which tends to continue into later life. An interactionist approach requires no 'models' to explain such effects. Once started on the path of timidity and close proximity-keeping this behaviour will tend to canalize itself. Isolate-reared rhesus would continue to show their self-contacting, self-directed attachment–security orientation patterns if subjected to trauma in later life. This they do when placed with other monkeys. If approach behaviour to other monkeys develops it should initially exhibit conflict. This is shown by the over-reactive approach–withdrawal of such monkeys and their aggressive reactions to other monkeys, e.g. Harlow and Harlow (1965), Sackett (1967), Mitchell (1970), Sackett and Ruppenthal (1973). Their inappropriate orientations in close contact will, of course, be the result of their lack of experience of such interactions, but their inability to acquire these adjustments rapidly perhaps suggests that there is a residual level of fear affect and a lasting effect of early experience. Where social interactions develop in isolate-reared monkeys they are less frequent, are usually dyadic, of unstable composition, with more play (orientation) rather than grooming, clasping and sex (contact behaviours) (cf. Anderson and Mason 1974). Such a conclusion supports the view that although distance orientation behaviours are being adjusted by experience the contact relationships are not, and these are the ones most central to affective states. In the case of less extreme early experience such as that of punitive mothering the subsequent social interactions may be marked by hyperaggressiveness, e.g. Mitchell, Arling and Møller (1967) and Mitchell (1970). This is understandable as a continuation of intense approach orientation with anticipated thwarting induced by the punitive mother. Again there is continuity of effect.

The extent to which early attachment orientations make impossible the later acquisition of any social behaviour will be considered later. But in the absence of such later development, the ultimate effect of orientation tendencies away from contact with species partners will be that sexual and parental behaviours will be unlikely. In fact isolate- and partially isolate-reared rhesus males fail to mate, e.g. Harlow and Harlow (1962, 1965, 1966), and females fail to show proper maternal care, being indifferent or aggressive to the infant, e.g. Seay, Alexander and Harlow (1964), and Harlow *et al*. (1966). Mason (1963) also describes how isolate-reared males on approaching a female may flee, attack, or try to mount in inappropriate orientations (see also Harlow and Harlow 1965). Erwin *et al*. (1974) have shown, by isolating rhesus during their second years, that continuity of social experience is also important for normal socio-sexual behaviour.

Again there are two possible influences of early experience. One is that early interactions set up specific contact interactions which can be employed in subsequent sexual and maternal interactions. The second is that contact with the mother establishes a pattern of contact which the species partner can fulfil to give a sense of security in which reproductive responses may be more likely to occur. Hollender (1969) has given evidence of just such a wish for, and feeling from, being held in adult humans. It appears to provide feelings of protection and comfort, and in men seems to lead to sexual responses. The work of Deutsch and Larsson (1974) is relevant, for they found that surrogate-reared rhesus males would display normal social and sexual behaviour towards a cloth-covered stationary model. They conclude that the movements of a normal female elicits passivity, withdrawal or aggression which disrupt the mating. This is the suggestion already made here and it is certainly true that independent movement of a social partner might remain a strong stimulus for flight since this kind of stimulation was totally lacking in their early experience. The rhesus infants reared with moving surrogates showed normal sex behaviour (Mason, Davenport and Menzel 1968) and this too supports the 'fear of movement' explanation. The same explanation applies to the motherless mothers of Harlow *et al*. (1966).

Although there is continuity of the effect of early experience in social adjustment which interactionist and learning explanations would expect, the resistance to social adaptation lends some support to modelling theories which suppose that the adaptability of neuronal modelling systems decreases in development. There are accumulating data that some rehabilitation of isolate-reared and deprived infants is possible. In man this more commonly involves recovery of cognitive functioning and the subject is well reviewed by Bronfenbrenner (1968). Casler (1965) describes the improvement that followed 20 min. per day of extra tactile stimulation in institutionalized infants (see also the report of Skeels 1966). On the whole, recovery occurs given compensatory experience, the earlier the better, with social adjustments accompanying the cognitive improvement. Beres and Obers (1950) describe what look like failed or aberrant attachment relations with a reasonable proportion recovering by adolescence. Alpert (1959) has described therapy involving the acquisition of an adult attachment figure by children with pathological behaviours resulting from aberrant early care. But again the non-human primates must provide the experimental data.

In his 1968 paper, Mitchell noticed that although isolate-reared rhesus showed increasing aggressiveness and declining fear toward age-mates, both behaviours declined toward infants. He suggested that rehabilitation might be helped by using less fear evoking or disturbing stimuli. Suomi, Harlow and McKinney (1972), and Suomi and Harlow (1972), used partners three months younger than six-month-old isolates for social therapy sessions and found that disturbed behaviours had nearly disappeared within six months. The younger monkeys initiated non-aggressive contact. Gomber and Mitchell (1974) have also confined isolate-reared males (in stages) with infants and obtained contact behaviours including grooming and play. More recently Novak and Harlow (1975) have reported recovery of species-typical social behaviours in four rhesus monkeys reared in isolation for twelve months and then exposed to graded interactions with younger 'therapist' monkeys. Suomi (1973) has also tried rehabilitating isolate rhesus by using surrogate models as the initial social partner. He was able to obtain both a reduction of abnormal behaviours and simple social interactions when the isolates were subsequently paired. But although they developed object contact experience, the lack of movement and perhaps interaction still inhibited responding to a species partner, i.e. an independently moving object was still not antecedent to adequate contact consequences. Subsequently Cummins and Suomi (1976) have reported that rehabilitated isolate-reared monkeys still show less social play than ones reared with a mother and peers. The importance of contact experience in the rehabilitation process is supported by the evidence on 'motherless-mother' rhesus reviewed by Ruppenthal et al. (1976). Intimate physical contact experience with peers in adolescence or with their own infants immediately after birth greatly reduced the probability of aberrant maternal behaviour in these mothers.

Finally there is evidence that the original attachment model can be replaced, i.e. that an attachment orientation preference can be reversed. In man the possible example is the multiple-peer attachment reported by Freud and Dann (1951). These children seemed to have successfully transferred to adult human attachment figures. In the rhesus, Mason and Kenney (1974) have shown that when mother, peer, or surrogate-reared infants up to ten months old were separated and confined with dogs they came to form strong attachments in the full manner, with the usual contact and proximity-maintaining behaviours. The dogs were used as 'secure bases' in the usual manner, and the first approaches and contacts occurred within a few hours. Most significantly these new attachments were specific – the infants discriminated and preferred their dog to a strange dog or to another rhesus of the same age, even the familiar peer in the case of peer-raised subjects. When rehoused with new dogs they quickly reattached once more. Mason and Kenney note that the characteristics of the attachment figures may determine the transfer so that monkeys will not reattach to surrogates (see also the discussions by Jensen 1975, Cairns 1977). Of course transfer at this equivalent early age clearly occurs in human infants where, following separation or loss of the parent, a substitute or adoptive parent can normally be accepted. Further the importance of optimal stimulus features both for distance and contact stimulation has already been discussed in describing the original attachment process through sensory homeostatic orientations operating with minimal intrinsic requirements or 'models'. The prescription for transfer or reversal has also been discussed (see also Salzen 1968). Graded treatment prevents orientation away and permits new modelling to occur – or new interactions to be learned.

In summary, then, this survey has considered the ways in which the effects of early experience on later behaviour may operate or be understood. It has been proposed that attachment behaviour is part of a general orientation for security that maintains a steady state of sensory input, a form of sensory homeostasis, and that the steady state goals, both social and environmental, are established by early experience. Attachment behaviour that is not directly orientation behaviour can be understood as responses to thwarting of orientation and are signalling behaviours which constitute the negative emotions of fear, anger and grief. The attainment of the steady state by approach and contact with the required stimulus sources corresponds with cessation of thwarting and may provide distinctive signals that constitute the positive emotions of pleasure and security.

The security orientation–affect system may operate in development as follows.

The orientation system adapts to the steady state input of the neonatal environment of contact–kinaesthetic stimulation. Adaptation to distance sensations is secondary to the contact adaptation and corresponds with social and environmental attachment. Social attachment may be dependent on the distance orientation culminating in satisfaction of the contact stimulus requirement. Changes in sensory input instigate orientation behaviours that remove the change or promote adaptation (exploration and curiosity). Adaptability decreases with maturation and experience.

The system has been used in an explanatory way as follows. Isolate- and surrogate-reared monkeys have adapted their contact requirements to their own bodies or to the surrogate, and orientation to these is elicited by the unfamiliar movements of a species partner. Adaptation can occur if this orientation can be suppressed and contact maintained; otherwise this orientation precludes the experience needed for normal social, sexual and parental interactions. Thus the security-orientation system must be in-active before sexual and parental patterns can be elicited (cf. Salzen 1966). This is consistent with the ethological view that courtship is conflict behaviour involving flight, attack, and sexual tendencies (cf. Kruijt 1962b, Baerends 1975). Early social experience ensures that the species partner becomes the source of maximum security allowing social interactions for physiological homeostatic needs and for later reproductive functions. Thus it might well be true to say that social attachment gives a sense of security – for life.

9.2. Understanding human development: limitations and possibilities in an ethological approach[1]

The idea that a child's early experience has profound and long-lasting implications for his subsequent development is an ancient one. Its ancestry reaches back at least to Plato, while John Locke's vision of the genesis of our mature beliefs ('the oracles of the nursery') and Freud's understanding of the forces which shape human personality still dominate psychological theory even today. In the last forty years the work of animal ethologists has influenced our ideas on the consequences of early experience in a number of different and important ways. The early ethologists studying the behaviour of animals in their natural habitat developed both a distinctive methodology, with their techniques of observation and description of naturally occurring behaviour, and a distinctive theoretical perspective, a perspective in which the function and survival value of the behaviour was of particular interest. When we consider the influence of ethology on the study of early experience in humans, it is clear that these two aspects of ethology have both been important, but important in rather separate ways. In this paper I shall discuss how ethological research has influenced thinking about human development, and argue that while they have been of considerable value in some respects, there are severe limits to the extent to which either the evolutionary perspective or the distinctive methodology developed by ethologists can help us to understand the significance of early events in human development. In conclusion, the question of how those who study children could most usefully learn from the intellectual skills of ethologists will be considered.

[1] I would like to thank Patrick Bateson, John Dunn and Robert Hinde for their very constructive comments on this paper.

The evolutionary perspective on infancy

It is possible to consider the importance of early experience in two distinctive ways. We can ask how general characteristics of early development are related to adult characteristics common to all individuals of the species – how, for example, the early interaction between mother and child is related to the development of language. We can also ask how *differences* in the early experience of the young are related to individual differences between adults. Within the framework of the first approach, recent interest in the adaptive importance of developments during infancy has been of particular value to our understanding of human infancy. The influence of ethology has been very direct here. For example, Frantz's work on perceptual skills (Frantz 1963) in infancy, which started a particularly important and productive wave of research on human infancy, stemmed from an ethological interest in innate perceptual preferences, an interest in the adaptive importance of predispositions in infancy. Our knowledge of the capabilities of the infant has been transformed by such studies, which have demonstrated not only the remarkable (and unsuspected) skills of newborn babies, but also their predisposition to attend to and learn about particular features of their environment. Babies are, for instance, especially sensitive to sounds which fall within the frequency range of the human female voice, and they are particularly interested in looking at objects that have features in common with the human face. The adaptive significance of these predispositions is clear, as is the significance of the newborn's remarkable capacity to learn how to adjust his behaviour to features of his environment. The contribution of animal studies to the understanding of the importance of the constraints on what a developing creature attends to, and learns about, has been of major importance (see Hinde and Stevenson-Hinde 1973).

The comparison of human infancy with that of other primates has also been extremely revealing: such comparison has drawn attention to the particularly long period of dependence on the mother in the human species, and it has supported the suggestion that the play and exchange between mother and child during this long dependency must be of especial importance in the development of human abilities to communicate and understand (Bruner 1974, Schaffer 1978). Heuristically, ethological interest in the adaptive value of behaviour has undoubtedly been of crucial importance in initiating and interpreting much of the research which has transformed our picture of infancy. The particular importance of the built-in capabilities and predisposition for social exchange for the development of language and cognitive development are discussed in other parts of this book; this paper will consider primarily the contribution which ethology has made to our conception of the consequences of early experience for the social development of individuals. (Since my brief is to examine the limitations of ethology, more space will be devoted to the particular problems which an ethological approach involves, than to its considerable contributions, which will be more briefly commented on.) This influence will be considered under four headings: the experimental manipulation of early experience, the extrapolation from studies of non-human primates, observation and methodology, and the study of interaction.

I. The experimental manipulation of early experience in animals

The experimental manipulation of early experience in animals, and the detailed analysis of its consequences, has dramatically demonstrated the long-term developmental effects of early events. We know that early experience can have a profound impact on a wide range of emotional behaviour, fear, withdrawal, fighting, on attachment and on sexual behaviour, and on learning more generally. These animal studies have by no means been exclusively ethological in orientation, but it is notable that where such work has been carried out within an ethological framework the studies have been particularly productive. For instance, in their examination of the effects of early separation experience on the young rhesus monkey, Hinde (1976) and colleagues were able to separate with elegance the effects of different aspects of the separation experience on mother and on infant, and to analyse the consequences of these for the development of the young monkey. It was because the animals were studied with the precision and the sensitivity born of the practice of detailed observation and of familiarity with the social behaviour of the group that an understanding of the *processes* involved in the disruption and rebuilding of the relationship between mother and infant was reached.

The study of early 'handling' of rodents provides another example. Initially studies had shown that if very young rodents were handled, even very briefly, by an experimenter, there were long-term effects on the growth rate and behaviour of the animals. Careful observation of the young with their mothers showed that in fact the mothers of such 'handled' young behaved differently to them, and that part of this long-term effect was attributable to a different pattern of interaction between mother and young (Richards 1967). The distinction between an ethological and a psychological approach to such experimental manipulation of early experience is of course now extremely blurred. Psychologists have become far more concerned to examine the broad effects of their interventions on the animal and its social companions.

How far and in what ways is it legitimate to extrapolate from studies of animals such as these, and from the rich field of research into the importance of early experience in birds, to the processes of human development? It is clear that even to compare social development in birds with that in mammals is fairly adventurous. (These two groups have, it should be remembered, been evolving independently for some 250 million years.) It is possible to argue that the similarities in some of the developmental problems which have faced the groups may well have produced a measure of evolutionary convergence in the development of comparable solutions. For instance, in discussing the importance of early experience in the development of sexual preference, Bateson argues that 'if strong evolutionary pressure promoted the involvement of learning in the development of birds' mating preferences, analogous processes would surely be expected in mammals, which have if anything a much greater capacity to learn than birds' (Bateson 1977).

But the move from one group to the other requires great caution. In the development of sexual preference, for instance, we find among birds that the species differ markedly in the extent to which sexual preferences are determined, and that even within a species the sexes may differ in the relative importance of early experience in determining sexual preferences. Little systematic work on these issues has yet been done on mammals, though there is much anecdotally based discussion (Bateson 1977). Nor can we assume, where parallel solutions to the evolutionary problems are found in birds and mammals, that the underlying processes or mechanisms are necessarily at all similar. The terms 'imprinting' and 'sensitive period', derived from the animal work of this character, have been widely used in discussions of human development (for instance, in the discussion of the consequences of early separation between mother and infant); but the vagueness with which these terms are used in the human context stands in marked contrast to the careful precision of the animal studies. The investigation of the processes in the development of birds and animals has enabled scientists to determine with precision the particular factors involved in imprinting and in sensitive periods (stimulus value, stage of development and its relationship with the responsiveness of the young animal, length of exposure, and so on), and it has made them very much aware of the importance of interaction between these factors. A particular danger in the loose borrowing of the terms imprinting and sensitive period from the careful animal work is that in the course of the borrowing the terms come to be used as if they were explanatory terms, as if they could in themselves contribute some deeper understanding of the processes involved. It is important that we should be clear that even in the study of birds the term 'sensitive period' is not in any sense explanatory, but simply a useful descriptive label. And it is clear that in every behavioural example where a sensitive period is invoked the particular factors which change with age, and which influence the onset and the termination of the period, must be identified separately (Hinde and White 1974).

The work on early experience in animals has provided unequivocal evidence that manipulation of experience at this time can have long-term effects of great importance, and the ethological work in particular has begun to show us something of the processes by which such effects are produced. These studies are extensively quoted by those discussing early human development: it is suggested that such studies should alert us to the possibility of parallel processes working in humans, to the possible importance of particular periods in development, and it is proposed that these studies may offer models of development appropriate to all animals, ourselves included. Possibly the most frequent form of extrapolation from animal to human studies is in terms of these 'principles' of development. It is suggested that such animal studies enable us to identify the principles which determine how early experience has its effects in animals, and that the identification of these principles will provide a valuable focus in our approach to the study of human development. We can indeed find examples where the parallels between human and animal development do appear striking. The work on filial imprinting in birds has indicated that filial responses, at first elicited by a wide range of stimuli, gradually become restricted to those presented by the mother. When we look at studies of the changes in babies' smiling behaviour, or in attentive responses to the mother, the parallel is clear (Ambrose 1961, Wolff 1963). But we should be careful about assuming that the processes are the same. Whether we can make that assumption will depend on the level of analysis employed. And it must be stressed that when the development of a response such as smiling is carefully studied, the complexity of its development, and of its range of possible meanings, rapidly becomes apparent. Babies smile in response to confirmed expectancies, at the mastery of tasks, and so on. While recent ethological work on development is particularly sensitive to the complexities of the development of single responses (e.g. Bateson 1973), and particularly illuminating in the way such developments are analysed, it is clear that to characterise the range of considerations involved in understanding such complex capabilities in human babies, specifically human categories will have to be employed – linguistic and intentional categories rather than behavioural.

We can also find examples of comparatively simple responses in which certain periods of development may be particularly important. If in the very first times that a baby is put to the breast he experiences difficulty in sucking (either because his nose is occluded, or because his mother's areola is insufficiently extensible), this experience may have a very marked effect on his willingness to accept the breast again, and may have very upsetting effects on the feeding relationship (Gunther 1955). At present we do not have good evidence for many such examples; indeed there is too little systematic study for us to judge how important these effects may be.

II. Extrapolation from studies of non-human primates

It was John Bowlby's work on attachment and the development of personality which brought ethological work centrally to the attention of those interested in human social development. In his discussion of the early relationship between mother and child Bowlby focussed on the adaptive function of the bond between the human mother and her child in an evolutionary context (Bowlby 1969). He stressed the biological advantage of a bond between mother and child which ensures proximity and contact, and thus protection of the young, during the long period of immaturity characteristic of the higher apes, and of humans in particular. Bowlby emphasised how far the behavioural system that brings the human mother and child together resembles that which links the non-human primate mother and her infant. The newborn primate is constantly in contact with the mother's body; he may be supported by the mother's hold, or he may maintain the contact by clinging and sucking the nipple. As he grows up he spends more time apart, but at any sign of danger, the mother will move towards him, and he towards her. This 'spatial' link was seen by Bowlby and by Ainsworth and Bell (1970) as the hallmark of attachment, a 'set-goal' of proximity to the mother that varies in different circumstances, and with infants of different ages. The human baby was seen as possessing built-in signals (crying, smiling) and responses (sucking, following, clinging) which form part of the behavioural system by which, with the appropriate response of the mother, physical closeness is ensured. Indeed the mother was seen as genetically programmed to respond appropriately to these signals (though an overlay of culturally learned responses may interfere with her naturally sensitive response). The consequences for the child's social development of mothering that failed to provide the appropriate and natural responses to the child's signals was seen as serious and long-lasting. The main implication drawn from this perspective was a stress on the danger of interfering with a process of attachment to which we are biologically adapted. In this way Bowlby added an evolutionary justification to the view which he had already developed of the function of attachment as an essential base for healthy adult social behaviour. He saw it as crucial to the mental health of a child to have a prolonged close relationship with a single mother-figure. Although in Bowlby's recent writing his emphasis has changed in a number of respects, it is the impact of his original approach which continues to be felt in ethological discussion of human development.

The evolutionary perspective of this earlier writing has had an especially strong influence upon the approach of those who study child-rearing in hunter-gatherer societies. DeVore and Konner (1974), for example, studying the !Kung bushmen, argue that the social organisation and behaviour of the !Kung reflect better the 'situation that Bowlby calls man's "environment of evolutionary adaptedness" than any other non-literate society for whom we have good information about infant care' (p. 135).

They regard the !Kung as representative of the way of life in which the human mother–infant relationship evolved, and from their observations of mothers and babies they suggest that Bowlby's emphasis on a prolonged nurturant relationship with a single mother-figure is 'appropriate'. !Kung mothering they observed to be characterised by continual contact between mother and baby, sensitive responsiveness of the mother to her baby's distress, and absolute indulgence towards his dependent behaviour. The essential features of an evolutionary argument, they maintain, must be to demonstrate the antiquity of a behaviour, its appearance in man's close relatives the non-human primates, and its presence in hunter-gatherer society. On these grounds they suggest that there is good support for the view that a prolonged attachment to a nurturant indulgent mother-figure is the form of early relationship to which we are biologically adapted.

Much of the interest in such studies of hunter-gatherer societies, and of non-human primates, has centred, then, on the picture this work might give us of the biological basis of human behaviour (a basis which is seen by some at least as being in some sense normative). The implication in some discussion of this issue is that recent cultural differences may have distorted or over-ridden the natural adaptation of man as an animal. It is clear that man's environment has indeed changed markedly from that to which he was originally adapted. It is very likely that some features of our behaviour reflect adaptations to an environment we no longer inhabit, and that some features of our behaviour reflect adaptation – non-genetic – to our more recent environment that would be quite inappropriate for the 'environment of evolutionary adaptedness'. But it is *not* clear that we can derive from studies of present-day hunter-gatherer societies any sweeping conclusions about human biological adaptations. Hunter-gatherer societies have flourished in a wide range of ecologies: each present-day hunter-gatherer society has its own long history, and we cannot assume that a particular group we choose to study will provide a sound basis for inferring the biological properties of human beings *in general*. Further, the argument that recent cultural differences have distorted or over-ridden the natural biological adaptation of man rests on a dichotomy between culture and nature which must not be presented in this way. Humans are cultural creatures, and in an important sense culture is not a mediator of nature, it *is* human nature (Pascal 1931). Patterns of social behaviour, even with a very young baby, are part of a culture, and the idea that there is a biological pattern of relationships which can be divorced from culture is misleading. There is a real danger that discussion of biology and culture will slide into an argument as sterile as the arguments about nature and nurture have proved. It has been noted that it is as pointless to ask about the extent to which a behavioural item is contributed to by inheritance, or by environment, as it is to ask whether there is a greater contribution to the area of a field from its length or its breadth (Hebb 1953). To suggest that some behavioural items in hunter-gatherer societies are more 'biological' than those in our own society has equally little meaning. We cannot treat any intentionally mediated behaviour as somehow 'culture-free'.

The early relationship between mother and baby, and the consequences of this for human development, has become an area of particular interest to those concerned with understanding the adaptedness of human behaviour, and with clarifying the extent to which cultures have distorted the 'natural' patterns of human behaviour. It is worth looking in some detail at the arguments and evidence here, as the questions raised highlight some of the most intractable issues in the understanding of human development.

The demonstration of antiquity and the wide phyletic range of some behaviour suggest, according to DeVore, that its appearance in the different species may be related to its genetic base. (It has been pointed out that ethologists disposed of this idea about two decades ago with the demonstration of the part played by non-genetic adaptation – individual experience – in behaviour that may appear similar or different between species (Lehrman 1970, Hinde 1968).) De Vore comments in fact that this in itself tells us nothing about the possible refractoriness to change of the behaviour in question, nor about the consequences of imposing change. This is surely a point of great importance. The fact that man has so rapidly evolved such a great range of social patterns in other cultural environments might well be taken as an argument against the view that biological adaptation to a hunter-gatherer existence can have been crucially important in human social development.

Let us look first at a comparatively simple example, breast-feeding: a natural process to which both mother and baby are clearly adapted, and a process seen as providing an ideal base for developing a warm relationship between mother and baby. What do we find when we look at breast-feeding in our own society? First, that the extent to which mothers succeed in, value, and enjoy breast-feeding is culturally determined. Many women do not even try to breast-feed, and of those who do, many fail. Cultural support influences their success to a dramatic extent (Rafael 1971). Second, we find that the reasons why mothers do what they do are not accessible to ethological methods. The study of 700 Nottingham mothers by the Newsons (1963) showed that the sort of reason given by mothers for giving up breast-feeding varied very much, from the 'practical' to the more emotional. The answers varied in part according to whether the interviewer was a professional health visitor or an ordinary mother, they varied according to the class and education of the mother, and so on. The whole issue of levels of interpretation of culturally mediated conduct is one which is necessarily beyond the scope of ethological methods.

It may at first sight seem puzzling that so many women have difficulty breast-feeding in our society, given the evident evolutionary pressure towards making the process problem-free. In fact a knowledge of biology coupled with information on what actually happens to mother and baby in the postnatal period in our own society can help us to understand at least part of the difficulty. In a study in Cambridge we found that the breast-fed babies woke and cried much more frequently than the bottle-fed babies, becoming restless and crying within two or three hours of the previous feed (Bernal 1972). Many women felt that a baby who was getting enough milk would sleep for about four hours between feeds (as indeed their medical advisors had indicated), and the frequent crying had a dramatic effect on the numbers of mothers who gave up the attempt to breast-feed. Now if the composition of the milk of various mammals is compared, we find that there is a relationship between the protein content of the milk and the frequency with which the mother feeds her young. With a high protein content, the time interval between feeds is long, and this association cuts across taxonomic relationships. If the different mammalian milks are arranged according to their protein content and the frequency of feeds, human breast milk with its comparatively low protein content places us among the species who are fed almost continuously (Ben Shaul 1962). Bottle milk, on the other hand, with its higher protein content, is comparable with the milk of those species that have a much longer feed interval. It is easy to understand then why the breast-fed babies, at least in the early days of lactation, demand frequent feeds, and why, when their mothers change to bottle-feeding, they sleep for much longer periods. (The middle-class mothers in the sample were more likely to persevere with breast-feeding in spite of the crying: their conviction that it was best for the baby was greater, and they were more likely to disregard the advice of medical authority regarding four-hourly feeds.)

By altering the content of the milk, we alter the pattern of contact between mother and baby. But as yet we have no knowledge of what the consequences of this alteration might be. When we look at patterns of mother–infant contact more generally in western societies, we find a disconcertingly wide difference from the pattern of intense and constant contact and immediate responsiveness of the !Kung mothers, and of the non-human primates. What do these differences, apparent distortions of the pattern to which mother and child are adapted, mean for the development of the child? The answer must be that we do not yet know; such striking contrasts should certainly make us cautious, and should remind us to take the differences seriously, when what may be at stake is so important. But it is by no means clear what these differences imply for the ways in which we should view our own caretaking patterns. In the first place we have already noted that it is dangerous to infer too readily from studies of present-day hunter-gatherers conclusions about human biological adaptation in general. It is probable that the child-rearing patterns and social organisation in the hunter-gatherer societies in different ecologies varied considerably.

Secondly, even if we had a considerably firmer base for our views on man's prehistory, it is quite unclear how this ought to affect our own child-rearing. Patterns of cuddling, feeding, talking and playing with a baby are part of the culture within which that baby will grow up. And it is not clear that parents who must function in an industrial society either could in practice bring up their children in a way that paralleled the constant physical contact and immediate responsiveness of !Kung parents, or ought to be making any such attempt. The !Kung mothers have both a great deal of leisure, and a supportive group of friends and relatives around them, not to mention a group of children who take over much of the caretaking of the child in his second year. We cannot isolate the mother–child dyad and treat them as a unit independent of the rest of their social group (a point which might well be drawn directly from ethological studies of primate groups).

Before we can judge just how seriously to take such differences in the early experience of babies, we need to know with more confidence what the consequences of variation in contact might be. The obvious difficulty in looking for differences in later personality or development between adults of different cultures, where babies are cared for and loved in different ways, is that the societies differ in so many other aspects that it would be impossible to link the child-rearing practices to any later differences with any precision. What we can begin to do is to look at the consequences of variation in early experience within a particular society, or in closely related societies. If we do examine the consequences of particular early events in this way, one finding that stands out is that these consequences depend to a very great extent on cultural factors. This point, of particular significance to our understanding of human development, is illustrated by the findings of studies which have followed up the development of children who have suffered perinatal trauma, or who have been kept in special care and thus been separated from their mothers in the postnatal weeks. The separation studies are of especial interest to ethologists, because their results have been interpreted in relation to the concept of a 'sensitive period'.

The pioneering studies here were carried out by Klaus and Kennell in a series of experiments in the US and in Guatemala (Kennell *et al.* 1974). They found that there were significant differences in the way the mothers behaved towards their babies at follow up visits at one month and one year: the mothers who had had more contact with their babies in the post-partum period showed more soothing behaviour towards their babies, more eye-to-eye contact and fondling than the 'separated' mothers. At two years of age, a comparison between five mothers from each group also found differences in the mothers' speech to the children, and at five years, the five 'extra contact' children had significantly higher IQ scores, better scores on a receptive language test, and better measures of comprehension. The Guatemalan results showed that the duration of breast-feeding increased in the 'extra contact' group, but were equivocal on other measures of mother-infant interaction. In several other studies similar results have now been reported for the early months, showing that both maternal attitude, and patterning of interaction between mother and baby, may be affected by early separation. However, in two series of studies, in Stanford (Leiderman and Seashore 1975) and in Oxford (Whiten 1977), these early effects disappeared after a few months, and it seems very likely that the fading of the effects was a function of the social background of the samples studied. The groups of mothers studied by Klaus and Kennell were extremely poor (in Cleveland they were very young, black and unmarried), and the conflicting results were reported for groups which were much better educated, in reasonable economic conditions, and married. It seems that there is then evidence for short-term effects of early separation of mother and baby on patterns of inter-action between them, and on the establishment of lactation, but that for effects continuing beyond the first year the picture is not at all clear, and certainly the consequences are heavily coloured by the social environment in which the child grows up (Sameroff and Chandler 1975).

In interpreting their findings, Klaus and Kennell used the term 'sensitive period' to describe the immediate post-partum period: 'a unique period in the human mother soon after delivery when she is especially sensitive to her baby and most ready to become attached' (Kennell, Trause and Klaus 1975).

The notion of sensitive period is of course being used here in a more metaphorical fashion than it is used by ethologists. No proposal is made as to what factors, intrinsic or extrinsic, might be involved in determining the onset or the termination of the period of special responsiveness. Indeed the results of the study are open to quite different interpretations. Richards (1978) has suggested that by intervening, the pediatricians have given the mothers not only much needed support, encouraging atten-tiveness to the babies, but also a different model of expectation for mothering than that experienced by similar mothers going through the hospital separation routine, and that this intervention, for these mothers living in such difficult circumstances, may be very important, important enough to account for noticeable differences in mothering later.

The point that must be emphasised is that the significance of particular early events for the baby, and for the mother, may be quite different for families in different cultural groups. This same point is further underlined by the findings of studies which follow up children who have suffered perinatal hazard. There is now a great deal of evidence that the long-term effects of perinatal difficulties are heavily influenced by the environment in which the child grows up. For instance, the prognosis for low birth weight babies is closely related to the social class of the parents (Sameroff and Chandler 1975). While human babies do show considerable capacity for recovery from perinatal complications, this recovery does seem to depend on the nature of the postnatal environment: the finding that poverty amplifies the effects of early difficulties is repeatedly reported in large scale surveys (Davie, Butler and Goldstein 1972).

There are striking parallels between this finding and those of a study we carried out on a medically low-risk sample in Cambridge. We were particularly interested in neonatal differences between babies, and in the early interaction between mothers and babies, and the seventy-seven families in the study were followed until the children were five and a half years old. We found that there were marked differences between the children in the neonatal period, and these were related to the birth histories of the babies, and to the later patterns of interaction between mother and child. This variation in neonatal patterns was unrelated to the assessments of behaviour and development made at four, five and five and a half years for the children from social classes I and II. However for the children from social classes III and IV there were associations between the neonatal differences and differences in the incidence of behaviour problems, in measures of distractibility, and in responsiveness to the person giving the tests, as well as in IQ. For the working-class children, then, a pattern of individual differences was consistent from the neonatal period, in marked contrast to the discontinuity in the pattern of individual variation among the middle-class children; the variation associated with neonatal factors was apparently swamped by sources of variation influencing the children's behaviour in their second and third years (Dunn 1978).

III. Observation and methodology

Ethological studies have been of considerable importance in influencing studies of child development at a very different level – that of methodology. There has been a great increase in observational studies of mothers and babies, and of children in group situations. This interest in observation and description of behaviour in 'natural' situations, or in semi-structured laboratory situations, is one that has grown very directly from a new awareness of ethological work. It is, of course, not a new interest. We have extensive diary accounts of children's behaviour and development from the nineteenth century on, and in the 1930s much research using description of children in groups took place. But it is striking how productive the approach has been in its recent form.

The most direct transposition from animal to human observation is found in studies such as those of Blurton Jones (1972a) and McGrew (1972), where attempts were made, on classical ethological grounds, to construct an 'ethogram' of children's behaviour, a comprehensive catalogue of behavioural items objectively described. A characteristic feature of the categorisation of behaviour used is that the observer avoids both descriptive units which imply motivational states (aggression, anxiety, etc.) and also global units such as 'attachment', at least at the level of initial data collection.

It was held that this rigorous restriction to 'objective' terms, about which different observers would agree (without extended training to achieve inter-rater reliability), 'frees' the information from the particular orientation of the psychologist observing the behaviour. Such techniques of recording behaviour do allow a wide variety of explicit treatment of the data which in the use of rating scales and larger predetermined scales is implicit and untested (Blurton Jones 1972b).

This approach was seen as having great advantages over descriptions of behaviour based on ratings of children's behaviour, or on interviews. Rating scales were criticised as being seldom based on empirically derived dimensions of behaviour, as difficult to validate, and as prone to halo effects. Interviewing was seen as a technique which cannot provide information on what mother and child actually do, either because the mother is unaware of or unwilling to report the child's behaviour in the sort of details and objectivity for which the ethologist strives, or because the interviewer's questions and the mother's answers involve problems of interpretation. Interviews were seen as particularly unsuitable for providing information on details of interaction.

There is, however, a serious difficulty with the view that ethological observation categories are 'objective'. These objective categories are specified by their appearance – they are visually given, and there cannot be categories for *human actions* which are solely visually given (which are imposed upon observers by phenomena, rather than imposed on phenomena by observers). *Action* involves the idea of intentionality; whether or not it is possible to describe the behaviour of animals in a way that does not imply interpretation, there is no way of describing human behaviour without implying interpretation of it (Dunn 1977). There is a particularly important issue here in the study of early human development. It is possible that with a newborn baby, categories of his behaviour that are visually specified would be appropriate; but to choose to employ categories of description that could not pick up on the baby's becoming *human* in the sense of his actions being intentional, and being interpreted as intentional, would clearly be absurd. One of the limitations in the view that places the evolutionary importance of the mother–child relationship primarily in terms of the physical protection it ensures is that it fails to consider the importance of the mother–child relationship in terms of the specifically human developments of language, communication and the development of self-consciousness. Early human development centrally includes the development of specifically human capacities. It can, as we have noted, be a very useful exercise to compare the early development and social behaviour of humans with other primates when it is these specifically human skills we are considering. The problems of understanding the beginnings of human communication and thought, and the further problems of understanding the effects of variation in early experience here, involve considering the origins of intentionality and self-consciousness. Recent elegant work with video and film analysis of the early interaction between mother and baby has shown just how important shared understanding and shared expectation may be to this development (Schaffer 1978, Newson 1974, Trevarthen 1974). Descriptive studies of this early exchange, then, can be extremely helpful in attempts to discover how the child 'learns how to mean', but these studies indicate that what is relevant in these exchanges for the development of intentionality, and communication, is not necessarily the overt behaviour, but what each partner expects or knows in common about the exchange. The latter necessarily has the status of an interpretative inference from behaviour.

There is a further difficulty with the idea of observational techniques as 'objective', and this involves the effects of the presence of an observer. It is likely that in group situations children take very little notice of an observer (Connolly and Smith 1972), but it is quite obvious that to think of an observer watching mother and child at home as non-participant in the situation is deeply misleading. This is not to suggest that the presence of an observer necessarily grossly distorts the style of interaction between mother and child, or that other methods of investigation can hope to circumvent the problem. It is, of course, likely that individuals will react differently to an interviewer, or to an experimental situation, just as they will to an observer. But we should be clear that what is observed in a family situation is inevitably affected by the presence of another person.

Another aspect of ethological methodology that has very general implications for those studying human development concerns the sort of causal inference which can be made about a given set of data. There are some instances where direct observation can be much more helpful in suggesting causal processes than information from a survey or interview can be. In a study of the effects of adult involvement on children's activities, we found that if the mother paid attention to what her child was doing, by looking and commenting in some way, not necessarily interrupting her own activity, then the length of time for which that child continued in the activity was much longer than the length of time for which that child played without such maternal attention. There were considerable differences between families in the amount of such joint attention that occurred, and the profile of attention patterns for the individual children varied very much in consequence (Dunn and Wooding 1977). There were also social class differences in the extent to which, and the context in which, the mothers paid attention to the children's activities. Now, a bald correlation between social class and distractibility in the class room could give us little idea about the underlying process producing such an association, whereas observation of family interaction does suggest how such an effect is mediated. What direct observation offers to us in this way is a far more sensitive heuristic procedure than is offered by other methods of enquiry. It is not, and cannot be, a means of guaranteeing the validity of the causal inferences to which it leads us. Causal inference remains causal *inference*.

IV. Principles for studying interaction

One area of enquiry in which ethological approach does offer major potential assistance to those studying human development is in the analysis of interaction. Here a considerable degree of sophistication has been reached in the analysis of mutual influences between two partners in a dyad, and between members of larger social groups. The general principles of interaction worked out for kittens (Rosenblatt 1975) or for mother and infant monkey (Hinde 1976) are important and relevant for the study of interaction between people. For instance, we have seen that in the discussion of attachment and its importance for the child's development, the experience of a responsive and sensitive mother was thought to be of central importance, a feature of the mother–child relationship to which both mother and child are biologically adapted. It is clearly of interest to examine the consequences for the child of variation in the sensitivity of mothering that it experiences. To do this we must be able to separate accurately measures of mothers' behaviour from measures of children's behaviour. Simple measures of what a mother does are inevitably confounded by what her child is doing. Those who study human mothers and their babies are only just beginning to realise the seriousness of this problem, and have much to learn from animal work. Similarly, those studying social behaviour of animals in groups have begun to develop methods of studying the interaction between several individuals within the group, in a way that may well produce useful analogies for those studying human beings.

Finally, I want to consider two general issues, which concern ways in which those studying the development of children could learn from ethologists.

1. Taking ethological methodology at a very general level it is clear that the ethological emphasis on studying the developing animal in its own habitat and social world is of crucial importance in the study of human development. We will only begin to understand human development if we study children in their real social world. We have to take account of the complexity of mutual influences within the family and social group in which the child grows up. Here we should learn not just from ethological sophistication in analysing mutual interaction between individuals within a larger group, but from a much wider psychological recognition of the complexity of family inter-relations. And further, the wider cultural and socio-economic setting of the family has profound effects on both the immediate behaviour and long-term development. A single example illustrates the complexity of factors which may be important here. A recent study of depression in women in London (Brown, Harris and

Copeland 1977) has shown that if a young girl loses her mother, this experience can greatly increase the likelihood of depression in adult life, *if* the individual experiences a combination of other events later. A combination of 'vulnerability' factors in addition to the early loss of mother (unsatisfactory relationship with husband, more than two children, not being employed) predicts the rate of depression in response to particular events with great accuracy. The issue is exactly that discussed in relation to perinatal complications: that the predictive importance of particular early events depends on a complex of features of the individual's later experience.

2. A second general issue which deserves some emphasis is the question of what models of development it is appropriate to employ in the analysis of early human experience. Much discussion of the significance of early experience in children carries the implicit assumption (heavily influenced by the animal studies mentioned in §II) that development proceeds rather as a tree grows, and that early events which affect the base or trunk of the tree have a more profound effect than later events. But biologists, and embryologists in particular, have developed far more sophisticated models of development, and these may prove to be of much value in thinking about human development. Evidence for the flexibility and adaptability of the developmental process has now accumulated from a number of different studies following up children who have suffered various difficulties early in life. Our models of development must be able to explain why, for example, children who have spent their first three years in residential nurseries specifically discouraging attachment to the nurses can indeed form warm and deep attachments to their adoptive parents when removed from the institution (Tizard and Rees 1975); they must be able to explain why an infancy spent in severely restricted circumstances does not necessarily preclude the development of intellectual ability later (Koluchova 1976). The flexibility of developmental processes, and the extent to which early development is buffered, is becoming increasingly clear, and it is not surprising that we find Waddington's epigenetic landscape discussed in contexts as different as the development of personality (Bowlby 1973) and cognitive development (Bower 1974). Ideas on homeostasis and self-regulation recently developed by Bateson (1977) in an ethological context may also prove helpful in understanding the human capacity to recover from early trauma.

In summary, it appears that the influence of ethology has been least fruitful where there has been disjointed and mechanical application of techniques in an inappropriate context; much more fruitful has been the more holistic perspective on studying a creature developing in the totality of its environment, and, particularly, the encouragement of careful sustained study, by human observers, of human beings. Gilbert White, in a letter of 1771, saw just how important such observation was for understanding animal behaviour:

Faunists, as you observe, are too apt to acquiesce in bare descriptions, and a few synonyms: the reason is plain; because all that may be done at home in a man's study, but the investigation of the life and conversation of animals, is a concern of much more trouble and difficulty, and is not to be attained but by the active and inquisitive, and by those that reside much in the country. (1977:136)

If faunists do have much to teach humanists, it is surely this lesson – the importance of sustained observation of our subjects in their own normal habitat.

Comments on papers by Salzen and Dunn

ROBERT A. HINDE

These papers involve two entirely different approaches, and I do not feel that it would be possible or proper to attempt to synthesize them. Instead, I shall try to emphasize a few questions which arise.

Eric Salzen's paper forms part of a long-standing tradition in ethology – a tradition of attempts to describe systems with considerable generality across species and types of behaviour. It is presented as a synthesizing system, with evidence drawn from species ranging from chicks to man, embracing behaviour, affect and their development. Its potential usefulness lies not so much in any of its elements as in the extent to which it provides a scheme to which diverse observations can be related. In the face of the diversity of data on the enormous range of species with which the ethologist is faced, the *possible* value of such an attempt is clear. The first question we must ask is whether such attempts are in fact useful in the present state of the study of behaviour? Have they been useful in the past? Are they likely to be in the future? Two requirements would seem to be necessary – an adequate accumulation of facts about the range of species the theory is to embrace, and adequate evidence that the species and types of behaviour are in fact sufficiently similar to be accommodated in one system. Is this true, for instance of the distress calls of chicks and the crying of the human infant? Or of imprinting and the attachment of the human infant to its mother?

A second question, qualifying the first, is the level of analysis at which such a system is likely to be useful. In general, in behaviour studies, the generality of a statement is likely to be inversely related to its precision. If we attempt broad syntheses, are we likely to be handling fundamental relationships with the flavour of e $= mc^2$, or are we likely to be left with

642

superficial trivialities? This is a real issue with a system that purports to explain a wide range of phenomena in terms of such variables as alternative tendencies to approach or withdraw.

One essential here is extreme clear-headedness about the concepts used, and clarification would be desirable on some issues. What, for instance, is the status of Salzen's three behaviour systems? Do examples of behaviour within each system share motivational factors, or are the systems classificatory devices based on similarity of mechanisms, or what? What exactly is meant by exploratory behaviour being *part of* orientation behaviour? Similar clarification for approach–withdrawal tendencies or many of the other concepts that he uses would be welcome.

Just because far ranging syntheses are likely to lack precision, there is a real danger that the concepts used will be able to explain almost any phenomena that might arise. It would, for instance, perhaps be a useful exercise to ask what sort of early behaviour could not be described in terms of approach–withdrawal tendencies, with orientation behaviour of higher and lower degrees. Interactions between two factors of varying strength can produce a very wide range of phenomena.

Another issue is the danger that complexities will be neglected. For instance, it will be seen by many that in the current account several of the complexities of imprinting – the diversity of learning processes involved and the occurrence of positive responses to discrepancy, for instance – receive scant mention. And accounts that bridge such a wide range of species are likely to do scant justice to differences in level of complexity between them.

Another issue that needs discussion in the context of such theories is the relation between description and explanation. I am sure Salzen would agree that Morris' categories of conflict behaviour lie well to the descriptive end of that continuum. But how far are we dealing with explanation and how far with description when we observe that, for instance, a number of species show behaviour to discrepancy that, at a certain level of precision, can be regarded as similar?

Here then are a number of general points about the type of approach Salzen has adopted. Judy Dunn's aims are more specific – she attempts to survey ways in which ethology has influenced thinking on human development, to delineate the limits of its usefulness, and to show how the ethologist's ways of thinking can be exploited to best advantage. I think a few points need further discussion.

In assessing the usefulness of extrapolation from non-human primates, Judy Dunn is concerned primarily with the impact of Bowlby's work on ethologists. It must be said immediately that Bowlby is a psychoanalyst, not an ethologist, so that she is concerned primarily with the misuses of a psychoanalyst's view of the ethology of the 1960s. She is in fact concerned primarily with the view of some anthropologists that, if man's behaviour can indeed be seen as having been adapted in an ecological sense, then the study of hunter-gatherer societies may give us some clue as to the nature of the social and physical environment to which they were adapted, and enable us to see the differences between that and the environment in which we now live. Here she argues that culture is ubiquitous in human societies, and that it is meaningless to argue that hunter-gatherer behaviour is more biological than our own. While I agree with the general point she is making, it is important to distinguish between culture and cultural differences. While some form of culture is part of human nature, cultures do differ, and it is not unreasonable to suppose that some are more distant from the social environments to which we were adapted than others. Furthermore, the argument that the diversity of present human cultures makes improbable the existence of adaptation to the particular hunter-gatherer mode neglects the relative time periods for which hunter-gatherer modes (admittedly in some degree diverse) and more recent cultures existed.

When it comes to understanding the factors controlling a particular type of behaviour, such as breast feeding, in a particular social environment, Judy Dunn is of course right in insisting that ethological methods as used for other species will take us only a part of the way. And she is right too in pointing out that we cannot isolate the mother–infant dyad from the culture in which they live. To put her argument in a slightly different form, in proposing 'what should be' we must distinguish between proposals that will fit the mother–infant dyad better to this culture, and proposals to change the culture that would in our view make it more congenial for them. That cultural and class differences may be crucial in determining the effects of early experience is now well established, but this seems to me to be primarily an indication of the complexity of the problem, and thus evidence only against the use of an over-simple ethological approach.

In discussing observations and methodology, Judy Dunn focusses on the Blurton Jones and McGrew attempts to construct ethograms of children's behaviour, arguing that their use of supposedly rigorous 'objective' categories of behaviour poses certain difficulties. She argues that human actions involve intentionality, and description of intentionality involves interpretation of the observed behaviour. Two points must be made. First, interpretation of intentionality is of course necessary not only for human behaviour. Second, whilst the micro-approach of Blurton Jones and McGrew can well be criticized as inappropriate for some problems, they themselves argue that categories based on observation could form the basis for interpretation in terms of higher level categories. Indeed, the recent demonstration by Sroufe and Waters (1977) that categories of 'attachment' are stable over time, even though the more molecular measures on which they are based may not be, demonstrates the importance of such interpretations.

In conclusion, perhaps I may express my own misgivings at the concept of human ethology. First, it implies a group of research workers studying *human* behaviour. Now, when the biological sciences were blossoming in the nineteenth and early twentieth century, it was convenient to divide up the subject matter on phyletic grounds. Biologists tended to be ornithologists, arachnologists, coleopterists or what have you. Of course that was not true of the great ones – Darwin wrote about organisms ranging from fungi to man – but as the knowledge grew the natural route for specialization was along the lines of the natural classification. Gradually, however, as the growth of knowledge demanded yet further specialization, a new type of division arose. Investigators became interested in particular aspects of the groups that they studied – there were specialists in the classification of butterflies, the behaviour of birds, the control of population in lemmings. Overlapping this, but lagging behind it, came the realization that the solution of such problems required that investigators should enlarge their scope beyond the phyletic group on which they were fixated: butterfly systematics required principles similar to those used in bird systematics; the same techniques and generalizations would serve for some aspects of insect and bird behaviour; the ecology of lemmings had something in common with that of crossbills. In short, investigators became primarily systematists, comparative psychologists, or ecologists, and only secondarily specialists in a particular phyletic group.

While I am not a historian of science and therefore not prepared to defend the precise accuracy of this account, I hope I have made my point: carving up science along phyletic lines smacks of a regression to nineteenth-century science. It can of course be argued that man is special, and deserves a special focus. I agree only partially with this view, and would be prepared to argue that even anthropologists and sociologists can profit by seeing some of the concepts they use put through their paces in the relatively simple case of non-human primates, and that they can gain insight into the role of institutions by comparing human societies with (relatively) institution-free non-human ones. But in any case 'human ethology' comes near to being a contradiction in terms. Whilst I am not going to get drawn into one of those futile discussions on 'What is ethology?', I think most of us would agree that it usually implies a comparative approach. Where is the comparison in 'human ethology'?

Now let us turn to the other aspect of 'human ethology'. The general view seems to be that some sort of characterization of ethology is possible in terms of subject matter, methods and/or attitudes. Now think where so-called human ethologists have come from. Some have escaped from the narrow constraints of Hullian theory, others from the Skinnerian mode. Some are reaching out from studies exclusively of children to see whether comparisons with other species will help. Others are finding that the experimental techniques in which they are versed need to be tempered with observation, and others have become conscious of biological constraints on what can be learned. Isn't the lesson that *any* strait jacket must be avoided at all costs? Isn't there a danger that, by erecting the shiny new banner of human ethology, shutting themselves off in a castle, they will fall into the old trap, and that as the banner tarnishes the castle will become another prison?

Is there an answer to this? If research workers by their nature must classify themselves, how can they form groups that will not subtly impede their efforts? This is where I am glad to be able to pay tribute to John Bowlby, from whom I learned an important lesson on this issue. In the fifties I was privileged to attend a weekly meeting which included, if I remember rightly, two varieties of psychoanalyst, a Hullian, a Skinnerian, a Piagetian, an ethologist, some psychiatric social workers, and even an anti-psychiatrist. The discussions were immensely fertile because we were all interested in a common problem – mother–child interaction. Some may not agree with all of Bowlby's conclusions, but none can deny that his achievement has arisen in part from his willingness to accept ideas from diverse sources – even if it led to embarrassment with his own colleagues – and focus them on a problem.

And that, I believe, must be the answer – to focus on a problem, and accept whatever material is relevant to it. The problem may of necessity be broadly defined, and what is and is not relevant may not always be easy to see. But if scientists or the products of their work are to be divided into groups, relevance to particular problems surely provides the best guide lines. In the case of child development, no one technique or theoretical approach will by itself prove sufficient. Comparative studies can certainly be of value. For instance, in successively focussing on the mother–infant relationship, on the importance of the infant as well as the mother in determining the nature of that relationship, on the importance of relationships with other social companions, and on the manner in which relationships affect relationships, primatologists have usually been one step ahead of most child developmentalists. That ethological observational methods can also be useful is now well proven. But the higher cognitive and moral levels of the human child, and the complexity of and cultural influences on its development, inevitably mean that the traditional ethological methods will not by themselves be sufficient.

Finally, since the precision of any generalization is inevitably inversely related to its range of applicability, my own preference is at the moment for tackling relatively limited problems: I doubt whether the time for any inevitably superficial synthesizing theories has yet come.

E. A. SALZEN: REPLY TO HINDE'S COMMENTS

I believe that the contribution of ethology to social attachment studies has been minimal. In general ethological theory has been used in post hoc discussions of studies that have been designed and conducted in the traditions of zoology and psychology and not with the methodology and approach of ethology. The ethological concept of imprinting may have had an influence through Bowlby, but Bowlby's use of a goal-corrected proximity-maintaining system involving central neural models was original since he did not make use of the only comparable imprinting model. Such goal-corrected behaviour is characteristic of taxis movements and appetitive behaviour which have received scant attention from ethologists compared with the fixed action pattern. In my paper, therefore, I attempted to apply ethological theory and thinking to the evidence on social attachment. I deliberately avoided using the classical imprinting concept because it can be misleading when applied to man.

First, my paper treated attachment behaviour as appetitive orientation behaviour for maintaining sensory homeostasis which has a protective function. This sensory homeostatic system clearly does have a separate motivating mechanism from the physiological homeostatic system and the reproductive system and this is explained in the paper. The sensory homeostatic system described is obviously not applicable to feeding and elimination behaviour of the infant. These three vertebrate behavioural systems are not simply classificatory groupings; they are distinct functional and evolutionary systems. The paper also describes in some detail an orientation mechanism that produces approach and withdrawal movements derived from extensor responses giving a forward vector, and flexor responses giving a turning component. A detailed analysis of orientation behaviour in structured stimulus fields where stimulus strength is a function of stimulus novelty is developed in the paper. Neonate orientation behaviour is shown to be a function of the developing familiarity of the environment and the two-component mechanism which necessarily produces approach to mild novelty. This causes the neonate first to orient to the attachment figure and later to explore increasingly distant objects and areas; being driven back to the attachment figure by highly novel events. A field theory analysis of typical social attachment situations and exploratory behaviour is presented. Thus there is a careful and detailed explanation of exploratory behaviour as part of the orientation mechanism. The mechanism is fully applicable to the positive responses to discrepancy seen in imprinting. I have applied this orientation system to the complexities of imprinting in previous papers and the present paper is not about imprinting studies.

Second, my paper treated the affective or emotional behaviour and feelings of attachment figure separation and reunion as being thwarted protective orientation behaviour (evolved as social distress signals) and the cessation of this thwarting (evolved as social pleasure signals) respectively. I do not think that the analysis of thwarting behaviours used is purely descriptive. On the contrary it is explanatory inasmuch as it represents systems on which natural selection and evolution have operated. Where species similarities are not actually homologous there could clearly be parallel evolution. The example of distress calls in chicks and squirrel monkeys is most apposite. And the early cries of the human infant are indeed similar in the characteristics common to these calls, as can be seen in the sound spectrographs given by Wolff (1969). Clearly the analysis of thwarting behaviours has specific implications for real behaviour mechanisms and the neurological systems of emotion. It presents a full theory of emotions both negative and positive and is far from superficial in both implications and applications.

Finally, in relation to Dunn's paper I think that modelling and interactionist approaches are complementary. The orientation and affect system I have described has the short-term effect of initiating and guiding the interactions, both individual and cultural, which Dunn has emphasized. These interactions may predominate over the long-term but there is some evidence from introspection and psycho-pathology that the basic orientation–affect may still operate under appropriate conditions. Thus we do not know for certain that cultural compensation restores deprived children to a state indistinguishable from normally experienced ones, as appears to be the case in the Cambridge study cited by Dunn. Perhaps the tests in such cases are not sensitive enough and the original epigenetic channel may not have been regained, but only simulated or paralleled. The difference between such epigenetic histories may only be revealed by particular circumstances or crises in later life. Dunn's example of breast feeding shows how a cultural practice over feeding-times may fail to meet the biological requirements of the infant. Although the cultural solution of bottle feeding with high protein milk may solve the particular problem of behaviour synchrony of mother and infant we do not know whether it leaves other biological patterns distorted or disrupted. And we do not know what the extent of these consequences may be – individually, socially, biologically or culturally. It is in this respect that the ethological approach is safer than the interactionist because it is less likely to underrate the potential effects of early experience. The value of the ethologically based theory which I have attempted to describe in some detail is that such synthesizing theories of foundational systems and mechanisms are a necessary guide for the meaningful data collection and analysis of the detailed microstructures of interactions and of more limited problems.

J. DUNN: REPLY TO HINDE'S COMMENTS

I would first like to make a brief comment on the question which Robert Hinde raised in discussing Eric Salzen's paper: Is the attempt to make a general model useful in the present state of the study of behaviour? In thinking and writing about the consequences of early experience for the development of children we are dealing with an urgent *practical* question. People have to make decisions about social policy and the care of children, and this puts a great responsibility on those who write about the consequences of early experience. Dalbir Bindra commented (§8 above) that good ideas in science come from many sources. In attempting to understand this particular issue, which is in practical terms such an urgent one, it is clearly important to use whatever good ideas may help us, from whatever source. In Eric Salzen's discussion of the longitudinal consequences of early relationships, the model which he used was so broad, encompassing as it did the development of chick and of human, that I did not feel that it brought out what we *do* know about the consequences of early experience in human development. If one is trying to understand the development of a species about which we already have a great deal of information, to which we have cognitive access, then it is likely that a scheme broad enough to include both chicks and humans may not provide us with much immediately explanatory help. We must surely make use of whatever advantages being *human* gives us in understanding human development. The complexity of the problem of predicting the consequences of early experience for humans is well understood now, but we do know something about which factors are most important, and about how these factors interact. We know which sorts of question seem to be the most useful to ask. This knowledge has come, of course, not primarily from ethological studies, but from epidemiological studies by psychiatrists and pediatricians, from the greater understanding we have of neonatal behaviour and vulnerability, and from sociological studies combined with medical and developmental studies.

The first point which Robert Hinde raised about my paper concerned the use made of ethological ideas by those studying hunter-gatherer societies. I agree with him that the borrowing of 'ethological' ideas via the early writing of Bowlby has often involved a gross distortion of recent ethological work. I commented on this use in the paper, because in much recent writing about early development it is *this* – the 'misuse of a psychoanalyst's view of ethology' – that forms the basis of discussion. As I hope I made clear in my paper, recent work by ethologists such as Bateson on early experience in other species has a great deal to teach us in terms of analytic precision. In reply to Robert Hinde's points I would emphasize first that hunter-gatherer societies occupied very diverse areas, including most of the world's surface except for the poles, and very different habitats. We do not know how representative the Kalahari Bushmen are of the way of life in which the human mother–infant relationship evolved. It is surely, then, unscientific to draw inferences about man's biological adaptation in general from the study of what may be an unrepresentative present-day hunter-gatherer society. My point was one of caution about the dangers of making sweeping inferences from such material. A second point was that even if we did know more about man's biological adaptation, that does not tell us what the consequences of changing the environment might be.

On the question about the interpretation of intentionality, I certainly did not mean to imply that this was a problem *only* for those studying humans. It was made clear by the discussion at the conference that it is a problem for animal watchers too. But I think that the complexity of possible human intentions (just because of the human powers of language and reflexive thought) means that it is a particularly hazardous business interpreting intentions when observing people. And the problem of interpreting intentions is particularly acute for those studying development. If you watch a child growing up, it is an exceedingly difficult and delicate business deciding *when* you are going to start calling the behaviour 'intentional'. One of Piaget's definitions involved noting when the child used a variety of means to gain a particular end. But what do you do about social behaviour when no objects are involved? At what point during development can we decide that, when a child cries and his mother comes, he is doing it on purpose?

References

Ainsworth, M. D. 1962. The effects of maternal deprivation: a review of findings and controversy in the context of research strategy. In *Deprivation of maternal care: a reassessment of its effects*. WHO Public Health Papers no. 14. Geneva.

1964. Patterns of attachment behavior shown by the infant in interaction with his mother. *Merrill-Palmer Quarterly*, 10:51–8.

1972. Attachment and dependency: a comparison. In J. L. Gerwirtz (ed.), *Attachment and dependency*. Washington D.C.: V. H. Winston.

Ainsworth, M. D. S. and Bell, S. M. 1970. Attachment, exploration and separation: illustrated by the behaviour of one-year-olds in a strange situation. *Child Development*, 41:49–67.

Ainsworth, M. D. S., Bell, S. M. and Stayton, D. J. 1974. Infant–mother attachment and social development: socialisation as a product of reciprocal responsiveness to signals. In M. P. M. Richards (ed.), *The integration of a child into a social world*, Cambridge: Cambridge University Press.

Ainsworth, M. D. S. and Wittig, B. A. 1969. Attachment and exploratory behavior of one-year-olds in a strange situation. In B. M. Foss (ed.), *Determinants of infant behaviour*, vol. IV. London: Methuen.

Alpert, A. 1959. Reversibility of pathological fixations associated with maternal deprivation in infancy. *Psychoanalytic Study of the Child*, 14:169–85.

Ambrose, J. A. 1961. The smiling and related responses in early human infancy: an experimental and theoretical study of their course and significance. Unpublished Ph.D. thesis, University of London.

Anderson, C. O. and Mason, W. 1974. Early experience and complexity of social organisation in groups of young rhesus monkeys (Macaca mulatta). *Journal of Comparative and Physiological Psychology*, 87:681–90.

Anderson, J. W. 1972. Attachment behaviour out of doors. N. G. Blurton Jones (ed.), *Ethological studies of child behaviour*, Cambridge: Cambridge University Press.

Andrew, R. J. 1963. Evolution of facial expression. *Science*, 142:1034–41.

1964. Vocalization in chicks, and the concept of 'stimulus contrast'. *Animal Behaviour*, 12:64–76.

Arnold, M. B. (ed.) 1970. *Feelings and emotions*. New York: Academic Press.

Baerends, G. P. 1975. An evaluation of the conflict hypothesis as an explanatory principle for the evolution of displays. In G. Baerends, C. Beer and A. Manning (eds.), *Function and evolution in behaviour*, London: Oxford University Press.

1976. A tentative model for the causation of neuroses. In H. M. van Praag (ed.), *Research in neurosis*. Utrecht: Bohn, Scheltema and Holkema.

Bateson, P. P. G. 1973. Internal influences on early learning in birds. In R. A. Hinde and J. Stevenson-Hinde (eds.), *Constraints on learning: limitations and predispositions*. London: Academic Press.

1976. Rules and reciprocity in behavioural development. In P. P. G. Bateson and R. A. Hinde (eds.), *Growing points in ethology*. Cambridge: Cambridge University Press.

1977. Early experience and sexual preferences. In J. B. Hutchison (ed.), *Biological determinants of sexual behaviour*. London: Wiley.

Ben Shaul, D. M. 1962. The composition of the milk of wild animals. *International Zoo Yearbook*, 4:333–42.

Beres, D. and Obers, S. J. 1950. The effects of extreme deprivation in infancy on psychic structure in adolescence: a study in ego development. *Psychoanalytic Study of the Child*, 5:212–35.

Berkson, G. 1968. Development of abnormal stereotyped behaviours. *Developmental Psychobiology*, 1:118–32.

Berkson, G., Mason, W. A. and Saxon, S. V. 1963. Situation and stimulus effects on stereotyped behaviors of chimpanzees. *Journal of Comparative and Physiological Psychology*, 56:786–92.

Berlyne, D. E. 1960. *Conflict, arousal and curiosity*. New York: McGraw-Hill.

Bernal, J. F. 1972. Crying during the first 10 days of life and maternal responses. *Developmental Medicine and Child Neurology*, 15:760–9.

1974. Attachment: some problems and possibilities. In M. P. M. Richards (ed.), *The integration of a child into a social world*. Cambridge: Cambridge University Press.

Birns, B., Blank, M. and Bridger, W. H. 1969. The effectiveness of various soothing techniques on human neonates. *Psychosomatic Medicine*, 28:316–22.

Blurton Jones, N. 1972a. Categories of child–child interaction. In N. Blurton Jones (ed.), *Ethological studies of child behaviour*, Cambridge: Cambridge University Press.

1972b. Characteristics of ethological studies of human behaviour. In N. Blurton Jones (ed.), *Ethological studies of child behaviour*, Cambridge: Cambridge University Press.

Bower, T. G. R. 1974. *Development in infancy*. San Francisco: Freeman and Co.

Bowlby, J. A. 1965. *Child care and the growth of love*. 2nd edn. Harmondsworth: Penguin.

1969. *Attachment and loss*, vol. I, *Attachment*. London: Hogarth Press.

1973. *Attachment and loss*, vol. II, *Separation: anxiety and anger*. London: Hogarth Press.

Bretherton, I. and Ainsworth, M. D. S. 1974. Responses of one-year-olds to a stranger in a strange situation. In M. Lewis and L. A. Rosenblum (eds.), *The origins of behavior* vol. II, *The origins of fear*. New York: Wiley.

Bridges, K. M. B. 1932. Emotional development in early infancy. *Child Development*, 3:324–41.

Bronfenbrenner, U. 1968. Early deprivation in mammals: a cross species analysis. In G. Newton and S. Levine (eds.), *Early experience and behavior*. Springfield, Illinois: C. C. Thomas.

Bronson, G. W. 1968. The development of fear in man and other animals. *Child Development*, 39:409–31.

1972. Infant's reactions to unfamiliar persons and novel objects. *Monographs on Social Research in Child Development*, 37(3) Serial no. 148.

Brown, G. W., Harris, T. and Copeland, J. R. 1977. Depression and loss. *British Journal of Psychiatry*, 130:1–18.

Bruner, J. S. 1974. The nature and uses of immaturity. In K. Connolly and J. S. Bruner (eds.), *The growth of competence*. London: Academic Press.

Cairns, R. B. 1977. Beyond social attachment: the dynamics of interactional development. In T. Alloway, P. Pliner and L. Krames (eds.), *Advances in the study of communication and affect*, vol. III. *Attachment behavior*. New York: Plenum Press.

Carmichael, L. 1970. The onset and early development of behavior. In P. H. Mussen (ed.), *Carmichael's manual of child psychology*. 3rd edn. New York: Wiley.

Casler, L. 1965. The effects of extra tactile stimulation in a group of institutionalized infants. *Genetic Psychology Monographs*, 71:137–75.

Coates, B., Anderson, E. P. and Hartup, W. W. 1972. Interrelations in the attachment behaviour of human infants. *Developmental Psychology*, 6:218–30.

Cohen, L. J. 1974. The operational definition of human attachment. *Psychological Bulletin*, 81:207–17.

Condon, W. S. and Sander, L. W. 1974. Neonate movement is synchronized with adult speech: interactional participation and language acquisition. *Science*, 183:99–101.

Connolly, K. and Smith, P. K. 1972. Reactions of preschool children to a strange observer. In N. Blurton Jones (ed.), *Ethological studies of child behaviour*, Cambridge: Cambridge University Press.

Corter, C. M. 1977. Brief separation and communication between infant and mother. In T. Alloway, P. Pliner and L. Krames (eds.), *Advances in the study of communication and affect*, vol. III, *Attachment behavior*. New York: Plenum Press.

Craig, W. 1918. Appetites and aversions as constituents of instincts. *Biological Bulletin*, 34:91–107.

Cross, H. A. and Harlow, H. F. 1965. Prolonged and progressive effects of partial isolation on the behavior of macaque monkeys. *Journal of Experimental Research in Personality*, 1:39–49.

Cummins, M. S. and Suomi, S. J. 1976. Long-term effects of social rehabilitation in rhesus monkeys. *Primates*, 17:43–51.

Darwin, C. 1872. *The expression of the emotions in man and animals*. London: John Murray.

Davenport, R. K. and Menzel, E. W. 1963. Stereotyped behavior of the infant chimpanzee. *Archives of General Psychiatry*, 8:99–104.

Davenport, R. K., Menzel, E. W. and Rogers, C. M. 1966. Effects of severe isolation on normal chimpanzees. *Archives of General Psychiatry*, 14:134–8.

Davie, R., Butler, N. R. and Goldstein, H. 1972. *From birth to seven*. London: Longmans.

DeVore, I. and Konner, M. J. 1974. Infancy on hunter-gatherer life: an ethological perspective. In N. J. White (ed.), *Ethology and psychiatry*, Toronto: University of Toronto Press.

Décarie, T. G. (ed.) 1974. *The infant's reaction to strangers*. New York: International Universities Press.

Deutsch, J. and Larsson, K. 1974. Model-oriented sexual behavior in surrogate-reared rhesus monkeys. *Brain, Behavior, Evolution*, 9:157–64.

Douglas, J. W. B. 1975. Early hospital admissions and later disturbances of behaviour and learning. *Developmental Medicine and Child Neurology*, 17:456–80.

Dunn, J. 1976. How far do early differences in mother-child relations affect later development? In P. P. G. Bateson and R. A. Hinde (eds.), *Growing points in ethology*. Cambridge: Cambridge University Press.

Dunn, John 1977. Practising history and social science on 'realist' assumptions. In C. Hookway and P. Pettitt (eds.), *Action and interpretation*. Cambridge: Cambridge University Press.

Dunn, J. F. 1978 (in press). The continuity of individual differences from the first year. In D. Shaffer and J. F. Dunn (eds.), *The first year of life: significance for later development*. London: Wiley.

Dunn, J. F. and Wooding, C. 1977. Play in the home and its implications for learning. In B. Tizard and D. Harvey (eds.), *The biology of play*. London: Heinemann Medical Books.

Eimas, P. D., Siqueland, E. R., Jusczyk, P. and Vigorito, J. 1971. Speech perception in infants. *Science*, 171:303–6.

Erwin, J., Maple, T., Mitchell, G. and Willott, J. 1974. Follow-up study of isolation-reared and mother-reared rhesus monkeys paired with preadolescent conspecifics in late infancy: cross-sex pairings. *Developmental Psychology*, 10:808–14.

Frantz, R. L. 1963. Pattern vision in newborn infants. *Science*, 140:296.

1967. Ontogeny of perception. In A. M. Schrier, H. F. Harlow and F. Stollnitz (eds.), *Behavior of non-human primates*, vol. II. New York: Academic Press.

Freedman, D. G. 1961. The infant's fear of strangers and the flight response. *Journal of Child Psychology and Psychiatry*, 1:242–8.

Freud, A. and Dann, S. 1951. An experiment in group upbringing. *Psychoanalytic Study of the Child*, 6:127–68.

Gewirtz, J. L. 1972. On the selection and use of attachment and dependence indices. In *Attachment and dependency*. Washington, DC: V. H. Winston.

Gibson, E. J. 1969. *Principles of perceptual learning and development*. New York: Appleton-Century-Crofts.

Gomber, J. and Mitchell, G. 1974. Preliminary report on adult male isolation-reared rhesus monkeys caged with infants. *Developmental Psychology*, 10:298.

Gunther, M. 1955. Instinct and the nursing couple. *Lancet* (19 March), 575–8.

Harlow, H. F. 1959. Love in infant monkeys. *Scientific American*, 200:68–74.

1960. Affectional behavior in the infant monkey. In M. A. B. Brazier (ed.), *The central nervous system and behavior*. New York: J. Macy Jr Foundation.

1969. Age-mate or peer affectional system. In D. S. Lehrman, R. A. Hinde and E. Shaw (eds.), *Advances in the study of behavior*, vol. II. New York: Academic Press.

Harlow, H. F., Dodsworth, R. O. and Harlow, M. K. 1965. Total social isolation in monkeys. *Proceedings of the National Academy of Sciences, New York*, 54:90–7.

Harlow, H. F., Gluck, J. P. and Suomi, S. J. 1972. Generalization of behavioral data between nonhuman and human animals. *American Psychologist*, 27:709–16.

Harlow, H. F. and Harlow, M. K. 1962. Social deprivation in monkeys. *Scientific American*, 207:137–46.

  1965. The affectional systems. In A. M. Schrier, H. F. Harlow and F. Stollnitz (eds.), *Behavior of non-human primates*, vol. II. New York: Academic Press.

  1966. Learning to love. *American Scientist*, 54:244–70.

  1969. Effects of various mother–infant relationships on rhesus monkey behaviours. In B. M. Foss (ed.), *Determinants of infant behaviour*, vol. IV. London: Methuen.

Harlow, H. F., Harlow, M. K., Dodsworth, R. O. and Arling, G. L. 1966. Maternal behavior of rhesus monkeys deprived of mothers and peer associations in infancy. *Proceedings of the American Philosophical Society*, 110:58–66.

Harlow, H. F. and Zimmerman, R. R. 1959. Affectional responses in the infant monkey. *Science*, 130:421–32.

Harlow, M. K. and Harlow, H. F. 1966. Affection in primates. *Discovery*, 27:11–19.

Hebb, D. O. 1953. Heredity and environment in mammalian behaviour. *British Journal of Animal Behaviour*, 1:43–7.

Heinicke, C. M. 1973. Parental deprivation in early childhood. In Scott and Senay 1973:141–60.

Hinde, R. A. 1968. Dichotomies in the study of development. In J. M. Thoday and A. S. Parkes (eds.), *Genetic and environmental influences on behaviour*. Edinburgh: Oliver and Boyd.

  1971. Development of social behaviour. In A. M. Schrier and F. Stollnitz (eds.), *Behavior of non-human primates*, vol. III. New York: Academic Press.

  1974. *Biological bases of human social behaviour*. New York: McGraw Hill.

  1976. Mother-infant separation, and the nature of inter-individual relationships: experiments with rhesus monkeys. *Proceedings of the Royal Society of London, Series B*, 196:29–50.

Hinde, R. A. and Spencer-Booth, Y. 1971. Effects of brief separation from mother on rhesus monkeys. *Science*, 173:111–18.

Hinde, R. A. and Stevenson-Hinde, J. (eds.) 1973. *Constraints on learning: limitations and predispositions*. London: Academic Press.

Hinde, R. A. and White, L. E. 1974. Dynamics of a relationship: rhesus mother–infant ventro-ventral contact. *Journal of Comparative and Physiological Psychology*, 86:8–23.

Hollender, M. H. 1969. The need or wish to be held. *Archives of General Psychiatry*, 22:445–53.

van Hooff, J. A. R. A. M. 1962. Facial expressions in higher primates. *Symposia of the Zoological Society of London*, 8:97–125.

  1972. A comparative approach to the phylogeny of laughter and smiling. In R. A. Hinde (ed.), *Non-verbal communication*. Cambridge: Cambridge University Press.

Hoppe, R. A., Milton, A. G. and Simmel, E. C. 1970. *Early experiences and the processes of socialization*. New York: Academic Press.

Howells, J. G. 1970. Fallacies in child care, 1. That 'separation' is synonymous with 'deprivation'. *Acta Paedopsychiatrica, 37*:3–14.

Hunt, J. McV. 1965. Intrinsic motivation and its role in psychological development. In D. Levine (ed.), *Nebraska Symposium on Motivation*. Lincoln: University of Nebraska Press.

Hutt, C. 1966. Exploration and play in children. *Symposia of the Zoological Society of London, 18*:61–81.

Hutt, S. J., Hutt, C., Lenard, H. C., Bernuth, H. V. and Muntjewerff, W. J. 1968. Auditory responsivity in the human neonate. *Nature, 217*:888–90.

Igel, G. J. and Calvin, A. D. 1960. The development of affectional responses in infant dogs. *Journal of Comparative and Physiological Psychology, 53*:302–5.

Jensen, G. D. 1975. Effects of modification of the social environment on young monkey development. *Biological Psychiatry, 10*:659–66.

Jensen, G. D., Bobbitt, R. A. and Gordon, B. N. 1973. Mother and infant roles in the development of independence of Macaca nemestrina. In C. R. Carpenter (ed.), *Behavioral regulators of behavior in primates*. Lewisburg: Bucknell University Press.

Johnston, C. M. and Deisher, R. W. 1973. Contemporary communal child rearing: a first analysis. *Pediatrics, 52*:319–26.

Kagan, J. 1970. Attention and psychological change in the young child. *Science, 170*:826–32.

1974. Discrepancy, temperament, and infant distress. In M. Lewis and L. A. Rosenblum (eds.), *The origins of behavior*, vol. II, *The origins of fear*. New York: Wiley.

Kaufman, I. C. 1960. Some ethological studies of social relationships and conflict situations. *Journal of the American Psychoanalytic Association, 8*:671–85.

1973. Mother-infant separation in monkeys. In Scott and Senay 1973: 33–52.

Kehrer, H. E. and Tente, D. 1969. Observations on displacement activities in children. *Journal of Child Psychology and Psychiatry, 10*:259–68.

Kennell, J. H., Jerauld, R., Wolfe, H., Chester, D., Kreger, N., McAlpine, W., Steffa, M. and Klaus, M. 1974. Maternal behaviour one year after early and extended post-partum contact. *Developmental Medicine and Child Neurology, 16*:172–9.

Kennell, J. H., Trause, M. A. and Klaus, M. 1975. Evidence for a sensitive period in the human mother. In M. O'Conner (ed.), *Parent–infant interaction*. Amsterdam: Elsevier.

Klaus, M., Jerauld, R., Kreger, N., McAlpine, N., Steffa, M. and Kennell, J. 1972. Maternal attachment – importance of the first post-partum days. *New England Journal of Medicine, 286*:460–3.

Koluchova, J. 1976. A report on the further development of twins after severe and prolonged deprivation. In A. M. and A. D. B. Clarke (eds.), *Early experience: myth and evidence*. London: Open Books.

Kruijt, J. P. 1962a. On the evolutionary derivation of wing display in Burmese Red Junglefowl and other Gallinaceous birds. *Symposia of the Zoological Society of London, 8*:25–36.

1962b. Imprinting in relation to drive interactions in Burmese red junglefowl. *Symposia of the Zoological Society of London, 8*:219–26.

Lehrman, D. S. 1970. Semantic and conceptual issues in the nature-nurture problem. In R. Aronson *et al.* (eds.), *Development and evolution of behavior*. San Francisco: Freeman.

Leiderman, P. H. and Seashore, M. J. 1975. Mother–infant separation: some delayed consequences. In M. O'Connor (ed.), *Parent–infant interaction*. Amsterdam: Elsevier.

Lewis, H. 1954. *Deprived children*. Oxford: Nuffield and Oxford University Press.

Lynch, J. J. 1970. Psychophysiology and development of social attachment. *Journal of Nervous and Mental Disease*, 151:231–44.

McGrew, W. C. 1972. Aspects of social development in nursery school children, with emphasis on introduction to the group. In N. Blurton Jones (ed.), *Ethological studies of child behaviour*. Cambridge: Cambridge University Press.

Mason, W. A. 1963. The effects of environmental restrictions on the social development of rhesus monkeys. In C. H. Southwick (ed.), *Primate social behavior*. New York: Van Nostrand.

1965. Determinants of social behavior in young chimpanzees. In A. M. Schrier, H. F. Harlow and F. Stollnitz (eds.), *Behavior of non-human primates*, vol. II. New York: Academic Press.

1967. Motivational aspects of social responsiveness in young chimpanzees. In H. W. Stevenson, E. H. Hess and H. L. Rheingold (eds.), *Early behavior*. New York: Wiley.

Mason, W. A. and Berkson, G. 1962. Conditions influencing vocal responsiveness of infant chimpanzees. *Science*, 137:127–8.

1975. Effects of maternal mobility on the development of rocking and other behaviors in rhesus monkeys: a study with artificial mothers. *Developmental Psychobiology*, 8:197–211.

Mason, W. A., Davenport, R. K. and Menzel, E. W. 1968. Early experience and the social development of rhesus monkeys and chimpanzees. In G. Newton and S. Levine (eds.), *Early experience and behavior*. Springfield, Ill.: C. C. Thomas.

Mason, W. A. and Green, P. C. 1962. The effects of social restriction on the behavior of rhesus monkeys: IV. responses to a novel environment and to an alien species. *Journal of Comparative and Physiological Psychology*, 55:363–8.

Mason, W. A. and Kenney, M. D. 1974. Redirection of filial attachments in rhesus monkeys: dogs as mother surrogates. *Science*, 183:1209–11.

Masters, J. C. and Wellman, H. M. 1974. The study of human infant attachment: a procedural critique. *Psychological Bulletin*, 81:218–37.

Miller, G. A., Galanter, E. and Pribram, K. H. 1960. *Plans and the structure of behavior*. New York: Holt, Rinehart and Winston.

Mitchell, G. D. 1968. Persistent behavior pathology in rhesus monkeys following early social isolation. *Folia Primatologica*, 8:132–47.

1970. Abnormal behavior in primates. In L. A. Rosenblum (ed.), *Primate behavior*, vol. I. New York: Academic Press.

Mitchell, G. D., Arling, G. L. and Møller, G. W. 1967. Long-term effects of maternal punishment on the behavior of monkeys. *Psychonomic Science*, 8:209–10.

Money, J., Hampson, J. G. and Hampson, J. L. 1957. Imprinting and the establishment of gender role. *Archives of Neurology and Psychiatry*, 77:333–6.

Moore, T. W. 1975. Exclusive early mothering and its alternatives: the outcome to adolescence. *Scandinavian Journal of Psychology*, 16:255–72.

Morris, D. 1956. The feather postures of birds and the problem of the origin of social signals. *Behaviour*, 9:75–113.

Mowbray, J. B. and Cadell, T. E. 1962. Early behavior patterns in rhesus monkeys. *Journal of Comparative and Physiological Psychology*, 55:350–7.

Murphy, G. 1947. *Personality. A biosocial approach to origins and structure.* New York: Harper.

Newson, J. 1974. Towards a theory of infant understanding. *Bulletin of the British Psychological Society*, 27:251–7.

Newson, J. and Newson, E. 1963. *Infant care in an urban community*. London: Allen and Unwin.

Novak, M. A. and Harlow, H. F. 1975. Social recovery of monkeys isolated for the first year of life: 1. Rehabilitation and therapy. *Developmental Psychology*, 11:453–65.

O'Connor, N. and Franks, C. 1961. Childhood upbringing and other environmental factors. In H. J. Eysenck (ed.), *Handbook of abnormal psychology*. New York: Basic Books.

Pascal, B. 1931. *Pensées*, nos. 92–4. London: Dent.

Passman, R. H. 1975. Mothers and blankets as agents for promoting play and exploration by young children in a novel environment: the effects of social and non-social attachment objects. *Developmental Psychology*, 11:170–7.

1976. Arousal reducing properties of attachment objects: testing the functional limits of the security blanket relative to the mother. *Developmental Psychology*, 12:468–9.

Prechtl, H. F. R. 1958. The directed head turning response and allied movements of the human baby. *Behaviour*, 13:212–42.

Quinton, D. and Rutter, M. 1976. Early hospital admission and later disturbances of behaviour: an attempted replication of Douglas' findings. *Developmental Medicine and Child Neurology*, 18:447–59.

Rafael, D. 1971. Effects of supportive behaviour on lactation. Paper presented at meeting of the American Anthropological Association, New York, November 1971.

Rheingold, H. L. 1969. The effect of a strange environment on the behaviour of infants. In B. M. Foss (ed.), *Determinants of infant behaviour*, vol. IV. London: Methuen.

Rheingold, H. L. and Eckerman, C. O. 1970. The infant separates himself from his mother. *Science*, 168:78–83.

1973. Fear of the stranger: a critical examination. *Advances in Child Development and Behavior*, 8:185–222.

Richards, M. P. M. 1967. Maternal behaviour in rodents and lagomorphs. In A. McLaren (ed.), *Advances in reproductive physiology*, vol. II. London: Logos/Academic Press.

1974. The pros and cons of breastfeeding. Paper presented for a meeting of the British Pediatric Association Council and Medical Education and Information Unit of the Spastics Society, Farnham, March 1974.

1978. Possible effects of early separation on later development of children a review. In F. S. W. Brimblecome, M. P. M. Richards and N. R. C. Roberton (eds.), *Separation and special care baby units*. London: SIMP/Heinemann Medical Books.

Roberts, A. R. (ed.) 1974. *Childhood deprivation*. Springfield, Ill.: C. C. Thomas.

Robinson, R. J. and Tizard, J. P. M. 1966. The central nervous system in the new-born. *British Medical Bulletin*, 22:49–56.

Rosenblatt, J. S. 1975. Prepartum and postpartum regulation of maternal behaviour in the rat. In R. Porter and M. A. O'Connor (eds.), *Parent–infant interaction*, CIBA Foundation Symposium 33. Amsterdam: Elsevier.

Rosenblatt, J. S., Turkewitz, G. and Schneirla, T. C. 1961. Early socialization in the domestic cat as based on feeding and other relationships between female and young. In B. M. Foss (ed.), *Determinants of infant behaviour*. London: Methuen.

Rosenblum, L. A. 1971. Infant attachment in monkeys. In H. R. Schaffer (ed.), *The origins of human social relations*. New York: Academic Press.

1973. Maternal regulation of infant social interactions. In C. R. Carpenter (ed.), *Behavioral regulators of behavior in primates*. Lewisburg: Bucknell University Press.

Rosenblum, L. A. and Harlow, H. F. 1963. Approach-avoidance conflict in the mother surrogate situation. *Psychological Reports*, 12:83–5.

Ruppenthal, G. C., Arling, G. L., Harlow, H. F., Sackett, G. P. and Suomi, S. J. 1976. A 10-year perspective of motherless-mother monkey behavior. *Journal of Abnormal Psychology*, 85:341–9.

Rutter, M. 1972. *Maternal deprivation reassessed*. Harmondsworth: Penguin.

Sackett, G. P. 1963. A neural mechanism underlying unlearned, critical period, and developmental aspects of visually controlled behavior. *Psychological Review*, 70:40–50.

1966. Monkeys reared in isolation with pictures as visual input: evidence for an innate releasing mechanism. *Science*, 154:1470–3.

1967. Some persistent effects of different rearing conditions on preadult social behavior of monkeys. *Journal of Comparative and Physiological Psychology*, 64:363–5.

1970. Unlearned responses, differential rearing experiences, and the development of social attachments by rhesus monkeys. In L. A. Rosenblum (ed.), *Primate behavior*, New York: Academic Press.

1973. Innate mechanisms in primate social behavior. In C. R. Carpenter (ed.), *Behavioral regulators of behavior in primates*. Lewisburg: Bucknell University Press.

Sackett, G. P., Porter, M. and Holmes, H. 1965. Choice behavior in rhesus monkeys: effect of stimulation during the first month of life. *Science*, 147:304–6.

Sackett, G. P. and Ruppenthal, G. C. 1973. Development of monkeys after varied experiences during infancy. In S. A. Barnett (ed.), *Ethology and development*. Clinics in developmental medicine no. 47. London: Heinemann.

Salzen, E. A. 1962. Imprinting and fear. *Symposia of the Zoological Society of London*, 8:199–217.

1963. Visual stimuli eliciting the smiling response in the human infant. *Journal of Genetic Psychology*, 102:51–4.

1966. The interaction of experience, stimulus characteristics and exogenous androgen in the behaviour of domestic chicks. *Behaviour*, 26:286–322.

1967. Imprinting in birds and primates. *Behaviour*, 28:232–54.

1968. The application of imprinting: discussion. *Science and Psychoanalysis*, 12:184–9.

1969. Contact and social attachment in domestic chicks. *Behaviour*, 33:38–51.

1970. Imprinting and environmental learning. In L. R. Aronson, E. Tobach, D. S. Lehrman and J. S. Rosenblatt (eds.), *Development and evolution of behavior*. San Francisco: W. H. Freeman.

Sameroff, A. J. and Chandler, M. J. 1975. Reproductive risk and the continuum of caretaking causality. In F. D. Horowitz, M. Hetherington, S. Scarr-Salapatek and G. Sregel (eds.), *Review of child development research*, vol. IV. Chicago: University of Chicago Press.

Schaffer, H. R. 1971. *The growth of sociability*. Harmondsworth: Penguin Books.

1978. Acquiring the concept of the dialogue. In M. H. Bornstein and W. Kessen (eds.) *Psychological development from infancy*. New York: Erlbaum.

Schaffer, H. R. and Emerson, P. E. 1964. The development of social attachments in infancy. *Monographs on Social Research in Child Development*, 29 (3), Serial no. 94.

Schaffer, H. R., Greenwood, A. and Parry, M. H. 1972. The onset of wariness. *Child Development*, 43:165–75.

Schneirla, T. C. 1959. An evolutionary and developmental theory of biphasic processes underlying approach and withdrawal. In M. R. Jones (ed.), *Nebraska symposium on motivation*. Lincoln: University of Nebraska Press.

1965. Aspects of stimulation and organization in approach/withdrawal processes underlying vertebrate behavioral development. In D. S. Lehrman, R. A. Hinde and E. Shaw (eds.), *Advances in the study of behavior*, vol. I. New York: Academic Press.

Scott, J. P. 1958. *Animal behavior*. Chicago: University of Chicago Press.

1969. The emotional basis of social behavior. *Annals of the New York Academy of Sciences*, 159:777–90.

Scott, J. P. and Senay, E. (eds.) 1973. *Separation and depression*. Washington DC: American Association for the Advancement of Science.

Seay, B., Alexander, B. K. and Harlow, H. F. 1964. Maternal behavior of socially deprived rhesus monkeys. *Journal of Abnormal and Social Psychology*, 69:345–54.

Seay, B., Hansen, E. W. and Harlow, H. F. 1962. Mother–infant separation in monkeys. *Journal of Child Psychology and Psychiatry*, 3:123–32.

Seay, B. and Harlow, H. F. 1965. Maternal separation in the rhesus monkey. *Journal of Nervous and Mental Disease*, 140:434–41.

Sherrington, G. S. 1906. *The integrative action of the nervous system*. 2nd edn. 1947. New Haven: Yale University Press.

Singh, M. 1975. Mother–infant separation in rhesus monkey living in natural environment. *Primates*, 16:471–6.

Skeels, H. M. 1966. Adult status of children with contrasting early life experiences: a follow-up study. *Monographs on Social Research in Child Development*, 31(3), Serial no. 105.

Sluckin, W. 1965. *Imprinting and early learning*. London: Methuen.

Sluckin, W. and Salzen, E. A. 1961. Imprinting and perceptual learning. *Quarterly Journal of Experimental Psychology*, 13:65–77.

Smith, P. K. 1974. Ethological methods. In B. M. Foss (ed.), *New perspectives in child development*. Harmondsworth: Penguin.

Sokolov, E. N. 1960. Neuronal models and the orienting reflex. In M. A. B. Brazier (ed.) *The central nervous system and behavior*. New York: J. Macey Jr Foundation.

Sroufe, L. A. and Waters, E. 1977. Attachment as an organizational construct. *Child Development*, 48:1184–99.

Stanley, W. C. 1965. The passive person as a reinforcer in isolated beagle puppies. *Psychonomic Science*, 2:21–2.

Stanley, W. C. and Elliot, O. 1962. Differential human handling as reinforcing events and as treatment influencing later social behavior in Basenji puppies. *Psychological Reports*, 10:775–88.

Strongman, K. T. 1973. *The psychology of emotion*. New York: Wiley.

Suomi, S. J. 1973. Surrogate rehabilitation of monkeys reared in total social isolation. *Journal of Child Psychology and Psychiatry*, 14:71–7.

1977. Development of attachment and other social behaviors in rhesus monkeys. In T. Alloway, P. Pliner and L. Krames (eds.), *Advances in the study of communication and affect*, vol. III. *Attachment behavior*. New York: Plenum Press.

Suomi, S. J., Eisele, C. D., Grady, S. A. and Tripp, R. L. 1973. Social preferences of monkeys reared in an enriched laboratory social environment. *Child Development*, 44:451–60.

Suomi, S. J. and Harlow, H. F. 1972. Social rehabilitation of isolate-reared monkeys. *Developmental Psychology*, 6:487–96.

Suomi, S. J., Harlow, H. F. and McKinney, W. T. 1972. Monkey psychiatrists. *American Journal of Psychiatry*, 128:927–32.

Tizard, B. and Rees, J. 1975. The effect of early institutional rearing on the behaviour problems and affectional relationships of 4 year old children. *Journal of Child Psychology and Psychiatry*, 16:61–73.

Tomkins, S. S. 1963. *Affect, imagery, consciousness*, vol. II. *The negative affects*. New York: Springer.

Trevarthen, C. 1974. Conversations with a two month old. *New Scientist*, 62:230–5.

Turkewitz, G., Birch, H. G., Moreau, T., Levy, L. and Cornwell, A. C. 1966. Effect of intensity of auditory stimulation on directional eye movements in the human neonate. *Animal Behaviour*, 14:93–101.

Waddington, C. H. 1956. *Principles of embryology*. London: Allen and Unwin.

White, G. 1977. *The natural history of Selbourne*. First published 1778–9. Harmondsworth: Penguin.

Whiten, A. 1977. Assessing the effects of perinatal events on the success of the mother–infant relationship. In H. R. Schaffer (ed.), *Studies in mother–infant interaction*. London: Academic Press.

Winter, P., Ploog, D. and Latta, J. 1966. Vocal repertoire of the squirrel monkey (*Saimiri sciureus*), its analysis and significance. *Experimental Brain Research*, 1:359–84.

Wolff, P. H. 1963. Observations on the early development of smiling. In B. M. Foss (ed.), *Determinants of infant behaviour*, vol. II. London: Methuen.

1969. The natural history of crying and other vocalizations in early infancy. In B. M. Foss (ed.), *Determinants of infant behaviour*, vol. IV. London: Methuen.

Yarrow, L. J. 1961. Maternal deprivation: toward an empirical and conceptual re-evaluation. *Psychological Bulletin*, 58:459–90.

1972. Attachment and dependency: a developmental perspective. In J. L. Gewirtz (ed.), *Attachment and dependency*. Washington DC: V. H. Winston.

Young, P. T. 1973. *Emotion in man and animal*. 2nd edn. New York: Wiley.

Zegans, S. and Zegans, L. S. 1972. Fear of strangers in children and the orienting reaction. *Behavioral Science*, 17:407–19.

10. Ontogeny of auditory perception[1]

10.1. Development of auditory perception in relation to vocal behavior[2]

PETER MARLER

Of the contributions of classical ethology to behavioral biology, none has had more far reaching consequences than the demonstration of innate factors in behavioral development, and particularly their influence on the ontogeny of responsiveness to environmental stimuli. Among vertebrates the emphasis on innate responsiveness has been especially strong in birds, as embodied in such notions as the 'releaser' and the 'innate release mechanism' – bringing to mind, for example, the now classical studies over a twenty-year period on feeding responses of gulls to visual stimulation (Tinbergen 1951, Tinbergen and Perdeck 1950, Hailman 1967, 1970). In theory, if not always in practice, ethologists have placed equal emphasis on the intercalation of innate factors with learning in the development of bird behavior. Those in neighboring disciplines are nevertheless prone to infer that the responsiveness of birds to stimuli is largely genetically programmed, except in such special situations as imprinting (e.g Gibson 1977). This is contrasted with the human situation, where innate influences are thought to play a minor, even vestigial, role. According to this view, non-human primates fall somewhere between these extremes. In fact little work has been done on the development of responsiveness in monkeys and apes to stimuli that control their

[1] The comments on this section (pp. 705–10) take account of the fact that auditory perception may be a subject less familiar to readers of this volume, and provide a brief overview of the experimental techniques.
[2] Research for this paper was supported by grants from NIMH (MH14651) and NSF (BNS7519431). The author is indebted to conference participants, especially to Dr Alvin Liberman and Dr Detlev Ploog for discussion and criticism, and to Dr Stephen Zoloth for reviewing the manuscript and adding new material.

behavior in nature, and the emphasis has been on the learnability of responsiveness. Actually there are hints of a significant degree of innate responsiveness, as for example in Sackett's (1966) studies of responses of infant monkeys to two-dimensional representations of facial expressions.

With such exceptions, there has been little attempt to explore the possibility of innate responsiveness of non-human primates to biologically significant stimuli in infancy. Nor has the possibility been explored of any special adult facility in learned perceptual processing of natural sign stimuli, irrespective of the richness or paucity of prior experience of them. The aim of this paper is to present new information on a study in progress on responsiveness of the Japanese macaque both to natural vocal stimuli and to synthetic stimuli molded on the natural vocabulary, and on a study of the intercalation of genetic and environmental influences in the development of responsiveness to vocal stimuli in birds.

The methodology of the animal studies I shall describe was stimulated by that used in recent investigations of the perceptual processing of speech stimuli by human adults and infants. As components in the revolution in our understanding of the perceptual capacities of human infants in the last fifteen years, these investigations have done much to establish a sensible balance between nativistic and empiricist views of the development of human perception. Just as ethology played its part in inspiring new approaches to the study of human behavior, I believe that the logic and sophistication of experimentation on human perceptual development has outpaced progress in ethological studies of animal perception. Ethologists can now learn much of benefit from human studies. I will illustrate this point with a brief review of an impressive, thought-provoking body of data on the development of speech perception that merits close attention from ethologists working on analogous problems with animals.

Approaching recent research on the structure of speech sounds as a novice, I was astonished to discover that cross-cultural descriptions of certain physical features of speech patterns reveal the existence of universals in the properties that define boundaries between some functionally distinct patterns of sounds. I can best illustrate the results from these comparative vocal 'ethograms' by reference to the distinction in many unrelated languages between critical pairs of voiced and unvoiced consonants. I have in mind the property known as 'voice-onset-time' (VOT), a focus of special study since it is one of the few characteristics of speech that can be reliably measured from the frequency–time sound spectrograms on which so many bioacoustical studies are based.

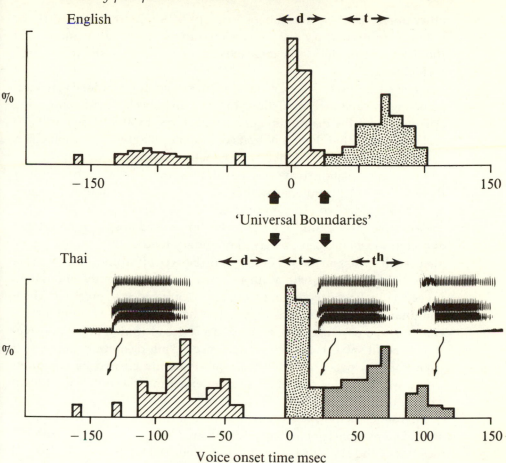

1. Measurements of speech sounds: histograms of voice-onset-times in stop consonants in English and Thai. The large arrows indicate the position of the perceived 'universal' boundaries. Inserts show three examples of synthetic speech with VOTs of −150 msec., +10 msec. and +100 msec. (After Lisker and Abramson 1964, Cutting and Eimas 1975.)

An example from English is shown in figure 1. The cross-cultural studies of Lisker and Abramson (1964) have shown that all languages studied employ voice-onset-time as one criterion for differentiating speech sounds, and that, when employed, the boundaries always fall in approximately the same places, at one of two locations (figure 1). Similar universals in speech sounds have been found in the patterns of formant onset that differentiate sounds produced at different points of articulation, labial, alveolar, and velar (e.g. [ba]-[da]-[ga]). There is a long list of other universals (e.g. Greenberg 1966, 1969, Studdert-Kennedy 1977), but the features of consonants I have mentioned have the advantage that they are specific and lend themselves to precise analysis and experimental control.

When such universals are discovered in ethograms of animal behavior, recurring in separate populations of the same species, and contrasting strikingly with the distribution of vocal dialects, local feeding traditions and the many other divergent traits of local populations, an ethologist is likely to entertain the possibility of genetic developmental controls.

A further revelation to me was that although we hear speech sounds as discretely distinct from one another, they are often distributed in actual speech in 'graded' continua rather than in discretely separate categories. For example, histograms of voice-onset-times used in speech reveal that although the values across a given boundary tend to be grouped separately, such as that on the VOT dimension between [pa] and [ba], there are nevertheless intermediate values. These occur frequently enough to invite us to ask why we are not more often confused as to precisely which consonant a speaker intends (figure 1). This implication was not lost on experimental psychologists, and led to a series of studies on responsiveness of adult subjects to such graded speech sound continua drawn first from natural speech patterns, and subsequently created by computer synthesis, with all characteristics under experimental control (Liberman 1957, Liberman et al. 1961, 1967).

Such series as the voice-onset-time continuum, in ten or twenty millisecond steps from [pa] to [ba] to [mba], created by the speech synthesis facilities of the Haskins Laboratories in New Haven, have provided the basis for many insights into the mysteries of speech perception. In particular, they have led to evidence for a distinctive mode of perceptual processing that has become known as 'categorical perception'. Although not unique to the perception of speech sounds (e.g. Cutting and Rosner 1974), nor restricted to the auditory modality (Pastore 1976), it is especially well exemplified by studies of responsiveness of human subjects to complex acoustic continua such as a voice-onset-time series. Asked to label sounds on such a continuum, an English-speaking subject divides the continuum into two parts, labelling one side [pa], the other [ba]. The sharp boundary between them coincides with the trough in voice-onset-time productions. This boundary recurs in different languages, though with subtle details that vary consistently from one to another. In some languages, such as Thai, there is a second boundary, around − 20 msec. VOT, shared by the speech pattern of many other cultures.

There is another characteristic of so-called 'categorical perception' of speech sound continua. Adult subjects, asked to discriminate between sound pairs differing by small increments on the VOT continuum, display greater sensitivity to variations in the zone of the boundary than to within-category variations under certain testing conditions (Studdert-Kennedy *et al*. 1970). They behave as though they were desensitized to within-category variations in this particular property of speech sounds, while being acutely sensitive to small changes at the boundary. This contrasts with the 'continuous' perception of other kinds of sound properties such as pitch or loudness. Categorical processing has the consequence of grouping stimuli in classes, imposing a particular kind of order on varying patterns of stimulation by a process of quantization. Although virtually unexplored by ethologists, we should seriously entertain the possibility that animals exhibit analogous perceptual phenomena. It is easy to imagine circumstances in which they could be of value, hence the genesis of some of the animal studies to be described shortly.

Much of what I have described about adult perception of speech could be thought of as a consequence of the rich perceptual and motor experience of speech that any adult brings to bear on a given task of speech-labelling or discrimination. Another set of recent findings suggests that special perceptual predispositions are also involved, irrespective of prior experience with speech. A variety of human infant response measures, including habituation of a sucking response, heart-rate changes and evoked brain potentials, indicate responsiveness to similar boundary values between functionally distinct speech sounds in subjects as young as one month of age (e.g. Dorman 1974, Eimas *et al*. 1971, Eimas 1975, Morse 1972, Wood, Goff and Day 1971). Figure 2 illustrates the kinds of results leading to this interpretation, derived from the work of Eimas. The early age at which these results are obtained led to the speculation that responsiveness to some of these boundary properties may be innate.

Evidence for an innate component was obtained by Lasky, Syrdal-Lasky and Klein (1975) in studies of speech perception of four-to-six-month-old infants living in a Spanish-speaking environment. There are slight but consistent differences in voice-onset-time boundaries in adult production and perception in English and Spanish. These led to the prediction that infants would demonstrate boundary limits different from those obtained by Eimas with children living in English-speaking environments, if these were acquired through infantile experience of speech patterns. The infants proved to be responsive to boundaries in both

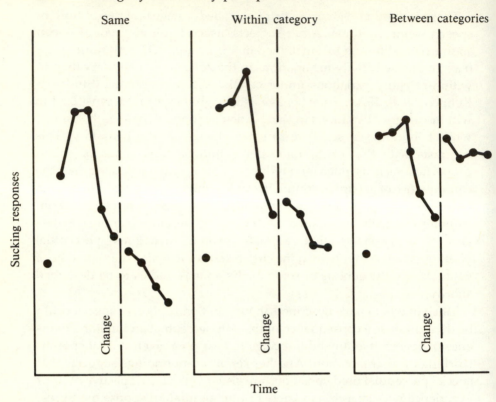

Sucking responses

Same   Within category   Between categories

Change   Change   Change

Time

2. A typical result of an experiment by Eimas and his colleagues on perception by a four-month-old infant of synthetic speech sounds varying in voice-onset-time. With repeated playbacks of a given sound triggered by the sucking response, habituation occurs. A new sound is then substituted. If the new sound is the same as the old one there is no change (same). If the new one is different, it evokes small or large response increases depending on whether it is on the same side (within category) or the opposite side (between categories) of the 'universal' VOT boundary at about 30 msec. (After Eimas *et al.* 1971.)

regions of the VOT continuum that are universals, the so-called 'English' and the 'Thai' boundaries, with no sign that experience of the distributions used in Spanish had affected their speech perception.

An innate component is implied by a study of Streeter (1975), although with evidence of acquired components as well. Infant perception of boundaries along the VOT continuum was studied in children exposed to Kikuyu in infancy. This language has only one labial stop consonant, with a VOT of about −60 msec. Perhaps as a consequence of exposure to the pattern of usage, two-month-old-infants were responsive to one boundary along the VOT continuum somewhere between 0 and −30 msec. They seemed more responsive to this boundary than the subjects Eimas had studied in an English-speaking environment. However, the Kikuyu-exposed infants, although lacking experience of anything equivalent to a [p], proved responsive to a boundary somewhere between +10 and +40 msec., thus resembling infants exposed to English and various other languages. Streeter concluded that there is evidence of interaction between nature and nurture, and that some phonetic or acoustic discriminations may be universal whereas others seem to require or are reinforced by previous relevant exposure.

Other studies have demonstrated responsiveness in infants between one and six months of age to the variations in second- and third-formant transitions in synthetic speech patterns that establish boundaries between the different articulation points distinguishing labial, alveolar and velar stop consonants. Infants also seem responsive to differences between vowel sounds.

The potential lability of predispositions that human infants may bring to segmentation of speech sound continua is clear. The [ra]–[la] distinction that Japanese adults find so difficult, unemployed in Japanese, is probably easier for infants, though only American subjects have been tested thus far (Eimas 1974). However, even though the stimulus patterns on which learned responsiveness in adulthood is based are likely to be more complex than those of infants, with more redundancy, perhaps involving configurational features, and sometimes so changed that the effective stimulus set no longer contains those that match the original predisposition, the latter must surely play an ontogenetic role in setting the trajectory for learning to respond to a more elaborate array of abstracted features.

Such possibilities are indicated in a study by Kuhl and Miller (1975). The formant patterns that distinguish different vowel sounds are complicated by variations in the fundamental frequency of different voices, likely to be a serious distraction for an infant learning to respond to speech. Given the importance of vowel coding in speech, we might expect a predisposition to focus more strongly on formant patterns than on pitch in early responses. By independently varying the two features in sounds presented to infants, Kuhl and Miller (1975) were able to show that variations in vowel pattern are indeed more salient or arresting for human infants than variations in pitch. This is not to say that they are unresponsive to pitch variations. However, the salience of pitch is lower than that of variations in vowel patterns, thus imposing some order in the process of learning to extract different features from the complex array of stimuli that speech sounds present.

Below I have summarized some of these findings about speech patterns, and speech perception in adults and infants, that seem to me of particular interest to biologists. They show that the human organism brings some well-defined perceptual predispositions to the task of developing responsiveness to the complex of sound stimuli that speech represents. Some are manifest in initial encounters, and are thus developed without prior experience of the stimuli involved.

(1) There are cross-cultural universals in acoustic properties defining boundaries between functionally distinct speech sounds.

(2) Some functionally distinct speech sounds are not discretely separated but connected by a continuous series of graded intermediates.

(3) Adults process graded speech sound continua 'categorically', by reference to boundaries, rather than 'continuously'.

(4) Pre-speech infants are sensitive to some of these same 'universal boundaries'.

However early in human development such predispositions are manifest, we are hardly likely to view them as developmental instructions for designing infants as automata. Instead it seems natural to think of them as initial instructions to set the trajectory for development of learned responsiveness to a more elaborate array of abstracted features. Eventually these are embodied in the centrally generated 'schemata' invoked by many psychologists in conceptualizing the development of human perceptions of complex stimuli (Marler 1977). I now want to present animal data from current experiments by Stephen Zoloth and myself and collaborators at the University of Michigan's Kresge Hearing Institute, suggesting that there are parallels in the perception of conspecific vocal sounds by both monkeys and birds.

One reason I was so intrigued to learn of the graded nature of speech sounds is that grading has proved to be an interesting characteristic of sounds of several higher primates. In addition to the rhesus monkey (Rowell 1962, Rowell and Hinde 1962), it has now been described in several other monkey species, as well as the chimpanzee (Marler 1976). Even some species originally thought to have discretely organized vocal repertoires, such as the squirrel monkey, are now known to exhibit more grading than had been originally thought (Winter, Ploog and Latta 1966, Schott 1975). It is virtually impossible to assay the communicative function of such sounds until we have some understanding of how they are processed during perception. The Japanese macaque has proved to be an ideal subject for further pursuit of this problem.

In a thorough study of the usage of sounds in wild Japanese macaques in relation to the circumstances of the vocalizer, Green (1975) has subjected the entire vocal repertoire to exhaustive analysis. Sound patterns intergrade freely in many parts of the repertoire. By subjecting the sounds to an arbitrary acoustical taxonomy, Green was able to show that even subtle variations in fine structure correlate well with varying circumstances of production, thus potentially encoding information of value to companions. One subsystem consists of a variety of coos, data for which are shown in figure 3.

A feature identified as significant by Green is the temporal position of a frequency rise, which may occur at any point in the coo. Early and late positions correlate with different circumstances of production. So-called 'smooth early highs' (SE) are contact coos given by isolated animals, by individuals in subgroups separated from the main group, or by young animals separated from regular companions within the group. Vocalizers are usually relatively calm, and smooth early highs seem to function mainly to maintain group cohesion.

Animals producing smooth late highs (SL) are more highly aroused. Though again the mood is affinitive, here the vocalizer is actively soliciting contact, as for example in the sexual solicitation of oestrous females in early stages of consortship. The call is typically given by a subordinate towards a dominant (see figure 3). A careful analysis of the position of 'highs' in natural usage reveals a distribution reminiscent of that for voice-onset-times, on the [pa]–[ba] continuum, for example (figure 4). As such it lends itself to similar kinds of questions about the perceptual processing by a species of its own vocal signals (Zoloth and Green, in press).

In the first publication from what is planned as a series of studies, Beecher *et al.* (1976) have trained both Japanese macaques and other monkeys in the laboratory to respond to playback of different classes of coo calls as cues, with one class as positive, the other negative. Eventually the monkeys will be exposed to intermediate forms, both natural and synthetic. Species differences in rates of generalization to new members of the classes of smooth early and smooth late highs bear directly on the theme of perceptual predispositions that are involved in learning to respond to biologically significant stimuli.

As in speech so in these monkey sounds certain physical features such as pitch and spectral composition vary in different renditions and from

| Coo type | Distinguishing criteria | | | |
Name	Midpoint pitch	Position of highest peak	Duration	Other features
Double	≤510 Hz	N.A.	N.A.	Two overlapping harmonic series
Long low	≤510 Hz	N.A.	≥0.20 sec	N.A.
Short low	≤590 Hz	≠1	≤0.19 sec	N.A.
Smooth early high	≥520 Hz	<2/3	N.A.	No dip
Dip early high	≥520 Hz	<2/3	N.A.	Dip
Dip late high	≥520 Hz	≥2/3	N.A.	Dip
Smooth late high	≥520 Hz	≥2/3	N.A.	No dip

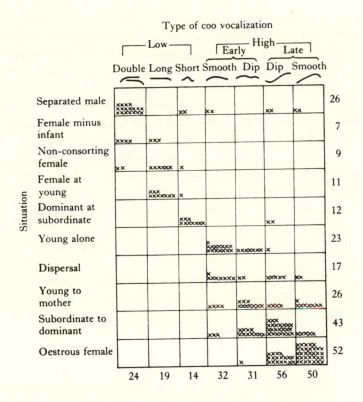

3. A taxonomy of different types of 'coo' calls of the Japanese macaque, together with a table of frequency of usage of each type in a variety of social situations. (After Green 1975.)

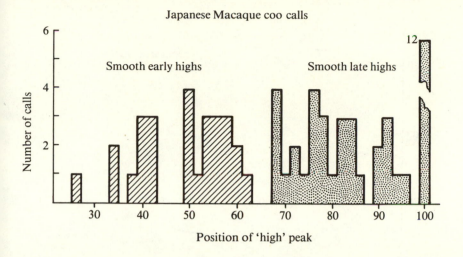

4. Distribution of frequency–peak positions in field recordings of Japanese macaque 'coo' calls. (After Zoloth and Green, in press.)

individual to individual. This variation seems to slow down the rate with which generalization occurs to new members of the two classes, when these are characterized by high position. Nevertheless, Japanese macaques proceed to achieve a high criterion of performance quite rapidly. The next step was a comparison with performance of two other species of monkeys with the same sounds. One, the vervet monkey, does not use coos. The other, a pig-tailed macaque, does have coo-type calls, but the details of its usage are unknown.

Members of these two control species had enormous difficulty in generalizing to new tokens of the two coo classes – smooth early highs and smooth late highs – in this situation (figure 5). This result is consistent with the notion that the SE–SL distinction is a conceptually relevant one for the Japanese macaque, and thus easy to demonstrate, but an alien one for the other species. Nevertheless, by exhaustive training the control species were eventually able to reach a similar level of performance to the Japanese macaques, showing that the task is not impossible for them, just harder.

In subsequent experiments the ability of Japanese macaques and the control species to group coo calls on the basis of either high position or pitch was compared. First two groups of coos were selected, smooth early

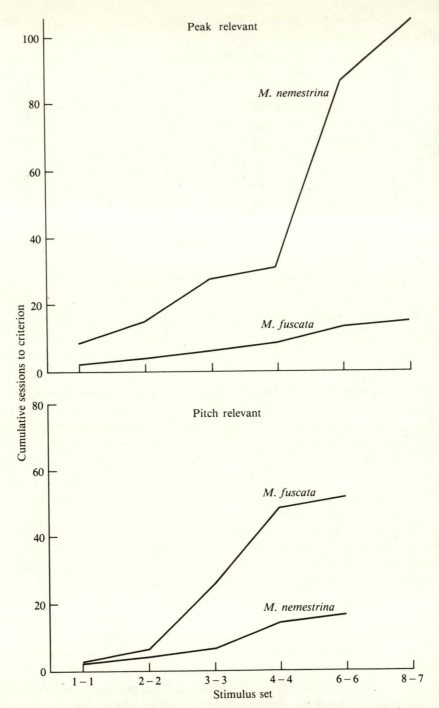

5. Generalization rates of two monkey species while being trained to discriminate between sets of natural calls that differ in frequency–peak position. With the 'peak relevant' task they had to discriminate on this basis while ignoring variations in starting pitch. The 'pitch relevant' task imposed the opposite requirement, obviously more difficult for *M. fuscata*. (By courtesy of Stephen Zoloth, after Beecher *et al*. 1976).

and smooth late highs, carefully counterbalanced for other acoustic variables such as pitch and duration. In this experiment, which replicated our
previous work, the three Japanese monkeys acquired the discrimination
faster than the three controls.

Next, we used the *same* coos but this time sorted on the basis of pitch.
The task for the animals was to distinguish high and low pitched calls,
and ignore high position. Since each group contained both smooth early
and smooth late highs, the position of the peak was not relevant to the
task. The result was in complete contrast to the previous experiment. The
Japanese macaques acquired the discrimination more slowly than the
other species. The pig-tailed macaques, for example, had no trouble at all
in classifying the Japanese macaque calls on the basis of starting pitch, a
relatively simple cue. Thus it appears that Japanese macaques are better
able to classify groups of coos when they are sorted by peak position than
by pitch, while the opposite was true for control species.

We assume that learning proceeds fastest when the discriminative
stimuli differ consistently along dimensions that are meaningful to the
subjects, and that for Japanese macaques classification according to the
position of the 'high' is an easier conceptual task. This reflects a predisposition to process the coos in a way that parallels their apparent
meanings. Of course it is too early to tell whether innate perceptual
mechanisms are involved. All subjects were wild-caught, with a history
of experience of reception and production of such sounds, experience
which the control species lack. Whatever the developmental basis, the
stimuli are clearly not equivalent to conspecific and alien adults, as
classical learning theory would have led us to expect. Further research
will tell if there is proneness to categorical divisions of these acoustic
continua, and whether some way can be found to ask similar questions of
infant monkeys.

Biological approaches to animal learning have in fact called several
assumptions of learning theory into question in recent years, especially
the principle of equipotentiality (Seligman and Hager 1972, Shettleworth
1972, Hinde and Stevenson-Hinde 1973). A feature of the song learning
process in which many male oscine birds engage in youth is its selectivity,
such that a male presented with a natural choice of songs of different
species to copy will selectively learn conspecific models. I present now an
example which parallels the results of human infant studies in some
respects, providing a more viable comparison than any non-human primate studies yet available on the ontogeny of auditorily controlled
behavior.

Song and swamp sparrows are closely related congeneric species whose male songs, although similar in duration, are very different in their temporal organization or 'syntax'. The simple song of the swamp sparrow consists of a slow trill of similar slurred liquid notes. That of the song sparrow is much more complex, with several distinct parts, consisting of many short diverse notes and a trill near the end (figure 6). Within these different, relatively stable, species-specific, syntactical patterns, both exhibit much individual variability in the acoustic structure of the so-called 'syllables' from which the songs are constructed.

Although the preferred micro-habitats of the two species differ, they are very often within earshot. Both engage in song learning, and the singing behavior of males reared in social isolation is significantly abnormal. Yet there is no evidence that the two species learn one another's song under field conditions, thus setting the stage for this experiment on selective learning (Marler and Peters 1977).

Our aim was to present male swamp sparrows in youth with both swamp and song sparrow songs to see if selective learning occurred. If so, we sought also to specify some of the acoustic parameters on which the selectivity is based. For this purpose, series of artificial songs were created by editing out distinctly different 'syllables' from tape recordings of normal local song of the two species and then splicing them together in a variety of simple but artificial syntactical patterns. These were chosen to explore the possible significance of some of the organizational features by which normal songs of the two species differ. Thus 'swamp-sparrow-like' patterns included sequences of identical syllables at various steady rates. 'Song-sparrow-like' features included variable rates of delivery of syllable sequences (accelerating, decelerating) and a multipartite structure (two parts), all features present in song sparrow song and lacking in that of the swamp sparrow. Ten such patterns were created, using sixteen different song sparrow syllables. Then an equivalent set was created from swamp sparrow syllables, again sixteen in all. The syllable types were sufficiently distinct that if imitation occurred we would be able to determine the temporal pattern from which each had been selected. Although there were more details to the design of stimuli, this outline will serve to illustrate the result which was striking and, to us, unexpected.

In the first experiment eight male swamp sparrows were taken from wild nests between three and ten days of age and reared by hand, together with female age mates, in small groups in acoustically shielded chambers. Song sparrows of a similar age were also present during

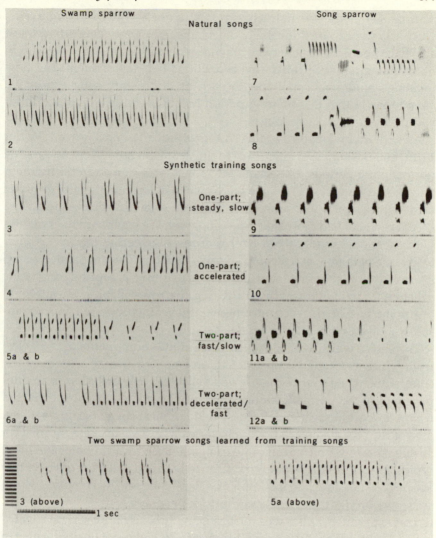

Swamp sparrow   Song sparrow

Natural songs

1

2

7

8

Synthetic training songs

One-part;
steady, slow

3

9

One-part;
accelerated

4

10

Two-part;
fast/slow

5a & b

11a & b

Two-part;
decelerated/
fast

6a & b

12a & b

Two swamp sparrow songs learned from training songs

3 (above)

5a (above)

1 sec

6. Sound spectrograms of natural song sparrow and swamp sparrow songs and artificial training songs. Natural songs are shown at the top. Syllables from these and others were assembled in synthetic songs, some created from swamp sparrow syllables (e.g. 3–6), some from song sparrow syllables (e.g. 9–12), some in 'swamp-sparrow-like' patterns (e.g. 3, 4, 9, 10), some in 'song-sparrow-like' patterns (e.g. 5, 6, 11, 12); syllables from songs 1 and 2 can be seen in songs 3 and 4, syllables from song 8 in songs 10 and 11. Only swamp sparrow syllables were learned. At the bottom are two songs of male swamp sparrows copied from training songs 3 and 5. A 1 sec. time marker is given at the bottom left, with a 500 Hz interval frequency scale.

rearing, so that they were freely exposed to one another's juvenile calls. The birds were trained for thirty days between twenty and fifty days of age. Each heard a set of the twenty synthetic songs arranged in bouts as in normal singing, with thirty-two repetitions per day of each song type totalling about 1000 exposures to each of the twenty song types. We already knew that this training period includes the sensitive period for vocal learning in this species.

As with other songbirds, such as the white-crowned sparrow (Marler 1970), male swamp sparrows learn to sing from memory. Kept on roughly normal photoperiods, they came into song some months after training. After songs had crystallized we were able to determine that the group of eight subjects produced altogether nineteen syllable types. As in nature each individual had more than one song type. We compared the syllables with the models and judged twelve of the nineteen to be close copies. Every one of them was a swamp sparrow syllable. Thus the male swamp sparrow exhibits extremely selective vocal learning, accepting conspecific syllables for imitation and rejecting song sparrow syllables. The interesting point is that this occurs whether they are presented in swamp-sparrow-like or song-sparrow-like patterns.

The choice is clearly made at the level of the components or 'syllables' from which the song is constructed, and not the overall pattern of the song. Thus while four of the learned syllables were extracted from one-part songs, the normal swamp sparrow pattern, eight were extracted from two-part models, much closer to the typical song sparrow pattern. Five of the accepted models were in series with a steady rate, normal for swamp sparrows, but seven came from a series with a variable rate, more typical of song sparrow patterns. Clearly the song syllables of these two species are not equivalent stimuli as a basis for vocal learning of swamp sparrows brought into the laboratory as nestlings.

This experiment still leaves the ontogenetic basis of the selective learning in doubt. What of the possibility that the few days of life in the nest in the wild before capture could provide a basis for selectivity? To test this possibility eggs were removed from the nests of wild swamp sparrows early in incubation and, with some difficulty, hatched and reared under canaries in the laboratory. These cross-fostered subjects were then trained from thirty to fifty days of age with synthetic songs like those used in the previous experiment. All subjects behaved similarly, selecting only swamp sparrow syllables for imitation, showing that an innate predisposition is involved. Obviously there is much in common with speech perception in human infants. In fact, many parallels can be struck between avian song learning and the development of the perception and the production of speech in human infants, as summarized below.

(1) Motor learning has dominant role in developing patterns of sound production
(2) Learning results in local vocal variants (dialects).
(3) All species members share some species-specific vocal characteristics (universals).
(4) Selective responsiveness to species-specific sounds during vocal learning (templates).
(5) Learning occurs most readily in certain life stages (sensitive periods).
(6) Extrinsic reinforcement (e.g. social or food) not prerequisite for vocal learning.
(7) Early deafness affects vocal development more than late deafness.
(8) Hearing important for access to external models and to monitor own vocalization (template matching).
(9) Progression from highly variable to more stereotyped sounds during vocal development (subsong and babbling).
(10) Lateralization of neural control (hypoglossal and hemispheric dominance).

Just as young of our own species are predisposed to respond selectively to particular aspects of speech sounds before themselves speaking, so some young songbirds are responsive to species-specific features of song before they themselves begin to sing. In both cases initial responsiveness is manifest to relatively simple, elementary properties with full appreciation of more complex aspects of adult sounds remaining to be shaped through learning. Such perceptual predispositions are valuable as biological constraints on the vocal learning process, serving to focus the young organism's attention on an appropriate set of complex sounds, and on particular properties that they exhibit. In the birds' case, they are guided to a set of conspecific models, focussing attention on a particular subset of properties that they exhibit, sufficient to reduce the potential hazard of learning the wrong song. This is achieved without sacrificing the ability to learn more complex features of natural song. Human infants stand to benefit not only from being encouraged to attend closely to sounds of speech, but also from guidance in embarking on its perceptual analysis. Speech sounds are enormously complex, and there is still controversy about which of the multitude of acoustic features exhibited are in fact the best purveyors of meaning. It could only benefit the infant to have guidance in the extraction of particularly meaningful features from the multitudes of varying reliability that speech presents.

I see great promise in unifying such classical ethological concepts as the 'releaser' and the 'innate release mechanism' with psychological concepts concerning perceptual development such as that of learned 'schemata'. To postulate innate responsiveness to certain stimuli in the young organism is by no means to commit it to a life of behavioral automaticity. On the contrary, it is likely that in animals, as in man, innate responsiveness in infancy will often become so heavily overlain and transformed by learning in the transition from youth to adulthood that its consequences will be difficult to detect. Nevertheless I believe that the consequences for behavioral ontogeny are likely to be considerable, tending to guide the young organism along certain species-specific developmental trajectories without necessarily sacrificing the many advantages that accrue from behavioral plasticity.

Such guidelines are likely to be especially important in the development of communicative behavior. While solitary behavioral innovations may be of immediate value in certain domains, such as feeding behavior, in communication there are special conditions to be satisfied before innovations can become effective. Participants must share some common rules in their behavior. I believe that, in our own species, innate constraints on development of the perception of stimuli generated by signalling behavior must aid in achieving this end, while still allowing the extraordinary diversity of culturally-determined behaviors that is diagnostic of the human condition.

Summary

A brief 'ethologist's' review has been presented of data on the development of speech perception in human infants, adult perception of natural and synthetic speech sounds, and descriptive 'ethograms' of the acoustic structure of speech. These demonstrate that there are universals in the placing of boundaries on the acoustic continua that occur in natural speech and that infants show innate predispositions to observe similar boundaries. The theme of perceptual predispositions brought to bear on learning tasks was then extended to animal studies. Japanese macaques confronted with discrimination tasks in which the cues are natural or synthetic calls of their own species learn to generalize much more quickly than other monkey species trained with the same Japanese monkey calls. Japanese monkeys seem predisposed to process their calls in the laboratory in ways that parallel their apparent natural meanings. Some songbirds show an innate selectivity in accepting acoustic models for song learning. In human and animal studies initial responsiveness seems to be focussed on elementary sound properties, with full appreciation of more complex aspects of sound signals of the species remaining to be shaped through learning. Innate perceptual predispositions guide the young organism in learning to extract meaningful features from complex sound stimuli. They will thus encourage the sharing of simple perceptual rules by species members, facilitating communication without sacrificing the advantages that accrue from the developmental plasticity of signalling behaviors and their perception.

10.2. An ethological approach to language through the study of speech perception[1]

A. M. LIBERMAN

Introduction

It is, I hope, appropriate to the purposes of this volume that my approach be the reverse of that taken by Peter Marler (chapter 10.1). Where he begins with the biology of communication in animals and looks toward man, I would begin with the biology of language in man and look toward the animals. I should emphasize that my aim is to complement what he has said, not to contradict it. Indeed, there is nothing I would want to contradict, for I find in his contribution the best hope we have for understanding certain aspects of human communication. I think especially in this connection of the seminal research on the learning of song by certain birds. That work has greatly enlightened us about the acquisition of language by children; more so, by a striking irony, than most of those vastly more numerous studies of language learning in humans that investigated the memorization of lists of unconnected (or unnaturally connected) words. Perhaps there is a lesson here for us human ethologists, which is that we can learn about language from birdsong if only because both are systems with biological function and biological integrity, whereas the rote learning of lists of words is not. But I will say little more about the work Peter Marler has described. I will only express my admiration, acknowledge my debt, and then take my own stance, which is, as I said, 180 degrees away.

[1] The preparation of this paper was aided by a grant to Haskins Laboratories from the National Institute of Child Health and Human Development.

Requirements for an ethology of language

To study language from an ethological point of view, we should meet at least two requirements. The first is to establish that language does have an ethology worth studying, for if we adopt certain views about language, we should conclude that it does not. Thus, we might suppose that language is an invention, as far removed from its biological base as the kinds of things people do when they build and use automobiles and sewing machines. That view is uncommon, perhaps, but we should understand nevertheless that there are aspects of language for which it is exactly right. Written language, for example, *is* an invention of sorts and, accordingly, not very interesting from an ethological point of view. In spoken language, on the other hand, an ethologist will surely find phenomena that are close to their biological roots, but he will just as surely encounter others that, like written language, represent cultural artifacts. At all events, the ethologist must make his way carefully, seeking out the former and avoiding the latter.

There is another, far more common way of looking at language that would also make us hesitate to study its ethology. In this view, language is seen, not as unnatural, but as secondary, the epiphenomenal result of more basic processes. Language has been so regarded by many psychologists, including some who are of very different, even opposite, theoretical persuasions. Thus, from the view of a 'cognitive' psychologist like Piaget, language is an aspect of those same processes that underlie cognitive activities in general (Piaget 1968). At the other extreme of psychological theory, a behaviorist like Skinner treats language as another set, albeit a large one, of conditioned responses (Skinner 1957). If we find reason to agree with either, then we should not want to investigate language, whether from an ethological point of view or from some other, but rather those more basic processes of which it is presumably a reflection. As for the communicative behavior of animals, we should then suppose that it differs from ours for reasons that have nothing to do with a faculty of language as such. We might, for example, even suppose that animals do not talk because they have nothing to say. In any case, we should want to study language from an ethological point of view only after we have, by appropriate research, found characteristics that distinguish it from nonlinguistic processes in human beings and, perhaps, from all processes in nonlinguistic animals.

A second, and even more obvious, requirement for an ethology of language is that its distinctive characteristics – or, at least, those we choose to study – be accessible to scientific investigation. It hardly suits our ethological purposes to have identified formal properties of syntax, for example, if we cannot determine how their underlying processes compare with those that result in the many other things that human creatures do. In the ideal case, indeed, we should want to determine in what form, if any, these same processes exist in nonhuman animals; and, in order to gain further insight into such biological predispositions to language as there may be, we should also want to be able to study these processes in human infants, including especially those who are too young to talk.

My aim is to suggest that both requirements can rather easily be met by putting our attention on speech perception. I use the term 'speech perception' in its narrowest sense to refer to just those events that occur when, on being presented with the sounds of speech, a listener perceives a string of consonants and vowels. There is nothing here of syntax or meaning, only the relation between acoustic signal and the phonetic message it conveys. In that relation we can, I think, find phenomena that imply the existence of biological specializations for language. These can be studied, not only in adult human beings, but also in presumably nonlinguistic animals and in patently prelinguistic (human) infants. For us ethologists, then, speech perception can be a window on language. Not perfectly transparent, to be sure, but likely nevertheless to afford a better view – at least for some purposes – than we can get by looking in at the more abstract levels of syntax or semantics. But we will best see what we are looking for if the biologically interesting characteristics of speech perception represent the special characteristics of language. Bear with me, then, while I say how language is special, at least in my view, and then how that is exemplified in speech. My colleagues and I have written on this matter at greater length in several papers (Liberman et al. 1967, Liberman 1970, Liberman and Studdert-Kennedy, in press); however, I cannot presume that these have been widely read, so I will offer a brief review.

A special characteristic of language and how speech partakes of it

Surely, the special characteristic of language is grammar, if by grammar we mean the peculiar codes that make sense of the relation between sound and meaning. So I will speak of grammatical codes, but instead of dealing with their form, which is what students of language most commonly worry about, I will ask rather about their function. For the moment, then, our concern is not with what those grammars are, but with what they do.

To appreciate the function of grammatical codes, it is helpful to see the nature and limits of agrammatic communication. In an agrammatic mode, which is common among animals and in man's nonlinguistic communication, the relation of message to signal is straightforward. Each message is directly linked to a signal, and each signal differs holistically from all others. There is no grammatical structure, only a list of all possible messages and their corresponding signals.

Notice, now, that if all human communication were of that kind, we should not have to wonder about distinctive linguistic processes. At the one end, the signals would have to be discriminated and identified, but that is what auditory perception is all about. At the other end, the messages to which those signals are so directly connected would have to be comprehended and stored, but that is the business of processes that lie squarely in the cognitive domain. So, if we knew all about auditory perception and all about cognition, we should understand perfectly the perception of agrammatic communication.

Such agrammatic communication would, of course, be quite limited, so much so that most of what we might want to say would be unsayable. For agrammatic communication would work well only if there were agreement in number between the messages we are capable of composing and the holistically different signals we can produce and perceive. But the number of messages we can generate and comprehend is uncountably large, or so we might immodestly assume, while, in contrast, our vocal tracts and ears can cope efficiently with only a relatively small number of signals. It is precisely there, in that incompatibility, that we see the function of grammar; for the need is to match the potentialities of the message-generating intellect to the limitations of the sound-transmitting vocal tract and sound-perceiving ear. In fact, that is what grammatical processes do. They restructure the message, often drastically, so as to make it differentially appropriate for the unmatched organs – those primarily associated with thinking, remembering, listening, and breathing–eating – that must deal with it, each in its own way.

To appreciate how very great that grammatical restructuring is, and what it does for you and me, consider what would happen if you were to try to recall what I have said thus far. Assuming even the best case – that is, that I have made sense – you could not possibly remember how I ordered phonetic segments into words, words into sentences, and sentences into coherent discourse. But, by using the grammatical processes of phonology and syntax, you could extract from my utterances such ideas as they might have contained. Those ideas, represented now in some presumably nonlinguistic form, you could store in (long-term) memory. On the occasion of recall you could once again use grammatical processes to restructure the ideas into transmittable language. But your language would be a paraphrase of mine. Your language and mine would both be metaphors, as it were, related to each other and to their (more or less) common meaning only by grammatical codes.

Thus, grammar serves to match a message generator, at the one extreme, to a transmitter and receiver at the other. In so doing, it makes human communication vastly more various and efficient than it would otherwise be. But the gain is achieved at a price, since grammar entails a peculiar complication in the relation between message and signal, and a need for correspondingly peculiar processes to deal with it. It is, I should think, in connection with those processes that the biological specializations for language exist.

What can we say, now, about the shape that those grammatical processes might take? Looking at the matter from the standpoint of the perceiver, we see that all the grammatical complications he must cope with are just those that he produces when he assumes the role of speaker. This is to say that the complications are internal to himself. But the same is not true for all other forms of perception. The complications of shape constancy, for example, are external to the perceiver, though he may have an internal model to deal with them; they are expressed, not in the rules of grammar, but in those of projective geometry. At all events, the special grammatical processes that are necessary to perceive language might be expected to have something in common with those that produce it. If so, the key to grammatical codes would lie in the manner of their production.

So much for grammatical codes in general. Now what about speech? Has the need for grammatical restructuring ended with the production of the abstract representations of consonants and vowels? Given that the processes of syntax and phonology have produced, finally, a string of phonetic segments, can those segments be effectively represented at the acoustic level in an agrammatic way, one acoustic segment for each phonetic segment? Plainly, they cannot. Indeed, we can see the need for grammatical restructuring even more clearly in speech than at the other levels of language. The difficulties that agrammatic communication would encounter at this level have been described in other papers (Liberman, Mattingly, and Turvey 1972, Liberman and Studdert-

Kennedy, in press). For our purposes here it is enough to speak of only one of these, and that but briefly. Consider, then, that the phonetic message is often transmitted at rates of twenty-five, or even thirty, segments per second, at least for short stretches. Surely, it would be impossible to speak that fast if the message segments were produced agrammatically by a string of discrete gestures, one for each segment and each in its proper turn. More to the point, given our emphasis on speech perception, is the fact that it would be impossible to listen that fast if each segment were, in similar fashion, represented by a unit sound, since twenty-five or thirty such sound units per second would far overreach the temporal resolving power of the ear.

In fact, the phonetic segments are not transmitted agrammatically. There is a kind of grammar that links the phonetic message to the acoustic signal; and, like the proper grammars of syntax and phonology, the grammar of speech serves to match the requirements of the one level to the limitations of the other. That is done, roughly speaking, in the following way. First, the message segments, of which there are most commonly about two to three dozen, are broken down into a somewhat smaller number of features. Each feature is assigned, as it were, to a gesture that can be made more or less independently of the others. The gestures are organized into units larger than a segment – the coding unit may be as long as a syllable or, in some cases, even longer – and then co-articulated in such a way that gestures corresponding to features of successive message segments are produced at the same time or else greatly overlapped.

By this means, a speaker can produce phonetic segments at rates several times faster than the rates at which he must change the state of any muscle. Moreover, by encoding information about several successive message segments into the same segment of the signal, he significantly reduces the number of acoustic segments per second that the listener's ear must resolve. But, as in the other grammatical conversions, these gains have a cost: there is no direct correspondence in segmentation between units of the message and units of the signal; also, the shape of the signal that carries the information for a given segment of the message will vary, often in apparently peculiar ways, depending on the nature of the other message segments that are simultaneously encoded with it.

Thus, in perception of speech, as in all of language, there is a peculiar complication in the relation between message and signal and, presumably, a need for an equally peculiar perceiver. Moreover, as will have been obvious by this time, the complications the perceiver must cope with are only those that were introduced by the speaker. Once again, then, the key to the code is in the manner of its production. We might expect, therefore, that the key would somehow be part of the perceptual process. If so, it would, I should think, be the biologically distinctive part.

Some comments on the claim that speech perception is biologically special

To suppose that speech perception is special is, of course, to imply that it is not ordinary. The view that speech perception is only ordinary sees it as an overlaid function, carried out by auditory processes no different from those we use when we hear the roar of a lion, the pattern of rain, or the clang of a bell. That view is the narrow analogue of the broader one, referred to earlier, that regards the whole of language as a more or less incidental result of processes of cognition or conditioning that are not specifically linguistic. The contrary view, which I present here, is that speech perception – and perhaps, the larger language system of which it is a part – depends on biological specializations. In the case of speech perception, these specializations can be of at least two kinds.

The first, which is perhaps the less interesting from an ethological point of view, would be a specialization of the auditory system. Thus, there may be devices specialized to respond to just those aspects of the acoustic signal that are phonetically relevant. Such devices would be useful for the purpose of extracting from the signal those physically inconspicuous parts – e.g. rapid frequency modulations – that are nevertheless of great importance from a phonetic point of view. If devices of that kind exist, they would represent auditory specializations, not phonetic (or linguistic) ones, though they would have developed in connection with speech. The distinction between auditory and phonetic specialization, which is, I think, an important one, has two aspects. First, the kind of auditory specialization I have imagined could only sharpen and clarify the signal; it could not manage the grammatical peculiarities of the relation between that signal and the phonetic message it encodes. Second, the specialized auditory mechanisms would be called into play in the processing of all sounds; hence, their perceptual consequences would be characteristic of all auditory perception, not just of the perception of speech. That is surely an important consideration, for if the specialization were extreme, then perception of other biologically important sounds would be altered and, perhaps, impaired.

The assumption of auditory specializations for speech has, of course, a counterpart for language in general – to wit, that the cognitive processes have undergone evolutionary changes that make them somehow better adapted for language. It is difficult even to imagine what such specializations would be like, but, simply to make the point, let us take account of the digital nature of language and suppose that the brain of a linguistic animal like man might be, in general, better adapted to digital processes. As in the auditory case, these cognitive specializations would apply in general and not just to those activities that are associated with language. Processes that are, perhaps, better carried out in an analogue mode – e.g. spatialization – might then be adversely affected.

In any case, there may be a class of specializations for speech perception that would properly be considered auditory. Unfortunately, we can find very little evidence that bears one way or the other on the matter (see Liberman and Studdert-Kennedy, in press), so, having remarked the possibility that special auditory devices might exist, we turn our attention to a second possible specialization for speech, one of potentially greater interest to ethologists.

This other specialization would serve to deal with the grammatical peculiarities in the relation between acoustic signal and phonetic message – in particular, the lack of correspondence in segmentation and the context-conditioned variation. It would presumably be called into play only in the perception of phonetic structures, leaving nonspeech perception entirely unaffected; and the result of its operation would be a distinctive mode of perception, the phonetic mode. Hence it would deserve to be called a phonetic specialization.

The analogous assumption for the other aspects of language is, of course, that they, too, depend on specialized grammatical processes and result in a distinct linguistic mode of perceiving or thinking. I should suppose, then, that, as I have already suggested, the phonetic device we are here considering would be an integral part of the larger specialization.

Following the argument of the earlier section, I will assume that the special characteristic of the phonetic device is a biologically based link between perception and production. Given such a link, speech perception is constrained as if by 'knowledge' of what a vocal tract does when it makes linguistically significant gestures. The development of that knowledge may depend in important ways on experience, much as the learning of song by some birds does, but we should suppose that, again as in the case of the birds, those effects of experience rest on a strong (and specialized) biological base. It is difficult, in the present state of our ignorance, to know how that biological base should be characterized. Putting the matter negatively, I should say that it seems hardly conceivable that, starting with a *tabula rasa*, the child could ever learn what he needs to know in order to make sense of the peculiarities of the speech code. For if he had only the speech signal, and no knowledge of vocal tracts, he could entertain an indefinitely large number of hypotheses about how the signal was produced, and a corresponding number of hypotheses about the nature of the coded relation to the message. To 'break' the code, the child would presumably need some biologically given limits on the kinds of hypotheses he should consider – that is, some biologically given 'knowledge' about what vocal tracts do. A somewhat similar argument has been made by Chomsky (1959) about the acquisition of syntax. The point of the argument is that there is no automatic 'discovery procedure' by which a child can infer the grammar of a language from the (mostly degenerate) examples he is offered. One supposes, then, that the child is biologically predisposed to entertain only certain kinds of hypotheses, presumably those that capture just the aspects of grammar that are universal. In the case of speech, I am tempted to assume, analogously, a special biological endowment that, given appropriate experience, enables the child to learn what he needs to know about the relation of sound to the manner of its production, and so to acquire the key to the code.

A few examples of putatively special phenomena of speech perception

The point of this paper, it will be recalled, is that there are phenomena of speech perception that can be shown to rest on specialized phonetic processes, and that these can be looked for and studied, not only in adult humans, but in human infants and nonhuman animals as well. I can offer only a few examples of such phenomena here, and even these I must deal with all too briefly. And, in order to keep technical phonetic and acoustic details to a minimum, I will limit the examples to those that deal with a single and simple acoustic cue: silence. The reader who may wish to find additional examples is referred to a recent review (Liberman and Studdert-Kennedy, in press) and to the studies cited there; he may also wish to see a short paper (Liberman and Pisoni 1977) written recently. Several of the examples I will use here have appeared in those papers, though I will also take advantage of some new data and examples.

Before presenting the examples, which derive entirely from studies of adult humans, I should say a word about how easy or difficult it might be to use them in research on animals and infants. To make it as easy as possible, I have chosen only those examples – generally very simple ones – for which it is possible to imagine straightforward behavioral tests. (Unfortunately, some of the most interesting phenomena of phonetic perception do not lend themselves to tests of that kind and can, therefore, only be investigated in adult humans. See Liberman *et al.* 1967, Liberman and Studdert-Kennedy, in press.) For some of the examples I will offer, it is quite likely that the appropriate tests can easily be made. Others may prove less feasible. Among the latter are those in which we may discover that the subject – in particular, the animal subject – lacks even the basic sensory capacity that is necessary (but presumably not sufficient) for the phenomenon we wish to study. In such cases we should hope to find animals that have the necessary sensory capabilities, or else develop other examples of the same general phenomenon that present fewer difficulties of a purely sensory sort. At all events, we ought, in one way or another, to be able to make the appropriate tests.

When silence sounds like sound

Articulatory gestures that produce linguistically significant contrasts (for example, 'rabid' versus 'rapid') typically have acoustic consequences that are numerous, diverse, and distributed over a considerable stretch of the acoustic signal. It is of interest from our point of view that these various acoustic consequences have an equivalence in phonetic perception. That equivalence is established by demonstrating that each such acoustic consequence – let us call it a 'cue' – is more or less sufficient (with all other cues held constant) to produce the perceived phonetic contrast. The rather considerable evidence bearing on that point is reviewed in Liberman and Studdert-Kennedy (in press). I will offer one example here.

Consider the contrast between the words 'slit' and 'split'. To articulate the stop consonant [p], which is the distinguishing segment in 'split', the speaker must close his vocal tract for 50 msec. or so after making the hissing noise associated with the fricative [s], and then open it as he undertakes the remaining (vocalic) section of the syllable. (Omitting the p in 'slit', the speaker does not completely close his vocal tract.) Among the acoustic consequences of the closing and opening are two – shown schematically in figure 1 – that will concern us here. One is the interval of silence between s-noise and the vocalic section that corresponds to the closure: relatively short silence for 'slit', relatively long silence for 'split'. The other is the effect on the acoustic spectrum at the beginning of the

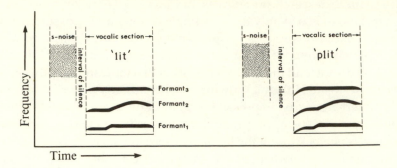

1. Schematic representations of the temporal (interval of silence) and spectral (initial formant transition) cues for the perceived distinction between 'slit' and 'split'. (From Erickson *et al.* 1977. A full account is in preparation.)

vocalic section that is a result of the subsequent opening of the vocal tract: the formants are initially level in 'slit', rapidly changing in 'split'.

Let us look first at the effect of the silence cue as shown in an experiment by Dorman, Raphael and Liberman (1976). They started with a (real speech) recording of the word 'lit'. To this they prefixed a brief patch of s-noise, separating it from 'lit' by intervals of silence that varied from 0 to 650 msec. These stimuli were randomized and presented to listeners for judgment as 'slit' or 'split'. The results are shown in figure 2, where we see that, with silent gaps from 0 to 60 msec., all listeners reported 'slit'; then, quite abruptly, they heard 'split'; finally, at 450 msec. of silence they began, though now rather slowly, to hear 'slit' once again. We will not concern ourselves here with the question: why 'split', not 'sklit' or 'stlit'? That is a separate issue, quite unrelated to our present interest, which is only in the presence or absence of a stop consonant. What we have seen in that connection is that appropriate variations in the amount of silence are sufficient to produce the perceived contrast between the absence of a stop in 'slit' and its presence in 'split'. If we suppose that the silence provides the phonetic information that the speaker did (or did not) close his vocal tract, and that the listener has a device specialized to make the appropriate interpretation, then silence proves to have just the sound we should expect it to have: it sounds like a stop consonant.

What, then, of the spectral cue? What does it sound like and how does it relate to the silence? For an answer, we turn to a recent experiment by Erickson *et al.* (1977), in which the effect of silence on the 'slit–split' contrast was investigated under each of two stimulus conditions. In one,

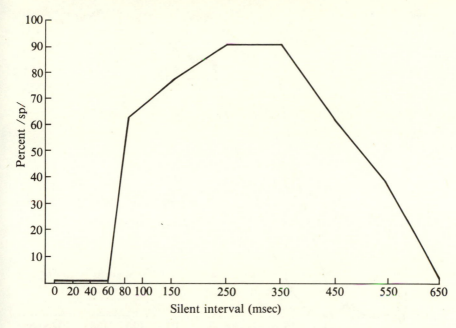

2. The effect of the interval of silence on the perceived distinction between 'slit' and 'split'. (From Dorman, Raphael and Liberman 1976: 203.)

illustrated by the example at the left of figure 1, there was a patch of (synthetic) s-noise, followed by a (silent) gap that varied in steps of 16 msec. from 8 to 152 msec., followed then by a (synthetic) vocalic section having at its onset straight formants appropriate for the syllable 'lit'. In the other set, illustrated by the example at the right of figure 1, all aspects of the stimuli were the same except that there were, at the onset of the vocalic section, formant transitions appropriate for the stop consonant [p] in the syllable 'plit'. These stimuli were randomized and presented to listeners for judgment. The results are shown in figure 3. There we see two almost parallel functions – one for s-noise plus 'lit', the other for s-noise plus 'plit' – that show the percentage of 'split' judgments plotted against the duration of the silent gap. The two functions are displaced with reference to each other in such a way as to indicate that, in order to convert 'slit' to 'split', 20 msec. less silence is necessary when the spectral cues appropriate for the stop [p] are present. In effect, then, there is, in this instance of phonetic perception, an equivalence between 20 msec. of silence, on the one hand, and, on the other, the presence or absence of certain transitions. Thus, a temporal cue sounds like a spectral cue.

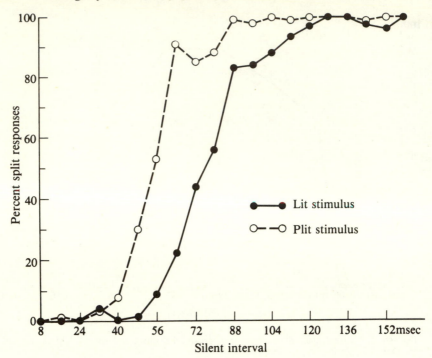

3. A trading relation in the perception of 'slit' and 'split' between temporal and spectral cues. (From Erickson *et al.* 1977.)

One is naturally led to ask why two such different physical events – and, indeed, it is difficult to imagine any two that would be more different – should sound the same. The answer is presumably to be found in the fact that these different acoustic cues are the distributed consequences of the same linguistically significant gesture. They sound alike, then, because both signal to a biologically specialized phonetic perceiver that the speaker did or did not close and open his vocal tract in a way appropriate for the production of 'split' (or 'slit').

Would such an equivalence exist in animals? On the basis of what we know about auditory systems in general, I should think it unlikely. In any case, we can find out, and, as we will see in a moment, by fairly simple procedures. Moreover, we can also test for the equivalence in human infants at various ages. We should especially want to do that because, given the repeated association of spectral and temporal cues in speech, we are tempted to suppose that the equivalence is learned. But could the learning of such phenomenological equivalence possibly be arbitrary?

That is, could it depend on the fact of association and nothing else? Surely, two different sounds that are frequently associated in the world will come to be associated in a listener's mind; on hearing one, he will expect to hear the other. Or, if they always signify the same thing, then each may become a sufficient sign. But will they, with any amount of association, come actually to sound alike, as in the case of the speech cues they clearly do? The experimental literature on 'acquired similarity' – as that possibility used to be called – together with the normal experience of all of us suggest that they will not. I should think, therefore, that, while experience may be necessary for establishing the perceived equivalence of the speech cues, it is not sufficient. In any case, we may hope to learn from research on infants whether the development of the equivalence comes so early and so suddenly as to imply a strong biological predisposition to profit from the experience in the particular and, perhaps, particularly human way that produces the effect we have observed in our experiments.

But let us look now at how we can, by simple behavioral tests, determine whether animals and infants hear the silence and spectral cues as we do. One possibly interesting experimental plan, drawn from the results shown in figure 3 and previously discussed, is sketched in figure 4. There we see four pairs of stimuli, the corresponding percepts, and the relevant characterization of the cues. Pairs I and II illustrate that the perceived contrast between 'slit' and 'split' can be produced by either of two acous-

Description of stimuli		Percept	Characterization of cues			
Gap	Vocalic		Temporal	Spectral	Temporal	Spectral
Pair I s-noise < -short – – – *lit* / -short – – – *plit*		*slit* / *split*	-p / -p	-p / +p } →	same	different
Pair II s-noise < -short – – – *lit* / -long – – – *lit*		*slit* / *split*	-p / +p	-p / -p } →	different	same
Pair III s-noise < -short – – – *lit* / -long – – – *plit*		*slit* / *split*	-p / +p	-p / +p } →	different	different
Pair IV s-noise < -short – – – *plit* / -long – – – *lit*		*split* / *split*	-p / +p	+p / -p } →	different	different

4. Diagrams illustrating the phonetically equivalent effects of spectral and temporal cues and, also, the phonetically different effects produced by the two ways in which those cues may be combined. (From Liberman and Studdert-Kennedy, in press; also in Liberman and Pisoni 1977.)

tic cues – one spectral, the other temporal. The patterns in each of these pairs differ by only one cue. Pairs III and IV illustrate the effects of combining the two cues, but in different ways and with different consequences. In Pair III, the spectral and temporal cues are combined in such a way as to 'add' to each other and so enhance the perceived difference between 'slit' and 'split'. In Pair IV, on the other hand, the two cues are combined so as to 'cancel' the perceived difference, with the result that listeners hear 'split' in both cases. Putting aside further discussion of what these patterns sound like, let us consider simply the relative difficulty that a human adult would have in discriminating them. That can only be inferred from the (phonetic) identification data of figure 3, but it has now been verified by direct measures of discriminability in an experiment by Fitch *et al.* (in preparation). In terms of increasing difficulty, the order is: Pair III (two-cue difference), Pairs I and II (one-cue difference), Pair IV (two-cue difference). The point to note is that the easiest and hardest discriminations have in common that the patterns differ by two cues. One of the pairs with two cues different (Pair IV) is harder to discriminate than either of the pairs that differ by only one cue (Pairs I and II). This is so, presumably, because the cues have, as it were, positive and negative signs, or vector-like directions, for the perceptions they induce; we should suppose that such signs, or such directions, exist only in the phonetic mode. If so, then animals should show a different order of relative difficulty. For them, Pairs III and IV ought to be of approximately equal difficulty, since the patterns in each differ by two cues; and both of these pairs should be easier than Pairs I and II, in which the patterns are distinguished by only one cue in each case. If the expected difference between adult humans and animals is found, we should want then to test infants at various ages. At all events, the test should be an easy one to make: the dependent variable is only ease of discrimination; the comparison to be made is only in the relative order of difficulty; and the expected result with animals (if obtained) cannot reasonably be attributed to inattention or lack of motivation.

When the sound of silence depends on how many are talking: phonetic constraints of an ecological sort

I have suggested that the biologically distinctive characteristic of phonetic perception is that it is governed as if by knowledge of what a vocal tract does when it makes linguistically significant gestures. We should ask now: whose vocal tract? A proper regard for the ecological realities suggests it can hardly be that of the listener, nor yet of the speaker; for if the listener is to cope with the fact that he is commonly exposed to several talkers simultaneously, he must make his perceptual calculations in terms of some abstract conception of the behavior of vocal tracts in general.

To see how that is, consider another example of the sound of silence. Suppose we record the sentence, 'You will please say *shop* again.' Now we introduce silence between the end of 'say' and the beginning of 'shop', and find, not surprisingly, that, with just the right amount of silence, listeners hear, 'You will please say *chop* again.' I say 'not surprisingly' because, to produce the affricate – that is, the stop-initiated fricative – in 'chop' instead of the fricative in 'shop', a speaker must close his vocal tract for a brief period and, in the process, introduce a brief period of silence (Dorman, Raphael and Liberman 1976). To a listener, that silence provides the information that the speaker closed his vocal tract just long enough to have said 'chop'; hence, 'chop' is what the listener perceives. But if there were two speakers, one saying 'You will please say', the other 'shop again', then the period of silence between the words 'say' and 'shop' (or 'say' and 'chop') would not, in principle, supply useful phonetic information: given intentional collaboration, or the accidents of speech when two are talking, one person might say 'You will please say' and the other 'chop again' with zero interval of silence between 'say' and 'chop'. Our experiments reveal that listeners behave as if they knew that perfectly well.

One of those experiments (Dorman, Raphael, and Liberman 1976; for a similar experiment, see Dorman *et al.* 1975) was performed with the utterance I have here used as an example. In one condition, we recorded a male speaker saying 'You will please say shop again.' In the other, we recorded a female saying 'You will please say' and joined that to the 'shop again' as previously recorded by the male. In both conditions, the experimental variable was the duration of silence between the words 'say' and 'shop'. The result was quite straightforward. In the one-voice condition, all listeners heard 'say shop' or 'say chop' depending on the presence (or absence) of the appropriate amount of silence. In the two-voice condition, on the other hand, listeners heard 'say shop' at all intervals of silence. Thus, they behaved as if, knowing that two vocal tracts can do what one vocal tract cannot, their perception of speech was governed by some quite abstract conception of vocal tracts in general. It would, I should think, be interesting from an ethological point of view to find out when infants begin to behave that way.

When the sound of silence depends on how fast the speaker is talking

One of the interesting problems that a speech perceiver must contend with is that which is created when speakers articulate at different rates. The problem is the more interesting because variations in rate do not affect all portions of the acoustic signal equally (Gaitenby 1965, Lehiste 1970, Huggins 1972): some portions are stretched (or compressed), others not, or not to the same degree. Presumably, then, the listener cannot make the necessary adjustment by, as it were, simply multiplying the acoustic signal by a constant factor. If he adjusts properly, it is as if he had some knowledge of the disproportionalities that are associated with rate variations, or, more generally, of the articulatory mechanisms that generate them. It would be particularly interesting, then, to know whether animals can make those adjustments, and at what age infants do so.

Unfortunately, the matter of adjustment for rate has been very little studied in adult human beings, so we do not have a large set of examples to choose from. There is, however, a recent study (Repp *et al.*, in press) that is particularly appropriate for our purposes if only because it deals with the same silence cue to which we have become accustomed.

In this study, we are concerned once more, then, with the role of silence in converting 'Please say shop again' to 'Please say chop again.' But this experiment adds two new variations: one is in the duration of the noise associated with the fricative [sh] in 'shop'; the other is in the rate at which the carrier sentence is articulated, more slowly in one condition and more rapidly in the other. (The several durations of the friction noise were the same in the two-rate conditions.) As I have implied, the experimental variable in all cases was the duration of silence between 'say' and 'shop'.

The results are shown in figure 5. There, the percentage of 'chop' judgments is plotted as a function of the duration of silence between 'say' and 'shop'. As usual, the silence cue is sufficient to produce the perceptual contrast between 'shop' and 'chop'. We also see that at both rates of articulation the amount of silence necessary for the affricate 'chop' is greater as the duration of the friction noise is longer. This is so because duration of friction noise is itself a cue to the fricative-affricate distinction – longer noise biases the perception toward the fricative [sh]. Thus, we have still another relation between different acoustic cues, similar in principle to the one between temporal and spectral cues described earlier. In this case, the relation establishes an equivalence in phonetic perception between durations of silence and durations of noise.

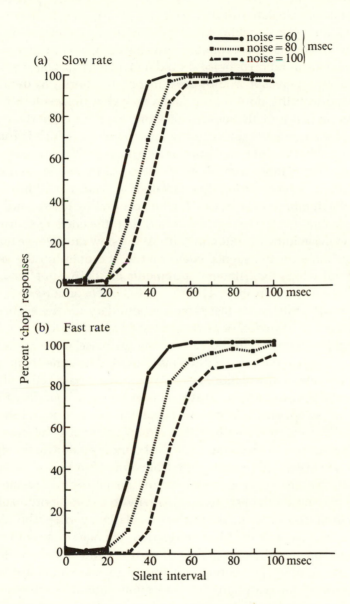

5. The effects on the perceived distinction between 'You will please say shop again' and 'You will please say chop again' of orthogonal variations in the duration of the silent interval (immediately preceding 'shop'), the duration of friction noise (in 'shop'), and the rate of articulation of the sentence frame. (From Repp *et al.*, in press; also in Liberman *et al*. 1977.)

More relevant to our present concern, however, is the variation in rate of articulation. There, we see an effect that is, apparently, paradoxical: when the rate of articulation of the carrier sentence is increased, while the duration of the noise is held constant, listeners require more silence to hear 'chop'. But perhaps that comparison is not altogether proper, since it assumes that the duration of noise should remain fixed as rate of articulation increases, whereas it would, presumably, be shorter as the rate is faster. So, perhaps the more appropriate way to view the results is to look at the different effects on the silence cue of the two ways of shortening the duration of the noise: within the same rate condition, which is roughly equivalent to what would have happened (to the noise) if the speaker had changed the articulation from 'shop' to 'chop'; or by moving across the rate conditions, which is roughly equivalent to what would have happened to the duration of the noise, if, while continuing to say 'shop', the speaker had simply speeded up. Consider, first, the effect of shortening the noise while holding the rate constant. At the slow rate, we see that the 'boundary' value for the silence cue – that is, the point on the silence continuum at which the listeners' judgments are 50% 'shop' and 50% 'chop' – goes down from about 41 msec. at 100 msec. of noise to 35 at 80 and then to 28 at 60; at the fast rate, the boundary for the silence cue moves from 50 at 100 msec. of noise to 42 at 80 and then to 37 at 60. But look now at the different effect of shortening the noise across rate conditions – that is, when the same reductions in noise durations are made by changing the rate of articulation. As the noise duration is reduced from 100 msec. at the slower rate to 80 at the faster rate, the boundary for the silence cue does not decrease at all; in fact, it increases very slightly from 41 msec. to 42 msec.; then, with further reduction in noise duration from 80 msec. (slower rate) to 60 (faster rate), the boundary value for the silence cue again increases slightly, this time from 35 to 37 msec.

I believe that the disproportionality in the perceptual results just described may reflect the listeners' sensitivity to a disproportionality in the acoustic effects of varying the rate of articulation: perhaps duration of the noise associated with the fricative generally changes more with rate of articulation than does the stop closure. If so, then we see here an instance of the rather complex perceptual adjustment to rate variation that we earlier wondered about and, in that connection, a demonstration of how very exact is the listener's knowledge of the particulars of vocal tract dynamics. But I hasten to say that, at this writing, we do not have definitive data about the acoustic effects of varying articulatory rate, so we can have no great confidence in that particular interpretation. Still, it is of interest from our point of view that the two ways of varying the duration of noise – by changing the phonetic segment, as it were, or by changing the rate of articulation – have different perceptual consequences for our adult listeners. How special are the calculations that underlie that distinction?

When the sound of silence is heard (or not) in one syllable depending on an acoustic cue in the next syllable

As I said in an earlier section of this paper, a very general and important characteristic of the speech code is that there is no direct correspondence in segmentation between segments of the phonetic message and segments of the acoustic signal. The rapid switches of sound source that occur during articulation often cause the information about a single phonetic segment to be spread through several acoustic segments; on the other hand, normal co-articulation often collapses information about several phonetic segments into a single segment of sound. A general consequence is that, at any given instant, the speech signal is likely to be carrying information about more than one phonetic segment. It is this characteristic that justifies our speaking of the relation between phonetic message and acoustic signal as a code rather than a cipher – or, indeed, as grammatical rather than agrammatical – and it is this same characteristic of speech that, perhaps more clearly than any other, would appear to be beyond the capacity of ordinary auditory devices. The task is not simply to respond to a complex acoustic pattern, but to recover a message from a signal in which it is peculiarly encoded. In that sense, perceiving speech is not so much a matter of complex pattern recognition as it is of crypt-analysis.

We should have no difficulty finding examples of the curious relation in segmentation between message and signal; their number is legion. The trick is rather to find some that lend themselves to relatively simple behavioral tests with animals and infants. A recent study (Liberman *et al.* 1977, and Repp *et al.* in press) presents a possibility, and happily for us, it deals yet again with the silence cue.

We begin with a recording of the sentence, 'He saw the gray ship.' The experimental variable is, as in all our other examples, the duration of silence – in this case, between the words 'gray' and 'ship'. The parameter of the experiment is the duration of the friction noise associated with the fricative [sh] in 'ship' (or the affricate [ch] in 'chip'). There were eleven durations of silence, ranging from 0 to 100 in steps of 10 msec.; the

durations of friction noise were set at 62, 102, 142, and 182 msec. The
resulting patterns were randomized and presented to listeners for judgment as '(He saw the) *gray ship*, *gray chip*, *great ship*, or *great chip*'. The
results are shown in figure 6, where the responses are plotted as a
function of duration of silence for each duration of friction noise. We see,
first, that at all noise durations the listeners reported hearing 'gray ship'
when the duration of silence was less than approximately 30 msec. That
is, when the silence was insufficiently long, listeners heard neither a stop

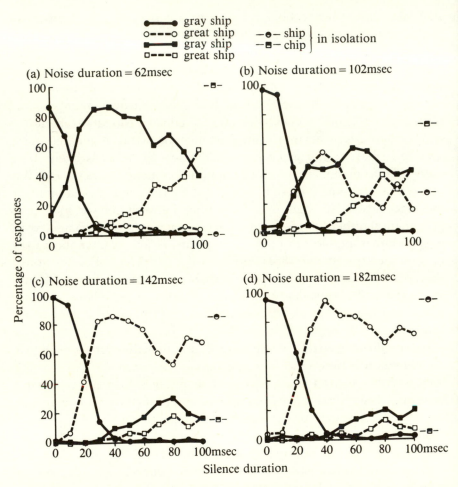

6. The relation between duration of silence and duration of friction noise in the perception
of fricative, affricate, and stop consonant, demonstrating how the perception of a phonetic
segment (the [t] of 'great') is determined by an acoustic cue (the duration of the friction noise
of 'ship') that lies in the following syllable. (From Repp *et al.*, in press; also in Liberman
et al. 1977.)

(as in 'great') nor a stop-initiated fricative (i.e. affricate, as in 'chip'), which is exactly what we should expect, given the results described earlier. If we look now at the results obtained with the shortest duration of noise (62 msec.), we see another familiar result: when the duration of the silence becomes long enough, listeners perceive a stop-like effect, reporting the affricate in 'gray chip' (instead of 'gray ship'). But consider now the result when the duration of fricative noise is long (182 msec.). To produce a stop-like effect in this condition, more silence is necessary, as it was indeed in the experiment described earlier. What is novel and particularly interesting, however, is that, under the particular conditions of this experiment, the stop-like effect is attached to the end of the 'gray' syllable: the listeners perceive, not 'gray chip', but 'great ship'. Thus, with all other aspects of the pattern held constant, it is possible to interconvert between the words 'gray' and 'great' – that is, to add or subtract the syllable-final stop consonant – by altering the duration of the noise associated with the fricative (affricate) in the next syllable. The effect is the more interesting, since adding the [t], which is commonly assumed to be a transient from an acoustic point of view, is accomplished by making the noise in the next syllable longer (that is, less transient).

It is not difficult to find a plausible explanation for the results just described. Consider, as we have before, that an appropriate interval of silence signals that the speaker closed his vocal tract, as he must to produce either a stop or an affricate. The listener will, as a consequence, tend to hear one or the other of those phones. But the duration of the friction noise is also an important cue for the affricate, distinguishing it from the corresponding fricative: relatively short noise for affricate, relatively long for fricative. Given a relatively short duration of noise at the onset of the second syllable, the listener takes the relatively long silence (hence closure) to mean an affricate: he hears 'gray chip'. But given a relatively long duration of noise at the onset of the second syllable, and the same relatively long silence as before, the listener perceives the fricative in 'ship', which accords with the long duration of the noise; then he adds a stop consonant [t] to the end of the previous syllable 'gray', which converts it to 'great' and allows him to take account of the vocal-tract closure that was signaled by the silence.

It is somewhat beside the point whether that account is exactly correct or not. For our purposes, the important fact is that a sufficient cue for the distinction 'gray' versus 'great' is in the duration of noise associated with the fricative (or affricate) at the beginning of the next syllable. Will animals decode the signal that way, and at what age will infants do it?

Summary

My aim has been to suggest that an ethologist might want to study the perception of speech because it is an integral and reasonably representative part of the language process, yet it can be investigated experimentally, not only in adult humans, but also in nonhuman animals and in human infants. Moreover, research on adult humans has already uncovered certain phenomena that strongly imply the existence of biological specializations for phonetic (as distinguished from auditory) perception. I have offered several examples of these, all taken from recent research on the role of silence in the perception of stop and affricate consonants.

Comments on papers by Marler and Liberman

D. PLOOG

The two papers by Peter Marler and Alvin Liberman which I will now review are papers with complementary approaches. They refer to different sets of experimental data but share similar aims. Marler focuses on animal communication, especially in monkeys and birds, and looks toward man, while Liberman focuses on language, and looks towards the animals.

I have the feeling that facts and concepts in the field of auditory perception are less well-known to ethologists, anthropologists, and psychologists and perhaps technically more difficult to understand than some other aspects of ethology with which this volume is concerned. Therefore I shall take the liberty of going into some technicalities. In the course of my comments you will, I hope, develop a feeling for the beauty of these experiments because of the precision of measurement that can be achieved, because of the reproducibility of the results, and because of the straightforward strategies that can be employed to ask specific questions.

One of the chief concerns in ethological research is the observation and, if possible, the quantification of motor behaviour. In the studies of auditory perception and speech perception discussed by Marler and Liberman a very specialized kind of motor behaviour, namely vocal behaviour, is used as stimulus material. Please note that we are dealing here with natural stimuli chosen from the species-specific vocal repertoire of monkeys, birds, and man.

On a sound spectrogram as in figure 1, the frequency modulation of a sound is usually plotted over time. However, the spectrogram does not show what the perceiver of a sound perceives. This is a key issue for the understanding of the experiments: the distribution of acoustic energy as

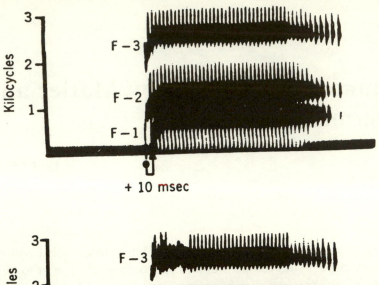

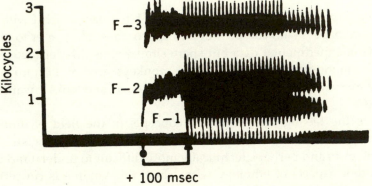

1. Spectrograms of synthetic speech showing two conditions of voice-onset-time (VOT): slight voicing lag in the upper figure and long voicing lag in the lower figure. The symbols F-1, F-2, and F-3 represent the first three formants, that is, the relatively intense bands of energy in the speech spectrum (Eimas *et al.* 1971).

reflected in the spectrogram does not correspond to the percept of the stimulus receiver. This is definitely so in the perception of speech sounds, as you will see in a moment. Whether this is also true for monkeys, birds, and other animals we do not know as yet, but for reasons which I will explain later it would be of great interest to find out.

The next thing one should know for the understanding of the experiments is the way in which a given vocal gesture – our stimulus configuration – can be technically manipulated. Listen to the sound shift from [pa] to [ba]: this series, and many such sounds, can be produced by a machine. Speech sounds and animal calls can be synthesized. Each parameter which contributes to the sound, such as frequency transitions, pauses in these transitions, and the duration of transitions, can be manipulated independently of the others, and the corresponding percept of the listener can be ascertained. In the [ba]–[pa] example, the one parameter that is systematically varied is the parameter called voice-onset-time (VOT). The VOT (see figure 1) is the time between the release of the consonant and the onset of voicing, or, to be more precise, the number of milliseconds by which the release of a consonant precedes voicing. Consonants with shorter VOTs are perceived as voiced (as in [ba]); consonants with longer VOTs are perceived as voiceless or, better, unvoiced.

This is, I think, all we need to know about the technicalities. Marler is very much intrigued by investigations of the perceptual processing of speech stimuli by human adults and infants. Such studies merit close attention from ethologists working on analogous problems with animals. Since the human data which Marler cites bear directly on Liberman's contribution – and are in fact either generated or incited by him – I will give you only one example for the human infant. Again I will use the [ba]–[pa] paradigm. One-month-old infants are exposed to the [ba]–[pa] sequence of speech sounds. The VOT is extended in 10- or 20-msec. steps from, say 10 to 60 msec. Neither these young infants nor adults who listen to such a VOT continuum perceive the continuum as such but rather as a sudden shift from [ba] to [pa]. The shift always occurs at a sharp boundary, about 40 msec. VOT. Before that time both infant and adult listeners hear [ba], thereafter they hear [pa]. I will not explain here how this sudden shift in the percepts can be precisely ascertained in young infants. I will merely state that this finding has been confirmed by several investigators with varying methods and different speech sounds. This evidence for a distinctive mode of perceptual processing has become known as categorical perception. Moreover, testing infants in very different linguistic environments has led to the same results, that speech sounds are perceived in the categorical mode. Obviously, categorical processing has the consequence of grouping stimuli into classes, imposing a particular kind of order on the varying acoustic patterns.

For the purpose of comparison let us now shift to monkeys. Although there are a number of studies on the vocalizations of various species of monkeys, very little is known about the functions of vocal signals. As Marler rightly states, it is virtually impossible to assay the communicative function of these signals until we have some understanding of how the signals are processed during perception.

Among the many graded calls of the Japanese macaque there is a variety of 'coos' on which I want to focus now (see figure 3, chapter 10.1

above). Steven Green has identified a significant feature within the variety of coos: the temporal position of a frequency rise. The rise may occur at any point of the coo (see 'Coo type', figure 3). Early and late frequency rises correlate with different circumstances of production. For example, the rises referred to as 'smooth early highs' are contact coos emitted by isolated animals; 'smooth late highs', on the other hand, are typically emitted by a subordinate monkey towards a dominant one. During one phase of experiments Japanese macaques were trained to respond conditionally to playback of different classes of coo calls. They achieved a high criterion of performance quite rapidly, whereas the two other species trained – the vervet monkey and the pig-tailed macaque – had enormous difficulty in generalizing to new tokens of the two classes. The smooth early–smooth late distinction appears to be a relevant distinction for the Japanese macaque but an alien one for the other species. One is tempted to argue that Japanese macaques exhibit a special predisposition to process coo sounds in a particular way that parallels their apparent meaning. The stimuli are clearly not equivalent to conspecific and alien adults, as classical learning theory would have led us to expect. That the principal of equipotentiality – one of the assumptions of learning theory – does not hold for a number of learning processes is beautifully demonstrated by Marler's experiments on song learning in swamp sparrows. A male of this species presented with a natural choice of songs of a congeneric species to copy will selectively learn conspecific models. There are surprising parallels between the song learning of birds and the development of the perception of speech in human infants. Just as our infants are predisposed to respond selectively to particular aspects of speech sounds before speaking themselves, so some young songbirds are responsive to species-specific features of song before they themselves begin to sing.

This might be a good point to turn back to the human case. In the studies on speech perception which I have discussed so far certain phenomena have come to light that strongly imply the existence of biological specializations for phonetic – as distinguished from auditory– perception. This is, in fact, the key issue of Liberman's paper, which is concerned with the relation between the acoustic signal and the phonetic message it conveys. There is a kind of grammar that links the phonetic message to the acoustic signal. How this transformation takes place will be exemplified in a few minutes. The transformational process involves the encoding of information about several successive message segments into the same signal, with the result that the speaker significantly reduces the number of acoustic segments per second that the listener's ear must resolve. As we shall see, the key to the phonetic code is in the manner of its production. To make things relatively easy, Liberman has concentrated on one striking phenomenon, the role of silence in the perception of consonants.

There is space for only one example. Suppose, he says, we record someone saying the sentence 'You will please say *shop* again.' Now we introduce silence between the end of 'say' and the beginning of 'shop'. How this is done in the right sequence you can see in figure 1 of chapter 10.2 above, although it is not the same example I am reporting now. With just the right amount of silence we find that listeners hear, 'You will please say *chop* again.' To produce the affricate in 'chop' instead of the fricative in 'shop' a speaker must close his vocal tract briefly, thus introducing a period of silence. To a listener, *that* silence provides the information that the speaker closed his vocal tract just long enough to have said 'chop'; so 'chop' is what the listener perceives. But if there were two speakers, one saying, 'You will please say', the other 'shop again', then the period of silence between the words 'say' and 'shop' (or 'say' and 'chop') would not, in principle, supply useful phonetic information. In experiments of this sort with one or two speakers and varying amounts of silence between 'say' and 'shop' the results were quite straightforward. In the one-voice condition, all listeners heard 'say shop' or 'say chop' depending on the presence or absence of the appropriate amount of silence. In the two-voice condition, on the other hand, listeners heard 'say shop', which was presented to them, at *all* intervals of silence. Thus, they behaved as if they knew that two vocal tracts can do what one vocal tract cannot. As Liberman says, it would be interesting to find out when infants begin to behave that way.

In my opinion the most important notion Liberman advances is the idea that the special characteristic of the phonetic device is a link between perception and production. Given such a link, he says, speech perception is constrained as if by innate 'knowledge' of what a vocal tract does when it makes linguistically significant gestures. For the language acquisition process this means that the child would need some biologically given 'knowledge' about what vocal tracts do.

Summing up the message of both papers, I should like to repeat that speech perception depends on biological specialization and is considered to be an integral part of the larger specialization for language. We may think of the perceptual predisposition in human infants as initial instructions to set the trajectory for development of learned responsiveness in the language acquisition process.

The comparative studies on monkeys and birds may remind us that the specialization in humans might be *one* special device among many for auditory perception. The study of speech perception seems to disclose the most pertinent ethological problems which we have been discussing here: the development of perception, a specialized stimulus–response relationship, selective learning through species-specific predisposition, and thereby the nature–nurture intercalation – all at a level of analysis which is very close to central nervous mechanisms, an aspect of speech perception which I cannot discuss here.

References

Beecher, M. D., Zoloth, S. R., Petersen, M., Moody, D. and Stebbins, W. 1976. Perception of conspecific communication signals by Japanese macaques (*Macaca fuscata*). *Journal of the Acoustical Society of America*, 60(1):89 (abstract).

Chomsky, N. 1959. Review of *Verbal behavior* by B. F. Skinner. *Language*, 36(1):26–58.

Cutting, J. E. and Eimas, P. D. 1975. Phonetic feature analyzers and the processing of speech in infants. In J. F. Kavanagh and J. E. Cutting (eds.), *The role of speech in language*. Cambridge, Mass.: MIT Press.

Cutting, J. E. and Rosner, B. 1974. Categories and boundaries of speech and music. *Perception and Psychophysics*, 16:564–70.

Dorman, M. F. 1974. Auditory evoked correlates of speech sound discrimination. *Perception and Psychophysics*, 15:215–20.

Dorman, M. F., Raphael, L. J. and Liberman, A. M. 1976. Further observations on the role of silence in the perception of stop consonants. *Haskins Laboratories Status Report on Speech Research*, SR–48:199–207.

Dorman, M. F., Raphael, L. J., Liberman, A. M. and Repp, B. 1975. Masking-like phenomena in speech perception. *Journal of the Acoustical Society of America*, 57 (Supplement 1: S48(A) (full text in *Haskins Laboratories Status Report on Speech Research*, SR–42/43, 265–76).

Eimas, P. D. 1974. Auditory and linguistic processing of the cues for speech: Discrimination of the r-l distinction by young infants. *Perception and Psychophysics*, 16:513–21.

1975. Infant perception. In L. B. Cohen and P. Salapatek (eds.), *Infant perception: from sensation to cognition*, vol. II. New York: Academic Press.

Eimas, P. D., Siqueland, E. R., Jusczyk, P. and Vigorito, J. 1971. Speech perception in infants. *Science*, 171:303–6.

Erickson, D. M., Fitch, H. L., Halwes, T. G. and Liberman, A. M. 1977. Trading relation in perception between silence and spectra. *Journal of the Acoustical Society of America*, 61 (Supplement 1): S46–S47(A).

Fitch, H. L., Erickson, D. M., Halwes, T. G. and Liberman, A. M. In preparation.

Gaitenby, J. H. 1965. The elastic word. *Haskins Laboratories Status Report on Speech Research*, SR–2:3.1–3.12.

711

Gibson, E. A. 1977. The development of perception as an adaptive process. In I. L. Janis (ed.), *Current trends in psychology*. Los Altos, California: William Kaufman Inc.

Green, S. 1975. Variation of vocal pattern with social situation in the Japanese monkey (*Macaca fuscata*): a field study. In L. A. Rosenblum (ed.), *Primate behavior*, vol. IV. New York: Academic Press.

Greenberg, J. H. 1966. *Language universals, with special reference to feature hierarchies*. The Hague: Mouton.

   1969. Language universals: a research frontier. *Science*, 166:473–8.

Hailman, J. P. 1967. Ontogeny of an instinct. *Behaviour Supplement*, 15:1–59.

   1970. Comments on the coding of releasing stimuli. In L. R. Aronson, E. Tobach, D. S. Lehrman and J. S. Rosenblatt (eds.), *Development and evolution of behavior*. San Francisco: Freeman.

Hinde, R. A. and Stevenson-Hinde, J. (eds.) 1973. *Constraints on learning*. New York: Academic Press.

Huggins, A. W. F. 1972. On the perception of temporal phenomena in speech. *Journal of the Acoustical Society of America*, 51:1279–90.

Kuhl, P. K. and Miller, J. D. 1975. Speech perception in early infancy: discrimination of speech sound categories. *Journal of the Acoustical Society of America*, 58 (Supplement 1): S56.

Lasky, R., Syrdal-Lasky, A. and Klein, R. 1975. VOT discrimination by four-to-six-month-old infants from Spanish environments. *Journal of Experimental Child Psychology*, 20:215–25.

Lehiste, I. 1970. *Suprasegmentals*. Cambridge: MIT Press.

Liberman, A. M. 1957. Some results of research on speech perception. *Journal of the Acoustical Society of America*, 29:117–23.

   1970. The grammars of speech and language. *Cognitive Psychology*, 1:301–23.

Liberman, A. M., Cooper, F. S., Shankweiler, D. P. and Studdert-Kennedy, M. 1967. Perception of the speech code. *Psychological Review*, 74:431–61.

Liberman, A. M., Harris, K. S., Kinney, J. and Lane, H. 1961. The discrimination of relative onset time of the components of certain speech and non-speech patterns. *Journal of Experimental Psychology*, 61:379–88.

Liberman, A. M., Mattingly, I. G. and Turvey, M. T. 1972. Language codes and memory codes. In A. W. Melton and E. Martin (eds.), *Coding processes in human memory*. Washington, DC: V. H. Winston.

Liberman, A. M. and Pisoni, D. B. 1977. Evidence for a special speech-perceiving subsystem in the human. In T. H. Bullock (ed.), *Recognition of complex acoustic signals*. Life Sciences Research Report 5. Berlin: Dahlem Konferenzen.

Liberman, A. M., Repp, B. H., Eccardt, T. and Pesetsky, D. 1977. Some relations between duration of silence and duration of friction noise as joint cues for fricatives, affricatives, and stops. *Journal of the Acoustical Society of America*, 62 (Supplement 1: S78(A).

Liberman, A. M. and Studdert-Kennedy, M. In press. Phonetic perception. In R. Held, H. Leibowitz, and H.-L. Teuber (eds.), *Handbook of sensory physiology*, vol. VIII, *Perception*. Heidelberg: Springer-Verlag Inc.

Lisker, L. and Abramson, A. S. 1964. A cross-language study of voicing of initial stops: acoustical measurements. *Word*, 20:384–422.

Marler, P. 1970. A comparative approach to vocal learning: song development in white-crowned sparrows. *Journal of Comparative and Physiological Psychology*, 71:1–25.

1976. Social organization, communication and graded signals: Vocal behavior of the chimpanzee and the gorilla. In P. Bateson and R. A. Hinde (eds.), *Growing points in ethology*. Cambridge: Cambridge University Press.

1977. Development and learning of recognition systems. In T. H. Bullock (ed.), *Recognition of complex acoustic signals*. Berlin: Dahlem Konferenzen.

Marler, P. and Peters, S. 1977. Selective vocal learning in sparrows. *Science*, 198:519–21.

Morse, P. A. 1972. The discrimination of speech and non-speech stimuli in early infancy. *Journal of Experimental Child Psychology*, 14:477.

Pastore, R. E. 1976. Categorical perception: a critical re-evaluation. In S. K. Hirsh et al. (eds.), *Hearing and Davis: Essays honoring Hallowell Davis*. St Louis, Missouri: Washington University Press.

Piaget, J. 1968. *The language and thought of the child*. 3rd edn. London: Routledge and Kegan Paul.

Raphael, L. J., Dorman, M. F. and Liberman, A. M. 1976. Some ecological constraints on the perception of stops and affricates. *Journal of the Acoustical Society of America*, 59 (Supplement 1): S25A.

Repp, B. H., Liberman, A. M., Eccardt, T. and Pesetsky, D. 1978 (in press). Perceptual integration of cries for stop, fricative, and affricative manner. *Journal of Experimental Psychology: Human Perception and Performance*, 4.

Rowell, T. E. 1962. Agonistic noises of the rhesus monkey. *Symposia of the Zoological Society of London*, 8:91–6.

Rowell, T. E. and Hinde, R. A. 1962. Vocal communication by the rhesus monkey (*Macaca mulatta*). *Proceedings of the Zoological Society of London*, 138:279–94.

Sackett, G. P. 1966. Monkeys reared in isolation with pictures as visual input: evidence for an innate releasing mechanism. *Science*, 154:1468–73.

Schott, D. 1975. Quantitative analysis of the vocal repertoire of squirrel monkeys (*Saimiri sciureus*). *Zeitschrift für Tierpsychologie*, 38:225–50.

Seligman, M. E. P. and Hager, P. L. 1972. *Biological boundaries of learning*. New York: Appleton-Century-Crofts.

Shettleworth, S. J. 1972. Constraints on learning. In D. S. Lehrman, R. A. Hinde and E. Shaw (eds.), *Advances in the study of behavior*. New York: Academic Press.

Skinner, B. F. 1957. *Verbal behavior*. New York: Appleton-Century-Crofts.

Streeter, L. A. 1975. Language perception of 2-month old infants shows effects of both innate mechanisms and experience. *Nature*, 259:39–41.

Studdert-Kennedy, M. G. 1977. Universals in phonetic structure and their role in linguistic communication. In T. H. Bullock (ed.), *Recognition of complex acoustic signals*. Berlin: Dahlem Konferenzen.

Studdert-Kennedy, M., Liberman, A. M., Harris, K. S. and Cooper, F. S. 1970. The motor theory of speech perception: a reply to Lane's critical review. *Psychological Review*, 77:234–49.

Tinbergen, N. 1951. *The study of instinct*. London: Oxford University Press.

Tinbergen, N. and Perdeck, A. C. 1950. On the stimulus situation releasing the begging response in the newly-hatched herring gull chick (*Larus a. argentatus* Pont.). *Behaviour*, 3:1–38.

Winter, P., Ploog, D. and Latta, J. 1966. Vocal repertoire of the squirrel monkey (*Saimiri sciureus*), its analysis and significance. *Experimental Brain Research*, 1:359–84.

Wood, C. C., Goff, W. P. and Day, R. S. 1971. Auditory evoked potentials during speech perception. *Science*, 173:1248–51.

Zoloth, S. and Green, S. In press. Perception of intergraded vocal signals by Japanese macaques. *Brain Behavior and Evolution*.

11. Language Development

11.1. Language origins[1]

DAVID McNEILL

Vocalization may not have been important initially in the origin of human language (Hewes 1973). In the ontogenesis of language vocalization is obviously important, but this importance exists mainly in the relation of vocalization to the simultaneous emergence of representational schemata. The distinctive ontogenetic process is the formation of *syntagmata*, which are the joint result of communicative movements on the one hand, and meaningful schemata or what I shall call *sensory-motor representations* on the other. These terms may not be familiar and I will explain them in the first two sections below. In this paper, I will consider the question of language origins from the point of view of the function of signs, and propose some uses of signs that could have provided a basis for the natural selection of syntagmata. Such an argument is compatible with a gestural origin of language, although it does not presuppose it.

Sensory-motor representations

Consider the following sentences. 'The sun rose on the frozen scene. The men stopped their cars beside the river. Bacon started to walk. He barely escaped a fierce winter storm.' In addition to relating a story, each of these sentences corresponds to the idea of an event. An event, according to von Wright (1963), is a change of state that takes place through an interval of time. One state, for example, is that the sun had not risen; then it had risen; and this change of state is an event. The representation of an event is an example of what I will refer to as a sensory-motor representation. Such representations can be traced back to a schematic organization of

[1] Preparation of this paper was supported by NIMH grant MH 26451–03.

715

action patterns, and take form when action schemes come to represent absent preceptions (Piaget 1954).

The presence of concrete sensory-motor representations in speech is a phenomenon that has received almost no attention from linguists or psychologists, and philosophers have discussed them only insofar as they wish to remove such ideas from the analysis of meanings. However, sensory-motor representations play a fundamental role in speech programming and articulation.

Sensory-motor representations occupy a unique position epistemologically. They are simultaneously part of action and part of meaning. Sensory-motor representations convey meanings which can be represented with action schemes. For example, the idea of an event (one kind of an event) can be represented in a causative action sequence involving an object and a person who is the agent of a change in state in the object. 'The men stopped their cars' is an event of this kind. This action scheme, when organized into a schematic pattern, can represent one type of an event. Other action schemes can represent actions, states, properties, entities, locations, etc.

Among the meanings which are representable in sensory-motor action schemes, together with a brief definition of the scheme itself, are the following:

> event – change of state
> action – the performance due to a performer
> state – condition before or after an event
> property – condition on an event or entity
> entity – the object concept (cf. Piaget)
> person – animate being (cf. Piaget)
> location – terminus or place of an event (cf. Piaget)

I have used these definitions to classify speech samples into segments which correspond to different sensory-motor representations. There is evidence that sensory-motor segments correspond in many cases to the units that speakers operate on in programming and producing speech output. This brings us to the second term introduced above, the syntagma.

The syntagma

The integration of speech output will be said to take place within syntagmata. This term has been used by Kozhevnikov and Chistovich (1965), who defined it as one meaning unit pronounced as a single output. It can be compared to Lashley's concept of an organizational scheme (Lashley

1951). The syntagma, as a theoretical concept, unites the articulation of speech with meaning. We shall say that the organization of speech articulation occurs within a single meaning structure. This is the syntagma. We should therefore expect that measures of output integration (phonemic clauses, maximization of temporal control, etc.) will coincide with meaning integration as speech is produced, and this result has been found. If speakers do generate speech output from syntagmata, we can describe the speaking process in the following terms. The speaker organizes and moves from one meaning unit to another. This includes sensory-motor meanings. As these new meanings are organized in the speaker's conceptions, fresh syntagmata become available. Hence there is an integrated articulation of speech output which coincides with the expression of meaning through sensory-motor representations.

In contrast to linguistic entities such as phrases, sentences, sentoids, etc., the syntagma is a unit of speech functioning. It may or may not correspond to the familiar structural units of linguistics, and it varies widely in size relative to linguistic levels of description. My assumption is that functional and structural units need not correspond in any fixed or obvious way, and that units of functioning must be approached without *a priori* expectation of a correspondence with linguistic units, on their own terms.

Origin of syntagmata in ontogenesis

To explain the function of sensory-motor representations within syntagmata further, it is necessary to consider the basis of these representations in the organization of action, and the basis of this organization in hierarchies of control over motor processes. According to Bernstein (1967) and other action theorists (Greene 1972), the performance of coordinated actions of any kind is the output of hierarchies of control processes. The most subordinate levels in these hierarchies are the localized actions of specific muscle groups. Higher levels are characterized by domains limited to activating and controlling the processes which are immediately below them. Successively higher levels are associated with increasing remoteness from the actual musculature and with increasing generality of the control mechanisms. At the most superordinate levels, the scale of generality can be equated with that of an action scheme, i.e. an overall plan of the action as one of a certain type, free of the details of actual operations. A scheme of this kind has been called the concept of the action by Turvey (1975).

An advantage of viewing action schemes in terms of hierarchies of control processes is that it becomes possible to see how two initially distinct hierarchies can be combined. This is possible, since the result can still be an action. For example, the lower levels of processes from hierarchy B can be inserted under the upper levels of processes of hierarchy A. This requires that the upper levels of A should be able to control only a few degrees of freedom in B. The result is a new action hierarchy, AB, the concept of which is A, and the motoric effect B.

During the sensory-motor period of a child's development (Piaget 1954), there is a convergence of two separate action systems, and the AB model appears to describe this situation. One system consists of sensory-motor action schemata of the type already mentioned. These schemata provide the principal basis of representation at the sensory-motor stage. We shall call this system A. The other system, B, is the basis of motor control over the speech musculature itself. This system passes through a complex development of its own during the same period (Jakobson 1941). Systems A and B are not isolated from each other during this time. Contacts occur quite early and there may be AB fusions even during the first year. However, these initial contacts are limited in scope and are not frequent. But during this time there gradually emerges what can be called a developmentally new form of action (speech) and meaning based on AB fusions, and by the end of the sensory-motor period the convergence is quite widespread. Sensory-motor representations have come to function as the highest levels of the control hierarchies of articulatory actions. These fusions make possible syntagmata in which meanings (sensory-motor representations) organize articulation and speech output; they form meaning units pronounced as single outputs. Meanings, represented in sensory-motor schemata, now activate and direct movements of the articulatory organs.

The motivation for this fusion of representational schemata with the control hierarchies of articulation is presumably innate in the species. There are no apparent alternate reasons why movements of the lips, jaw, tongue, velum, uvula, larynx, etc., should be connected with sensory-motor representational schemes. A universal connection, which always appears in ontogenesis at approximately the same time, is plausibly treated as an innate characteristic. This may have evolved due to selection pressures that have little to do with the functional organization of human communication, or there may have been some gain in efficiency by shifting to syntagmata expressed through articulatory movements (an example of 'ritualization'). According to the gestural theory of language origins, in any case, these vocal AB fusions emerged in a second stage of evolution, following an initial stage in which the B part of the fusion was manual and closer to the domain of sensory-motor representations. It is because of some such 'natural affinity' of gestures with sensory-motor representations of meaning that the gesture theory appears plausible.

The gesture theory of the origin of language

Hewes (1973) has revitalized the gesture theory of the origin of language. This theory states that the original mode of linguistic communication in hominids was manual, not vocal. Vocalizations appeared later and were grafted onto a gestural system already evolved to some degree. Hewes cites the following evidence against vocalization as the first channel of linguistic communication (by 'linguistic' is meant communication that is capable of propositionalizing and denoting). (1) Primate calls are mainly 'emotional' or reactive to events, and only weakly denotative or propositional. (2) These calls are not under close voluntary control or inhibition, and are thus quite unlike the manipulative behavior of the same primates. (3) Electrical stimulation of monkey brain can elicit natural sounding calls, but the brain sites do not correspond to the speech areas of the human brain. (4) Human language decoding and encoding depend on linkages between the auditory input areas, the limbic system, and the motor speech centers usually in the left cerebral hemisphere. (5) Auditory-visual connections are weak or absent in monkeys and apes, and therefore are not likely to have been established early in the evolution of hominids. (6) There is evidence, based on the reconstruction of the articulatory tract of a Neanderthal specimen, that the full range of human speech sounds has been reached only recently. These various points of evidence may be open to differing interpretations in some cases, but taken together they add to the plausibility of the central assumption of the gesture theory, that initially human linguistic communication was not primarily vocal.

That it may have been primarily manual is less well established. Hewes relies heavily on an analogy with the successful attempts by Premack (1976), Gardner and Gardner (1971), and others to have chimpanzees use systems of manual communication that possess some of the properties of language. Early hominids could have evolved equivalent manual systems (over vastly longer periods of time). (Hewes, of course, does not propose that these hypothetical systems would have in any way resembled the manual systems that have been used in modern experiments.)

Two other indirect forms of evidence can be added to strengthen this conclusion. One is the invention without tutelage of a gestural system of communication by deaf children (Goldin-Meadow 1975). The other is the manner of integration of gestures with speech by normal adults (Kendon 1975).

Goldin-Meadow has observed the development of a means of gestural communication used by several unacquainted deaf children. These children have hearing parents who are committed to oralist principles of education, so they were taught no manual signs. Therefore, the children's use of manual gestures is an almost pure situation of a communication system emerging without linguistic input. There was, of course, communicative interaction with parents, but the parents rarely produced sequences of gestures, as the children did. (The children received concurrent speech training, but at least initially there was little chance of this affecting the system of gestures, since the latter developed much more rapidly.) In all cases, the deaf children were seen to have devised their own manual signs. Many of these were based on actual movements. And they combined signs into sequences with relatively stable 'word' order preferences. The most rapidly developing child eventually made use of such sophisticated devices as clausal embeddings. The steps in the development of these sign systems occur in a regular sequence, and at times which resemble the development of vocal speech by hearing children.

It seems from Goldin-Meadow's results that human children can use manual systems of communication which have linguistic properties. This capacity appears in the linguistic vacuum produced by deafness. That there is such a capacity appearing under these conditions is consistent with the theory that vocal speech overlies an ability for manual communication. When vocal speech is blocked the original gestural system remains.

Kendon (1975) has written as follows:

Our observations suggest that gesture is not so much a common accompaniment to speech but that it is an integral part of the whole act of uttering; that it is not just a kinesic paralanguage but that it may be employed, even in the apparently highly verbal situations we have studied, to encode many different aspects of the ideas being given expression. The notion that gesture may convey nuances, emphasis, or contradiction is correct. However, it also may encode the most central and abstract ideas also being encoded in speech.   (Kendon 1975:366)

In support of this conclusion I can mention some observations of my own. These show that the spontaneous gestures which accompany speech tend to coincide with sensory-motor segments in the speech output. In one conversation, for example, 86% of 500 gestures which were analyzed coincided with the expression of sensory-motor content, and another 8% may have done so. ('Coincide' means operationally the following: the intention movements marking the beginning of a gesture occur within a syllable or less, within 180 msec., of the onset of a speech segment which corresponds to a sensory-motor representation. Also, the gesture ends within a syllable of the termination of this speech segment, either because a new gesture begins or the hand starts to move to a rest position. These observations must be made from video records.) In other words, even with adult speakers, there remains a close synchrony of hand movements and articulation plans. Such a degree of synchronization (which may not be limited to the hands) is consistent with the idea that both the speech output and the gestures involve a common process, as the gesture theory of language would predict.

Extension of the gesture theory

This theory, however, is inadequately formulated, since it lacks any notion of representation. The sense in which movements become gestures is accordingly not stated. It is at this point that I wish to connect the earlier discussion of syntagmata with the present one of the gesture theory of language origins.

Even assuming that the gesture theory of language origins is correct, the use of gestures is not the first step that we should explain. The key step is the use of sensory-motor representations as the basis of syntagmata (gestural and/or vocal). The representation of information about the world in the form of schemata based on actions makes gestures into signs; they cease to be mere actions. The gestures arise from the same schemata as organize the actions and represent information about the world. Hence the gestures can refer to this information. Because the movements summarized in schemata and the gestural movements which result from schemata can be similar, gestures are a plausible initial form of original linguistic output (whereas acoustic broadcast transmission is a more plausible ultimate form, once there has been selection for its greater efficiency, advantages for communication during manipulation, etc.). A back and forth sawing motion is a gesture that arises from the same sensory-motor scheme which represents the operation of sawing wood. Thinking in terms of this action scheme, one can mentally represent the action of sawing wood. Making the gesture based on this scheme, one can refer to this action. The production of the gesture can be organized from a syntagma in which the representational part A is the sensory-motor scheme of the action of sawing, and the motoric part B is the back and forth movement of the hand.

In another study of gestures (McNeill 1975), I had adult speakers describe the process of mental paper folding. For example, they were presented with the diagram in figure 1 and told that it is a cut-out sheet of paper, creased where shown, and that they were to imagine folding it into a three dimensional cube. (The arrows meet when this is done and the shaded square is at the bottom.)

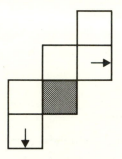

1. Mental paper folding (after Shepard and Feng 1972).

Although not instructed to do so, the speakers nearly always performed gestures as they described this process. These movements simulated the movements which would have been made if an actual paper cut-out had been folded, and the gestures were synchronized with the speech. For example, one person said 'I'll fold the left side up', and his left hand simultaneously moved from a position parallel to the table top to an upright position perpendicular to it. This movement began concurrently with the articulation of 'I'. There are many other such examples.

Logically, we should try to explain the ability to form such syntagmata based on sensory-motor representations. What functional advantages are there in such a communication system, compared to a system (for example) based on reactions to present stimuli?

Advantages of a communication system based on sensory-motor representations

The following proposals do not comprise an exhaustive list. They do reflect advantages of sensory-motor representations in situations which have been proposed by others as being of importance in the evolution of man; and in these situations sensory-motor representations seem to be uniquely advantageous. Such advantages may have led to the natural selection of a hereditary capacity to use syntagmata in communicative systems (gestural and/or vocal).

These advantages reside outside the communication system itself. They are not primarily defined as *improvements* in communication. This is not to say that an ability to use language-like communication did not also evolve under pressures which may have worked primarily on the process of communication itself. A shift to vocal from gestural communication might be an example of this kind of natural selection. But the advantages listed below are more fundamental. They could have caused the selection of the basic type of communication system, either gestural or vocal; that is, one which rests on the use of syntagmata. All are applications of the same principle, which is that signs based on sensory-motor represen- tations can function as *vicarious actions*. Therefore, anything which selects the actions for which they substitute should tend to select the ability to form signs based on sensory-motor representations at the same time.

1. The use of sensory-motor representations extends and replaces imitation

With signs that are based on sensory-motor representations, it is possible for an adult to give, through gestures or speech, the same kind of instruc- tion as can be given by a demonstration. The same or nearly the same action schemata are inculcated by the adult's gestures or utterances as by demonstrations of the actions themselves. This advantage would exist for both the teacher and the learner. One does not actually have to saw wood to demonstrate or imitate the process of sawing. If the communication system uses sensory-motor representations one can make a back and forth movement of the hands in the air or say something which means 'saw', and activate the same or approximately the same action scheme. The learner can practice in the sign mode rather than in an actual behavior mode, and the effect on the action scheme would tend to be the same as doing the real thing.

Whatever advantages arise from a capacity to imitate, therefore, could transfer to a capacity to form signs based specifically on sensory-motor representations. If imitation was selected, these syntagmata could have been too, as a superior method of imitation. Imitation is a form of 'envi- ronment tracking' (Wilson 1975), and is particularly well developed in certain of the primates, man included. It is involved in play, tool use,

724   Language development

social learning, and many other functions besides. This role of imitation has been documented in a variety of psychological studies of children, and has been shown in chimpanzees by van Lawick-Goodall (1971).

2. The use of sensory-motor representations allows a convergence of play with signs onto play with materials

Play with signs may be important for the development of language skill itself in children, but the advantage I have in mind under this heading is the same as that of playing with nonlinguistic materials. The advantages of being able to play with physical objects, social interactants, and other things in the environment could transfer to play with signs if these are based on sensory-motor representations. Specifically, the part of play which is correlated with the development of action schemata could be transferred. Play is thought to be crucial for the development of skills, social interactions, an individual's place in the social matrix, and so forth (see Bruner, Jolly, and Silva 1976 for a survey of play and its functions). It is possible, to some degree, to play at these activities, although in fact only signs are being played with. (An entire industry of children's entertainment is based on this premise.)

Most collections of children's linguistic games are organized for the purpose of showing that their play contributes to the development of linguistic skill (e.g. Weir 1962, Cazden 1976). Nonetheless, if we look at these examples in a different way, we can often see how the same games could contribute to play in a wider sense as well, via a sensory-motor basis of linguistic signs. The following examples, mentioned by Weir, are from her two and a half year old son, who was in the habit of engaging in prolonged monologues before falling asleep. In these examples and all others below, the child was recorded alone in his bedroom. Weir's son was not deaf, and the examples are of speech, not gestures.

I go up there
I go up there
I go
she go up there

This is a game of pronominal replacement (Weir's interpretation), but at the level of sensory-motor representation it is also a game of alternation between actors. Another example is this:

I'm fixing the door
Door's open
I'm locking

There is practice here at substituting differently marked verbs (Weir), but also play at the level of sensory-motor representation with a clear sequence of events.

Practically any example of children's linguistic play can be seen simultaneously as vicarious play with social or physical materials at the representational level. This possibility of vicarious play could have been an advantage for the sensory-motor form of representation which led to the selection of an ability to form these kinds of syntagma as a superior kind of play (or at least as another, quite different kind).

Bruner (1976b) describes some of the functions served by play with objects and other things in the environment. Each of these could be served vicariously by playing with signs. (1) Play is 'a means of minimizing the consequences of one's actions and of learning, therefore, in less risky situations' (p. 38). The examples quoted above from Weir could be regarded as instances of this function, and they are produced in an even less risky form than play with real objects. (2) Play allows the young a chance to try out combinations of behavior that would not otherwise be attempted. Bruner cites examples such as a chimpanzee's play with sticks, licking the ends, poking them into holes, and the like. A linguistic analogue mentioned by Weir, which would seem to serve a combinatorial function vicariously and far more spectacularly than play with real objects, is this:

lock the door
mail all the letter
mailman
doggie can bite the mailman
bite all the letters
mailman have a bite
bite the letters.

Bruner argues that an association between play and tool use may have been built in during hominid evolution (this is noticeable in chimpanzees also), because play helps the process of mastering the use of tools. The same argument points to the conclusion that a capacity to form syntagmata based on sensory-motor representations would also be selected at the same time, since this capacity likewise helps in the mastery of tools, by simulating play and imitation. This would be an explanation of why there is a connection between tool use and language-like communication. It is not only that language is a kind of tool, but that the capacity to use signs with sensory-motor representations contributes to the capacity to master tools of various kinds.

The type of linguistic play which could do this is illustrated by the following examples from Weir. The first is a sequence of actions which corresponds to components of object manipulation:

it took it
bring it back
took them
took it down
he took it

The following examples, not necessarily contiguous in the child's discourse (though they occurred in the same session), show parallels with object manipulation:

Daddy give it
milk in the bottle
I spilled it
let Daddy have it
take off
turn around
pick up the [dɔn]
I can pick up
I can
put on a record for you
what Daddy got
Daddy got
I put this in here
see the doggie here

3. The use of sensory-motor representations aids development and rehearsal of plans

A complex goal-directed action consists of two or more parts. These parts are actions which can be regarded as modular in that they may be learned and practiced separately from one another. They are combined into new actions under the headings provided by goals. This description more or less corresponds to that found in Miller, Galanter and Pribram (1960) under the designation of plans. When complex, plans require development and may require practice. Whatever advantages there are which would have selected a capacity to develop and practice complex plans could have selected sensory-motor based syntagmata at the same time.

The individual can assemble and try out different combinations of action modules in the sign mode, and the effect of doing this approximates doing the same with real actions. For example, one can gesture (to himself or someone else) with a back and forth movement; then perform a lifting movement; and finally point to the woodshed (or say something which means these things). And all of these actions arranged in this order lay down a plan which can guide behavior without one actually having to perform real actions (thus there may be savings in terms of energy expenditure and risk). The same gestures and utterances obviously lend themselves to group planning.

Some examples from the presleep monologues of Weir's son seem to show the planning of complex actions in the sign mode. For instance:

I hope so

clean out the drawer

excuse me

and also:

Bobo has a hat

take off the hat

hat for Anthony and Bobo

for Bobo, not Anthony

hat for Anthony

(Anthony was the child's name.) In each of these, there are different sensory-motor representations which correspond to action modules directed toward goals (cleaning out the drawer; getting the hat). Whatever advantages exist in such practice and development of complex action sequences could have transferred to a communication system based on syntagmata.

Conclusion

The advantages of sensory-motor representations for human communication are such that selection pressures causing an evolution toward greater imitation, play, and purposiveness in general could have selected a system which rests on syntagmata at the same time. This argument does not explain the appearance of sensory-motor representations in the first place, though it explains how such representations could have become part of the communication system.

Other species which are capable of sensory-motor representations could be expected to feel the same natural selection pressures. Chimpanzees, for one, appear to have the ability to form sensory-motor representations. They also have evolved imitation, play, and goal-directed behavior; and they have proven capable of forming syntagmata as well, as shown by Premack (1976) and Gardner and Gardner (1971). However, they seem not to have undergone the further development of vocal syntagmata.

Chimpanzees may therefore serve as a model of the communication potentialities of the hominid which evolved into man, at the origin of language (Hewes 1973). According to this model, evolution has selected the ability to produce syntagmata – defined as behavior sequences which are programmed on the basis of meaning (sensory-motor representations). Such behavior sequences are of the same kind as the action schemata from which the sensory-motor representations themselves are derived (i.e. they are mostly manual movements). There is, at the same time, a parallel but underutilized vocal channel which is involved in a quite separate vocal communication system, reactive and not propositional.

The recruitment of this vocal channel by the system of syntagmata apparently has not taken place in the chimpanzee. The most straight-forward proposal for what may have transpired in the case of man is that the evolutionary development of vocalization was an example of the process of ritualization. (The name trivializes the significance of this shift.) According to this proposal, the use of syntagmata exploited pre-existing connections between and within the motor areas of the brain for the hands and the mouth articulators and the auditory input areas (Sherrington 1947, Penfield and Rasmussen 1952). The advantages of the vocal channel over the manual for purposes of efficient communication ('display') have been described by Wilson (1975) and Hewes (1973). Once the vocalization process was underway, further evolutionary changes might have taken place both in the brain and in the mouth; the mouth may have been structurally modified for communication use (Lieberman and Crelin 1971). We observe a pattern in man today which is consistent with this picture. Speech overlies a substrate of gestures (Kendon 1975), and gestures have sufficient linguistic structural properties to assume some of the duties of language communication in the absence of speech (Goldin-Meadow 1975).

11.2. Language acquisition: a human ethological problem?[1]

KLAUS FOPPA

Whatever the function of human language may be, its communicative possibilities are obvious. Since many nonhuman species also dispose of very effective and differentiated communication systems, one could easily be led to assume that there must exist evolutionary connections between one or the other animal communication system and human language. If both systems have common structural or functional features, certain aspects of language behavior could be homologized with structural elements of nonhuman communicative behavior, or one could look for convergent developments, i.e. for analogies (von Cranach 1976).

Despite the impressive research with chimpanzees (Gardner and Gardner 1971, Premack and Premack 1972, Fouts 1975) it is to be doubted that the trained ASL-using chimp resembles speaking man in its essential features (Limber 1977) or manifests the link between linguistic and non-linguistic animals. It is not only that 'the development of human speech represents a quantum jump', as Wilson points out (1975:556), but that the differences between *spontaneously developing* human and nonhuman communication systems are enormous. To mention only a few: human language is extremely flexible with respect to its form as well as to its content; it has a time perspective, which means that one can speak about past and future events; it is independent of the concrete situation (i.e. one can deal verbally with actually not present or nonexistent objects as well as with abstract contents); it allows for the expression of logical relations

[1] I am grateful to Marie-Louise Kaesermann for critical comments on an earlier version of this paper and for technical assistance; and to Roger Masters who went through a preliminary draft for stylistic corrections.

and for metacommunication (i.e. one can communicate about language with lingual means).

Most important in our context, however, is the fact that language behavior develops gradually. During a period of several years the child achieves relative control over the language that is spoken in his environment. It has to be stressed, however, that it is not simply German, English or Chinese which the child learns but specific idiolects, sociolects and dialects. Usually the older child disposes of at least two different codes. A Swiss-German infant, for example, not only has to learn the dialect of his region (in the specific idio- and sociolectic form spoken in his family), but to acquire High-German (after all, another language) for reading, writing and 'official' communication.

Neither this bi- or multilingualism, nor any of the above mentioned discriminative features of human language, immediately suggest the possibility that the process of language acquisition could be treated as a biological problem in general or as a human ethological one in particular. But instead of aiming at a premature answer, I shall try to highlight some aspects of the ontogenesis of language which are frequently neglected by developmental psycholinguists, and to discuss some of the preliminary results from studies of the Bernese Group of Language Development. One or the other of them will, I hope, shed some light on our question.

Communication and language development[2]

Mothers are not only eager to respond to the infant's first cries in the appropriate way, but later they try to 'understand' what his babbling 'means'. Months before the first sequences of sounds (similar to the language's phonemes and to a certain word's structure and meaning) are consistently used, the child is able to point to things that he wants. It is important to note that this is no one-way communication and that there are not only 'communicative moments' in the mother–child interaction. As Papoušek and Papoušek (1975:254) emphasize: 'The most impressive feature of the interaction between infant and mother is the continuous sequence of short scenes in which the two members *mutually* stimulate and reinforce one another.'

It is held that this relatively effective form of communication is not only important for the child's cognitive development (Papoušek and Papoušek 1975, Trevarthen, chapter 8.2 above), but that it is also essential for his

[2] See e.g. Francescato 1973, Bruner 1976a, Moerk 1977.

later abilities. Nevertheless it is quite unclear why and how the child's preverbal communicative behavior is transformed into his later speaking behavior. Moerk (1977), for example, describes the process in the following rather unspecific way: 'The expressive function of communication is inborn and can be found from birth on as reflexive-instinctual crying which expresses a general form of excitement. *Soon, however, the communication of the infant becomes more and more differentiated, approaches stepwise the endstate of linguistic communication*' (my italics). However, nonverbal and paralingual means of information-transmission (intonation, rhythm of speech etc.) continue to be indispensable elements of face-to-face communication even when the linguistic abilities are fully developed.

Transcribed spoken language is often almost incomprehensible as long as contextual information and paralingual and nonverbal concomitants are missing:

(1) /Well far as I could see well I don't know how to begin you know because my father he never had it you know too easy you know ah childhood. . . ./[3]

The better sentences are formed, the less their intelligibility depends on nonlinguistic cues. Take, for example, a stratified version of (1). While (1) is hard to understand without knowledge of context, intonation and stress, (2) is readily comprehensible.

(2) /Well, as far as I can see my father never had too easy a childhood. . ./

This is especially important with respect to child language. Since children's utterances are mostly incorrect and incomplete even when the speakers are well beyond Brown's Stage I (Brown 1973), the effectiveness of communication between the child and his social environment depends on additional information.

Take, for example, the following utterances spoken by a twenty-three month old boy (Kaesermann 1978):

(3) /Eto do miuch/ (Eto – the boy's name, correctly 'Reto' – there milk) which is hard to understand. Even with intonation marks

(3a)   /Eto do miuch/

it is not quite clear if the boy wants to *get* some milk into his cup or if the utterance is meant to be a proposition:/I *have* milk there in my

[3] Data from L. Alberti, personal communication.

cup/. Only the following utterances make clear what the boy's intentions are:

(4) /Eto do di/ (Eto there in *or* into)

and after his mother does not understand:

(5) /Eto tinke/ (Eto drink)

(By the way, all three sentences are incorrect and incomplete Bernese German sentences with respect to syntax and/or grammar and/or word form.) Interestingly enough, the child seems to dispose of some knowledge of paralingual cueing well before he actually begins to speak. As Aebi (1977) has shown in a thorough analysis of 'dialogues' between mothers and their babbling children, there are clear cut indications that the mean length of their switching pauses converges over the months. Beyond that it is well known that at the age of about seven months infants' babblings are marked by different intonation contours, similar to adults' intonation patterns (e.g. Tonkova-Jampolskaja 1973). All this presupposes a relatively early comprehension of certain distinctive features of dialogic interactions. In fact, as Aebi (1977) has demonstrated, the mean length of vocalizations in monologic situations is significantly longer than in dialogues even with four month old infants.

Variability of children's utterances

If one scans the literature on developmental psycholinguistics, one gets the impression that the language behavior of the child can be characterized as relatively stable. That means that the child, able to produce utterances of a certain kind, will preserve these patterns as long as he remains in the respective stage of development. Any variation should therefore be a symptom of a developmental step, and hence the new linguistic form should be less deficient than the old one. This is by no means the case. Within half an hour or less you may hear many variations of one and the same word or utterance.

Take, for example, the following transcription of an unsuccessful discourse between mother and child (Kaesermann 1978). Mother and child are sitting side by side; mother is looking at an illustrated newspaper. To the picture of a grape she gives the Bernese German name: 'Trübu' (*Traube*). After a while the boy wants to go back to that picture but is unable to pronounce the word correctly. His trials read as follows (mother's questions are omitted; they would have to be placed after each line of child's utterances):

(6) /díbu/   /dibu/
     /díbu/   /díbu/
     /dóbu/   /debu/   /díbu/
     /díbuch/ /dubu/   /díbu/
     /dóbu/
     /dóbu/
     /dóbuch/
     /dóbu/   /dóbu/
     /dóbu/
     /díbu/

The recordings of a monologue of one of Weir's sons (1966) are very similar:

(7)   [əːnč], [əɪndž], [əɪdž], [ənts]
        (all items are variations of the word 'orange')

We shall have to return to these examples; suffice it to say for the moment that this tendency to vary one's utterances in case of an uncomprehending partner might be a very effective strategy. By enlarging the sample of variant forms of realization of one and the same communicative intention, the probability of a correct interpretation by the partner should rise. On a much more elaborate level, we as adults proceed in a very similar manner: suspecting that our partner has not correctly understood what we intended to say, we try to explain it with other words. The child's verbal variations in communicative situations seem to serve the same goals. However, this cannot be the whole story. As Weir's example clearly demonstrates, variations do occur independently of any actual communicative intent. We shall deal with this problem a little bit later.

Children's communicative intentions and language development

The variability of language behavior within one stage of development should not obscure the fact that it is the variations across the stages which usually interest the developmental psycholinguist. This is important to note, because it helps to explain why certain problems are stressed at the expense of others. There are many studies of the syntactic (structural) or the semantic (pragmatic) transformations in children's language through the years, or of the cognitive presuppositions for certain linguistic achieve-ments. The respective merits of these approaches will not be discussed. I only want to stress the fact that other more general problems have been neglected on account of these dominant interests of psycholinguists.

For example, why is there language acquisition at all? The child's effective preverbal communication seems (as mentioned above) to render any further communicative development unnecessary. Of course, one could assume that the ontogenesis of speech is due to maturational processes. But this assumption would not explain very much, and would not take into account the definite influences of the child's social environ-ment on the process of language acquisition (e.g. Dunn, chapter 9.2 above). As one of the very few who realizes the existence of this problem, Brown (1973:410) writes:

What impels the child to 'improve' his speech at all remains something of a mystery. We can take 'improve' simply to mean 'bring into closer approximation to the speech of older persons around the child'. It is surprising that there should be any mystery about forces impelling improvement because it is just this aspect of the process that most people imagine that they understand. Surely the improvement is a response to selection pressures of various kinds; ill-formed or incomplete utterances must be less effective than well-formed and complete utterances in accomplishing the child's intent; parents probably approve of well-formed utterances and disapprove or correct the ill-formed. These ideas sound sensible and may be correct but the still scant evidence available does not support them.

And further on: 'In sum, then, we do not presently have evidence that there are selection pressures of any kind operating on children to impel them to bring their speech into line with adult models' (p. 412).

Whereas Brown considers the child's communicative intention at least a possible factor in language development (even if its influence is not yet demonstrated), for Lenneberg it is inadmissible to state that the child begins to speak because it has a need to communicate (1967:125). He explicitly describes the eighteen month old as making 'no attempt at communicating information and (showing) no frustration for not being understood' (p. 129). But is the child really not interested in getting some message through? Are there in fact no communicative intentions and no selection pressures operating? Would it not be hard to understand why, for example, the boy in (6) is desperately trying to make clear what he wants? For Lenneberg and Brown the existence of something like com-municative intentions is either not possible to prove at all or at least not yet proved. The proof, however, should not be impossible.

It was Kaesermann's (1978) idea that if the child were interested in making himself understood (at least when he addresses a partner), situations where the partner does not understand should provoke variations of utterances similar to those in (6). Plausible as this was, there were two difficulties to overcome: first, there are not many instances of spontaneous lack of understanding of children's utterances by mothers; second, one can not always be quite sure if the mother has understood or not. It was Amstutz (another member of the Bernese Group of Language Development) who proposed a very simple but effective operationalization (1977): if one instructs the child's partner from time to time to show signs of incomprehension by simply asking 'mhm?' 'what?' etc. after an utterance, this should provoke the intended language variations. If so, Kaesermann concluded, one could assume that the child has in fact – contrary to Lenneberg's conviction – communicative intentions which could possibly explain the selective pressures responsible for the instigation of language development.

Currently there are five studies under way, all using the same technique. Different kinds of subjects are used: children of different age, children of different social class, bilinguals, and children with language disturbances. Up to now it can be stated that independent of age, social class, etc., there is a strong tendency to modify the utterance if the child gets the impression that he or she is not being understood. Over the different subjects and the different situations 80–90% of the 'mhm?' interventions are reacted upon with a modification of the immediately preceding utterance. These variations may affect prosodic features (intonation, stress), the characteristics of individual sounds or of sound structure, and/or words or word sequences. There are different operations possible: elements (sounds, words, word sequences) can be added, extinguished, substituted or reordered. Which of these operations are used seems to depend primarily on the complexity of the preceding utterances. (8), (9) and (10) are examples of the different operations (see Kaesermann):

(8) /ändli/ (dimunitive form of *Hand*, hand)
    Mother: *He?* (What?)
    /do ändli so/ (means something like 'there hand – this way')
    (*addition*)

(9) /nägge duffe nägge/ ('nägge' is a reduced form of *Schnecke*, snail;
                         'duffe' means something like 'on there')
    Mother: *Wie?* (What?)
    /fe nägge/
    (*extinction*)

(10) /Loki au ditue das/ ('Loki' is a diminutive form of *Lokomotive*,
                          locomotive; 'au ditue das' means something
                          like 'that too put into')

Mother: *Wie?* (What?)
/das au loki ditue/
(*reordering*)

(For an example of the operation of substitution see (3), (4) and (5).)

These observations suggest a rather simple model of language acquisition: the child, while intending to communicate certain messages to his
social environment, modifies his utterances as long as he gets the impression that he is not understood. The necessity to enlarge his linguistic
knowledge would result from changes in his life space: as soon as he is
able to move around, the 'need' could arise to identify objects not present
in the immediate physical environment (e.g. a toy in the next room) or to
communicate with partners not experienced with the meaning of the
child's nonverbal sign system. By the child's tendency to vary communicative acts which are unsuccessful with respect to his intentions, the
basis for a selection process would be provided: only the successful forms
(which would have to be more and more complex) would be selected and
remembered – a view rather akin to Skinner's basic assumptions (1957).
Furthermore, since language acquisition would be a close analogue to
evolution, it could be treated as a human ethological problem by applying
biological theories and methods to phenomena of human behavior –
according to Eibl-Eibesfeldt's definition (chapter 1.1 above).

Variability of children's utterances and the approximation of standards

Impressive as the child's tendency is to modify his uncomprehended
utterances, we have to take into account some evidence which contradicts
a simple selection-pressure view. First of all, we need to recognize the fact
that the child's adult interaction partners are experts in interpreting
incorrect or incomplete utterances. Certainly, there *are* situations in
which mothers react in a way which resembles the instructed 'mhm?'
interactions (as in (6) above). But far more often mothers *understand* what
their children intend to say. Therefore, the child is frequently successfully
communicating by inadequate verbal means. If those linguistically false
forms were selected, the child would never learn to speak correctly (a
point which seems to me a critical argument against Skinner). Second,
the child's modifications (variations) are by no means a random sample of
the population of the actually possible variations. Take, for example, (6):

the seventeen items produced are clearly *approximations* to the standard
form with respect to the word length (two syllables) as well as to the
overall sound pattern. The only possible exceptions /dibuch/ and
/döbuch/ are provoked by one of the mother's responses: while trying to
understand what the boy says, she asks: 'was isch dibuch?' (what does
dibuch mean?). Immediately afterwards the child utters /dibuch/. Weir's
(1966) observations demonstrate, furthermore, that the concept of random variation is definitely untenable (see (7) above). Otherwise it would
be completely impossible for the child to try – even for *himself* – to produce
a certain sound pattern. Such an attempt presupposes a more or less
definite idea of what is to be aimed at. However, we are not restricted to
this rather vague conception. We are, at least in principle, able to detect
the features of the child's linguistic ideas (and therefore to explicate his
actual linguistic knowledge). The range of produced variations displays
at least partly what are admissible verbal forms for the child, given a
certain communicative context. It can be supposed that there is a continuous change of the various models: while the range of possible realizations
should be large at the beginning it should be continually reduced as the
child's communicative experience increases. Moreover, there should be
the same mechanism operating while the child is learning the correct
articulation of a single word as while he is acquiring the production of
well-formed sentences. Just as he has to detect rules for the pronunciation
of a single word (or words in general), he should be forced to 'formulate'
rules for sentences (not in the sense of Transformational Grammar). This
does not mean that language development could be viewed as a simple
shaping process (see above). Instead, the generation of the production
models for words and sentences seems to resemble the essential characteristics of concept formation.

Conclusion

Questions asked in the title of a paper should be answered. However, I
am unable to decide whether language acquisition can or should be
treated as a human ethological problem or not. Certainly, there are
selection pressures at work, but they alone cannot explain the course of
language development. They are to be supplemented by a principle of
modelling. How this principle works in detail is not at all clear. The
problem can be stated as follows: the child not only has to represent the
standard form in some way or another, but he also has to match his own
production with this model. Since the frequency range of adult speech is

quite different from that of the child's sound production, and since he himself hears his own utterances also through bone conduction, the involved mechanisms have to be rather complicated (chapters 10.1 and 10.2 above). The details of the cognitive control are far from being known. I wonder if human ethology can be of any help for the solution of these problems. Nevertheless, there could be an advantage of a more biologically oriented analysis of language development. As far as I can see, it seems to be necessary to stress the possible functional value of the achievements in the child's language. Possibly these functional aspects can only be dealt with adequately in the broader frame of a biologically tuned science of man.

Comments on papers by McNeill and Foppa

The origins of language and language awareness

WILLEM J. M. LEVELT

Both papers in this final section are about the origins of language. It was with great hesitation that I agreed to be a referee, since discussion about the origins of language, which are as old as our culture, have mostly been absolutely futile and a sheer waste of time. In order to protect its own members, the Linguistic Society of Paris prohibited any communications about the origins of language in 1866. However, this did not help for long. Darwin's *The descent of man* was published in 1871, and it produced a new era of discussion, in which we are still involved.

This century of discussion has, again, taught us very little about the phylogeny of language. The main finding, which was certainly unexpected in the Darwinian framework, was that all primitive peoples turned out to have full-fledged vocal languages. Both the full-fledged and the vocal were surprising. If language evolution did develop gradually by natural selection, no trace of this process can now be found. A one-step mutation, as implied by Chomsky (1968), is biologically untenable in view of the complexity of the behavioral patterns involved. The vocal modality of all human language was a surprise because the general feeling after Darwin was that language must have been gestural in origin. Many philosophers, linguists and biologists have argued this long before McNeill's contribution to this volume. I mention, for instance, Bulwer, who in 1644 called gesturing the 'onlely speech that is naturall to Man',

739

also Rousseau (1782), Wundt (1900), and there are many others. Again, although gesture is everywhere important in language communication, no tribe was ever found where language was essentially gestural,[1] in spite of expectations to the contrary (see 'observations' made by Kingsley (1897) and dismissed by Langer (1942)). There are, moreover, no other anthropological sources of evidence for a gradual transition from gestural to vocal language in the human species. And the arguments by Hewes to which McNeill refers are without force. Tylor concluded in 1878 that 'The idea that the gesture-language represents a distinct separate stage of human utterance, through which man passed before he came to speak, has no support from facts.' This conclusion is still valid.

So McNeill cannot use evolutionary findings as an argument for his gestural theory of language origins. Rather, McNeill's phylogenetic claims are no more than hypotheses which are exclusively based on evidence from ontogenesis and from experimental psychology. The evidence is interesting, but inconclusive, as I will argue in a moment. The main point, however, is the futility of such discussions: what can be gained by inferences from ontogeny to phylogeny, as long as anthropology leaves us, a century after Darwin, fully in the dark about the evolution of human language? Since claims about the phylogeny of human language can at best be paraphrases of other empirical findings, the only gain is a false suggestion of additional support to such findings. And this happens in McNeill's paper where he cites Goldin-Meadow's work. She found spontaneous development of gestural language in deaf children. McNeill concludes that this 'is consistent with the theory that vocal speech overlies an ability for manual communication. When vocal speech is blocked the original gestural system remains.' It is, however, equally consistent with other theories, notably the one which claims that if the vocal channel is blocked, the most flexible alternative will be used for linguistic communication. In deaf-blinds, for instance, gesture language is also impossible, and a manual-tactual replacement is developed, but it seems far-fetched to conclude from this that this must be the evolutionary more primitive form of linguistic communication. Since I see no evidence whatsoever for McNeill's gesture theory, I need not ask him why he didn't deal with the main problem of this theory, namely, if gesture is such a natural system, why did the human species switch at all to the horrors of a vocal language?

[1] It is true that gesture languages have been found, but vocal language is always the main mode (e.g. Plains Indians, Amazon Indians, Bushmen, see Stokoe 1974).

So much for the gestural origins of language. Let us now move to the essence of McNeill's paper, his syntagma theory. It says, if I understand it well, that the ontogenesis of language is based on the unique human capacity to link the articulation system to the system of sensory motor representations. In my view McNeill touches an essential point here. The fact that humans, and also chimpanzees for that matter (e.g. Premack 1977), can communicate linguistically about things, states, actions, or events not present is in full agreement with present-day cognitive psychology, in that one has to suppose elaborate systems of internal representation of such things, states, actions, or events. Major experimental evidence for the structure of such internal representations, and for operations within such systems, comes from various sources, among them from reaction time studies. By the way, this method is – to my knowledge – not frequently practiced in ethology. This is regrettable in view of the high precision by which otherwise elusive behavior patterns can be measured.

McNeill stresses the enormous adaptive value of using such systems, i.e. of being able to perform 'vicarious actions'. This is the ability to do internal or covert computations on internal representations, instead of having to perform overt actions to check out the consequences of one's behavior. If a linguistic signalling system of vocal or gestural signs is attached to such internal representations and operations, this would allow for very easy transmission of action plans, directions, etc. within a community. But again, McNeill comes close to circularity in his exposé, this time because of the use of rather ill-defined terms. I would like to mention one example of this. McNeill argues that the syntagma theory would predict that output integration should coincide with meaning integration, and he does not hesitate to add that 'this result has been found'. There is much here that the reader has to take on trust. On the one hand McNeill leaves undefined what is meant by 'a single meaning structure', and how it could be manipulated independently. On the other hand, McNeill doesn't tell us what units of speech articulation are. Are they related to Ekman's 'punctuation' (see chapter 3.1 above), or to what Goffman called 'topical runs' (chapter 3.2 above)? According to McNeill, they are not the familiar linguistic units such as sentence or clause, and one is left with the impression that they are really those stretches of speech that correspond to single meaning units. But this would make the argument fully circular. Since Professor McNeill cannot have meant that, I would like to ask him to define his constructs in such a way that I can understand what is meant by 'this result has been found'. It might especially be helpful if he could give reference to empirical work on which his statements are based.

In McNeill's paper the articulation system is sketched as a late and somewhat arbitrary addition to the system of sensory motor representations, and it is left undiscussed. Foppa's contribution is a good complement to McNeill's in that it centers around the ontogenesis of articulated speech. Foppa starts out by sketching how little ethology can tell us about the evolution of human language, especially since it is so very different from spontaneously developing communication systems in animals. So, Foppa has also to restrict himself to ontogenetic evidence. The ethological question as to the role of natural selection shrinks to the question as to whether there is a mechanism of Skinnerian shaping in the child's language acquisition. Again, the answer to the latter question will, in my opinion, tell us nothing about the former, in spite of possible analogies. Foppa is wise enough not to try this route seriously.

The main issue in Foppa's paper is the issue of self-correction in children's speech. Here, Foppa and his co-workers have developed a method which can metaphorically be called 'ethological'. The adult says 'mhm?', suggesting that he doesn't understand the child, and the child's repeat performance is registered. As usual, the method is not really new. I have seen similar ideas in a 1914 paper by Bohn, and similar experiments in recent papers by Grimm (1975), Stokes (1976, 1977), Cherry (in press), and Garvey (in press).

I think this type of work is very important: it stresses a rather typical human aspect of language acquisition, and it might be of inspiration to anthropology, and even to ethology. I will finish my introduction by sketching a more general framework for this research, and my question to Professor Foppa is whether he agrees to be placed in this pigeon hole.

The framework is called 'metacognition'. One talks about metacognition if there is evidence that a person has knowledge about his own cognitive processes. A typical case is metamemory: the person knows that he is going to forget and therefore he makes notes, or constructs a mnemonic. Meta-activities are very general in humans, and the issue is not really different from what philosophers have called 'self-consciousness'. Especially Flavell (1976, 1977) and Brown (1977) have done empirical work here, and this has led them to distinguish different levels of metacognition. The lowest level, which is apparent early in ontogenesis, is *self-monitoring*: making self-corrections, either spontaneously, or as a response to specific stimulation. The highest level is explicit *reflection* on one's own cognitive activities and products, such as explaining how one solved a problem.

Metalinguistic behavior is a special case of metacognition. Foppa mentions one higher level of this which he calls 'metacommunication', but limits his study to the lowest level: self-monitoring in the child's speech. The important question to ask about metacognition is: what function does it fulfill in the acquisition of cognitive skills, i.e. in language development? Skinner has little to say about this, and Foppa suggests that it might help to establish internal standards in a process similar to concept learning. One function of linguistic awareness in the child might be to shape his internal representations of linguistic tools by vicarious action, to use McNeill's terminology. The case described by Weir, and cited in both papers, is an example of this shaping of linguistic tools. Nothing much is known about the growth and functions of linguistic awareness in the child, but I can refer to a book which we recently edited in our Max-Planck project-group (Sinclair, Jarvella and Levelt 1978).

Metacognition is probably universal in humans, but detailed anthropological work is needed to determine its bounds and cultural variations. A first anthropological paper in metalinguistics has been written by Heeschen (1978); it analyzes the linguistic means by which the stone-age Eipo can refer to their own language.

Back to Foppa's specific case: the child says something to the adult, and the adult feigns not to understand. The child is aware of the failure of his utterance and makes a new one, expressing the same intention.

It seems that, psychologically speaking, linguistic awareness arises out of devices for finding faults. These cognitive devices could do two things: (i) detect that a fault has occurred, and (ii) specify what sort of fault it was. An intriguing analysis of such devices can be found in a paper by Marshall and Morton (1978), from which most of the following notions and examples are derived.

Fault-finding devices operate both in the production and the perception of language. Foppa's examples concern *production*. Normally, the child would formulate his intended message and receive feedback that he has been understood. No specific awareness needs to be involved. If the feedback (or absence of it) signals that the utterance has failed, the child will send the same message into his formulating system again, and a new utterance arises. This new utterance may differ from the original one either through random variability in the formulating system, or through systematic attempts by the child to change the structure of his formulator. Foppa's cases are examples of fault-detection, but fault-specification can also occur in language production, for instance in spontaneous self-correction, such as: (child, age 2; 2): 'Look, look. A caterpillar . . . helicopter (laugh).' Such self-corrections are frequent in early speech and need explanation. In the example, the child becomes aware that the meaning of the word his formulator produced (caterpillar) is different from the meaning he intended to express (that of helicopter). One has to assume that the child monitors its speech by extracting the real meaning of caterpillar after it has been produced, then compares this meaning to the intended meaning and finds the fault. This involves, therefore, a feedback loop and a comparison device.

Very clear cases of such early linguistic awareness can be seen in the child's *perception* of language. One example (again from Marshall and Morton) should suffice. The child (age 4; 7) comes home from school, and enters the very noisy kitchen.

> Adult: Did you enjoy yourself?
> Child: What?

At this point the child has detected a fault. There was speech input, but no meaning-output. The continuation of the conversation shows that the child has moreover identified the sort of fault:

> Adult: Did you have a good time at. . .?
> Child: No, no, *say* it again!

The adult guessed that the problem was one of lexical understanding, but the child's answer makes it clear that his problems were merely acoustic. The child was thus able to locate the source of the communication failure, showing awareness of stages in the process of speech perception.

What sort of functions could be fulfilled by such metalinguistic devices? First, they seem to improve the *ad hoc* communication, which is certainly advantageous. But secondly, they may also have a specific function in language learning. The mentioned feedback loop from perceptual parser to formulator may be an important channel for the parser to 'teach' the formulator, so that the perceptual detection of a fault leads to a permanent change in the formulator. The young child's capability of language perception is far ahead of his production competence. Linguistic awareness might help him bridge this gap.

Similar mechanisms of awareness may be involved in the acquisition of other cognitive skills as well, and an interesting question for ethology is whether such phenomena can also be observed in animals. The closest may be the acquisition of skills through play – play is an outstanding case of becoming aware of a tool, be it a physical or a cognitive tool. But could one observe the use of meta-devices in the acquisition of a communication system? A non-natural case is Premack's effective use of the metalin-guistic label 'name of' in teaching a language to his chimpanzees. One wonders whether phenomena of fault-finding and self-correction can be observed in the spontaneous acquisition of communication patterns such as bird song.

D. McNEILL: REPLY TO LEVELT'S COMMENTS

Levelt is skeptical of attempts to reconstruct, however tentatively, what may have been the origin of human language activity. He cites the famous incident of the 1860s when, for self-protection, the Linguistic Society of Paris banned further discussion of language origins. However, there has been more than a century of scientific advancement in linguistics and psychology since that memorable event, including several developments that are regarded as revolutionary in importance; in particular in this field, there is the great corpus of Piagetian psychology, and the advances of Chomsky and his followers in transformational generative grammar. In view of these new developments and others, it seems not amiss to examine the problem of language origins anew in a contemporary framework.

Turning over the question of language origins, however, merely to see if anything new can be said about it, is not a promising line of attack and is not my main justification for writing on this subject. Levelt asks 'What can be gained?' and my answer is this. Carefully thought out speculations about language origins can suggest places where evidence bearing on the basic or primitive form of language might be sought. For example, if a gestural theory of language origins is plausible, then it is in the gestural mode of signal emission that we should search for a graded series of steps leading up to language, not only in the vocal mode where this search has largely been carried out heretofore (animal vocalizations, birdsong, etc.). The value of speculation in this situation, it seems to me, comes from the possibility of establishing the prima facie relevance of new lines of inves-tigation. Levelt is of course right; we cannot expect such reasoning to lead to new *facts* about the origin of language, but that is not my purpose and I should not wish my paper to be read in that way.

Levelt also raises a number of criticisms of the gestural theory itself. I am less willing to defend this theory than I am to try to establish the usefulness of considering (in a responsible way) language origins in the first place, but his remarks still should not pass without some form of comment. I see that I have four points.

1. The syntagma theory is in no sense dependent on the gesture theory. The two theories are compatible, that is all. When one considers the possible sources of syntagmata in the sensory-motor coordination of actions, the 'distance' (if I can speak this way) between the resulting form of representation and the gestural mode of output is generally less than would exist with a vocal mode of output. This is because many (though not all) sensory-motor schemata themselves arise from coordinations of hand movement, thus already apply to the same output channel that carries the gestures as well. But the syntagma theory describes just as well the organization of vocal output, and in fact was developed to explain speech, not gesture communication.

2. Levelt maintains that no human group has been found by anthropologists or anyone else where language is primarily gestural. I wonder, however, why this is considered to be relevant? The fact that all human groups use primarily the vocal mode merely suggests that all are fully evolved *Homo sapiens*, and this does not seem to be evidence one way or the other concerning the gestural theory. This theory, as I understand it, refers to an earlier stage of *biological* (*not* cultural) evolution of man. The proper comparative groups are not other human societies, but other animal species, of which the chimpanzee seems the foremost example. It is most important in this context that chimpanzees seemingly *are able to form syntagmata* with manual outputs. This may be relatable to human evolution via the gestural theory (expanded to include the concept of representation).

3. When Levelt describes the tactile communication of deaf-blind people, it sounds as if the gestural theory now opens the way for a whole troop of basic communicative capacities to follow. But these deaf-blind cases are really further examples of *gestural communication* emerging when speech is blocked. The communication of deaf-blind people employs manual output, just as gestural communication does, and appears to be organized along similar lines. A common means of communication for the deaf-blind is to manipulate the hands of the recipient, forming conventional deaf-mute signs (Wade 1904). I do not see that any principles beyond those of gestural communication by the deaf are required to understand this performance.

4. Two points of view have been expressed regarding the question of vocalization supplanting gesticulation in an evolutionary sequence as the primary output channel. On the one hand, we have Levelt's question – if gesticulation is so 'natural', why did vocal language emerge at all? On the other hand, we have the question arising in general discussion – since

vocal language is so much more efficient, why should a gesture modality ever have emerged? Before I am bisected trying to answer both questions, I should point out that there are two distinct steps which must not be confused. One is the origin of syntagmata and the other is the selection of an optimal output channel. The conditions for these steps may have been different. Thus, for example, the gestural mode would seem to have certain advantages in forming syntagmata in the first place, because it requires moving a smaller distance from the sensory-motor level of representation. The vocal mode, however, would have had several advantages in becoming the optimal channel (as Wilson 1975 has summarized, speech is energetically efficient, it flows around obstacles, permits high rates of transmission, and is generated with a single out-of-the-way organ). The gestural theory of language origins, to preserve its identity, need only assert that these two output modes have differential advantages with respect to origin and selection of the optimal channel. It does not have to say that the two steps were even temporally distinct, although Hewes seems to suppose that they were, in fact, successors.

Levelt has asked for clarification of the concept of a syntagma and its empirical basis. At the risk of appearing to avoid the most difficult questions, I will refer the reader to a book I have just completed on this subject (McNeill 1978). If Levelt had known of the extensive discussion in this work on the empirical basis of syntagmata, I am sure that he would not have raised the bogey of circularity. The definition of a syntagma, that is, one meaning unit pronounced as a single output, places two categories (meaning and pronunciation) into correspondence in a certain way. In the book referred to, independent classifications of these categories have been made for actual utterances and the two compared. The results show an 80% to 100% correlation of sensory-motor segments with phonemic clauses (a phonemic clause is a purely phonological measure, cf. Trager and Smith 1951), for example, suggesting that the output of speech is organized in terms of meaning units, i.e. within syntagmata. (The definition of a meaning unit can be formalized by use of graph theory.)

References

Aebi, Elisabeth. 1977. *Eine empirische Analyse der Sprachproduktion aus Dialogen zwischen Müttern und ihren Kindern.* Unpublished M.A. thesis, University of Bern.

Amstutz, Beatrice. 1977. *Sprachmodifikationen bei Zweisprachigen.* Unpublished M.A. thesis, University of Bern.

Bernstein, Nicholas. 1967. *The co-ordination and regulation of movements.* Oxford: Pergamon.

Bohn, W. E. 1914. First steps in verbal expression. *Pedagogical Seminary*, 21:578–95.

Brown, A. L. 1977. Knowing when, where, and how to remember: A problem of metacognition. In R. Glaser (ed.), *Advances in instructional psychology.* Hillsdale: Erlbaum.

Brown, R. 1973. *A first language. The early stages.* Cambridge, Mass.: Harvard University Press.

Bruner, J. S. 1976a. From communication to language. A psychological perspective. *Cognition*, 3:255–87.

1976b. Nature and uses of immaturity. In Bruner, Jolly and Silva 1976.

Bruner, Jerome S., Jolly, Allison and Silva, Kathy (eds.) 1976. *Play: its role in development and evolution.* Harmondsworth: Penguin.

Bulwer, J. 1644. *Chirologia: on the naturall language of the hand.* London.

Cazden, Courtney B. 1976. Play with language and meta-linguistic awareness: one dimension of language experience. In Bruner, Jolly and Silva 1976.

Cherry, L. In press. The role of adult's requests for clarification in the language development of children. In R. O. Freedle (ed.), *Discourse processing: multidisciplinary perspectives*, vol. II. Hillsdale: Ablex.

Chomsky, N. 1968. *Language and mind.* New York: Harcourt Brace.

von Cranach, M. (ed.) 1976. *Methods of inference from animal to human behaviour.* The Hague: Mouton.

Darwin, C. 1871. *The descent of man.* London: Murray.

Flavell, J. H. 1976. Metacognitive aspects of problem solving. In L. B. Resnick (ed.), *The nature of intelligence.* Hillsdale: Erlbaum.

748

1977. Metacognitive development. Paper for NATO Advanced Study Institute on Structural/Process Theories of Complex Human Behavior, Banff, Alberta, Canada.

Fouts, R. S. 1975. Communication with chimpanzees. In G. Kurth and I. Eibl-Eibesfeldt (eds.), *Hominisation und Verhalten. Hominisation and Behavior*. Stuttgart: G. Fischer.

Francescato, G. 1973. *Spracherwerb und Sprachstruktur beim Kinde*. Stuttgart: Klett.

Gardner, B. T. and Gardner, R. A. 1971. Two-way communication with an infant chimpanzee. In A. M. Schrier and F. Stollnitz (eds.), *Behavior of non-human primates*. New York: Academic Press.

Garvey, C. In press. Contingent queries and their relations in discourse. In E. D. Keenan (ed.), *Studies in linguistic pragmatics*. New York: Academic Press.

Goldin-Meadow, Susan J. 1975. The representation of semantic relations in a manual language created by deaf children of hearing parents: a language you can't dismiss out of hand. Unpublished Ph.D. thesis, Department of Psychology, University of Pennsylvania.

Greene, Peter. 1972. Problems of organization of motor systems. In R. Rosen and F. M. Snell (eds.), *Papers in theoretical biology*, vol. II. New York: Academic Press.

Grimm, H. 1975. Analysis of short-term dialogues in 5–7 year olds: Encoding of intentions and modifications of speech acts as a function of negative feedback. Paper for Third International Child Language Symposium, London.

Heeschen, V. 1978. The metalinguistic vocabulary in a speech community in the Highlands of Irian Jaya (West New Guinea). In Sinclair, Jarvella and Levelt 1978.

Hewes, Gorden W. 1973. Primate communication and the gestural origin of language. *Current Anthropology*, 14:5–11.

Jakobson, Roman. 1941. *Kindersprache, Aphasie, und allgemeine Lautgesetze*. Uppsala: Almgvist and Wiksell.

Kaesermann, Marie-Louise. 1978. Interaktion und Spracherwerb. Unpublished Ph.D. thesis, University of Bern.

Kendon, Adam. 1975. Gesticulation, speech, and the gesture theory of language origins. *Sign Language Studies*, 9:349–73.

Kingsley, M. H. 1897. *Travels in West Africa: Congo Français, Corisco and Cameroons*. London/New York: Macmillan.

Kozhevnikov, V. A. and Chistovich, L. A. 1965. Speech: articulation and perception. *National Technical Information Service* (Washington), 30:543.

Langer, S. K. 1942. *Philosophy in a new key*. Cambridge, Mass.: Harvard University Press.

Lashley, Karl. 1951. The problem of serial order in behavior. In L. A. Jeffress (ed.), *Cerebral mechanisms in behavior*. New York: Wiley.

van Lawick-Goodall, Jane. 1971. *In the shadow of man*. Boston: Houghton Mifflin.

Lenneberg, E. H. 1967. *Biological foundations of language*. New York: Wiley.

Lieberman, Philip and Crelin, Edmund. 1971. On the speech of Neanderthal Man. *Linguistic Inquiry*, 11:203–22.

Limber, J. 1977. Language in child and chimp? *American Psychologist*, 32:280–95.

McNeill, David. 1975. Semiotic extension. In R. Solso (ed.), *Information processing and cognition*. Hillsdale: Erlbaum.

1978 (in press). The conceptual basis of language. Hillsdale: Erlbaum.

Marshall, J. and Morton, J. 1978. On the mechanisms of Emma. In Sinclair, Jarvella and Levelt 1978.

Miller, G. A., Galanter, E. and Pribram, K. H. 1960. *Plans and the structure of behavior.* New York: Holt.

Moerk, E. L. 1977. *Pragmatic and semantic aspects of early language development.* Baltimore: University Press.

Papoušek, H. and Papoušek, M. 1975. Cognitive aspects of preverbal social interaction between human infants and adults. In G. Kurth and I. Eibl-Eibesfeldt (eds.), *Hominisation und Verhalten. Hominisation and Behavior.* Stuttgart: G. Fischer.

Penfield, Wilder and Rasmussen, Theodore. 1952. *The cerebral cortex of man: a clinical study of localization of function.* New York: Macmillan.

Piaget, Jean. 1954. *The construction of relativity in the child.* New York: Basic Books.

Premack, A. J. and Premack, D. 1972. Teaching language to an ape. *Scientific American*, 227:92–9.

Premack, D. 1977. *Intelligence in ape and man.* New York: Halsted.

Rousseau, J. J. 1782. *Essai sur l'origine des langues.* Geneva.

Shepard, Roger and Feng, C. A. 1972. A chronometric study of mental paper folding. *Cognitive Psychology*, 3:228–43.

Sherrington, C. S. 1947. *The integrative action of the nervous system.* Cambridge: Cambridge University Press.

Sinclair, A., Jarvella, R. and Levelt, W. J. M. (eds.) 1978. *The child's conception of language.* Heidelberg: Springer.

Skinner, B. F. 1957. *Verbal behavior.* New York: Appleton-Century-Crofts.

Stokes, W. 1976. Children's replies to requests for clarification: An opportunity for hypothesis testing. Paper for First Annual Boston University Conference on Language Development.

1977. Motivation and language development: The struggle towards communication. Paper for the Biennial Meeting of the Society for Research in Child Development, New Orleans.

Stokoe, W. C. 1974. Classification and description of sign languages. In T. A. Sebeok (ed.), *Current trends in linguistics*, vol. XII, part 1. The Hague and Paris: Mouton.

Tonkova-Jampolskaja, R. V. 1973. Development of speech intonation in infants during the first two years of life. In C. A. Ferguson and D. Slobin (eds.), *Studies of child language development.* New York: Holt, Rinehart and Winston.

Trager, G. and Smith, H. L. 1951. *Outline of English structure.* Norman, Oklahoma: Battenburg.

Turvey, Michael, 1975. Preliminaries to a theory of action with reference to vision. *Haskins Laboratories Status Report on Speech Research, SR–41* (Jan.–March).

Tylor, E. B. 1878. *Researches into the early history of mankind and the development of civilization.* London: J. Murray.

Wade, W. 1904. *The blind-deaf.* Indianapolis: Hecker.

Weir, Ruth H. 1962. *Language in the crib.* The Hague: Mouton.

1966. Some questions on the child's learning of phonology. In F. Smith and

G. A. Miller (eds.), *The genesis of language*. Cambridge, Mass.: MIT Press.

Wilson, Edward O. 1975. *Sociobiology: the new synthesis*. Cambridge, Mass.: Harvard University Press.

von Wright, Georg H. 1963. *Norm and action*. London: Routledge and Kegan Paul.

Wundt, W. 1900. *Die Sprache*. Leipzig: Engelman.

Index